Daily
Learning
Drills

Grade 5

McGraw-Hill Children's Publishing

Columbus, Ohio

 **Children's Publishing**

Copyright © 2004 McGraw-Hill Children's Publishing.

Printed in the United States of America. All rights reserved. Except as permitted under the United States Copyright Act, no part of this publication may be reproduced or distributed in any form or by any means, or stored in a database or retrieval system, without prior written permission from the publisher, unless otherwise indicated.

Send all inquiries to:
McGraw-Hill Children's Publishing
8787 Orion Place
Columbus, OH 43240-4027

ISBN 0-7696-3095-2

1 2 3 4 5 6 7 8 9 10 MAZ 08 07 06 05 04 03

The *McGraw·Hill* Companies

Table of Contents

Name _____

Everything Has Its Place

Rewrite each of the four lists on this page and the next in alphabetical order.

List 1

adamant	a c c e l e r a t e
arrogant	a d a m a n t
allies	a l l i e s
anticlimax	a m o R
automatic	a n t i c l i m a x
accelerate	a r r o g a n t
amok	a u t o m a t i c

I REMAIN adamant aBoUT MY ARROGANT allies EVEN THOUGH I'M WEARING THIS SillY HAT!

List 2

mute	m u c k
nasturtium	m u v i s h
qualm	m u t e
muck	n a s t o r t i u m
ordinance	o m e r
omen	o r d i n a n c e
mulish	q u a l m

Name _____

Everything Has Its Place

List 3

pommel	p o _9_ m n e l	
regaled	p o o _6_ t e r	
scrimmage	r a b b l e	
pouter	r e _17_ g a c e d	
rove	r i p e	
rabble	r o v e	
ripe	s _5_ c r i m m a g e	

List 4

tack	s p i e _12_ l
tersely	s p _7_ a r r a n
trowel	s a v e e m i s h _11_
thwarted	t a c k
sporran	t e r s e l y
squeamish	t h _13_ w a r t e d
spiel	t _1_ r o w e l

Now write the letters from the numbered blanks on the spaces at the bottom to answer the question.

Question:
When Omri asked Matron if Little Bear could ride his horse, what did she reply?

Answer:

t h a t s u p t o t h e
_1_ _2_ _3_ _4_ _5_ _6_ _7_ _8_ _9_ _10_ _11_ _12_

h o r s e !
_13_ _14_ _15_ _16_ _17_

Name _____

Color Time

Count the syllables in each word and color each space as follows:

1 syllable – green
4 syllables – yellow

2 syllables – brown
5 syllables – red

3 syllables – blue

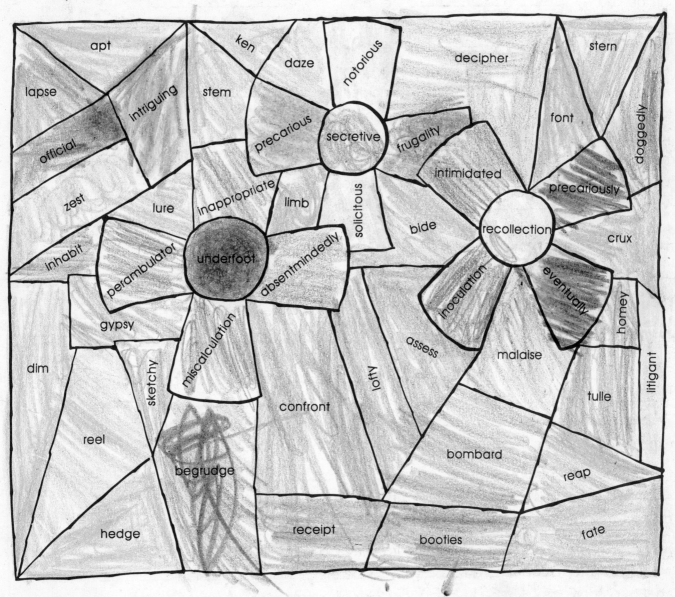

Challenge   Make flashcards of these words to use with a partner. Use a dictionary to write a simple definition on the back of each card.

Break It Up

Name _____

Divide the words below into syllables. You may use your dictionary.

amusement	a - muse - ment	antagonistic	an-tag-o-nis-tic
antiquated	an-ti-quat-ed	blimey	blim-ey
conservatory	con-ser-va-to-ry	conversation	con-ver-sa-tion
creatures	crea-ture	evasive	eva-sive
extricate	extri-cate	gingerly	gin-ger-ly
horrendous	hor-ren-dous	incidentally	In-ci-den-tal-ly
minute	mi-note	remotely	re-mote-ly
reverently	rever-ent-ly	ruthless	ruth-less
self-respecting	self-re-spect-ing	suspect	sus-pect
unshod	un-shod	vanished	van-ished
varmint	var-mint	wrathful	wrath-ful

Use the syllables from above and your keen intellect to complete the following article.

5¢ Extra! / Extra! 5¢

An Editorial
from The Newton Conservatory for Boys
May 8, 1989

Beware of the {e-_vas_-sive} rascal who kicks cats with his {_un_-shod} foot merely for {_a_-muse-_ment_}. No {self-_re_spect_ing_} person at the {Con-_con ser_-va-_to_-ry} would share a {con-_ver_-sa-_tion_} with this {_ruth_-less} and {wrath-_ful_} child. Most of our classmates would treat all pets {rev-_er_-ent-_ly_} and handle them more {gin-_ger_-ly}.

One student who observed this {_hor_-ren-_dous_} action was heard to exclaim, "{Bli-_mey_}! Who is this {_var_-mint} who looks {re-_mote_-ly} like a human?

{In-_cid_-den-tal-_ly_} the International Humane Society hopes to {ex-_extri_-cate} all {crea-_tures_} from this lad's immediate vicinity. While we hope he will change his {an-_ti_-quat-_ed_} beliefs and {_an_-tag-_an_-nis-tic} behavior soon, we {_sus_-pect} that this child's {mi-_nute_} sensibilities have {_van_-ished}.

With disappointment,
Mel N. Kolly

Name _____

What Beautiful Islands!

Rule and Example There are four types of sentences.

1. A **declarative** sentence makes a statement.
   Tuesday was a chilly day.
2. An **interrogative** sentence asks a question.
   Was Tuesday a chilly day?
3. An **imperative** sentence gives a command or makes a request.
   Be at my house at 11 o'clock.
4. An **exclamatory** sentence expresses excitement or strong feeling.
   What a terrible storm!

Exercise Identify each type of sentence.

1. The Hawaiian Islands are really mountain tops. _____

2. Were those mountains once active volcanoes? _____

3. Read the article in the magazine that Sid brought. _____

4. What beautiful pictures that article has! _____

5. Hawaii is made up of a chain of 132 islands in the Pacific Ocean. _____

6. Bring your lei to school tomorrow. _____

7. Which island has the most people living on it? _____

8. I just can't believe that the small island of Oahu does! _____

9. I'm astonished that the average temperature is 75 degrees! _____

10. It rains frequently for short periods of time. _____

11. What is the capital of Hawaii? _____

12. Get the United States map so we can find out. _____

• Rewrite each sentence so that it is the type asked for in parentheses.

1. Were the Polynesians the first people on Hawaii? (declarative)

   _____

2. An English explorer, Captain James Cook, named the islands the "Sandwich Islands." (interrogative) _____

   _____

3. Will you bring me a present from Hawaii? (imperative)

   _____

Name _____

Food for Thought

Rule Every sentence is made up of two parts: a **complete subject** and a **complete predicate**.
- The **complete subject** is made up of all the words that tell whom or what the sentence is about.
- The **simple subject** is the **main word** in the complete subject.
- The **complete predicate** is made up of all the words that tell what the subject is or does.
- The **simple predicate** is the **verb** in the complete predicate.

Example

complete subject	complete predicate
<u>People</u> around the world	<u>eat</u> a variety of foods.
↑	↑
simple subject	simple predicate

Exercise Draw a vertical line between the complete subject and the complete predicate. Then circle the simple subject and the simple predicate.

1. Certain foods have been eaten for many centuries.
2. The Earl of Sandwich invented the sandwich in the early 1700's.
3. Early colonists ate popcorn at the first Thanksgiving dinner.
4. Peanut butter was used by a doctor in the 1800's to treat a patient's stomach disorder.
5. People ate potato chips during the time of the Civil War.
6. The ice-cream cone was served for the first time at the 1904 Exposition in St. Louis.
7. The Romans made the first pies with two crusts.
8. A person's diet depends on available foods.
9. Customs and religion also influence eating patterns.
10. Bird's nest soup is considered a delicacy in some countries.
11. Some people in the Far East make a flour of dried, powdered grasshoppers.
12. Certain groups in Iran enjoy eating sheep's eyes.
13. Tea leaves are eaten as a salad in Burma.

Name _____

We Agree

Rule A sentence with a **singular** subject must have a **singular** verb. A sentence with a **plural** subject must have a **plural** verb.

Example *The **ocean** **contains** salt.*
singular   singular
subject   verb

*The **waves** **crash** against the shore.*
plural   plural
subject   verb

Exercise Underline the simple subject and circle the verb in each sentence. If the subject and verb agree, write **agree**. If they do not, write **don't agree**.

1. The ocean contains salt, which is made of sodium and chlorine. _____

2. The ocean waters covers about 71% of the earth's surface. _____

3. Wind creates most waves in the ocean near the shore. _____

4. The depth of the Pacific Ocean average about 14,000 feet. _____

5. Numerous sea animals lives in the ocean waters of the earth. _____

6. A starfish grow a new leg if one is pulled off. _____

7. Earthquakes can generates tidal waves, or *tsunamis*. _____

8. High tides occur twice a day. _____

• Complete each sentence below using a form of the verb in parentheses.

1. Surfers (glide) _____ .

2. Driftwood (float) _____ .

3. Ocean vessels (zoom) _____ .

4. Seaweed (taste) _____ .

5. Volcanic islands (form) _____ .

6. Seashells (wash) _____ .

7. Ocean waves (splash) _____ .

8. Water (evaporate) _____ .

9. A killer whale (jump) _____ .

10. The dolphins (play) _____ .

Name _____

A Whale of an Activity

Rule Some words may be used as both nouns and verbs.

Example *Fish* are good to eat. *(noun)*
We *fish* every Saturday in the summer. *(verb)*

Exercise Read the paragraphs below. Decide if each bold, numbered word is used as a noun or a verb. Write your answers on the lines.

A whale is a mammal that does not live on **land**.[1] It would be impossible to **land**[2] a whale with ordinary fishing gear. A whale would not **attack**[3] a boat unless the whale was injured. However, an **attack**[4] by an injured whale could be very dangerous. Whales can **dive**[5] into the sea to a depth of more than one-half of a mile. Their powerful tails make such a **dive**[6] possible. Whales do not **fight**[7] among themselves. A **fight**[8] with a whale would be a losing battle! The skeleton of a whale is not strong enough to **support**[9] the whale's weight. Water provides the extra **support**[10] needed to hold up such huge bodies. Whales **swim**[11] across entire oceans searching for food. Such a long **swim**[12] is not unusual for a whale.

Whalers **hunt**[13] for whales in many countries of the world. In the old days, sailing ships might stay at sea for two or three years on a whale **hunt**.[14] Men would **race**[15] to get into small boats. It was a **race**[16] to see who could get to the whale first. Now, whaling boats may **catch**[17] just a few whales each year. Their **catch**[18] may not include mother whales with calves. Whalers have had to **part**[19] with old ways. They may no longer catch whales in every **part**[20] of the ocean.

1. _____
2. _____
3. _____
4. _____
5. _____
6. _____
7. _____
8. _____
9. _____
10. _____
11. _____
12. _____
13. _____
14. _____
15. _____
16. _____
17. _____
18. _____
19. _____
20. _____

Name _____

Hawaii and Alaska

Rule A **compound subject** always takes a **plural verb**.

Example

Hawaii and Alaska <u>were</u> the last states to join the Union.
**compound   plural
subject   verb**

Exercise Circle the correct form of the verb in parentheses so that it agrees with the compound subject.

1. Hawaii, Maui, Oahu, Kauai, Molokai, Lanai, Niihau, and Kahoolawe (is, are) the names of the eight main islands that make up the state of Hawaii.

2. Delaware, Pennsylvania, and New Jersey (was, were) the first three states to enter the Union.

3. Arizona, Alaska, and Hawaii (was, were) the last states to join.

4. Alaska and Texas (ranks, rank) the largest in area of all the states.

5. Delaware and Rhode Island (is, are) the smallest states in the U.S.

6. Both Missouri and New York (has, have) the bluebird as the state bird.

7. Mount McKinley in Alaska and Death Valley in California (contains, contain) the highest and lowest points of the United States.

8. California, Arizona, New Mexico, and Texas (borders, border) the country of Mexico.

9. Kansas and Missouri (is, are) located in the center of the United States.

10. Wisconsin and Michigan (is, are) partially bordered by the Great Lakes.

11. Florida and Georgia (is, are) almost the same size in square miles.

12. California and New York (is, are) the most populated states in the U.S.

Name _____

More About Pronouns

Rule The **subject pronoun** and the **verb** of the sentence must always agree in gender and number.

Example

We visit Lake Champlain when we go to Vermont. *(plural pronoun and verb)*

He visits Lake Champlain when he goes to Vermont. *(singular pronoun and verb)*

Exercise Choose a verb from the Word Bank to complete each sentence below. Make sure the subject pronoun and verb agree.

1. When they _____ in San Francisco, they always go first to Fisherman's Wharf.

2. After we _____ New York City, it's always fun to flag down a taxi.

3. I _____ to go to the top of the Space Needle when we visit Seattle, Washington.

4. He always _____ to Colorado but never gets used to the beauty of the Rocky Mountains.

5. If you _____ to climb down the Grand Canyon in Arizona, it's best to go there in winter while it's cooler.

6. If she _____ Chicago, she should go to the top of the Sears Tower.

Word Bank					
tour	arrive	travel	decide	visit	love
tours	arrives	travels	decides	visits	loves

Rule and Example Some **contractions** are made by combining pronouns and verbs.

Pronoun + Verb = Contraction

we + *have* = *we've*

you + *are* = *you're*

Exercise Combine the verb and the pronoun in parentheses to form a contraction. Write it in the blank.

1. (I will) _____ be traveling to Charleston, South Carolina.

2. (You are) _____ going to enjoy visiting the ocean beaches along the Oregon coastline.

3. (We have) _____ visited Niagara Falls in New York State before.

4. (She will) _____ just love visiting with all of the Native American artists in Santa Fe, New Mexico.

5. (He is) _____ planning on riding down the Mississippi River.

Name _____

Snack on These!

Rule A **subject pronoun** is a pronoun used as the subject of a sentence. **Subject pronouns: I, you, he, she, it, we, they**

Example *We just love to munch on celery filled with peanut butter.*

I think that carrots are delicious.

Exercise Replace the noun subject in each sentence with a subject pronoun.

1. Jerry can't wait to crunch on another fresh string bean. _____

2. Martha really enjoys the taste of persimmons. _____

3. Gary and Tammy will bring oranges in their lunch today. _____

4. Rochele eats red bell peppers like apples. _____

5. Samuel's dog loves the biscuits we gave him! _____

6. Bill and I eat peanut butter and banana sandwiches all the time. _____

7. The cats love chasing after the bubbles we blow. _____

8. Monica always puts noodles in her cottage cheese. _____

9. My hamster loves to chew on wood. _____

10. The apricot tree provides us with fruit every year. _____

Rule A **subject pronoun** can be used after a linking verb.

Example *The greatest consumers of vegetables are Lindsey and **he**.*

*The one with the most colorful hat is **she**.*

Exercise Underline the correct subject pronoun.

1. The one who loves spinach the best is (he, him).

2. The healthiest people are (they, them).

3. The first to try the French onion dip was (she, her).

4. The best cook in our house was (I, me).

5. The only people eating the zucchini were (we, us).

Pets and More

Name _____

Rule **Object pronouns** can be used as **direct objects** of action verbs. Object pronouns: **me, you, him, her, it, us, them**

Example *I'll see you later at the pet store.*
Jane helped me with my cat.

Exercise Underline the correct pronoun in each sentence.

1. Jared's Dalmatian puppy amused (we, us).

2. We found (he, him) under the couch.

3. Sandy's rabbit followed (we, us) all around the house.

4. Becky's Golden Retriever loved (her, she).

5. David's Great Dane scared (them, they).

6. Travis's dog bit (I, me) on the hand.

7. Eva found (they, them) in the back yard.

8. The beautiful macaw noticed (she, her).

9. Amanda showed (we, us) where to find the ducks on the pond.

10. The puppy saw (she, her) from the window.

Rule **Object pronouns** can also be used as **objects of prepositions**.

Example
preposition ↓
The sheep walked quietly behind us.
↑ object pronoun

preposition ↓
The South American frog leaped over them.
↑ object pronoun

Exercise Complete each sentence below with an object pronoun.

1. The elephant walked beside _____ in the circus ring.

2. The horses went around _____ .

3. The birds flew over _____ .

4. The waves splashed on _____ .

5. The fish jumped near _____ while we stood at the bank of the river.

6. Birds were singing beautiful songs right above _____ .

7. The crickets were chirping beside _____ in the flower garden.

Name _____

Whom or What Are You Referring To?

A pronoun takes the place of another word. The word the pronoun refers to is the referent. In each sentence below, circle the referent(s) for the pronoun that is underlined. Draw a line to connect the words.

1. Jeff Miller enjoyed learning the Indian traditions of the Tommie family. He visited the camp often.

2. Billie, Jeff, and Charlie went frog gigging together. They had quite an exciting trip.

3. Billie and Jeff thought they had fooled Billie's grandfather when Sihoki gave Jeff the stew to eat.

4. Billie visited the Miller family. He thought they ate unusual food.

5. Mrs. Kelly helped Billie to teach Charlie how to read. She gave them flash-cards and books to use.

6. Mush Jim entertained tourists by wrestling alligators and giving airboat rides. They gave him money for these services.

7. The hurricane destroyed the Tommie family camp. It was one of the worst hurricanes to hit the area.

8. Grandfather Abraham was very special to Billie. He will keep Grandfather's spirit alive by teaching the white man about the Indian ways.

Use five of the pronouns in sentences of your own telling about the story. Circle the words they refer to.

_____

_____

_____

_____

Name _____

Pick an Apostrophe

Rule • A **proper noun** names a specific person, place, or thing. All other nouns are **common nouns**.
- Most **plural nouns** end in **-s** or **-es**. Some plural nouns are irregular.
- The **possessive** of a noun is formed by adding an apostrophe (') or an apostrophe and an **s** ('s).
- Do not use apostrophes with **possessive pronouns**.
- Do not confuse **subject pronouns** with **object pronouns**.

Exercise

• Tell if the nouns below are **common** or **proper**.

1. Mexico _____
2. airplane _____
3. Amanda _____

4. beauty _____
5. story _____
6. kindness _____

7. peace _____
8. Star Wars _____
9. jacket _____

• Write the correct **plural** form of each noun below.

1. ox _____
2. baby _____
3. foot _____

4. wife _____
5. moose _____
6. turkey _____

7. fish _____
8. chair _____
9. glass_____

• Copy each phrase below. Use the correct **possessive** form of the noun in parentheses.

1. the (children) shoes

_____

2. my (parents) house

_____

3. the (dog) dish

_____

4. the (passengers) tickets

_____

5. one (tree) leaves

_____

6. the (players) uniforms

_____

• Underline the **possessive noun**. Replace it with a **possessive pronoun**.

1. Is that Jane's red hair? _____
2. Bill's sweater is torn. _____
3. Where is Sam and Ed's project? _____
4. The cat's dish is empty. _____

• Circle the correct **pronoun**.

1. (We, Us) saw (they, them) at the restaurant.
2. (He, Him) asked (her, she) for a menu.
3. Mother ordered dinner for Sue and (I, me).

Now or Later?

Name _____

Rule • A verb in the **present tense** shows action that is happening **now**.
• A verb in the **past tense** shows action that happened in the **past**.
• A verb in the **future tense** shows action that will happen in the **future**.

Example

Present: Eva **works** on the class mural every day.
Past: She **worked** on the mural yesterday.
Future: She **will work** on the mural tomorrow after school.

Exercise At the end of each sentence, write the tense of the underlined verb.

1. Jamie <u>painted</u> a watercolor of the pasture behind her house. _____
2. The majestic Arabian horse <u>will move</u> if we get too close. _____
3. Jimmy <u>carved</u> a mountain lion out of his block of wood. _____
4. Tom <u>mixes</u> a lot of colors when he paints with oils. _____
5. Mark <u>will create</u> a collage using photographs tomorrow. _____
6. Andy <u>arranged</u> seashells to create a very interesting mosaic. _____
7. Roger <u>decided</u> to collect driftwood for his sculpture. _____
8. Cheryl <u>sketches</u> pictures of her friends. _____
9. Steven <u>will draw</u> a picture of the horse in the field. _____
10. The horse <u>galloped</u> through the woods. _____
11. Sandra <u>studies</u> the flowers in the vase. _____
12. She <u>works</u> with oil paint. _____

• Write the correct tense of the verb in parentheses.

1. Jim _____ (crunch) on carrots while he watches his brother draw cartoons.
2. Kathy _____ (make) a big mess tomorrow when she creates her papier mâché parrot during art class.
3. Bill _____ (invent) incredible designs when he tie-dyes shirts.
4. Peter _____ (design) a very colorful salad plate yesterday.
5. Monica _____ (form) an incredible vase using clay last week.

Name _____

Garden Variety

Rule A **direct object** is used with an **action verb**. A noun that tells who or what receives the action of the verb is a direct object.

Example

direct object
↓
*Sarah **planted** a **garden**.*
↑
action verb

Exercise Circle the action verb and underline the direct object in each sentence. Then fill in the chart.

1. Nicki prepared the soil.
2. Monica chose seeds for her garden.
3. Mark planted his garden by the fence.
4. Heather wants herbs in her garden.
5. Eva plants tomato plants in the garden.
6. Gwen saves seeds from all the fruit and vegetables her mom buys.
7. She dries the seeds in the sun.
8. Tammy loves fresh lettuce.
9. David planted carrots in his garden.
10. Michele shared vegetables with the local food bank.

	Action Verb	Direct Object
1.		
2.		
3.		
4.		
5.		
6.		
7.		
8.		
9.		
10.		

• Complete each sentence below with a direct object.

1. Dick planted _____.
2. Joan bought _____.
3. Steven designed _____.
4. Samuel shared _____.
5. Cheryl used _____.
6. The gardener picked _____.

LANGUAGE ARTS

Name _____

The Circus Was Born

Rule A **verb phrase** is made up of a main verb and one or more helping verbs. The main verb names the action. The helping verbs tell the time of the action.

Example Helping verbs used in the present tense:
am swimming *is* fishing *are* racing
Helping verbs used in the past tense:
was swimming *was* fishing *were* racing

Exercise Write the main verb and helping verb from each sentence in the chart below. Tell the tense.

1. The Ringling Brothers were living in Iowa.
2. The boys are playing on the river bank today.
3. They were laughing when they saw the circus boat.
4. "The circus is coming!" stated the advertisements.
5. The boys are talking about owning a circus someday.
6. The brothers are hiring many circus acts.
7. One day John said, "I am hiring a real clown."
8. Otto said, "We are buying both of these elephants."
9. Alf T. commented, "We are training many performers."
10. From a small circus, they were growing to a huge size.

Helping Verb	Main Verb	Tense	Helping Verb	Main Verb	Tense
1.			6.		
2.			7.		
3.			8.		
4.			9.		
5.			10.		

• Use a helping verb and a form of the verb shown to form each tense.

race
1. The boys _____. (present)
   The boys _____. (past)

walk
2. The elephants _____. (present)
   The elephants _____. (past)

dance
3. The horse _____. (present)
   The horse _____. (past)

laugh
4. The crowd _____. (present)
   The crowd _____. (past)

Butterflies and Spiders

Rule **Linking verbs** link the subject to a word in the predicate. The linking verbs most often used are **am**, **is**, **are**, **was**, and **were**.

Example *We **were** happy about the outcome.*

Rule A **linking verb** may be followed by a **predicate noun**, which renames the subject, or a **predicate adjective**, which describes the subject.

Example *Harry is a **teacher**. (predicate noun)*
*Harry is **confident**. (predicate adjective)*

Exercise Finish each sentence with a predicate noun.

1. Sarah is a _____ .

2. Her best friend was a _____ .

3. The other people at the party are _____ .

4. Their party was a _____ .

• Circle each predicate noun. Underline the noun or pronoun in the subject that is renamed.

1. The children were actors.
2. The setting of the play was a garden.
3. Butterflies are main characters in the play.
4. Ralph is the star.
5. He is an actor.
6. All the children are drama club members.

• Finish each sentence with a predicate adjective.

1. Today's weather is _____ .   3. Tom will be _____ .
2. The clouds are _____ .   4. The picnic was _____ .

• Circle each predicate adjective. Underline the noun or pronoun in the subject that is described.

1. The trap-door spider is clever.
2. Its building skills are amazing.
3. The house's shell is narrow and tube-like.
4. The plaster on the walls was wet and smooth.
5. The webs covering the walls were soft and silky.

Name _____

Slightly Irregular!

Rule Verbs that do not add **-ed** to show the past tense are called **irregular verbs**. Below are some commonly used irregular verbs.

Example

Present	Past	Past with helpers
begin	began	(has, have) begun
see	saw	(has, have) seen
drive	drove	(has, have) driven

Exercise Fill in the blanks on the chart. You may refer to a dictionary.

Present	Past	Past with helpers
speak		
		taken
		ridden
choose		
	rang	
	went	
drink		
		driven
	drew	
know		
		eaten
do		

• Underline the correct verb in the sentences below.

1. Martha has (began, begun) her research project.
2. First she (chose, chosen) the topic.
3. She (drove, driven) many places to locate information.
4. Martha made a list of the interviews she had (did, done).
5. She (spoke, spoken) to people of many ages.
6. Many (knew, known) a great deal about the subject.
7. Martha (rang, rung) many doorbells during the interviews.
8. While interviewing people, Martha had (took, taken) notes.

• Write sentences for the verbs below on another paper.

1. swim (past)
2. wear (past with helper)
3. blow (past)
4. eat (past with helper)
5. tear (past)
6. drink (past with helper)

Name _____

To Be a Polar Bear

Rule   Some forms of the verb **be** can be used as linking or helping verbs. Three forms of **be** cannot be used alone as verbs: **be, being,** and **been**. These must always be used with helping verbs.

Example   *Polar bears **are** carnivores. (**be** as linking verb)*
*The polar bear **is** hunting the seal. (**be** as helping verb)*
*A polar bear **has been** seen near here. (**be** with helping verb)*

Exercise   Complete each sentence below with the correct form of the verb **be** found in parentheses. Add helping verbs where needed. Forms of **be**: **am, is, are, was, were, be, being, been**

1. Polar bears _____ excellent swimmers. (is, are)

2. The polar bear _____ seen running at a speed of 35 miles per hour. (was, being)

3. Polar bears _____ found in the Arctic regions of the world. (is, are)

4. I _____ sure I saw a polar bear swimming in the water. (am, are)

5. Polar bears _____ seen swimming many miles from shore. (been, have been)

6. The polar bear _____ protected by law in the countries where it lives. (being, is being)

7. The polar bear's fur _____ white to help the bear blend in with ice and snow. (be, is)

Rule and Example   The verbs **do** and **have** can be used as main verbs or as helping verbs.
*I **have** traveled to Canada to see polar bears. (**helping verb**)*
*I **did** my report on polar bears yesterday. (**main verb**)*
Forms of do: *do, did, done*   Forms of have: *have, has, had*

Exercise   Complete the story below using the correct forms of the verbs **do** and **have**.

I _____ believe polar bears are very beautiful. I _____ seen them along the coast of Alaska. I _____ see one come up to our tour bus. By the age of 8-10 years, a male polar bear _____ grown to its full size. Countries around the Arctic have _____ a very good job of trying to save the polar bear from extinction. Polar bears _____ beautiful coats which _____ attracted hunters. Now the bears _____ protection from hunters by law.

Name _____

I'm Confused

Rule   Don't confuse verbs that have similar meanings.

> **Lay** means "put" or "place."
> **Lie** means "rest" or "recline."
>
> **Set** means "put something somewhere."
> **Sit** means "sit down."
>
> **Let** means "allow."
> **Leave** means "let to remain."
>
> **Teach** means "show how."
> **Learn** means "find out."
>
> **Lend** means "give to someone."
> **Borrow** means "get from someone."

Exercise   Choose the correct verb to go in each blank below.

"Mark, did you _____ (set, sit) the saddle on the fence?" David asked.

"Yes, David. I was going to _____ (let, leave) it in the barn, but it was heavy.

Did you _____ (teach, learn) how to throw the saddle onto your horse's

back yet?" Mark asked.

"Yes, and then I needed to _____ (lay, lie) down and rest," David answered.

"I was going to _____ (lend, borrow) you a hand, but I was too busy trying to

_____ (teach, learn) how to rope," David remarked.

"Will you _____ (let, leave) me _____ (lend, borrow) your horse

tomorrow morning?" Mark inquired.

"Sure, Mark. I'm going to just _____ (set, sit) under a tree and read a book

tomorrow morning," David responded.

• Choose the correct verb in parentheses for each sentence.

1. Tell your dog to _____ (lay, lie) down in front of the barn.

2. Please, _____ (lay, lie) that saddle down in front of the stall and
   _____ (set, sit) the bridle on the table.

3. _____ (Set, Sit) on that bale of hay and rest your tired legs.

4. Will you _____ (let, leave) me wear your boots tomorrow?

5. Don't _____ (let, leave) those oats there.

6. I want to _____ (teach, learn) how to trim my horse's hooves.

7. We will certainly be happy to _____ (teach, learn) you.

8. May I _____ (lend, borrow) a brush to comb my horse's mane?

Name _____

The Hairy Spider

Rule   **Adjectives** describe, or modify, nouns. Adjectives answer these questions about nouns: **Which one? What kind? How many?**

Exercise   Circle the adjectives in the sentences below. Underline the nouns they modify.

1. Timid Miss Muffet was frightened by a hairy spider.
2. This is an ordinary reaction when someone meets an unfamiliar creature.
3. Actually, spiders have an important role in pest control.
4. The daily diet of spiders includes many insects that harm crops.
5. Few spiders are of a dangerous variety.
6. The hairy tarantula can be tamed to make a wonderful pet.
7. Although spiders aren't insects, they belong to the same family.
8. Insects have six legs and a three-part body.
9. Spiders have eight legs and a two-part body.
10. In warm weather, look for spiders under large rocks.
11. Finding spiders shouldn't be a difficult task even for a beginning collector.

• Reread the sentences and fill in the charts below.

	Adjective	Noun Modified	Question Answered		Adjective	Noun Modified	Question Answered
1.				7.			
2.				8.			
3.				9.			
4.				10.			
5.				11.			
6.							

Name _____

That Beet, Those Berries

Rule The adjectives **this** and **that** are singular. The adjectives **these** and **those** are plural. **This** and **these** refer to things that are nearby. **That** and **those** refer to things that are farther away.

Example

This *apple is the crunchiest of them all.*
That *cherry on the far branch is ripe.*

These *apples here are crunchy, too.*
Those *cherries growing on the tree look delicious!*

Exercise Complete the chart below using **this, that, these**, or **those** before each noun.

Nearby	Farther Away
_____ carrots	_____ stalk of celery
_____ watermelon	_____ heads of lettuce
_____ persimmons	_____ string beans
_____ turnip	_____ red bell pepper
_____ navel oranges	_____ pumpkin
_____ kumquats	_____ bunch of radishes
_____ beans	_____ stalks of corn
_____ bunch of asparagus	_____ tangelo
_____ wild strawberries	_____ nectarine
_____ apricots	_____ peanut plants

• Complete each quotation below with **this, that, these**, or **those**.

1. "The size of_____ grapefruit you're holding is simply incredible!" exclaimed David.

2. "Please go and pick _____ bell peppers back in the third row for me," Eva requested.

3. Monica laughed, "Can you believe the size of _____ blackberries I just picked?"

4. "_____ garden over there is the largest I've ever seen," Mark commented.

5. "Look at _____ ears of corn over by the barn," Katelyn said.

Carefully Prepared

Rule   Adverbs describe **verbs**, **adjectives**, or **other adverbs**. They answer these questions: **When? Where? How? How much?**

Exercise   Underline the adverbs. Circle the verbs, adjectives, or adverbs they modify. Then fill in the chart using the words from the sentences.

1. The cook <u>carefully</u> (prepared) a large banana cream pie.
2. The high school student wrote the term paper yesterday.
3. The scientist handled the explosive liquid delicately.
4. Soon the carpenters will complete the house.
5. The children raced outside to see the jagged lightning.
6. The painter covered the walls thoroughly with paint.
7. Old Professor James hobbled slowly to his laboratory.
8. The attorney was extremely nervous as he spoke to the jury.
9. The beaver was very busy building a new dam on the river.
10. The architect carefully drew the plans for the new house.
11. The audience enthusiastically applauded the performance.

	Adverb	Modified Word	Question Answered
1.	*carefully*	*prepared*	*How?*
2.			
3.			
4.			
5.			
6.			
7.			
8.			
9.			
10.			
11.			

Name _____

About Eagles . . .

Rule You have learned that adverbs modify verbs. An **adverb** can also modify **adjectives** and **other adverbs**. These adverbs usually answer the question **how much** or **to what degree**.

Example *The eagle's descent was **very** steep.*
(modifies "steep," an adjective)
*The eagle attacked the fish **quite** suddenly.*
(modifies "suddenly," an adverb)

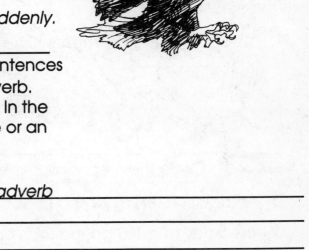

Exercise Underline only the adverbs in the sentences below that modify an adjective or another adverb. Draw an arrow to the word that each modifies. In the blank, write if the modified word is an adjective or an adverb.

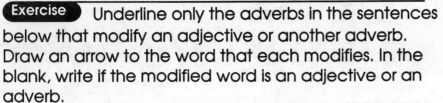

1. The eagle spread its wings very wide. ___*adverb*_____

2. It had to fly quite far to the lake. _____

3. The eagle is an extremely graceful bird. _____

4. It is much larger than most birds. _____

5. Its hooked beak is rather sharp. _____

6. The eagle watched the lake very carefully. _____

7. A large trout is really tasty food for the eagle. _____

8. A beautiful rainbow trout jumped quite suddenly out of the water. _____

9. The eagle has extremely sharp eyesight. _____

10. It swooped almost instantly toward the fish. _____

• Complete each sentence below with an adverb that modifies the adjective or adverb.

1. The eagle flew _____ low over the water's surface.

2. Then it flew _____ high into the blue summer sky.

3. It landed in its nest _____ gently.

4. The eagle is a _____ majestic bird.

5. It has to be _____ patient as it hunts for food.

Name _____

Of the Human Body

Rule A **prepositional phrase** is a group of words that begins with a preposition and ends with the object of the preposition.

Example *Water makes up about 65 percent* ***of the human body****.*

Exercise Circle the prepositional phrases in the sentences.

1. An adult skeleton consists of about 200 bones.

2. The body of a 160-pound man contains about 5 quarts of blood.

3. People who live in high altitudes may have more blood flowing in their veins.

4. Our skin helps protect our inner tissues from the outside world.

Rule If a prepositional phrase modifies a noun or pronoun, it acts as an **adjective**. If a prepositional phrase modifies a verb, it acts as an **adverb**.

Example *Fluids* ***in the inner ear*** *help us maintain our balance.* **(adjective)**
The doctors talked ***in loud voices****.* **(adverb)**

Exercise Circle the prepositional phrase in each sentence. Then identify it as **adjective** or **adverb** on the line.

1. The muscles in the human body number 600. _____

2. All adults should brush their 32 teeth with great care. _____

3. Our skin might burn in the hot sun. _____

4. Every person on the earth is warm-blooded. _____

5. The man went through the hospital doors. _____

6. The temperature inside the body is about 98.6°. _____

Name _____

What Is It?

Rule Some words can be used as **prepositions** or as **adverbs**.

Example *Preposition: The wagon traveled **down** the mountain.*
Adverb: *The rain came **down** and soaked the wagon.*

Exercise Tell whether the underlined word is a preposition or an adverb.

1. The horses weren't complaining <u>about</u> the wagons full of hayriders. _____

2. The trees seemed to smile as we passed <u>by</u>. _____

3. The hay kept us warm as we rode <u>beneath</u> the stars. _____

4. The stars seem to shine so brightly when city lights aren't <u>around</u>. _____

5. The sky stretched <u>above</u> as we sang our funny songs. _____

6. It felt great sitting <u>beside</u> the fire. _____

7. The horses pulled faithfully <u>along</u> the dusty trail. _____

8. The horses seemed thirsty as they waded <u>across</u> the stream. _____

9. I was a little frightened, but my horse went <u>through</u> just fine. _____

10. Traveling seems more peaceful when you leave your car <u>behind</u>. _____

• Change the following adverbs into prepositions by completing each sentence below.

1. The wagon creaked <u>along</u> _____ .

2. We rode <u>past</u> _____ .

3. Falling stars streaked the sky <u>above</u> _____ .

4. Happy faces were all <u>around</u> _____ .

5. Darkness fell <u>outside</u> _____ .

6. We all gathered <u>around</u> _____ .

7. Everyone walked <u>along</u> _____ .

8. We went <u>inside</u> _____ .

9. The wagon went <u>down</u> _____ .

Name _____

The Lizard

Rule and Example **A, an,** and **the** are special
kinds of adjectives called **articles**.
- Use **a** before singular words that begin
  with a consonant sound.
  a lizard
- Use **an** before singular words that
  begin with a vowel sound or a silent **h**.
  an insect
- Use **the** before singular or plural words
  beginning with any letter.
  the lizards

Exercise Use either **a, an,** or **the** in the blanks to complete the paragraph.

There are almost 3,000 different kinds of lizards. _____ lizard may have _____

tail that is much longer than its body. _____ lizard may even leave its tail behind

when escaping from _____ enemy. _____ lizard then grows _____ new

tail. "Dinosaur" is _____ word that means *terrible lizard*. Both _____ dinosaur

and _____ lizard are in _____ reptile family. Most lizards hatch from _____

leathery egg. _____ chameleon is _____ type of lizard that actually changes

color for many different reasons. _____ chameleon may change color if it is

frightened. It also changes color in response to _____ change in temperature or

light. _____ chameleon gets close enough to shoot out its tongue to capture

_____ insect to eat. _____ chameleon's tongue may be as long as its body.

Lizards are truly _____ interesting type of animal!

- Complete each sentence below using **a, an,** or **the**.

1. _____ insect would not taste as good to me as it does to lizards!

2. _____ lizard could lose its tail while escaping from its enemies.

3. _____ chameleon's eyes can actually move in two different directions at
   one time.

4. Some geckos make _____ loud sound.

5. _____ claws of some gecko lizards can be drawn in like a cat's.

Name _____

Jack, the Janitor

Rule and Example Use commas to set off an **appositive**, a noun or phrase that explains or identifies the noun it follows.
Jack, the janitor, walked down the hall.

- Use commas to separate words or phrases in a **series**.
He ate the apple, the peach, and the plum.

- Use commas after **introductory** words or phrases.
Yes, I'm going to the fair.
By the way, did you bring a camera?

- Use commas to set off a **noun of address**, the name of the person being addressed or spoken to.
Caroline, will you come with me?

- Use commas to set off **interrupting** words or phrases.
He was, as you know, an actor before he was elected.

Exercise Add commas to these sentences where they are needed. On the line, explain why you added the comma by writing **appositive, series, introductory, noun of address,** or **interrupting**.

1. Maryanne the new girl in school is a very good cook. _____

2. My favorite snacks are red apples pretzels and popcorn. _____

3. My skills however do not include cooking. _____

4. I know Sally that you love to cook. _____

5. That was in my opinion the best meal ever served. _____

6. After they finished the books Tom and Larry wrote the report. _____

7. Thomas Edison an inventor had failures before each success. _____

8. Mr. Barker the principal of the school spoke to our class. _____

9. Pete our best soccer player won't be here for the big game. _____

10. No I won't be seeing the movie. _____

11. The puppy the kitten and the bunny were all lovable. _____

12. The coating on the pecans was sweet sugary and crisp. _____

13. That is if I'm not mistaken my yellow and green pencil. _____

14. I have by the way done your chores as well as mine. _____

Name _____

On July 4, 1776 . . .

Rule When writing a date, use a comma to separate the day of the week from the month. A comma also separates the date from the year.

Example *Tuesday, September 27, 1994*
Friday, October 13, 1556

Exercise Write these dates correctly. Add commas and capitalize days of the week and months of the year.

monday october 12 1492

_____

wednesday july 4 1776

_____

sunday march 18 1965

_____

tuesday january 23 1994

_____

saturday april 14 2000

_____

saturday march 17 1497

_____

tuesday july 23 1991

_____

friday june 13 1536

_____

thursday august 16 1999

_____

wednesday may 15 1732

_____

Rule When a date is written in a sentence, a comma follows each part of the date except the month.

Example *On Tuesday, April 1, 1991, I will be taking a space flight. The space shuttle will leave on March 13, 1993, with five passengers.*

Exercise Write these sentences correctly using commas where they are needed.

1. On Thursday October 4 1957 the U.S.S.R. put the first satellite into orbit.

_____

2. On Sunday January 31 1958 the U.S. orbited a smaller satellite.

_____

3. On Saturday November 3 1957 a dog became the first living animal in space.

_____

Name _____

Bats at Night

Rule Remember to always capitalize the following:

1. first word in a sentence
2. first word in a direct quotation
3. first word in every line of poetry
4. pronoun I
5. names of people
6. names of pets

7. initials
8. proper nouns
9. proper adjectives

Exercise Underline each word that should begin with a capital letter. Put the number of the reason it should be capitalized above the word. Some will have more than one reason.

one summer night, seth and tony noticed a bat flying overhead.

"did you know that bats help control insects?" remarked tony.

seth replied, "somehow i always think of dracula when i see a bat."

"long ago, people of slavic countries believed in vampires, but a bat isn't really scary," laughed tony. "a brown bat weighs only about half an ounce."

"i haven't seen one up close," admitted seth.

"a good place to see bats is the carlsbad caverns in new mexico. a colony of mexican free-tailed bats lives in one of the caves. at dusk, hundreds of thousands of bats fly out to hunt. many american tourists visit there to see this amazing sight."

edwin gould studied the eating habits of bats in cape cod, massachusetts. donald r. griffin photographed bats eating. one tiny bat caught 175 mosquitoes in fifteen minutes of hunting! fredric a. webster discovered that bats catch insects with their tail membranes.

most north american bats hibernate during december, january and february. when early insects come out in march or april, the bats awaken.

Bats

bats come out at night

catching insects in their flight.

furry little mammal brown

found in country, village, and town.

Name _____

Major Marks

For each sentence, add quotation marks where they belong and underline the letters that should be capitalized twice.

Example: p̲aul asked, "h̲ow did you learn to juggle, t̲om?"

1. peering out the car window, larry blurted, i hope this place is as good as palo alto.

2. you said i'd have a backboard when we left california, the punk reminded dad.

3. looking around the new house, mom exclaimed, look at all those trees, frank. we're really in the woods.

4. paul pitched a perfect game against santa barbara in the state tournament, bragged the pest.

5. hey, kid, why don't you pitch anymore? questioned monk.

6. paul warned, you better borrow that pitcher's mitt, monk.

7. guys in our league don't even throw curves yet, said abels.

8. paul, could you and larry come in now? called my father quietly from the house steps.

9. i'd rather look at the ceiling from the top bunk than see your rear end, i teased the punk.

10. mom cried, how long would it have been before that team dragged you onto their team, paul?

Write four sentences of dialogue that you had with another person today.

_____

_____

_____

_____

_____

Name _____

Quotation Quiz

Add quotation marks where needed to these sentences. Draw two lines under the letters that should be capitalized. The first one has been done for you.

1. "you are lying to me, uncle henrik," said annemarie suddenly.

2. i'm so sorry your aunt birte died, murmured ellen sadly.

3. the bearded man whispered, god keep you safe.

4. who died? questioned the soldier harshly.

5. it will be very cold, remarked Peter. put on your coats.

6. peter joked, don't grow much more, little longlegs, or you will be taller than i am.

7. fiercely ellen whispered, i'll be back someday, i promise.

8. annemarie, you should have seen your proper mama crawling inch by inch! said

   mrs. johansen with a wry look.

9. mama, what is this? asked annemarie as she reached into the grass at the foot of

   the steps.

10. uncle henrik doesn't even like fish, giggled annemarie.

11. the young soldier barked, stop crying, you idiot child!

12. they took my bread, eh? said uncle henrik. i hope they choke on it.

13. uncle henrik! the god of thunder has fallen into the milk pail! shrieked annemarie.

14. mama shook her head sadly as she murmured, they were all so young.

Challenge: Make up an amusing conversation between two animals or two objects.
Use quotation marks.

Name _____

Fancy Figuring

Write the word for each phonetic spelling. Then find each word in the wordsearch.

1. /păd´ lŏk/ _____
2. /sab´ ə täzh/ _____
3. /lăng´ kē/ _____
4. /troo sō´/ _____
5. /fē´ än sā/ _____
6. /snŭg´ əl/ _____
7. /ŭn roo´ lē/ _____
8. /krō´ n ə r/ _____
9. /někst/ _____
10. /stoopt/ _____
11. /kûr´ fyoo/ _____
12. /ĕm broi´ d ə r/ _____
13. /bə -boosh´kə/ _____

14. /kă fā´/ _____
15. /rŭk´ săk/ _____
16 /ûrbz/ _____
17. /krō shā´/ _____
18. /trŭj/ _____
19. /dā ´ nĭsh/ _____
20. /prăngk/ _____
21. /dôd´ əl/ _____
22. /răsh´ ən/ _____
23. /hô´ tē/ _____
24. /tôr mĕnt´/ _____
25. /dĭ fī´ ənt lē/ _____

```
T R O U S S E A U T K I
E U N G N C T H R X I E
H C H E U R S O K E C L
C K A T G N U R O N T D
O S U N G A O L A P Y W
R A G E L N T I Y L E A
C C H M E H F O T M I D
U K T R F A E N B A N A
R C Y O A I A R S A R N
F O A T C I O L B V S I
E L E R F I Y B A S R S
W D A E D V P R A N K H
E A D E B A B U S H K A
M P R A N E G D U R T Y
```

The remaining letters of the wordsearch spell a message. Write the letters in order starting in the upper left-hand corner and working across.

Message:

_____

_____

_____

Sound It Out

Name _____

Write the word for each phonetic spelling given. Then use the words to complete the crossword.

1. /tawt/   _____
2. /shah'mən/   _____
3. /sŭt/   _____
4. /wîr/   _____
5. /kwahn' sit/   _____
6. /foi' ər/   _____
7. /pĭn'ə k ə l/   _____
8. /dĭ měn' shən/   _____

9. /kăm pān'/   _____
10. /sĭn' yū/   _____
11. /ī' d ə r/   _____
12. /wēn/   _____
13. /rīth/   _____
14. /bĭ lī'/   _____
15. /prā/   _____
16. /gawnt/   _____

Clues

Across
4. sea duck
6. black material formed by incomplete combustion
8. work toward an organized purpose
10. prove false
11. tight
12. entrance hall
13. medicine man
14. mountain peak

Down
1. length, width, height
2. twist in pain
3. shelter of corrugated metal
5. to withhold mother's milk
7. thin and bony
9. low dam built in river
13. a tendon
14. hunt

Name _____

A Message to Learn

Write a synonym from the Word Bank for each vocabulary word.

Word Bank

concentrated	ancestors	protected	convince
memorial	delicious	heavenly	heroine
patiently	recovered	attempt	nervous

1. calmly ☐ _ _ _ _ _ _ _ _ _

2. remembrance _ ☐ _ _ _ _ _ _ _

3. forefathers ☐ _ _ _ _ _ _ _ _

4. persuade ☐ _ _ _ _ _ _ _

5. appetizing _ ☐ _ _ _ _ _ _ _

6. focused _ ☐ _ _ _ _ _ _ _ _ _ _

7. legendary female _ _ _ _ _ ☐ _

8. jittery _ ☐ _ _ _ _ _

9. try ☐ _ _ _ _ _ _

10. regained ☐ _ _ _ _ _ _ _

11. sheltered _ _ _ ☐ _ _ _ _ _

12. celestial ☐ _ _ _ _ _ _ _

Read down the boxes to find Sadako's hidden message.

Name _____

Certainly Similar Synonyms

Synonyms are words that have almost the same meaning. Match the underlined word in the sentence with the word that has almost the same meaning by drawing a line.

1. Grandfather Abraham looked at Billie <u>sorrowfully</u> when Billie did not know the Indian legend.

   ominous

2. Billie's dark brown eyes were one of his <u>striking</u> features.

   penetrating

3. The dog moved about the camp looking <u>downcast</u>.

   consoling

4. Mrs. Kelly tried to tell Billie that both sides suffered from <u>terrible things</u> in the Seminole War.

   doleful

5. The pilot's arm was found in a <u>very distorted</u> manner.

   prominent

6. Alice Tommie told Grandfather of Grandmother's hospital stay in a very <u>comforting</u> manner.

   mournfully

7. The dog's howl had a <u>piercing</u> sound when Grandfather died.

   atrocities

   grotesque

8. Mush Jim's sign made intruding tourists believe the camp was <u>restricted from visitors</u>.

   inaudibly

9. Billie read the words <u>silently</u>.

   quarantined

10. The hurricane gave a <u>threatening</u> feel to the air.

Name _____

A Criss-Cross Puzzle

Use the Word Bank to write an antonym by each word. Then write each pair of words where they fit in the puzzle.

1. tumult   _____
2. surmise   _____
3. persist   _____
4. dejected   _____
5. dawdle   _____
6. accelerate   _____
7. perilous   _____
8. adept   _____
9. lavish   _____
10. sanity   _____

Word Bank

certainty   stop
hurry   foolishness
delay   hopeful
safe   sparing
bungling   quiet

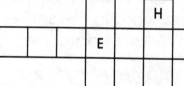

Boom!

Name _____

Draw a green dollar sign ($) over each word that is a synonym of the first word. Draw an orange bomb () over each word that is its antonym.

forfeit	choose	generous	gain	lose
adjacent	sudden	nearby	clean	remote
pompous	modest	festive	noisy	proud
nosegay	unhappy	bouquet	puncture	weeds
exquisite	careful	beyond	hideous	delightful
impeccable	flawed	perfect	scarce	painful
wary	alert	brittle	unguarded	tired
harry	furry	attract	annoy	soothe
despondently	happily	elegantly	crazily	unhappily
interrogate	cross-examine	dislike	persecute	hush
cull	answer	charge	select	scatter
elude	confront	scold	avoid	frighten

Name _____

Like It or Not

Choose synonyms and antonyms from the Word Bank to match the words below.
Feel free to use a dictionary!

Word Bank						
calm	tart	daydream	raise	noise	wretched	make dull
strong	fearful	weak	brave	sugary	ghost	small
quietude	free	solemnity	virtuous	human	huge	imprison
nightmare	disturb	sharpen	lower	merrymaking		

	Synonym	Antonym
hoist		
whet		
incubus		
wraith		
saccharine		
stout		
valiant		
revelry		
liberate		
din		
prodigious		
vile		
appease		

Name _____

On Your Mark, Get Set, Go!

Race to the finish by following the directions on each column to name the winners in the story. Start at the same time as a partner and see who gets finished with their worksheet first.

1. Write soften without the "s."
   _____

2. Remove the "of" to make a number.
   _____

3. Remove a consonant and add one vowel and one consonant to make a synonym for chew. _____

4. Remove a consonant and a vowel to form a pronoun. _____

5. Add a vowel to the beginning and two silent consonants to make the sum of 4 + 4. _____

6. Add two consonants and drop the "e" to form a noun similar to "flying."
   _____

7. Remove a consonant to make an antonym of dark. _____

8. Add "sun" to make a compound word.
   _____

9. Remove "sun" and replace with "porch."
   _____

10. Replace "porch" with "search."
    _____

The winner is _____

1. Write a past form of sing.
   _____

2. Change the first consonant to make a vampire tooth. _____

3. Remove the "f" and add a two-letter suffix to make a synonym of wrath.
   _____

4. Add a "d" to make a warning.
   _____

5. Change "d" to "r" to make a forester's friend. _____

6. Change the first vowel to "i."
   _____

7. Change "i" to "o," add "w" to the beginning and drop the "er."
   _____

8. Replace "w" with "st."
   _____

9. Add "box" to make a compound word.
   _____

10. Replace "b" with "f," "g" with "e" and remove the "r." _____

The winner is _____

Why is one of the racers a winner even though he did not cross the finish line first? _____

_____

Name _____

Mixed-Up Information

Miss Freed decided to play a trick on her students. She wrote a bunch of information on the board about The Pleistocene Epoch, and then started asking the students questions about the information. None of them could answer because the information was all mixed up.

Help Miss Freed's students sort out the information on prehistoric animals. See if you can put the sentences below in order so that they make sense.

It included a period called the Ice Age. The giant ground sloth was as big as an elephant and used long, hooklike claws to pull down tree branches. The Pleistocene Epoch is the geologic time beginning about 1-¾ million years ago and ending about 10,000 years ago. It was during the Ice Age that the last of the prehistoric animals, like the giant ground sloth, the woolly rhinoceros and the mastodon, died out. The mastodon was also an elephantlike creature with a thick coat of reddish-brown hair and 8-9 foot long tusks. The woolly rhinoceros, or "hollow-tooth," ate small bushes and poor grass and looked much like the rhinoceros that live in Africa today.

_____

_____

_____

_____

_____

_____

_____

_____

_____

_____

•SOMETHING EXTRA•

What do you think our world would be like today if these creatures were still around?

Name _____

"Speak Fitly or Be Silent Wisely"

Unscramble the letters on the right to find the simple word or phrase for these complex expressions on the left.

1. female practitioner in the art of conjuration _____ ctihw

2. officer of a law-enforcement government agency _____ aceilmnop

3. monarch's province of dominion _____ dgikmno

4. starchy tubers crushed into a pulpy mass _____ adehms aeoopstt

5. oratory address _____ pehsce

6. contentious argument _____ aelqrru

7. insertion of specified marks to clarify meaning _____ acinnopttuu

8. day of natal remembrance _____ abdihrty

9. most delectable and scrumptious aroma _____ cdeiilosu ellms

10. sugary pastry coating _____ cgiin

Challenge   Be as wordy as the king's advisers. Use another sheet of paper to write complex descriptions for each of these words.

1. car
2. school
3. city
4. meal

Name _____

Up a Tree

Match these expressions with their meanings.

_____ all the personality of wallpaper paste   a. without question

_____ a piece of my mind.   b. consider clearly

_____ what got into you?   c. becoming wild

_____ running amok   d. gather up great quantities

_____ beyond a shadow of a doubt   e. misunderstand the problem

_____ think straight   f. a very bland disposition

_____ ace in the hole   g. strong opinion

_____ seize the wrong horn of the dilemma   h. from a bad situation to a worse one

_____ shop like a bear about to hibernate   i. why are you bothered?

_____ out of the frying pan and into the fire   j. special advantage

Write two of the above expressions in sentences of your own.

Example: When my teacher asked me to give the answer, I couldn't think straight.

_____

_____

_____

Name _____

Just Bust Out Laughin'

Make your own matching exercise! In the blank boxes below write, in *random* order, the meaning of each underlined expression. Then give your worksheet to a partner to match the expressions with the meanings by writing the correct letter in each space.

Idiom	Meanings	Partner's Answers
a. Addie knew that <u>the old goat</u> owed her dad some money.		_____
b. When the girls received their food, they <u>wolfed it down</u>.		_____
c. Carla Mae told Addie she was <u>cracked</u> to consider giving Mr. Rehnquist a Thanksgiving dinner.		_____
d. After the funeral, Addie dashed to her room; she didn't want to be in the kitchen for the <u>fireworks</u>.		_____
e. Addie felt that Cousin Henry was <u>poison</u>.		_____
f. Mr. Rehnquist and Pearlie used to sing <u>at the top of their lungs</u>.		_____
g. With <u>a straight face</u>, Addie told Carla Mae that it wouldn't take Mr. Rehnquist long to shoot them.		_____
h. When he was a boy, Mr. Rehnquist would <u>split his sides</u> because of Pearlie's antics.		_____
i. Addie's dad was quick to <u>blow his top</u>.		_____
j. Grandma, who was getting old, had already <u>raised</u> two families.		_____
k. The girl tried to brush Treasure and quickly <u>got the the hang of it</u>.		_____
l. The lawyer <u>dropped a bomb in the lap of</u> Addie's familiy.		_____

Name _____

When Aslan Comes

Write an **X** in front of all the sentences that show elements of fantasy.

_____ 1. Lucy heals the wounded warriors with her cordial.

_____ 2. It's always winter but never Christmas.

_____ 3. The Professor wonders what is taught in school these days.

_____ 4. Aslan returns to life.

_____ 5. Peter holds a shield that has a red lion for its insignia.

_____ 6. Spring flowers come into bloom.

_____ 7. A faun invites Lucy for tea.

_____ 8. The children enter Narnia through a wardrobe.

_____ 9. Mr. Beaver shows his dam to the children.

_____ 10. The Queen creates an enchanted Turkish Delight for Edmund.

_____ 11. Edmund loves Turkish Delight.

_____ 12. Mrs. Macready leads tourists through the Professor's house.

_____ 13. Because it rains, the four children must remain indoors.

_____ 14. The beaver builds his dam using trees and mud.

_____ 15. The Queen's wand is used to turn creatures to stone.

_____ 16. The giant tears down the Queen's gate and tower with his club.

_____ 17. Edmund is hurt in battle.

_____ 18. The dwarf becomes like a stump.

Decode the prophecy.

Write the letters which are underlined twice in order here.

_____ . . .

Write the letters which are underlined once in order here.

_____ .

Name _____

What Would You Do?

Circle the best answer. For help, look up the key underlined words in the dictionary.

1. What would you do with a <u>telly</u>?
   a. pet it
   b. climb it
   c. watch it

2. What would you do with a <u>mackintosh</u>?
   a. ride it
   b. wear it
   c. shoot it

3. What would you do if you <u>queued up</u>?
   a. raise your hand
   b. call the police
   c. get in line

4. How would you move on a <u>lift</u>?
   a. up or down
   b. in a circle
   c. forward or backward

5. What would you do with a <u>dustbin</u>?
   a. put garbage in it
   b. wear it in the garden
   c. fly it in a breeze

6. What would you do if you <u>mucked about</u>?
   a. gather eggs
   b. waste time
   c. scrape out dirty pots and pans

7. What would you do with a <u>quid</u>?
   a. spend it
   b. swim away from it
   c. step on it

8. What would you do if you were <u>knackered</u>?
   a. carry a load and take a hike
   b. make a face
   c. lie down and rest

9. What would you do with <u>petrol</u>?
   a. feed pigeons
   b. fill a tank
   c. trim a hedge

As Easy As Falling Off a Log

Name _____

List the two things that are compared in each sentence.

1. A butterfly as big as my hand fluttered across the path.

   _____

2. It was the loneliest sound I'd ever heard, as lonely as a ghost who had been lying alone in the dark for 100 years.

   _____

3. As quickly as a cat, Heather wriggled away from me.

   _____

4. A gust of wind lifted the vines and sent them billowing toward us like outstretched arms.

   _____

5. Like a prisoner on her way to a beheading, Heather walked sullenly when we came to the creek.

   _____

6. Michael's worried face made him look like a little old man.

   _____

7. Do you think death is like going to sleep and never waking up?

   _____

8. Finally Helen's image wavered like a reflection on the water.

   _____

Complete these comparisons.

1. In the kitchen, Molly's hands became as warm as _____

   _____

2. Heather's cry was like a _____

   _____

3. Helen walked as quietly as _____

   _____

4. Walking into the cemetery was like _____

   _____

5. The new mystery was as scary as _____

   _____

6. Michael dashed down the path as quick as _____

   _____

Name _____

DeCree's Dictionary

LANGUAGE ARTS

Decode each word in DeCree's Dictionary by substituting the letter that comes before each letter in the nonsense words given. Write the word on the line in the first column. Then complete the dictionary by finishing each simile in the second column.
Hint: Z comes before A.

as			as
as	BOOPZJOH	ANNOYING	as
as	CVNQZ	BUMPY	as
as	DSBOLZ	CRANKY	as
as	EFMJDJPVT	DELICIOUS	as
as	FYBTQFSBUJOH	EXASPERATING	as
as	GBUUFOJOH	FATTENING	as
as	HSPVDIZ	GROUCHY	as
as	IVOHSZ	HUNGRY	as
as	JUDIZ	ITCHY	as
as	KPMMZ	JOLLY	as
as	LJOEIFBSUFE	KINDHEARTED	as
as	MBAZ	LAZY	as
as	NBEEFOJOH	MADDENING	as
as	OFSWPVT	NERVOUS	as
as	PME	OLD	as
as	QPXFSGVM	POWERFUL	as
as	RVJDL	QUICK	as
as	SPVOE	ROUND	as
as	TJMMZ	SILLY	as
as	UBMM	TALL	as
as	VTFGVM	USEFUL	as
as	WBMVBCMF	VALUABLE	as
as	XFBMUIZ	WEALTHY	as
as	FYDJUJOH	EXCITING	as
as	ZPVUIGVM	YOUTHFUL	as
as	ABOZ	ZANY	as

As Fast As Lightning

Name _____

List the two things that are compared in each sentence.

1. When Mother and Aunt Mildred's bicycle crashed into the reviewing stands, it died like a worn-out horse.

   _____

2. Aunt Mildred would sweep into our house like a whirlwind.

   _____

3. At Uncle John's funeral, Louis and I were as good as homemade bread.

   _____

4. The funeral was as exciting as three-day-old milk.

   _____

5. The casket's body and Uncle John were as different as ducks and owls.

   _____

6. Mother's Beetle Eater glowed like a ship from outer space.

   _____

7. When bugs touched it, they sparked like miniature fireworks.

   _____

8. Ol' Vergil looked like a pile of dirty laundry when he slept.

   _____

9. Like a dropped load of bricks, Vergil's body would fall in slumber.

   _____

Complete these similes.
1. Our family car was as noisy as _____
2. Aunt Blanche was as pretty as _____
3. People said that Louis was as bright as _____
4. We feared that Janine would cry like _____
5. The pieces of worms squirmed like _____
6. Cousin Lloyd looked like _____
7. Father thought Mother's family was as crazy as _____
8. Louisa May's smile was like _____

Name _____

Championship Categories

Circle the one word in each group that does not fit with the others. Name the category that describes the remaining words.

1.
snowy
wintry
spring
blustery
_____

2.
asks
tells
inquires
questions
_____

3.
Indian
table
chair
sofa
_____

4.
inferno
hot tub
heat wave
blizzard
_____

5.
plural
single
many
multitude
_____

6.
two
solitaire
solo
singular
_____

7.
lamp
TV
seeds
VCR
_____

8.
ugly
homely
hideous
beautiful
_____

9.
boy
lady
widow
queen
_____

10.
big
red
little
tall
_____

11.
demon
devil
enemy
angel
_____

12.
found
discovered
lost
recovered
_____

13.
plant
ocean
sea
river
_____

14.
life
birth
death
existence
_____

15.
girl
man
boy
male
_____

Write the circled words from above in the matching numbered blanks to complete the paragraph.

The old _____ legend about the _____ fern _____ how an
                3   10   2

Indian _____ and _____ were _____ in a _____
          9   15   12   4

and had frozen to _____. In the _____ a _____ red fern had
                       14   1   8

grown between their _____ bodies. The legend says that only an _____
                         6   11

could _____ the _____ of a red fern.
          13   7

Name _____

Odd Word Out

Circle the word in each line below which does not belong.

1.	ee<u>r</u>ie	un<u>c</u>anny	<u>v</u>indictive	pec<u>u</u>liar
2.	b<u>a</u>rricade	me<u>n</u>ace	<u>p</u>eril	thr<u>e</u>at
3.	mi<u>m</u>ic	str<u>o</u>ll	<u>s</u>camper	a<u>m</u>ble
4.	f<u>a</u>re	slee<u>p</u>	cha<u>r</u>ge	f<u>ee</u>
5.	shrie<u>k</u>	scr<u>ea</u>m	str<u>i</u>ke	sque<u>a</u>l
6.	cra<u>m</u>	skitte<u>r</u>	stuff	<u>j</u>am
7.	b<u>a</u>rge	intru<u>d</u>e	e<u>n</u>ter	utt<u>e</u>r
8.	un<u>c</u>onventional	o<u>p</u>aque	biza<u>r</u>re	pec<u>u</u>liar
9.	t<u>i</u>nker	<u>f</u>idget	to<u>y</u>	tr<u>o</u>t
10.	rec<u>k</u>on	sur<u>m</u>ise	calc<u>u</u>late	im<u>p</u>ress
11.	em<u>b</u>arrassed	bash<u>f</u>ul	<u>c</u>owardly	shee<u>p</u>ish
12.	acu<u>t</u>e	mem<u>o</u>rable	<u>i</u>ntense	k<u>ee</u>n
13.	<u>h</u>ull	peel	s<u>k</u>in	ba<u>r</u>
14.	c<u>l</u>atter	offe<u>n</u>d	commo<u>t</u>ion	<u>r</u>attle

List in order the underlined letters of the circled words to spell two words.

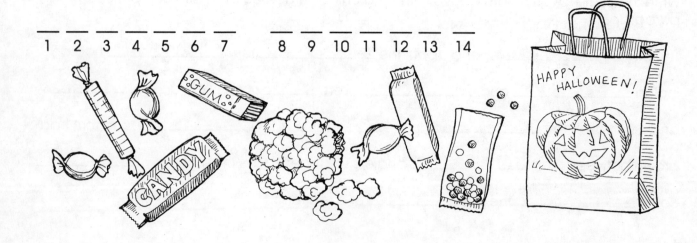

___ ___ ___ ___ ___ ___ ___   ___ ___ ___ ___ ___ ___ ___
 1   2   3   4   5   6   7   8   9 10 11 12 13 14

Excerpts from Annemarie's Diary

Circle the word which best completes each sentence.

1. I ___ for the frosted cupcakes which we had not been able to bake for so many years.
   longed   lessened   concealed

2. When Ellen ___ a queen's costume, she seemed royal herself.
   executed   devastated   donned

3. As the pounding raindrops began to ___ , Kirsti and I entertained thoughts of a walk.
   glower   subside   lattice

4. I feared that Ellen would be unable to ___ her necklace from the soldiers.
   give   conceal   distort

5. We wished the rude soldiers would leave the house quietly. Mama ___them to go.
   expected   urgency   implored

6. The suspicious officer___ watched us board the train at Copenhagen.
   sleepily   haughtily   warily

7. As the boat pulled ___on its lines, we could hear it creaking.
   condescendingly   taut   quaver

8. Uncle Henrik hoisted the nets from which many ___fell onto the deck.
   churns   herring   trousseau

9. A ___ brought Great-aunt Birte's casket to our home for the wake.
   hearse   clasp   fiancé

10. Poor Birte died from ___ , Mama says.
    typhus   kroner   herring

11. The rapping on our door that evening made a ___ sound like the burst of machine gun fire.
    gnarled   staccato   chatterbox

12. The foreign bully ordered us to our seats in a ___ voice.
    stricken   caustic   distracted

13. I feared that Peter's pistol would ___ from his waistband.
    reside   wedge   protrude

14. The package was too ___ to conceal inside Ellen's rucksack.
    ruffled   distracted   bulky

15. I helped Mama___ into the house early that morning.
    hobble   saunter   intricate

Challenge   On another sheet of paper write a definition for each circled word.

Name _____

What's the Row?

Carefully read each sentence and write the number of the correct definition for each underlined word.

	Definitions		
file:	1) a line of people	2) to arrange in a useful order	3) to sharpen, smooth or grind
party:	1) an assembly of people	2) a fun occasion	
passage:	1) a journey	2) a hallway	3) a segment of a writing
row:	1) a straight line	2) to move by using oars	3) a noisy quarrel
spectacles:	1) displays	2) eyeglasses	
wind:	1) to turn	2) moving air	3) hear (get wind of)

_____ 1. The children and the beavers made their way in single <u>file</u> to the Stone Table.

_____ 2. The beavers did not need to <u>row</u> across the springtime streams.

_____ 3. The Professor's <u>spectacles</u> slipped down his nose in a comical manner.

_____ 4. There could be no Christmas <u>party</u> without Father Christmas.

_____ 5. The children heard Mrs. Macready and her visitors in the <u>passage</u>.

_____ 6. The path through the woods would <u>wind</u> often because of the rocky ground.

_____ 7. The Queen <u>filed</u> her nails to a fine point.

_____ 8. In a later novel Lucy will take a <u>passage</u> aboard the "Dawn Treader."

_____ 9. Susan feared that Peter and Edmund would have a <u>row</u>.

_____ 10. The children wished to travel in a small <u>party</u>.

_____ 11. The warm <u>wind</u> helped melt the slushy snow.

_____ 12. What a <u>spectacle</u> greeted the children when they awoke!

_____ 13. Mr. Beaver hoped that the Queen did not get <u>wind</u> of the children's visit.

_____ 14. A <u>party</u> of visitors gathered to meet Mrs. Macready.

_____ 15. The stone figures appeared to stand in a <u>row</u>.

_____ 16. Peter <u>filed</u> the information in his mind for later reference.

Name _____

Criss-Cross

Complete each sentence below using words from the Word Bank. Then use these words to complete the criss-cross.

Word Bank	confer congregation refugee	cockeyed poinsettia Vaseline	colic pierce	collapsible charitable	pews dress

1. In many churches people sit on _____, which are long benches.

2. If people wish to wear earrings, they should go to a professional who will _____ their ears.

3. Alice Wendleken put_____ on her eyelids to make them sparkle.

4. The people who gather in a church to worship are called the _____ .

5. A person who leaves home to find greater safety in a foreign land is called a _____ .

6. An organization is _____ if it raises money or material to help those in need.

7. The _____ plant has red or white leaves and is often used for holiday decorations.

8. When people suffer from _____ , they have severe stomach or intestinal pain.

9. Often people in plays and pageants try to wear their costumes in the last practice which they call the _____ rehearsal.

10. A _____ stroller can be folded up to be stored more easily.

11. You may need to turn your head to one side to see a picture which hangs on the wall in a _____ manner.

12. People _____ with one another to discuss issues and make decisions.

Name _____

Take Me Out to the Ball Game

Using the diagram, answer these questions.

1. Who plays left field?   _____
2. How far is it from first to second base?   _____
3. Does Monk Lawler play the outfield?   _____
4. How many innings are played in Little League?   _____
5. If a batter hits a triple, how many feet will he run?   _____
6. What position does Cliff Borton play?   _____
7. How far is Paul Mather from home plate?   _____
8. Can a 10-year-old child play Little League ball?   _____
9. How long may a bat be?   _____
10. What position does Jim Hakken play?   _____
11. Who is Stu closer to, Monk or Kenny?   _____

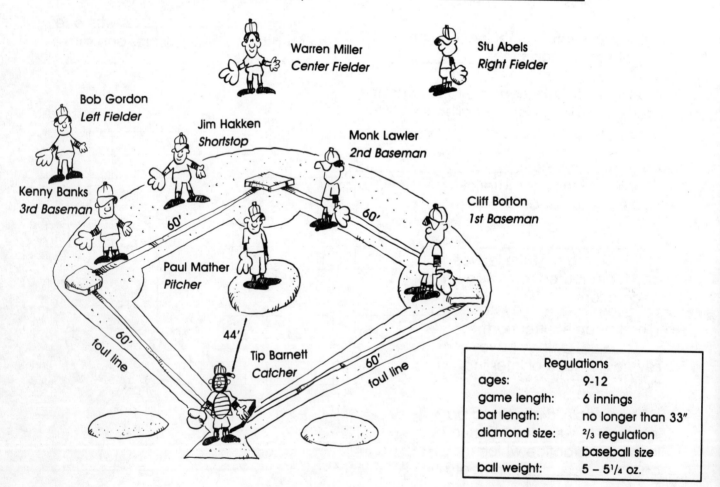

Warren Miller
Center Fielder

Stu Abels
Right Fielder

Bob Gordon
Left Fielder

Jim Hakken
Shortstop

Monk Lawler
2nd Baseman

Kenny Banks
3rd Baseman

Cliff Borton
1st Baseman

Paul Mather
Pitcher

60'

60'

60'

44'

foul line

foul line

Tip Barnett
Catcher

Regulations	
ages:	9-12
game length:	6 innings
bat length:	no longer than 33"
diamond size:	2/3 regulation baseball size
ball weight:	5 – 5 1/4 oz.

Name _____

A Feverish Task

Read each paragraph. Underline the topic sentence. Then circle the letter of the best title.

1. Did you think mosquitoes were to blame for malaria? Actually the culprits are tiny one-celled creatures named plasmodia. If a person is bitten by an Anepholes mosquito, one of about 3,000 kinds of mosquitoes, and the saliva of that particular mosquito contains plasmodia that person can contract malaria. So the mosquito only acts as the carrier for plasmodia, the *real* cause of malaria.

   A. Mosquitoes bite people
   B. Plasmodia cause malaria
   C. 3,000 species of mosquitoes

2. When the Anopheles bites a person, it leaves some of its saliva behind. If the saliva contains plasmodia, these tiny creatures find their way through the body until they find the liver. There they stay for around 10 days until they have multiplied into the thousands. At that time many of them return to the blood stream and try to kill red blood cells. Other plasmodia remain in the liver and continue to reproduce.

   A. How plasmodia spread
   B. Ten days in the liver
   C. Plasmodia kill red blood cells

3. Most people who contract malaria have the following symptoms. About 14 days after the plasmodia enter the body, the person may experience a day of headaches, fatigue and nausea. Then comes a 12- to 24-hour period in which malaria shows itself more strongly. The person starts having chills, enters a period of high fever with sweating and ends with a reduced body temperature. If the victim does not receive medical treatment, these attacks may continue for years. However, the body begins to fight the infection and the attacks occur less frequently.

   A. Why people get headaches
   B. How the body fights malaria
   C. The symptoms of malaria

Name _____

What's the Idea?

Circle the number of the sentence which best expresses the main idea for each pararaph.

Edmund began to question whether or not the lion in the Queen's courtyard was alive. The large creature looked as if it were about to pounce on a dwarf. But it did not move. Then Edmund noticed the snow on the lion's head and back. Only a statue would be covered like that!
1. The statue is snow-covered.
2. Edmund wonders if the lion is alive.
3. The lion is ready to jump out.

The resting party of children and beavers heard the sound of jingling bells. Mr. Beaver dashed out of his hiding place and soon called the others to join him. He could hardly contain himself with excitement. Father Christmas is here!
1. Mr. Beaver is a brave animal.
2. The group hears a jingling sound.
3. Father Christmas has come to Narnia.

Poor Edmund! Because he came to the Queen, he expected her to reward him gratefully with Turkish Delight. After all he had traveled so far and had suffered miserably in the cold. When the Queen finally commanded that he receive food and drink, the cruel dwarf brought Edmund a bowl of water and a hunk of dry bread.
1. Edmund is not rewarded as he expected.
2. Edmund receives bread and water.
3. The young boy suffered from the cold.

Peter knew he must rescue Susan from the wolf. When the wolf charged, Susan climbed up a nearby tree. The wolf's snapping and snarling mouth was inches away. When Peter looked more closely, he realized that his sister was about to faint. Rushing in with his sword, Peter slashed at the beast.
1. Peter kills the wolf.
2. The wolf snarls at Susan.
3. Peter realizes he must save his sister.

Now choose one of the following sentences as your main idea and write a paragraph.
1. The Queen demands that Edmund be returned to her.
2. Aslan's army loses the Queen and her dwarf.
3. Father Christmas gives gifts to the beavers and the three children.

_____
_____
_____
_____

Name _____

Try to Groove It

Write **M** if the sentence gives the main idea.
Write **D** if the sentence gives detail.
Hint: Each set of sentences has only one
main idea.

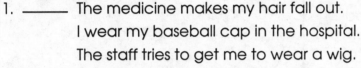

1. _____ The medicine makes my hair fall out.
I wear my baseball cap in the hospital.
The staff tries to get me to wear a wig.

2. _____ I can hardly imagine what it's like to breathe the fresh air.
I can tell the difference between people's footsteps.
I feel like I've been in the hospital for years.

3. _____ Parents and other spectators often bring their own chairs and blankets to games in Arborville.
In California we played in miniature big league parks.
The playing fields are not as elaborate here as they were in California.
Here, games are usually played on junior high or elementary school diamonds.

4. _____ I notice that I'm the center of attention as I warm up.
Even the Ace players gawk at me like I'm some strange animal.
Our whole team stops warming up to watch Tip and me.

5. _____ He felt naked and lonely playing up so close to the batter.
Kenny was reluctant to move in closer.
I tried to coax him in but he barely budged.

6. _____ Red kept glancing at me from the pitcher's mound.
He seemed to hear every noise and wisecrack.
Was Red too easily distracted?

7. _____ I knew I had to touch first.
Inch by inch I crawled toward it.
I knew the baseman was running back toward me with the ball.
Finally I lunged and fell forward.

8. _____ I held Jim for support.
We attracted a crowd of Daily players.
The three of us made an unusual sight.
I turned so Dad would sign his name using my back as a table.

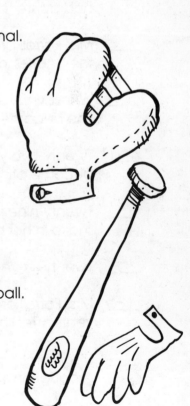

Name _____

This Is Your Life!

Principal's Day is this week. All of the classes are doing something special for their principal, Mrs. Farrell. The fifth grade decided to do a "This Is Your Life" type of skit. In order to do this, they had to ask Mrs. Farrell a lot of questions.

Help the fifth graders put the information below into chronological order. **Note:** Read all of the clues before you begin. This will help you determine the years in which the events happened.

____ Mrs. Farrell gave birth to triplet sons two years after she and Mr. Farrell got married.

____ Twenty-five years after Mrs. Farrell was born, she got the chicken pox for the first time with her sons.

____ Mrs. Farrell was born in 1951 in Dukwilma. She has a brother two years older than her and a sister one year younger.

____ Mrs. Farrell broke her arm rollerblading with her sons three years after she tried to kill the "snake" in her backyard.

____ When Mrs. Farrell was 9, she and her family went on a vacation to the Grand Canyon. She became lost, and the rangers had to search for her.

____ Twenty-two years after she tripped on the steps at her graduation, Mrs. Farrell became principal of Dukwilma Elementary.

____ Twenty-nine years after Mrs. Farrell became lost in the Grand Canyon, she tried to kill a snake in her backyard that turned out to be a stick.

____ Twenty-six years before she became principal, Mrs. Farrell married Mr. Farrell.

____ Mrs. Farrell organized the first "Kids Are Great Day" at Dukwilma Elementary twenty years after she married Mr. Farrell.

____ Mrs. Farrell tripped on the steps going up to receive her diploma at her high school graduation 18 years after she was born.

•SOMETHING EXTRA• Make a time line of your life in chronological order.

Name _____

It's All a Matter of Timing

Use the time line to circle the correct event in each numbered pair.

Which happens first?

1. Omri travels through the chest *or* Bright Stars shows her infant to the villagers

2. The tepee begins to burn *or* Patrick returns to the present

3. The villagers pack to leave *or* an owl call is heard

4. The Algonquins build a large fire *or* the baby is born

5. Bright Stars leaves with the villagers *or* Patrick travels through the chest

Which happens last?

1. Bright Stars shows her infant *or* the baby is born

2. An owl call is heard *or* Boone notices he is in the Iroquois village

3. Omri travels through the chest *or* Boone fires his revolver

4. The tepee begins to burn *or* the villagers pack

5. Patrick returns to the present *or* the Algonquins build a fire

Time Line

Start

— Patrick travels through the chest with Boone and Bright Stars.

— The baby is born.

— Patrick returns to the present.

— Omri travels through the chest.

— Boone notices he is in the Iroquois village.

— Bright Stars shows her infant to the villagers.

— The villagers pack to leave.

— Bright Stars and the baby leave with the villagers.

— An owl call is heard.

— The Algonquins build a large fire.

— The tepee begins to burn.

— Boone fires his revolver.

End

Name _____

Get the Facts, Max

Skim this paragraph to answer the questions below.

The islands of Aruba, Bonaire and Curacao, sometimes known as the ABC islands, are part of the Netherlands Antilles. They lie 50 miles north off the coast of Venezuela. Three more islands, Saint Eustatius, Saba and Saint Martin (the northern half of which belongs to France), are approximately 500 miles northeast of the ABC islands.

Until 1949 the islands were known as the Dutch West Indies or "Curacao Territory." In 1986 Aruba separated to become a self-governing part of the Netherlands realm.

On the island of Curacao most food is imported. Because it is so rocky, little farming is possible. The island is the largest and most heavily populated of the Netherlands Antilles. Its oil refineries, among the largest in the world, give its people a relatively high standard of living. Today most people of Curacao work either in the shipping, refining or tourist industry.

Netherlands Antilles – Other Facts

Area

Aruba	75	square miles
Bonaire	111	square miles
Curacao	171	square miles
Saba	5	square miles
Saint Eustatius	11	square miles
Saint Martin	13	square miles

Capital
   Willemstad

Major Languages
   Dutch, Papiamento (a mixture of Spanish, Dutch, Portuguese, Carib and English), English, Spanish

---

1. Name the capital of the Netherlands Antilles. _____

2. What industry gives the people a high standard of living? _____

3. Name the ABC islands. _____

4. What is Papiamento? _____

5. Why must food be imported to Curacao? _____

6. Which island is smallest? _____

7. Which two islands are the largest? _____

8. Which island belongs in part to France? _____

9. In what year did Aruba become self-governing? _____

Name _____

Deep Magic

Fill in the missing letters to complete each word.

Meanings	Words
a slow, ignorant person	D __ __ __ E
to go at some risk	V __ __ __ __ __ E
to regard with excessive satisfaction	G __ __ __ T
musty	F __ __ __ __ __ Y
a stimulating liquid	C __ __ __ __ __ __ L
a pest	V __ __ __ N
a member of a council	C __ __ __ __ __ __ __ __ R
a coniferous tree which sheds its needles yearly	L __ __ __ H
to move restlessly	F __ __ __ __ T
slender	L __ __ __ E
an evergreen shrub with flat, dark green needles	Y __ W
a man-eating giant	O __ __ E
to give up	F __ __ __ __ __ T
to desire	C __ __ __ E
a type of early spring flower	C __ __ __ __ S
a poisonous mushroom	T __ __ __ __ __ __ __ L

Find each word in the puzzle.

```
C G S V E N T U R E
O R C Y M T A O L G
U L O O T S D A O T
N V I C R S Y A L E
C N T T U D W L H G
I O I D H S E O C D
L D E M U E Y U R I
L W F O R N A O A F
O G R E M E C B L N
R S O C R A V E I G
T U F L A I D R O C
```

Name _____

Sing of Change

Read the clues and fill in the blanks using the words in the Word Bank. Then decipher the code below.

Word Bank
bestial
caper
indigo
plumage
abeyance
predator
engulf
annex
totem
hostile
resonant
wax
aurora
wrest
cauldron
advent
preen
plaintive
crescendo
frigid

Clues

meat-eating hunter — — — — — — — —
             10

dark blue — — — — — —
            8

increase in volume — — — — — — — — — —
                 20

primp — — — — —
   17

unfriendly — — — — — — —
   4

brutal — — — — — — —
    7

temporary inaction — — — — — — — —
        14

confiscate — — — — —
  1

large kettle — — — — — — — —
      12

sorrowful — — — — — — — — —
      13

feathers — — — — — — —
    6

freezing — — — — — —
 11

northern lights — — — — — —
 15

spirit symbol — — — — —
    16

arrival — — — — — —
    3

grow — — —
 21

addition — — — — —
  5

rich, lasting sound — — — — — — — —
     18

overwhelm — — — — — —
    2

antic — — — — —
    19

— — —   — — — — — — — — — —   — — —   — — — — — — — —
16 4 7   18 17 13 19 13 16 18   20 11   16 4 7   15 5 13 6 15 12 18

— — —   — — — — — — —   — — — —.
15 19 7   17 15 18 18 13 5 8   15 1 15 14

— — —   — — — — — —   — — —   — — — — —   — — —
16 4 7   4 20 2 19 20 11   16 4 7   1 20 12 11   15 5 10   16 4 7

— K — — —   — — — — —.
7 18 13 6 20   13 18 20 3 7 19

Name _____

A Terrific Idea

Complete the crossword with words from the Word Bank.

Word Bank

finicky	feud	smug	vigorously	skeptically	misanthrope
lash	gimpy	dodo	shamble	accomplish	kingdom come
conch	pinto	raspy	cornucopia	disheveled	bittersweet
garret	groom	deter	waddle	bungalow	freehand

Across
2. to bind with a cord or string
6. energetically
10. to walk awkwardly, sloppily
12. fussy
14. with a harsh, irritating sound
16. a large, clumsy bird now extinct
18. house space just below a sloping roof; attic
20. horn-shaped container which represents a very good harvest
21. to walk like a duck
22. done by hand, without the aid of devices
23. disorderly

Down
1. to clean and brush
3. to succeed in doing
4. with a limp
5. a one-story home
7. to hinder
8. afterlife
9. one who hates humans
10. doubtfully
11. a plant with red seeds
13. a spotted horse
15. a large, spiral seashell
17. self-satisfied (complacent or self-righteous)
19. lasting conflict

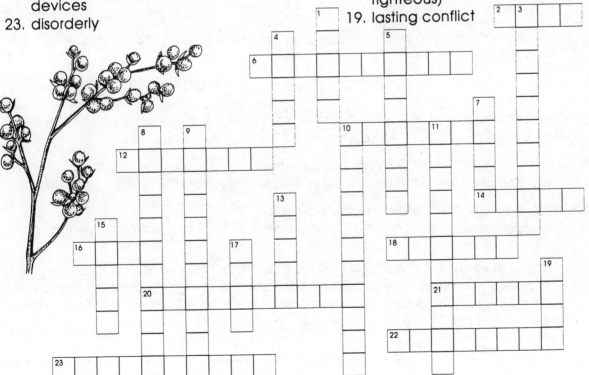

Score Chore

Name _____

Circle the phrase which you feel best completes each statement. You may want to check your work with a dictionary.

1. If Miyax's ulo is *versatile*, it . . .
   can do many tasks.   is made of bone.   must be a complex tool.

2. If the wolf pups are *tawny*, they must have . . .
   glossy coats.   well-formed muscles.   tan coloring.

3. If Miyax's stew has a *savory* smell, it . . .
   should be thrown out.   is very pleasing.   is hot enough.

4. When the sun has reached its *apogee*, it . . .
   can go no higher.   is just above the horizon.   cannot be seen.

5. When the adult wolves *regurgitate* food, they . . .
   belch.   swallow loudly.   spit it up.

6. Miyax *quelled* her feelings of despair, and she . . .
   panicked.   could not sleep.   quieted down.

7. Because the wolf pup's tail was *conspicuous*, the young girl . . .
   cut it off.   feared he was ill.   could find him.

8. When wolf calls *undulate*, they . . .
   move up and down in pitch.   create disturbances.   take turns.

9. If Miyax *solicits* for food, she is . . .
   asking earnestly.   hunting vigorously.   searching frantically.

10. The wolves glanced *warily* at Miyax, because they . . .
    were hungry.   were tired.   were cautious.

11. If you dig into the *permafrost*, you will certainly find . . .
    a natural refrigerator.   ancient Viking artifacts.   bones of the wooly mammoth.

12. If Jello is an *incorrigible* creature, he must be . . .
    a vicious and bloodthirsty monster.   a weakling.   impossible to change.

Scoring: If you guessed 1-4 phrases correctly, you are a "likeable lemming." If you guessed 5-7 correctly, you become a "brave bunting." If you are fortunate to have guessed 8-10 correctly you earn the title "fabulous fox." Those with scores of 11 or 12 are "wondersome wolves."

Score _____   **Title** _____

Name ____________________

Don't Be a Sissy

What is the most frightening spot in Learning? Complete the puzzle and read down the darkened row of boxes to find out.

Clues

1. highly agitated
2. impossible to read
3. showing proper manners
4. spirit, pluck
5. a celebration
6. pertaining to the stomach
7. nearly
8. to take more than one's share
9. tobacco juice container
10. aromatic seed of a tropical tree
11. to pretend
12. a difficult problem
13. sharp, irritating smell
14. a mischievous adventure
15. shabby, worthless
16. order of importance
17. to escape
18. generously, freely
19. long chat
20. brownish yellow
21. heavy
22. rough, disorderly
23. stealthy action

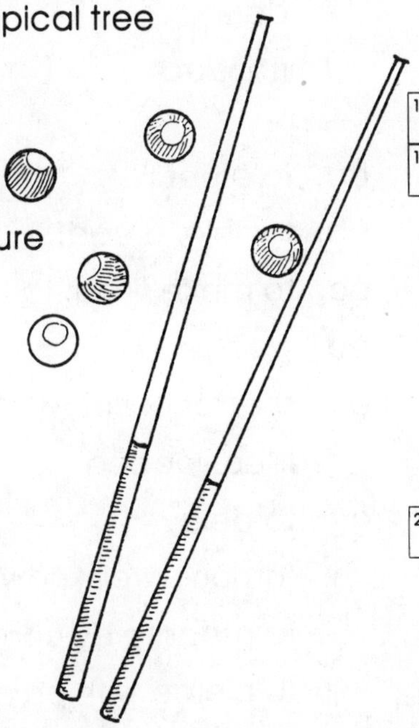

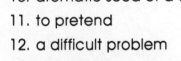

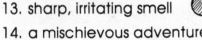

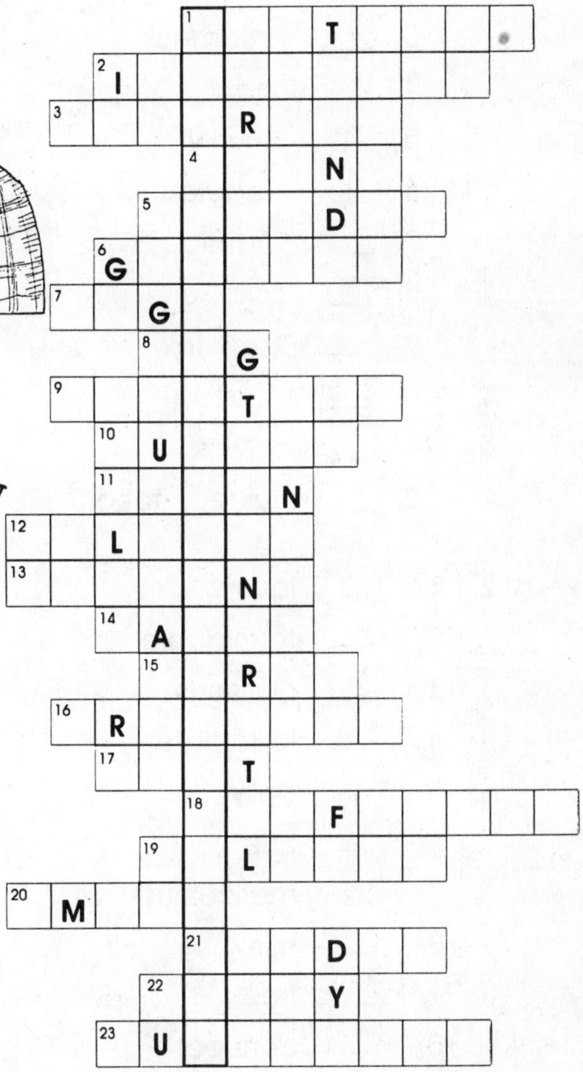
1 T
2 I
3 R
4 N
5 D
6 G
7 G
8 G
9 T
10 U
11 N
12 L
13 N
14 A
15 R
16 R
17 T
18 F
19 L
20 M
21 D
22 Y
23 U

Word Bank

priority	amber	pungent	spittoon	feign
rowdy	spunk	dilemma	furtively	bolt
decorous	shindig	palaver	nutmeg	hog
caper	nigh	profusely	seething	sorry
gastric	illegible	leaden		

With Little Tea and Just Rice for All

Match each word on the left with its meaning on the right.

List 1

1. ___ emanate
2. ___ torso
3. ___ infamous
4. ___ hoist
5. ___ murky
6. ___ regale
7. ___ frantic
8. ___ crimson
9. ___ kow-tow
10. ___ oust
11. ___ civics
12. ___ pigeon-toed

a. to show deep respect or to bow
b. to entertain
c. the trunk of the body
d. to lift
e. deep red
f. with toes turned inward
g. the study of government
h. to proceed, go out
i. to force out
j. having a terrible reputation
k. dark
l. frenzied

List 2

1. ___ jaunty
2. ___ formidable
3. ___ illustrious
4. ___ intimidate
5. ___ dally
6. ___ hue
7. ___ meticulous
8. ___ spew
9. ___ frail
10. ___ concoct
11. ___ fraught
12. ___ spike

aa. to erupt
bb. terrible, dreadful
cc. to make timid; to threaten
dd. weak
ee. a color or tint
ff. filled, loaded
gg. to delay
hh. famous, well-known
ii. to prepare by combining diverse ingredients
jj. to pierce with points
kk. lively or sporty
ll. careful, attending to details

Challenge: On another sheet of paper, write a sentence using four of the words from the lists above. Then draw a picture which illustrates your sentence. For example: The *jaunty* young man with a *crimson* umbrella was *formidable* as he *ousted* the mosquitoes from the room.

Name _____

Put a Minotaur in Your Tank

Decode the names of creatures. Then use a dictionary to match the names with their meanings.

a. _____ ____ a creature with a man's upper body but a horse's body and legs

b. _____ ____ a ghost

c. _____ ____ the leader of the satyrs; a chubby old man with pointed ears

d. _____ ____ a river nymph

e. _____ ____ a faun; woodland god or demon

f. _____ ____ a small, evil spirit

g. _____ ____ a creature with a man's body and bull's head

h. _____ ____ a creature with human body but ears, tail and hindlegs of a goat

i. _____ ____ a sea nymph whose song lures sailors to wreck their ships

j. _____ ____ any nature goddess

k. _____ ____ a horse-like creature with one horn coming out from its forehead

l. _____ ____ the god of wine and merrymaking

m. _____ ____ an evil grave-robbing spirit

n. _____ ____ a creature with an eagle's head and wings and a lion's body

o. _____ ____ a man-eating giant

p. _____ ____ a wood nymph

One of a Kind

Name _____

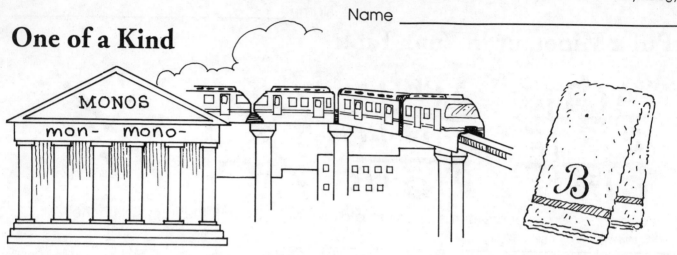

The prefixes **mon-** and **mono-** come from the Greek word **monos** which means *one, alone,* or *single.* Write the correct word from the Word Box in each sentence below.

Word Box

monarchy	monarch	monastery	monologue
monocle	monogram	monolingual	monolithic
monopolize	monorail	monosyllabic	monotone

1. Queen Elizabeth is the _____ of England.

2. Our city has a high-speed _____ train.

3. Uncle Ralph wears a _____ on one eye.

4. The lecture was boring because the speaker spoke in a _____ .

5. One, two, and three are examples of _____ words.

6. A monk lives a religious life in a _____ .

7. Betsy will embroider her _____ on the towels.

8. I don't want to _____ all of your time, but will you go to the museum with me?

9. The United States has never been a _____ like some European countries.

10. The _____ structure stands in the center of the town square.

11. Gail is _____ – she speaks only English.

12. The actor's _____ was absolutely spellbinding.

Name _____

Add-a-Letter

Make new words by adding a letter from the Letter Bank
to each word below. The letter may be added anywhere.

Letter Bank
c e e g h i l m
n r t t u u v w

Word	Letter	New Word	Clue
Example: room	g	groom	to brush
1. sob	—	_____	one who looks down on others as inferior
2. pro	—	_____	a formal school dance
3. save	—	_____	wooden strip forming the side of a barrel
4. beet	—	_____	a soft, flat cap
5. ringer	—	_____	a machine for squeezing out water
6. hears	—	_____	the vehicle which carries the dead
7. trade	—	_____	a scolding speech
8. state	—	_____	that which a person owns
9. diver	—	_____	to turn aside from a course
10. action	—	_____	a sale in which items go to highest bidder
11. oat	—	_____	a promise
12. ape	—	_____	a point of land which juts into the water
13. fare	—	_____	to burst into flame or activity
14. arose	—	_____	to excite
15. aid	—	_____	eager

Guidelines

Name _____

For each search word below fill in the circle by the correct guide word pair.

Search Words	Guide Word Pairs		
1. pick	○ piece/pigpen	○ pheasant/picture	○ pinch/pink
2. woolly	○ wooden/wordy	○ with/wonky	○ which/wild
3. villain	○ veto/vinegar	○ volcano/vulcan	○ valiant/vapor
4. withdrew	○ warble/web	○ whittle/wizard	○ weekly/weigh
5. impress	○ imperfect/import	○ implore/impulse	○ ideal/ill
6. crooked	○ collide/crib	○ chalk/clear	○ creep/croquet
7. lobby	○ livery/lob	○ long/lotus	○ loathe/logjam
8. bewildered	○ bent/bike	○ belly/beret	○ bewitch/bid
9. welfare	○ wharf/winter	○ weir/west	○ warrior/weevil
10. penitentiary	○ physics/pickerel	○ pelt/penguin	○ peddler/penny
11. privet	○ poncho/private	○ people/phony	○ privateer/prune
12. intermediate	○ immigrant/invent	○ issue/ivory	○ ilk/immediate
13. coordinator	○ crop/cupola	○ contract/coronet	○ conduct/console
14. contribution	○ consider/coop	○ count/crease	○ chum/cog
15. bazaar	○ barbecue/batter	○ bacteria/band	○ bay/bean
16. ancestor	○ along/antic	○ ace/acting	○ antique/apart
17. resin	○ rend/rhubarb	○ rectangle/reflect	○ rewind/roomy
18. manger	○ margin/material	○ mangy/mantel	○ man/manicure
19. fresh	○ fierce/flip	○ freight/fuddle	○ forage/freeze
20. program	○ pathetic/pavilion	○ piffle/platypus	○ preside/pucker
21. insane	○ inhabit/instant	○ invalid/ion	○ impartial/Inca
22. traction	○ temper/that	○ touch/train	○ tin/toothache

Write three sentences using some of the above words.

_____

_____

_____

Name _____

Dictionary Pitch

Below each sentence are three guide word pairs. Circle the pair which would be on the same page as the underlined word.

1. "That was some pitch," croaked Monk <u>approvingly</u>.

   archangel/arctic   apprehension/aptitude   apocryphal/apostrophe

2. I had three <u>autographed</u> baseballs in my hospital room.

   Austria/avail   attach/audible   auk/auspices

3. Dad might have blown his <u>stack</u> if Larry continued to pester him.

   stalk/stampede   staple/starve   stab/stagger

4. We drove up the <u>winding</u> driveway to our new house.

   whine/widow   wimble/wink   wise/witness

5. To loosen up my arm, I <u>lobbed</u> the ball to Monk.

   longhand/lore   llama/loch   lode/longevity

6. The force of the throw <u>bowled</u> him over.

   boundary/box   boxwood/breathe   boon/bough

7. Monk <u>grimaced</u> as he shook his glove hand in pain.

   grill/grotto   gratuity/grenadier   gridiron/griffin

8. My dad is a <u>geology</u> professor at the university.

   general/genteel   gentle/geranium   gesture/gimlet

9. Wilson Dairy would need a huge <u>rally</u> to win this game.

   radiator/ragged   ragman/rajah   rake/random

10. Larry and I were being <u>unreasonable</u> with Mom and Dad that day.

    unveil/urn   unpack/unseat   unseen/unto

Use a dictionary to write the guide words for each of these words.

Name of dictionary _____

squat	_____	pronouncement _____
maneuver	_____	fraternity _____
agenda	_____	microphone _____

Name _____

Where's the Key?

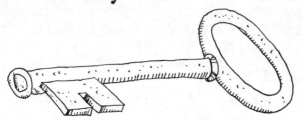

Underline the key word in each question. Then write the encyclopedia volume number you would use to answer each one.

A	B	C-Ch	Ci Cz	D-E	F	G	H	I	J-K	L	M	N-O	P	Q-R	S-Sn	So-Sz	T	U-V	W-Z
1	2	3	4	5	6	7	8	9	10	11	12	13	14	15	16	17	18	19	20

1. Where are the jaeger's nesting grounds?   _____

2. What land masses are found along the Chukchi Sea?   _____

3. How is peat created and what is it used for?   _____

4. For how long will a wolf nurse her young?   _____

5. What materials are used in the construction of a kayak?   _____

6. What plants are found in a tundra region?   _____

7. What product is Alaska's chief export?   _____

8. What other name is given to reindeer?   _____

9. Is the igloo the most common home for Eskimos?   _____

10. How far does the Brook's Range extend?   _____

11. What are the wolf's greatest weapons?   _____

12. Why is Barrow, Alaska, an important town?   _____

13. What is the life expectancy of a lemming?   _____

14. Are caribou found in Uruguay?   _____

15. How are mosquitoes able to survive in the Arctic?   _____

Challenge   Use an encyclopedia index to find as many references as possible for one of these topics. Then write a report.

gray wolf	Alaskan history	Eskimo clothing	kayak	caribou
lemming	Eskimo housing (past and present)		seals of the Arctic	
Alaskan hunting methods (past and present)			Alaskan pipeline	

A Sleuth for Truth

Name _____

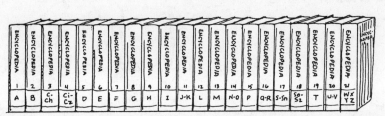

Underline the key word in each sentence and write the encyclopedia volume number you would use to answer these questions.

____ 1. When did children first practice trick-or-treating on Halloween?

____ 2. How did chocolate become a common treat?

____ 3. Which poisons affect the nervous system?

____ 4. What is a vampire?

____ 5. What are the dangers associated with barbiturates?

____ 6. What are the rules for soccer?

____ 7. How does catnip taste?

____ 8. What is the largest city on the continent of Africa?

____ 9. How long have pumpkins grown in North America?

____ 10. What are the eight phases of the moon?

____ 11. How many different kinds of teeth are there?

____ 12. Where are Brussels sprouts best grown, and what is their nutritional value?

____ 13. When were witches first persecuted in the United States?

____ 14. From what story does the name "jack-o'-lantern" come?

Challenge: On another sheet, form nine different words using these letters:

H A L L O W E E N

Flowers 'R Us

Name _____

Use the index to answer the questions.

Index

African violet
care – 16
watering – 17
disease – 18
insects – 20
light – 22

begonia
disease – 32
light – 31
pruning – 33
watering – 35

gladiolus
breeding – 46
disease – 47
harvesting – 48
history – 50
watering and weeding – 48-49

larkspur
coloration – 67
history – 68
stem length – 66

petunia
light – 83
planting time – 85
use in vertical gardening – 83-84

rose
harvesting – 100
history – 105
insects and disease – 101-102
nutrition and watering – 99
pruning – 103

What page would you turn to if you wish to research . . .

1. the history of the larkspur? _____
2. how much water an African violet requires? _____
3. the diseases common to the gladiolus plant? _____
4. how to prune roses? _____
5. how to create a vertical garden for petunias? _____
6. insect problems of the African violet? _____
7. the lighting needed for begonia care and growth? _____
8. the problems with breeding gladioli? _____
9. nutritional needs of the rosebush? _____
10. where the larkspur originated? _____

Challenge Research two of the flowering plants given in the index. Draw pictures showing the parts of each. Then state one important fact about each one.

Name _____

Help Me!

Circle the reference book you would use to answer each question.

1. Which source would you use to learn to make flapjacks?
   a. dictionary   b. atlas   c. cookbook

2. Which source might show you where Treegap is?
   a. dictionary   b. atlas   c. thesaurus

3. Which source would describe the peacock?
   a. book on insects   b. encyclopedia   c. newspaper

4. Which source would tell you about the sounds a cricket makes?
   a. book on insects   b. thesaurus   c. atlas

5. Which source would give the meaning of "constable"?
   a. newspaper   b. dictionary   c. atlas

6. Which source would tell about the most recent world events?
   a. newspaper   b. encyclopedia   c. thesaurus

7. Which source would tell you how to divide "accommodations" into syllables?
   a. thesaurus   b. book on insects   c. dictionary

8. Which source could give you a synonym for "push"?
   a. thesaurus   b. cookbook   c. encyclopedia

9. Which source might describe what a trout eats?
   a. encyclopedia   b. cookbook   c. atlas

10. Which source might best forecast tomorrow's weather?
    a. encyclopedia   b. atlas   c. newspaper

Challenge   Use sources from school or home to answer the following questions:

Which countries border Nepal?

Answer: _____

Source: _____

Page #: _____

What are the headlines in today's paper?

Answer: _____

Source: _____

Page #: _____

Name _____

The Right Stuff

Circle the resource book you would use to find . . .

1. A recipe for baking homemade bread –
   encyclopedia   cookbook   *The Life of a Beaver*

2. A description of how beavers make dams –
   almanac   *The Life of a Beaver*   *The Guinness Book of World Records*

3. Another word for "route" –
   thesaurus   math textbook   world atlas

4. A map of the United Kingdom –
   thesaurus   world atlas   *The Guinness Book of World Records*

5. The ingredients for Turkish Delight –
   The Life of a Beaver   world atlas   cookbook

6. The difference between a muffler and a mantle –
   dictionary   science textbook   cookbook

7. Information about the author, C.S. Lewis –
   almanac   encyclopedia   *Guidebook for Art Instructors*

8. The membership of major world religions –
   math textbook   almanac   cookbook

9. Which is the world's most massive dam –
   The Guinness Book of World Records   dictionary   thesaurus

10. The oldest words in the English language –
    almanac   atlas   *The Guinness Book of World Records*

11. Another word for "trouble" –
    almanac   cookbook   thesaurus

12. Why a beaver slaps its tail –
    dictionary   *The Life of a Beaver*   atlas

13. The pronunciation of "courtier" –
    The Hobbit   dictionary   almanac

14. What camphor is used for –
    dictionary   *The Life of a Beaver*   thesaurus

15. What land is closest to England –
    atlas   cookbook   spelling workbook

16. How to bake trout –
    The Life of a Beaver   dictionary   cookbook

Name _____

Day of Reckoning

At what time does Paul ask for his mirror?_____

Which happens first? Do Red and Paul shake hands or does Paul greet Toddy?

_____

What is the earliest time shown on the time line?_____

Which happens last? Does Brophy give Paul his medication or does the game begin?

_____

What is the final score of the game?_____

At what time does the game end?_____

When do Brophy and Paul's dad get Paul back into bed?_____

How many Dairy players walk in the 4th inning?_____

In the 4th inning which happens first? Does Jim walk or does Tip hit a home run?

_____

How many hours does this time line cover? Be careful!_____

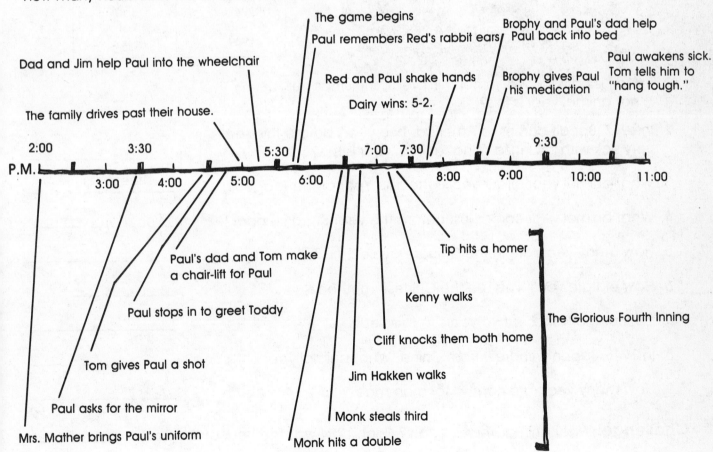

Name _____

What Year Is It?

Use the information on this page to answer the questions below. Answer the questions using the Chinese name for the year.

The Chinese calendar works in 12-year cycles. The first year is the Year of the Rat; the last is the Year of the Boar.

Because the Chinese use cycles of the moon to set up their calendars, New Year's Day does not fall on January 1 every year as it does with the Western calendar. It falls somewhere between mid-January and mid-February.

In Chinese thinking, a person is a year old when born and gains another year when the New Year arrives.

Western Year	Chinese Name of the Year
1936	Rat
1937	Ox
1938	Tiger
1939	Rabbit
1940	Dragon
1941	Snake
1942	Horse
1943	Sheep
1944	Monkey
1945	Rooster
1946	Dog
1947	Boar
1948	Rat
1949	Ox

1. Bandit is born in 1938. In her third year, she stubs her toe. What animal year is this? _____

2. In 1947, Bandit comes to America. Two years before this, she is very sick with influenza. What animal year is this? _____

3. What animal year is four years after the Year of the Dragon? _____

4. What animal year comes just before the year Bandit is born? _____

5. How many years are in the Chinese cycle? _____

6. How old are you if you use the Chinese method? _____

7. Year of the Horse + two years − five years = _____

8. In 1945, Japan withdrew from China. What animal year is this? _____

9. How many years are named for mammals? _____

Challenge: What animal year is it now? (Hint: 1984 was the Year of the Rat.) _____

Name _____

"My Country, 'Tis of Thee"

Choose a country. Review and write down some of the outstanding characteristics of this land.

_____

_____

_____

_____

_____

_____

_____

_____

A tanka is made up of 31 syllables in five lines. The syllabic scheme is as follows:

River Life
The Nile streams northward   (5 syllables)
It carries life to Egypt   (7 syllables)
The Nile is our life   (5 syllables)
We will live because of it   (7 syllables)
We will grow in its goodness   (7 syllables)

Now write your own. Take one main idea from your notes (such as your country's beauty) and fashion it into a tanka.

Title _____

_____

_____

_____

_____

_____

Name _____

Write Away

The title of an acrostic poem is printed in a column on the left. Each letter is used as the first letter of a phrase or sentence which describes the title. For example:

Birdbath

B ehemoth-like concrete object
I n which birds soak.
R ather peculiar purchase item and
D ifficult to haul home in Mother's taxi.
B ought by fringed and beaded
A unt Mildred whose
T axi was already full with
H er other market purchases.

Write an acrostic poem using one of the topics given here.

Young Chauffeur	Baby Talk	Parade Day	Tandem Bicycle
Prize Winner	Flower Shows	A Drink of Worms	Beetle Eater

(Title) _____

_____ _____
_____ _____
_____ _____
_____ _____
_____ _____
_____ _____
_____ _____
_____ _____
_____ _____
_____ _____
_____ _____
_____ _____
_____ _____
_____ _____

Name _____

LANGUAGE ARTS

See the Islands

Research an island of the Caribbean. Then make a travel brochure to convince others that they should visit your island. Include photos or illustrations and descriptions of places to visit, with a map of the island. Last give phone numbers to call for travel information, history and interesting facts.

Tourist Attractions
include:

COME TO
BEAUTIFUL

_____

FOR FURTHER info, call:

Name _____

The Home Front

Imagine being involved in the following war-time situations. Read each section and answer the questions.

1. Imagine you live on a farm. Because the armed forces need so much food, farms are asked to produce large quantities. Citizens are only permitted to buy a certain amount of meat. There is such a food shortage that "price ceilings" are used to keep food affordable. One day a stranger arrives on your farm and offers you twice as much money for three cows as you can get in the market. It is illegal for you to sell him the beef at these prices, but you could use the money. What do you do?

_____

_____

_____

2. Your family is permitted to drive 140 miles per month. Your parents work together at a factory 23 days each month. What changes in lifestyle will you have to make?

factory - 5 miles round trip   grocery store   - 1 mile round trip
school - 1 mile round trip (no bus) place of worship - 2 miles round trip
beach - 16 miles round trip   movie theater - 1 mile round trip

_____

_____

_____

3. Why did the U.S. government ban the production of all new cars in late January, 1942? Why do you think the speed limit was set at 35 miles per hour?

_____

_____

4. After Japan took possession of the islands of the East Indies, the U.S. could obtain only about 8% of the natural rubber that it needed. If you were in Congress, what laws would you pass to be certain to have enough rubber for your war industry and still be fair to the country's citizens?

_____

_____

_____

Name _____

Create a Constellation!

For centuries, stargazers have made pictures by connecting the stars with imaginary lines. Many of these pictures were based on stories about gods and mythology. Over the years, many groups of people saw the same groups of stars as the same constellation, but gave it different shapes, names and stories.

The star pattern on this page is an actual constellation. Connect the stars in a new configuration to create your own unique constellation. Give the new constellation a title, and write your own story about it.

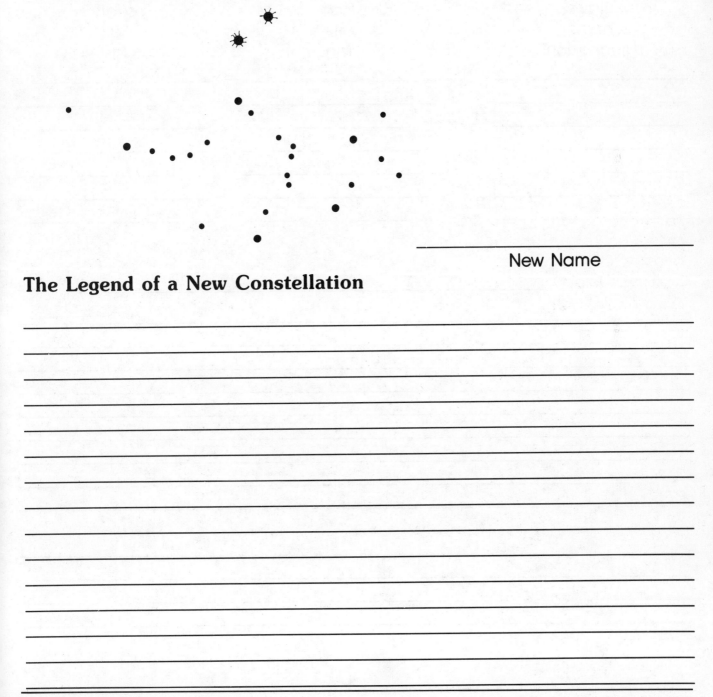

New Name _____

The Legend of a New Constellation

_____
_____
_____
_____
_____
_____
_____
_____
_____
_____
_____
_____
_____
_____

Creative Cretaceous Writing

Study the dinosaurs that lived during the Cretaceous Period. Complete the lists of words below that you associate with these dinosaurs. Then use the words to compose a poem or short story about these dinosaurs. A few examples are given under each heading to get you started. You may write your own compositions or share your ideas with other students and write a group composition. Then, read your composition to the class.

Nouns	Verbs	Adjectives
claws	roar	scaly
horns	bite	tall
Iguanodon	run	fast

Title: _____

_____

Name _____

Ghostly Problems

What do you call a noisy ghost? Follow the directions below to find out.

1. Put an A above number 2 if 31,842 rounded to the nearest thousand is 31,000.

2. Put an E above number 8 if 62 rounded to the nearest ten is 60.

3. Put an S above number 10 if 4,234 rounded to the nearest hundred is 4,200.

4. Put an L above number 3 if 677 rounded to the nearest hundred is 700.

5. Put an E above number 5 if 345 rounded to the nearest ten is 350.

6. Put an A above number 9 if 5,499 rounded to the nearest thousand is 6,000.

7. Put a B above number 1 if 94 rounded to the nearest ten is 100.

8. Put an O above number 2 if 885 rounded to the nearest hundred is 900.

9. Put a T above number 11 if 521 rounded to the nearest ten is 520.

10. Put an R above number 6 if 76 rounded to the nearest ten is 80.

11. Put an I above number 9 if 3,291 rounded to the nearest thousand is 3,000.

12. Put a T above number 4 if 258 rounded to the nearest hundred is 300.

13. Put a T above number 7 if 615 rounded to the nearest ten is 610.

14. Put a P above number 1 if 198 rounded to the nearest hundred is 200.

15. Put a G above number 7 if 6,817 rounded to the nearest thousand is 7,000.

___ ___ ___ ___ ___ ___ ___ ___ ___ ___ ___
 1   2   3   4   5   6   7   8   9 10 11

Name _____

Rounding to Skull Island

Shade correctly rounded answers to find the path to Skull Island.

9999 1000	7659 9000	6650 6000	239 300	9764 8000	4596 4000	9327 9000	3794 2000
3653 4000	5931 6000	5100 5000	4398 4000	8781 9000	59589 60000	3479 3000	6743 8000
7010 7000	3426 4000	7900 6000	4533 4000	9700 9000	1234 2000	6349 7000	4576 4000
2395 2000	1876 2000	6289 6000	2895 3000	16793 20000	1324 1000	55721 60000	87888 90000
9746 1000	3625 5000	3296 4000	5697 4000	7896 9000	4567 4000	8235 9000	27681 30000
92116 90000	7759 8000	66656 70000			2975 1000	76950 70000	751 800
63825 60000	237 300	5235 6000			2975 2000	1099 2000	8479 8000
31326 30000	1097 100	7659 7000	89657 80000	3974 3000	7695 9000	3265 2000	18618 20000
9191 9000	6253 7000	421 400	6667 7000	4989 5000	965 100	7543 7000	396 400
7861 8000	8235 9000	92381 90000	367 300	23515 20000	73921 70000	52352 50000	35479 40000
333 300	3457 4000	563 600	6295 7000	4325 5000	9234 10000	765 700	4326 5000
793 800	42431 40000	77216 80000	3279 4000	1099 2000	4976 4000	7695 7000	6959 6000

Name _____

Average Shelters

Find the average score for each group of numbers.

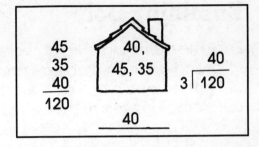

45
35
40
120

40,
45, 35

40
3⟌120

40

202,85
172

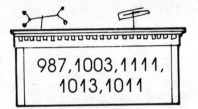

987,1003,1111,
1013,1011

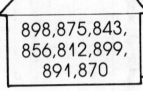

898,875,843,
856,812,899,
891,870

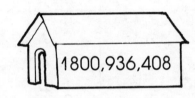

1800,936,408

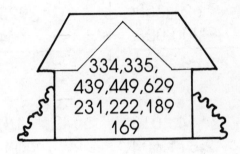

334,335,
439,449,629
231,222,189
169

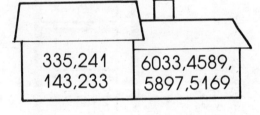

335,241
143,233

6033,4589,
5897,5169

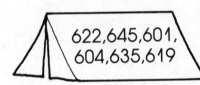

622,645,601,
604,635,619

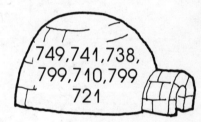

749,741,738,
799,710,799
721

185,167,95
125,59,154,146

536,584,555,
525,563,548,
585,464,

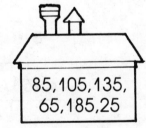

85,105,135,
65,185,25

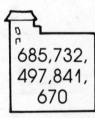

685,732,
497,841,
670

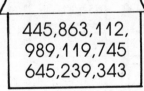

445,863,112,
989,119,745
645,239,343

1005,995,
1010,998,
992

11,45,83,55,
69,74,3,12,
16,22

799,739,941,
899,845,697,
1045,955

Name _____

Bumbling Bob

Bob, the bumbling burglar, wants to get up this fire escape to pull a heist. Solve the following addition problems and shade in the answers on the ladder. If any numbers are not shaded when all the problems have been done, Bob gets caught while going up. Some answers may not be on the ladder.

1.
$$\begin{array}{r} 986,145 \\ 621,332 \\ +\ 200,008 \\ \hline \end{array}$$

2.
$$\begin{array}{r} 1,873,402 \\ 925,666 \\ +\ \quad 4,689 \\ \hline \end{array}$$

3.
$$\begin{array}{r} 506,328 \\ 886,510 \\ +\ 342,225 \\ \hline \end{array}$$

4.
$$\begin{array}{r} 43,015 \\ 2,811,604 \\ +\ \quad 987,053 \\ \hline \end{array}$$

5.
$$\begin{array}{r} 18,443 \\ 300,604 \\ +\ 999,999 \\ \hline \end{array}$$

6.
$$\begin{array}{r} 8,075 \\ 14,608 \\ +\ 33,914 \\ \hline \end{array}$$

7.
$$\begin{array}{r} 9,162 \\ 7,804 \\ +\ 755,122 \\ \hline \end{array}$$

8.
$$\begin{array}{r} 88,714 \\ 213,653 \\ +\ 5,441,298 \\ \hline \end{array}$$

9.
$$\begin{array}{r} 3,244,662 \\ 1,986,114 \\ +\ \quad 521,387 \\ \hline \end{array}$$

10.
$$\begin{array}{r} 4,581 \\ 22,983 \\ +\ 5,618,775 \\ \hline \end{array}$$

11.
$$\begin{array}{r} 818,623 \\ 926 \\ +\ 3,260,004 \\ \hline \end{array}$$

12.
$$\begin{array}{r} 80,436 \\ 9,159 \\ +\ 3,028,761 \\ \hline \end{array}$$

13.
$$\begin{array}{r} 25,004 \\ 862,010 \\ +\ \quad 9,302 \\ \hline \end{array}$$

14.
$$\begin{array}{r} 5,043,666 \\ 4,589,771 \\ +\ 8,711,229 \\ \hline \end{array}$$

15.
$$\begin{array}{r} 432,188 \\ 900,000 \\ +\ 611,042 \\ \hline \end{array}$$

Ladder:
- 1,319,046
- 2,803,757
- 5,743,665
- 3,118,356
- 56,597
- 4,079,553
- 1,807,485
- 2,943,230
- 18,344,666
- 1,735,063
- 5,752,163
- 896,316
- 3,841,672
- 5,646,339

Does Bob make it? _____

Name _____

We Can Do It!

Add.

1.	508,209	2.	986,412	3.	870,304	4.	7,007,421
	41,642		79,843		90,427		3,900,340
	9,021		2,764		8,002		740,070
	100		963		734		5,422,009
+	395	+	229	+	895	+	7,080

5.	305,208	6.	7,002,350	7.	5,003,820	8.	8,007,730
	70,040		408,902		408,502		408,403
	4,040		75,700		42,700		71,900
	721		8,060		7,060		9,090
+	603	+	476	+	921	+	520

9.	904,501	10.	8,395	11.	64,153	12.	21,987
	621,423		21,987		2,934		46,832
	72,432		96,374		34,900		92,138
	8,290		34,910		63,280		31,629
+	726	+	84,795	+	23,962	+	4,796

13.	239,600	14.	34,762	15.	92,436	16.	92,138
	84,795		29,788		96,842		31,629
	294,100		39,979		21,943		47,962
	64,739		68,394		76,429		34,316
+	83,271	+	72,591	+	10,402	+	18,213

MATH

Name _____

TV Time

Tune into this cross number.

Tune
Time

Across

2. 826,298
   − 358,126

5. 603,435
   − 200,874

6. 969,751
   − 400,979

9. 997,776
   − 101,223

11. 785,848
    − 785,562

12. 712,637
    − 500,963

16. 382,537
    − 339,884

17. 908,465
    − 907,731

18. 674,371
    − 574,433

19. 781,893
    − 772,896

Down

1. 595,337
   − 287,455

2. 100,915
   − 100,874

3. 999,836
   − 844,622

4. 946,116
   − 920,447

7. 528,668
   − 447,522

8. 372,818
   − 298,863

10. 675,261
    − 668,833

13. 856,673
    − 842,995

14. 107,222
    − 31,774

15. 983,529
    − 973,932

92 Daily Learning Drills Grade 5

Name _____

Happy Birthday!

Which cartoon character turned 30 in 1990?

To find this answer, solve the following subtraction problems and find the answers in the TV set. Put the letter above the corresponding problem number at the bottom.

1. 3,000,000
    − 259,268
    2,740,732

2. 68,200
    − 53,925
    14,275

3. 900,000
    − 863,211
    36,789

4. 10,000,000
    − 640,925
    9,359,075

5. 9,900
    − 503
    9,397

6. 70,027
    − 62,098
    7,979

7. 80,006
    − 4,427
    75,379

8. 20,000,000
    − 19,986,215
    10,013,785

9. 19,600
    − 44
    19,556

10. 700,000
    − 381,332
    318,668

11. 56,004
    − 39,578
    16,426

12. 80,109
    − 63,247
    16,862

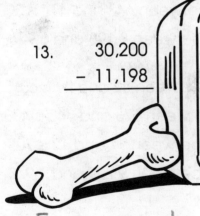

13. 30,200
    − 11,198

E = 30,122   L = 7,929
E = 36,789   N = 13,785
I = 75,579   N = 19,002
O = 16,862   R = 14,275
D = 9,359,075   S = 318,668
F = 9,397   T = 16,426
F = 2,740,732   T = 19,556

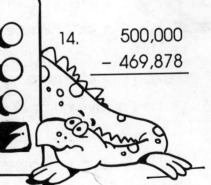

14. 500,000
    − 469,878

F r e d   F __ __ __ __ __ __ __ __ __
1 2 3 4   5 6 7 8 9 10 11 12 13 14

Name _____

Camel Trivia

What kind of camel has two humps? To find out, follow the directions below.

1. Put a C above number 3 if the estimated difference between 286 and 98 is 200.

2. Put an E above number 2 if the estimated difference between 919 and 522 is 300.

3. Put an I above number 6 if the estimated difference between 72 and 49 is 20.

4. Put an N above number 8 if the estimated difference between 88 and 23 is 70.

5. Put an O above number 7 if the estimated difference between 7,628 and 3,333 is 4,000.

6. Put a K above number 4 if the estimated difference between 618 and 285 is 400.

7. Put a T above number 5 if the estimated difference between 92 and 68 is 30.

8. Put a U above number 4 if the estimated difference between 472 and 114 is 300.

9. Put a B above number 1 if the estimated difference between 9,428 and 1,579 is 7,000.

10. Put an E above number 7 if the estimated difference between 2,910 and 1,150 is 1,000.

11. Put an S above number 5 if the estimated difference between 891 and 444 is 400.

12. Put an M above number 8 if the estimated difference between 52 and 39 is 20.

13. Put an I above number 2 if the estimated difference between 642 and 414 is 300.

14. Put an R above number 5 if the estimated difference between 8,198 and 3,926 is 4,000.

15. Put an L above number 1 if the estimated difference between 82 and 29 is 60.

16. Put a T above number 4 if the estimated difference between 673 and 348 is 400.

17. Put an A above number 7 if the estimated difference between 77 and 12 is 70.

18. Put an A above number 2 if the estimated difference between 9,249 and 1,973 is 7,000.

___ ___ ___ ___ ___ ___ ___ ___
 1   2   3   4   5   6   7   8

Name _____

Wah! Wah!

Solve the following multiplication problems.
Connect the correct problems to make
a path from the baby to her bottle.

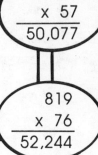

863
x 24
21,712

904
x 93
85,072

6,520
x 74
582,480

199
x 98
19,502

663
x 54
53,802

392
x 28
11,976

485
x 53
24,605

925
x 68
62,900

4,516
x 22
98,352

566
x 74
41,884

2,576
x 92
236,992

466
x 18
8,388

1,530
x 93
152,290

534
x 34
28,156

5,563
x 35
194,705

719
x 82
69,958

239
x 15
4,585

329
x 16
5,624

861
x 57
50,077

1,344
x 49
65,856

671
x 68
45,628

793
x 81
64,233

651
x 83
34,738

819
x 76
52,244

2,316
x 27
62,532

1,524
x 43
65,532

4,110
x 28
125,080

Name _____

Puzzling Cross Number

Dive into this cross number!

Across

1. 462
    x 212

5. 234
    x 101

7. 926
    x 815

8. 624
    x 783

11. 832
    x 458

13. 336
    x 817

14. 801
    x 101

Down

2. 634
    x 755

3. 208
    x 422

4. 672
    x 833

6. 547
    x 900

9. 926
    x 950

10. 698
    x 741

12. 111
    x 111

Name _____

Happy Remainders

Work problems. Give the clowns with remainders a happy face 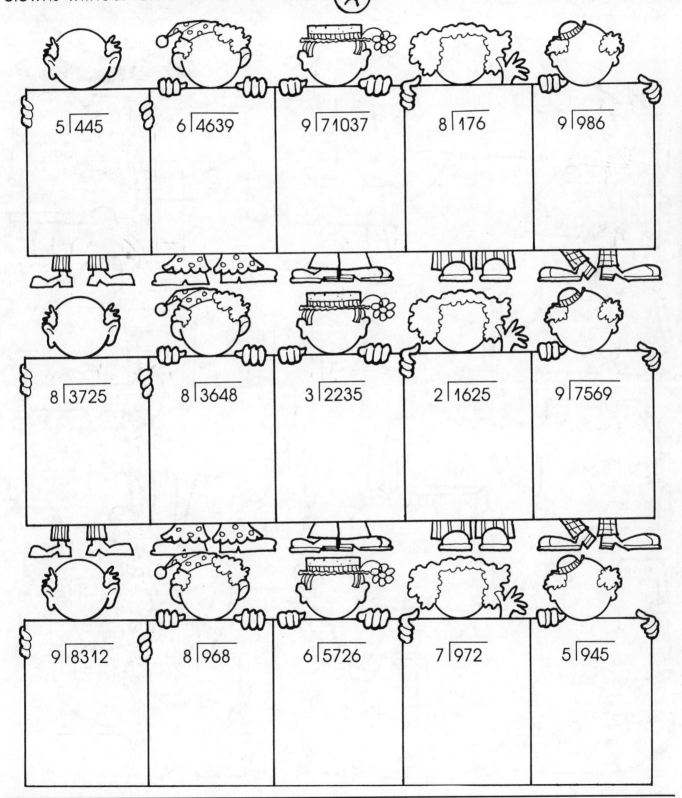. Give the clowns without remainders a sad face.

5)445   6)4639   9)71037   8)176   9)986

8)3725   8)3648   3)2235   2)1625   9)7569

9)8312   8)968   6)5726   7)972   5)945

Name _____

Mousy Maze

Lead the mouse to the trap by connecting the quotients in order starting at 795.

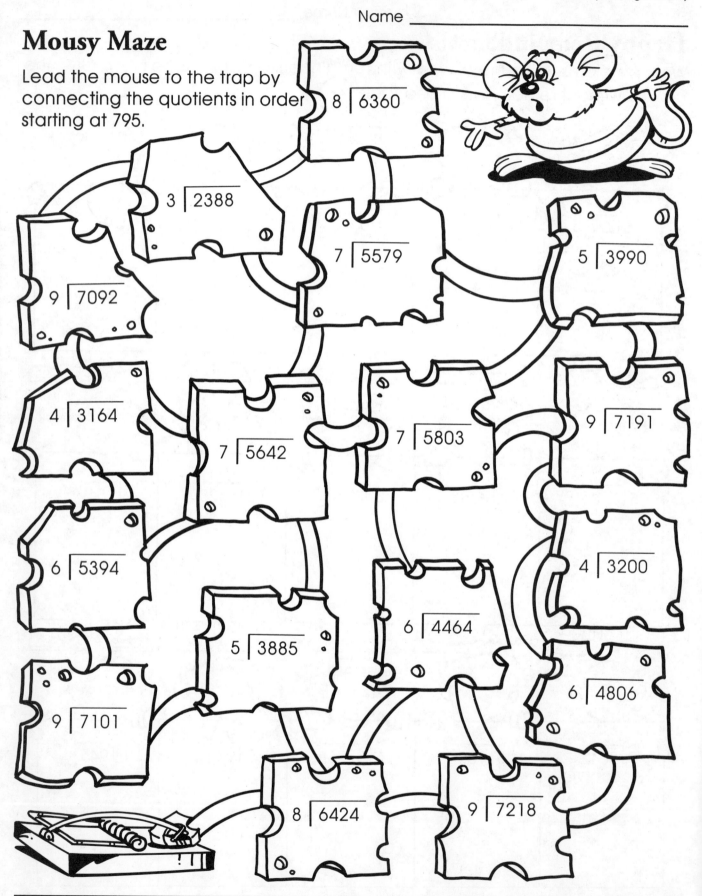

8) 6360

3) 2388

7) 5579

5) 3990

9) 7092

4) 3164

7) 5642

7) 5803

9) 7191

6) 5394

5) 3885

6) 4464

4) 3200

9) 7101

6) 4806

8) 6424

9) 7218

Name _____

Divisors in the Clouds

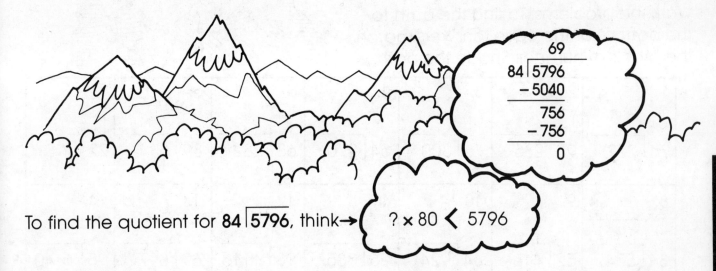

To find the quotient for 84⟌5796, think→ ? × 80 < 5796

1.
40⟌2560

2.
50⟌2150

3.
31⟌9362

4.
62⟌12,400

5.
51⟌1020

6.
35⟌1050

7.
84⟌6720

8.
26⟌1638

9.
12⟌372

10.
29⟌2465

11.
90⟌7020

12.
60⟌4560

13.
30⟌2460

14.
49⟌294

15.
80⟌640

16.
7⟌210

MATH

Name _____

Spelunking

Work the problems. To find the path to
the bottom of the cave, answers match
the problem number. Shade the path.

1. 74⟌222	2. 95⟌285	3. 75⟌300	4. 54⟌270	5. 63⟌252	6. 89⟌534	7. 22⟌198
8. 84⟌504	9. 52⟌416	10. 84⟌924	11. 35⟌385	12. 93⟌1116	13. 69⟌897	14. 95⟌1140
15. 63⟌882	16. 35⟌525	17. 21⟌357	18. 73⟌1314	19. 36⟌648	20. 34⟌782	21. 44⟌792
22. 66⟌1386	23. 99⟌2277	24. 24⟌576	25. 38⟌874	26. 84⟌2268	27. 28⟌672	28. 33⟌858
29. 37⟌962	30. 35⟌1050	31. 46⟌966	32. 27⟌837	33. 21⟌987	34. 29⟌928	35. 16⟌736
	36. 63⟌2268	37. 62⟌2294	38. 13⟌494	39. 18⟌774	40. 78⟌3276	
		41. 78⟌3432	42. 24⟌1008	43. 53⟌2544		

Name _____

Wisconsin's Nickname

What is Wisconsin known as?

To find out, solve the division problems below. Then, find the answers at the bottom of the page and put the corresponding letter on the line above the answer.

T. $14\overline{)1218}$ E. $23\overline{)1633}$ S. $53\overline{)2756}$

A. $38\overline{)1596}$ A. $61\overline{)5185}$ E. $18\overline{)1764}$

T. $22\overline{)1628}$ R. $40\overline{)2520}$ D. $55\overline{)4400}$

G. $31\overline{)1364}$ B. $12\overline{)780}$

$\overline{}$ $\overline{}$ $\overline{}$ $\overline{}$ $\overline{}$ $\overline{}$ $\overline{}$ $\overline{}$ $\overline{}$ $\overline{}$ $\overline{}$
 65   85   80   44   71   63   52   74   42   87   98

Name _____

Prehistoric Problems

Work the problems. Shade in the letters of those problems that have remainders to reveal the "ancient one."

A. 42)8799   B. 33)9278   C. 72)38952   D. 43)28939   E. 52)336

F. 26)16822   G. 58)22388   H. 27)743   I. 57)20406   J. 35)296

K. 62)984   L. 42)5761   M. 38)8056   N. 36)28404   O. 35)7623

P. 62)6735   Q. 26)1664   R. 46)419   S. 84)6552   T. 17)9741

U. 52)4628   V. 17)6145   W. 41)8173   X. 39)5304   Y. 66)6930

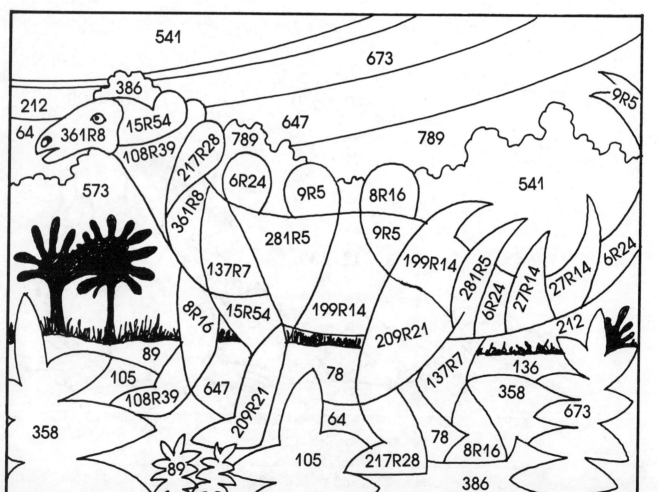

Name _____

Just Ducky!

Divide each problem. Draw a line connecting each problem to its answer.

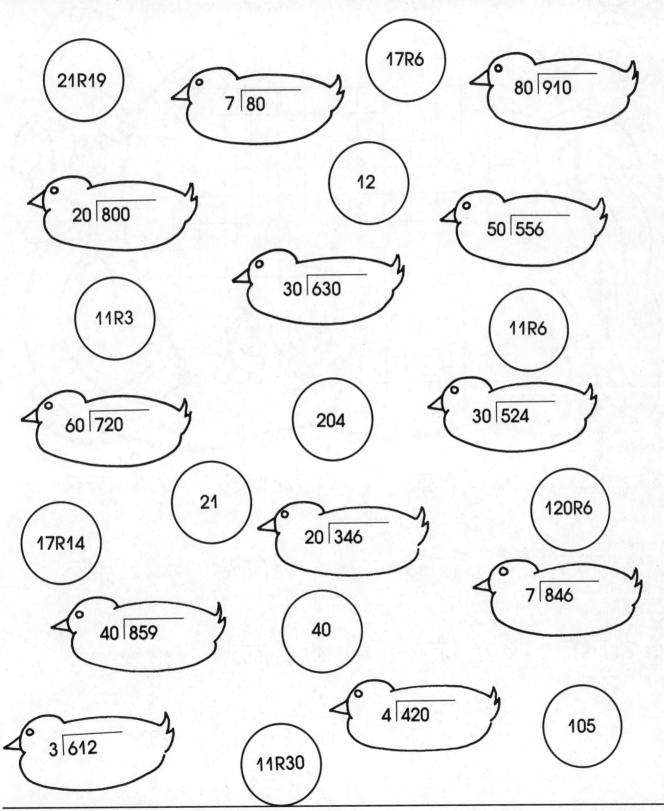

21R19

7⟌80

17R6

80⟌910

20⟌800

12

50⟌556

30⟌630

11R3

11R6

60⟌720

204

30⟌524

21

120R6

17R14

20⟌346

7⟌846

40⟌859

40

3⟌612

4⟌420

105

11R30

Name _____

Octopus Crossword

Try to disarm this crossword by writing in the remainders in word form.

Across

3. 23 ⟌1313

4. 41 ⟌3501

7. 18 ⟌1733

8. 35 ⟌2706

10. 64 ⟌4618

12. 51 ⟌4746

13. 70 ⟌5881

14. 32 ⟌2132

Down

1. 45 ⟌2389

2. 60 ⟌3786

3. 28 ⟌1076

4. 33 ⟌1360

5. 55 ⟌3533

6. 72 ⟌6128

9. 84 ⟌7494

11. 16 ⟌1497

12. 22 ⟌1088

Production Line

Work each problem, starting at the top of each machine, working down.

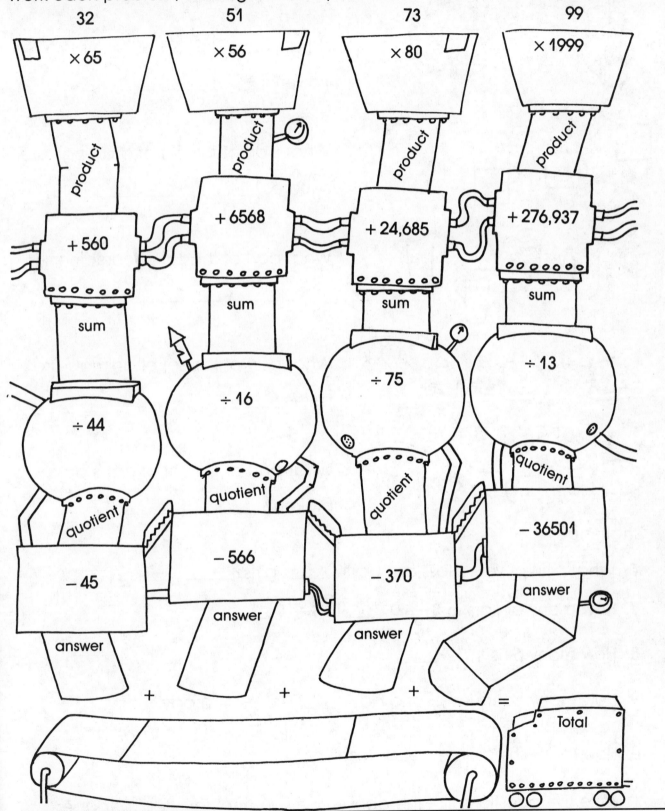

MATH

Name _____

Get Set
Write a fraction to answer each question.

1. What part of this set of plants is a flower? _____

2.  What part of this set of drawings are squares? _____

3.  What part of this set of containers is full? _____

4. What part of this set of animals are cats? _____

5. What part of this set of eggs are broken? _____

Challenge:

6. What part of your class are boys? _____ girls? _____

7. How many dollars in $\$\frac{18}{6}$? _____ In $\$\frac{30}{6}$? _____

8. How many 6ths in 1? _____

9. How many hours in $\frac{5}{12}$ of a day? _____ In $\frac{7}{12}$ of a day? _____

10. How many things in $\frac{11}{12}$ of a dozen? _____

☆ Write five questions like the above ones on another sheet of paper.

Name _____

OK, Everyone Reduce!

$\frac{6}{20}$	largest number that will divide evenly into both $\frac{6}{20} \div \frac{2}{2} = \frac{3}{10}$	$\frac{6}{20} = \frac{3}{10}$

Reduce to lowest terms.

$\frac{5}{20} = \frac{}{4}$ $\qquad$ $\frac{8}{20} = $ _____ $\qquad$ $\frac{3}{15} = $ _____ $\qquad$ $\frac{12}{20} = $ _____

$\frac{2}{8} = $ _____ $\qquad$ $\frac{12}{16} = $ _____ $\qquad$ $\frac{14}{16} = $ _____ $\qquad$ $\frac{4}{8} = $ _____

$\frac{9}{12} = $ _____ $\qquad$ $\frac{5}{10} = $ _____ $\qquad$ $\frac{6}{10} = $ _____ $\qquad$ $\frac{10}{15} = $ _____

$\frac{2}{4} = $ _____ $\qquad$ $\frac{4}{8} = $ _____ $\qquad$ $\frac{6}{24} = $ _____ $\qquad$ $\frac{6}{8} = $ _____

$\frac{8}{16} = $ _____ $\qquad$ $\frac{2}{12} = $ _____ $\qquad$ $\frac{2}{10} = $ _____ $\qquad$ $\frac{8}{12} = $ _____

$\frac{4}{20} = $ _____ $\qquad$ $\frac{3}{12} = $ _____ $\qquad$ $\frac{9}{15} = $ _____ $\qquad$ $\frac{4}{12} = $ _____

$\frac{10}{24} = $ _____ $\qquad$ $\frac{6}{20} = $ _____ $\qquad$ $\frac{10}{12} = $ _____ $\qquad$ $\frac{12}{24} = $ _____

$\frac{4}{10} = $ _____ $\qquad$ $\frac{8}{10} = $ _____ $\qquad$ $\frac{2}{10} = $ _____ $\qquad$ $\frac{6}{12} = $ _____

MATH

Name _____

Which Is Longer?

Match the pairs of equivalent fractions.

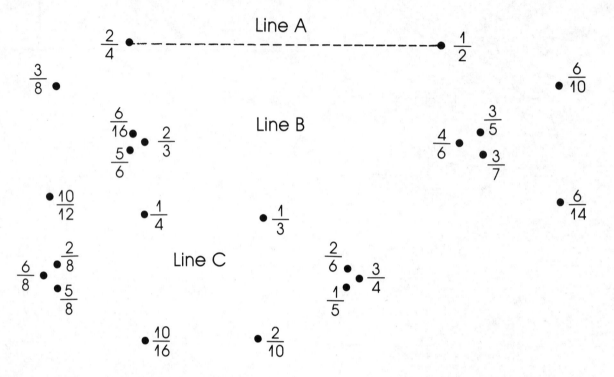

Line A

$\frac{2}{4}$ • — — — — — — — • $\frac{1}{2}$

$\frac{3}{8}$ •   • $\frac{6}{10}$

$\frac{6}{16}$• • $\frac{2}{3}$ Line B $\frac{4}{6}$ • • $\frac{3}{5}$

$\frac{5}{6}$ •   • $\frac{3}{7}$

• $\frac{10}{12}$ • $\frac{1}{4}$ • $\frac{1}{3}$ • $\frac{6}{14}$

$\frac{6}{8}$ • • $\frac{2}{8}$ Line C $\frac{2}{6}$ • • $\frac{3}{4}$

• $\frac{5}{8}$ $\frac{1}{5}$•

• $\frac{10}{16}$ • $\frac{2}{10}$

Which line is longer? **A**, **B** or **C**.

• $\frac{2}{3}$

• $\frac{2}{6}$ Line A

$\frac{2}{16}$•   • $\frac{3}{4}$ $\frac{1}{3}$ • • $\frac{1}{2}$

• $\frac{5}{8}$ • $\frac{3}{8}$

Line B

• $\frac{10}{16}$ • $\frac{6}{16}$

$\frac{3}{12}$ •   • $\frac{9}{12}$ • $\frac{1}{8}$ $\frac{1}{4}$ • • $\frac{5}{10}$

Line C

• $\frac{4}{6}$

Which line is longer? **A**, **B** or **C**.

Name _____

Going for the Gold

Change fractions to mixed numbers. Shade in each answer to find the path to the pot of gold.

1. $\frac{11}{9} =$

2. $\frac{8}{3} =$

3. $\frac{8}{7} =$

4. $\frac{11}{6} =$

5. $\frac{7}{3} =$

6. $\frac{7}{6} =$

7. $\frac{9}{4} =$

8. $\frac{8}{5} =$

9. $\frac{4}{3} =$

10. $\frac{7}{2} =$

11. $\frac{3}{2} =$

12. $\frac{6}{5} =$

13. $\frac{7}{4} =$

14. $\frac{9}{2} =$

15. $\frac{11}{8} =$

16. $\frac{5}{2} =$

17. $\frac{9}{7} =$

18. $\frac{11}{4} =$

19. $\frac{17}{12} =$

20. $\frac{13}{12} =$

 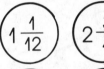     

Name _____

Cactus Fractions

Draw lines from the mixed numbers to the correct improper fractions.

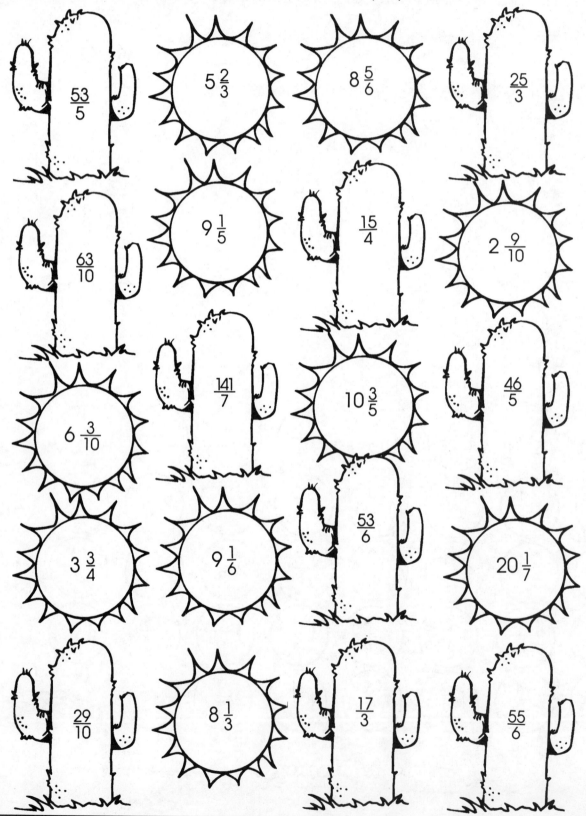

$\frac{53}{5}$

$5\frac{2}{3}$

$8\frac{5}{6}$

$\frac{25}{3}$

$\frac{63}{10}$

$9\frac{1}{5}$

$\frac{15}{4}$

$2\frac{9}{10}$

$6\frac{3}{10}$

$\frac{141}{7}$

$10\frac{3}{5}$

$\frac{46}{5}$

$3\frac{3}{4}$

$9\frac{1}{6}$

$\frac{53}{6}$

$20\frac{1}{7}$

$\frac{29}{10}$

$8\frac{1}{3}$

$\frac{17}{3}$

$\frac{55}{6}$

Name _____

A Real Gem!

Add problems to find the real gem. Shade in answer gems. The one left is the real gem.

$\dfrac{3}{8}$
$+\dfrac{2}{8}$
_____

$\dfrac{4}{7}$
$+\dfrac{1}{7}$
_____

$\dfrac{4}{6}$
$+\dfrac{1}{6}$
_____

$\dfrac{1}{3}$
$+\dfrac{1}{3}$
_____

$\dfrac{1}{4}$
$+\dfrac{1}{4}$
_____

$\dfrac{1}{8}$
$+\dfrac{1}{8}$
_____

$\dfrac{1}{6}$
$+\dfrac{2}{6}$
_____

$\dfrac{1}{8}$
$+\dfrac{4}{8}$
_____

$\dfrac{3}{20}$
$+\dfrac{4}{20}$
_____

$\dfrac{4}{10}$
$+\dfrac{3}{10}$
_____

$\dfrac{1}{5}$
$+\dfrac{3}{5}$
_____

$\dfrac{4}{12}$
$+\dfrac{5}{12}$
_____

$\dfrac{5}{15}$
$+\dfrac{4}{15}$
_____

$\dfrac{14}{20}$
$+\dfrac{5}{20}$
_____

$\dfrac{3}{16}$
$+\dfrac{5}{16}$
_____

$\dfrac{1}{8}$
$+\dfrac{6}{8}$
_____

$\dfrac{2}{5}$
$+\dfrac{1}{5}$
_____

$\dfrac{7}{12}$
$+\dfrac{2}{12}$
_____

$\dfrac{2}{13}$
$+\dfrac{5}{13}$
_____

$\dfrac{5}{17}$
$+\dfrac{8}{17}$
_____

$\dfrac{9}{18}$
$+\dfrac{8}{18}$
_____

$\dfrac{3}{15}$
$+\dfrac{5}{15}$
_____

$\dfrac{5}{12}$
$+\dfrac{2}{12}$
_____

$\dfrac{5}{14}$
$+\dfrac{4}{14}$
_____

$\dfrac{1}{7}$
$+\dfrac{5}{7}$
_____

$\dfrac{6}{16}$
$+\dfrac{7}{16}$
_____

$\dfrac{7}{21}$
$+\dfrac{8}{21}$
_____

$\dfrac{5}{10}$
$+\dfrac{4}{10}$
_____

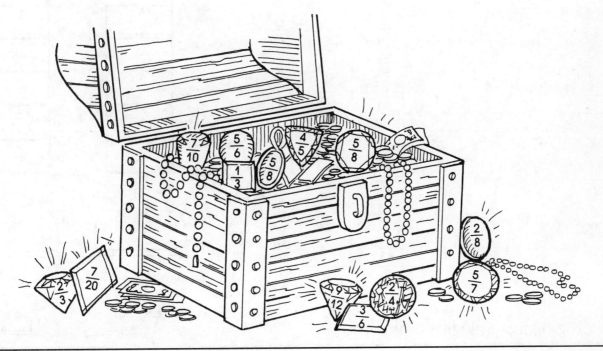

Name _____

How High?

Work the problems. Shade in the answers in the boxes above balloon **A** or **B** to see how high each balloon flew.

$$\begin{array}{r}\frac{1}{10}\\\frac{4}{10}\\+\frac{3}{10}\\\hline\end{array}\qquad\begin{array}{r}\frac{1}{5}\\\frac{2}{5}\\+\frac{1}{5}\\\hline\end{array}\qquad\begin{array}{r}\frac{1}{7}\\\frac{1}{7}\\+\frac{1}{7}\\\hline\end{array}\qquad\begin{array}{r}\frac{4}{9}\\\frac{1}{9}\\+\frac{2}{9}\\\hline\end{array}$$

$$\begin{array}{r}\frac{1}{4}\\\frac{1}{4}\\+\frac{1}{4}\\\hline\end{array}\qquad\begin{array}{r}\frac{1}{10}\\\frac{7}{10}\\+\frac{1}{10}\\\hline\end{array}\qquad\begin{array}{r}\frac{3}{7}\\\frac{2}{7}\\+\frac{1}{7}\\\hline\end{array}\qquad\begin{array}{r}\frac{2}{8}\\\frac{1}{8}\\+\frac{2}{8}\\\hline\end{array}$$

$$\begin{array}{r}\frac{3}{9}\\\frac{3}{9}\\+\frac{2}{9}\\\hline\end{array}\qquad\begin{array}{r}\frac{5}{15}\\\frac{3}{15}\\+\frac{4}{15}\\\hline\end{array}\qquad\begin{array}{r}\frac{1}{10}\\\frac{5}{10}\\+\frac{1}{10}\\\hline\end{array}\qquad\begin{array}{r}\frac{5}{11}\\\frac{1}{11}\\+\frac{4}{11}\\\hline\end{array}$$

$$\begin{array}{r}\frac{3}{12}\\\frac{5}{12}\\+\frac{1}{12}\\\hline\end{array}\qquad\begin{array}{r}\frac{4}{7}\\\frac{1}{7}\\+\frac{1}{7}\\\hline\end{array}\qquad\begin{array}{r}\frac{7}{14}\\\frac{2}{14}\\+\frac{4}{14}\\\hline\end{array}\qquad\begin{array}{r}\frac{6}{20}\\\frac{7}{20}\\+\frac{4}{20}\\\hline\end{array}$$

$$\begin{array}{r}\frac{3}{8}\\\frac{2}{8}\\+\frac{1}{8}\\\hline\end{array}\qquad\begin{array}{r}\frac{9}{21}\\\frac{5}{21}\\+\frac{4}{21}\\\hline\end{array}\qquad\begin{array}{r}\frac{2}{13}\\\frac{1}{13}\\+\frac{7}{13}\\\hline\end{array}\qquad\begin{array}{r}\frac{7}{16}\\\frac{3}{16}\\+\frac{5}{16}\\\hline\end{array}$$

A	B
$\frac{3}{8}$	$\frac{14}{15}$
$\frac{8}{11}$	$\frac{11}{14}$
$\frac{19}{21}$	$\frac{13}{16}$
$\frac{13}{15}$	$\frac{9}{13}$
$\frac{5}{7}$	$\frac{9}{11}$
$\frac{6}{9}$	$\frac{11}{15}$
$\frac{3}{5}$	$\frac{7}{8}$
$\frac{15}{16}$	$\frac{4}{7}$
$\frac{9}{10}$	$\frac{2}{4}$
$\frac{10}{13}$	$\frac{3}{4}$
$\frac{8}{10}$	$\frac{17}{20}$
$\frac{10}{11}$	$\frac{5}{8}$
$\frac{13}{14}$	$\frac{7}{10}$
$\frac{8}{9}$	$\frac{12}{15}$
$\frac{6}{8}$	$\frac{18}{21}$
$\frac{3}{7}$	$\frac{4}{5}$
$\frac{9}{12}$	$\frac{6}{7}$
$\frac{6}{7}$	$\frac{7}{9}$

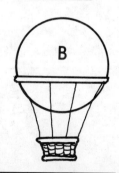

Which balloon flew the highest? _____

Name _____

Bat Adding

Don't let this crossword puzzle drive you batty!

Across

1. $\frac{7}{10} + \frac{9}{10}$ = one and three ____

2. $\frac{5}{6} + \frac{5}{6}$ = one and ____ thirds

6. $\frac{1}{8} + \frac{5}{8}$ = three ____

9. $\frac{7}{15} + \frac{4}{15}$ = ____ fifteenths

10. $\frac{2}{9} + \frac{5}{9}$ = ____ ninths

11. $\frac{11}{16} + \frac{7}{16}$ = one and one ____

13. $\frac{3}{11} + \frac{7}{11}$ = ____ elevenths

16. $\frac{4}{9} + \frac{2}{9}$ = two ____

18. $\frac{14}{15} + \frac{4}{15}$ = one and one ____

21. $\frac{1}{18} + \frac{5}{18}$ = one ____

22. $\frac{5}{7} + \frac{6}{7}$ = one and ____ sevenths

Down

1. $\frac{1}{15} + \frac{13}{15}$ = fourteen ____

3. $\frac{7}{12} + \frac{7}{12}$ = one and ____ sixth

4. $\frac{7}{10} + \frac{2}{10}$ = ____ tenths

5. $\frac{13}{20} + \frac{13}{20}$ = one and three ____

7. $\frac{15}{16} + \frac{13}{16}$ = one and ____ fourths

8. $\frac{4}{7} + \frac{2}{7}$ = ____ sevenths

9. $\frac{7}{9} + \frac{1}{9}$ = ____ ninths

12. $\frac{1}{12} + \frac{5}{12}$ = one ____

14. $\frac{8}{9} + \frac{2}{9}$ = one and one ____

15. $\frac{4}{18} + \frac{17}{18}$ = one and one ____

17. $\frac{3}{11} + \frac{2}{11}$ = ____ elevenths

19. $\frac{1}{10} + \frac{7}{10}$ = ____ fifths

20. $\frac{3}{4} + \frac{3}{4}$ = one and one ____

Name _____

Climbing to New Heights

Name _____

Pizza Pie

Work problems. Shade in answers on pizzas to show which pieces have been eaten.

$$\frac{1}{10} + \frac{4}{5}$$ $$\frac{3}{12} + \frac{1}{6}$$ $$\frac{1}{2} + \frac{1}{3}$$ $$\frac{3}{4} + \frac{1}{5}$$ $$\frac{1}{5} + \frac{1}{3}$$ $$\frac{2}{3} + \frac{1}{4}$$ $$\frac{5}{12} + \frac{1}{6}$$

$$\frac{2}{5} + \frac{9}{20}$$ $$\frac{1}{3} + \frac{2}{9}$$ $$\frac{3}{5} + \frac{1}{10}$$ $$\frac{1}{4} + \frac{1}{2}$$ $$\frac{1}{8} + \frac{1}{4}$$ $$\frac{1}{10} + \frac{1}{5}$$ $$\frac{2}{3} + \frac{1}{5}$$

$$\frac{1}{8} + \frac{1}{3}$$ $$\frac{1}{4} + \frac{1}{5}$$ $$\frac{3}{8} + \frac{1}{5}$$ $$\frac{9}{16} + \frac{3}{8}$$ $$\frac{2}{8} + \frac{9}{16}$$ $$\frac{1}{5} + \frac{1}{9}$$

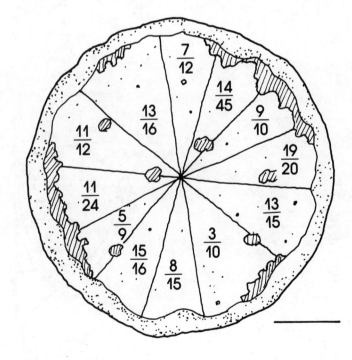

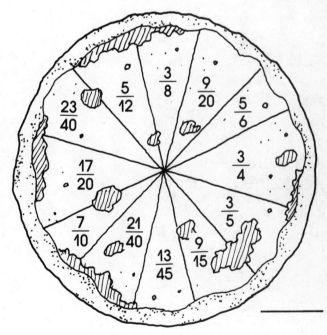

Which fractional part of each pizza has been eaten?

Name _____

All Mixed Up

$$3\frac{1}{5} = 3\frac{2}{10}$$
$$+\ 2\frac{7}{10} = 2\frac{7}{10}$$
$$\overline{\phantom{+\ 2\frac{7}{10} = }\ 5\frac{9}{10}}$$

$$5\frac{1}{4} = 5\frac{3}{12}$$
$$+\ 1\frac{1}{6} = 1\frac{2}{12}$$
$$\overline{\phantom{+\ 1\frac{1}{6} = }\ 6\frac{5}{12}}$$

1. $8\frac{1}{3}$
$+\ 7\frac{1}{4}$

2. $6\frac{3}{4}$
$+\ 2\frac{1}{8}$

3. $9\frac{7}{10}$
$+\ 8\frac{1}{15}$

4. $8\frac{7}{10}$
$+\ 1\frac{1}{5}$

5. $5\frac{5}{6}$
$+\ 3\frac{1}{12}$

6. $4\frac{1}{2}$
$+\ 7\frac{1}{3}$

7. $5\frac{1}{2}$
$+\ 2\frac{1}{3}$

8. $7\frac{1}{6}$
$+\ 8\frac{1}{4}$

9. $5\frac{1}{3}$
$+\ 3\frac{4}{9}$

10. $6\frac{1}{5}$
$+\ 1\frac{7}{10}$

11. $1\frac{1}{7}$
$+\ 5\frac{3}{7}$

12. $3\frac{1}{2}$
$+\ 4\frac{1}{4}$

Challenge—
Solve the equations.

$$3\frac{7}{8} + 1\frac{3}{4} = 5 + n$$

$$15\frac{3}{8} + 29\frac{5}{6} = 45 + n$$

Name _____

Can Captain Kook Subtract?

Help Captain Kook find his hidden treasure by shading in the path of the incorrect subtraction problems.

$\frac{8}{9} - \frac{2}{9} = \frac{2}{3}$	$\frac{4}{15} - \frac{1}{15} = \frac{1}{5}$	$\frac{8}{9} - \frac{1}{9} = \frac{2}{3}$	$\frac{71}{100} - \frac{27}{100} = \frac{1}{2}$	$\frac{4}{5} - \frac{1}{5} = \frac{7}{10}$	$\frac{13}{14} - \frac{1}{14} = \frac{6}{7}$
$\frac{5}{6} - \frac{1}{6} = \frac{1}{3}$	$\frac{3}{7} - \frac{1}{7} = \frac{2}{7}$	$\frac{11}{15} - \frac{1}{15} = \frac{3}{4}$	$\frac{11}{25} - \frac{6}{25} = \frac{1}{5}$	$\frac{11}{12} - \frac{5}{12} = \frac{2}{5}$	$\frac{7}{15} - \frac{2}{15} = \frac{1}{3}$
$\frac{4}{7} - \frac{2}{7} = \frac{1}{3}$	$\frac{5}{18} - \frac{1}{18} = \frac{2}{9}$	$\frac{9}{10} - \frac{7}{10} = \frac{2}{5}$	$\frac{4}{5} - \frac{3}{5} = \frac{1}{5}$	$\frac{3}{25} - \frac{2}{25} = \frac{1}{50}$	$\frac{7}{10} - \frac{5}{10} = \frac{1}{5}$
$\frac{7}{10} - \frac{3}{10} = \frac{3}{5}$	$\frac{3}{8} - \frac{1}{8} = \frac{1}{4}$	$\frac{5}{12} - \frac{1}{12} = \frac{1}{4}$	$\frac{7}{20} - \frac{1}{20} = \frac{3}{10}$	$\frac{9}{14} - \frac{1}{14} = \frac{5}{7}$	$\frac{11}{19} - \frac{3}{19} = \frac{8}{19}$
$\frac{7}{12} - \frac{5}{12} = \frac{3}{12}$	$\frac{4}{9} - \frac{2}{9} = \frac{2}{9}$	$\frac{10}{11} - \frac{5}{11} = \frac{1}{2}$	$\frac{2}{7} - \frac{1}{7} = \frac{1}{7}$	$\frac{5}{11} - \frac{2}{11} = \frac{1}{4}$	$\frac{7}{8} - \frac{1}{8} = \frac{3}{4}$
$\frac{3}{5} - \frac{1}{5} = \frac{3}{5}$	$\frac{11}{15} - \frac{7}{15} = \frac{4}{15}$	$\frac{9}{20} - \frac{3}{20} = \frac{1}{5}$	$\frac{9}{10} - \frac{3}{10} = \frac{3}{5}$	$\frac{5}{8} - \frac{1}{8} = \frac{5}{16}$	$\frac{9}{22} - \frac{5}{22} = \frac{2}{11}$
$\frac{7}{8} - \frac{1}{8} = \frac{1}{4}$	$\frac{17}{20} - \frac{3}{20} = \frac{7}{10}$	$\frac{23}{25} - \frac{11}{25} = \frac{1}{2}$	$\frac{8}{9} - \frac{1}{9} = \frac{7}{9}$	$\frac{13}{16} - \frac{3}{16} = \frac{1}{2}$	$\frac{18}{25} - \frac{3}{25} = \frac{3}{5}$
$\frac{8}{9} - \frac{4}{9} = \frac{2}{3}$	$\frac{11}{12} - \frac{5}{12} = \frac{5}{12}$	$\frac{31}{40} - \frac{10}{40} = \frac{1}{2}$	$\frac{6}{7} - \frac{2}{7} = \frac{4}{7}$	$\frac{11}{18} - \frac{5}{18} = \frac{1}{4}$	$\frac{11}{12} - \frac{5}{12} = \frac{1}{2}$
$\frac{2}{3} - \frac{1}{3} = \frac{1}{3}$	$\frac{11}{14} - \frac{9}{14} = \frac{1}{7}$	$\frac{5}{8} - \frac{1}{8} = \frac{1}{2}$	$\frac{13}{18} - \frac{5}{18} = \frac{4}{9}$	$\frac{7}{15} - \frac{1}{15} = \frac{3}{5}$	$\frac{3}{5} - \frac{1}{5} = \frac{2}{5}$
$\frac{19}{20} - \frac{1}{20} = \frac{9}{10}$	$\frac{7}{9} - \frac{4}{9} = \frac{1}{3}$	$\frac{5}{6} - \frac{1}{6} = \frac{2}{3}$	$\frac{3}{4} - \frac{1}{4} = \frac{1}{2}$	$\frac{9}{10} - \frac{3}{10} = \frac{2}{5}$	$\frac{5}{6} - \frac{1}{6} = \frac{5}{12}$

MATH

Name _____

Sandwich Solutions

Who invented the sandwich?

To find out, solve the following subtraction problems and put the letter before each problem above its answer at the bottom.

A. $\frac{3}{5} - \frac{1}{4}$ A. $\frac{5}{6} - \frac{1}{3}$ E. $\frac{9}{16} - \frac{1}{4}$

I. $\frac{7}{10} - \frac{3}{5}$ D. $\frac{1}{2} - \frac{5}{12}$ C. $\frac{7}{8} - \frac{3}{4}$

W. $\frac{13}{18} - \frac{1}{6}$ N. $\frac{2}{3} - \frac{1}{12}$ H. $\frac{19}{20} - \frac{4}{5}$

F. $\frac{18}{25} - \frac{2}{5}$ L. $\frac{8}{9} - \frac{1}{6}$ R. $\frac{5}{8} - \frac{3}{16}$

O. $\frac{4}{5} - \frac{2}{3}$ S. $\frac{1}{7} - \frac{1}{14}$

$\frac{5}{16}$ $\frac{7}{20}$ $\frac{7}{16}$ $\frac{13}{18}$ $\frac{2}{15}$ $\frac{8}{25}$ $\frac{1}{14}$ $\frac{1}{2}$ $\frac{7}{12}$ $\frac{1}{12}$ $\frac{5}{9}$ $\frac{1}{10}$ $\frac{1}{8}$ $\frac{3}{20}$

Name _____

Subtracting Fractions

Example—

$3\frac{1}{2} = 3\frac{3}{6}$

$-2\frac{2}{6} = 2\frac{2}{6}$

$\overline{\qquad 1\frac{1}{6}}$

Subtract. Show all work.

1. $3\frac{4}{7}$
    $-1\frac{1}{14}$
    $\overline{\qquad}$

2. $8\frac{5}{6}$
    $-3\frac{3}{8}$
    $\overline{\qquad}$

3. $7\frac{7}{8}$
    $-2\frac{1}{4}$
    $\overline{\qquad}$

4. $6\frac{1}{2}$
    $-1\frac{5}{12}$
    $\overline{\qquad}$

5. $7\frac{3}{8}$
    $-6\frac{1}{6}$
    $\overline{\qquad}$

6. $9\frac{1}{2}$
    $-6\frac{1}{12}$
    $\overline{\qquad}$

7. $8\frac{2}{3}$
    $-4\frac{1}{6}$
    $\overline{\qquad}$

8. $5\frac{1}{2}$
    $-2\frac{1}{4}$
    $\overline{\qquad}$

9. $9\frac{4}{5}$
    $-1\frac{3}{10}$
    $\overline{\qquad}$

10. $9\frac{2}{5}$
    $-2\frac{4}{15}$
    $\overline{\qquad}$

11. $6\frac{7}{12}$
    $-1\frac{1}{2}$
    $\overline{\qquad}$

12. $9\frac{1}{3}$
    $-8\frac{1}{4}$
    $\overline{\qquad}$

Name _____

Jibber Jabber

Take a "jab" at this crossword!

Across

1. $9 - 8\frac{1}{11}$ = ten ____

3. $3\frac{3}{4} - 1\frac{1}{5}$ = two and eleven ____

5. $14\frac{3}{10} - 2\frac{1}{2}$ = eleven and four ____

8. $5\frac{1}{2} - \frac{4}{5}$ = four and seven ____

10. $15 - 11\frac{17}{20}$ = three and ____ twentieths

11. $15\frac{1}{3} - 2\frac{1}{2}$ = twelve and ____ sixths

12. $7\frac{7}{9} - 3\frac{1}{9}$ = four and ____ thirds

13. $12\frac{3}{5} - 2\frac{1}{10}$ = ____ and one half

14. $8 - 2\frac{1}{8}$ = five and ____ eighths

16. $10\frac{3}{8} - 1\frac{5}{8}$ = eight and three ____

17. $17\frac{1}{5} - 7\frac{7}{10}$ = nine and one ____

18. $18 - 11\frac{1}{6}$ = six and five ____

Down

2. $6\frac{3}{4} - 3\frac{1}{3}$ = three and five ____

3. $10\frac{1}{5} - 2\frac{1}{3}$ = seven and ____ fifteenths

4. $8\frac{2}{9} - 2\frac{1}{3}$ = five and ____ ninths

6. $4 - 1\frac{1}{3}$ = two and two ____

7. $9\frac{17}{18} - 3\frac{7}{9}$ = ____ and one sixth

9. $6\frac{7}{9} - 1\frac{2}{3}$ = five and one ____

11. $7\frac{1}{20} - 3\frac{1}{4}$ = three and ____ fifths

13. $10\frac{1}{12} - 6\frac{3}{4}$ = three and one ____

15. $9\frac{1}{2} - 4\frac{1}{8}$ = five and three ____

Name _____

Puzzling Fractions

Multiply the problems in the puzzle.

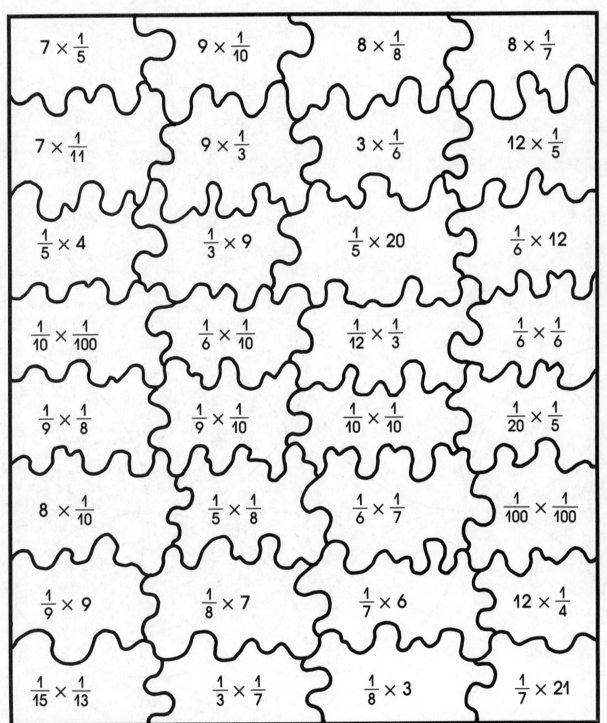

$7 \times \frac{1}{5}$ $9 \times \frac{1}{10}$ $8 \times \frac{1}{8}$ $8 \times \frac{1}{7}$

$7 \times \frac{1}{11}$ $9 \times \frac{1}{3}$ $3 \times \frac{1}{6}$ $12 \times \frac{1}{5}$

$\frac{1}{5} \times 4$ $\frac{1}{3} \times 9$ $\frac{1}{5} \times 20$ $\frac{1}{6} \times 12$

$\frac{1}{10} \times \frac{1}{100}$ $\frac{1}{6} \times \frac{1}{10}$ $\frac{1}{12} \times \frac{1}{3}$ $\frac{1}{6} \times \frac{1}{6}$

$\frac{1}{9} \times \frac{1}{8}$ $\frac{1}{9} \times \frac{1}{10}$ $\frac{1}{10} \times \frac{1}{10}$ $\frac{1}{20} \times \frac{1}{5}$

$8 \times \frac{1}{10}$ $\frac{1}{5} \times \frac{1}{8}$ $\frac{1}{6} \times \frac{1}{7}$ $\frac{1}{100} \times \frac{1}{100}$

$\frac{1}{9} \times 9$ $\frac{1}{8} \times 7$ $\frac{1}{7} \times 6$ $12 \times \frac{1}{4}$

$\frac{1}{15} \times \frac{1}{13}$ $\frac{1}{3} \times \frac{1}{7}$ $\frac{1}{8} \times 3$ $\frac{1}{7} \times 21$

Name _____

Multiplying Fractions

Work problems. Use code to color the design: B-blue, Y-yellow, O-orange, G-green.

$\frac{5}{6} \times \frac{3}{4} =$ ___ B $\frac{7}{10} \times \frac{3}{5} =$ ___ Y $\frac{2}{3} \times \frac{7}{8} =$ ___ G $\frac{3}{4} \times \frac{3}{5} =$ ___ O

$\frac{5}{6} \times \frac{4}{5} =$ ___ Y $\frac{3}{8} \times \frac{8}{10} =$ ___ Y $\frac{9}{16} \times \frac{5}{6} =$ ___ O $\frac{4}{7} \times \frac{1}{6} =$ ___ G

$\frac{5}{9} \times \frac{3}{5} =$ ___ Y $\frac{7}{12} \times \frac{5}{6} =$ ___ B $\frac{2}{5} \times \frac{1}{3} =$ ___ B $\frac{9}{10} \times \frac{2}{3} =$ ___ Y

$\frac{5}{8} \times \frac{3}{5} =$ ___ B $\frac{1}{3} \times \frac{4}{5} =$ ___ Y $\frac{3}{4} \times \frac{5}{8} =$ ___ O $\frac{5}{6} \times \frac{3}{8} =$ ___ B

$\frac{2}{5} \times \frac{5}{8} =$ ___ Y $\frac{5}{6} \times \frac{1}{3} =$ ___ O $\frac{7}{9} \times \frac{1}{4} =$ ___ O $\frac{3}{8} \times \frac{5}{12} =$ ___ O

$\frac{3}{7} \times \frac{14}{15} =$ ___ G $\frac{3}{4} \times \frac{2}{3} =$ __ B $\frac{2}{7} \times \frac{3}{7} =$ ___ G $\frac{5}{6} \times \frac{1}{10} =$ ___ Y

$\frac{2}{3} \times \frac{4}{5} =$ ___ O $\frac{7}{10} \times \frac{5}{8} =$ ___ O $\frac{1}{6} \times \frac{5}{6} =$ ___ B $\frac{3}{4} \times \frac{4}{5} =$ ___ B

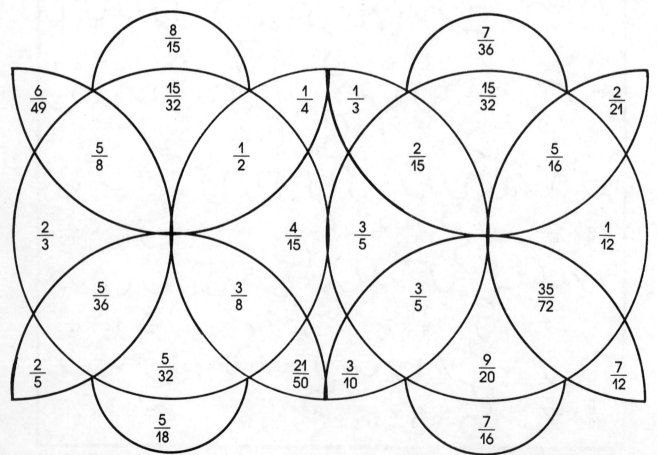

Name _____

Daredevil Danny

Daredevil Danny has many dangerous pastimes. Solve the following multiplication problems and find the answers in his wheels. Put the corresponding letter above that problem's number at the bottom of the page to find out Danny's favorite pastime.

1. $3\frac{1}{2} \times \frac{4}{6}$

2. $\frac{3}{19} \times 4\frac{2}{9}$

3. $\frac{3}{4} \times 5\frac{1}{7}$

4. $4\frac{1}{5} \times \frac{3}{4}$

5. $\frac{7}{10} \times 3\frac{3}{4}$

6. $\frac{4}{15} \times 6\frac{7}{8}$

7. $\frac{10}{11} \times 1\frac{1}{2}$

8. $3\frac{1}{3} \times \frac{3}{5}$

9. $8\frac{3}{8} \times \frac{4}{5}$

10. $2\frac{2}{7} \times \frac{7}{10}$

11. $5\frac{1}{3} \times \frac{1}{4}$

12. $\frac{2}{3} \times 5\frac{1}{4}$

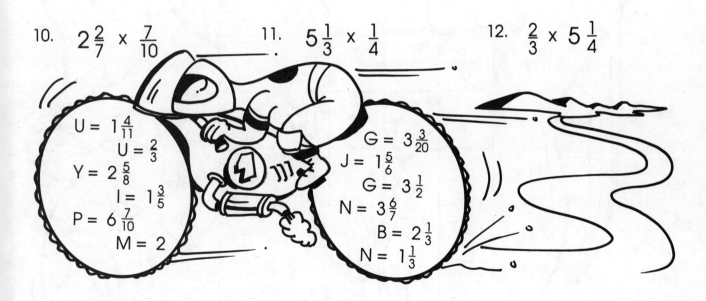

$U = 1\frac{4}{11}$
$U = \frac{2}{3}$
$Y = 2\frac{5}{8}$
$I = 1\frac{3}{5}$
$P = 6\frac{7}{10}$
$M = 2$

$G = 3\frac{3}{20}$
$J = 1\frac{5}{6}$
$G = 3\frac{1}{2}$
$N = 3\frac{6}{7}$
$B = 2\frac{1}{3}$
$N = 1\frac{1}{3}$

___ ___ ___ ___ ___   ___ ___ ___ ___ ___ ___ ___
 1   2   3   4   5   6   7   8   9   10 11 12

Name _____

"Corny" Number Sentences

$$\frac{10}{11} \div \frac{2}{5} = $$

$$\div$$

$$\frac{2}{9} \div \frac{4}{5} = $$

$$\div \qquad = $$

$$\frac{1}{3} \div \qquad = $$

$$= $$

$$\div \frac{8}{15} = $$

$$\div$$

$$\frac{1}{18} \div \frac{1}{6} = $$

$$\div \qquad = \qquad \div$$

$$\frac{4}{9} \qquad \qquad \frac{1}{10}$$

$$= \qquad \qquad = $$

Name _____

Geometrical Fractions

Work problems. Shade boxes with whole number.

$\frac{4}{5} \div \frac{2}{5}$	$1\frac{1}{2} \div 18$	$0 \div \frac{2}{3}$	$\frac{1}{2} \div \frac{1}{4}$
$1 \div 7\frac{1}{2}$	$\frac{9}{10} \div \frac{1}{5}$ $\quad 6 \div \frac{1}{2}$ $4\frac{1}{2} \div 18$ $\quad \frac{1}{4} \div \frac{2}{5}$	$1 \div \frac{1}{2}$	$4\frac{2}{5} \div \frac{1}{4}$
$4\frac{1}{3} \div 1$	$\frac{2}{3} \div 8$ $\quad 3\frac{5}{8} \div 8$ $\frac{9}{10} \div \frac{9}{10}$ $\quad 1 \div \frac{1}{8}$		$3\frac{2}{5} \div \frac{2}{3}$
$6 \div 1\frac{1}{2}$	$3\frac{5}{8} \div 1$	$1 \div 7\frac{1}{3}$	$\frac{1}{2} \div \frac{1}{12}$

Name _____

A Mere Fraction

Work problems. Arrange your work this way:

$$6 \div \frac{1}{4} = \frac{6}{1} \div \frac{1}{4} = \frac{6}{1} \times \frac{4}{1} = \frac{24}{1} = 24$$

$7 \div \frac{1}{3} =$	$8 \div \frac{1}{2} =$
$16 \div \frac{1}{3} =$	$6 \div \frac{1}{2} =$
$5 \div \frac{1}{6} =$	$18 \div \frac{1}{7} =$
$8 \div \frac{1}{5} =$	$7 \div \frac{1}{9} =$
$15 \div \frac{1}{6} =$	$2\frac{1}{2} \div \frac{1}{2} =$
$3\frac{1}{9} \div \frac{1}{3} =$	$5\frac{1}{4} \div \frac{3}{8} =$

 Daily Learning Drills Grade 5

Name _____

Decimal Delight

Kooky Claude Clod, the cafeteria cook, has some strange ideas about cooking. He does not understand fractions—only decimals. Help Claude convert these measurements to decimals so he can get cooking!

Mix together and sauté:

$\frac{9}{20}$ cup minced cat whiskers

$\frac{7}{8}$ cup crushed snails

$\frac{3}{5}$ cup toothpaste

$\frac{3}{4}$ tablespoon vinegar

$\frac{11}{25}$ cup pig slop

Simmer 93 $\frac{1}{2}$ days.

Gradually fold in:

$\frac{1}{5}$ teaspoon soot

$\frac{3}{8}$ cup car oil

$\frac{9}{10}$ tablespoon lemon juice

$\frac{11}{20}$ cup chopped poison ivy

6 $\frac{1}{4}$ rotten eggs

Brew for 1,500 $\frac{24}{25}$ years. Enjoy!

Mix together and sauté:

_____ cup minced cat whiskers

_____ cup crushed snails

_____ cup toothpaste

_____ tablespoon vinegar

_____ cup pig slop

Simmer _____ days

Gradually fold in: _____ teaspoon soot

_____ cup car oil

_____ tablespoon lemon juice

_____ cup chopped poison ivy

_____ rotten eggs

Brew for _____ years. Enjoy!

Name _____

Crack That Whip!

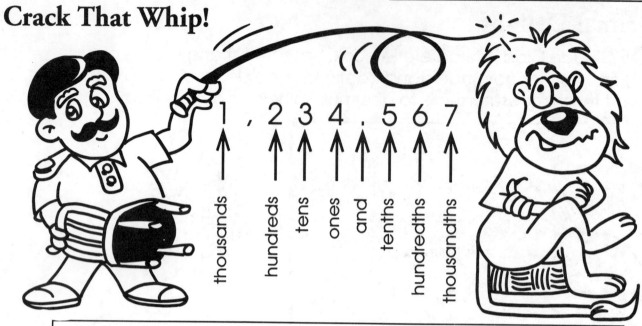

Decimal	Word Name
26.157	twenty-six and one hundred fifty-seven thousandths
3,004.08	three thousand four and eight hundredths
916.4	nine hundred sixteen and four tenths
8.002	eight and two thousandths
0.12	twelve hundredths

Write the word name for each decimal. The first one is started for you.

1. 2.06 = two and six _____

2. 17.009 = _____

3. 2,010.8 = _____

4. 555.55 = _____

5. 68.123 = _____

6. 4.38 = _____

7. 218.1 = _____

8. 5,002.09 = _____

9. 620.813 = _____

10. 6,190.007 = _____

Name _____

More Puzzling Problems

Down

1. 6.5 = six and five _____

2. .428 = four hundred _____ thousandths

3. 8,100.1 = eight _____ one hundred and one tenth

4. 3.02 = three and two _____

8. .685 = six hundred _____ thousandths

11. 50.19 = fifty and _____ hundredths

14. .015 = _____ thousandths

16. 430.7 = four hundred thirty and seven _____

17. 73.4 = seventy-three and four _____

Across

3. 7.333 = seven and three hundred thirty-three _____

5. 67.02 = sixty-seven and _____ hundredths

6. 490.1 = four hundred _____ and one tenth

7. .512 = five _____ twelve thousandths

9. 8.06 = eight and _____ hundredths

10. .007 = _____ thousandths

12. 11.3 = _____ and three tenths

13. 300.12 = _____ hundred and twelve hundredths

15. 62.08 = sixty-two and _____ hundredths

18. 70.009 = _____ and nine thousandths

19. 9.3 = _____ and three tenths

20. 10.51 = _____ and fifty-one hundredths

21. 1,000.02 = one thousand and two _____

Name _____

Andy Is Awesome!

Aussie Andy has a ratlike pet that is a marsupial. What is this "down under" animal called? Solve the problems below to find out.

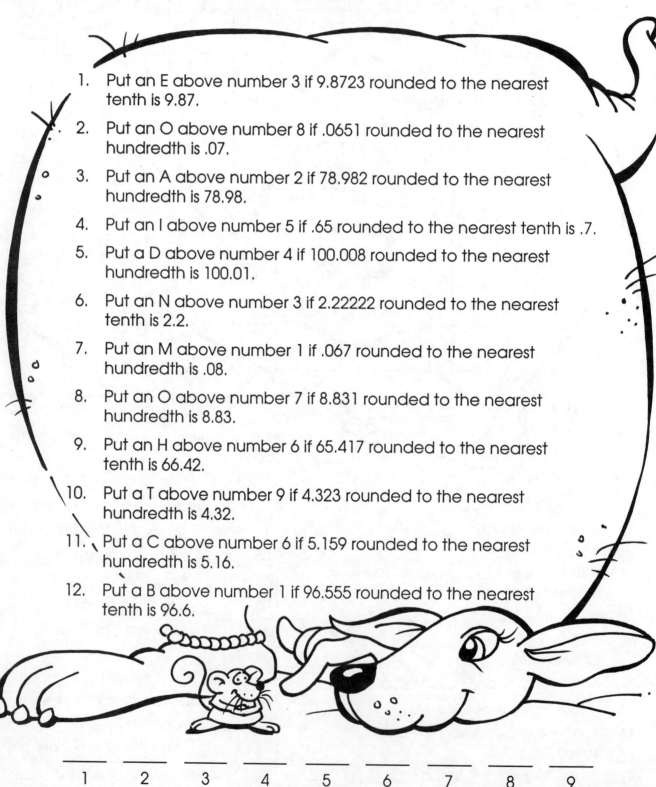

1. Put an E above number 3 if 9.8723 rounded to the nearest tenth is 9.87.

2. Put an O above number 8 if .0651 rounded to the nearest hundredth is .07.

3. Put an A above number 2 if 78.982 rounded to the nearest hundredth is 78.98.

4. Put an I above number 5 if .65 rounded to the nearest tenth is .7.

5. Put a D above number 4 if 100.008 rounded to the nearest hundredth is 100.01.

6. Put an N above number 3 if 2.22222 rounded to the nearest tenth is 2.2.

7. Put an M above number 1 if .067 rounded to the nearest hundredth is .08.

8. Put an O above number 7 if 8.831 rounded to the nearest hundredth is 8.83.

9. Put an H above number 6 if 65.417 rounded to the nearest tenth is 66.42.

10. Put a T above number 9 if 4.323 rounded to the nearest hundredth is 4.32.

11. Put a C above number 6 if 5.159 rounded to the nearest hundredth is 5.16.

12. Put a B above number 1 if 96.555 rounded to the nearest tenth is 96.6.

_1_ _2_ _3_ _4_ _5_ _6_ _7_ _8_ _9_

Name _____

My Name Is . . .

Decimals are names for fractional numbers. Write each fraction as a decimal.

1. $\frac{7}{10}$ = _____

2. $\frac{2}{10}$ = _____

3. $\frac{78}{100}$ = _____

4. $38\frac{1}{10}$ = _____

5. $3\frac{2}{100}$ = _____

6. $4\frac{36}{100}$ = _____

7. $\frac{3}{10}$ = _____

8. $\frac{4}{100}$ = _____

9. $\frac{21}{1000}$ = _____

10. $8\frac{103}{1000}$ = _____

11. $7\frac{16}{100}$ = _____

12. $1\frac{8}{10}$ = _____

13. $\frac{2}{10}$ = _____

14. $14\frac{8}{10}$ = _____

15. $38\frac{1}{10}$ = _____

16. $\frac{6}{10}$ = _____

17. $7\frac{6}{10}$ = _____

18. $\frac{3}{10}$ = _____

19. $15\frac{6}{10}$ = _____

20. $\frac{4}{10}$ = _____

21. $\frac{1}{4}$ = _____

22. $\frac{3}{8}$ = _____

23. $\frac{5}{8}$ = _____

24. $\frac{1}{40}$ = _____

25. $\frac{200}{400}$ = _____

26. $\frac{50}{125}$ = _____

27. $\frac{7}{8}$ = _____

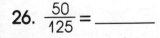

MATH

Name _____

How Do We Add Up?

Add problems.

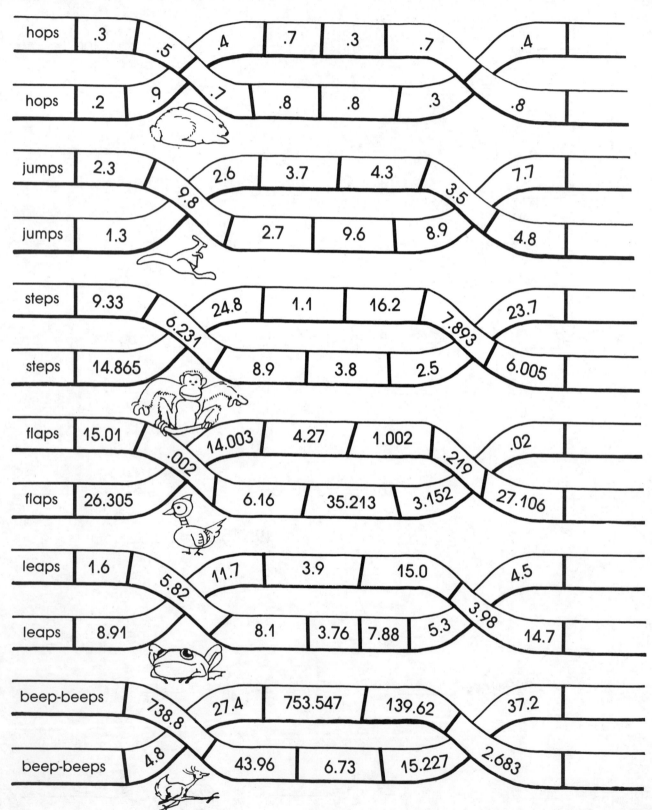

| hops | .3 | | .4 | .7 | .3 | | .7 | | .4 | |
| hops | .2 | .5 .9 .7 | | .8 | .8 | | .3 | | .8 | |

| jumps | 2.3 | | 2.6 | 3.7 | 4.3 | | | | 7.7 | |
| jumps | 1.3 | 9.8 | | 2.7 | 9.6 | 8.9 | 3.5 | | 4.8 | |

| steps | 9.33 | | 24.8 | 1.1 | 16.2 | | | 23.7 | |
| steps | 14.865 | 6.231 | | 8.9 | 3.8 | 2.5 | 7.893 | 6.005 | |

| flaps | 15.01 | | 14.003 | 4.27 | 1.002 | | | .02 | |
| flaps | 26.305 | .002 | | 6.16 | 35.213 | 3.152 | .219 | 27.106 | |

| leaps | 1.6 | | 11.7 | 3.9 | 15.0 | | | 4.5 | |
| leaps | 8.91 | 5.82 | | 8.1 | 3.76 | 7.88 | 5.3 | 3.98 | 14.7 | |

| beep-beeps | | 738.8 | 27.4 | 753.547 | 139.62 | | | 37.2 | |
| beep-beeps | | 4.8 | 43.96 | 6.73 | 15.227 | | 2.683 | |

Blast Off!

Name _____

Have a blast with this crossnumber! Hint: Decimal points take up their own square.

Down

1. 33.333
    + .896

2. 2.587
    + 3.191

3. 5.78
    + 1.09

7. 22.05 + 15.91

9. 2.057 + .008

10. .531 + .19

11. 7.852 + 1.489

13. 3.012 + 1.025

Across

3. 1.068
    + 5.086

4. .444
    + .53

5. 521.8
    + 312.4

6. 7.32 + .99

8. .502 + .191

12. 40.389 + 38.076

14. 270.85 + 90.57

15. .033 + .066

16. 8.749 + 3.388

Name _____

Your Turn to Subtract

Subtract. Check all problems.

1. 2.4 − .6	**2.** .79 − .08	**3.** 18.24 − 7.56	**4.** 38.57 − 16.83
5. 1.9 − .7	**6.** 13.5 − 7.3	**7.** 29.6 − 19.8	**8.** 42.6 − 8.1
9. 98.21 − 6.43	**10.** 2.7 − .7	**11.** 48.9 − 9.8	**12.** 63.29 − 9.43
13. 6.34 − 4.57	**14.** 12.6 − 6.5	**15.** 93.21 − 9.43	**16.** 691.98 − 42.69
17. 4.26 − .02	**18.** 98.6 − 7.8	**19.** 26.43 − 1.49	**20.** 987.23 − 8.97
21. 7.2 − 6.7	**22.** 88.7 − 43.8	**23.** 95.7 − 8.6	**24.** 143.29 − 86.74

Name _____

Firefighter Fred's Fate

Fred the Firefighter is trying to put out this fire and save the math books on the top floor. Solve the following subtraction problems and shade in the answers on the ladder. Some answers may not be on the ladder. At the end, if any numbers on the ladder are not shaded, Fred doesn't make it.

Does Fred save the math books? _____

1. 26.52
    – 19.48

2. 8.37
    – .98

3. .045
    – .011

4. 79.03
    – 78.52

5. 3.48
    – 2.49

6. .131 – .104

7. 6.678 – 6.566

8. 52.83 – 45.92

9. 8.61 – 1.83

10. 6.423 – 5.211

11. 2.47 – .56

12. .68 – .56

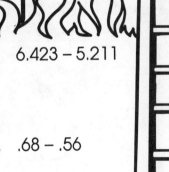

Ladder: .034, 6.78, 1.91, .99, .51, .123, 6.91, .027, 7.39, .112, 7.04

Name _____

Historical Harry

Harold is a history buff — thus his nickname, Historical Harry. Here is his trivia question to you: What were the large cannons used by Germany in World War I called? Solve the following subtraction problems and find the answers in the cannon. Put the corresponding letter above the problem's number at the bottom of the page to spell out the answer to this historical trivia question. This will be a good stumper for your parents!

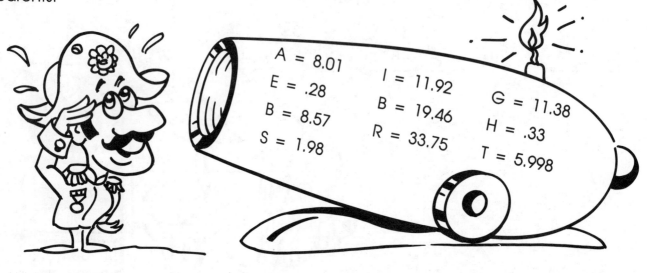

A = 8.01
E = .28
B = 8.57
S = 1.98
I = 11.92
B = 19.46
R = 33.75
G = 11.38
H = .33
T = 5.998

1. 9 – .43

2. 12 – .08

3. 15 – 3.62

4. 20 – .54

5. 1 – .72

6. 46 – 12.25

7. 6 – .002

8. 21 – 20.67

9. 9 – .99

10. 4 – 2.02

___ ___ ___   ___ ___ ___ ___   ___ ___ ___
 1   2   3   4   5   6   7   8   9   10

Name _____

Mogul Multiplication

Help Nancy the Novice get down this difficult mogul course by solving the multiplication problems. Start at the top and draw her path down by connecting the correct answers.

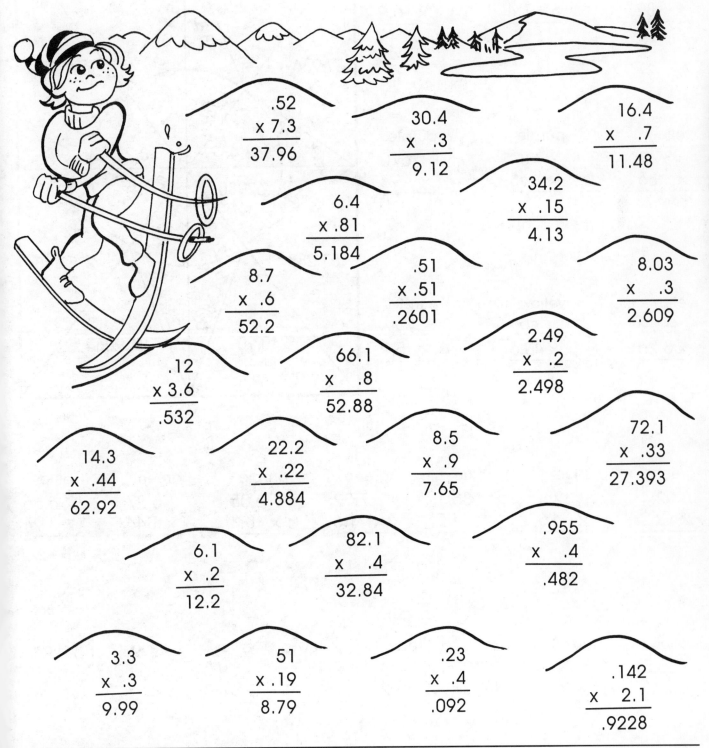

MATH

$$
\begin{array}{r}
.52 \\
\times\ 7.3 \\
\hline
37.96
\end{array}
$$

$$
\begin{array}{r}
30.4 \\
\times\ .3 \\
\hline
9.12
\end{array}
$$

$$
\begin{array}{r}
16.4 \\
\times\ .7 \\
\hline
11.48
\end{array}
$$

$$
\begin{array}{r}
6.4 \\
\times\ .81 \\
\hline
5.184
\end{array}
$$

$$
\begin{array}{r}
34.2 \\
\times\ .15 \\
\hline
4.13
\end{array}
$$

$$
\begin{array}{r}
8.7 \\
\times\ .6 \\
\hline
52.2
\end{array}
$$

$$
\begin{array}{r}
.51 \\
\times\ .51 \\
\hline
.2601
\end{array}
$$

$$
\begin{array}{r}
8.03 \\
\times\ .3 \\
\hline
2.609
\end{array}
$$

$$
\begin{array}{r}
.12 \\
\times\ 3.6 \\
\hline
.532
\end{array}
$$

$$
\begin{array}{r}
66.1 \\
\times\ .8 \\
\hline
52.88
\end{array}
$$

$$
\begin{array}{r}
2.49 \\
\times\ .2 \\
\hline
2.498
\end{array}
$$

$$
\begin{array}{r}
14.3 \\
\times\ .44 \\
\hline
62.92
\end{array}
$$

$$
\begin{array}{r}
22.2 \\
\times\ .22 \\
\hline
4.884
\end{array}
$$

$$
\begin{array}{r}
8.5 \\
\times\ .9 \\
\hline
7.65
\end{array}
$$

$$
\begin{array}{r}
72.1 \\
\times\ .33 \\
\hline
27.393
\end{array}
$$

$$
\begin{array}{r}
6.1 \\
\times\ .2 \\
\hline
12.2
\end{array}
$$

$$
\begin{array}{r}
82.1 \\
\times\ .4 \\
\hline
32.84
\end{array}
$$

$$
\begin{array}{r}
.955 \\
\times\ .4 \\
\hline
.482
\end{array}
$$

$$
\begin{array}{r}
3.3 \\
\times\ .3 \\
\hline
9.99
\end{array}
$$

$$
\begin{array}{r}
51 \\
\times\ .19 \\
\hline
8.79
\end{array}
$$

$$
\begin{array}{r}
.23 \\
\times\ .4 \\
\hline
.092
\end{array}
$$

$$
\begin{array}{r}
.142 \\
\times\ 2.1 \\
\hline
.9228
\end{array}
$$

Daily Learning Drills Grade 5

Name _____

A Multiple Design

Work the problems. Find the answers in the design and color correctly.

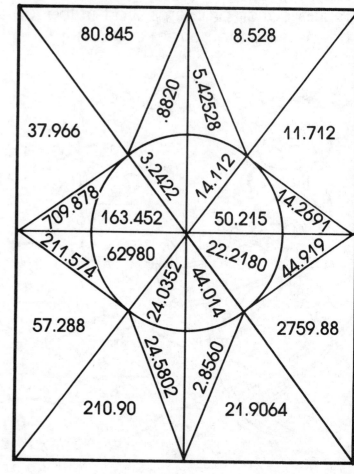

green	blue	red
.463	28.5	6.51
× 82	× 7.4	× 6.9

yellow	purple	purple
39.2	7.54	.670
× .36	× .43	× .94

yellow	yellow	purple
64.9	.592	7.46
× 3.26	× 40.6	× 5.9

Numbers in design: 80.845, 8.528, .0820, 5.42528, 37.966, 11.712, 3.2422, 14.112, 709.878, 163.452, 50.215, 14.2691, 211.574, .62980, 22.2180, 44.919, 24.0352, 44.014, 57.288, 2759.88, 24.5802, 2.8590, 210.90, 21.9064

green	blue	blue	green	purple	green	blue
92.4	32.8	85.1	7.32	6.05	3.27	5.56
× .62	× .26	× .95	× 1.6	× 8.3	× 844	× 3.94

yellow	red	red	red	yellow	yellow	yellow	yellow
80.5	5.77	95.8	.784	2.57	29.3	6.80	.245
× .276	× 4.26	× 7.41	× 6.92	× 63.6	× .487	× .42	× 3.6

Name _____

Decimal Review

Work problems. Shade in each answer to find the path to the bug.

```
   .43          35.1          377.5         4.289        13.190
   .06        475.11        × 1.53        × 67.3       −  5.734
   .28          .54
   .77          .3
 + 1.01       +  1.5
```

```
  .4392         5.03          .8627         5.621        3.108
 ×.216          .371        × .456        × 4.87       × .539
                .51
               1.22
             + 1.3
```

```
 10.3500        5.764         8.879          3.6         13.066
 − 2.3844      + .49        − 2.933       +6.938       −  4.214
```

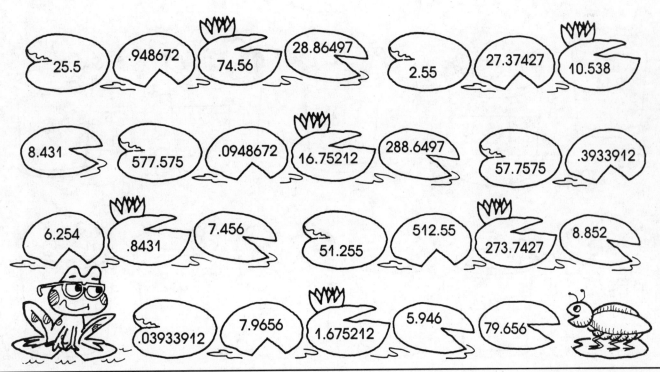

Name _____

The Perfect Sweet-Treat Solution

Solve each division problem. Draw a line from the popcorn (problem) to the correct drink (answer).

$3\overline{)7.95}$

6.84

$11\overline{)3.322}$

$5\overline{).31}$

2.65

.905

$9\overline{)2.196}$

.395

.302

$2\overline{).016}$

$7\overline{)47.88}$

.063

$5\overline{)11.4}$

.244

$4\overline{)15.48}$

1.135

$8\overline{)7.24}$

.008

$2\overline{).79}$

3.87

2.28

$8\overline{).504}$

.062

$6\overline{)6.81}$

Name _____

Note in a Bottle

Work problems. Unscramble the letters to find the secret message.

M
2.1) 8.4   = 21.) 84.

A
0.36) 1.872

S
1.24) 0.4712

R
8) 1.12

R
0.3) 17.7

L
6) 126.

A
.80) 16.00

E
6.1) 32.33

A
0.3) 0.234

E
.082) 0.3772

H
0.2) 6.34

C
9) 81.9

D
7.4) 103.6

D
.87) .5307

I
5.5) 3.025

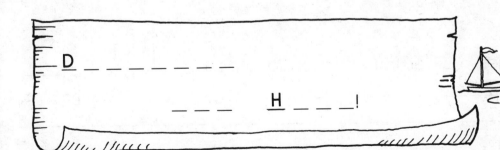

D _ _ _ _ _ _

_ _ _ H _ _ _ !

Name _____

I'm 100 Percent!

To write a decimal as a percent, move the decimal two places to the right and add a % sign.

.95 _____

7.21 _____

.08 _____

3.25 _____

.6 _____

.1576 _____

9.25 _____

.4 _____

.12 _____

1.90 _____

.240 _____

.60 _____

.03 _____

.56 _____

.609 _____

.02 _____

2.5 _____

.156 _____

.05 _____

.09 _____

.88 _____

42.5 _____

9.21 _____

.8 _____

.42 _____

1.00 _____

.63 _____

1.21 _____

.9 _____

1.5 _____

Rewrite the percentages in order, from smallest to largest. _____

_____

Name _____

Addition of Time

60 seconds	= 1 minute (min)	7 days	= 1 week (wk)
60 minutes	= 1 hour (h)	4 weeks	= 1 month (mo)
24 hours	= 1 day (d)	12 months or 52 weeks	= 1 year (y)

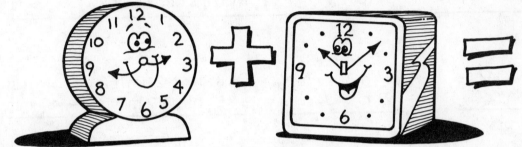

Complete.

1.
```
   2 h   14 min
 + 3 h   31 min
 _____
```

2.
```
   5 h   24 min
 + 7 h   19 min
 _____
```

3.
```
   3 min  14 s
 + 4 min  18 s
 _____
```

4.
```
   5 min  41 s
 + 3 min  29 s
 _____
```

5.
```
   3 h   43 min
 + 2 h   51 min
 _____
```

6.
```
   3 h   14 min
 + 6 h   72 min
 _____
```

7.
```
   2 min  18 s
 + 7 min  58 s
 _____
```

8.
```
   9 h   30 min
 + 3 h   31 min
 _____
```

9.
```
   1 min  49 s
 + 2 min  27 s
 _____
```

10.
```
   3 h   41 min
 + 4 h   59 min
 _____
```

11.
```
   8 min  29 s
 + 3 min  46 s
 _____
```

12.
```
   2 h   39 min
 + 5 h   41 min
 _____
```

13.
```
   5 wk  2 d
 + 2 wk  4 d
 _____
```

14.
```
   3 h   16 min
 + 1 h   48 min
 _____
```

15.
```
   2 d   4 h
 + 3 d   15 h
 _____
```

16.
```
   3 d   15 h
 + 4 d   10 h
 _____
```

17.
```
   6 wk  3 d
 + 1 wk  9 d
 _____
```

18.
```
   16 h  51 min
 + 4 h   8 min
 _____
```

19.
```
   5 min  27 s
 + 14 min  33 s
 _____
```

20.
```
   3 y   8 mo
 + 2 y   6 mo
 _____
```

Name _____

Subtraction of Time

60	seconds	= 1 minute (min)	7	days	= 1 week (wk)
60	minutes	= 1 hour (h)	4	weeks	= 1 month (mo)
24	hours	= 1 day (d)	12	months or 52 weeks	= 1 year (y)

Complete.

1.
```
   7  min  42 s
 - 3  min  29 s
```

2.
```
   5  h    49 min
 - 2  h    34 min
```

3.
```
   8  h    24 min
 - 5  h    19 min
```

4.
```
   4  min  47 s
 - 3  min  28 s
```

5.
```
   8  h    14 min
 - 3  h    25 min
```

6.
```
   7  h    29 min
 - 2  h    38 min
```

7.
```
   9  min  23 s
 - 8  min  51 s
```

8.
```
   4  min  21 s
 - 2  min  53 s
```

9.
```
   12 min  19 s
 -  8 min  42 s
```

10.
```
   5  h    14 min
 - 3  h    29 min
```

11.
```
   16 min  42 s
 -  8 min  25 s
```

12.
```
   3  h    12 min
 - 1  h    46 min
```

13.
```
   5  d    9 h
 - 2  d    10 h
```

14.
```
   3  wk   4  d
 - 1  wk   5  d
```

15.
```
   16 d    14 h
 -  9 d     7 h
```

16.
```
   6  y    4  mo
 - 3  y    6  mo
```

17.
```
   5  min  21 s
 - 2  min  22 s
```

18.
```
   8  d    7  h
 - 5  d    21 h
```

19.
```
   5  wk   3  d
 - 2  wk   6  d
```

20.
```
   13 h    14 min
 -  7 h    48 min
```

21.
```
   8  y    9  mo
 - 2  y    10 mo
```

22.
```
   4  d    13 h
 - 1  d    17 h
```

23.
```
   21 h    10 min
 -  8 h    54 min
```

24.
```
   4  min  32 s
 - 2  min  47 s
```

       Daily Learning Drills Grade 5

Name _____

Good Timing

Complete the wheels beginning at the center and adding or subtracting using the rule given.

Name _____

What Time Is It?

Complete.

_____ minutes after _____

_____ minutes before _____

_____ minutes after _____

_____ minutes before _____

_____ minutes after _____

_____ minutes before _____

_____ minutes after _____

_____ minutes before _____

_____ minutes after _____

_____ minutes before _____

_____ minutes after _____

_____ minutes before _____

_____ minutes after _____

_____ minutes before _____

_____ minutes after _____

_____ minutes before _____

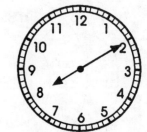

_____ minutes after _____

_____ minutes before _____

_____ minutes after _____

_____ minutes before _____

_____ minutes after _____

_____ minutes before _____

Name _____

Time Conversion

60 seconds	= 1 minute (min)	7 days	= 1 week (wk)	
60 minutes	= 1 hour (h)	4 weeks	= 1 month (mo)	
24 hours	= 1 day (d)	12 months or 52 weeks	= 1 year (y)	

Complete.

1.

50 h = ____ d ____ h

2.

72 s = ____ min ____ s

3.

12 min 12s = ____ s

4.

9 d = ____ wk ____ d

5.

2 d 6 hr = ____ h

6.

26 h = ____ d ____ h

7.

129s = ____ min ____ s

8.

37 d = ____ wk ____ d

9.

189 min = ____ h ____ min

10.

4 d 4 hr = ____ h

11.

53 d = ____ wk ____ d

12.

78 h = ____ d ____ h

13.

5 min 14 s = ____ s

14.

484 min = ____ h ____ min

15.

6 wk 2 d = ____ d

16.

65 d = ____ wk ____ d

17.

369 s = ____ min ____ s

18.

2 wk 6 d = ____ d

19.

3 mo 2 wk = ____ wk

20.

55 wk = ____ y ____ wk

21.

16 mo = ____ y ____ mo

22.

88 d = ____ wk ____ d

23.

50 d = ____ wk ____ d

24.

39 wk = ____ mo ____ wk

Name _____

Elapsed Time
How much time has gone by?

1. **From**   **To**

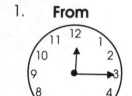

     P.M.   **P.M.**

_____ minutes

2. **From**   **To**

     A.M.   **P.M.**

_____ hours _____ minutes

3. **From**   **To**

     A.M.   **P.M.**

_____ hours _____ minutes

4. **From**   **To**

     A.M.   **P.M.**

_____ hours _____ minutes

5. **From**   **To**

     A.M.   **P.M.**

_____ hours _____ minutes

6. **From**   **To**

     P.M.   **A.M.**

_____ hours _____ minutes

7. **From**   **To**

     A.M.   **P.M.**

_____ hours _____ minutes

8. **From**   **To**

     P.M.   **A.M.**

_____ hours _____ minutes

Name _____

Addition of Elapsed Time

Figure the elapsed time.

1.

+ 50 minutes

Time: _____

2.

+ 1 hour 5 minutes

Time: _____

3.

+ 2 hours 40 minutes

Time: _____

4.

+ 25 minutes

Time: _____

5.

+ 30 minutes

Time: _____

6.

+ 4 hours 35 minutes

Time: _____

7.
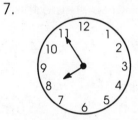

+ 2 hours 20 minutes

Time: _____

8.
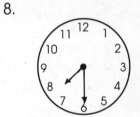

+ 4 hours

Time: _____

9.

+ 3 hours 15 minutes

Time: _____

10.

+ 20 minutes

Time: _____

11.
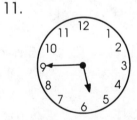

+ 6 hours 30 minutes

Time: _____

12.

+ 3 hours 30 minutes

Time: _____

13.

+11 hours

Time: _____

14.

+ 24 hours 5 minutes

Time: _____

MATH

Name _____

More Addition of Time

Determine the sum total.

STUDIO
A

A. Geneva worked on her sculpture this week:

Monday:	2 h	14 min
Tuesday:		30 min
Wednesday:	1 h	16 min
Thursday:	3 h	25 min
Friday:	1 h	45 min

Sum total: _____ _____

B. Monica's choir practice this week:

Monday:		55 min
Tuesday:		45 min
Wednesday:		30 min
Thursday:		50 min
Friday:	1 h	20 min

Sum total: _____ _____

C. David's swim practice this week:

Monday:	1 h	25 min
Tuesday:		43 min
Wednesday:	1 h	59 min
Thursday:	3 h	29 min
Friday:	1 h	37 min

Sum total: _____ _____

D. Eva's rollerblade club met for five Saturdays in a row:

Saturday #1:	2 h	12 min
Saturday #2:	3 h	51 min
Saturday #3:	1 h	43 min
Saturday #4:	3 h	49 min
Saturday #5:	2 h	29 min

Sum total: _____ _____

E. Michele went horseback riding with her friends for five Saturdays in a row:

Saturday #1:	1 h	50 min
Saturday #2:	2 h	5 min
Saturday #3:	3 h	10 min
Saturday #4:	1 h	42 min
Saturday #5:	1 h	27 min

Sum total: _____ _____

F. Mark's model rocket club met and built rockets for 5 Saturdays in a row:

Saturday #1:	2 h	35 min
Saturday #2:	3 h	21 min
Saturday #3:	2 h	41 min
Saturday #4:	1 h	56 min
Saturday #5:	3 h	29 min

Sum total: _____ _____

Name _____

More Elapsed Time

Complete.

	Time Now	Add this Elapsed Time	Future Time (Include Day and Time)
1.	Monday, 9:00 a.m.	2 days, 4 hours	_____
2.	Saturday, 4:00 p.m.	3 days, 5 hours, 32 minutes	_____
3.	Tuesday, 6:00 a.m.	6 days, 7 hours, 45 minutes	_____
4.	Sunday, 1:00 p.m.	1 day, 9 hours, 56 minutes	_____
5.	Thursday, 2:45 p.m.	5 days, 2 hours, 45 minutes	_____
6.	Wednesday, 4:00 a.m.	8 days, 12 hours, 29 minutes	_____
7.	Monday, 7:00 a.m.	14 days, 7 hours, 39 minutes	_____
8.	Friday, 7:00 p.m.	2 days, 3 advanced time zones	_____
9.	Monday, 5:00 p.m.	4 days, 25 hours	_____
10.	Saturday, 12:00 a.m.	6 days, 13 hours, 1 minute	_____
11.	Tuesday, 5:00 p.m.	12 days, 14 hours, 23 minutes	_____
12.	Sunday, 2:00 a.m.	3 days, 26 hours	_____
13.	Monday, 1:00 p.m.	2 weeks, 4 days, 35 minutes	_____
14.	Saturday, 6:00 a.m.	74 hours	_____
15.	Sunday, 8:00 a.m.	21 days, 2 hours	_____
16.	Wednesday, 4:00 a.m.	15 days, 12 hours, 45 minutes	_____
17.	Friday, 3:00 p.m.	5 days, 3 hours, 128 minutes	_____
18.	Thursday, 6:00 p.m.	3 days, 4 earlier time zones	_____

Complete. Give the elapsed time in days and hours.

1. Monday, 4:00 a.m. to Wednesday, 5:00 a.m. _____
2. Wednesday, 12:00 p.m. to Saturday, 2:00 p.m. _____
3. Friday, 5:00 a.m. to Sunday, 4:00 p.m. _____
4. Thursday, 7:00 p.m. to Friday, 9:00 a.m. _____
5. Saturday, 6:00 p.m. to Monday, 5:00 a.m. _____
6. Tuesday, 3:00 p.m. to Friday, 6:00 p.m. _____
7. Saturday, 8:00 p.m. to Sunday, 3:00 a.m. _____
8. Monday, 4:00 p.m. to Wednesday, 8:00 a.m. _____

Name _____

Dog and Jog Graphs

Answer the questions using the graphs indicated.

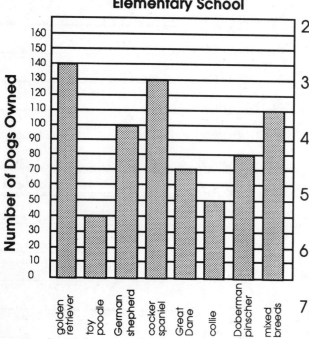

Dog Owners at Petumalot Elementary School

Number of Dogs Owned

golden retriever, toy poodle, German shepherd, cocker spaniel, Great Dane, collie, Doberman pinscher, mixed breeds

1. How many students own Great Danes at Petumalot Elementary School? _____

2. Which dog listed is owned by the least number of students? _____

3. Which breed is owned by the most number of students? _____

4. What is the mean number of dogs owned? _____

5. What is the range between golden retrievers and toy poodles? _____

6. How many students own Doberman pinschers? _____

7. How many more students own German shepherds than collies? _____

1. Which class jogged the most during a one-week period? _____

2. Which class jogged the most miles during this four-week period? _____ What was the difference between classes? _____

3. Which week had the greatest range between the two classes? _____

4. Which week had the smallest range? _____

5. What was the mean number of miles jogged by Mrs. Singalot's class? _____

6. What was the range for Mr. Explainitwell's class during these four weeks? _____

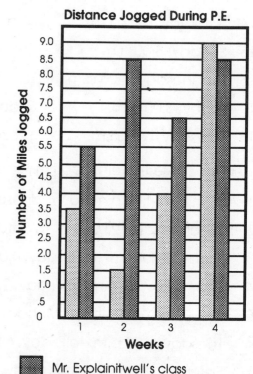

Distance Jogged During P.E.

Number of Miles Jogged

Weeks

■ Mr. Explainitwell's class
□ Mrs. Singalot's class

Name _____

Recreation Spots and Food Drives

Lowell Lake's Busiest Summer Recreation Spots

Total Visitors This Year: 15,300

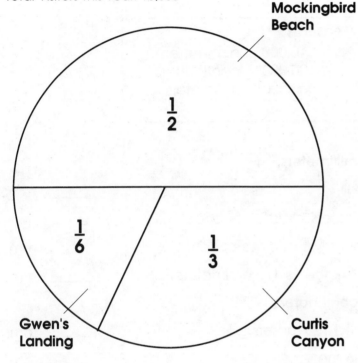

Mockingbird Beach

$\frac{1}{2}$

$\frac{1}{6}$

$\frac{1}{3}$

Gwen's Landing

Curtis Canyon

1. Which spot at Lowell Lake had the least amount of visitors?_____

2. How many people in all visited Mockingbird Beach? _____

3. What fraction of the people visited Gwen's Landing and Curtis Canyon combined?_____

Earlridge Community's Annual Food Drive

Total Pounds Collected: 183,200 pounds

1. In which time period was the greatest amount of food collected?

   _____

2. How many pounds of food were collected in the first two weeks? _____

3. How many pounds of food were collected in the first four weeks? _____

4. In which time period was the least amount of food collected?_____

5. What fraction of the food was collected during the first two weeks and the last three weeks of the drive?_____

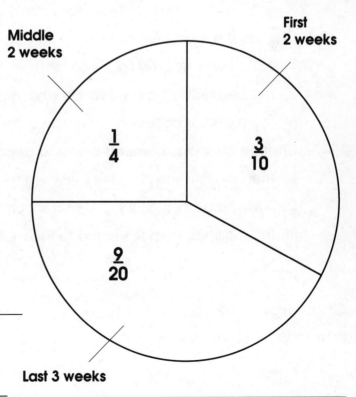

Middle 2 weeks

First 2 weeks

$\frac{1}{4}$

$\frac{3}{10}$

$\frac{9}{20}$

Last 3 weeks

Name _____

Metric Madness

Use the chart to convert these metric measurements.

Equal Measures			
1	kilometer	10,000	decimeters
10	hectometers	100,000	centimeters
100	dekameters	1,000,000	millimeters
1,000	meters		

I.   Change the measurements below to millimeters.

1. Rudy's chess king is 5 centimeters tall.   _____ mm

2. The camp's baseballs are 23 centimeters in circumference.   _____ mm

3. The camp's baseball bats are all roughly 8 decimeters long.   _____ mm

4. The distance between Mr. Warden's knees is 41 centimeters.   _____ mm

II. Change the measurements below to centimeters.

1. Rudy's longest home run ball traveled 123 meters.   _____ cm

2. Algonkian's tennis courts are each 6 meters wide.   _____ cm

3. The world record for the javelin throw is just over 94 meters.   _____ cm

III. Change the measurements below to decimeters.

1. Algonkian's hockey field is 86 meters long.   _____ dm

2. The beaver built a dam which was about 8 meters across.   _____ dm

3. The distance between the camp office and the mess hall is 150 meters. _____ dm

IV. Change the measurements below to dekameters.

1. The trail distance from the mess hall to the garbage area is 220 meters. _____ dkm

2. Rudy naturally won the 200-meter hurdles.   _____ dkm

3. The distance from the island to the mainland is 2 kilometers.   _____ dkm

Challenge: The island has 9,123 meters of coastline.

How many millimeters is this? _____

Name _____

Up and Away

Hint: If it's .5 or greater, round up to the next cm.
If it's less than .5, round down.

$$1 \text{ cm} = 10 \text{ mm}$$

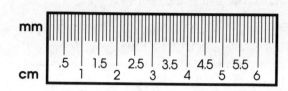

A. Complete each conversion.

30 mm = _____ cm   8.5 cm = _____ mm   50 mm = _____ cm

80 mm = _____ cm   38 mm = _____ cm   5.9 cm = _____ mm

14.2 cm = _____ mm   4.7 cm = _____ mm   900 mm = _____ cm

65 mm = _____ cm   3.2 cm = _____ mm   2.9 cm = _____ mm

B. Measure each section of this rocket in millimeters.

A = _____ mm
B = _____ mm
C = _____ mm
D = _____ mm
E = _____ mm
F = _____ mm
G = _____ mm

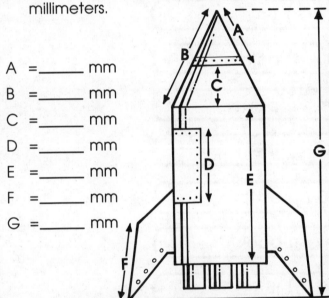

C. Measure each section of this hot air balloon to the nearest centimeter.

A = _____ cm
B = _____ cm
C = _____ cm
D = _____ cm
E = _____ cm
F = _____ cm

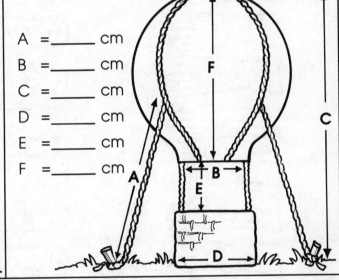

D. Measure in millimeters and to the nearest centimeter.

1. Width of your thumbnail – _____ mm _____ cm
2. Distance between your eyes – _____ mm _____ cm
3. Length of the pencil you're using right now – _____ mm _____ cm
4. Thickness of your front door – _____ mm _____ cm
5. Length of a book – _____ mm _____ cm
6. Length of a mailbox – _____ mm _____ cm
7. Width of your favorite photograph – _____ mm _____ cm
8. Length of your shoe – _____ mm _____ cm

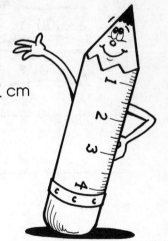

Name _____

Metric Match Magic

Use the chart to help you match the metric equivalents. Then, write the word beside each answer on the line and follow the directions.

km	hm	dam	m	dm	cm	mm
1,000 m	100 m	10 m	1 m	.1 m	.01 m	.001 m

1.  2 m •

2.  900 cm •

3. 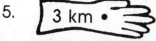 4,000 m •

4.  700 cm •

5. 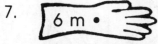 3 km •

6. 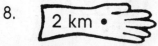 5,000 m •

7.  6 m •

8.  2 km •

9. 800 cm •

10. 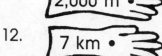 5 m •

11. 2,000 m •

12. 7 km •

- 7 m) of
- 600 cm) draw
- 500 cm) very
- 200 cm) on
- 7,000 m) animal
- 5 km) paper
- 9 m) the
- 2,000 m) a
- 4 km) back
- 3,000 m) this
- 8 m) magician's
- 2 km) favorite

_____1_____   _____2_____   _____3_____   _____4_____

_____5_____   _____6_____   _____7_____   _____8_____

_____9_____   _____10_____   _____11_____   _____12_____

Name _____

Metric Units of Mass

| 1,000 mg | = | 1 g |
| 1,000 g | = | 1 kg |

A. Astronauts aboard the spacecraft "Moon Crater" accidentally left the gravity machine off when they bunked down for the night. What mass would each of these floating items have on earth? milligram (**mg**), gram (**g**), or kilogram (**kg**)

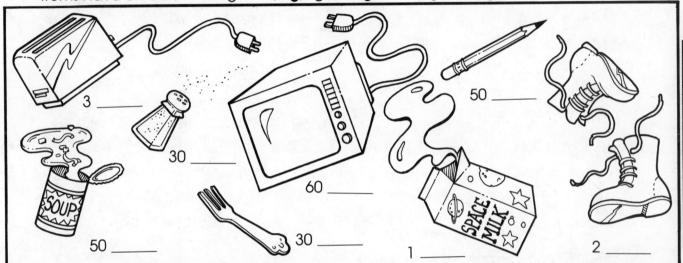

3 _____   30 _____   50 _____   60 _____   30 _____   1 _____   2 _____   50 _____

B. Solve the following problems.

1. Kelly's dog "Barksinger" weighs a total of 40 kg while soaking wet during a bath. After drying off, he loses 3,000 g. How much does Barksinger now weigh? _____

2. Carolyn picks 10 kg of oranges from her tree. After squeezing out the juice, she discovers that the leftover rinds weigh 2,000 g. How many kilograms of juice are there? _____

3. On Wednesday, Al ran a magnet through the sand to extract iron filings. He collected a total of 720 g of iron. On Thursday, he extracted another 1,280 g. How many kilograms did he extract altogether? _____

4. Marnie picked 82,000 g of watermelon for the family picnic. How many kilograms does this equal? _____

C. Circle the appropriate unit of mass.

1. Katy poured 350 (**mg g kg**) of salt on her steak.

2. Casandra lugged home 4 (**mg g kg**) of books in her backpack today.

3. Jonathan was pleased to find 10 (**mg g kg**) of black olives on his pizza.

4. Brittainy was happy to find that her new skates only weighed 2 (**mg g kg**).

Name _____

How Long?

12 in = 1 ft	3 ft = 1 yd	5,280 ft = 1 mi	1,760 yd = 1 mi

A. Complete.

9 ft = _____ yd   6 yd = _____ ft

3 mi = _____ yd   18 ft = _____ in

3 mi = _____ ft   27 ft = _____ yd

39 in = _____ ft _____ in   5,280 ft = _____ mi

10,560 ft = _____ mi   6 ft = _____ in

7 yd = _____ ft   144 in = _____ ft

5 mi = _____ yd   48 in = _____ ft

14 ft = _____ yd _____ ft   5,286 ft = _____ mi _____ yd

B. Measure each picture to the nearest eighth inch.

ice-cream cone: _____ in

big shoe: _____ in

long bow: _____ in

telescope: _____ in

very happy fish: _____ in

A. Circle the correct unit of measure.

1. Width of a calculator is 3 (**in   ft   yd   mi**).

2. Length of your arm is _____ (**in   ft   yd   mi**).

3. Distance from one side of town to the other is 10 (**in   ft   yd   mi**).

4. Length of a guitar is 3 (**in   ft   yd   mi**).

5. The approximate distance from Earth to the planet Mars is 50,000,000 (**in   ft   yd   mi**).

6. Distance sound travels in one hour is approximately 750 (**in   ft   yd   mi**).

7. Distance light travels in one second is 186,000 (**in   ft   yd   mi**).

8. Distance from your feet to the top of your head is _____ (**in   ft   yd   mi**).

Name _____

Take a Gander!

| 1 pt = 2 c | 1 qt = 2 pt | 1 gal = 4 qt |

What is the name for a group of geese?

To find out, follow the directions below.

1. Put a G above number 1 if 50 fl oz = 6 c.

2. Put an E above number 7 if 11 pt = 22 c.

3. Put a G above number 1 if 24 c = 12 qt.

4. Put an A above number 1 if 6 gal = 24 qt.

5. Put an L above number 7 if 7 pt = 220 fl oz.

6. Put an H above number 6 if 32 fl oz = 32 c.

7. Put a G above number 4 if 28 c = 14 pt.

8. Put a G above number 5 if 16 pt = 8 qt.

9. Put an E above number 1 if 21 gal = 168 qt.

10. Put an O above number 3 if 35 fl oz = 2 pt.

11. Put an A above number 3 if 16 qt = 64 c.

12. Put a G above number 3 if 7 pt = 110 fl oz.

13. Put an E above number 2 if 15 gal = 122 c.

14. Put an H above number 6 if 30 fl oz = 4 c.

15. Put an L above number 6 if 5 qt = 20 c.

16. Put a G above number 2 if 128 fl oz = 16 c.

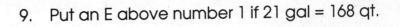

___ ___ ___ ___ ___ ___ ___
 1   2   3   4   5   6   7

Name _____

Units of Weight

A. Complete.

1 lb = 16 oz
1 T = 2,000 lb

32 oz = _____ lb   4 T = _____ lb

8,000 lb = _____ T   7 lb = _____ oz

60,000 lb = _____ T   3,000 lb = _____ T

32,000 oz = _____ T   240 oz = _____ lb

3 T = _____ lb   1,920 oz = _____ lb

96 oz = _____ lb $2\frac{1}{2}$ lb = _____ oz

48 oz = _____ lb $1\frac{3}{4}$ lb = _____ oz

1,000 lb = _____ T   5 lb = _____ oz

B. Circle the heavier amount.

1. 1 T   3,000 lb   6. 7 lb   113 oz

2. 3 lb   46 oz   7. 61,000 lb   30 T

3. 5,000 lb   2 T   8. 150 oz   9 lb

4. 6 T   11,000 lb   9. 2 lb 2 oz   35 oz

5. 64 oz   3 lb   10. 6 lb 4 oz   101 oz

C. Circle the correct unit of measurement.

1. Curt purchased 4 (**oz lb T**) of balsa wood to build his model airplane.

2. Diana and her friends collected 3 (**oz lb T**) of shells in 2 bags.

3. Mark and his family discovered that their furniture in the moving van weighed about 3 (**oz lb T**)!

4. Sharon purchased a 12 (**oz lb T**) bag of roasted peanuts at the circus.

5. Eva found that each of the baby rabbits in her back yard weighed 6 (**oz lb T**)!

6. Chase carried the 10 (**oz lb T**) sack of apples up to the house.

7. Megan could not believe her mother had just purchased 70 (**oz lb T**) of groceries at the store.

8. Crystal's brand new earrings weighed 3 (**oz lb T**).

Name _____

Orville's Orchards

Mrs. Appleton's class went on a field trip to Orville's Orchards. It was apple-pickin' time and the students were going to get apples for their families and for their class. Help them figure out how many apples they need. Use the chart to the right to help you.

> 1 peck = 18 apples
> 1 bushel = 4 pecks

1. Jimmy and Tommy told Mrs. Appleton that their moms wanted enough apples for 6 pies each. Orville said that 8 apples are needed for each pie. Altogether, how many apples did Jimmy and Tommy need? _____ How many pecks? _____ How many apples will be left over? _____ How many bushels? _____ How many apples left over? _____

2. Sarah's mom makes apple butter each year. This year, she is going to make 50 jars to give to family and friends as gifts. Each batch makes 10 jars and she needs 24 apples per batch. How many apples does Sarah need to buy her mom? _____ What is the best way to buy the apples so there are few left over? _____

_____

3. Mrs. Appleton told her students she wanted each student to pick 9 apples for classroom activities. There are 27 students in her class. How many bushels will this be? _____ How many apples will be left over? _____ How many pecks will this be? _____

4. Orville counted up one group's apples. Two boys had 2 pecks each, 4 girls each had 3 pecks, and 7 students had 1 peck each. How many apples did they buy? _____ How many bushels was this? _____ How many pecks was this? _____

5. Altogether, Mrs. Appleton's class bought 13 bushels, 3 pecks and 7 apples. How many apples did they buy? _____

6. Students could buy a peck of apples for $3.28, a bushel for $12.25 and one apple for 16¢. How much in all did Mrs. Appleton's class spend? _____

7. Orville told all the students that he'd give them each 4 free apples for every 20 rotten apples they gathered. If Mrs. Appleton's students gathered 363 rotten apples, how many free apples did Orville give away? _____ What is the average number of apples each student picked? _____

Fascinating Fact! Did you know that every year, each person in the U.S. uses up enough items made from wood to equal a 100-foot tall, 16-inch wide tree?

Name _____

Geometric Figures

Find the perimeter of each figure.

Perimeter is the distance around an area.

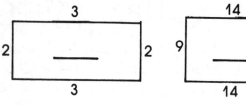
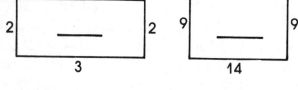
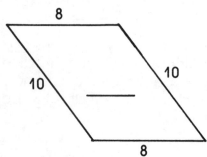
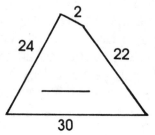
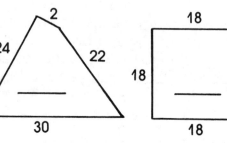
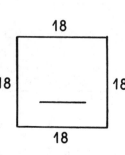
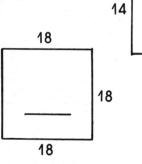
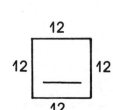
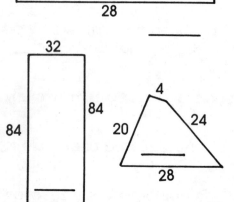
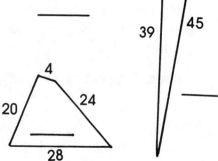
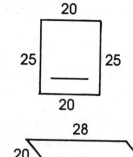
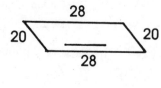
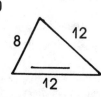
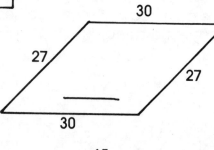
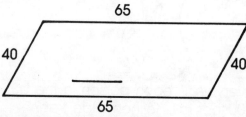
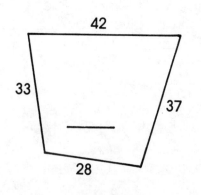

Name _____

Area and Perimeter

Use drawings to answer puzzles.

Across

1.

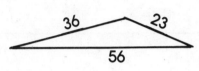

3.

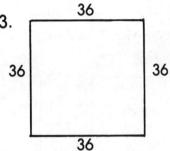

5.

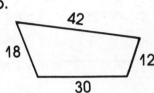

Down

1.

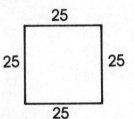

2.

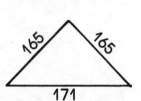

3.

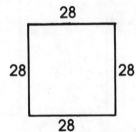

4.

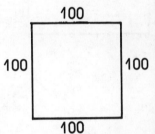

Perimeter

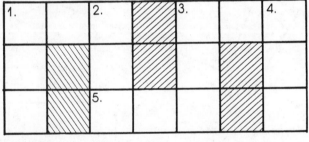

Across

1.

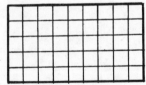

2.

3.

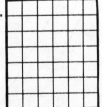

4.

5.

Down

1.

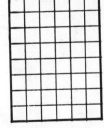

3.

2.

Area

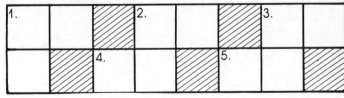

Name _____

So Many Stomachs!

> What holiday animal has six stomachs and can give milk?

To find out, find the areas of the following shapes at the bottom of the page and put the corresponding letter above each answer.

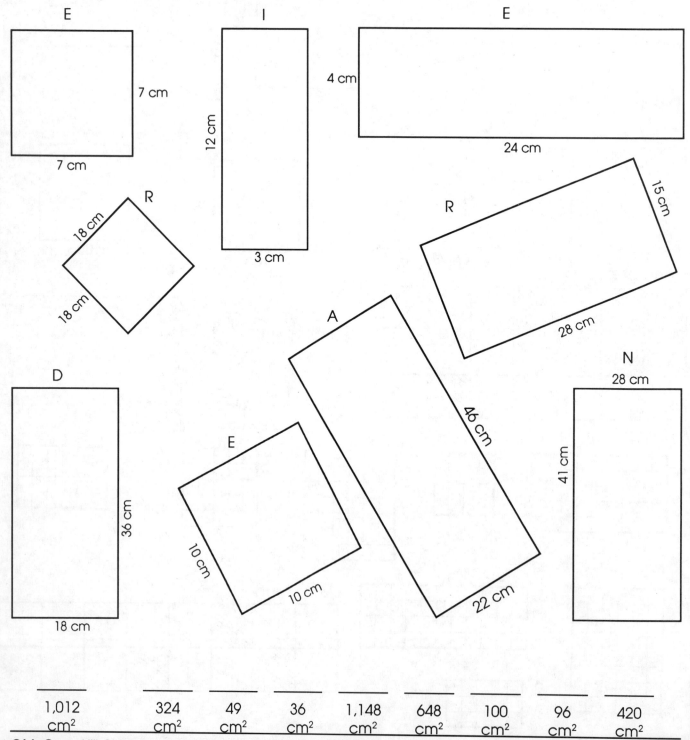

E — 7 cm, 7 cm

I — 12 cm, 3 cm

E — 4 cm, 24 cm

R — 18 cm, 18 cm

R — 15 cm, 28 cm

A — 46 cm, 22 cm

D — 36 cm, 18 cm

E — 10 cm, 10 cm

N — 28 cm, 41 cm

1,012 cm²	324 cm²	49 cm²	36 cm²	1,148 cm²	648 cm²	100 cm²	96 cm²	420 cm²

Name _____

Area

A. Find the area of each figure.
   A = Length x width

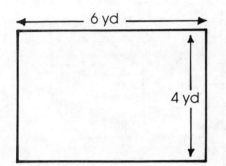

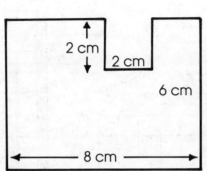

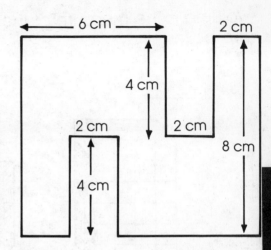

A = _____ yd²   A = _____ cm²   A = _____ cm²

B. Find the area of each triangle.
   A = 1/2 (b x h)

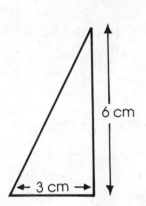

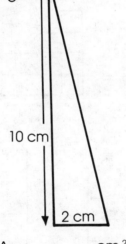

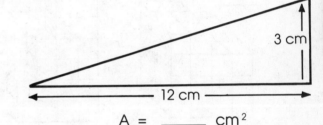

A = _____ cm²

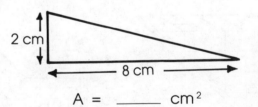

A = _____ cm²   A = _____ cm²   A = _____ cm²

C. Find the area of each circle.
   A = π x r²   (π = 3.14)

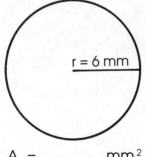

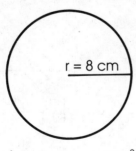

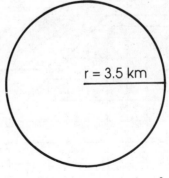

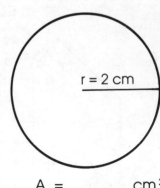

A = _____ mm²   A = _____ cm²   A = _____ km²   A = _____ cm²

Name _____

Volume

Volume is the measure of the inside of a space figure. Find the volume. Count the boxes.

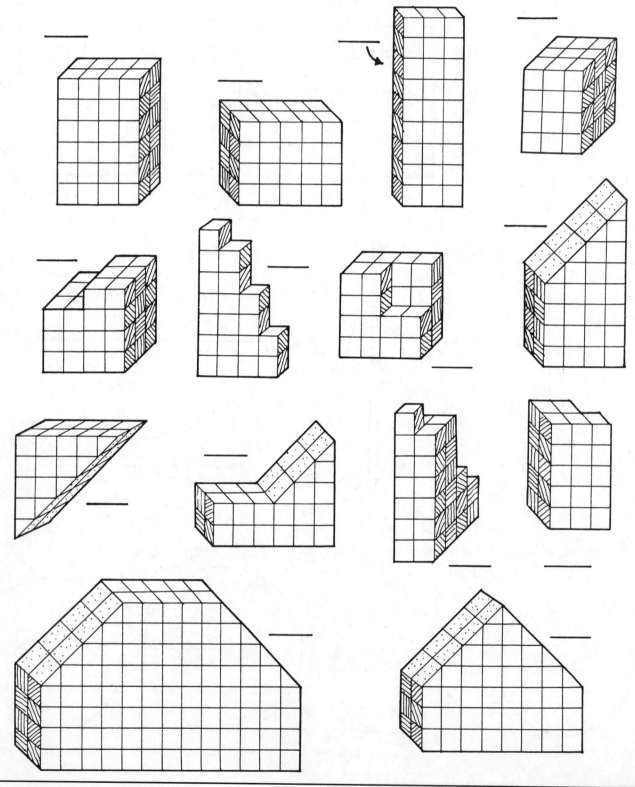

Name _____

Figure It

Find the volume of each figure.

$$V = length \times width \times height$$

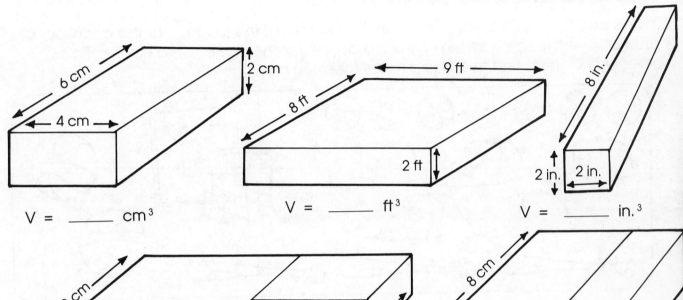

V = _____ cm³

V = _____ ft³

V = _____ in.³

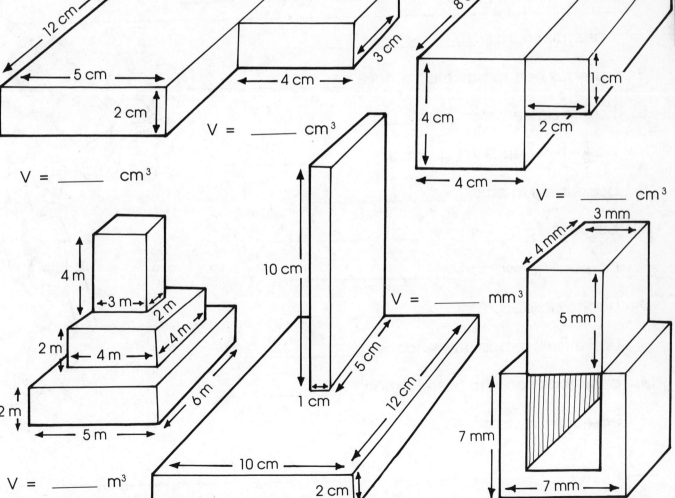

V = _____ cm³

V = _____ cm³

V = _____ cm³

V = _____ m³

V = _____ mm³

ratios

Name _____

What a Backward Bird!

| What bird can fly backwards? |

To find out, find the following ratios at the bottom of the page. Put the corresponding letter above the ratio. When you have answered the riddle, write each ratio two other ways. Then, find two equal ratios for each one.

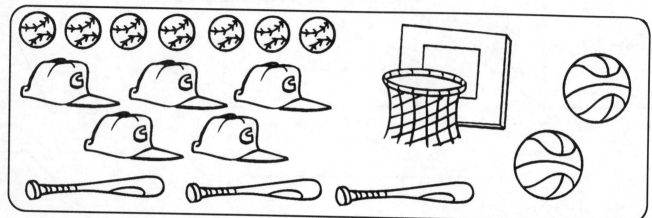

M. baseballs to bats _____

B. baseball hats to basketball hoops _____

U. bats to basketballs _____

N. basketball hoops to baseballs _____

R. basketballs to bats _____

G. baseballs to basketballs _____

H. baseball hats to bats _____

D. bats to baseballs _____

I. basketballs to basketball hoops _____

M. basketball hoops to baseball hats _____

I. baseball hats to baseballs _____

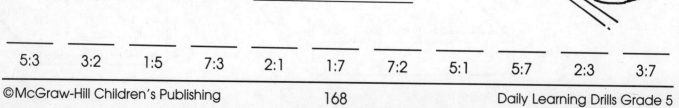

___ ___ ___   ___ ___ ___ ___ ___ ___ ___ ___
5:3   3:2   1:5   7:3   2:1   1:7   7:2   5:1   5:7   2:3   3:7

©McGraw-Hill Children's Publishing   168   Daily Learning Drills Grade 5

Name _____

Geometric Figures

Point S = •S	Ray XY = $\overrightarrow{XY}$
Line CD = $\overleftrightarrow{CD}$	Line segment BC = $\overline{BC}$

Match.

1. 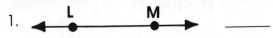 _____

2. Q _____

3. 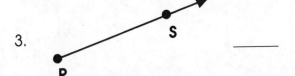 _____

4.  _____

5. 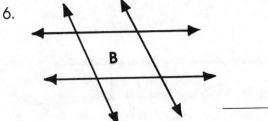 _____

6. B _____

7. X _____

8. _____

9. 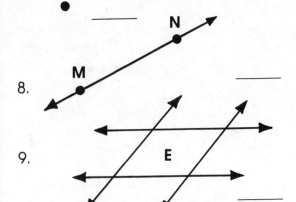 _____

10. P   Q _____

11. G   H _____

12. H   I _____

13. A _____

14. P   O _____

15. Q   R _____

16. D _____

17. J   K 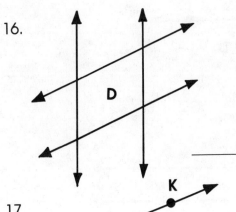 _____

A. $\overrightarrow{GH}$

B. Point Q

C. Plane E

D. Plane D

E. Point A

F. $\overrightarrow{OP}$

G. $\overleftrightarrow{LM}$

H. $\overline{YZ}$

I. $\overleftrightarrow{MN}$

J. $\overleftrightarrow{HI}$

K. $\overrightarrow{JK}$

L. $\overrightarrow{RS}$

M. $\overleftrightarrow{PQ}$

N. $\overrightarrow{TU}$

O. Point X

P. $\overline{QR}$

Q. Plane B

MATH

Name _____

More Geometric Figures

$\overleftrightarrow{AB}$ is perpendicular to $\overleftrightarrow{CD}$ = $\overleftrightarrow{AB} \perp \overleftrightarrow{CD}$ $\overline{AB}$ is parallel to $\overline{CD}$ = $\overline{AB} \parallel \overline{CD}$

Circle the correct name for each figure.

1.
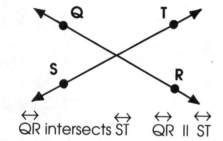

$\overleftrightarrow{QR}$ intersects $\overleftrightarrow{ST}$ $\overleftrightarrow{QR} \parallel \overleftrightarrow{ST}$

2.
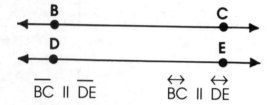

$\overline{BC} \parallel \overline{DE}$ $\overleftrightarrow{BC} \parallel \overleftrightarrow{DE}$

3.
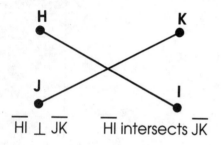

$\overline{HI} \perp \overline{JK}$ $\overline{HI}$ intersects $\overline{JK}$

4.
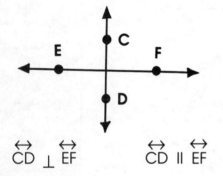

$\overleftrightarrow{CD} \perp \overleftrightarrow{EF}$ $\overleftrightarrow{CD} \parallel \overleftrightarrow{EF}$

5.
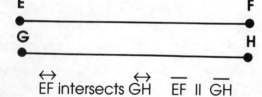

$\overleftrightarrow{EF}$ intersects $\overleftrightarrow{GH}$ $\overline{EF} \parallel \overline{GH}$

6.
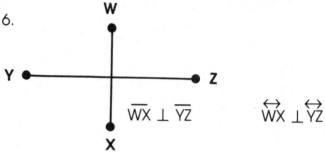

$\overline{WX} \perp \overline{YZ}$ $\overleftrightarrow{WX} \perp \overleftrightarrow{YZ}$

7.
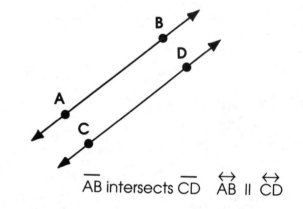

$\overline{AB}$ intersects $\overline{CD}$ $\overleftrightarrow{AB} \parallel \overleftrightarrow{CD}$

8.
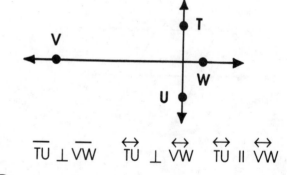

$\overline{TU} \perp \overline{VW}$ $\overleftrightarrow{TU} \perp \overleftrightarrow{VW}$ $\overleftrightarrow{TU} \parallel \overleftrightarrow{VW}$

9.
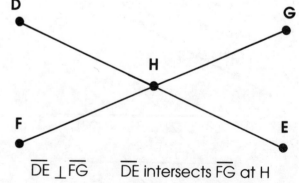

$\overline{DE} \perp \overline{FG}$ $\overline{DE}$ intersects $\overline{FG}$ at H

Name _____

Naming Figures

Use this figure to answer the questions below.

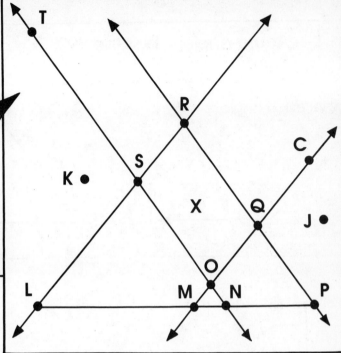

1. Name the plane in this figure. _____

2. Point K is inside which angle? _____

3. Name three triangles in this figure. _____

4. Point J is inside which angle? _____

5. Name three angles for which Q is the vertex. _____

6. Which points make up the parallelogram in this figure? _____

7. Name the largest triangle in this figure. _____

8. How many other angles can be named inside ∠ LNT? _____

9. Name all the angles that contain a side on $\overleftrightarrow{LR}$. _____

_____

10. How many points are on $\overleftrightarrow{MC}$? _____ Name them. _____

11. Name the point at which $\overleftrightarrow{LR}$ and $\overleftrightarrow{NT}$ intersect. _____

12. Name the vertex for ∠SNL. _____

13. Are lines $\overleftrightarrow{TN}$ and $\overleftrightarrow{RP}$ perpendicular or parallel? _____

14. Are lines $\overleftrightarrow{LR}$ and $\overleftrightarrow{MC}$ perpendicular or parallel? _____

Name _____

What's Your Angle?

Acute Angle: Less than 90°
Right Angle: 90°

Obtuse Angle: Greater than 90°,
less than 180°

Label each angle.

1.
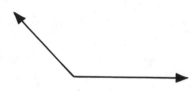

_____

2.

_____

3.
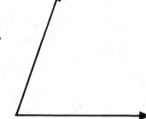

_____

4.
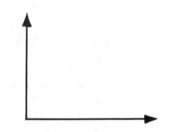

_____

5.

_____

6.
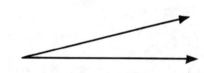

_____

7.
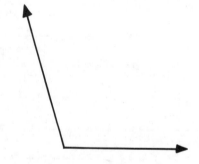

_____

8.
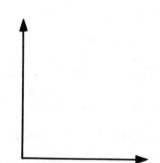

_____

9.

_____

10.
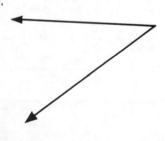

_____

11.
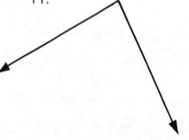

_____

12.
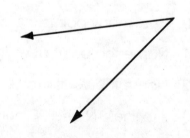

_____

Name _____

Angle Measurement

The **degree** is the unit used to measure angles.

Measure the following angles using a protractor.

1. 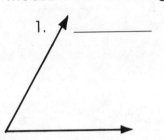 _____

2. _____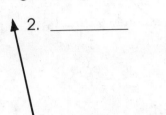

3. _____

4. _____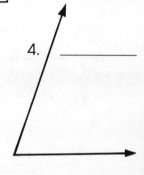

5. _____

6. _____

7. _____

8. _____

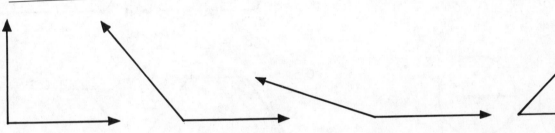 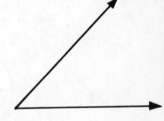

Draw the angles given using a protractor.

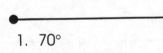

1. 70°

2. 120°

3. 40°

4. 90°

5. 150°

6. 110°

MATH

Name _____

Congruent Figures

Are these congruent? Write **yes** or **no**.

1.

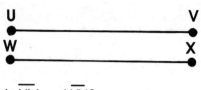

Is $\overline{UV} \cong \overline{WX}$? _____

2.

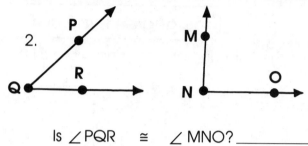

Is $\angle PQR \cong \angle MNO$? _____

3.

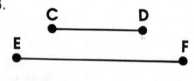

Is $\overline{CD} \cong \overline{EF}$? _____

4.

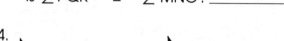

Is $\angle B \cong \angle L$? _____

5.

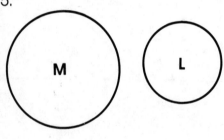

Is $M \cong L$? _____

6.

Is $Q \cong X$? _____

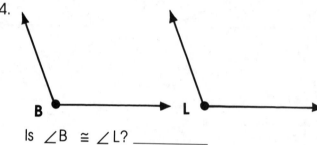

7.

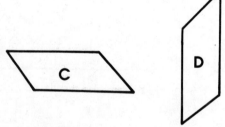

Is $C \cong D$? _____

8.

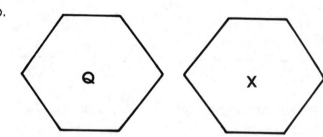

Is $\angle S \cong \angle T$? _____

9.

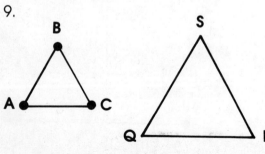

Is $\triangle ABC \cong \triangle QRS$? _____

10.

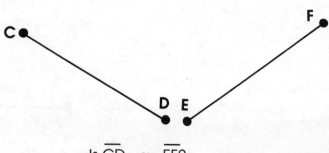

Is $\overline{CD} \cong \overline{EF}$? _____

Name _____

Think Fast!

The time it takes for your ears to send a message to your brain, and your body to respond is called **reaction time.**

Let's try an experiment to test your reaction time. Find a partner and take turns helping one another with the experiment.

Materials: 30 cm metric ruler

Procedure:

1. Place your left arm on a table with your hand over the edge.

2. Space your thumb and index fingers about 4 cm apart.

3. Have a partner hold the "30 cm end" of the ruler, with the other end just above your open thumb and index finger.

4. Your partner will say "set," and drop the ruler.

5. Catch the ruler with your thumb and index finger as quickly as possible.

6. Check the distance fallen by taking a reading at the bottom of the index finger.

7. Record your results.

8. Repeat the procedure 10 times with each hand.

Are you right-handed, or left-handed? Which of your hands was the quickest?

_____

Did others find the same results? _____

Form a group of 5 or 6 students. Make a graph depicting your results.

Trial #	Reaction Distance	
	Left Hand	Right Hand
1.		
2.		
3.		
4.		
5.		
6.		
7.		
8.		
9.		
10.		

SCIENCE

Name _____

The Circulatory System

As you read the information given below, underline the two main functions and the main organ of the circulatory system. Then, answer the questions.

The circulatory system is responsible for transporting materials throughout the body and for regulating body temperature.

As a transportation network, the heart is vital to the circulatory system. It pumps blood to all parts of the body. The blood then carries nutrients and other important materials to your cells. Blood also carries waste products away from cells to disposal sites like the liver, lungs and kidneys. The circulatory system also acts as a temperature control for your body. Warmer blood from the center of your body is brought to the surface to be cooled. On a cold day, your blood vessels contract very little allowing little blood to flow through. This is why your skin might appear pale, or even blue. However, in hot weather, blood vessels widen and more blood is able to flow through them to increase the loss of heat. Thus, your skin looks pinker and feels warmer.

1. What are the two main functions of the circulatory system?

_____

2. The blood carries important nutrients to the _____.
3. Blood carries _____ away from cells to the
_____, _____ and _____.
4. Warmer blood is brought from the _____ of the body to the
_____ of the body to be cooled.
5. In cold weather, why does your skin appear pale, or even blue?

_____

A "Hearty" Experiment

To learn more about the circulatory system, do the experiment below.

Materials needed: tennis ball   watch with a second hand

• Hold the tennis ball in your strongest hand and give it a hard squeeze. This is about the strength it takes your heart muscle to contract to pump one beat.
• Squeeze the ball as hard as you can and release it 70 times in one minute.

Record how your hand feels._____

Conclusion: _____

Fascinating Fact! Did you know that if your blood vessels were laid end to end, they would encircle the globe twice over?

Name _____

Feel the Beat

When the heart pumps, it forces blood out into the arteries. The walls of the arteries expand and contract to the rhythm of the heart which creates a **pulse.**
You can feel your pulse where the arteries are close to the surface of the skin. Two good places to feel a pulse are on the inside of the wrist, and on the neck to the side of the windpipe.

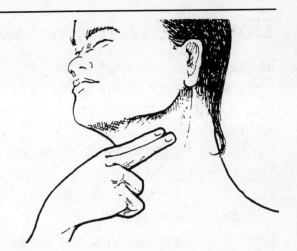

The type of activity you are doing can greatly affect the rate of your pulse. Try the experiment below and complete the chart by –
1. counting the number of heartbeats in 15 seconds.
2. multiplying that number by 4 to get the pulse rate for one minute.

Study your results. Explain how each type of activity affected your pulse rate.

Activity	Pulse Rate for 15 sec.	X 4 =	Pulse Rate per minute
Sitting still for 10 minutes			
Running in place for 3 minutes			
Just after finishing your lunch or dinner			
While still in bed in the morning			
Just after getting ready for school			

SCIENCE

Fascinating Fact! The heart pumps about 1,250 gallons of blood each day.

Name _____

How Your Digestive System Works

In your digestive system, enzymes, special kinds of chemicals produced by the salivary glands in the walls of your stomach, break food up so it can pass through the wall of your small intestine into your blood. You cannot see inside to watch these enzymes work, but you can do the activity below to help you better understand what they do.

The following experiment will show you the effect enzymes can have on proteins. Enzymes that break down proteins do not become active until the food reaches the stomach.

Materials needed: 4 small bowls, meat tenderizer, small amount of hamburger

Procedure:

1. Mark bowls #1, #2, #3 and #4.
2. Make 4 equal marble-sized pieces of hamburger.
3. Put one piece of hamburger in bowl #1 and another in bowl #3.
4. Break the other 2 pieces of hamburger up into small pieces and put one in bowl #2 and one in bowl #4.

5. Cover the meat in bowl #1 and #2 with meat tenderizer and a few drops of water.
6. Cover the meat in bowls #3 and #4 with the same amount of water only.
7. Let the bowls stand in a warm place for a few days.

Results:

Bowl #1: _____

Bowl #2: _____

Bowl #3: _____

Bowl #4: _____

Conclusions: _____

_____

_____

_____

Fascinating Fact!

Borborygmi is the rumbling noise your digestive system makes.

Name _____

Enlightening Environmental Information

An **environment** includes all living and nonliving things with which an organism interacts. These living and nonliving things are **interdependent**, that is, they depend on one another. The living things in an environment (plants, animals, etc.) are called **biotic factors** and the nonliving things and factors (soil, light, temperature, etc.) are called **abiotic factors**. **Ecology** is the study of the relationships and interactions of living things with one another and their environment.

Living things inhabit many different environments. A group of organisms living and interacting with each other in their nonliving environment is called an **ecosystem**. The living part of an ecosystem, all the organisms that live together in an area, is called a **community**. In a community, each kind of living thing makes up a **population**.

Follow the directions below.

1. Label two biotic factors and two abiotic factors in the picture.
2. Explain the relationships between the living things in the environment shown in the picture.
3. At the top of the picture, write the type of ecosystem pictured.
4. Circle all the members of the community.
5. Write how the organisms in this environment are dependent on one another.
6. List the types of populations that live in the environment.
7. Define *ecology* in your own words on the back of the page.

Name _____

Pond Water

Some of the organisms found in pond water are so small that you need a microscope to see them. To make the following observations, you will need a sample of pond water, a microscope, and a microscope slide. (If you cannot bring in a small container of pond water, your teacher will furnish it.)

1. Put a drop of pond water on your slide. Look at it with your microscope under low power.

2. Mark the circle below which looks like the approximate number of organisms you can see in your sample.

☐ ☐ ☐ ☐

3. Turn your microscope to high power and find an organism. Watch it carefully. Make a sketch of it below. If it looks like any of the organisms to the right, write its name in the blank under your sketch.

_____ (If not, try to identify it later by looking in the encyclopedia or biology book.) Does it have any special features such as a tail or hairs to help it move? _____

4. Look for other organisms. Do you see any that are different from your first organism? _____ Sketch two of them on another paper. As time progresses, many of the smaller ones will be eaten by the larger ones, such as the water flea or copepod.

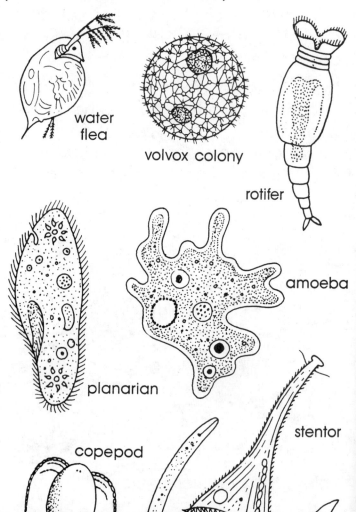

water flea

volvox colony

rotifer

amoeba

planarian

stentor

copepod

roundworm

paramecium

Name _____

File Up, Phylums!

Scientists separate animals according to their differences and group them according to their likenesses.

Draw a line from the phylum in the first column to the correct picture and then to the characteristics. The first one is done for you.

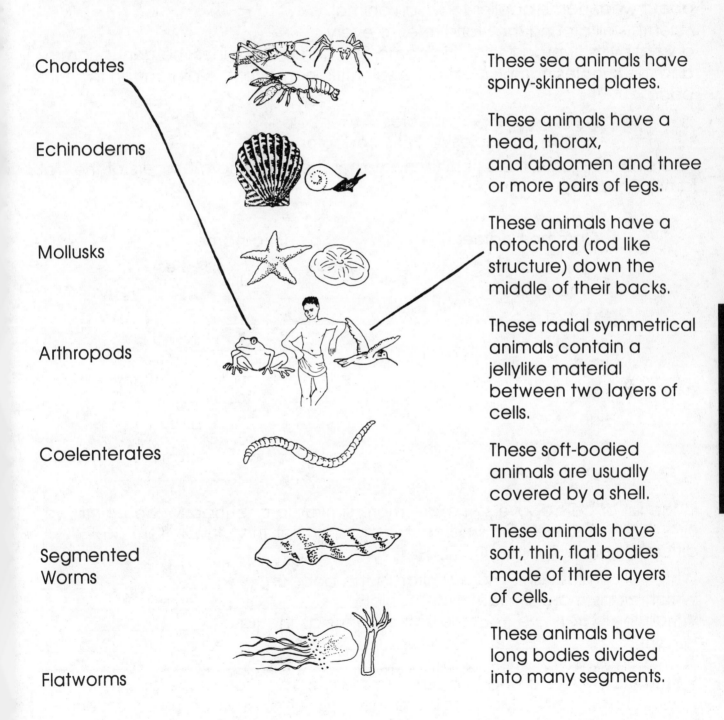

Chordates

Echinoderms

Mollusks

Arthropods

Coelenterates

Segmented Worms

Flatworms

These sea animals have spiny-skinned plates.

These animals have a head, thorax, and abdomen and three or more pairs of legs.

These animals have a notochord (rod like structure) down the middle of their backs.

These radial symmetrical animals contain a jellylike material between two layers of cells.

These soft-bodied animals are usually covered by a shell.

These animals have soft, thin, flat bodies made of three layers of cells.

These animals have long bodies divided into many segments.

SCIENCE

Mixed-Up Names

Name _____

What is the name for this cat? Is it a puma, mountain lion, panther, or cougar? Most people use common names when referring to an animal, but it's easy to be confused about what name applies to which animal. Scientists all around the world refer to every animal by its two-part scientific name. This name combines the **genus name** and the **species name**. What is the scientific name for the big cat on this page?

> genus = Felis   species = concolor
> genus + species = **Felis concolor**

Find and compare the scientific names of the following members of the cat family. (Felidae)

Common name	Scientific name (genus + species)	
domestic cat	_____	_____
bobcat	_____	_____
ocelot	_____	_____
jaguar	_____	_____
lynx	_____	_____
lion	_____	_____
tiger	_____	_____
panther	_____	_____

In the list of cats above some are more similar to one than to the other. Two cats with the same genus name are more similar than those from two different genus names.

Which cat in the list is more similar to the bobcat? _____
Which cat is more similar to the ocelot?_____
Which three cats are from the same genus as the tiger? _____

_____

Find Out: Make a chart comparing the classification of the domestic cat with the domestic dog. Compare the kingdoms, phyla, classes, orders, genus and species of each.

Name _____

Invertebrates

Just three groups of the many kinds of invertebrates are listed below. The first group are **arthropods.** Arthropods are invertebrates with jointed legs. Insects, spiders, and crustaceans, like lobsters and crabs, belong to this group. **Worms** are slender, creeping animals with soft bodies and no legs. The last group are **mollusks.** Mollusks are also soft-bodied, but most have shells for protection. Some mollusks, like the octopus, do not have shells.

Using the words from the word bank, find some examples of invertebrates in the puzzle below. Then list them under the group they belong to.

```
M F T A P E W O R M F
C R A Y F I S H O S L
L O B S T E R D U O A
A P L Q C M C H N C T
M T I U W O R A D T W
S N A I L T A J W O O
S K N D B H B E O P R
A N T O Y S T E R U M
E A R T H W O R M S O
```

Word Bank

ant	crayfish	lobster	oyster	squid
clam	earthworm	moth	roundworm	tapeworm
crab	flatworm	octopus	snail	

Arthropods   **Worms**   **Mollusks**

_____   _____   _____

_____   _____   _____

_____   _____   _____

_____   _____   _____

_____   _____   _____

SCIENCE

Fun Fact

The longest known species of giant earthworm is found in South Africa and is 136 cm long!

Name _____

Orderly Insects

There are more than 25 different orders of insects. Seven of the most common orders are listed below. Write the name of the insects pictured under the correct order.

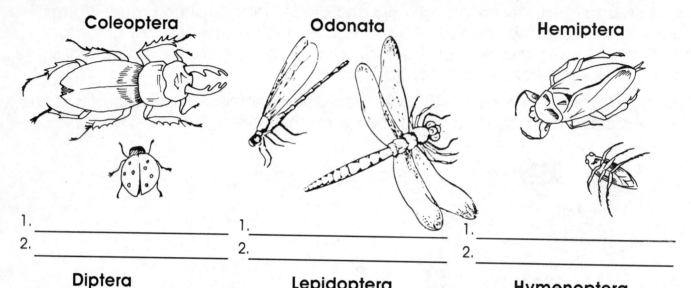

Coleoptera

1. _____
2. _____

Odonata

1. _____
2. _____

Hemiptera

1. _____
2. _____

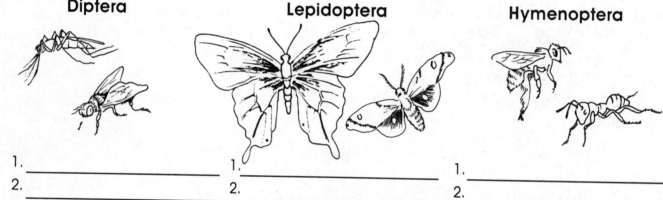

Diptera

1. _____
2. _____

Lepidoptera

1. _____
2. _____

Hymenoptera

1. _____
2. _____

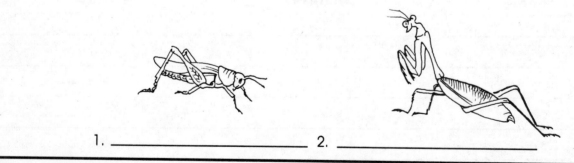

Orthoptera

1. _____   2. _____

WORD BANK

stag beetle	grasshopper	damsel fly	dragonfly
butterfly	mosquito	giant water bug	back swimmer
honeybee	ant	silkworm moth	housefly
ladybug	praying mantis		

Name _____

Friend or Foe?

Insects play a very important role in the balance of nature. Insects eat many kinds of plants and animals, but they also are a source of food for many other kinds of plants and animals. Complete the list of ways that insects can be harmful and helpful.

HELPFUL

_____
_____
_____
_____
_____
_____
_____

HARMFUL

_____
_____
_____
_____
_____
_____
_____

Insect Control

Man has used many different methods for insect control. One method is the use of chemicals called insecticides. One such insecticide that is commonly used throughout the world is **DDT**. DDT is a very effective insecticide, but it was found to also be very harmful to man and the environment. This insecticide has been banned in the United States, but it is still used in many other parts of the world.

Read about the uses and effects of DDT. Pretend that you are writing an editorial in an international newspaper that would convince the other nations of the world that they, too, should ban the use of DDT.

SCIENCE

International News Editorial

DDT — Helpful or Harmful?

_____
_____
_____
_____

Continue on the back of your paper.

Name _____

Worms, Worms, Worms

There are thousands of different kinds of worms. Each kind belongs to one of the four major groups of worms.

Draw a line from each pictured worm to the group to which it belongs.

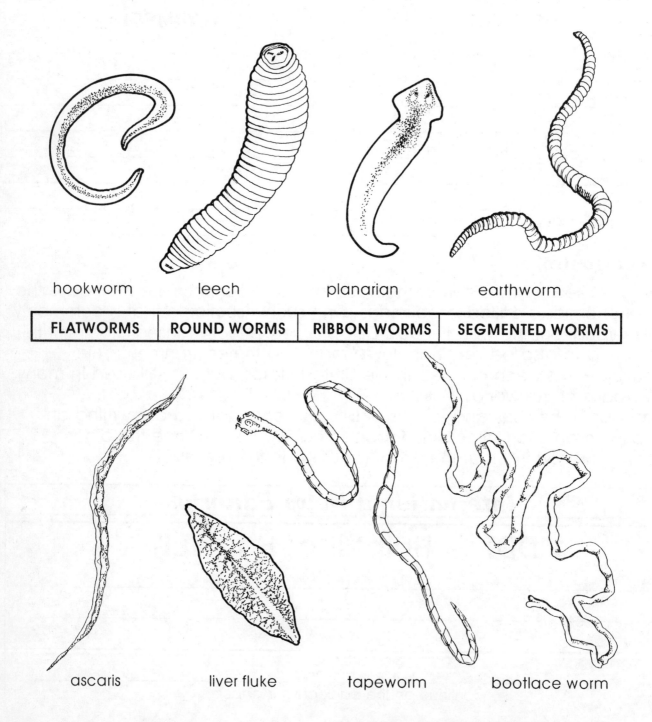

hookworm   leech   planarian   earthworm

| FLATWORMS | ROUND WORMS | RIBBON WORMS | SEGMENTED WORMS |

ascaris   liver fluke   tapeworm   bootlace worm

• On a sheet of paper, explain each of the four worm groups.

Name _____

Vertebrates

The more than five groups of vertebrates have many characteristics that are similar. Complete the chart below.

	Fish	Amphibians	Reptiles	Birds	Mammals
Warm-blooded or Cold-blooded					
Type of Body Covering					
Born Alive or Hatched					
Feed Young with Milk (Yes/No)					
Air, Land or Water Habitat					
Type of Appendages					

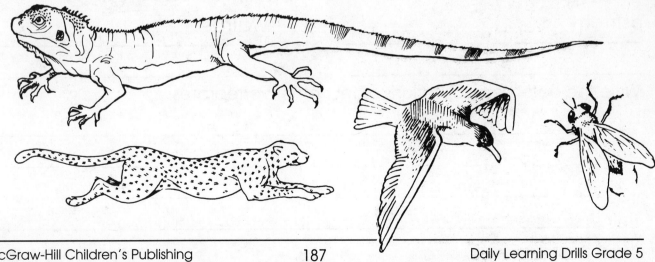

SCIENCE

Name _____

Defensive Adaptations

In nature, animals hunt and eat other animals so that they can survive. All animals struggle to stay alive. Some animals hide from predators while others have built-in weapons that other animals fear.

Over the years, each animal has changed to give itself more protection. This is known as defensive adaptation. Some of these adaptations are very strange and unusual.

Identify and explain the adaptation for each vertebrate pictured below.

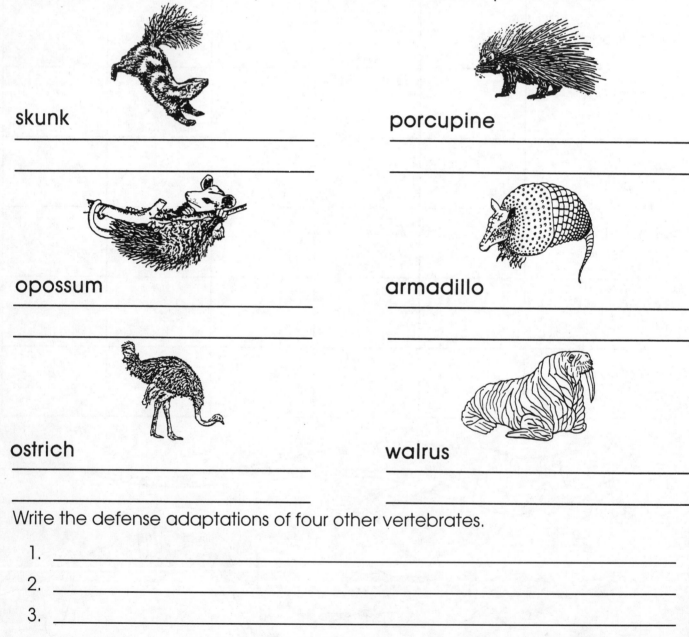

skunk
_____
_____

porcupine
_____
_____

opossum
_____
_____

armadillo
_____
_____

ostrich
_____
_____

walrus
_____
_____

Write the defense adaptations of four other vertebrates.

1. _____
2. _____
3. _____
4. _____

Name _____

Fishy Business

What do a porpoise and a perch have in common? You might answer that they both live in the water, they both have fins and they are both fish. Only two out of your three answers are correct. A porpoise is not a fish. It is a mammal.

Make a comparison between the porpoise and the perch. You can find resource books in your library to help you make this comparison.

	Porpoise	Perch
Body covering		
"Fins" (Kinds)		
Skeleton		
Respiratory System		
Reproduction		
Feeding of Young		
Body Temperature		

SCIENCE

Name _____

Marine Life

The ocean is filled with thousands of different kinds of animals. Some of these creatures are so small that they can be seen only with the help of a microscope. Others are over 100 feet long and can weigh over 100 tons. Their habitats, diets, defense systems, and litter size may vary as much as their size.

Use reference books from your library and other sources to research the marine animals listed below.

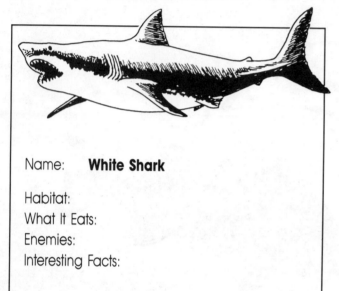

Name: **White Shark**

Habitat:
What It Eats:
Enemies:
Interesting Facts:

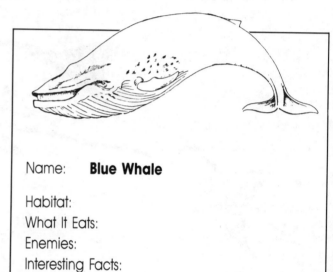

Name: **Blue Whale**

Habitat:
What It Eats:
Enemies:
Interesting Facts:

Name: **Sea Horse**

Habitat:
What It Eats:
Enemies:
Interesting Facts:

Name:

Habitat:
What It Eats:
Enemies:
Interesting Facts:

Research a marine creature of your choice.

Name _____

A Whale of a Story

Below is information about whales. Make a whale glossary of terms using the words that are in bold. Write a definition of the bold words using the context of the story. Then, use as many of the words as possible to write a poem or story.

Whales belong to a group of animals called **Cetaceans**. There are two major types of whales, **baleen whales** and **toothed whales**. Baleen whales have no teeth. They have hundreds of thin plates made of material similar to human fingernails. These **baleen plates** filter out food from the water. **Krill**, small, shrimplike animals, are the main food of baleen whales. There are ten kinds of baleen whales. These are further divided into three groups. One group, the **rorquals**, have long grooves on their throats and chests and include the largest whale, the blue whale.

There are about 65 kinds of toothed whales that are divided into five groups. One group, the **beluga** and narwhal, measures 10-15 feet long. Belugas are milk-white when fully grown and are often called white whales.

Whales are shaped like torpedoes. They have a **blowhole**, a nostril on top of their head, through which they breathe. Also on top of the body is a **dorsal fin** that stands upright and helps whales steer. **Flippers** also are used for steering and for balance. Whales' **flukes** are two triangular lobes that are part of its tail. The flukes beat up and down to move the whale through the water. Beneath their skin, whales have a layer of fat called **blubber**. Blubber helps keep whales warm, and when food is scarce whales can live off their blubber for a long time.

Whales are the most intelligent of all animals. They communicate with one another by making a variety of sounds called **phonations**, or **whale songs**. These songs consist of groans, moans, roars, sighs, high-pitched squeaks, and chirps.

Other interesting facts about whales include: Whales perform impressive leaps from the water called **breaching**. Many also **migrate**, sometimes thousands of miles every year, to spend the winter in warm water and the summer in cold water. Whales use a method of navigation called **echolocation**. Whales emit sounds and then listen for an echo produced when objects reflect the sounds. From the echoes, they can determine the distance and direction of an object.

Whaling has become so efficient that some whales are **endangered**. **Whalers**, people who hunt whales, realized that some species were almost extinct. In 1946, the International Whaling Committee (IWC) was formed to protect the whales' future.

SCIENCE

Life on a Rotting Log

Name _____

pin cushion moss

pixie-cup lichen

jack-ó-lantern mushroom

pale-shield lichen

ant larvae

earthworm

red-backed salamander

The forest community is not limited to animals and plants that live in or near living trees. As the succession of the forest continues, many trees will die and fall to the ground. As the "dead" log lies on the forest floor, the actions of plants, animals, bacteria, lichens and the weather help break it down and return its components to the forest soil. Notice the many different varieties of life found on the rotting log.

1. List the different kinds of plant life that are found on the rotting log. _____
_____

2. How do the small plants help this log to decay? _____

3. What do the plants get from the log? _____

4. What kinds of small animals are found in or on the rotting log? _____

5. How do these animals help the log to decay? _____
_____

Find Out! — The lichen found on the rotting log is a very interesting kind of plant. It is actually two organisms that are living together. What two organisms form lichen? What does each of these organisms need to live? How do organisms help each other?
_____
_____

Name _____

Endangered

Many of the animals in the grassland community are very rare, and some are in danger of becoming extinct. The American buffalo was once one of those animals. In 1889, only 551 of them could be found. Today, after laws were established to protect them, there are about 15,000 of them in the U.S.

The black-footed ferret, which lives in the western Great Plains of North America, is an endangered species. Complete the chart below and color the picture. You will need to find information from an encyclopedia or other source to help you. When you have finished, complete the activity at the bottom of the page.

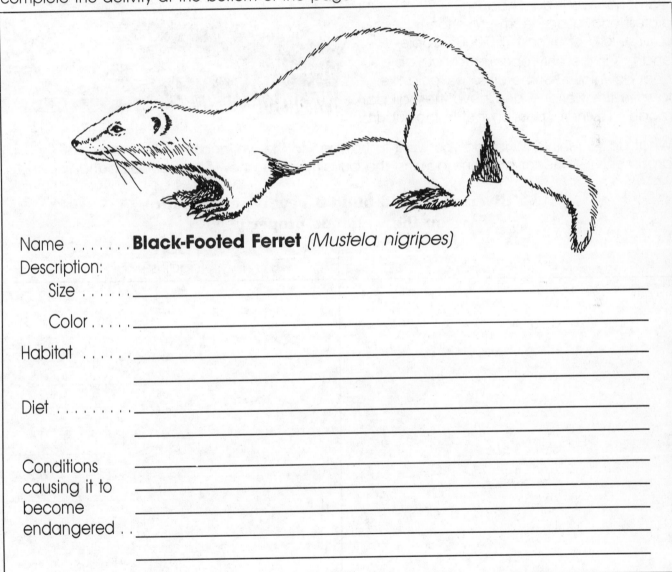

Name . . . . **Black-Footed Ferret** *(Mustela nigripes)*
Description:
    Size . . . . . . _____
    Color . . . . . _____
Habitat . . . . . . _____
_____
Diet . . . . _____
_____

Conditions _____
causing it to _____
become _____
endangered . . _____
_____

Below is a list of grassland animals that have become rare. Pick one or choose one of your own and do research to find out more about the animal. Then, write a news story voicing your opinion about protecting the animal.

African elephant   white rhinoceros   prairie dog   kangaroo   bald eagle

Name _____

The Great Debate

Close to downtown Riverton are 300 acres of wetlands. This area of marshes and ponds is the home of a countless number of species of plants and animals. A group of citizens from the city of Riverton wants to build a new baseball stadium on this land. Riverton has never had a professional baseball team, nor has it ever had any professional sports teams. Riverton is a large city of almost 750,000 people, and this is the only open land available near downtown. Some citizens would like to save this wetland and have the ball park made elsewhere, possibly out in the suburbs.

What do you think? What do you want to happen to the wetlands? Make two lists of arguments — one for and one against the building of the new Riverton ball park.

"Riverton should build a new baseball park on the wetlands property."

Pro (for)	**Con** (against)
1.	1.
2.	2.
3.	3.
4.	4.
5.	5.
6.	6.

Name _____

The Prairie Food Web

In complex grassland communities, like the prairie community, the flow of food and energy cannot be described by just looking at simple food chains. Instead, you must look at the interlocking of food chains in a community called a **food web**. The many kinds of producers and consumers available in the prairie community allow animals to select from a wide variety of food sources.

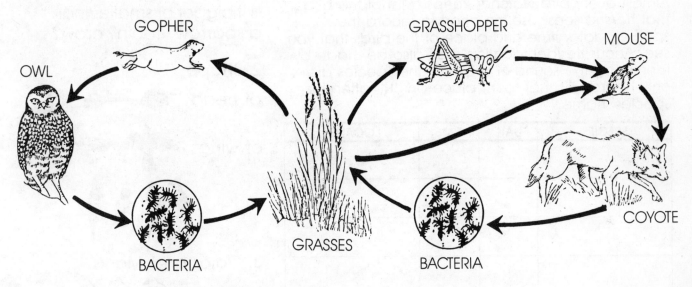

GOPHER   GRASSHOPPER   MOUSE

OWL

GRASSES

BACTERIA   BACTERIA   COYOTE

1. Name at least four relationships shown in the food web pictured above.

   1. _____   3. _____

   2. _____   4. _____

2. If there were no coyotes left in the prairie community, what would happen to the mouse
   population? Why? _____

   _____

   _____

3. If there was a decrease in the owl population, what would happen to the gopher
   population? Why? _____

   _____

   _____

4. If the prairie grasses were destroyed by fire, what would happen to the coyote population?
   Why? _____

   _____

   _____

5. What does it mean when we say, "The death of one species in a food web upsets the
   rest of the web"? _____

   _____

   _____

SCIENCE

Name _____

Bird Watcher's List

Observer _____
Date _____

Almost every bird watcher keeps a list of the birds that he/she sees. Use the chart to record the species, date, time and place of the birds that you see. Accurate identification may also be made by identifying the sound of a bird. If the species are only heard and not seen, place an "H" after the species' name.

SPECIES	DATE	TIME	LOCALITY

What bird did you see?
Look at the following.

1. Size
Is it bigger or smaller than a sparrow? robin? crow?

2. Shape
of head

of wings

of tail

3. Color and Marks
on body

on tail

on head

on wings

4. Habitat and Behaviors

What was it doing?

Where was it?

How does it fly?

Name _____

Adopt a Bird

There are probably more than one hundred different kinds of birds that live in your region. Select one species of bird and become an expert. Research your species of bird and complete the profile below.

Common Name _____
Scientific Name _____

Description

Size:

Body shape:

Wing shape:

Tail shape:

Color and field marks:

Flight pattern:

Picture of Male

Behaviors

Description of Habitat: _____
_____
_____

Food and Feeding Habits: _____
_____
_____

Migration (if applicable): _____
_____
_____

Name _____

Clues from the Past

Fossil clues of dinosaurs and other prehistoric animals are used in forming images of these animals. When only parts of a skeleton have been found, the clues must be pieced together in order to describe the size, habitat, strength, speed and family patterns of the animal. From the clues listed below, make some of your own inferences about the animals.

1. extremely large rib cage and stomach _____
_____

2. long, stiff tails _____
_____

3. long, hollow nasal bones from snout to back of jaws _____
_____

4. thousands of tiny, flat teeth in back of jaws _____
_____

5. moveable spines and plates on back _____
_____

6. thick, rounded bone on top of skull _____
_____

7. large, saucer-shaped mud mounds of eggs spaced exact distances apart
_____
_____

8. nostrils on top of skull _____
_____

9. large, strong hind leg bones; short, weak front leg bones _____
_____

10. jagged or serrated teeth _____
_____

Name _____

Dinosaur Acrostic

Write the answers to the following definitions in the spaces provided. The circled letters are used as clues for your answers.

The middle period of the Age of Dinosaurs   _ _ _ _ Ⓢ _ _ _

The climate of the middle period   _ _ Ⓣ

Another name for carnosaur   _ _ Ⓔ _ - _ _ _ _ _

A supercontinent that continued to separate   _ _ _ Ⓖ _ _ _

One of the largest and longest dinosaurs   _ _ _ Ⓞ _ _ _ _

Dinosaur with bony plates on its back   _ _ _ Ⓢ _ _ _ _

The oldest bird known   _ _ _ _ Ⓐ _ _ _ _ _ _ _

A fast, hollow-tailed dinosaur   _ _ _ _ Ⓤ _ _ _

One of the first large, meat-eating dinosaurs   _ _ _ _ _ _ Ⓡ _ _ _

A dinosaur better known as Brontosaurus   _ _ _ _ _ _ _ Ⓤ _ _

Shallow water that covered much of Europe   Ⓢ _ _ _

SCIENCE

Name _____

Cretaceous Crossword

Solve the crossword puzzle using words found in the Word Bank.

Across

2. Meaning of the word "dinosaur"
3. Dinosaur with three horns on its head
6. Province of Canada in which many fossils of dinosaurs have been found
9. This type of plant flourished during this period.
10. A large group of dinosaurs that traveled together
11. The teeth of this dinosaur were discovered in England by Mary Ann Mantell.
12. A hadrosaurid, or dinosaur with a broad, toothless beak
13. Marine reptiles with flippers; much like dolphins today

Down

1. The third period of time in the Age of Dinosaurs
2. "Tyrant lizard" dinosaur
4. Long-necked marine reptiles
5. "Bird imitator" dinosaur; resembled today's ostrich
7. Dinosaur with massive skull bone used in fighting
8. Flying reptiles such as Pteranodon and Rhamphorhynchus

Word Bank

Terrible Lizard		Plesiosaurs
Tyrannosaurus	Ichthyosaurs	Ornithomimus
Pterosaurs	herd	bonehead
duckbilled	Triceratops	Alberta
Cretaceous	flowering	Iguanodon

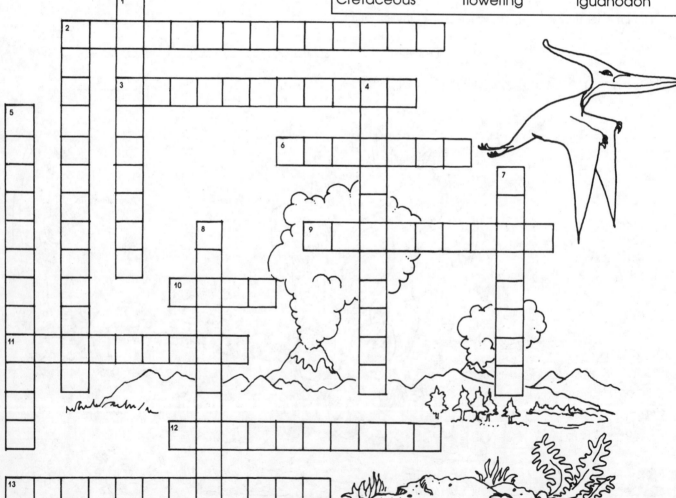

Name _____

Making Fossils

Real fossils of plants and animals are recovered from mud, rock layers and tar pits. In this activity, you will make your own fossil tracks. Read the directions before gathering your supplies.

What to use: small cardboard boxes or milk cartons, plaster of Paris, stirring stick, water, plastic or paper cup, nonstick cooking spray, newspapers, nail, nail file or paper clip

What to do:
1. Select a small box or carton for your fossil mold.
2. Select a small object, such as a shell, bone or leaf, that will fit easily into the box.
3. Fill a cup half full with water. Add plaster of Paris to the water and stir until you have a thin mixture.
4. Pour about half of this mixture into the bottom of the box.
5. Carefully place the object on top of the plaster. Spray a small amount of the nonstick cooking spray on the object.
6. Quickly add the remainder of the plaster mixture to fill the box.
7. Set aside until the next day.
8. After the plaster has hardened, carefully peel the cardboard away from the plaster. Place the hardened plaster on newspaper.
9. Now you are ready to discover your fossil! With an instrument such as a nail, nail file or paper clip, begin to scrape away the top of the plaster carefully until you discover some evidence of a fossil deposit. Continue to work until you have fully uncovered the "fossil."
10. Remove the fossil from the plaster. Examine the depression it has left in the underlying plaster. Is the cast of the object a good copy of the fossil?

Questions to answer:

1. How has this activity demonstrated the actual discovery and removal of fossil remains from a site? _____
_____

2. Why are the complete skeletons of some animals never found at a site? _____
_____

3. What precautions do paleontologists take to preserve the fossils and remove them from a site without damage? _____
_____

4. What can we learn from the discovered fossils of plants and animals? _____
_____
_____

SCIENCE

Name _____

Mysteries of the Ice Age

Many of the mysteries of the Pleistocene Epoch are still to be solved. Many of the puzzling questions are still to be answered.

Use reference books to help you form your own hypotheses or answers to these questions.

1. Why have fossils of some animals been found all over the world? _____
_____
_____
_____

2. How did animals migrate from one continent to another? _____
_____
_____

3. What changes in the climate occurred during this epoch? _____
_____
_____

4. What changes in the land masses occurred during this epoch? _____
_____
_____

5. Why did large sheets of ice appear in the Northern Hemisphere? _____
_____
_____

6. Why were there periods of alternating glacial and warm conditions on Earth during the Pleistocene Epoch? _____
_____
_____
_____
_____
_____.

Name _____

Classification of Dinosaurs

Refer to the encyclopedia or a book on dinosaurs to locate the dinosaurs pictured below. Think of the ways in which you could classify these animals under different headings, such as bird-hipped, meat eater, Cretaceous Period.

In the spaces at the bottom of the page, list the Classification Headings and the numbers of the dinosaurs you would place under each of these headings.

1. Plateosaurus
2. Allosaurus
3. Apatosaurus
4. Coelophysis
5. Stegosaurus
6. Iguanodon
7. Triceratops
8. Archaeopteryx
9. Corythosaurus
10. Tyrannosaurus
11. Diplodocus
12. Pachycephalosaurus

SCIENCE

Name _____

River System

Using resource materials and the Word Bank below, label the parts of the river system. After labeling each part, write the description of each word in the space provided.

Word Bank

waterfall _____
_____
_____

meander _____
_____
_____

rapids _____
_____
_____

flood plain _____
_____
_____

delta _____
_____
_____

oxbow lake _____
_____
_____

tributary _____
_____
_____

lake _____
_____
_____

alluvial fan _____
_____
_____

Name _____

The Earth as a Puzzle

Use the Word Bank to complete the word puzzle.

Across

2. Uneven ridges of gravel, sand and rock deposited by a melting glacier
4. Material deposited by wind, water and melting glaciers
7. Molten rock that is deposited on Earth's surface
9. S-shaped loop formed by a river
10. The thin, outermost layer of Earth from where magma flows
11. The action of wearing down Earth's surface by wind and water

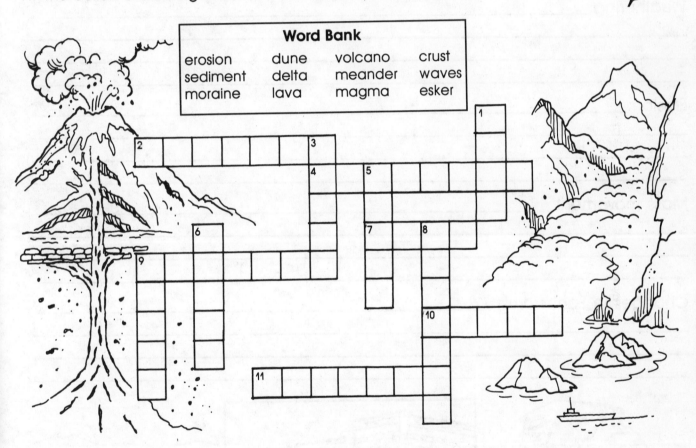

Word Bank

erosion	dune	volcano	crust
sediment	delta	meander	waves
moraine	lava	magma	esker

Down

1. Sand carried by the wind and deposited in mounds forms a _____.
3. Long ridge of gravel or sand deposited by a stream that flows in a tunnel under a melting glacier
5. Fan-shaped channels formed by a river depositing sediment at its mouth
6. Pounding force that causes erosion along the seashore
8. Mountain formed from molten rock and other erupted material
9. Molten rock within Earth's surface

SCIENCE

Name _____

How the Earth Changes

Earth changes continuously. Some changes, such as an earthquake, take only a few minutes. Others, such as the wearing away of the Grand Canyon, take place over millions of years.

Four kinds of changes affect Earth's surface: weathering, erosion, mass movement and changes in Earth's crust.

With the help of your science book, an encyclopedia or some other source, write a description of each of the four kinds of changes.

Weathering _____
_____
_____
_____

Erosion _____
_____
_____
_____

Mass movement _____
_____
_____
_____

Changes in Earth's crust _____
_____
_____
_____

Name _____

The Rock Cycle

With the help of heat, pressure, and weathering, one kind of rock can be changed into a new kind of rock. For example, beautiful marble is formed from limestone, and slate comes from shale and clay.

The changing of rocks is an ongoing cycle. There is no true beginning, but it might be easier to understand by beginning with magma. Complete the rock cycle diagram pictured below.

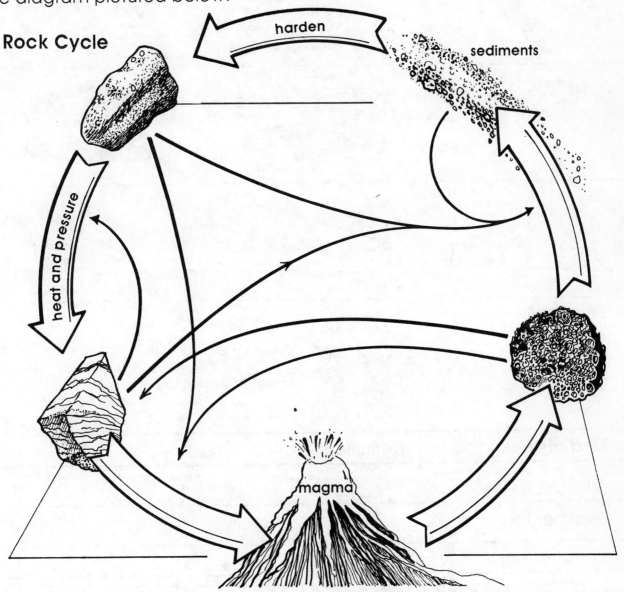

Rock Cycle

harden

sediments

heat and pressure

magma

WORD BANK

sedimentary rock	igneous rock	metamorphic rock
melting	weathering	cooling and hardening

Name _____

Classy Rocks

There are three main groups of rock: **igneous** rock, **metamorphic** rock, and **sedimentary** rock. Each of the rocks pictured on this page belongs to one of these groups. Fill in the definitions. Then, in the space below each picture, tell which group each rock belongs to.

 granite

 gneiss

 marble

 limestone

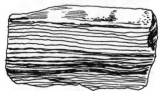 shale

 basalt

 sandstone

 slate

 obsidian

conglomerate

Kind of Rock	Definition
Igneous	
Sedimentary	
Metamorphic	

Word Bank	Definitions
igneous metamorphic sedimentary	• layers of loose material which solidified • cooled magma • rock that has been changed into a new rock

Name _____

Good News – Bad News

As the edges of Earth's plates bump, grind, slip and slide, they can bring good news and bad news. The good news is that these areas of activity are valuable sources of geothermal energy that man is just beginning to use. The bad news is that great destruction in the forms of earthquakes or volcanic eruptions can also occur in these same areas.

You are the reporter. Using the headlines below, write two news articles that show the good news and the bad news brought about by the forces inside Earth.

Middle Earth News

vol. 2   Thursday, February 20 $1.25

New Unlimited Energy Source

Shake, Rattle and Roll

SCIENCE

Name _____

Inside Earth

Using the Word Bank below, label the Earth's layers. Then, complete the paragraph. Some words will be used twice.

The structure of Earth is sometimes compared to that of a _____ . Just like the fruit, Earth also has _____ layers. They are the _____ , _____ and _____ . The innermost layer of Earth is the _____ . This is the _____ part of Earth. Scientists think it is about 1,400 miles thick and is made mostly of _____ and _____ . Beneath the crust is the _____ . It is very hot, solid _____ . The crust is the _____ layer of Earth. This layer is very _____ and is made of three kinds of _____ — _____ , _____ , and _____ .

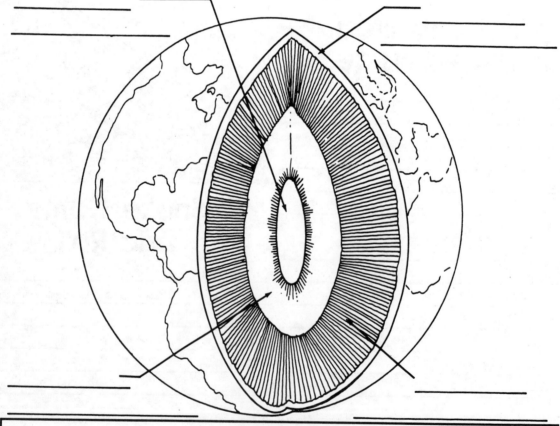

WORD BANK							
iron	rock	three	hottest	sedimentary	peach	crust	nickel
mantle	core	first	igneous	metamorphic	thin		

Name _____

How a Volcano Forms

Mount Vesuvius was dormant for hundreds of years before it erupted in 79 A.D. and buried several ancient Roman cities. On August 24, pressure from gases inside the mountain caused its top to blow off. Hot ashes, cinders, and dust shot into the air. Pliny the Younger recorded this disaster in a letter.

Read the paragraph below. Then write the words in bold in the correct place on the diagram.

When the heat in the center of the Earth is so very hot, it melts the rock in the **mantle**, the thick rock layer just below the **crust**. The melted rock is called **magma**. A volcano begins as magma. When rock melts, gases form that mix with magma. Gas-filled magma rises through weakened places in the Earth because it is now lighter than the solid rock around it. It forms a **magma chamber** below the crust. The pressure of the solid rock around the chamber causes the magma to melt a **channel** through the crust up into the mountain. When the gas-filled magma nears the peak and the pressure is too great, it is released through an opening called the **central vent**. Most magma and other volcanic materials like **ashes** and **cinders** fly into the air. When the eruption is over, a **crater** is formed. The central vent is at the bottom of the crater.

Read about another volcano. Write about it.

_____

_____

_____

_____

SCIENCE

Name _____

Volcanic Cones

Volcanic cones can be classified by their shapes. Label the three different kinds of volcanic cones pictured below. Label the parts of the volcanoes.

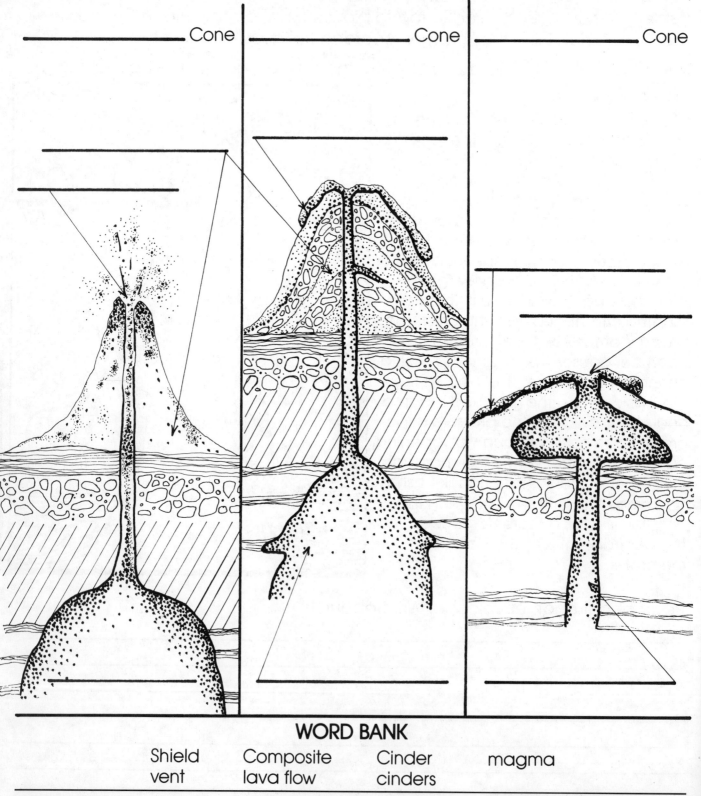

_____ Cone   _____ Cone   _____ Cone

WORD BANK

Shield	Composite	Cinder	magma
vent	lava flow	cinders	

Name _____

Fascinating, Terrifying Eruptions

People have always been fascinated and terrified by the spectacle of volcanic eruptions and their tremendous power. Some of the worst disasters in the world have been caused by volcanic eruptions, which can result in thousands of deaths and entire towns destroyed.

Research a volcanic eruption such as Vesuvius or Mount St. Helens. Write a magazine article about it on another piece of paper as if you were an eyewitness. Include the volcano's location, date of eruption, and other interesting facts. Below, use colored pencils to draw a picture of the volcano erupting. Make a caption for your drawing as if it were the illustration for your article.

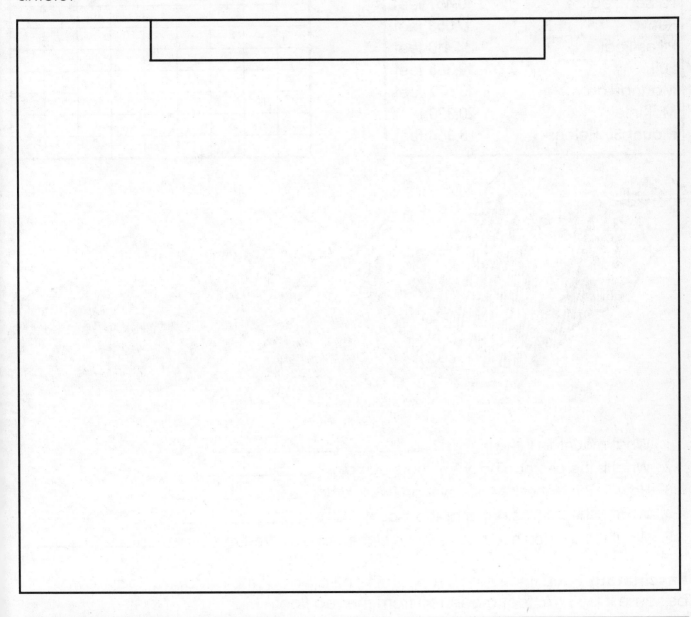

SCIENCE

Name _____

Majestic Mountains

The word *mountain* means different things to different people. Some people who live on vast, level plains consider a small hill a mountain. Others who live in the mountains would not consider a region mountainous unless it was very high and rugged.

Listed below are eight famous mountains. Graph each mountain's height. On the bottom of the graph, put the mountain's name and on the side of the graph, put its height. When you have finished graphing, use the results to answer the questions below.

Name	Height
Everest	29,028 feet
Lassen Peak	10,457 feet
Kenya	17,058 feet
Pikes Peak	14,110 feet
Fuji	12,388 feet
Mauna Loa	13,677 feet
McKinley	20,320 feet
Mount St. Helens	8,364 feet

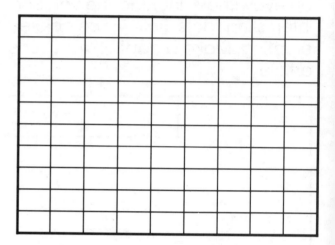

1. What mountain is the highest? _____
2. What is the average height of the mountains? _____
3. How much higher is McKinley than Pikes Peak? _____
4. What is the total height of all the mountains? _____
5. What is the difference between the highest and shortest mountain? _____

Fascinating Fact! The highest mountain on Earth is actually Mauna Kea, Hawaii, because it is 33,476 feet measured from the sea floor.

Soil Profile

Study the soil profile pictured here. Identify the layer or layers where each of the following is found.

_____ live animals

_____ rock

_____ minerals

_____ live plants

_____ organic matter

_____ top layer

_____ middle layer

_____ lowest layer

_____ topsoil

_____ subsoil

_____ tree roots

_____ boulders

SCIENCE

Name _____

Mysterious Sand

Sand is any earthy material that consists of loose grains of minerals or rocks that are smaller than gravel. Most grains of sand are parts of solid rocks that have been crumbled away by waves battering and grinding down rocky cliffs. Many types of minerals are found in sand, and this determines the color of the sand. Some beaches are a mixture of colors, while others have sand of one color. Some examples are given in the box. Sand has many uses: quartz sand is used to make chemicals and glass, sandpaper is made by gluing loose sand onto heavy paper, and mortar and concrete are also made with sand. Try the experiment below to learn more about sand.

Color	Made of
black	lava
light brown/tan	granite, quartz
yellow	quartz
gold	mica
red	garnet
white	coral, seashells, quartz

Materials Needed:

beach sand or sand
   from a building supply store
pan
paper

magnifying lens
Popsicle stick
newspaper
measuring cup

hot plate
cornstarch
small milk cartons
water

Experiment:

1. Spread a few grains of sand on the paper and examine them with a magnifying lens.

2. Sketch some of the grains on the back of this page.

3. Do all the grains look exactly alike? _____

4. Are all the grains the same color? _____

5. What were these grains of sand originally? _____

6. Your teacher will now assist you with the following:
   a. Mix 2 cups of sand, 1 cup of water, and
      1 cup of cornstarch with a Popsicle stick.
      Pour mixture into pan.
   b. Heat mixture slowly until it thickens.
   c. Pour mixture into individual milk cartons to
      cool and harden.
   d. Peel away the sides of the carton.
   e. Working on newspaper, carve sea animals,
      plants, shells, coral, or sea sculptures with the Popsicle stick.
   f. Display the work in your class or school media center.

Name _____

What Am I?

The solar system contains many different objects that travel around the sun. Use the encyclopedia and other sources to explore the solar system and solve the following "What Am I?" riddles.

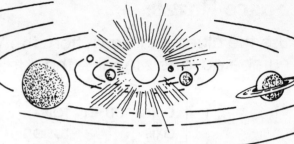

1. I am the largest planet. _____
2. I am the planet best known for my rings. _____
3. I am the planet known for my "Great Red Spot." _____
4. I am the smallest planet. _____
5. I am the planet closest to the sun. _____
6. I am known as the "Red Planet." _____
7. Voyager 2 discovered new moons and rings around me in 1989. _____
8. Until 1999, I am the planet farthest from the sun. _____
9. I am the planet closest in size to Earth. _____
10. I am the planet with the shortest rotation time. _____
11. My moon, Titan, is larger than the planet, Mercury. _____
12. I am the planet with the rotation time most similar to Earth's. _____
13. I am the planet with the most natural satellites. _____
14. My buddies and I form a belt between Mars and Jupiter. _____
15. I am the largest object in the solar system. _____
16. I am the brightest planet in the sky. _____
17. I am the only planet known to support life. _____
18. I am the planet that orbits the sun "on my side." _____
19. I am known as "Earth's Twin." _____
20. People once thought that there were canals on my surface, but they were wrong. _____
21. I am the brightest object in the night sky. _____
22. I am often called a "snowball in space." _____
23. I am also known as a "shooting star." _____
24. My surface temperature is about 10,000° F. _____
25. I am the most distant planet that can be seen with the unaided eye. _____

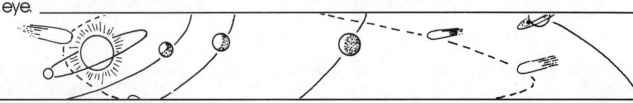

SCIENCE

Name _____

Space Puzzle

Use the clues and words from the Word Bank to complete the puzzle. Use the numbered letters to solve the riddle at the bottom of the page.

Word Bank				
astronomer	fall	Mercury	Pluto	sun
axis	fusion	meteorite	red	
Centauri	hydrogen	moon	rotation	
Earth	maria	orbit	shuttle	

1. A star's energy comes from nuclear __ __ __ __ __ __.
   1

2. The only planet with life is __ __ __ __ __.
   2

3. The path of a planet around the sun is its __ __ __ __ __.
   3

4. Earth's largest satellite is the __ __ __ __.
   4

5. The autumnal equinox is the first day of __ __ __ __.
   5

6. The planet farthest away from the sun is __ __ __ __ __.
   6

7. The closest planet to the sun is __ __ __ __ __ __ __.
   7

8. A meteor that lands on the earth is a __ __ __ __ __ __ __ __ __.
   8

9. A scientist who studies the Universe is an __ __ __ __ __ __ __ __ __ __.
   9

10. A star's fuel is __ __ __ __ __ __ __ __.
    10

11. The star closest to the earth is the __ __ __.
    11

12. Oceans on the moon are called __ __ __ __ __.
    12

13. A space __ __ __ __ __ __ __ is a reusable space craft.
    13

14. The closest star to our solar system is Proxima __ __ __ __ __ __ __ __.
    14

15. The color of a dying star is __ __ __.
    15

16. The spinning movement of a planet is its __ __ __ __ __ __ __ __.
    16

17. The imaginary line from the North Pole to the South Pole is the Earth's

    __ __ __ __.
    17

• How do creatures from outer space drink their tea?

__ __ __ __ __ __ __ __ __ __ __ __ __ __ __ __ __!
 1 2 3 4   5 6 7 8 9 10 11 12 13 14 15 16 17

Name _____

Mars—Then and Now

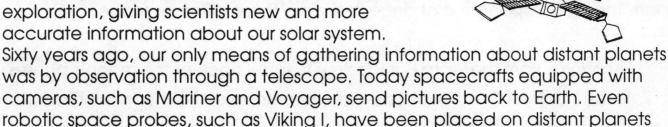

Many advances have been made in space exploration, giving scientists new and more accurate information about our solar system. Sixty years ago, our only means of gathering information about distant planets was by observation through a telescope. Today spacecrafts equipped with cameras, such as Mariner and Voyager, send pictures back to Earth. Even robotic space probes, such as Viking I, have been placed on distant planets to transmit high-quality pictures and analyze soil samples.

Early information about the planets was very inaccurate and led people to believe many things that have been proven untrue. An example is the belief that little green men, called Martians, lived beneath the surface of Mars. The Mariner space probe found no evidence to support this idea.

Write two articles that compare our knowledge of the planet Mars. In your first article, pretend that you are a newspaper reporter in the early 1900s reporting on the life and evidence of life on Mars. Your article may refer to the "canals" and intelligent life on the planet. Your second article should reflect what scientists have learned through the most recent space probes.

Use the two headlines below for your articles. Cut out the headlines and paste them on another sheet of paper. Write your articles.

SCIENCE

The New York Times
Monday, March 5, 1918
Intelligent Life on Mars

The New York Times
Monday, March 5
Space Probe Visits Mars

Name _____

The Moon's Many "Faces"

As the moon orbits Earth, we see different amounts of the moon's lighted part. The moon appears to change its shape. These different shapes are called phases.

1. Use words from the Word Bank below to label each of the moon's phases.

2. In the box next to each phase, draw the shape of the moon's lighted part that is visible from Earth.

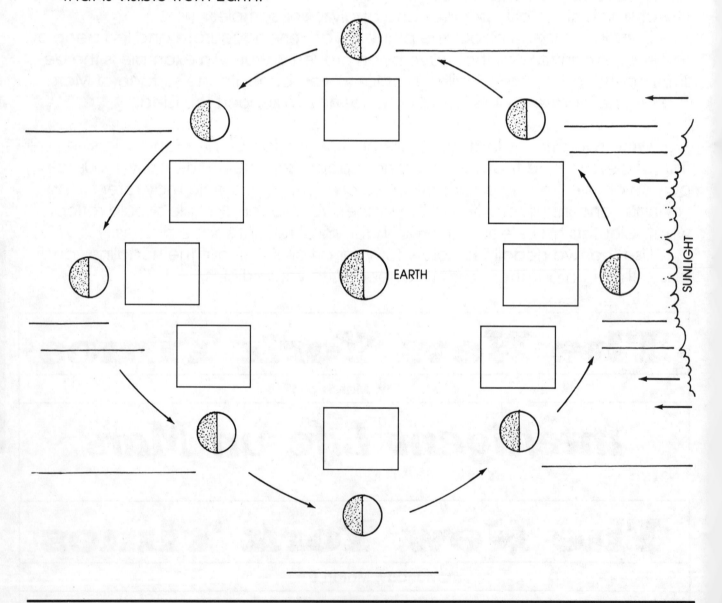

WORD BANK

new moon	waning crescent	waning gibbous	first quarter
waxing gibbous	waxing crescent	last quarter	full moon

Name _____

Comets—Dirty Snowballs

Use words from the Word Bank to label the diagram and complete the following description of a comet.

Word Bank

Sun   nucleus   coma   dust tail   gas tail   rocks   dust   gases   orbits   tail

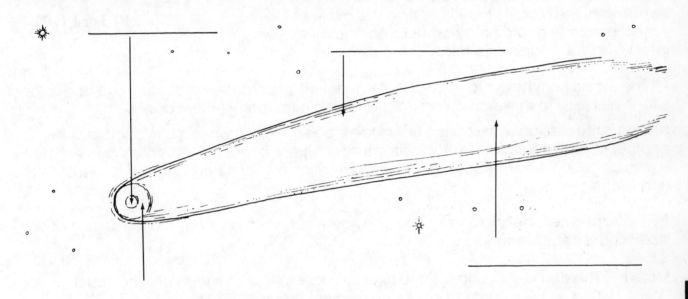

An astronomer once described a comet as a dirty snowball. Its tiny nucleus, measuring less than 10 miles in diameter, is made of _____ and _____ cemented together by frozen _____ . Comets travel in long, cigar-shaped _____ that take them from the outermost regions of the solar system toward the _____ . As the comet approaches the sun, the ice changes into a huge, hazy gas cloud called a _____ . The solar wind pushes on the coma to form a long, thin _____ that is millions of miles long and glows in the sunlight.

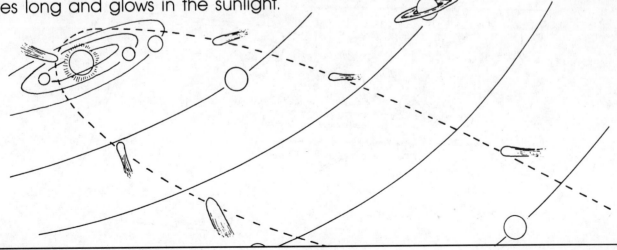

SCIENCE

Name _____

Ford and Friction

Can you imagine if one out of every two people who own cars in the U.S. were driving cars made by the same company? Well, from 1908 to 1927, more than half of the cars sold in the United States were Fords.

In 1903, Henry Ford organized the Ford Motor Company. At first, it produced only expensive cars. However, Ford's invention of the Model T in 1908 helped the average American family afford an automobile not too many years later. Can you imagine life today without cars?

Model T Ford 1908

Try the experiment below to learn about one scientific principle Ford may have had to deal with in his quest to make an automobile affordable for many Americans.

Friction is the resistance an object has against being moved when it is in contact with another object or surface. Reducing friction is of great concern to scientists and engineers, especially when they are dealing with the operation of machinery and the movement of heavy objects.

Try the experiment below to see if you can figure out when and why friction is greater or lesser under certain conditions.

Materials Needed: rubber band (Size 32 is ideal.)   sheets of sandpaper
                        box of crayons or straws   tape   ruler

Student Directions

Investigate
1. Wrap a long rubber band around the front cover of a book. Put half of the rubber band against the inside binding and the other half on the outside of the binding.
2. Pull the rubber band just until the book starts to move.
3. Use a ruler to measure the distance the rubber band was stretched just before the book moved. Measure from the spine of the book to the end of the rubber band in your fingers. How many inches did it stretch? _____

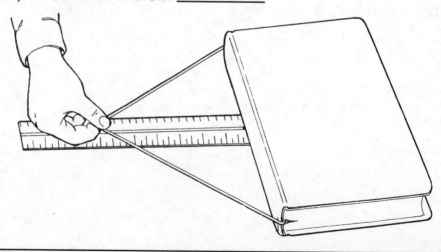

Name _____

Ford and Friction (cont.)

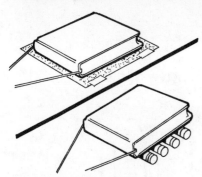

Extending the Concept

1. Place the book on a piece of sandpaper taped to the desk. Pull the rubber band until the book starts to move. How many inches did the rubber band stretch?_____

2. Place the book on a row of crayons or straws. Pull the rubber band until the book starts to move. How many inches did the rubber band stretch? _____

Drawing Conclusions

Fill in the blanks in the sentences below using the words in the box to make some statements about friction.

1. Friction is greatest when one of the surfaces in contact is _____ as evidenced when the _____ was used. When this occurs, the rubber band will be stretched _____ than if the surface was smooth.

2. Friction is less when one of the surfaces in contact is _____ .

3. Even less friction is produced when _____ or crayons are used as _____ under the book. The rubber band will be stretched _____ when this occurs.

| farther | sandpaper | rollers | minimally | straws | rough | smooth |

Chart Keeping

To further understand the principle of friction, use the rubber band and the ruler to measure the number of inches the rubber band stretches when pulling each of the objects in the chart. Fill in the chart below.

Object	Inches Stretched		
	on the desk	on sandpaper	on crayons
a box of crayons			
a second book			
large scissors			

Drawing Conclusions

Write two facts you have learned about friction.

1. _____

2. _____

Personality Plus Design a car. Draw a picture and write a description of how fast it can go, what it runs on, different gadgets it has, and so on.

SCIENCE

Name _____

Panpipes

Facts to Know

Sound is produced by vibrations. A column of air will vibrate when you blow across it. A short column of air will have a high pitch. A long column of air will have a low pitch.

Materials

20" of clear flexible tubing (purchase from building supply or hardware store) or straws, tape

Making the Panpipes

Take five pieces of tubing that are the following lengths: 6 inches, 5 inches, 4 inches, 3 inches and 2 inches. Lay the tubes in a row, arranging them from longest to shortest, about 1 inch apart. With the tops even, tape them together.

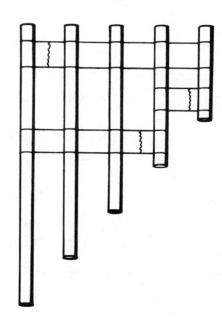

Playing the Panpipes

Blow across the top of each tube, like a flute player. Listen to the sounds. Which tube has the highest pitch?

Blow across the tubes again going first in one direction and then the other. Describe the sound.

_____

What do you think makes the pitch change?

_____

What would happen if you added and blew on a tube which is 1 inch longer than the longest tube already on your pipes? _____

_____

Name _____

Egg Drop

Facts to Know
Gravity is the force which pulls all objects toward earth. Some materials can insulate and cushion an object from the impact of gravity. Paper, Styrofoam, cloth, and similar materials are good insulators.

Materials
Collect as many of these materials as possible before beginning the project: newspaper, Styrofoam pieces or "peanuts," pantyhose, pieces of cloth, string. In addition, one or more raw eggs and a shoe-box or cardboard carton will be needed.

Investigate
The goal of this investigation is to have an egg survive from the highest possible height. Use all of the collected packaging materials to protect the egg inside the cardboard carton or shoe box. Be as creative as you can in wrapping the egg. Let your teacher hold the package as high as possible or use a ladder to stand on. He or she will drop the package. Check your egg. Did it break? _____ If your egg didn't break the first time, have your teacher drop it from a higher point. Did it break this time? _____ From how high do you think it can be dropped before it breaks? _____

SCIENCE

Name _____

Making a Periscope

Facts to Know

Light travels in a straight line. Mirrors reflect light in a straight line. The slanted mirrors in a periscope allow the user to see above a normal field of view.

Materials

shoebox
poster board
two mirrors

Making the Periscope

Stand your box vertically, take the lid off your box and cut a 1-inch-square hole on one side of the top. Cut another hole on the bottom of the box on the opposite side. Fold a long, narrow piece of poster board into fourths. Overlap and tape two of the folded sides to make a triangle. Trim the triangle so that it will fit into the bottom of the box opposite the hole. Make another triangle the same size and shape and fit it into the top of the box opposite the top hole. Use tape or glue to attach both triangles. Attach one mirror onto the slanting side of the bottom triangle and the other mirror onto the top triangle. Make sure each mirror slants at the same angle and that both mirrors face into the box. Place the lid back on your box.

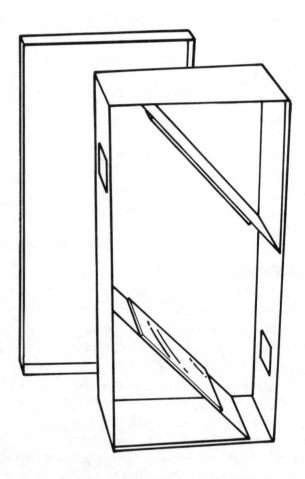

Using the Periscope

Kneel beside your desk or sit underneath it. Hold the tip of the periscope over the side of your desk. Look through the bottom hole at the mirror. What do you see? _____

_____

Why do you think the periscope works? _____

_____

What do the mirrors do? _____

Draw a picture on the back of this sheet to show one thing you saw through the periscope.

Modifying the Investigation

Change the angle of your triangles. Does this change what you see? _____

Name _____

Simple Machines

There are six simple machines which are the basic units of all complex machines: the lever, the wheel and axle, the wedge, the pulley, the inclined plane and the screw.

Recognizing Simple Machines

Which simple machines can you find in each of the tools listed below?

hammer _____   scissors _____

doorstop _____   drill _____

saw _____   screwdriver _____

crowbar _____   monkey wrench _____

Bicycle Parts

Study a bicycle carefully. Which simple machines can you find? Fill in the blanks.

tire _____   parking stand _____

caliper brakes _____   handlebars _____

chain and sprocket _____   gearshift _____

pedal and shaft _____   fork _____

other _____

       Daily Learning Drills Grade 5

Name _____

Newton's Cradle

Fact to Know

Every action has an equal and opposite reaction.

Materials

ruler   paper clips   beads
pencil or dowel   thread or fish line

Making Newton's Cradle

Use a ruler and measure an unsharpened pencil or dowel at the following points: 1 inch, 2 inches, inches, 4 inches, 5 inches and 6 inches. Use scissors to score a circle around the wood at each mark. Thread an 8-inch piece of fish line through a round bead. Knot one end to a paper clip so that the bead will not slip out. Thread the other fish lines through the other beads and tie them the same way. Tie each of the five fish lines to a mark on the pencil. Then tighten the lines. Line up all the beads so that they hang exactly even.

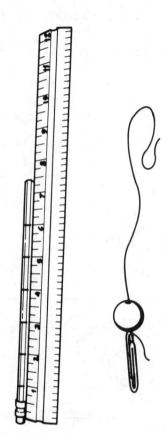

Using Newton's Cradle

Carefully pull back the farthest bead at one end of the cradle and let it strike the next bead. What happened? _____
_____
_____

Try it again. Did the same thing happen?
_____

Why do you think this happens? _____
_____
_____

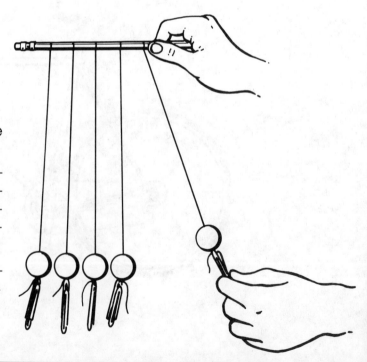

Name _____

Cartesian Diver

Materials

large jar   eyedropper   balloon
rubber band   water

Making the Cartesian Diver

Fill a large clear jar almost full with water. Fill an eyedropper about half full with water. Place the eyedropper in the water. It should barely float. Stretch a piece of balloon across the top of the jar. Use a tight rubber band to hold the rubber balloon firmly in place.

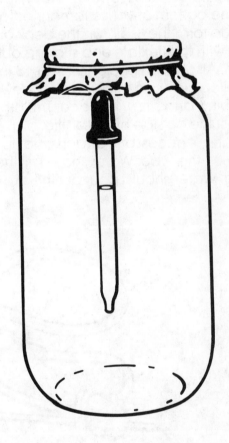

Using the Cartesian Diver

Press down on the rubber balloon.
Did the eyedropper sink? _____
If it didn't, put more water in the eyedropper until pressing down on the balloon causes it to sink.

Expanding the Concept

Take out the eyedropper. Put some water in a small cup. Add a few drops of food coloring. Fill the eyedropper with colored water so that it just floats in the jar again. Cover the jar with the rubber again. Press down on the cover. What happened to the water in the eyedropper? ____
_____
_____

Making Hypotheses

What do you think happened to the air when more water went into the eyedropper?
_____
What do you think makes the Cartesian Diver work? _____
_____
What could you use instead of an eyedropper? _____

Name _____

Making a Submarine

Facts to Know
A submarine rises by pumping water out of its tanks. It sinks by pumping water into its tanks.

Materials
four crayons   tape   18" thin tubing
plastic packing   small plastic bottle   modeling clay

Building the Submarine

Use plastic packing tape to attach four crayons to the side of a small plastic bottle to form the bottom of your submarine. Tape a piece of stiff plastic to the other side of the bottle to form the "sail" on the deck of your submarine. Insert a flexible straw into the bottle with the flexible end sticking out of the mouth of the bottle and pointing down as shown. Also, insert one end of an 18-inch piece of thin tubing into the bottle. Use modeling clay or a thick wad of chewing gum to seal the mouth of the bottle and hold the tubing and straw in place. The other end of the tubing can be held firmly by taping it against the outside of the bottle. Make sure the top tube stays in place. Set the bottle in the water. If necessary, attach additional crayons to improve the sub's balance. Suck gently on the tube. Water should fill the bottle, and the sub should sink. Blow firmly into the tubing. Water should pour out the straw, and the sub should rise.

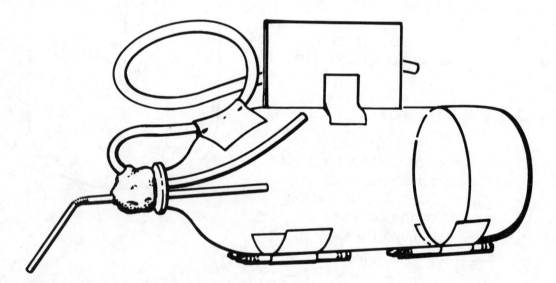

Making Hypotheses

How and why does air pressure make the submarine rise and sink?

_____
_____
_____

Name _____

Telephone Tactics

Can you imagine life without the telephone? Did you know that our first 17 Presidents ran our country without the use of a telephone? Thanks to Alexander Graham Bell, the telephone was invented in 1876. Try the experiment below to better understand the basics behind this very necessary invention. Note: The project is best done with two people.

Materials Needed: tin cans   paper clips   hammer   nail
                      30-foot pieces of string or fish line (10 pound test or higher)

Student Directions:

1. Punch a hole in the centers of the bottoms of two tin cans using a hammer and a nail.

2. Thread one end of the string or fish line through the hole in one can. Pull it inside.

3. Tie a paper clip securely to the end of the string on the inside and pull the string until it stops. Do the same with the other end.

4. You and your partner should each take one of the tin cans and walk away from each other until the string is pulled very tight.

5. Have your partner talk into his/her can. You should put your can over your ear. Can you hear what your partner is saying? Now you speak into the can and let your partner listen. Note: String must always be taut and only one person can talk at a time.

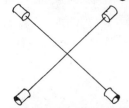

Extra: Make a 4-way party line with the tin can telephones. To do this, stretch one pair of phones tight and keep them in place. Have a second pair of phones going the other way at right angles to the first pair of phones. Hook the second pair of phones' string around the first pair's string and stretch both strings tight. Remember only one person can talk at a time!

Define the following terms: vibration, diaphragm, molecules, eardrum, party line. Then, on the back of this page, use them to explain the process of the telephone in relation to sound, objects, vibration and distance. _____

_____

_____

_____

1. What would your life be like today without the telephone? _____

_____

2. How do you think this invention changed the office of the President? _____

_____

Presidential Plus Find another important invention that you think made the role of the President easier. Tell when it was invented, how it changed the role of the President, etc. Share it with the class.

SCIENCE

Name _____

What Are You All About?

Create a **web** on this page that explains who you are.

To start, place your name in the oval. This is the center of the web. Draw three lines branching out from the center and draw a circle at the end of each branch. In each circle, write a word to describe yourself. Draw a branch out from each of these three circles and then draw three larger circles. In each one, write a sentence telling why the word you chose describes you. For example, if one of the words you chose to describe yourself is *smart*, you might write: I am smart because I study.

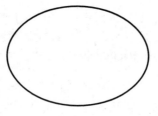

Once you have your ideas down, use construction paper or unlined white paper to create your web for display. Use markers for drawing and/or cut pictures from a magazine to make your web as interesting and creative as possible.

On another sheet of paper, write a sentence using each branch of the web (e.g., "I am smart because I study.") Then, write one more sentence to explain each of these sentences. (I study before tests. I study each night to make sure I understand the topic.)

What's Your Slogan?

Write a slogan about yourself and tell why you chose this slogan. It can be a group of words like Encyclopedia Brown's that tell what you can or will do ("No case too small"), or a group of words that tells people what you are best at.

Slogan: _____

_____

_____

Now, describe yourself as a sleuth. What might your nickname be? Why?

_____

_____

_____

Jot down several ideas on the lines below to use in creating a poster advertising your sleuthing skills. Then, make your poster.

- _____
- _____
- _____
- _____
- _____

SOCIAL STUDIES

Name _____

"Give Me Your John Hancock"

Below are sentences describing different people. Have someone matching each description sign your sheet in the appropriate space. A person may sign your sheet only once.

1. _____ is someone
who is my height.

2. _____ is someone
who is shorter than I am.

3. _____ is someone
who has the same hair color as I do.

4. _____ is someone
who likes dogs.

5. _____ is someone whose name has been in the newspaper.

6. _____ is someone who loves to read mysteries.

7. _____ is someone who loves to solve mysteries.

8. _____ is someone
who has the same number of family members
as mine.

9. _____ is someone
who can tell a joke. (Let him/her tell it to you.)

10. _____ is someone
who loves to play a sport.

11. _____ is someone
who plays a musical instrument.

12. _____ is someone
who likes to play board games.

Name _____

Logical Fun

Below is a Venn diagram. Venn diagrams are used to compare and contrast 2 or more subjects. The area in each circle that is not overlapped contains characteristics unique to one subject. The overlapped areas contain characteristics common to 2 or more subjects.

Follow the directions to complete the Venn diagram.

1. List the names of the students in your class who have blue eyes in area #1.
2. List the names of the students who wear glasses in area #2.
3. List the names of any students who have blue eyes and wear glasses in area #3.
4. List the names of any students who have brown hair in area #7.
5. List the names of any students who have brown hair and blue eyes in area #4.
6. List the names of any students who have brown hair and wear glasses in area #6.
7. List the names of any students who have blue eyes, wear glasses and have brown hair in area #5.

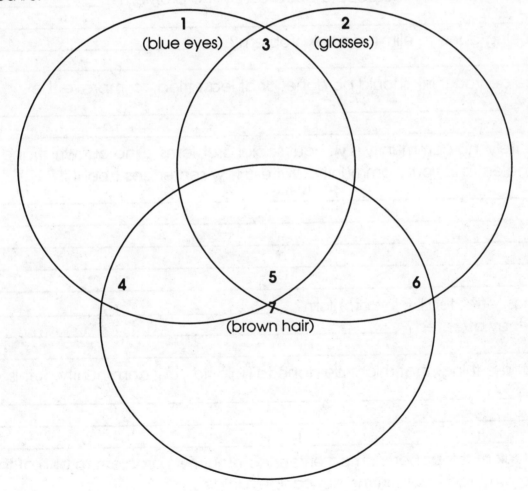

Try this comparing yourself to your favorite sleuth. Note: You will only be using 2 circles.

Name _____

Social Problems

Look at newspaper articles that tell of various social problems around the world. List what some of these problems are. _____
_____
_____

Select one problem from the articles and answer the following questions:
What is the problem? _____
_____

Where is the problem occurring? _____
Who is affected by the problem? _____
How are they affected? _____
_____

What is being done for the people affected by the problem? _____
_____

What is being done to eliminate the problem? _____
_____

What else do you think should be done, or at least tried, to improve the situation? _____
_____

Unfortunately, no community is without social problems. Find out what one social problem is in your community. Write a few sentences about it.
_____
_____
_____
_____
_____

Who is most affected by this problem? _____
How are they affected? _____
_____

Suggest some things that might be done to help rid your community of this problem. _____
_____
_____

On the back of this paper, compare your community's problem to one of the problems you read about in the newspaper articles.

Name _____

Similarities and Differences

Interpret each of the following sayings. Include an example.

"a chip off the old block" _____

_____

_____

"like night and day" _____

_____

_____

"two peas in a pod" _____

_____

_____

Compare yourself to one person.

Write the name of the person to whom you will compare yourself. _____

Write all the similarities you and that person share. _____

_____

_____

_____

_____

_____

_____

_____

_____

Write the ways in which you and the person are different. _____

_____

_____

_____

_____

_____

_____

_____

SOCIAL STUDIES

Name _____

Getting to Know the Newspaper

Look over a newspaper's flag (headline). Describe what it contains in the box below.

```
┌──────────────────────────────────────────────────────────┐
│                                                            │
│                                                            │
│                                                            │
│                                                            │
│                                                            │
└──────────────────────────────────────────────────────────┘
```

Take a few minutes to look through the paper. List the news articles, features, photographs, and advertisements that interested you the most.

1. _____
2. _____
3. _____
4. _____
5. _____

Answer the following questions about this specific issue of the newspaper.

What is the lead story about? _____

_____

Write the titles for two stories that came from a wire service.

1. _____
2. _____

Write the names of three reporters and the title of each one's article.

Reporter	**Title**
_____	_____
_____	_____
_____	_____

Write the title of an article that has a dateline. _____

_____

What is its dateline? _____

On which page will you find the Crossword Puzzle? ____ Obituaries? ____ Television Schedule? ____ Comics? ____ Classified Advertising? ____

Which part of the paper helped you know where to find the above? _____

Look back at one of the items you listed as interesting you the most. Write which one it is.

_____

Read it thoroughly. On the back of this page, write what it was about or what you liked about it.

Name _____

What Building Am I?

Find out as many facts as you can about one building in your community.

★ The building is _____ ★

1. Is the building the first to stand on its site? _____ If not, what was there before? _____
2. When was the building built? _____ How old is it? _____
3. Who built the building? _____
4. For what reason was the building built? _____
   For what is the building used now? _____
5. Who are the building's tenants? _____
6. Other information: _____
   _____

Write 20 facts about the building above without naming it. Write the clues (facts) beginning with the vaguest, or most difficult, and progressing to the easiest, or the "dead giveaway." These clues will be used to play "Get a Clue!"

★ What Building Am I? ★

1. _____ 11. _____
2. _____ 12. _____
3. _____ 13. _____
4. _____ 14. _____
5. _____ 15. _____
6. _____ 16. _____
7. _____ 17. _____
8. _____ 18. _____
9. _____ 19. _____
10. _____ 20. _____

★ The building is _____ ★

SOCIAL STUDIES

Name _____

The Beginning of Greece

The first major civilization in Greece began on the island of Crete in about 3000 B.C. It is known as the Minoan culture because of its legendary founder, King Minos. It was not the Minoans, however, that settled the mainland of Greece. This area was settled by Greek-speaking peoples from the north who settled in small farming villages around 2000 B.C. By 1600 B.C., fortified towns had been built and the Mycenaean culture had begun. In 1450 B.C., Crete fell into the power of the Mycenaeans. Their power lasted only until about 1200 B.C.

When was your city or town founded? Who were the first people here? Do some research to answer the questions below. Be sure to keep a record of the sources you use. Remember: Senior citizens who grew up in your city are great resources. Include pictures if possible.

Name of city/town _____ Date founded _____

Who founded it? _____

Why was it founded? _____

Why did it grow? _____

Important events in its history:

1. _____

2. _____

3. _____

4. _____

5. _____

Changes you have seen _____

_____

_____

Changes you predict in the future _____

_____

_____

Every city/town has its own flag. To the right is a space in which you can design your own flag for your city or town. On the back of this page, tell why you designed the flag the way you did.

Name _____

Place Poems

Write an acrostic poem about one of the world's major cities. First, do some research on the city. Get to know its attractions, landmarks, and people. To find this information, skim books, magazines, travel brochures, and the encyclopedia, or view a video about the city. After you have gathered the information you need, prepare to write your poem. Study the example below.

Parade down the Champs Élysées
Art masterpieces in the Louvre
Ride to the top of the Eiffel Tower
Imagine eating in a sidewalk café
Seine River boat ride.

Now it's your turn to write your poem.

_____
_____
_____
_____
_____
_____
_____

SOCIAL STUDIES

Name _____

Styles of Dress

Throughout history people in different regions have worn different kinds of clothes. Today, more and more people dress in a similar fashion. They wear what is referred to as Western dress. It is a style of dress common in the United States, Canada, and Western Europe.

In some parts of the world people still prefer to wear traditional clothing. Traditional styles of clothing vary because of climate, available materials, and the customs of a region. Let's examine some different types of clothing.

You will need:
magazines (*National Geographic* magazines are great!)
2-3 copies per student of *Clothing Around the World* (page 243)
glue, scissors, markers

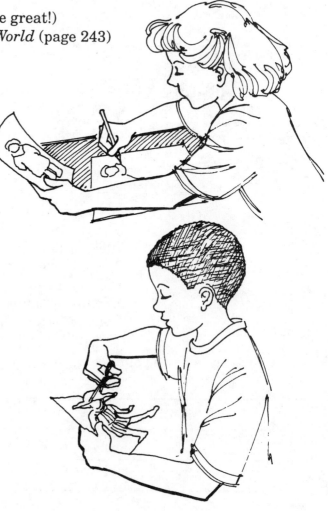

Directions:

1. Look through magazines to find examples of different kinds of clothing worn in various regions around the world.

2. Cut out the pictures and glue them to the copies of *Clothing Around the World* (page 243), or make drawings of clothing on the worksheet. Complete one worksheet for each picture or drawing.

3. Design a cover and staple all the pages together to make a booklet.

clothing

Name _____

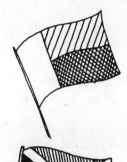

Clothing Around the World

Country _____

Description of clothing: _____
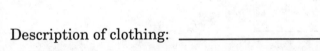
_____
_____
_____

Purpose for wearing this type of clothing: _____
_____
_____
_____

SOCIAL STUDIES

Name _____

"Made in . . ."

Most of the products that we use are not made in our own community. Many are not even made in our own country. Products that are brought into a country are called **imported** products. Products that leave a country are called **exported** products. Most imported products, and the packages in which they are sent, are labeled with the words *Made in . . . .*

Look around your home for imported products. Complete the chart by writing the names of the exporting countries and the products you found that came from each country.

The Great Import Hunt

Made in _____   Made in _____

_____   _____

_____   _____

_____   _____

Made in _____   Made in _____

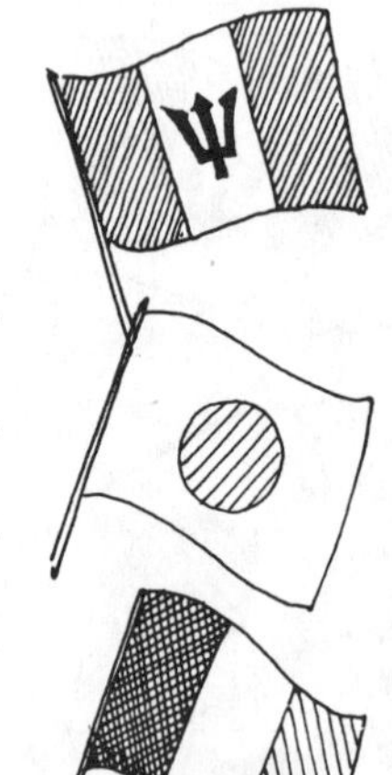

_____   _____

_____   _____

_____   _____

Made in _____   Made in _____

_____   _____

_____   _____

Name _____

Cookbook Geography

Linguini, sukiyaki, burrito—food speaks
the languages of the world. Without
leaving your own town you can probably
sample foods from all around the world.

With the help of restaurant menus or ethnic cookbooks, make a list of foods from other countries.
(Many families also have favorite recipes that great grandparents brought with them from the
"old country" when they immigrated to America.) Write the name of the food and its country of
origin.

Foods from Around the World

Food	Country
_____	_____
_____	_____
_____	_____
_____	_____
_____	_____
_____	_____
_____	_____
_____	_____
_____	_____

SOCIAL STUDIES

Name _____

Home Sweet Home

Shelter, in one form or another, is one of life's necessities that is shared by people around the globe. The types of homes people live in depend on the climate, available building materials, building methods, economy, available living space, and tradition.

Look at the two examples of shelter that are pictured on this page. Draw examples of two more kinds of shelter. Then complete the chart.

Shelter	Where would you expect to find this kind of shelter?	Advantages of this type of construction.	Disadvantages of this type of construction.

Name _____

Greek City-States

Ancient Greece was made up of city-states by about the 700's B.C. Most of the citizens in a city-state spoke the same Greek dialect, practiced the same customs and religion and came from common ancestors. The members were like one large family.

Each city-state was governed mainly by a few wealthy men until the 500's B.C. This type of government is called oligarchy. During the 500's, however, some city-states began to move toward democracy.

Did you know that the U.S. government is based on the same type of government the Greek city-states used over 2,300 years ago? However, many countries still do not have a democratic form of government.

Write some advantages and disadvantages of a democracy. Then, choose another type of government to compare it to. Tell which country(s) use this type of government. On a separate sheet of paper, write an essay giving your views on the best type of government for the U.S.

Democracy	
Advantages:	**Disadvantages:**

_____
name of government

Advantages:	**Disadvantages:**

country(s):

SOCIAL STUDIES

Name _____

On the Diplomatic Trail

Eleanor Roosevelt was an unusual President's wife. She worked hard for many human rights programs. As chairman of the United Nations Human Rights Commission, she helped write the Universal Declaration of Human Rights which said, "All people are born free and equal in dignity and rights."

Write a mini Declaration of Human Rights for your school.

_____
_____
_____
_____
_____
_____

John Foster Dulles wore many hats. He was a lawyer, diplomat, senator and author. He negotiated several treaties for the United States and helped form the United Nations. He once said that in order to have peace, you must take chances, just as you must take chances in war.

Select one of today's world situations (i.e. the future of the Soviet Union) and tell what chances you might take to solve the problem. _____

_____
_____
_____
_____
_____

As President Nixon's Secretary of State, Henry Kissinger never stopped traveling around the world. He negotiated secretly with the North Vietnamese to end the war. He made several trips to the Middle East as a negotiator between Israel, Egypt and Syria - the three countries involved in the 1973 Arab-Israeli War. He visited China and Russia and paved the way for the President's visits to the two Communist nations.

Be a diplomat. Whenever sports teams are chosen, Jonathan is always last. After school, a bunch of your classmates are teasing him about it. Write what you would do about the situation. _____

_____
_____
_____
_____
_____

Name _____

They Were in Command

Three military leaders during World War II are quoted below. After reading the quotes, answer the questions.

General Eisenhower had these words for his troops before they invaded Europe. "The hopes and prayers of liberty-loving people everywhere march with you."

What kind of a man do you think he was? _____

_____

What values/beliefs make you think and act as you do? _____

_____

_____

_____

When President Roosevelt ordered General MacArthur and his family to leave Corregidor Island in the Philippines in 1942 because they were in great danger, he made a pledge, "I shall return."
How do you think he felt about leaving? _____

_____

What do you think he said when he did return in 1944 and eventually recaptured the islands in the next nine months? _____

_____

_____

_____

General George S. Patton, Jr., had a tough approach to war as expressed in the following quote. "Wars may be fought with weapons, but they are won by men."
What do you think he meant by this remark? _____

_____

What kind of a soldier would do well under Patton? _____

For which of the above generals would you rather fight? _____

Why? _____

If you were a general and were in charge of a battalion of men about to go into a highly dangerous battle situation, what would you say to them? _____

_____

_____

Personality Plus   Write a one-page paper about what you think a day in a battlefield would be like. Include sounds, smells, feelings, etc. Share it with the class.

SOCIAL STUDIES

Name _____

Contributing Factors

The following people played an important role in our country's history. Fill in the blank in front of each event with the correct year from the time line below to learn exactly how these people affected our lives. Hint: Read all the clues before you begin.

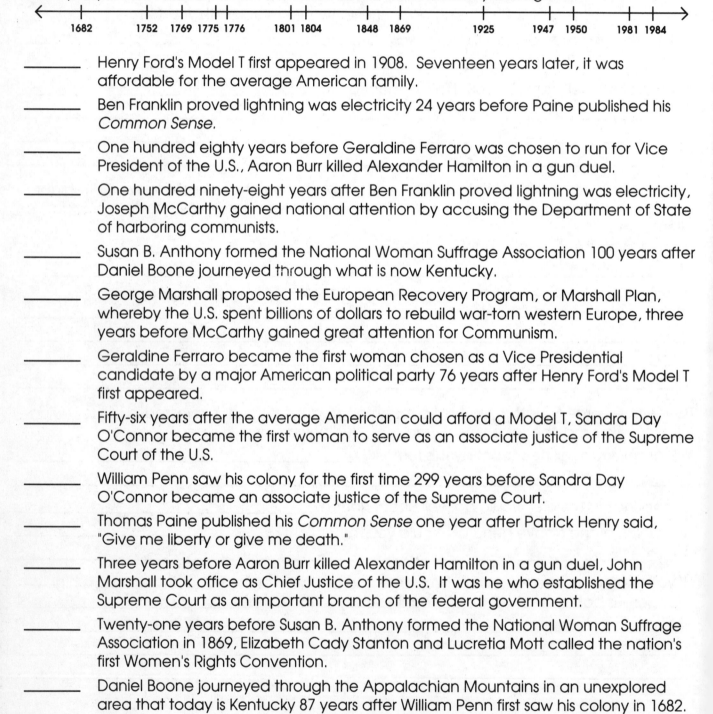

1682   1752 1769 1775 1776   1801 1804   1848 1869   1925   1947 1950   1981 1984

_____ Henry Ford's Model T first appeared in 1908. Seventeen years later, it was affordable for the average American family.

_____ Ben Franklin proved lightning was electricity 24 years before Paine published his *Common Sense.*

_____ One hundred eighty years before Geraldine Ferraro was chosen to run for Vice President of the U.S., Aaron Burr killed Alexander Hamilton in a gun duel.

_____ One hundred ninety-eight years after Ben Franklin proved lightning was electricity, Joseph McCarthy gained national attention by accusing the Department of State of harboring communists.

_____ Susan B. Anthony formed the National Woman Suffrage Association 100 years after Daniel Boone journeyed through what is now Kentucky.

_____ George Marshall proposed the European Recovery Program, or Marshall Plan, whereby the U.S. spent billions of dollars to rebuild war-torn western Europe, three years before McCarthy gained great attention for Communism.

_____ Geraldine Ferraro became the first woman chosen as a Vice Presidential candidate by a major American political party 76 years after Henry Ford's Model T first appeared.

_____ Fifty-six years after the average American could afford a Model T, Sandra Day O'Connor became the first woman to serve as an associate justice of the Supreme Court of the U.S.

_____ William Penn saw his colony for the first time 299 years before Sandra Day O'Connor became an associate justice of the Supreme Court.

_____ Thomas Paine published his *Common Sense* one year after Patrick Henry said, "Give me liberty or give me death."

_____ Three years before Aaron Burr killed Alexander Hamilton in a gun duel, John Marshall took office as Chief Justice of the U.S. It was he who established the Supreme Court as an important branch of the federal government.

_____ Twenty-one years before Susan B. Anthony formed the National Woman Suffrage Association in 1869, Elizabeth Cady Stanton and Lucretia Mott called the nation's first Women's Rights Convention.

_____ Daniel Boone journeyed through the Appalachian Mountains in an unexplored area that today is Kentucky 87 years after William Penn first saw his colony in 1682.

_____ Patrick Henry said, "Give me liberty or give me death," urging the Virginia militia to be prepared to defend the colony against England one year before the Declaration of Independence was adopted in 1776.

Name _____

Numbers, Figures, and Graphs

Answer the word problems below to learn more about these American personalities.

1. Benedict Arnold became the most famous traitor in U.S. history when he corresponded with the British during the Revolutionary War. Upon joining the British army, he demanded 20,000 pounds from them. However, he only received 6,315 pounds. If the British pound is worth $1.75, how many dollars would Arnold have received if he had gotten 20,000 pounds? _____ How many dollars did he actually receive? _____

2. Lewis and Clark started up the Missouri River from St. Louis and traveled almost 7,700 miles to the Pacific Coast. If one mile is equal to 1.6 kilometers, approximately how many kilometers did they travel? _____

3. During the 1850's, Harriet Tubman helped about 300 slaves escape. If a reward for Tubman totaled $40,000, about how much was offered per slave?

_____

During the Civil War, she helped more than 750 slaves escape. How many slaves did Tubman help free altogether? _____

4. Edward R. Murrow was an American radio and TV broadcaster. He narrated the programs, "See It Now" from 1951 to 1958 and "Person to Person" from 1953 to 1959. He served as director of the U.S. Information Agency from 1961 to 1964. On the graph below, shade in the years Murrow narrated 2 programs at the same time.

1951 1952 1953 1954 1955 1956 1957 1958 1959 1960 1961 1962 1963 1964

5. Babe Ruth was the first great home run hitter in baseball history. In 1927, Ruth set a record of 60 home runs in a 154-game season. Since then, Roger Maris of the Yankees hit 61 home runs in 1961 in a 162-game season. Ruth hit a total of 714 home runs during his career - a record that wasn't broken until Henry Aaron hit his 715th home run in 1974! Between Aaron and Ruth, how many home runs did they hit? _____ Who really has a better record, Ruth or Maris? Why? _____

_____

6. William Randolph Hearst, a famous American publisher of newspapers and magazines, had one of the most lavish private dwellings in the U.S. It included 240,000 acres of land, 50 miles of ocean frontage, four castles and a priceless art collection. If 2.5 acres is equal to one hectare (metric system), how many hectares of land did Hearst own? _____ How many kilometers of ocean frontage did he own? _____

Personality Plus Choose 3 famous people. Make up a math word problem concerning them and/or events in their lives. Trade your problems with a friend.

SOCIAL STUDIES

Name _____

What If ?

Think about what the world was like before Wilbur and Orville Wright flew the first motor-powered airplane in 1903. List five ways their invention changed the world.

_____

_____

_____

_____

_____

Albert Einstein is considered to be one of the fathers of the atom age. When he formed his theory of relativity, $E=mc^2$, he laid the basis for controlling the release of energy (E) from the atom. In 1939, he wrote to President Franklin Roosevelt and urged him to budget monies for studying the release of nuclear energy. He warned that Germany might already be building the atom bomb. Do you think President Roosevelt should have taken Einstein's advice? Why or why not?

_____

_____

_____

_____

_____

Thomas Edison had only three months of formal education, but he had 1,093 inventions patented in his lifetime. Two of his inventions that are very much a part of our lives today are the light bulb and the phonograph. Write a paragraph that tells what life would be like now if Edison had not created his wonderful inventions.

_____

_____

_____

_____

_____

Personality Plus   What invention do you think is the best? Write who invented it, when it was invented, etc. and tell why you think it is so great.

Name _____

Inventions

An inventor needs to have an understanding of a problem and an ability to create a device that will alleviate or reduce the problem. Choose and research a problem so you will know all you can about it and will be better able to answer the questions below and "invent" a device to eliminate or reduce the problem.

Describe precisely what the problem is. _____

_____

_____

_____

What needs to be done about the problem? _____

_____

_____

_____

Tell how you would do what needs to be done to alleviate or reduce the problem. Tell how your device would work.

_____

_____

_____

_____

_____

_____

_____

_____

_____

_____

_____

_____

_____

_____

Draw a picture of your device to the right.
Label its parts.

SOCIAL STUDIES

Name _____

Sorting the Facts

The fifth grade students are making history books about famous Americans. Every day, Miss Freed puts some facts on the board. The students copy each fact on a separate piece of paper and then illustrate each page. Once the pages are done, the students put them in chronological order so the information makes sense.

Try your hand at making a history book about Ben Franklin. Number the information in each box below in chronological order to learn about this famous man. Then cut them apart and make your own book.

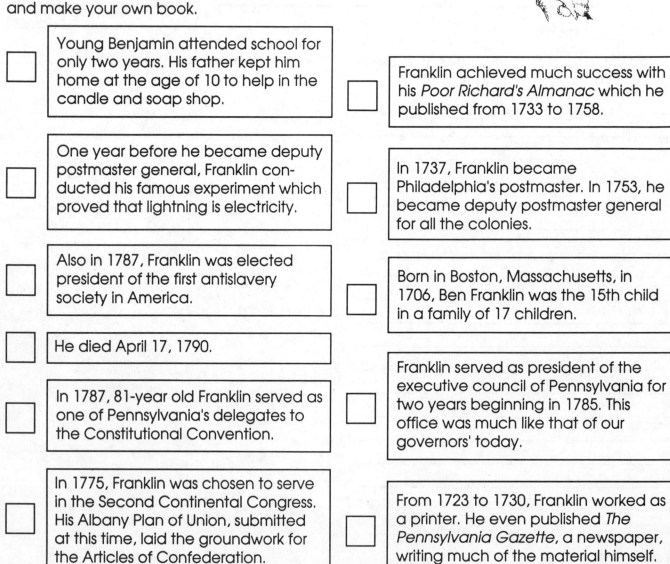

| | Young Benjamin attended school for only two years. His father kept him home at the age of 10 to help in the candle and soap shop. |

| | One year before he became deputy postmaster general, Franklin conducted his famous experiment which proved that lightning is electricity. |

| | Also in 1787, Franklin was elected president of the first antislavery society in America. |

| | He died April 17, 1790. |

| | In 1787, 81-year old Franklin served as one of Pennsylvania's delegates to the Constitutional Convention. |

| | In 1775, Franklin was chosen to serve in the Second Continental Congress. His Albany Plan of Union, submitted at this time, laid the groundwork for the Articles of Confederation. |

| | Franklin achieved much success with his *Poor Richard's Almanac* which he published from 1733 to 1758. |

| | In 1737, Franklin became Philadelphia's postmaster. In 1753, he became deputy postmaster general for all the colonies. |

| | Born in Boston, Massachusetts, in 1706, Ben Franklin was the 15th child in a family of 17 children. |

| | Franklin served as president of the executive council of Pennsylvania for two years beginning in 1785. This office was much like that of our governors' today. |

| | From 1723 to 1730, Franklin worked as a printer. He even published *The Pennsylvania Gazette*, a newspaper, writing much of the material himself. |

Name _____

What Would You Say?

When John Tyler's horse died, he wrote the following epitaph for the tombstone on the horse's grave.

> "Here lies the body of my good horse, The General. For twenty years he bore me around the circuit of my practice, and in all that time he never made a blunder. Would that his master could say the same."
>
> John Tyler

Write an epitaph for an animal that you know (or knew) for its tombstone.

_____

_____

_____

_____

When Coolidge decided not to run again for another term, he called reporters into his summer vacation office in the high school in Rapid City, South Dakota, and surprised them and the nation with the announcement. He had written on it, "I do not choose to run for President in 1928."

If you were President and did not want to run again, how would you handle it and what would you say?

_____

_____

_____

_____

Nine Vice Presidents have filled the Presidency when it was vacated by death, assassination or resignation. Each has said something about taking the oath. President Arthur said, "Men may die, but the fabrics of our free institutions remain unshaken. No higher proof could exist of the strength of popular government than the fact that, though the chosen of the people be struck down, his constitutional successor is peacefully installed without shock or strain."

What might you say if you succeeded to the Presidency?

_____

_____

_____

_____

Presidential Plus Pretend you were just elected President of the United States. Write your acceptance speech. Deliver it to your class.

SOCIAL STUDIES

Name _____

Hindsight Is 20/20!

A President is faced with making many decisions. Some of them are easier to make than others. Some decisions are popular with the citizens. Some are not. Harry Truman wrote in his memoirs, "To be President of the United States is to be lonely, very lonely at times of great decision." When Truman succeeded to the Presidency, America had been at war for over four years. He made the decision to drop the atom bomb which soon brought an end to World War II, but the bomb changed the world and involved it in a race for nuclear power.

What do you think President Truman should have done and why? _____

_____
_____
_____
_____
_____
_____
_____

President Carter also said it was not easy to make decisions, but he expressed it differently. He said, "I've learned that only the most complex and difficult tasks come before me in the Oval Office. No easy answers are found there - because no easy questions come there." In November 1979, several Iranian Revolutionaries took over the United States Embassy in Teheran and held several people hostage until President Reagan was inaugurated, January 20, 1981. President Carter tried to obtain the hostages' freedom by banning imports from Iran, cutting off diplomatic relations and authorizing a rescue mission.

What would you have done if you had been President and how would you have done it?

_____
_____
_____
_____
_____
_____

Presidential Plus

In 1991, President George Bush made the decision to go to war with Iraq and thus, the War in the Persian Gulf began. What would you have done if you were President Bush? Do you agree with his decision? Why?

Name _____

The Presidency

As the chief executive of the United States, the President helps shape and enforce laws, directs foreign policy, is responsible for national defense, presides at ceremonial affairs, and leads his Party. He does not control the Legislative and Judicial Branches, but he can influence law making, and he does appoint justices to the Supreme Court. No one man can assume all the duties of the president, and so he appoints assistants. They form the White House Office. It is their job to keep the President informed about the many departments of the government. They may advise and influence the president in his decisions. The members of the White House office do not need congressional approval, nor must they answer to the Congress. The Cabinet, consisting of thirteen department heads called secretaries, is also appointed by the President to advise and assist him. However, Cabinet members must be approved by Congress and must answer to the Legislative Branch whenever asked.

Label the diagram below to show the various departments and officials running the government. Use the words from the word box to complete the diagram.

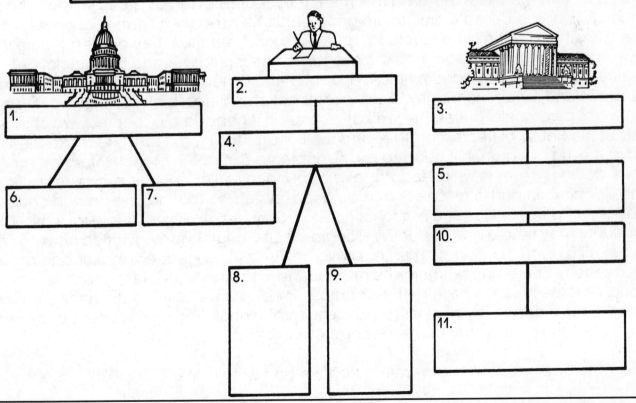

PRESIDENT	WHITE HOUSE STAFF	JUSTICES
LEGISLATIVE BRANCH	CABINET	EXECUTIVE BRANCH
SENATE	JUDICIAL BRANCH	CHIEF JUSTICE
HOUSE OF REPRESENTATIVES	SUPREME COURT	

1.
2.
3.
4.
5.
6.
7.
8.
9.
10.
11.

SOCIAL STUDIES

Name _____

Three Branches of Government

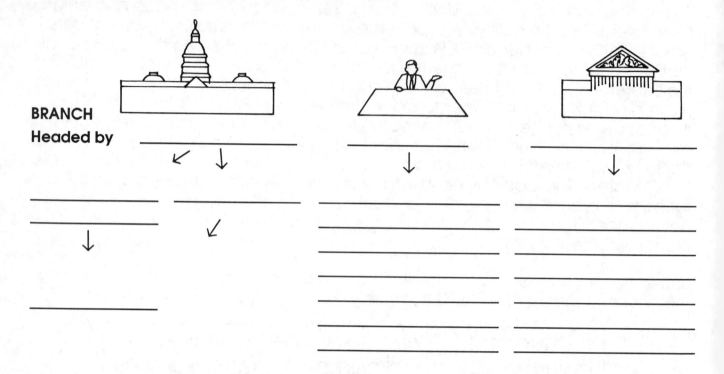

BRANCH

Headed by _____

The Founding Fathers did not want all the powers given to the government to be controlled by one man, or even just a few men. They feared if a small group was given too much power, the United States would once again be ruled by a tyrannical government like it had been under England. To avoid such a situation they divided the new government into three branches: the executive, the legislative, and the judicial. The executive branch is headed by the President of the United States who carries out federal laws and recommends new ones, directs national defense and foreign policy, and performs ceremonial duties. The legislative branch is headed by Congress, which consists of the House of Representatives and the Senate. Their main task is to make the laws. The judicial branch is headed by the Supreme Court. This branch interprets the laws, decides cases in which federal laws apply, and settles troubles between states. The Constitution built in a "check and balance" system so that no one branch could become too powerful. Each branch is controlled by the other two in several ways. The President may veto a law passed by Congress, but Congress may override his veto with a two-thirds vote. The Senate must approve any treaty the President makes and approve many of the appointments he makes. Any money the President needs for national defense must come from the Congress. The Supreme Court may check the Congress or the President by declaring a law unconstitutional. And the Court is appointed by the other two and may be impeached by Congress.

Label the branches of the government above and write in their Constitutional duties.

Name _____

Reading the Constitution

Look at a copy of the entire Constitution. It is only 4,300 words long. After you have looked at it, answer the questions or fill in the blanks below.

The Constitution is divided into _____ main parts.

They are the _____, _____ and _____.

What is the purpose of the Preamble? _____

_____

_____

There are ____ Articles in the Constitution. Many of them have several sections. Tell which article provides for the following services or laws.

United States court system _____

The nation's debts and upholding the Constitution _____

The lawmaking body or the government _____

What must be done for the Constitution to be law _____

(That process was called _____.)

Explains the duties of the President _____

Allows for changes to be made in the Constitution _____

(That process is called _____.)

Tells what the states can do and what the federal government can do_____

There are ____ Amendments in the Constitution.

What makes the Constitution a usable document today? _____

_____

_____

Which Article has allowed it to be an up-to-date document? _____

Define the following words as they relate to the Constitution.

ARTICLE _____

AMENDMENT _____

RATIFY _____

SOCIAL STUDIES

Name _____

The Preamble

The first sentence of the Preamble to the Constitution could be written simply, "We the people of the United States do ordain and establish this Constitution for the United States of America." But between "We the people of the United States" and "do ordain ....." are six reasons explaining why the Constitution was written. Read the Preamble below and write what the six reasons for its establishment are after each "To" below the Preamble. Then write what each reason means and give an example of why it is included or what it is meant to accomplish or prevent.

We the people of the United States, in order to form a more perfect Union, establish justice, insure domestic tranquility, provide for the common defense, promote the general welfare, and secure the blessings of liberty to ourselves and our posterity, do ordain and establish this Constitution for the United States of America.

Reasons for establishment of Constitution:

To _____

_____

_____

To _____

_____

_____

To _____

_____

_____

To _____

_____

_____

To _____

_____

_____

To _____

_____

_____

Name _____

State Fact Sheet

My state is _____

Date state entered Union _____

It was the _____ state to join the Union.

How many years has it been one of the United States? _____

How many states were already part of the Union when your state
entered it? _____

How many states joined the Union after your state? _____

Total area in square miles _____

Rank in size among states _____

How many states are smaller than your state? _____

How many states are larger than your state? _____

Population _____

Rank in population among states _____

How many other states have more people living in them? _____

How many other states have less peole living in them? _____

Write the names of the state's five largest cities and each
one's population.

City	Population
_____	_____
_____	_____
_____	_____
_____	_____
_____	_____

Is the state capital one of the five largest cities? _____

How many people live in these five cities altogether? _____

How many people live in the rest of the state? _____

Write the names of several famous people from your state. _____

_____

_____

Select one of these people about whom to write a few sentences.

   Daily Learning Drills Grade 5

SOCIAL STUDIES

Name _____

State Government

Fill in the names of the people currently holding the elected positions listed below in the executive branch of your state.

Governor _____ Lieutenant Governor _____

Write the names of the people currently representing you (your district) in the legislative branch of the state government.

Senator _____ Representative _____

The executive and legislative branches of the state government make laws that affect every citizen in the state. What kinds of laws can you think of that, if enacted by the legislature, might affect everyone in the state?

_____

_____

What law would you like to see passed that might improve a condition (problem) for everyone in the state?

_____

_____

Write a letter to the governor of your state, your senator or your representative suggesting such a law and giving reasons for it. Write the letter on the stationery below.

Name _____

states

From Billings to Boston

Use a U.S. map or an encyclopedia to locate these state stumpers.

1. Which seven letters of the alphabet do not begin the names of any states? _____
2. Name the nine states with double letters in their names.

    _____

    _____

3. Which state name has only one syllable? _____
4. Name the only letter not used in a state's name. _____
5. When listed in alphabetical order, which state comes first? _____
6. When listed in alphabetical order, which state comes last? _____
7. In what state is the letter **i** used the most? _____
8. Which state name has the most **o**'s? _____
9. Which state name has the most **a**'s? _____
10. Which state name has the most **e**'s? _____
11. Name four states whose names end with **o**. _____
12. Name the ten states with two words in their names.

    _____

    _____

13. Name four states that start and end with the same letter. _____

    _____

14. Which two letters are the first letters of more states than any others? _____
15. Which two states have only one consonant in their names? _____
16. Which was the first state to become part of the United States? _____
17. Which state was last? _____

SOCIAL STUDIES

What's in a Name?

Name _____

Over half of the United States' names came from Indian words. Some of the states' Indian names are listed below followed by their postal abbreviation in parentheses. Write the name of each state as we know it today.

Mnishota (MN) _____   Teysha (TX) _____

KwEnihtEkot (CT) _____   Arizonac (AZ) _____

Tanasi (TN) _____   Illini (IL) _____

KaNze (KS) _____   Mitchisawqyegan (MI) _____

alaschka (AK) _____   Ohiiyo (OH) _____

Mesatsuset (MA) _____   kentake (KY) _____

Niboapka (NE) _____   micizibi (MS) _____

maugh-wauwame (WY) _____   Ookanasa (AR) _____

Other states' names were derived from rivers that flowed through them, from people important to the region or from the geography of the region. Read each clue below and write the name of the state you think it is telling about. The postal abbreviation appears in parentheses.

1. It is a Latin word for "mountainous." (MT) _____

2. The state's name might have come from the French word "ouragan" meaning hurricane. (OR) _____

3. The name of this state honors the King of France, Louis XIV. (LA) _____

4. In 1610, Capt. Samuel Argall was blown off-course near this state. He named it for the man who had sponsored his journey, Thomas West Lord De La Warr. (DE) _____

5. It was the presence of Indians that caused a land development company to name the area. (IN)_____

6. In 1602, a Spanish expedition named a stream in the region of this state using a Spanish word to describe the reddish-brown color of the water. The word was later used to name the state and its big river. (CO) _____

7. This state is named in honor of King George II. (GA) _____

8. Its green mountains, or "verts monts," as written in slightly incorrect French, give this state its name. (VT) _____

9. This colony's founder named it after his king's wife, Henrietta Maria. It was known once as Mary's Land. (MD) _____

10. Its name may have come from several sources. Its size was once described as, "about the bigness of the Island of Rhodes," a Greek Island. A Dutch sea captain thought the red clay in some of its shoreline made it look fiery and named it "Roodt Eylandt." _____ (RI)

©McGraw-Hill Children's Publishing

Daily Learning Drills Grade 5

Name _____

The "Maine" Event

Discover facts about Maine by following the instructions below. An encyclopedia or atlas may be used.

1. Label the state capital on the map.
2. Label the four main rivers:
   Saco, Androscoggin, Kennebec and Penobscot. Color the river lines blue.
   Write "rivers" on the key.
3. Label the White Mountains. Color them brown and write "mountains" on the key.
4. Label the Atlantic Ocean. Draw blue and green waves.
5. Label all points on the compass rose.
6. Outline the state border in red. Write the state's name in any empty space on the map.

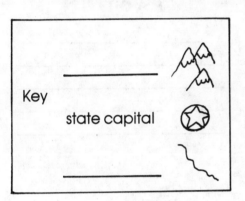

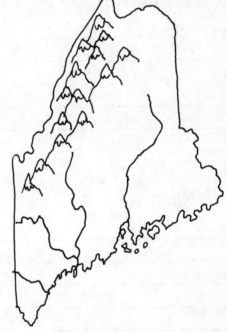

Now travel further into the encyclopedia or atlas and list the following Maine facts.

7. State bird: _____
8. State flower: _____
9. State tree: _____
10. Date Maine became a state: _____
11. State motto: _____
12. State song: _____

Bonus

Make a poster of Maine. Draw the state map as well as pictures of the state bird, flower, etc. Research famous people from Maine, events, and products manufactured by the state.

SOCIAL STUDIES

Name _____

U.S. Products and Natural Resources

The United States is one of the world's largest producers of manufactured goods because it is very rich in natural resources.

A study of the *U.S. Products and Natural Resources Map* (p. 267) will indicate which states are the chief suppliers of certain products and natural resources.

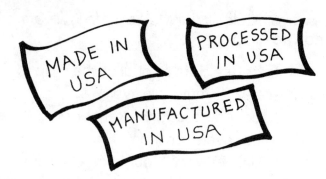

For each product and natural resource listed below, use the map on page 267 to name the states that are major suppliers.

Coal
_____
_____
_____
_____

Iron Ore
_____
_____
_____
_____

Oil
_____
_____
_____
_____

Corn
_____
_____
_____
_____

Wheat
_____
_____
_____
_____

Cotton
_____
_____
_____
_____

Dairy
_____
_____
_____
_____

Lumber
_____
_____
_____
_____

Beef
_____
_____
_____
_____

Name _____

U.S. Products and Natural Resources
(Use with page 266.)

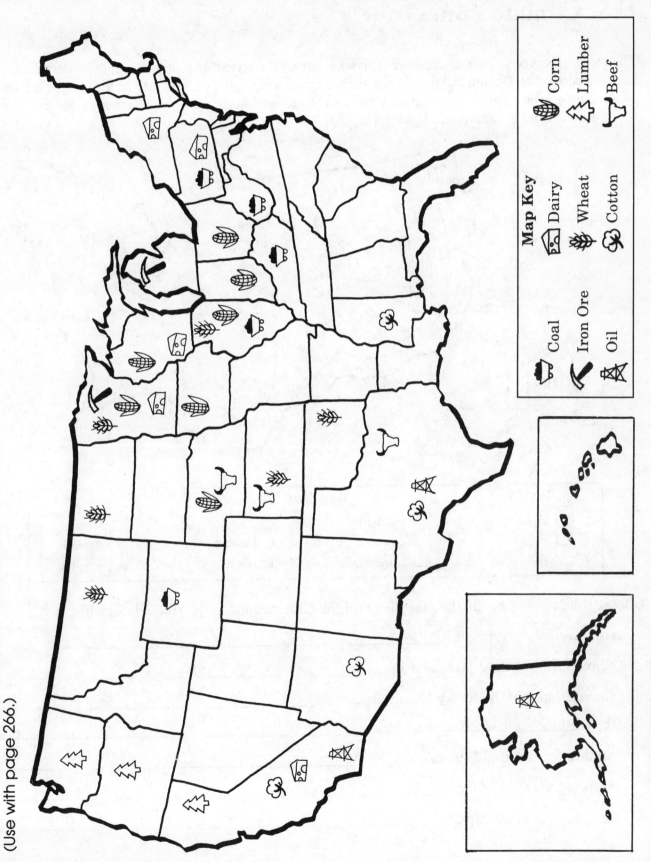

Map Key

Corn
Lumber
Beef

Dairy
Wheat
Cotton

Coal
Iron Ore
Oil

SOCIAL STUDIES

Name _____

U.S. Climate Zones

The word **climate** is used to describe the weather in a particular place over a long period of time. Because the United States covers such a large area, it has a number of different climate zones. Some areas have long, cold winters and short, cool summers, while other areas are always warm in both the summer and the winter.

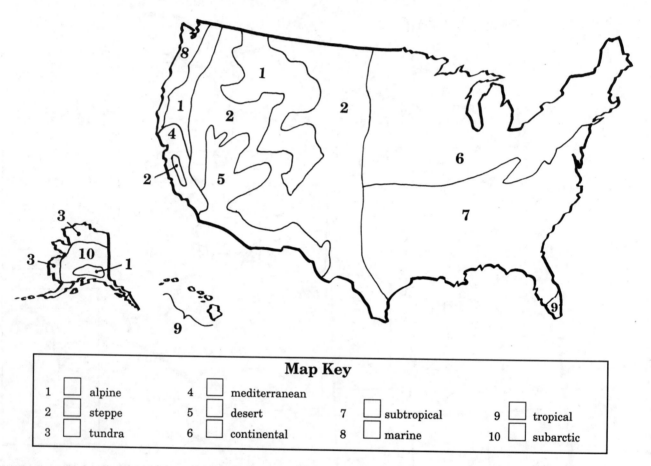

Map Key

1	☐ alpine	4	☐ mediterranean			7	☐ subtropical	9	☐ tropical
2	☐ steppe	5	☐ desert			8	☐ marine	10	☐ subarctic
3	☐ tundra	6	☐ continental						

Choose colors to color-code the Map Key and the climate zone map. Then, determine the . . .

climate zone you live in. _____

climate zone of the Northeast. _____

climate zones of the Rocky Mountains. _____

three climate zones found in Alaska. _____

climate zones found in Texas. _____

climate zones of Florida. _____

climate zone of Michigan. _____

Name _____

Temperature Ranges

What is the average January temperature where you live? The average monthly temperature is figured using the daily temperatures for the whole month. This information can be found in most almanacs and encyclopedias. Why would it be helpful to know the average temperature of a city?

_____

_____

Use an almanac or encyclopedia to find the average high and low temperatures for January and July listed below.

State	City	Average Monthly Temperatures (F°)			
		January		July	
		High	Low	High	Low
Alaska					
California					
Colorado					
Florida					
Iowa					
Michigan					
New York					
North Dakota					
South Carolina					
Texas					
Wisconsin					
State of your choice:					

Circle the highest temperature in each "high" column and the lowest temperature in each "low" column.

SOCIAL STUDIES

Name _____

Natural Wonders of the U.S.A.

Listed below are ten natural physical features found in the United States.

Use an encyclopedia, atlas, or other source to complete the chart. Write the number of each feature on a copy of the U.S. Political Map (page 271) in its correct location.

Natural Feature	State	Description
1. Devil's Tower		
2. Grand Canyon		
3. Mount McKinley		
4. Everglades		
5. Mount St. Helens		
6. Kilauea		
7. Carlsbad Caverns		
8. Cape Cod		
9. Badlands National Park		
10. Mojave Desert		

Name _____

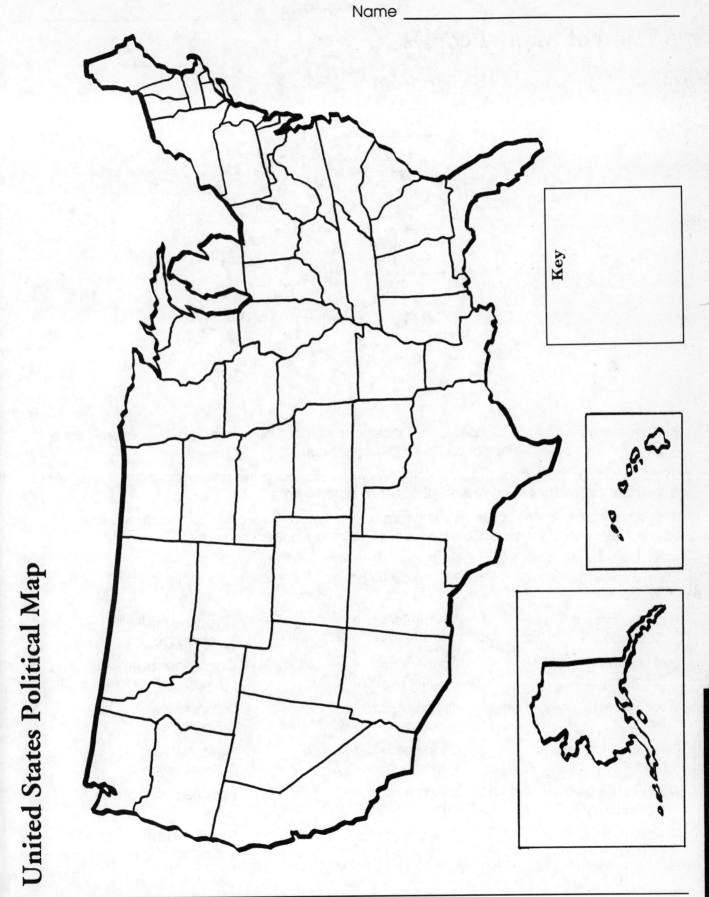

United States Political Map

Key

SOCIAL STUDIES

Name _____

A Land of Many Peoples

The Iroquois were a group of tribes joined together by a common language. Their enemies, the Algonquin, were several tribes of another language group.

Listed below are the names of some North American tribes and the states who claim them. Please remember that Indians often moved about from state to state.

Write each tribe's name in or by its state name on the map. Then color each state the color beside the name of the tribe. Colors symbolize common language groups.

Ojibwa (green)	Nez Perce (lt. blue)	Iroquois (red)
Wisconsin	Idaho	New York
Arapaho (green)	Yakima (lt. blue)	Cherokee (red)
Colorado	Washington	Tennessee
Leni Lenape (green)	Sioux (yellow)	Chickasaw (blue)
Delaware	South Dakota	Mississippi
Illinois (green)	Osage (yellow)	Seminole (blue)
Illinois	Kansas	Florida
Penobscot (green)	Crow (yellow)	Navaho (orange)
Maine	Montana	New Mexico
Algonquin (green)	Ute (tan)	Apache (orange)
Massachusetts	Utah	Texas
Powhatan (green)	Shoshoni (tan)	Shasta (violet)
Virginia	Wyoming	California

Name _____

North America

Use this map and a political map of North America to do the following:

1. On another sheet of paper, number from 1–17. Then identify these places in North America.
2. Next list the letters A–G. Write the correct name for each body of water after each letter.

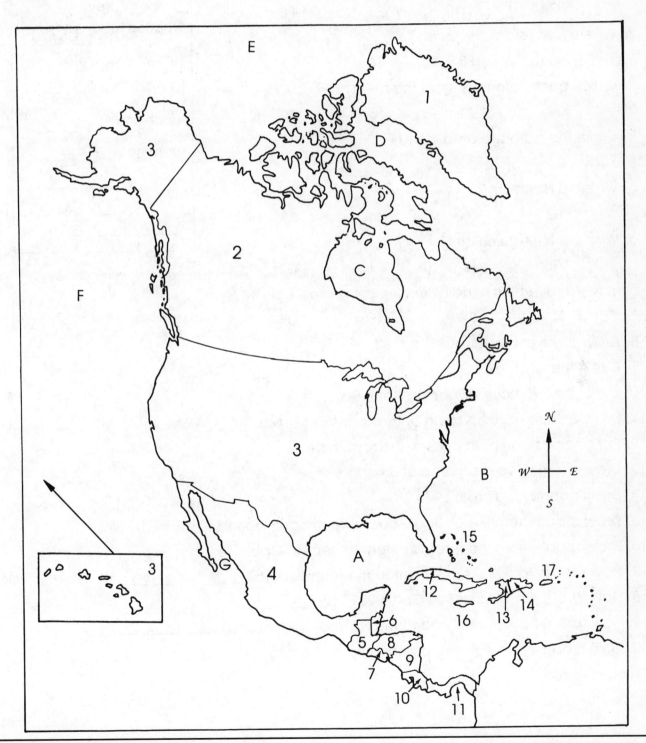

Name _____

Case the Joint (Use with page 275.)

Use the map to answer these questions.

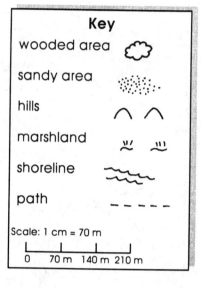

Key

wooded area

sandy area

hills

marshland

shoreline

path

Scale: 1 cm = 70 m

0   70 m   140 m 210 m

1. Where is the camp's track?

      C4   D10   E3   F8

2. Where is the swimming area?

      G6   F5   E4   F7

3. Which cabin is farthest from the mess hall?

      7   21   16   12

4. Circle the garbage area in red.

5. Where is North Bay?

      E2   B4   C10   E9

6. Where is McKenzie Point?

      A5   H2   C10   G1

7. In which direction is the swimming pier from Cabin 13?

      N   SW   NE   SE

8. Draw a green picnic table near B2.

9. Circle the swamp at G2.

10. Draw the two boys' sailboat in North Bay.

11. Draw a swimming raft south of the swimming area.

12. Put goalposts on both ends of the soccer field.

13. Draw a large, wooded area at B5 and B6.

14. Draw a sandy region at E9.

15. Draw a path from the obstacle course to the compound.

16. Draw a path from the track and tennis areas to Cabin 16.

17. How far is it from McKenzie Point to the tennis courts?_____

18. How far is it from Cabin 5 to Cabin 20?   _____

19. How far is it from the SW end to the NE end of the island?_____

20. Give a name to the creek, a peninsula and a large hill. _____

Name _____

Case the Joint (cont.)

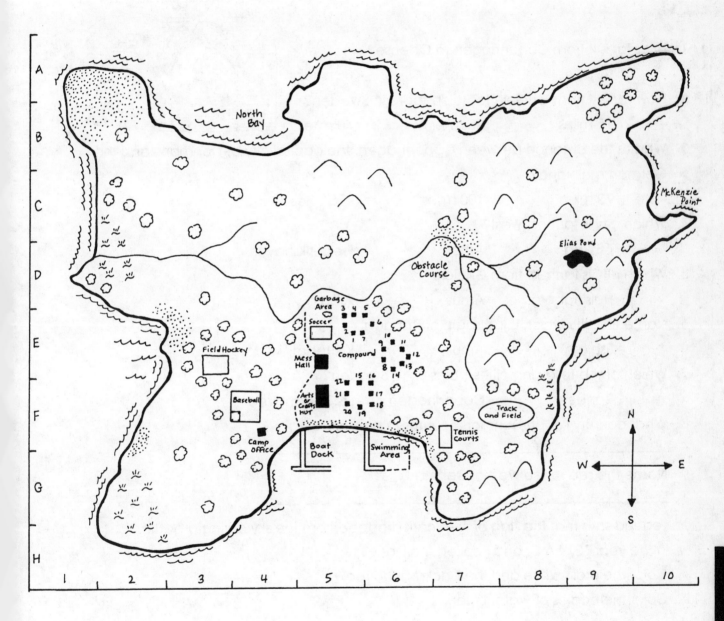

SOCIAL STUDIES

Name _____

Occupied Denmark

Use the map on page 277 to answer the questions below.

1. How far is it from Copenhagen to Odense?

         25 miles   60 miles   85 miles

2. How far is it from Gilleleje to Halsingborg in Sweden?

         15 miles   25 miles   40 miles

3. What is the distance between Copenhagen, the capital city of Denmark, and the German mainland?

         70 miles   100 miles   175 miles

4. Which city is farthest west?

         Esbjerg   Arhus   Frederikshaven

5. Which city is farthest from Gilleleje?

         Halsingborg   Arhus   Alborg

6. Name the city which is just south of Randers.

         Esbjerg   Arhus   Kattegat

7. Which of the following cities is closest to Sweden?

         Randers   Copenhagen   Frederikshaven

8. What country lies on Denmark's southern border?

    _____

9. Name the sea to the west of Denmark.

    _____

10. Legend says that the flag of Denmark dropped from the sky during a battle in the year 1219 A.D. and inspired the Danes to victory.
    Color the cross white and the background red.

11. Color the bodies of water blue.

12. Color Denmark red.

13. Color Sweden green.

14. Color Germany orange.

Name _____

Occupied Denmark (cont.)

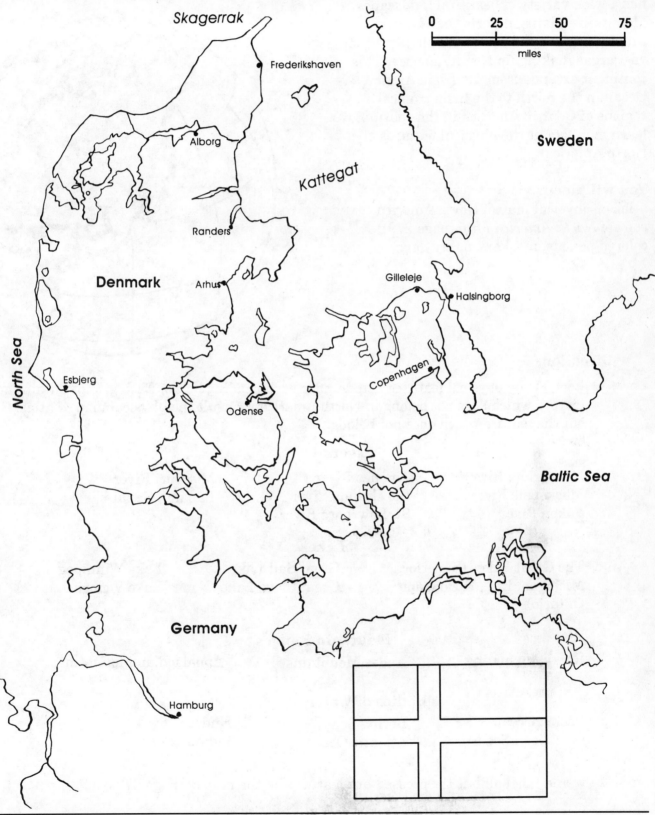

Name _____

North America

North America, the third-largest continent, has a wide variety of beautiful landscapes. Mountains, plains, deserts, rainforests, tundra, and rugged coasts are all part of the vast areas making up North America. This continent extends from the frigid Arctic Ocean in the north to the lush, tropical regions of Central America in the south. Let's learn more about the physical features of North America.

You will need:
atlas or physical map of North America
copy of *North America Map* (page 279)
colored pencils, markers, or crayons

Directions:

1. Look at the physical features listed under each heading below. Each group contains one feature which does not belong in North America. Consult the physical map or atlas. Cross out the feature which does not belong.

Rivers

Mississippi River	Thames River	Missouri River
Mackenzie River	Rio Grande River	Panama Canal
Yukon River	St. Lawrence River	

Lakes

The Great Lakes (Superior, Michigan, Erie, Huron, and Ontario)	Great Salt Lake	Lake Winnipeg
	Great Slave Lake	Lake Victoria

Mountain Ranges

Rocky Mountains	Andes Mountains	Appalachian Mountains

Bodies of Water

Pacific Ocean	Bering Sea	Hudson Bay
Caribbean Sea	Atlantic Ocean	Indian Ocean

2. Draw and label all but the crossed-out features on the map on page 279.

Name _____

North America
(Use with page 278.)

SOCIAL STUDIES

Name _____

Landform Regions of the United States

The continental United States can be divided into several major landform regions. Label each region using the list found in the **Word Bank**.

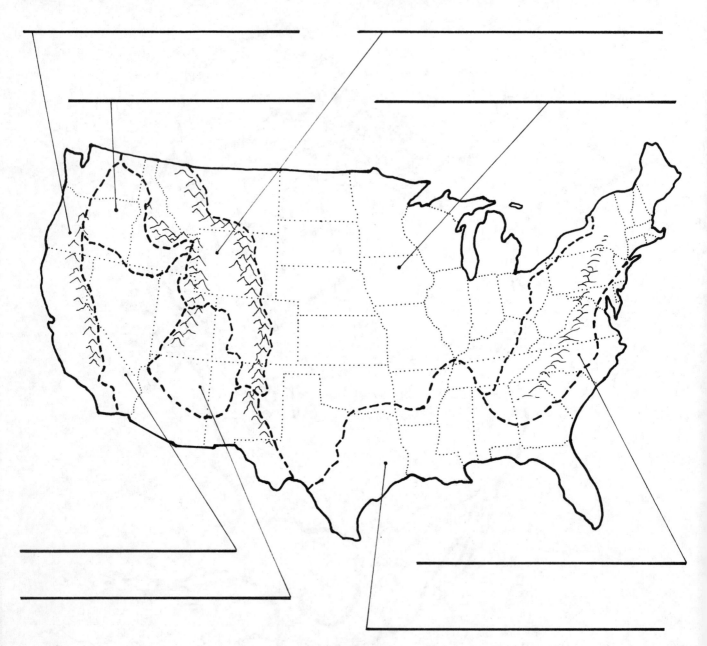

WORD BANK

Interior Plains
Great Basin
Pacific Ranges and Lowlands

Columbia Plateau
Colorado Plateau
Appalachian Highlands

Rocky Mountains
Coastal Lowlands

Name _____

Hemispheres

The earth is a sphere. When the earth is cut in half either vertically or horizontally, hemispheres are created. If the earth is cut in half along the **equator**, the **Northern Hemisphere** and the **Southern Hemisphere** are formed. If the earth is cut in half from the North Pole to the South Pole along the **prime meridian**, the **Eastern Hemisphere** and the **Western Hemisphere** are formed.

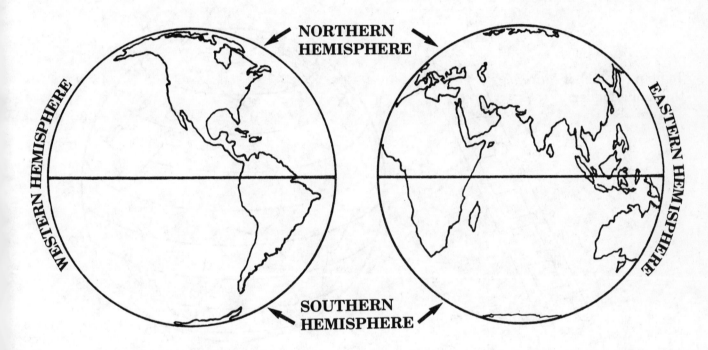

Examine the illustration of the hemispheres. Decide in which two hemispheres (Eastern or Western, and Northern or Southern) each of the following countries is located. (**Example:** United States is in the Northern and Western Hemispheres) You may need to use a more detailed globe or map to find the exact locations of the countries.

1. Australia _____

2. India _____

3. Japan _____

4. Italy _____

5. Argentina _____

6. Ethiopia _____

7. South Africa _____

8. Mexico _____

9. China _____

10. Canada _____

11. Israel _____

12. Chile _____

13. Iraq _____

14. Peru _____

SOCIAL STUDIES

Name _____

Lines of Latitude

The lines on a globe help you find where places are located. The lines that go around the globe from east to west are called **lines of latitude,** or **parallels**. The lines of latitude tell you how far north or south of the **equator** (0°) you are.

All lines of latitude are measured from the equator in degrees. Everything north of the equator is labeled N for **north**, and everything south of the equator is S for **south**.

To help remember *latitude,*
think of a ladder.

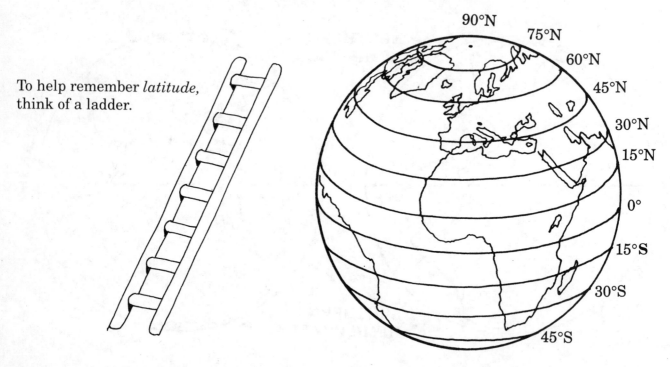

Use a globe or map to find the latitude for each of the following cities. Remember to indicate both the number of degrees and whether it is north or south of the equator.

1. Baghdad, Iraq _____

2. Madrid, Spain _____

3. LaPaz, Bolivia _____

4. San Jose, Costa Rica _____

5. Quito, Ecuador _____

6. Canberra, Australia _____

7. Oslo, Norway _____

8. Prague, Czechoslovakia _____

9. Reykjavik, Iceland _____

10. Mexico City, Mexico _____

11. Lisbon, Portugal _____

12. Frankfurt, Germany _____

13. Johannesburg, South Africa _____

14. Athens, Greece _____

15. Helsinki, Finland _____

16. Karáchi, Pakistan _____

Name _____

Lines of Longitude

The lines on a globe help you find where places are located. The lines that go from the North Pole to the South Pole are called **lines of longitude**, or **meridians**. The lines of longitude tell how far east or west of the **prime meridian** (0°) you are.

All lines of longitude are measured from the prime meridian in degrees. Everything west of the prime meridian is labeled W for **west**, and everything east of the prime meridian is labeled E for **east**.

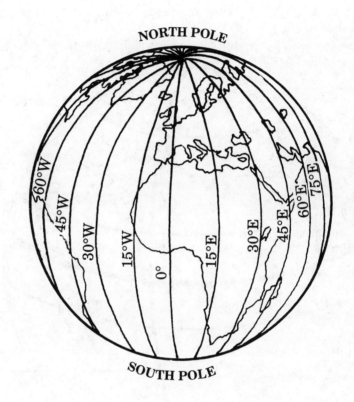

Use a globe or map to find the longitude for each of the following cities. Remember to indicate both the number of degrees and whether it is east or west of the prime meridian.

1. Los Angeles, U.S.A. _____

2. London, United Kingdom _____

3. Wellington, New Zealand _____

4. Tokyo, Japan _____

5. Bangkok, Thailand _____

6. Santiago, Chile _____

7. Nairobi, Kenya _____

8. Tehran, Iran _____

9. Paris, France _____

10. Glasgow, United Kingdom _____

11. Rome, Italy _____

12. Buenos Aires, Argentina _____

13. Anchorage, Alaska _____

14. Calcutta, India _____

15. Cairo, Egypt _____

16. Shanghai, China _____

SOCIAL STUDIES

Name _____

What's My Line?

There are several important lines of latitude on the globe which have special names.

Use a map, globe, or other resource to identify the special lines on the illustration of the globe below.

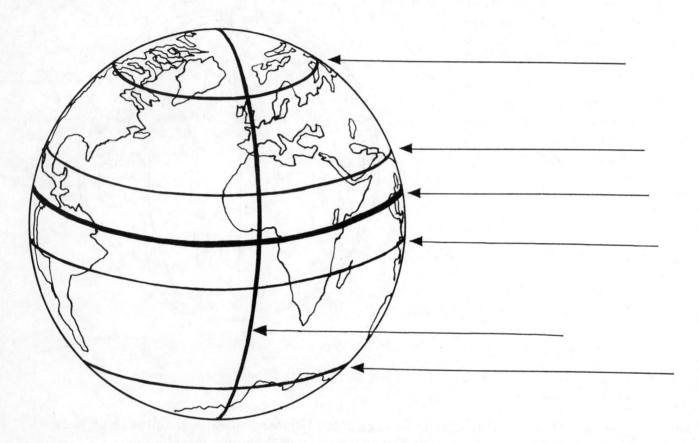

Name the imaginary line that . . .

passes through Mexico. _____

is 0° latitude. _____

passes through Alaska. _____

is 0° longitude. _____

divides the Northern and Southern hemispheres. _____

passes through Botswana. _____

Name _____

Pinpointing Your Location

A specific location can be "pinpointed" by using latitude and longitude together. The number of degrees latitude will tell you how far it is north or south of the equator. The number of degrees longitude will tell you how far it is east or west of the prime meridian.

Grand Rapids
42°N 85°W

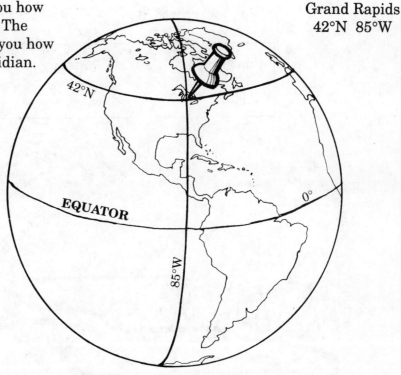

Locate each of the cities listed below on a map. Write the latitude and longitude coordinates in the blanks. Remember to write both the number of degrees and the direction north or south from the equator, and east or west of the prime meridian.

	Latitude	**Longitude**
1. Mexico City, Mexico	_____	_____
2. Buenos Aires, Argentina	_____	_____
3. New Delhi, India	_____	_____
4. Seoul, South Korea	_____	_____
5. Chicago, U.S.A.	_____	_____
6. Beijing, China	_____	_____
7. Paris, France	_____	_____
8. Sydney, Australia	_____	_____

SOCIAL STUDIES

Name _____

The Story of a River

The river systems of the world provide people with transportation, energy, fertile soil, and water for drinking, washing, and irrigation. The terms below are used when telling the story of a river system. Learn the meanings of these terms, and then label the parts of the river on the illustration.

flood plain	tributary	lake
delta	rapids	levee
mouth	swamp	source

Name _____

Famous Rivers of the World

Use an atlas, encyclopedia, or almanac to learn about ten important rivers listed below. Complete the chart on this page.

River	Continent	Length	Outflow
Amazon			
Colorado			
Danube			
Ganges			
Niger			
Mississippi			
Nile			
Rhine			
Volga			
Yangtze			

Daily Learning Drills Grade 5

SOCIAL STUDIES

Name _____

River Cities

Many of the world's great cities began as small towns and settlements along major rivers. Communities near water were easily accessible. Water was readily available for drinking, cooking, washing, irrigation, obtaining food, etc.

Use an atlas, almanac, or encyclopedia to help you complete the chart.

River	City	Country	Continent
Mississippi			
	New York		
	Rome		
Nile			
	London		
	Buenos Aires		
Seine			
	Shanghai		

Answer Key

Everything Has Its Place
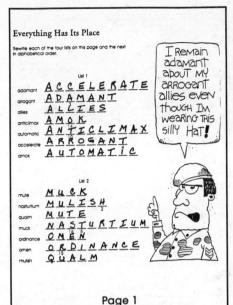
Rewrite each of the four lists on this page and the next in alphabetical order.

List 1
adamant	ACCELERATE
arrogant	ADAMANT
allies	ALLIES
anticlimax	AMOK
automatic	ANTICLIMAX
accelerate	ARROGANT
amok	AUTOMATIC

I remain adamant about my arrogant allies even though I'm wearing this silly hat!

List 2
mute	MUCK
nasturtium	MULISH
qualm	MUTE
muck	NASTURTIUM
ordinance	OMEN
omen	ORDINANCE
mulish	QUALM

Page 1

Everything Has Its Place

List 3
pommel	POMMEL
regaled	POUTER
scrimmage	RABBLE
pouter	REGALED
rove	RIPE
rabble	ROVE
ripe	SCRIMMAGE

List 4
tack	SPIEL
tersely	SPORRAN
trowel	SQUEAMISH
thwarted	TACK
sporran	TERSELY
squeamish	THWARTED
spiel	TROWEL

Now write the letters from the numbered blanks on the spaces at the bottom to answer the question.

Question:
When Omri asked Matron if Little Bear could ride his horse, what did she reply?

Answer: THAT'S UP TO THE HORSE

Page 2

Color Time
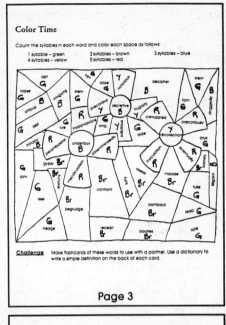
Count the syllables in each word and color each space as follows:

1 syllable – green   2 syllables – brown   3 syllables – blue
4 syllables – yellow   5 syllables – red

Challenge Make flashcards of these words to use with a partner. Use a dictionary to write a simple definition on the back of each card.

Page 3

Break It Up
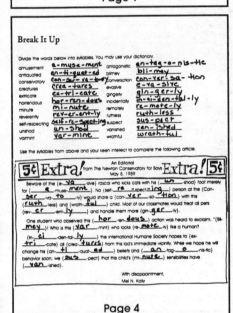
Divide the words below into syllables. You may use your dictionary.

amusement	a-muse-ment
antiquated	an-ti-quat-ed
conservatory	con-ser-va-to-ry
creatures	crea-tures
extricate	ex-tri-cate
horrendous	hor-ren-dous
minute	mi-nute
reverently	rev-er-ent-ly
self-respecting	self-re-spect-ing
unshod	un-shod
varmint	var-mint
antagonistic	an-tag-o-nis-tic
blimey	bli-mey
conversation	con-ver-sa-tion
evasive	e-va-sive
gingerly	gin-ger-ly
incidentally	in-ci-den-tal-ly
remotely	re-mote-ly
ruthless	ruth-less
suspect	sus-pect
vanished	van-ished
wrathful	wrath-ful

Use the syllables from above and your keen intellect to complete the following article.

5¢ Extra! Extra! 5¢

An Editorial from The Newton Conservatory for Boys
May 8, 1989

Beware of the (e-va-sive) rascal who kicks cats with his (un-shod) foot merely for (a-muse-ment). No (self-re-spect-ing) person at the (Con-ser-va-to-ry) would share a (con-ver-sa-tion) with this (ruth-less) and (wrath-ful) child. Most of our classmates would treat all pets (rev-er-ent-ly) and handle them more (gin-ger-ly).

One student who observed this (hor-ren-dous) action was heard to exclaim, "(Bli-mey)! Who is this (var-mint) who looks (re-mote-ly) like a human?

(In-ci-den-tal-ly), the International Humane Society hopes to (ex-tri-cate) at (crea-tures) from this lad's immediate vicinity. While we hope he will change his (an-ti-quat-ed) beliefs and (an-tag-o-nis-tic) behavior soon, we (sus-pect) that this child's (mi-nute) sensibilities have (van-ished).

With disappointment,
Mel N. Kelly

Page 4

What Beautiful Islands!
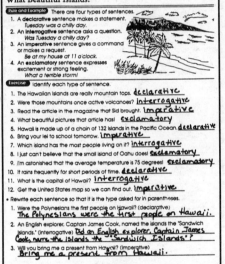
Rule and Example There are four types of sentences.
1. A **declarative** sentence makes a statement.
   Tuesday was a chilly day.
2. An **interrogative** sentence asks a question.
   Was Tuesday a chilly day?
3. An **imperative** sentence gives a command or makes a request.
   Be at my house at 11 o'clock.
4. An **exclamatory** sentence expresses excitement or strong feeling.
   What a terrible storm!

Exercise Identify each type of sentence.

1. The Hawaiian Islands are really mountain tops. **declarative**
2. Were those mountains once active volcanoes? **interrogative**
3. Read the article in the magazine that Sid brought. **imperative**
4. What beautiful pictures that article has! **exclamatory**
5. Hawaii is made of a chain of 132 islands in the Pacific Ocean. **declarative**
6. Bring your lei to school tomorrow. **imperative**
7. Which island has the most people living on it? **interrogative**
8. I just can't believe that the small island of Oahu does! **exclamatory**
9. I'm astonished that the average temperature is 75 degrees! **exclamatory**
10. It rains frequently for short periods of time. **declarative**
11. What is the capital of Hawaii? **interrogative**
12. Get the United States map so we can find out. **imperative**

- Rewrite each sentence so that it is the type asked for in parentheses.
1. Were the Polynesians the first people on Hawaii? (declarative)
   The Polynesians were the first people on Hawaii.
2. An English explorer, Captain James Cook, named the islands the "Sandwich Islands." (interrogative) Did an English explorer, Captain James Cook, name the islands the "Sandwich Islands"?
3. Will you bring me a present from Hawaii? (imperative)
   Bring me a present from Hawaii.

Page 5

Food for Thought
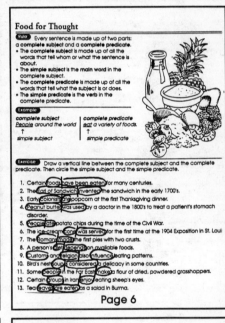
Rule Every sentence is made up of two parts: a **complete subject** and a **complete predicate**.
- The complete subject is made up of all the words that tell whom or what the sentence is about.
- The **simple subject** is the main word in the complete subject.
- The complete predicate is made up of all the words that tell what the subject is or does.
- The **simple predicate** is the verb in the complete predicate.

Example
complete subject	complete predicate
People around the world	ate a variety of foods.
↑	↑
simple subject	simple predicate

Exercise Draw a vertical line between the complete subject and the complete predicate. Then circle the simple subject and the simple predicate.

1. Certain foods have been eaten for many centuries.
2. The Earl of Sandwich invented the sandwich in the early 1700's.
3. Early colonists ate popcorn at the first Thanksgiving dinner.
4. Peanut butter was used by a doctor in the 1800's to treat a patient's stomach disorder.
5. People ate potato chips during the time of the Civil War.
6. The ice-cream cone was served for the first time at the 1904 Exposition in St. Louis.
7. The Romans made their pies with two crusts.
8. A person's diet depends on available foods.
9. Customs and religion also influence eating patterns.
10. Bird's nest soup is considered a delicacy in some countries.
11. Some people in the Far East make a flour of dried, powdered grasshoppers.
12. Certain groups in Iran enjoy eating sheep's eyes.
13. Tea leaves are eaten as a salad in Burma.

Page 6

We Agree
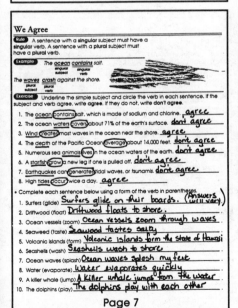
Rule A sentence with a **singular subject** must have a **singular verb**. A sentence with a plural subject must have a **plural verb**.

Example
The *ocean* *contains* salt.
(singular subject / singular verb)
The *waves* *crash* against the shore.
(plural subject / plural verb)

Exercise Underline the simple subject and circle the verb in each sentence. If the subject and verb agree, write *agree*. If they do not, write *don't agree*.

1. The ocean contains salt, which is made of sodium and chlorine. **agree**
2. The ocean waters cover about 71% of the earth's surface. **don't agree**
3. Wind creates most waves in the ocean near the shore. **agree**
4. The depth of the Pacific Ocean average about 14,000 feet. **don't agree**
5. Numerous sea animals lives in the ocean waters of the earth. **don't agree**
6. A starfish grow a new leg if one is pulled off. **don't agree**
7. Earthquakes can generate tidal waves, or tsunamis. **don't agree**
8. High tides occur twice a day. **agree**

- Complete each sentence below using a form of the verb in parentheses. (Answers will vary.)
1. Surfers (glide) Surfers glide on their boards.
2. Driftwood (float) Driftwood floats to shore.
3. Ocean vessels (zoom) Ocean vessels zoom through waves.
4. Seaweed (taste) Seaweed tastes salty.
5. Volcanic islands (form) Volcanic islands form the state of Hawaii.
6. Seashells (wash) Seashells wash to shore.
7. Ocean waves (splash) Ocean waves splash my feet.
8. Water (evaporate) Water evaporates quickly.
9. A killer whale (jump) A killer whale jumps from the water.
10. The dolphins (play) The dolphins play with each other.

Page 7

A Whale of an Activity
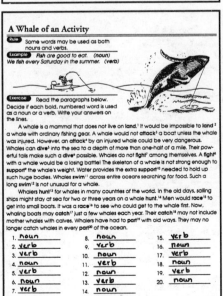
Rule Some words may be used as both nouns and verbs.

Example Fish are good to eat. (noun)
We fish every Saturday in the summer. (verb)

Exercise Read the paragraphs below. Decide if each bold, numbered word is used as a noun or a verb. Write your answers on the lines.

A whale is a mammal that does not live on land.[1] It would be impossible to land[2] a whale with ordinary fishing gear. A whale would not attack[3] a boat unless the whale was injured. However, an attack[4] by an injured whale could be very dangerous. Whales can dive[5] into the sea to a depth of more than one-half of a mile. Their powerful tails make such a dive[6] possible. Whales do not fight[7] among themselves. A fight[8] with a whale would be a losing battle! The skeleton of a whale is not strong enough to support[9] the whale's weight. Water provides the extra support[10] needed to hold up such huge bodies. Whales swim[11] across entire oceans searching for food. Such a long swim[12] is not unusual for a whale.

Whalers hunt[13] for whales in many countries of the world. In the old days, sailing ships might stay at sea for two or three years on a whale hunt.[14] Men would race[15] to get into small boats. It was a race[16] to see who could get to the whale first. Now, whaling boats may catch[17] just a few whales each year. Their catch[18] may not include mother whales with calves. Whales have had to part[19] with old ways. They may no longer catch whales in every part[20] of the ocean.

1. noun	8. verb	15. verb
2. verb	9. verb	16. noun
3. verb	10. noun	17. verb
4. noun	11. verb	18. noun
5. verb	12. noun	19. verb
6. noun	13. verb	20. noun
7. noun	14. noun	

Page 8

Hawaii and Alaska
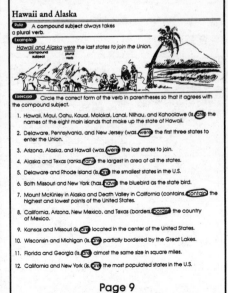
Rule A **compound subject** always takes a plural verb.

Example
Hawaii and Alaska *were* the last states to join the Union.
(compound subject / plural verb)

Exercise Circle the correct form of the verb in parentheses so that it agrees with the compound subject.

1. Hawaii, Maui, Oahu, Kauai, Molokai, Lanai, Niihau, and Kahoolawe (is, **are**) the names of the eight main islands that make up the state of Hawaii.
2. Delaware, Pennsylvania, and New Jersey (was, **were**) the first three states to enter the Union.
3. Arizona, Alaska, and Hawaii (was, **were**) the last states to join.
4. Alaska and Texas (**rank**, ranks) the largest in area of all the states.
5. Delaware and Rhode Island (is, **are**) the smallest states in the U.S.
6. Both Missouri and New York (has, **have**) the bluebird as the state bird.
7. Mount McKinley in Alaska and Death Valley in California (contains, **contain**) the highest and lowest points of the United States.
8. California, Arizona, New Mexico, and Texas (**border**, borders) the country of Mexico.
9. Kansas and Missouri (is, **are**) located in the center of the United States.
10. Wisconsin and Michigan (is, **are**) partially bordered by the Great Lakes.
11. Florida and Georgia (is, **are**) almost the same size in square miles.
12. California and New York (is, **are**) the most populated states in the U.S.

Page 9

More About Pronouns

Rule The **subject pronoun** and the **verb** of the sentence must always agree in gender and number.

Example

We visit Lake Champlain when we go to Vermont. (plural pronoun and verb)
He visits Lake Champlain when he goes to Vermont. (singular pronoun and verb)

Exercise Choose a verb from the Word Bank to complete each sentence below. Make sure the subject pronoun and verb agree.

1. When they __arrive__ in San Francisco, they always go first to Fisherman's Wharf.
2. After we __tour__ New York City, it's always fun to flag down a taxi.
3. I __love__ to go to the top of the Space Needle when we visit Seattle, Washington.
4. He always __travels__ to Colorado but never gets used to the beauty of the Rocky Mountains.
5. If you __decide__ to climb down the Grand Canyon in Arizona, it's best to go there in winter while it's cooler.
6. If she __visits__ Chicago, she should go to the top of the Sears Tower.

Word Bank					
tour	arrive	travel	decide	visit	love
tours	arrives	travels	decides	visits	loves

Rule and Example Some **contractions** are made by combining pronouns and verbs.

Pronoun + Verb = Contraction
we + have = we've
you + are = you're

Exercise Combine the verb and the pronoun in parentheses to form a contraction. Write it in the blank.

1. (I will) __I'll__ be traveling to Charleston, South Carolina.
2. (You are) __You're__ going to enjoy visiting the ocean beaches along the Oregon coastline.
3. (We have) __We've__ visited Niagara Falls in New York State before.
4. (She will) __She'll__ just love visiting with all of the Native American artists in Santa Fe, New Mexico.
5. (He is) __He's__ planning on riding down the Mississippi River.

Page 10

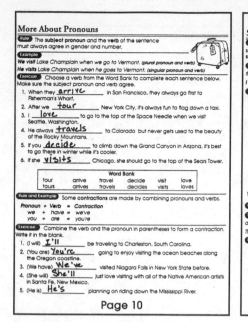

Snack on These!

Rule A **subject pronoun** is a pronoun used as the subject of a sentence. **Subject pronouns: I, you, he, she, it, we, they**

Example *We just love to munch on celery filled with peanut butter.*
I think that carrots are delicious.

Exercise Replace the noun subject in each sentence with a subject pronoun.

1. Jerry can't wait to crunch on another fresh string bean. __He__
2. Martha really enjoys the taste of persimmons. __She__
3. Gary and Tammy will bring oranges in their lunch today. __They__
4. Rochele eats red bell peppers like apples. __She__
5. Samuel's dog loves the biscuits we gave him! __It__
6. Bill and I eat peanut butter and banana sandwiches all the time. __We__
7. The cats love chasing after the bubbles we blow. __They__
8. Monica always puts noodles in her cottage cheese. __She__
9. My hamster loves to chew on wood. __It__
10. The apricot tree provides us with fruit every year. __It__

Rule A **subject pronoun** can be used after a linking verb.

Example *The greatest consumers of vegetables are Lindsey and he.*
The one with the most colorful hat is she.

Exercise Underline the correct subject pronoun.

1. The one who loves spinach the best is (he, him).
2. The healthiest people are (they, them).
3. The first to try the French onion dip was (she, her).
4. The best cook in our house was (I, me).
5. The only people eating the zucchini were (we, us).

Page 11

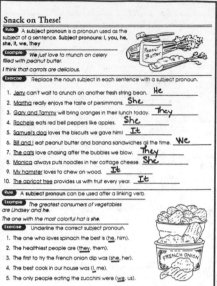

Pets and More

Rule **Object pronouns** can be used as **direct objects** of action verbs. Object pronouns: **me, you, him, her, it, us, them**

Example *I'll see you later at the pet store.*
*Jane helped **me** with my cat.*

Exercise Underline the correct pronoun in each sentence.

1. Jared's Dalmation puppy amused (we, us).
2. We found (he, him) under the couch.
3. Sandy's rabbit followed (we, us) all around the house.
4. Becky's Golden Retriever loved (her, she).
5. David's Great Dane scared (them, they).
6. Travis's dog bit (I, me) on the hand.
7. Eva found (they, them) in the back yard.
8. The beautiful macaw noticed (she, her).
9. Amanda showed (we, us) where to find the ducks on the pond.
10. The puppy saw (she, her) from the window.

Rule **Object pronouns** can also be used as **objects of prepositions.**

Example *The sheep walked quietly behind us.* (preposition: behind; object pronoun: us) *The South American frog leaped over them.* (preposition: over; object pronoun: them)

Exercise Complete each sentence below with an object pronoun.

1. The elephant walked beside __him__ in the circus ring.
2. The horses went around __it__.
3. The birds flew over __you__.
4. The waves splashed on __me__.
5. The fish jumped near __us__ while we stood at the bank of the river.
6. Birds were singing beautiful songs right above __them__.
7. The crickets were chirping beside __her__ in the flower garden.

(Answers will vary.)

Page 12

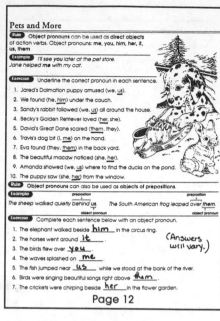

Whom or What Are You Referring To?

A pronoun takes the place of another word. The word the pronoun refers to is the referent. In each sentence below, circle the referent(s) for the pronoun that is underlined. Draw a line to connect the words.

1. (Jeff Miller) enjoyed learning the Indian traditions of the Tommie family. He visited the camp often.
2. (Billie, Jeff, and Charlie) went frog gigging together. They had quite an exciting trip.
3. (Billie and Jeff) thought they had fooled Billie's grandfather when Sihoki gave Jeff the stew to eat.
4. (Billie) visited the Miller (family). He thought they ate unusual food.
5. (Mrs. Kelly) helped (Billie) to teach (Charlie) how to read. She gave them flash-cards and books to use.
6. (Mush Jim) entertained (tourists) by wrestling alligators and giving airboat rides. They gave him money for these services.
7. The (hurricane) destroyed the Tommie family camp. It was one of the worst hurricanes to hit the area.
8. Grandfather Abraham was very special to (Billie). He will keep Grandfather's spirit alive by teaching the white man about the Indian ways.

Use five of the pronouns in sentences of your own telling about the story. Circle the words they refer to.

Answers will vary

Page 13

Pick an Apostrophe

Rule
- A **proper noun** names a specific person, place, or thing. All other nouns are **common nouns.**
- Most **plural nouns** end in **-s** or **-es**. Some plural nouns are irregular.
- The **possessive** of a noun is formed by adding an apostrophe (') or an apostrophe and an **s** ('s).
- Do not use apostrophes with **possessive pronouns.**
- Do not confuse **subject pronouns** with **object pronouns.**

Exercise
- Tell if the nouns below are common or proper.

1. Mexico __proper__	4. beauty __common__	7. peace __common__
2. airplane __common__	5. story __common__	8. Star Wars __proper__
3. Amanda __proper__	6. kindness __common__	9. jacket __common__

- Write the correct plural form of each noun below.

1. ox __oxen__	4. wife __wives__	7. fish __fish__
2. baby __babies__	5. moose __moose__	8. chair __chairs__
3. foot __feet__	6. turkey __turkeys__	9. glass __glasses__

- Copy each phrase below. Use the correct **possessive** form of the noun in parentheses.

1. the (children) shoes __the children's shoes__
2. my (parents) house __my parents' house__
3. the (dog) dish __the dog's dish__
4. the (passengers) tickets __the passengers' tickets__
5. one (tree) leaves __one tree's leaves__
6. the (players) uniforms __the players' uniforms__

- Underline the **possessive noun.** Replace it with a **possessive pronoun.**

1. Is that Jane's red hair? __her__
2. Bill's sweater is torn. __his__
3. Where is Sam and Ed's project? __their__
4. The cat's dish is empty. __Its__

- Circle the correct pronoun.

1. (We, Us) saw (they, them) at the restaurant.
2. (He, Him) asked (her, she) for a menu.
3. Mother ordered dinner for Sue and (I, me).

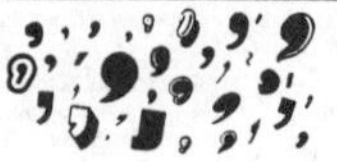

Page 14

Now or Later?

Rule
- A verb in the **present tense** shows action that is happening now.
- A verb in the **past tense** shows action that happened in the **past.**
- A verb in the **future tense** shows action that will happen in the **future.**

Example
*Present: Eva **works** on the class mural every day.*
*Past: She **worked** on the mural yesterday.*
*Future: She **will work** on the mural tomorrow after school.*

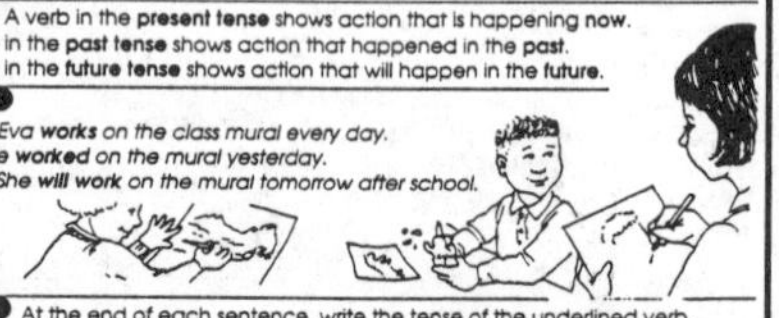

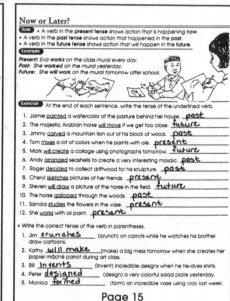

Exercise At the end of each sentence, write the tense of the underlined verb.

1. Jamie painted a watercolor of the pasture behind her house. __past__
2. The majestic Arabian horse will move if we get too close. __future__
3. Jimmy carved a mountain lion out of his block of wood. __past__
4. Tom mixes a lot of colors when he paints with oils. __present__
5. Mark will create a collage using photographs tomorrow. __future__
6. Andy arranged seashells to create a very interesting mosaic. __past__
7. Roger decided to collect driftwood for his sculpture. __past__
8. Cheryl sketches pictures of her friends. __present__
9. Steven will draw a picture of the horse in the field. __future__
10. The horse galloped through the woods. __past__
11. Sandra studies the flowers in the vase. __present__
12. She works with oil paint. __present__

- Write the correct tense of the verb in parentheses.

1. Jim __crunches__ (crunch) on carrots while he watches his brother draw cartoons.
2. Kathy __will make__ (make) a big mess tomorrow when she creates her papier mâché parrot during art class.
3. Bill __invents__ (invent) incredible designs when he tie-dyes shirts.
4. Peter __designed__ (design) a very colorful salad plate yesterday.
5. Monica __formed__ (form) an incredible vase using clay last week.

Page 15

Garden Variety

Rule A **direct object** is used with an **action verb.** A noun that tells who or what receives the action of the verb is a direct object.

Example *Sarah planted a garden.* (action verb: planted; direct object: garden)

Exercise Circle the action verb and underline the direct object in each sentence. Then fill in the chart.

1. Nick (prepared) the soil.
2. Monica (chose) seeds for her garden.
3. Mark (planted) his garden by the fence.
4. Heather (wants) herbs in her garden.
5. Eva (plants) tomato plants in the garden.
6. Gwen (saves) seeds from all the fruit and vegetables her mom buys.
7. She (dries) the seeds in the sun.
8. Tammy (loves) fresh lettuce.
9. David (planted) carrots in his garden.
10. Michele (shared) vegetables with the local food bank.

Action Verb	Direct Object
1. prepared	soil
2. chose	seeds
3. planted	garden
4. wants	herbs
5. plants	plants
6. saves	seeds
7. dries	seeds
8. loves	lettuce
9. planted	carrots
10. shared	vegetables

- Complete each sentence below with a direct object.

1. Dick planted __pumpkin seeds__
2. Joan bought __fresh peas__
3. Steven designed __his own garden__
4. Samuel shared __his watermelon__
5. Cheryl used __sunflower seeds to feed the birds__
6. The gardener picked __beans__

(Answers will vary)

Page 16

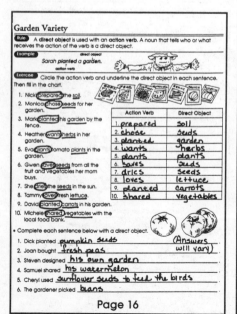

The Circus Was Born

Rule A **verb phrase** is made up of a main verb and one or more helping verbs. The main verb names the action. The helping verbs tell the time of the action.

Example Helping verbs used in the present tense:
***am** swimming* ***is** fishing* ***are** racing*
Helping verbs used in the past tense:
***was** swimming* ***was** fishing* ***were** racing*

Exercise Write the main verb and helping verb from each sentence in the chart below. Tell the tense.

1. The Ringling Brothers were living in Iowa.
2. The boys are playing on the river bank today.
3. They were laughing when they saw the circus boat.
4. "The circus is coming!" stated the advertisements.
5. The boys are talking about owning a circus someday.
6. The brothers are hiring many circus acts.
7. One day John said, "I am hiring a real clown."
8. Otto said, "We are buying both of these elephants."
9. Alf T. commented, "We are training many performers."
10. From a small circus, they were growing to a huge size.

Helping Verb	Main Verb	Tense	Helping Verb	Main Verb	Tense
1. were	living	past	6. are	hiring	present
2. are	playing	present	7. am	hiring	present
3. were	laughing	past	8. are	buying	present
4. is	coming	present	9. are	training	present
5. are	talking	present	10. were	growing	past

- Use a helping verb and a form of the verb shown to form each tense.

1. (race) The boys __are racing__. (present) The boys __were racing__. (past)
2. (walk) The elephants __are walking__. (present) The elephants __were walking__. (past)
3. (dance) The horse __is dancing__. (present) The horse __was dancing__. (past)
4. (laugh) The crowd __is laughing__. (present) The crowd __was laughing__. (past)

Page 17

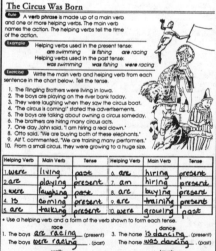

Butterflies and Spiders

Rule **Linking verbs** link the subject to a word in the predicate. The linking verbs most often used are **am, is, are, was,** and **were.**

Example *We were happy about the outcome.*

Rule A **linking verb** may be followed by a **predicate noun,** which renames the subject, or a **predicate adjective,** which describes the subject.

Example *Harry is a **teacher**. (predicate noun)*
*Harry is **confident**. (predicate adjective)*

Exercise Finish each sentence with a predicate noun. (Answers may vary.)

1. Sarah is a __singer__.
2. Her best friend was a __dancer__.
3. The other people at the party are __actors__.
4. Their party was a __success__.

- Circle each predicate noun. Underline the noun or pronoun in the subject that is renamed.

1. The children were (actors).
2. The setting of the play was a (garden).
3. Butterflies are main (characters) in the play.
4. Ralph is the (star).
5. He is an (actor).
6. All the children are drama club (members).

- Finish each sentence with a predicate adjective. (Answers may vary.)

1. Today's weather is __sunny__.
2. The clouds are __white__.
3. Tom will be __happy__.
4. The picnic was __amusing__.

- Circle each predicate adjective. Underline the noun or pronoun in the subject that is described.

1. The trap-door spider is (clever).
2. Its building skills are (amazing).
3. The house's shell is (narrow) and (tube-like).
4. The plaster on the walls was (wet) and (smooth).
5. The webs covering the walls were (soft) and (silky).

Page 18

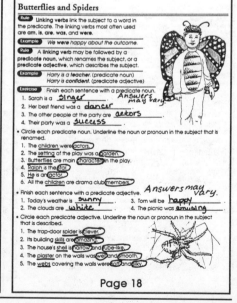

Slightly Irregular!

Rule Verbs that do not add **-ed** to show the past tense are called **irregular verbs.** Below are some commonly used irregular verbs.

Example

Present	Past	Past with helpers
begin	*began*	*(has, have) begun*
see	*saw*	*(has, have) seen*
drive	*drove*	*(has, have) driven*

Exercise Fill in the blanks on the chart. You may refer to a dictionary.

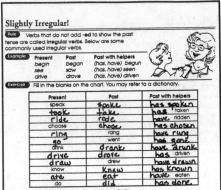

Present	Past	Past with helpers
speak	spoke	has spoken
took	take	has taken
ride	rode	have ridden
choose	chose	has chosen
ring	rang	have rung
go	went	has gone
drink	drank	have drunk
drive	drove	has driven
draw	drew	have drawn
know	Knew	has Known
ate	eat	have eaten
do	did	has done

• Underline the correct verb in the sentences below.

1. Martha has (began, begun) her research project.
2. First she (chose, chosen) the topic.
3. She (drove, driven) many places to locate information.
4. Martha made a list of the interviews she had (did, done).
5. She (spoke, spoken) to people of many ages.
6. Many (knew, known) a great deal about the subject.
7. Martha (rang, rung) many doorbells during the interviews.
8. While interviewing people, Martha had (took, taken) notes.

• Write sentences for the verbs below on another paper.

1. swim (past)
2. wear (past with helper)
3. blow (past)
4. eat (past with helper)
5. tear (past)
6. drink (past with helper)

Page 19

To Be a Polar Bear

Rule Some forms of the verb **be** can be used as linking or helping verbs. Three forms of **be** cannot be used alone as verbs: **be, being,** and **been.** These must always be used with helping verbs.

Example *Polar bears* ***are*** *carnivores. (be as linking verb)*
The polar bear ***is*** *hunting the seal. (be as helping verb)*
A polar bear ***has been*** *seen near here. (be with helping verb)*

Exercise Complete each sentence below with the correct form of the verb **be** found in parentheses. Add helping verbs where needed. Forms of **be: am, is, are, was, were, be, being, been**

1. Polar bears are excellent swimmers. (is, are)
2. The polar bear was seen running at a speed of 35 miles per hour. (was, being)
3. Polar bears are found in the Arctic regions of the world. (is, are)
4. I am sure I saw a polar bear swimming in the water. (am, are)
5. Polar bears have been seen swimming many miles from shore. (been, have been)
6. The polar bear is being protected by law in the countries where it lives. (being, is being)
7. The polar bear's fur is white to help the bear blend in with ice and snow. (be, is)

Rule and Example The verbs **do** and **have** can be used as main verbs or as helping verbs.
I ***have*** *traveled to Canada to see polar bears. (helping verb)*
I ***did*** *my report on polar bears yesterday. (main verb)*
Forms of do: *do, did, done* **Forms of have:** *have, has, had*

Exercise Complete the story below using the correct forms of the verbs **do** and **have.**

I do believe polar bears are very beautiful. I have seen them along the coast of Alaska. I did see one come up to our tour bus. By the age of 8-10 years, a male polar bear has grown to its full size. Countries around the Arctic have done a very good job of trying to save the polar bear from extinction. Polar bears have beautiful coats which have attracted hunters. Now the bears have protection from hunters by law.

Page 20

I'm Confused

Rule Don't confuse verbs that have similar meanings.

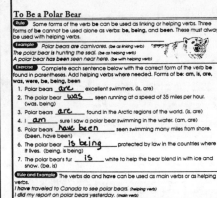

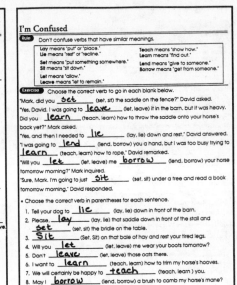

Lay means "put" or "place."
Lie means "rest" or "recline."
Set means "put something somewhere."
Sit means "sit down."
Let means "allow."
Leave means "let to remain."
Teach means "show how."
Learn means "find out."
Lend means "give to someone."
Borrow means "get from someone."

Exercise Choose the correct verb to go in each blank below.

"Mark, did you set (set, sit) the saddle on the fence?" David asked.
"Yes, David. I was going to leave (let, leave) it in the barn, but it was heavy. Did you learn (teach, learn) how to throw the saddle onto your horse's back yet?" Mark asked.
"Yes, and then I needed to lie (lay, lie) down and rest." David answered. "I was going to lend (lend, borrow) you a hand, but I was too busy trying to learn (teach, learn) how to rope," David remarked.
"Will you let (let, leave) me borrow (lend, borrow) your horse tomorrow morning?" Mark inquired.
"Sure, Mark. I'm going to just sit (set, sit) under a tree and read a book tomorrow morning," David responded.

• Choose the correct verb in parentheses for each sentence.

1. Tell your dog to lie (lay, lie) down in front of the barn.
2. Please, lay (lay, lie) that saddle down in front of the stall and set (set, sit) the bridle on the table.
3. Sit (Set, Sit) on that bale of hay and rest your tired legs.
4. Will you let (let, leave) me wear your boots tomorrow?
5. Don't leave (let, leave) those oats there.
6. I want to learn (teach, learn) how to trim my horse's hooves.
7. We will certainly be happy to teach (teach, learn) you.
8. May I borrow (lend, borrow) a brush to comb my horse's mane?

Page 21

The Hairy Spider

Rule **Adjectives** describe, or modify, nouns. Adjectives answer these questions about nouns: **Which one? What kind? How many?**

Exercise Circle the adjectives in the sentences below. Underline the nouns they modify.

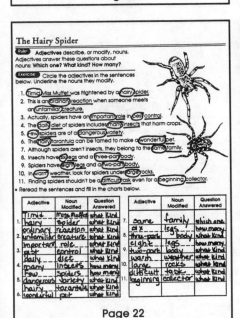

1. Timid Miss Muffet was frightened by a hairy spider.
2. This is an ordinary reaction when someone meets an unfamiliar creature.
3. Actually, spiders have an important role in pest control.
4. The daily diet of spiders includes many insects that harm crops.
5. Few spiders are of a dangerous variety.
6. The hairy tarantula can be tamed to make a wonderful pet.
7. Although spiders aren't insects, they belong to the same family.
8. Insects have six legs and a three-part body.
9. Spiders have eight legs and a two-part body.
10. In warm weather, look for spiders under large rocks.
11. Finding spiders shouldn't be a difficult task even for a beginning collector.

• Reread the sentences and fill in the charts below.

	Adjective	Noun Modified	Question Answered
1.	Timid	Miss Muffet	what kind
	hairy	spider	what kind
2.	ordinary	reaction	what kind
	unfamiliar	creature	what kind
3.	important	role	what kind
	pest	control	what kind
4.	daily	diet	what kind
	many	insects	how many
5.	Few	spiders	how many
	dangerous	variety	what kind
6.	hairy	tarantula	what kind
	wonderful	pet	what kind

	Adjective	Noun Modified	Question Answered
7.	same	family	which one
8.	six	legs	how many
	three-part	body	what kind
9.	eight	legs	how many
	two-part	body	what kind
10.	warm	weather	what kind
	large	rocks	what kind
11.	difficult	task	what kind
	beginning	collector	what kind

Page 22

That Beet, Those Berries

Rule The adjectives **this** and **that** are singular. The adjectives **these** and **those** are plural. **This** and **these** refer to things that are nearby. **That** and **those** refer to things that are farther away.

Example
This apple is the crunchiest of them all. *These apples here are crunchy, too.*
That cherry on the far branch is ripe. *Those cherries growing on the tree look delicious!*

Exercise Complete the chart below using **this, that, these,** or **those** before each noun.

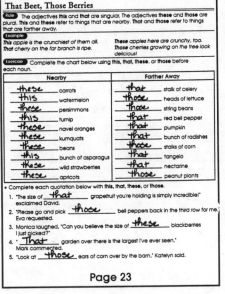

Nearby		Farther Away	
these	carrots	that	stalk of celery
this	watermelon	those	heads of lettuce
these	persimmons	those	string beans
this	turnip	that	red bell pepper
these	navel oranges	that	pumpkin
these	kumquats	that	bunch of radishes
these	beans	those	stalks of corn
this	bunch of asparagus	that	tangelo
these	wild strawberries	that	nectarine
these	apricots	those	peanut plants

• Complete each quotation below with **this, that, these,** or **those.**

1. "The size of that grapefruit you're holding is simply incredible!" exclaimed David.
2. "Please go and pick those bell peppers back in the third row for me," Eva requested.
3. Monica laughed, "Can you believe the size of these blackberries I just picked?"
4. "That garden over there is the largest I've ever seen," Mark commented.
5. "Look at those ears of corn over by the barn," Katelyn said.

Page 23

Carefully Prepared

Rule **Adverbs** describe **verbs, adjectives,** or **other adverbs.** They answer these questions: **When? Where? How? How much?**

Exercise Underline the adverbs. Circle the verbs, adjectives, or adverbs they modify. Then fill in the chart using the words from the sentences.

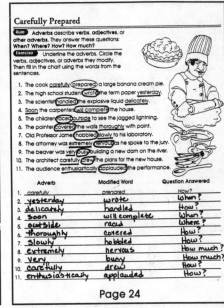

1. The cook carefully prepared a large banana cream pie.
2. The high school student wrote the term paper yesterday.
3. The scientist handled the explosive liquid delicately.
4. Soon the carpenters will complete the house.
5. The children raced outside to see the jagged lightning.
6. The painter covered the walls thoroughly with paint.
7. Old Professor James hobbled slowly to his laboratory.
8. The attorney was extremely nervous as he spoke to the jury.
9. The beaver was very busy building a new dam on the river.
10. The architect carefully drew the plans for the new house.
11. The audience enthusiastically applauded the performance.

	Adverb	Modified Word	Question Answered
1.	*carefully*	*prepared*	*How?*
2.	yesterday	wrote	When?
3.	delicately	handled	How?
4.	Soon	will complete	When?
5.	outside	raced	Where?
6.	thoroughly	covered	How?
7.	slowly	hobbled	How?
8.	extremely	nervous	How much?
9.	very	busy	How much?
10.	carefully	drew	How?
11.	enthusiastically	applauded	How?

Page 24

About Eagles . . .

Rule You have learned that adverbs modify verbs. An **adverb** can also modify **adjectives** and **other adverbs.** These adverbs usually answer the question **how much** or **to what degree.**

Example *The eagle's descent was* ***very*** *steep.*
(modifies "steep," an adjective)
The eagle attacked the fish ***quite*** *suddenly.*
(modifies "suddenly," an adverb)

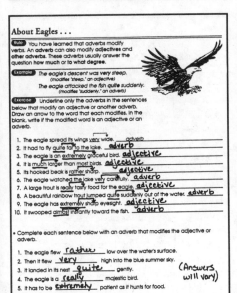

Exercise Underline only the adverbs in the sentences below that modify an adjective or another adverb. Draw an arrow to the word that each modifies. In the blank, write if the modified word is an adjective or an adverb.

1. The eagle spread its wings very wide. *adverb*
2. It had to fly quite far to the lake. adverb
3. The eagle is an extremely graceful bird. adjective
4. It is much larger than most birds. adjective
5. Its hooked beak is rather sharp. adjective
6. The eagle watched the lake very carefully. adverb
7. A large trout is really tasty food for the eagle. adjective
8. A beautiful rainbow trout jumped quite suddenly out of the water. adverb
9. The eagle has extremely sharp eyesight. adjective
10. It swooped almost instantly toward the fish. adverb

• Complete each sentence below with an adverb that modifies the adjective or adverb.

1. The eagle flew rather low over the water's surface.
2. Then it flew very high into the blue summer sky.
3. It landed in its nest quite gently.
4. The eagle is a really majestic bird.
5. It has to be extremely patient as it hunts for food.

(Answers will vary)

Page 25

Of the Human Body

Rule A **prepositional phrase** is a group of words that begins with a preposition and ends with the object of the preposition.

Example *Water makes up about 65 percent* ***of the human body.***

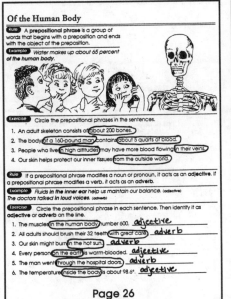

Exercise Circle the prepositional phrases in the sentences.

1. An adult skeleton consists of about 200 bones.
2. The body of a 160-pound man contains about 5 quarts of blood.
3. People who live in high altitudes may have more blood flowing in their veins.
4. Our skin helps protect our inner tissues from the outside world.

Rule If a prepositional phrase modifies a noun or pronoun, it acts as an **adjective.** If a prepositional phrase modifies a verb, it acts as an **adverb.**

Example *Fluids* ***in the inner ear*** *help us maintain our balance. (adjective)*
The doctors talked ***in loud voices.*** *(adverb)*

Exercise Circle the prepositional phrase in each sentence. Then identify it as **adjective** or **adverb** on the line.

1. The muscles in the human body number 600. adjective
2. All adults should brush their 32 teeth with great care. adverb
3. Our skin might burn in the hot sun. adverb
4. Every person on the earth is warm-blooded. adjective
5. The man went through the hospital doors. adverb
6. The temperature inside the body is about 98.6°. adjective

Page 26

What Is It?

Rule Some words can be used as **prepositions** or as **adverbs.**

Example ***Preposition:*** *The wagon traveled* ***down*** *the mountain.*
Adverb: *The rain came* ***down*** *and soaked the wagon.*

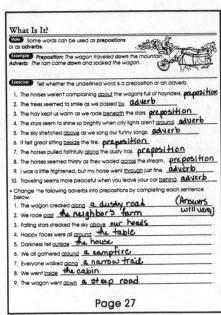

Exercise Tell whether the underlined word is a preposition or an adverb.

1. The horses weren't complaining about the wagons full of hayriders. preposition
2. The trees seemed to smile as we passed by. adverb
3. The hay kept us warm as we rode beneath the stars. preposition
4. The stars seem to shine so brightly when city lights aren't around. adverb
5. The sky stretched above as we sang our funny songs. adverb
6. It felt great sitting beside the fire. preposition
7. The horses pulled faithfully along the dusty trail. preposition
8. The horses seemed thirsty as they waded across the stream. preposition
9. I was a little frightened, but my horse went through just fine. adverb
10. Traveling seems more peaceful when you leave your car behind. adverb

• Change the following adverbs into prepositions by completing each sentence below. (Answers will vary)

1. The wagon creaked along a dusty road
2. We rode past the neighbor's farm
3. Falling stars streaked the sky above our heads
4. Happy faces were all around the table
5. Darkness fell outside the house
6. We all gathered around a campfire
7. Everyone walked along a narrow trail
8. We went inside the cabin
9. The wagon went down a steep road

Page 27

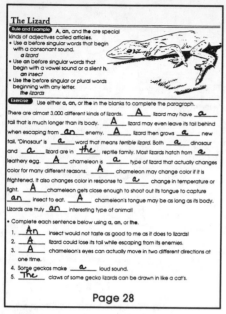

The Lizard

Rule and Example **A**, **an**, and **the** are special kinds of adjectives called **articles**.

- Use **a** before singular words that begin with a consonant sound.
  a lizard
- Use **an** before singular words that begin with a vowel sound or a silent **h**.
  an insect
- Use **the** before singular or plural words beginning with any letter.
  the lizards

Exercise Use either **a**, **an**, or **the** in the blanks to complete the paragraph.

There are almost 3,000 different kinds of lizards. A lizard may have a tail that is much longer than its body. A lizard may even leave its tail behind when escaping from an enemy. A lizard then grows a new tail. "Dinosaur" is a word that means *terrible lizard*. Both a dinosaur and a lizard are in the reptile family. Most lizards hatch from a leathery egg. A chameleon is a type of lizard that actually changes color for many different reasons. A chameleon may change color if it is frightened. It also changes color in response to a change in temperature or light. A chameleon gets close enough to shoot out its tongue to capture an insect to eat. A chameleon's tongue may be as long as its body. Lizards are truly an interesting type of animal!

- Complete each sentence below using **a**, **an**, or **the**.

1. An insect would not taste as good to me as it does to lizards!
2. A lizard could lose its tail while escaping from its enemies.
3. A chameleon's eyes can actually move in two different directions at one time.
4. Some geckos make a loud sound.
5. The claws of some gecko lizards can be drawn in like a cat's.

Page 28

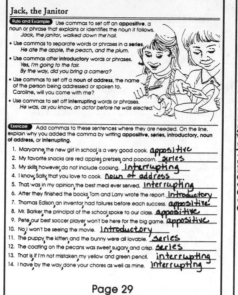

Jack, the Janitor

Rule and Example Use commas to set off an **appositive**, a noun or phrase that explains or identifies the noun it follows.
Jack, the janitor, walked down the hall.

- Use commas to separate words or phrases in a **series**.
  He ate the apple, the peach, and the plum.
- Use commas after **introductory** words or phrases.
  Yes, I'm going to the fair.
  By the way, did you bring a camera?
- Use commas to set off a **noun of address**, the name of the person being addressed or spoken to.
  Caroline, will you come with me?
- Use commas to set off **interrupting** words or phrases.
  He was, as you know, an actor before he was elected.

Exercise Add commas to these sentences where they are needed. On the line, explain why you added the comma by writing **appositive**, **series**, **introductory**, **noun of address**, or **interrupting**.

1. Maryanne, the new girl in school, is a very good cook. appositive
2. My favorite snacks are red apples, pretzels, and popcorn. series
3. My skills, however, do not include cooking. interrupting
4. I know, Sally, that you love to cook. noun of address
5. That was, in my opinion, the best meal ever served. interrupting
6. After they finished the books, Tom and Larry wrote the report. introductory
7. Thomas Edison, an inventor, had failures before each success. appositive
8. Mr. Barker, the principal of the school, spoke to our class. appositive
9. Pete, our best soccer player, won't be here for the big game. appositive
10. No, I won't be seeing the movie. introductory
11. The puppy, the kitten, and the bunny were all lovable. series
12. The coating on the pecans was sweet, sugary, and crisp. series
13. That is, if I'm not mistaken, my yellow and green pencil. interrupting
14. I have, by the way, done your chores as well as mine. interrupting

Page 29

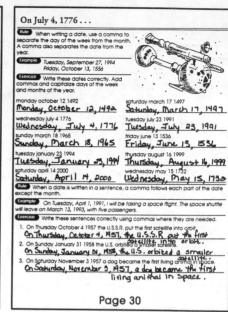

On July 4, 1776 . . .

Rule When writing a date, use a comma to separate the day of the week from the month. A comma also separates the date from the year.

Example *Tuesday, September 27, 1994*
Friday, October 13, 1556

Exercise Write these dates correctly. Add commas and capitalize days of the week and months of the year.

monday october 12 1492 — Monday, October 12, 1492
saturday march 17 1497 — Saturday, March 17, 1497
wednesday july 4 1776 — Wednesday, July 4, 1776
tuesday july 23 1991 — Tuesday, July 23, 1991
sunday march 18 1965 — Sunday, March 18, 1965
friday june 13 1536 — Friday, June 13, 1536
tuesday january 23 1994 — Tuesday, January 23, 1994
thursday august 16 1999 — Thursday, August 16, 1999
saturday april 14 2000 — Saturday, April 14, 2000
wednesday may 15 1732 — Wednesday, May 15, 1732

Rule When a date is written in a sentence, a comma follows each part of the date except the month.

Example *On Tuesday, April 1, 1991, I will be taking a space flight. The space shuttle will leave on March 13, 1993, with five passengers.*

Exercise Write these sentences correctly using commas where they are needed.

1. On Thursday October 4 1957 the U.S.S.R. put the first satellite into orbit.
   On Thursday, October 4, 1957, the U.S.S.R. put the first satellite into orbit.
2. On Sunday January 31 1958 the U.S. orbited a smaller satellite.
   On Sunday, January 31, 1958, the U.S. orbited a smaller satellite.
3. On Saturday November 3 1957 a dog became the first living animal in space.
   On Saturday, November 3, 1957, a dog became the first living animal in space.

Page 30

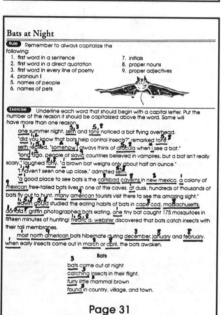

Bats at Night

Rule Remember to always capitalize the following:

1. first word in a sentence
2. first word in a direct quotation
3. first word in every line of poetry
4. pronoun I
5. names of people
6. names of pets
7. initials
8. proper nouns
9. proper adjectives

Exercise Underline each word that should begin with a capital letter. Put the number of the reason it should be capitalized above the word. Some will have more than one reason.

one summer night, seth and tony noticed a bat flying overhead.
"did you know that bats help control insects?" remarked tony.
seth replied, "somehow I always think of dracula when i see a bat."
"long ago, people of slavic countries believed in vampires, but a bat isn't really scary," laughed tony. "a brown bat weighs only about half an ounce."
"i haven't seen one up close," admitted seth.
"a good place to see bats is the carlsbad caverns in new mexico. a colony of mexican free-tailed bats lives in one of the caves. at dusk, hundreds of thousands of bats fly out to hunt. many american tourists visit there to see this amazing sight."
edwin gould studied the eating habits of bats in cape cod, massachusetts. donald r. griffin photographed bats eating. one tiny bat caught 175 mosquitoes in fifteen minutes of hunting! frederic a. webster discovered that bats catch insects with their tail membranes.
most north american bats hibernate during december, january and february. when early insects come out in march or april, the bats awaken.

Bats

bats come out at night
catching insects in their flight.
furry little mammal brown
found in country, village, and town.

Page 31

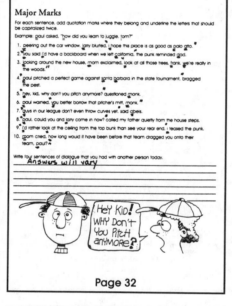

Major Marks

For each sentence, add quotation marks where they belong and underline the letters that should be capitalized twice.

Example: paul asked, "how did you learn to juggle, tom?"

1. peering out the car window, larry blurted, "i hope this place is as good as palo alto."
2. "you said i'd have a backboard when we left california," the punk reminded dad.
3. looking around the new house, mom exclaimed, "look at all those trees, frank. we're really in the woods."
4. paul pitched a perfect game against santa barbara in the state tournament, bragged the pest.
5. "hey, kid, why don't you pitch anymore?" questioned monk.
6. paul warned, "you better borrow that pitcher's mitt, monk."
7. "guys in our league don't even throw curves yet," said obeis.
8. "paul, could you and larry come in now?" called my father quietly from the house steps.
9. "i'd rather look at the ceiling from the top bunk than see your rear end," i teased the punk.
10. mom cried, "how long would it have been before that team dragged you onto their team, paul?"

Write four sentences of dialogue that you had with another person today.

Answers will vary

Page 32

Quotation Quiz

Add quotation marks where needed to these sentences. Draw two lines under the letters that should be capitalized. The first one has been done for you.

1. "you are lying to me, uncle henrik," said annemarie suddenly.
2. "i'm so sorry your aunt birte died," murmured ellen sadly.
3. the bearded man whispered, "god keep you safe."
4. "who died?" questioned the soldier harshly.
5. "it will be very cold," remarked Peter. "put on your coats."
6. peter joked, "don't grow much more, little longlegs, or you will be taller than i am."
7. fiercely ellen whispered, "i'll be back someday, i promise."
8. "annemarie, you should have seen your proper mama crawling inch by inch!" said mrs. johansen with a wry look.
9. "mama, what is this?" asked annemarie as she reached into the grass at the foot of the steps.
10. "uncle henrik doesn't even like fish," giggled annemarie.
11. the young soldier barked, "stop crying, you idiot child!"
12. "they took my bread, eh?" said uncle henrik. "i hope they choke on it."
13. "uncle henrik! the god of thunder has fallen into the milk pail!" shrieked annemarie.
14. mama shook her head sadly as she murmured, "they were all so young."

Challenge: Make up an amusing conversation between two animals or two objects. Use quotation marks.

Page 33

Fancy Figuring

Write the word for each phonetic spelling. Then find each word in the wordsearch.

1. /păd' lŏk/ padlock
2. /săb' ə täzh/ sabotage
3. /lăng' kē/ lanky
4. /trōō sō'/ trousseau
5. /fē' ŏn sā/ fiance
6. /snŭg' əl/ snuggle
7. /ŭn rōō' lē/ unruly
8. /krō' nər/ kroner
9. /nĕkst/ next
10. /stōōpt/ stooped
11. /kûr' fyōō/ curfew
12. /ĕm broi' dər/ embroider
13. /bə·bōōsh'kə/ babushka
14. /kă fā'/ cafe
15. /rŭk' săk/ rucksack
16. /ûrbz/ herbs
17. /krō shā'/ crochet
18. /trŭj/ trudge
19. /dă' nĭsh/ danish
20. /prăngk/ prank
21. /dôd' əl/ dawdle
22. /răsh' ən/ ration
23. /hô' tē/ haughty
24. /tôr mĕnt'/ torment
25. /dī' ənt lē/ defiantly

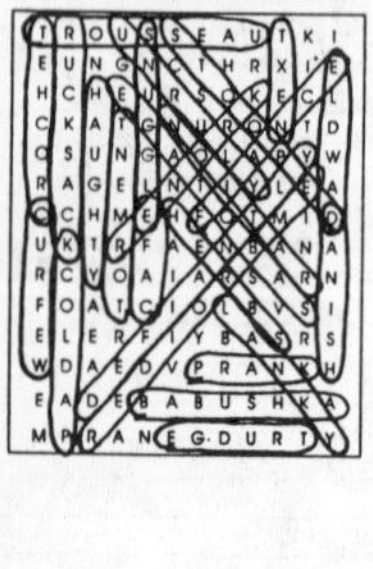

The remaining letters of the wordsearch spell a message. Write the letters in order starting in the upper left-hand corner and working across.

Message: King Christian is a very brave man.

Page 34

Sound It Out

Write the word for each phonetic spelling given. Then use the words to complete the crossword.

1. /tawt/ taut
2. /shah'mən/ shaman
3. /sŭt/ soot
4. /wēr/ weir
5. /kwahn' sĭt/ quonset
6. /foi' ər/ foyer
7. /pin'ə kəl/ pinnacle
8. /dĭ mĕn' shən/ dimension
9. /kăm pān'/ campaign
10. /sĭn' yū/ sinew
11. /ĭl' dər/ elder
12. /wēn/ wean
13. /rīth/ writhe
14. /bī lī'/ belie
15. /prā/ prey
16. /gawnt/ gaunt

Clues

Across
4. sea duck
6. black material formed by incomplete combustion
8. work toward an organized purpose
10. prove false
11. tight
12. entrance hall
13. medicine man
14. mountain peak

Down
1. length, width, height
2. twist in pain
3. shelter of corrugated metal
5. to withold mother's milk
7. thin and bony
9. low dam built in river
13. a tendon
14. hunt

Page 35

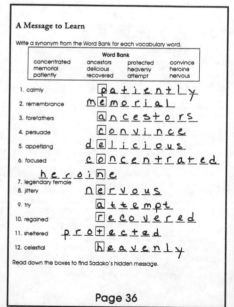

A Message to Learn

Write a synonym from the Word Bank for each vocabulary word.

Word Bank			
concentrated	ancestors	protected	convince
memorial	delicious	heavenly	heroine
patiently	recovered	attempt	nervous

1. calmly — patiently
2. remembrance — memorial
3. forefathers — ancestors
4. persuade — convince
5. appetizing — delicious
6. focused — concentrated
7. legendary female — heroine
8. jittery — nervous
9. try — attempt
10. regained — recovered
11. sheltered — protected
12. celestial — heavenly

Read down the boxes to find Sadako's hidden message.

Page 36

Page 37

Certainly Similar Synonyms

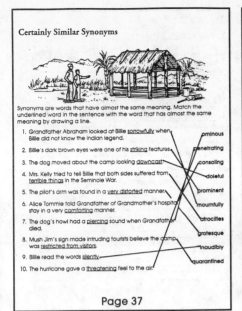

Synonyms are words that have almost the same meaning. Match the underlined word in the sentence with the word that has almost the same meaning by drawing a line.

1. Grandfather Abraham looked at Billie sorrowfully when Billie did not know the Indian legend.
2. Billie's dark brown eyes were one of his striking features.
3. The dog moved about the camp looking downcast.
4. Mrs. Kelly tried to tell Billie that both sides suffered from terrible things in the Seminole War.
5. The pilot's arm was found in a very distorted manner.
6. Alice Tommie told Grandfather of Grandmother's hospital stay in a very comforting manner.
7. The dog's howl had a piercing sound when Grandfather died.
8. Mush Jim's sign made intruding tourists believe the camp was restricted from visitors.
9. Billie read the words silently.
10. The hurricane gave a threatening feel to the air.

- ominous
- penetrating
- consoling
- doleful
- prominent
- mournfully
- atrocities
- grotesque
- inaudibly
- quarantined

Page 37

Page 38

A Criss-Cross Puzzle

Use the Word Bank to write an antonym by each word. Then write each pair of words where they fit in the puzzle.

1. tumult — quiet
2. surmise — certainty
3. persist — stop
4. dejected — hopeful
5. dawdle — hurry
6. accelerate — delay
7. perilous — safe
8. adept — bungling
9. lavish — sparing
10. sanity — foolishness

Word Bank: certainty, hurry, delay, safe, bungling, stop, foolishness, hopeful, sparing, quiet

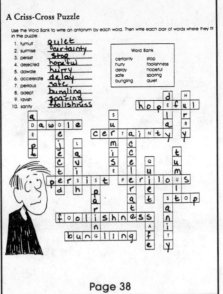

Page 38

Page 39

Boom!

Draw a green dollar sign ($) over each word that is a synonym of the first word. Draw an orange bomb () over each word that is its antonym.

forfeit	choose	generous	gain	lose
adjacent	sudden	nearby	clean	remote
pompous	modest	festive	noisy	proud
nosegay	unhappy	bouquet	puncture	weeds
exquisite	careful	beyond	hideous	delightful
impeccable	flawed	perfect	scarce	painful
wary	alert	brittle	unguarded	tired
harry	furry	attract	annoy	soothe
despondently	happily	elegantly	crazily	unhappily
interrogate	cross-examine	dislike	persecute	hush
cull	answer	charge	select	scatter
elude	comfort	scold	avoid	frighten

Page 39

Page 40

Like It or Not

Choose synonyms and antonyms from the Word Bank to match the words below. Feel free to use a dictionary!

Word Bank: calm, tart, fearful, daydream, raise, noise, sugary, wretched, ghost, make dull, strong, weak, solemnity, brave, virtuous, human, small, quietude, free, sharpen, lower, merrymaking, huge, imprison, nightmare, disturb

	Synonym	Antonym
hoist	raise	lower
whet	sharpen	make dull
incubus	nightmare	daydream
wraith	ghost	human
saccharine	sugary	tart
stout	strong	weak
valiant	brave	fearful
revelry	merrymaking	solemnity
liberate	free	imprison
din	noise	quietude
prodigious	huge	small
vile	wretched	virtuous
appease	calm	disturb

Page 40

Page 41

On Your Mark, Get Set, Go!

Race to the finish by following the directions on each column to name the winners in the story. Start at the same time as a partner and see who gets finished with their worksheet first.

1. Write soften without the "s." — often
2. Remove the "of" to make a number. — ten
3. Remove a consonant and add one vowel and one consonant to make a synonym for chew. — bite
4. Remove a consonant and a vowel to form a pronoun. — it
5. Add a vowel to the beginning and two silent consonants to make the sum of 4 + 4. — eight
6. Add two consonants and drop the "e" to form a noun similar to "flying." — flight
7. Remove a consonant to make an antonym of dark. — light
8. Add "sun" to make a compound word. — sunlight
9. Remove "sun" and replace with "porch." — porch light
10. Replace "porch" with "search." — search light

The winner is

1. Write a past form of sing. — sang
2. Change the first consonant to make a vampire tooth. — fang
3. Remove the "f" and add a two-letter suffix to make a synonym of wrath. — anger
4. Add a "d" to make a warning. — danger
5. Change "d" to "r" to make a forester's friend. — ranger
6. Change the first vowel to "i." — ringer
7. Change "i" to "o," add "w" to the beginning and drop the "er." — wrong
8. Replace "w" with "st." — strong
9. Add "box" to make a compound word. — strong box
10. Replace "b" with "t," "g" with "e" and remove the "r." — stone tor

The winner is

Why is one of the racers a winner even though he did not cross the finish line first? _____

Page 41

Page 42

Mixed-Up Information

Miss Freed decided to play a trick on her students. She wrote a bunch of information on the board about The Pleistocene Epoch, and then started asking the students questions about the information. None of them could answer because the information was all mixed up.

Help Miss Freed's students sort out the information on dinosaurs. See if you can put the sentences below in order so that they make sense.

It included a period called the Ice Age. The giant ground sloth was as big as an elephant and used long, hooklike claws to pull down tree branches. The Pleistocene Epoch is the geologic time beginning about 1-¾ million years ago and ending about 10,000 years ago. It was during the Ice Age that the last of the prehistoric animals, like the giant ground sloth, the woolly rhinoceros and the mastodon, died out. The mastodon was also an elephantlike creature with a thick coat of reddish-brown hair and 8-9 foot long tusks. The woolly rhinoceros, or "hollow-tooth," ate small bushes and poor grass and looked much like the rhinoceros that live in Africa today.

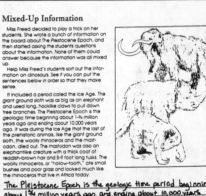

The Pleistocene Epoch is the geologic time period beginning about 1¾ million years ago and ending about 10,000 years ago. It included a period called the Ice Age. It was during the Ice Age that the last of the prehistoric animals, like the giant ground sloth, the woolly rhinoceros, and the mastodon, died out. The giant ground sloth was as big as an elephant and used long hooklike claws to pull down tree branches. The mastodon was also an elephantlike creature with a thick coat of reddish-brown hair and 8-9 foot long tusks. The woolly rhinoceros, or "hollow-tooth," ate small bushes... and looked much like the rhinoceros that live in Africa today.

SOMETHING EXTRA! What do you think our world would be like today if these creatures were still around?

Page 42

Page 43

"Speak Fitly or Be Silent Wisely"

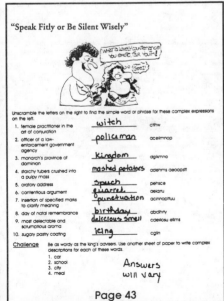

Unscramble the letters on the right to find the simple word or phrase for these complex expressions on the left.

1. female practitioner in the art of conjuration — witch — cithw
2. officer of a law-enforcement government agency — policeman — aceimnop
3. monarch's province of dominion — kingdom — dgiknmo
4. starchy tubers crushed into a pulpy mass — mashed potatoes — adehms aeoopstt
5. oratory address — speech — pehsce
6. contentious argument — quarrel — aelqru
7. insertion of specified marks to clarify meaning — punctuation — acinnoptuu
8. day of natal remembrance — birthday — abdihty
9. most delectable and scrumptious aroma — delicious smell — cdeilosu elims
10. sugary pasty coating — icing — cgiin

Challenge: Be as wordy as the king's advisers. Use another sheet of paper to write complex descriptions for each of these words.
1. car
2. school
3. city
4. meal

Answers will vary

Page 43

Page 44

Up a Tree

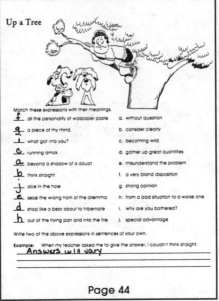

Match these expressions with their meanings.

f. all the personality of wallpaper paste
g. a piece of my mind.
i. what got into you?
a. running amok
a. beyond a shadow of a doubt
b. think straight
j. ace in the hole
e. seize the wrong horn of the dilemma
d. shop like a bear about to hibernate
h. out of the frying pan and into the fire

a. without question
b. consider clearly
c. becoming wild
d. gather up great quantities
e. misunderstand the problem
f. a very bland disposition
g. strong opinion
h. from a bad situation to a worse one
i. why are you bothered?
j. special advantage

Write two of the above expressions in sentences of your own.

Example: When my teacher asked me to give the answer, I couldn't think straight.

Answers will vary

Page 44

Page 45

Just Bust Out Laughin'

Make your own matching exercise! In the blank boxes below write, in random order, the meaning of each underlined expression. Then give your worksheet to a partner to match the expressions with the meanings by writing the correct letter in each space.

Idiom	Meanings	Partner's Answers
a. Addie knew that the old goat owed her dad some money.	Answers will vary	___
b. When the girls received their food, they wolfed it down.		___
c. Carla Mae told Addie she was cracked to consider giving Mr. Rehnquist a Thanksgiving dinner.		___
d. After the funeral, Addie dashed to her room; she didn't want to be in the kitchen for the fireworks.		___
e. Addie felt that Cousin Henry was poison.		___
f. Mr. Rehnquist and Pearlie used to sing at the top of their lungs.		___
g. With a straight face, Addie told Carla Mae that it wouldn't take Mr. Rehnquist long to shoot them.		___
h. When he was a boy, Mr. Rehnquist would split his sides because of Pearlie's antics.		___
i. Addie's dad was quick to blow his top.		___
j. Grandma, who was getting old, had already raised two families.		___
k. The girl tried to brush Treasure and quickly got the hang of it.		___
l. The lawyer dropped a bomb in the lap of Addie's family.		___

Page 45

When Aslan Comes

Write an X in front of all the sentences that show elements of fantasy.

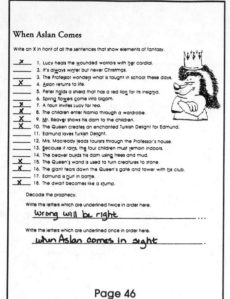

- X 1. Lucy heals the wounded warriors with her cordial.
- ___ 2. It's always winter but never Christmas.
- ___ 3. The Professor wonders what is taught in school these days.
- X 4. Aslan returns to life.
- ___ 5. Peter holds a shield that has a red lion for its insignia.
- ___ 6. Spring flowers come into bloom.
- X 7. A faun invites Lucy for tea.
- X 8. The children enter Narnia through a wardrobe.
- X 9. Mr. Beaver shows his dam to the children.
- X 10. The Queen creates an enchanted Turkish Delight for Edmund.
- ___ 11. Edmund loves Turkish Delight.
- ___ 12. Mrs. Macready leads tourists through the Professor's house.
- ___ 13. Because it rains, the four children must remain indoors.
- ___ 14. The beaver builds his dam using trees and mud.
- X 15. The Queen's wand is used to turn creatures to stone.
- X 16. The giant tears down the Queen's gate and tower with his club.
- ___ 17. Edmund is hurt in battle.
- X 18. The dwarf becomes like a stump.

Decode the prophecy.

Write the letters which are underlined twice in order here.

Wrong will be right ...

Write the letters which are underlined once in order here.

when Aslan comes in sight.

Page 46

What Would You Do?

Circle the best answer. For help, look up the key underlined words in the dictionary.

1. What would you do with a telly?
   a. pet it
   b. climb it
   c. watch it
2. What would you do with a mackintosh?
   a. ride it
   b. wear it
   c. shoot it
3. What would you do if you queued up?
   a. raise your hand
   b. call the police
   c. get in line
4. How would you move on a lift?
   a. up or down
   b. in a circle
   c. forward or backward
5. What would you do with a dustbin?
   a. put garbage in it
   b. wear it in the garden
   c. fly it in a breeze
6. What would you do if you mucked about?
   a. gather eggs
   b. waste time
   c. scrape out dirty pots and pans
7. What would you do with a quid?
   a. spend it
   b. swim away from it
   c. step on it
8. What would you do if you were knackered?
   a. carry a load and take a hike
   b. make a face
   c. lie down and rest
9. What would you do with petrol?
   a. feed pigeons
   b. fill a tank
   c. trim a hedge

Page 47

As Easy As Falling Off a Log

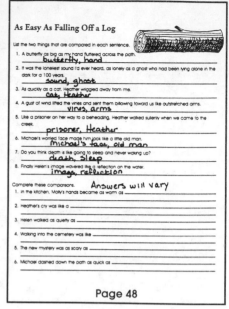

List the two things that are compared in each sentence.

1. A butterfly as big as my hand fluttered across the path.
   butterfly, hand
2. It was the loneliest sound I'd ever heard, as lonely as a ghost who had been lying alone in the dark for a 100 years.
   sound, ghost
3. As quickly as a cat, Heather wriggled away from me.
   cat, Heather
4. A gust of wind lifted the vines and sent them billowing toward us like outstretched arms.
   vines, arms
5. Like a prisoner on her way to a beheading, Heather walked sullenly when we came to the creek.
   prisoner, Heather
6. Michael's worried face made him look like a little old man.
   Michael's face, old man
7. Do you think death is like going to sleep and never waking up?
   death, sleep
8. Finally Helen's image wavered like a reflection on the water.
   image, reflection

Complete these comparisons. Answers will vary

1. In the kitchen, Molly's hands became as warm as ______
2. Heather's cry was like a ______
3. Helen walked as quietly as ______
4. Walking into the cemetery was like ______
5. The new mystery was as scary as ______
6. Michael dashed down the path as quick as ______

Page 48

DeCree's Dictionary

Decode each word in DeCree's Dictionary by substituting the letter that comes before each letter in the nonsense words given. Write the word on the line in the first column. Then complete the dictionary by finishing each simile in the second column.
Hint: Z comes before A.

as BOOPZJOH	annoying	as ______
as CVNQZ	bumpy	as ______
as DSBOLZ	cranky	as ______
as EFMJDJPVT	delicious	as ______
as FYBTQFSBUJOH	exasperating	as ______
as GBUUFOJOH	fattening	as ______
as HSPVDIZ	grouchy	as ______
as IVOHSZ	hungry	as ______
as JUDIZ	itchy	as ______
as KPMMZ	jolly	as ______
as LJOEIFBSUFE	kindhearted	as ______
as MBAZ	lazy	as ______
as NBEEFOJOH	maddening	as ______
as OFSWPVT	nervous	as ______
as PME	old	as ______
as QPXFSGVM	powerful	as ______
as RVJDL	quick	as ______
as SPVOE	round	as ______
as TJMMZ	silly	as ______
as UBMM	tall	as ______
as VTFGVM	useful	as ______
as WBMVBCMF	valuable	as ______
as XFBMUIZ	wealthy	as ______
as FYDJUJOH	exciting	as ______
as ZPVUIGVM	youthful	as ______
as ABOZ	zany	as ______

Answers will vary

Page 49

As Fast As Lightning

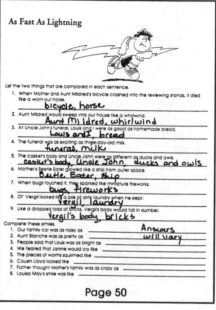

List the two things that are compared in each sentence.

1. When Mother and Aunt Mildred's bicycle crashed into the reviewing stands, it died like a worn-out horse.
   bicycle, horse
2. Aunt Mildred would sweep into our house like a whirlwind.
   Aunt Mildred, whirlwind
3. At Uncle John's funeral, Louis and I were as good as homemade bread.
   Louis and I, bread
4. The funeral was as exciting as three-day-old milk.
   funeral, milk
5. The casket's body and Uncle John were as different as ducks and owls.
   casket's body, Uncle John, ducks and owls
6. Mother's Beetle Eater glowed like a ship from outer space.
   Beetle Eater, ship
7. When bugs touched it, they sparked like miniature fireworks.
   bugs, fireworks
8. Ol' Vergil looked like a pile of dirty laundry when he slept.
   Vergil, laundry
9. Like a dropped load of bricks, Vergil's body would fall in slumber.
   Vergil's body, bricks

Complete these similes. Answers will vary

1. Our family car was as noisy as ______
2. Aunt Blanche was as pretty as ______
3. People said that Louis was as bright as ______
4. We feared that Janine would cry like ______
5. The pieces of worms squirmed like ______
6. Cousin Lloyd looked like ______
7. Father thought Mother's family was as crazy as ______
8. Louisa May's smile was like ______

Page 50

Championship Categories

Circle the one word in each group that does not fit with the others. Name the category that describes the remaining words. Category names may vary.

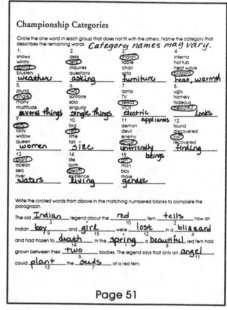

1.	2.	3.	4.
snowy	asks	**Indian**	inferno
wintry	**tells**	table	hot tub
spring	inquires	chair	heat wave
blustery	questions	sofa	**blizzard**
weather	asking	furniture	heat, warmth
5.	**6.**	**7.**	**8.**
plural	**two**	lamp	ugly
single	solitaire	TV	homely
many	solo	**seeds**	hideous
multitude	singular	VCR	**beautiful**
several things	single things	electric appliances	looks
9.	**10.**	**11.**	**12.**
boy	big	demon	found
lady	**red**	devil	discovered
widow	little	enemy	**lost**
queen	tall	**angel**	recovered
women	size	unfriendly beings	finding
13.	**14.**	**15.**	
plant	life	**girl**	
ocean	birth	man	
sea	**death**	boy	
river	existence	male	
waters	living	gender	

Write the circled words from above in the matching numbered blanks to complete the paragraph.

The old Indian (3) legend about the red (10) fern tells (2) how an Indian boy (9) and girl (15) were lost (12) in a blizzard (4) and had frozen to death (14). In the spring (1) a beautiful (8) red fern had grown between their two (6) bodies. The legend says that only an angel (11) could plant (13) the seeds (7) of a red fern.

Page 51

Odd Word Out

Circle the word in each line below which does not belong.

1.	eerie	uncanny	**vindictive**	peculiar
2.	**barricade**	menace	peril	threat
3.	**mimic**	stroll	scamper	amble
4.	fare	**sleep**	charge	fee
5.	shriek	scream	**strike**	squeal
6.	cram	**skitter**	stuff	jam
7.	barge	intrude	enter	**utter**
8.	unconventional	**opaque**	bizarre	peculiar
9.	tinker	fidget	toy	**trot**
10.	reckon	surmise	calculate	**impress**
11.	embarrassed	bashful	**cowardly**	sheepish
12.	acute	**memorable**	intense	keen
13.	hull	peel	skin	**bar**
14.	clatter	**offend**	commotion	rattle

List in order the underlined letters of the circled words to spell two words.

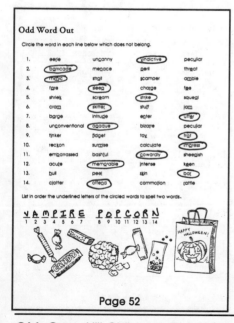

V(1) A(2) M(3) P(4) I(5) R(6) E(7) P(8) O(9) P(10) C(11) O(12) R(13) N(14)

Page 52

Excerpts from Annemarie's Diary

Circle the word which best completes each sentence.

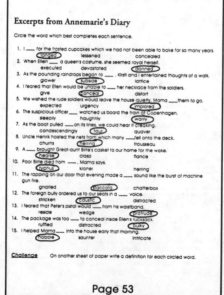

1. I ___ for the frosted cupcakes which we had not been able to bake for so many years.
   longed lessened concealed
2. When Ellen ___ a queen's costume, she seemed royal herself.
   executed devastated **donned**
3. As the pounding raindrops began to ___ , Kirsti and I entertained thoughts of a walk.
   glower **subside** lattice
4. I feared that Ellen would be unable to ___ her necklace from the soldiers.
   give **conceal** distort
5. We wished the rude soldiers would leave the house quietly. Mama ___ them to go.
   expected urgency **implored**
6. The suspicious officer ___ watched us board the train at Copenhagen.
   sleepily haughtily **warily**
7. As the boat pulled ___ on its lines, we could hear it creaking.
   condescendingly **taut** quaver
8. Uncle Henrik hoisted the nets from which many ___ fell onto the deck.
   churns **herring** trousseau
9. A ___ brought Great-aunt Birte's casket to our home for the wake.
   hearse clasp fiance
10. Poor Birte died from ___ , Mama says.
    typhus kroner herring
11. The rapping on our door that evening made a ___ sound like the burst of machine gun fire.
    gnarled **staccato** chatterbox
12. The foreign bully ordered us to our seats in a ___ voice.
    stricken **caustic** distracted
13. I feared that Peter's pistol would ___ from his waistband.
    reside wedge **protrude**
14. The package was too ___ to conceal inside Ellen's rucksack.
    ruffled distracted **bulky**
15. I helped Mama ___ into the house early that morning.
    hobble saunter intricate

Challenge On another sheet of paper write a definition for each circled word.

Page 53

What's the Row?

Carefully read each sentence and write the number of the correct definition for each underlined word.

Definitions			
file:	1) a line of people	2) to arrange in a useful order	3) to sharpen, smooth or grind
party:	1) an assembly of people	2) a fun occasion	
passage:	1) a journey	2) a hallway	3) a segment of a writing
row:	1) a straight line	2) to move by using oars	3) a noisy quarrel
spectacles:	1) displays	2) eyeglasses	
wind:	1) to turn	2) moving air	3) hear (get wind)

- 1 — 1. The children and the beavers made their way in single file to the Stone Table.
- 2 — 2. The beavers did not need to row across the springtime streams.
- 2 — 3. The Professor's spectacles slipped down his nose in a comical manner.
- 2 — 4. There could be no Christmas party without Father Christmas.
- 2 — 5. The children heard Mrs. Macready and her visitors in the passage.
- 1 — 6. The path through the woods would wind often because of the rocky ground.
- 3 — 7. The Queen filed her nails to a fine point.
- 1 — 8. In a later novel Lucy will take a passage aboard the "Dawn Treader."
- 3 — 9. Susan feared that Peter and Edmund would have a row.
- 1 — 10. The children wished to travel in a small party.
- 2 — 11. The warm wind helped melt the slushy snow.
- 1 — 12. What a spectacle greeted the children when they awoke!
- 3 — 13. Mr. Beaver hoped that the Queen did not get wind of the children's visit.
- 1 — 14. A party of visitors gathered to meet Mrs. Macready.
- 1 — 15. The stone figures appeared to stand in a row.
- 2 — 16. Peter filed the information in his mind for later reference.

Page 54

Criss-Cross

Complete each sentence below using words from the Word Bank. Then use these words to complete the criss-cross.

Word Bank					
confer	cockeyed	colic	collapsible	pews	
congregation	poinsettia	pierce	charitable	dress	
refugee	Vaseline				

1. In many churches people sit on **pews** which are long benches.
2. If people wish to wear earrings, they should go to a professional who will **pierce** their ears.
3. Alice Wendleken put **Vaseline** on her eyelids to make them sparkle.
4. The people who gather in a church to worship are called the **congregation.**
5. A person who leaves home to find greater safety in a foreign land is called a **refugee**
6. An organization is **charitable** if it raises money or material to help those in need.
7. The **poinsettia** plant has red or white leaves and is often used for holiday decorations.
8. When people suffer from **colic**, they have severe stomach or intestinal pain.
9. Often people in plays and pageants try to wear their costumes in the last practice which they call the **dress** rehearsal.
10. A **collapsible** stroller can be folded up to be stored more easily.
11. You may need to turn your head to one side to see a picture which hangs on the wall in a **cockeyed** manner.
12. People **confer** with one another to discuss issues and make decisions.

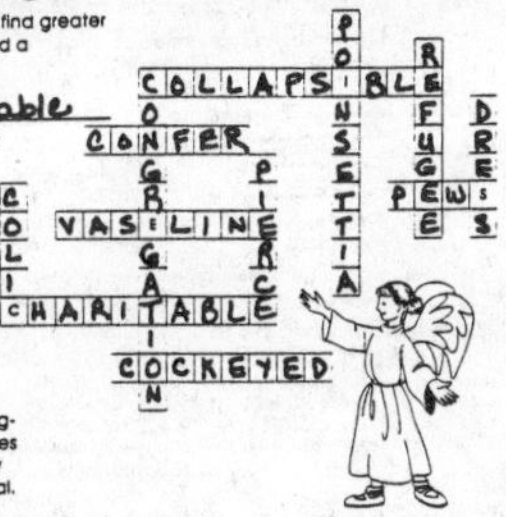

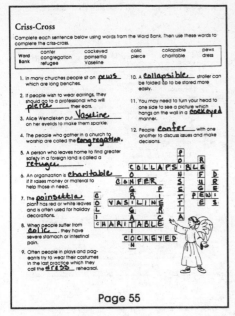

Page 55

Take Me Out to the Ball Game

Using the diagram, answer these questions.

1. Who plays left field? **Bob Gordon**
2. How far is it from first to second base? **60 feet**
3. Does Monk Lawler play the outfield? **no**
4. How many innings are played in Little League? **six**
5. If a batter hits a triple, how many feet will he run? **180 feet**
6. What position does Cliff Borton play? **first base**
7. How far is Paul Mather from home plate? **44 feet**
8. Can a 10-year-old child play Little League ball? **yes**
9. How long may a bat be? **33 inches**
10. What position does Jim Hakken play? **Shortstop**
11. Who is Stu closer to, Monk or Kenny? **Monk**

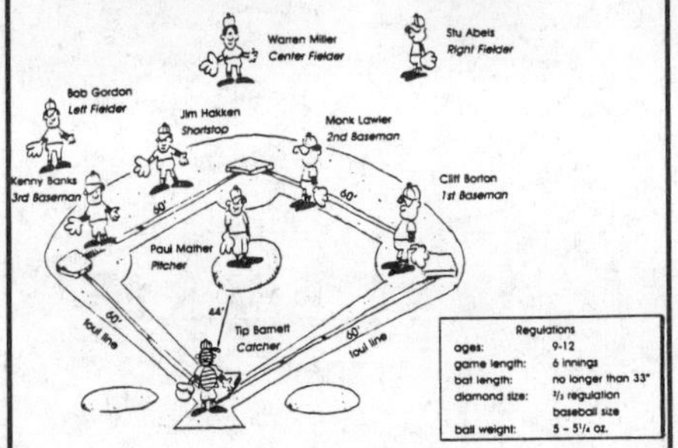

Regulations	
ages:	9-12
game length:	6 innings
bat length:	no longer than 33"
diamond size:	$^2/_3$ regulation baseball size
ball weight:	5 – $5^1/_4$ oz.

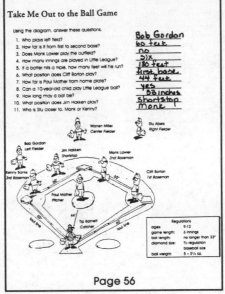

Page 56

A Feverish Task

Read each paragraph. Underline the topic sentence. Then circle the letter of the best title.

1. Did you think mosquitoes were to blame for malaria? Actually the culprits are tiny one-celled creatures named plasmodia. If a person is bitten by an Anepholes mosquito, one of about 3,000 kinds of mosquitoes, and the saliva of that particular mosquito contains plasmodia that person can contract malaria. So the mosquito only acts as the carrier for plasmodia, the *real* cause of malaria.
   A. Mosquitoes bite people
   (B.) Plasmodia cause malaria
   C. 3,000 species of mosquitoes

2. When the Anopheles bites a person, it leaves some of its saliva behind. If the saliva contains plasmodia, these tiny creatures find their way through the body until they find the liver. There they stay for around 10 days until they have multiplied into the thousands. At that time many of them return to the blood stream and try to kill red blood cells. Other plasmodia remain in the liver and continue to reproduce.
   (A.) How plasmodia spread
   B. Ten days in the liver
   C. Plasmodia kill red blood cells

3. Most people who contract malaria have the following symptoms. About 14 days after the plasmodia enter the body, the person may experience a day of headaches, fatigue and nausea. Then comes a 12- to 24-hour period in which malaria shows itself more strongly. The person starts having chills, enters a period of high fever with sweating and ends with a reduced body temperature. If the victim does not receive medical treatment, these attacks may continue for years. However, the body begins to fight the infection and the attacks occur less frequently.
   A. Why people get headaches
   B. How the body fights malaria
   (C.) The symptoms of malaria

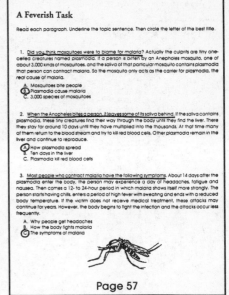

Page 57

What's the Idea?

Circle the number of the sentence which best expresses the main idea for each pararaph.

Edmund began to question whether or not the lion in the Queen's courtyard was alive. The large creature looked as if it were about to pounce on a dwarf. But it did not move. Then Edmund noticed the snow on the lion's head and back. Only a statue would be covered like that!
1. The statue is snow-covered.
(2.) Edmund wonders if the lion is alive.
3. The lion is ready to jump out.

The resting party of children and beavers heard the sound of jingling bells. Mr. Beaver dashed out of his hiding place and soon called the others to join him. He could hardly contain himself with excitement. Father Christmas is here!
1. Mr. Beaver is a brave animal.
2. The group hears a jingling sound.
(3.) Father Christmas has come to Narnia.

Poor Edmund! Because he came to the Queen, he expected her to reward him gratefully with Turkish Delight. After all he had traveled so far and had suffered miserably in the cold. When the Queen finally commanded that he receive food and drink, the cruel dwarf brought Edmund a bowl of water and a hunk of dry bread.
(1.) Edmund is not rewarded as he expected.
2. Edmund receives bread and water.
3. The young boy suffered from the cold.

Peter knew he must rescue Susan from the wolf. When the wolf charged, Susan climbed up a nearby tree. The wolf's snapping and snarling mouth was inches away. When Peter looked more closely, he realized that his sister was about to faint. Rushing in with his sword, Peter slashed at the beast.
1. Peter kills the wolf.
2. The wolf snarls at Susan.
(3.) Peter realizes he must save his sister.

Now choose one of the following sentences as your main idea and write a paragraph.
1. The Queen demands that Edmund be returned to her.
2. Aslan's army loses the Queen and her dwarf.
3. Father Christmas gives gifts to the beavers and the three children.

Answers will vary

Page 58

Try to Groove It

Write M if the sentence give the main idea.
Write D if the sentence gives detail.
Hint: Each set of sentences has only one main idea.

1. **M** The medicine makes my hair fall out.
   I wear my baseball cap in the hospital.
   The staff tries to get me to wear a wig.
2. **D** I can hardly imagine what it's like to breathe the fresh air.
   I can tell the difference between people's footsteps.
   I feel like I've been in the hospital for years.
3. **D** Parents and other spectators often bring their own chairs and blankets to games in Arborville.
   In California we played in miniature big league parks.
   The playing fields are not as elaborate here as they were in California.
   Here, games are usually played on junior high or elementary school diamonds.
4. **M** I notice that I'm the center of attention as I warm up.
   Even the Ace players gawk at me like I'm some strange animal.
   Our whole team stops warming up to watch Tip and me.
5. **D** He felt naked and lonely playing up so close to the batter.
   Kenny was reluctant to move in closer.
   I tried to coax him in but he barely budged.
6. **D** Red kept glancing at me from the pitcher's mound.
   He seemed to hear every noise and wisecrack.
   Was Red too easily distracted?
7. **M** I knew I had to touch first.
   Inch by inch I crawled toward it.
   I knew the baseman was running back toward me with the ball.
   Finally I lunged and fell forward.
8. **D** I held Jim for support.
   We attracted a crowd of Daily players.
   The three of us made an unusual sight.
   I turned so Dad would sign his name using my back as a table.

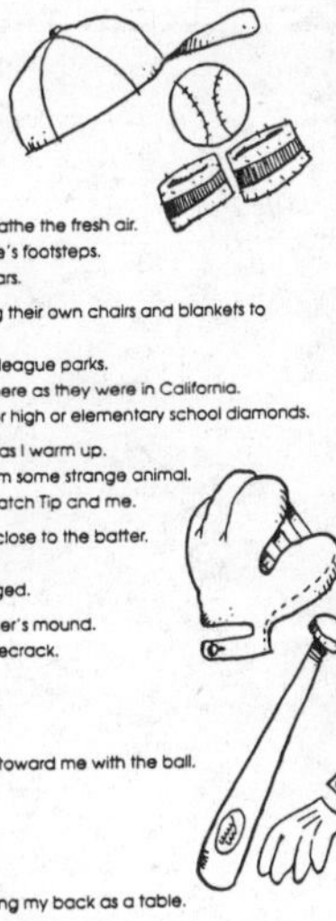

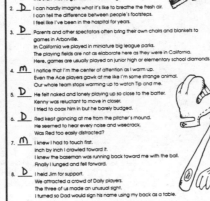

Page 59

This Is Your Life!

Principal's Day is this week. All of the classes are doing something special for their principal, Mrs. Farrell. The fifth grade decided to do a 'This Is Your Life' type of skit. In order to do this, they had to ask Mrs. Farrell a lot of questions.

Help the fifth graders put the information below into chronological order. **Note:** Read all of the clues before you begin. This will help you determine the years in which the events happened.

5 Mrs. Farrell gave birth to triplet sons two years after she and Mr. Farrell got married.
6 Twenty-five years after Mrs. Farrell was born, she got the chicken pox for the first time with her sons.
1 Mrs. Farrell was born in 1951 in Dukwilma. She has a brother two years older than her and a sister one year younger.
10 Mrs. Farrell broke her arm rollerblading with her sons three years after she tried to kill the 'snake' in her backyard.
2 When Mrs. Farrell was 9, she and her family went on a vacation to the Grand Canyon. She became lost, and the rangers had to search for her.
7 Twenty-two years after she tripped on the steps at her graduation, Mrs. Farrell became principal of Dukwilma Elementary.
8 Twenty-nine years after Mrs. Farrell became lost in the Grand Canyon, she tried to kill a snake in her backyard that turned out to be a stick.
4 Twenty-six years before she became principal, Mrs. Farrell married Mr. Farrell.
9 Mrs. Farrell organized the first 'Kids Are Great Day' at Dukwilma Elementary twenty years after she married Mr. Farrell.
3 Mrs. Farrell tripped on the steps going up to receive her diploma at her high school graduation 18 years after she was born.

•SOMETHING EXTRA• Make a time line of your life in chronological order.

Page 60

It's All a Matter of Timing

Use the time line to circle the correct event in each numbered pair.

Which happens first?
1. (Omri travels through the chest) or Bright Stars shows her infant to the villagers
2. The tepee begins to burn or (Patrick returns to the present)
3. (The villagers pack to leave) or an owl call is heard
4. The Algonquins build a large fire or (the baby is born)
5. Bright Stars leaves with the villagers or (Patrick travels through the chest)

Which happens last?
1. (Bright Stars shows her infant) or the baby is born
2. (An owl call is heard) or Boone notices he is in the Iroquois village
3. Omri travels through the chest or (Boone fires his revolver)
4. (The tepee begins to burn) or the villagers pack
5. Patrick returns to the present or (the Algonquins build a fire)

Time Line

Start
- Patrick travels through the chest with Boone and Bright Stars.
- The baby is born.
- Patrick returns to the present.
- Omri travels through the chest.
- Boone notices he is in the Iroquois village.
- Bright Stars shows her infant to the villagers.
- The villagers pack to leave.
- Bright Stars and the baby leave with the villagers.
- An owl call is heard.
- The Algonquins build a large fire.
- The tepee begins to burn.
- Boone fires his revolver.

End

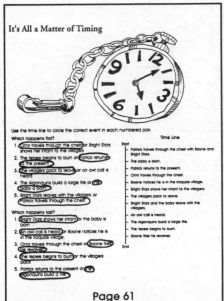

Page 61

Get the Facts, Max

Skim this paragraph to answer the questions below.

The islands of Aruba, Bonaire and Curacao, sometimes known as the ABC islands, are part of the Netherlands Antilles. They lie 50 miles north off the coast of Venezuela. Three more islands, Sint Eustatius, Saba and St. Martin (the northern half of which belongs to France), are approximately 500 miles northeast of the ABC islands.

Until 1949 the islands were known as the Dutch West Indies or "Curacao Territory." In 1986 Aruba separated to become a self-governing part of the Netherlands Realm.

On the island of Curacao most food is imported. Because it is so rocky, little farming is possible. The island is the largest and most heavily populated of the Netherlands Antilles. Its oil refineries, among the largest in the world, give its people a relatively high standard of living. Today most people of Curacao work either in the shipping, refining or tourist industry.

Netherlands Antilles – Other Facts

Area:			Capital:
Aruba	75	square miles	Willemstad
Bonaire	111	square miles	**Major Languages:**
Curacao	171	square miles	Dutch, Papiamento (a mixture of
Saba	5	square miles	Spanish, Dutch, Portuguese, Carib and
Sint Eustatius	11	square miles	English), English, Spanish
St. Martin	13	square miles	

1. Name the capital of the Netherlands Antilles. **Willemstad**
2. What industry gives the people a high standard of living? **Oil refining**
3. Name the ABC islands. **Aruba, Bonaire, Curacao**
4. What is Papiamento? **a language.**
5. Why must food be imported to Curacao? **It is too rocky to farm**
6. Which island is smallest? **Saba.**
7. Which two islands are the largest? **Bonaire, Curacao**
8. Which island belongs in part to France? **St. Martin**
9. In what year did Aruba become self-governing? **1986**

Page 62

Deep Magic

Fill in the missing letters to complete each word.

Meanings	Words
a slow, ignorant person	D **U N C** E
to go at some risk	V **E N T U R** E
to regard with excessive satisfaction	G **L O A** T
musty	F **R O W S T** Y
a stimulating liquid	C **O R D I A** L
a pest	V **E R M I** N
a member of a council	C **O U N C I L L O** R
a coniferous tree which sheds its needles yearly	L **A R C** H
to move restlessly	F **I D G E** T
slender	L **I T H** E
an evergreen shrub with flat, dark green needles	Y **E** W
a man-eating giant	O **G R** E
to give up	F **O R F E I** T
to desire	C **R A V** E
a type of early spring flower	C **R O C U** S
a poisonous mushroom	T **O A D S T O O** L

Find each word in the puzzle.

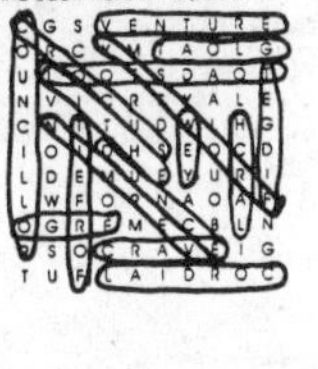

Page 63

Sing of Change

Read the clues and fill in the blanks using the words in the Word Bank. Then decipher the code below.

Word Bank
bestial, caper, indigo, plumage, abeyance, predator, engulf, annex, totem, hostile, resonant, wax, aurora, wrest, cauldron, advent, preen, plaintive, crescendo, frigid

Clues

meat-eating hunter	P R E D A T O R
dark blue	I N D I G O
increase in volume	C R E S C E N D O
primp	P R E E N
unfriendly	H O S T I L E
brutal	B E S T I A L
temporary inaction	A B E Y A N C E
confiscate	W R E S T
large kettle	C A U L D R O N
sorrowful	P L A I N T I V E
feathers	P L U M A G E
freezing	F R I G I D
northern lights	A U R O R A
spirit symbol	T O T E M
arrival	A D V E N T
grow	W A X
addition	A N N E X
rich, lasting sound	R E S O N A N T
overwhelm	E N G U L F
antic	C A P E R

THE SPIRITS OF THE ANIMALS ARE PASSING AWAY THE HOUR OF THE WOLF AND THE ESKIMO IS OVER

Page 64

A Terrific Idea

Complete the crossword with words from the Word Bank.

Word Bank
finicky, feud, smug, vigorously, skeptically, misanthrope, lash, gmoy, dodo, shamble, accomplish, kingdom come, conch, pinto, raspy, cornucopia, disheveled, bittersweet, garret, groom, deter, waddle, bungalow, freehand

Across
2. to bind with a cord or string
6. energetically
10. to walk awkwardly, sloppily
12. fussy
14. with a harsh, irritating sound
16. a large, clumsy bird now extinct
18. house space just below a sloping roof; attic
20. horn-shaped container which represents a very good harvest
21. to walk like a duck
22. done by hand, without the aid of devices
23. disorderly

Down
1. to clean and brush
3. to succeed in doing
4. with a limp
5. a one-story home
7. to hinder
8. afterlife
9. one who hates humans
10. doubtfully
11. a plant with red seeds
13. a spotted horse
15. a large, spiral seashell
17. self-satisfied (complacent or self-righteous)
19. lasting conflict

Page 65

Score Chore

Circle the phrase which you feel best completes each statement. You may want to check your work with a dictionary.

1. If Miyax's ulo is versatile, it . . .
   (can do many tasks) is made of bone. must be a complex tool.
2. If the wolf pups are tawny, they must have . . .
   glossy coats. well-formed muscles. (tan coloring.)
3. If Miyax's stew has a savory smell, it . . .
   should be thrown out. (is very pleasing.) is hot enough.
4. When the sun has reached its apogee, they . . .
   (can go no higher.) is just above the horizon. cannot be seen.
5. When the adult wolves regurgitate food, they . . .
   belch. swallow loudly. (spit it up.)
6. Miyax quelled her feelings of despair, and she . . .
   panicked. could not sleep. (quieted down.)
7. Because the wolf pup's tail was conspicuous, the young girl . . .
   cut it off. feared he was ill. (could find him.)
8. When wolf calls undulate, they . . .
   (move up and down in pitch.) create disturbances. take turns.
9. If Miyax solicits for food, she is . . .
   (asking earnestly.) hunting vigorously. searching frantically.
10. The wolves glanced warily at Miyax, because they . . .
    were hungry. were tired. (were cautious.)
11. If you dig into the permafrost, you will certainly find . . .
    a natural refrigerator. ancient Viking artifacts. (bones of the wooly mammoth.)
12. If Jello is an incorrigible creature, he must be . . .
    a vicious and bloodthirsty monster. a weakling. (impossible to change.)

Scoring: If you guessed 1-4 phrases correctly, you are a "likeable lemming." If you guessed 5-7 correctly, you become a "brave bunting." If you are fortunate to have guessed 8-10 correctly you earn the title "fabulous fox." Those with scores of 11 or 12 are "wondersome wolves."

Score _____ Title _____

Page 66

Don't Be a Sissy

What is the most frightening spot in Learning? Complete the puzzle and read down the darkened row of boxes to find out.

Clues
1. highly agitated
2. impossible to read
3. showing proper manners
4. spirit, pluck
5. a celebration
6. pertaining to the stomach
7. nearly
8. to take more than one's share
9. tobacco juice container
10. aromatic seed of a tropical tree
11. to pretend
12. a difficult problem
13. sharp, irritating smell
14. a mischievous adventure
15. shabby, worthless
16. order of importance
17. to escape
18. generously, freely
19. long chat
20. brownish yellow
21. heavy
22. rough, disorderly
23. stealthy action

1. SEETHING
2. ILLEGIBLE
3. DECOROUS
4. SPUNK
5. SHINDIG
6. GASTRIC
7. NIGH
8. HOG
9. SPITTOON
10. NUTMEG
11. FEIGN
12. DILEMMA
13. PUNGENT
14. CAPER
15. SORRY
16. PRIORITY
17. BOLT
18. PROFUSELY
19. PALAVER
20. AMBER
21. LEADEN
22. ROWDY
23. FURTIVITY

Word Bank
priority, amber, pungent, spittoon, bolt, rowdy, spunk, dilemma, furtivity, hog, decorous, shindig, palaver, nutmeg, sorry, caper, nigh, profusely, seething, gastric, illegible, leaden, feign

Page 67

With Little Tea and Just Rice for All

Match each word on the left with its meaning on the right.

List 1
1. H emanate
2. C torso
3. J infamous
4. D hoist
5. K murky
6. B regale
7. L frantic
8. E crimson
9. A kow-tow
10. I oust
11. G civics
12. F pigeon-toed

a. to show deep respect or to bow
b. to entertain
c. the trunk of the body
d. to lift
e. deep red
f. with toes turned inward
g. the study of government
h. to proceed, go out
i. to take out
j. having a terrible reputation
k. dark
l. frenzied

List 2
1. KK jaunty
2. BB formidable
3. HH illustrious
4. CC intimidate
5. GG dally
6. EE hue
7. LL meticulous
8. AA spew
9. DD frail
10. II concoct
11. FF fraught
12. JJ spike

aa. to erupt
bb. terrible, dreadful
cc. to make timid; to threaten
dd. weak
ee. a color or tint
ff. filled, loaded
gg. to delay
hh. famous, well-known
ii. to prepare by combining diverse ingredients
jj. to pierce with points
kk. lively or sporty
ll. careful, attending to details

Challenge: On another sheet of paper, write a sentence using four of the words from the lists above. Then draw a picture which illustrates your sentence. For example: The jaunty young man with a crimson umbrella was formidable as he ousted the mosquitoes from the room.

Page 68

Put a Minotaur in Your Tank

Decode the names of creatures. Then use a dictionary to match the names with their meanings.

	Name	
a.	faun	H
b.	Silenus	G
c.	Bacchus	B
d.	nymph	F
e.	dryad	D
f.	naiad	M
g.	satyr	I
h.	centaur	A
i.	ghoul	N
j.	minotaur	J
k.	spectre	C
l.	unicorn	O
m.	goblin	K
n.	siren	L
o.	griffin	P
p.	ogre	E

H. a creature with a man's upper body but a horse's body and legs
G. a ghost
B. the leader of the satyrs; a chubby old man with pointed ears
F. a river nymph
D. a faun; woodland god or demon
M. a small, evil spirit
I. a creature with a man's body and bull's head
A. a creature with human body but ears, tail and hindlegs of a goat
N. a sea nymph whose song lures sailors to wreck their ships
J. any nature goddess
C. a horse-like creature with one horn coming out from its forehead
O. the god of wine and merrymaking
K. an evil grave-robbing spirit
L. a creature with an eagle's head and wings and a lion's body
P. a man-eating giant
E. a wood nymph

Page 69

One of a Kind

The prefixes mon- and mono- come from the Greek word monos which means one, alone, or single. Write the correct word from the Word Box in each sentence below.

Word Box
monarchy, monarch, monastery, monologue, monocle, monogram, monolingual, monolithic, monopolize, monorail, monosyllabic, monotone

1. Queen Elizabeth is the **monarch** of England.
2. Our city has a high-speed **monorail** train.
3. Uncle Ralph wears a **monocle** on one eye.
4. The lecture was boring because the speaker spoke in a **monotone.**
5. One, two, and three are examples of **monosyllabic** words.
6. A monk lives a religious life in a **monastery.**
7. Betsy will embroider her **monogram** on the towels.
8. I don't want to **monopolize** all of your time, but will you go to the museum with me?
9. The United States has never been a **monarchy** like some European countries.
10. The **monolithic** structure stands in the center of the town square.
11. Gail is **monolingual** – she speaks only English.
12. The actor's **monologue** was absolutely spellbinding.

Page 70

Add-a-Letter

Make new words by adding a letter from the Letter Bank to each word below. The letter may be added anywhere.

Letter Bank
c e e g h i l m n r t t u u v w

Word	Letter	New Word	Clue
Example: room	g	groom	to brush
1. sob	n	snob	one who looks down on others as inferior
2. pro	m	prom	a formal school dance
3. save	t	stave	wooden strip forming the side of a barrel
4. beet	r	beret	a soft, flat cap
5. ringer	w	wringer	a machine for squeezing out water
6. hears	e	hearse	the vehicle which carries the dead
7. trade	i	tirade	a scolding speech
8. state	e	estate	that which a person owns
9. diver	t	divert	to turn aside from a course
10. action	u	auction	a sale in which items go to highest bidder
11. oat	h	oath	a promise
12. ape	c	cape	a point of land which juts into the water
13. fare	l	flare	to burst into flame or activity
14. arose	u	arouse	to excite
15. aid	v	avid	eager

Page 71

Guidelines

For each search word below fill in the circle by the correct guide word pair.

Search Words	Guide Word Pairs		
1. pick	○ piece/pigpen	● pheasant/picture	○ pinch/pink
2. woolly	● wooden/wordy	○ with/wonky	○ which/wild
3. villain	○ veto/vinegar	● volcano/vulcan	○ valiant/vapor
4. withdrew	○ warble/web	● whittle/wizard	○ weekly/weigh
5. impress	○ imperfect/import	● implore/impulse	○ ideal/ill
6. crooked	○ collide/crib	○ chalk/clear	● creep/croquet
7. lobby	● livery/lob	○ long/lotus	○ loathe/logjam
8. bewildered	○ bent/bike	● belly/beret	○ bewitch/bid
9. welfare	○ wharf/winter	● weir/west	○ warrior/weevil
10. penitentiary	○ physics/pickerel	● pelf/penguin	○ peddler/penny
11. privet	○ poncho/private	● people/phony	○ privateer/prune
12. intermediate	● immigrant/invent	○ issue/ivory	○ ilk/immediate
13. coordinator	○ crop/cupola	○ contract/coronet	● conduct/console
14. contribution	● consider/coop	○ count/crease	○ chum/cog
15. bazaar	○ barbecue/batter	● bacterial/band	○ bay/bean
16. ancestor	● along/antic	○ ace/acting	○ antique/apart
17. resin	○ rend/rhubarb	● rectangle/reflect	○ rewind/roomy
18. manger	○ margin/material	● mangy/mantel	○ man/manicure
19. fresh	● fierce/flip	○ freight/fuddle	○ forage/freeze
20. program	○ pathetic/pavilion	● piffle/platypus	○ preside/pucker
21. insane	● inhabit/instant	○ invalid/ion	○ impartial/inca
22. traction	● temper/that	○ touch/train	○ tin/toothache

Write three sentences using some of these words to describe the Christmas pageant.

Answers will vary

Page 72

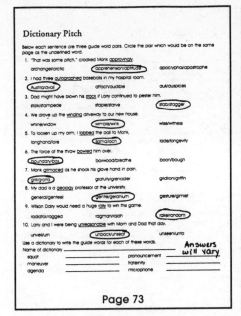

Dictionary Pitch

Below each sentence are three guide word pairs. Circle the pair which would be on the same page as the underlined word.

1. "That was some pitch," croaked Monk approvingly.
   archangel/arctic   (apprehension/aptitude)   apocryphal/apostrophe
2. I had three autographed baseballs in my hospital room.
   (Austria/avail)   attach/audible   auk/auspices
3. Dad might have blown his stack if Larry continued to pester him.
   stalk/stampede   staple/starve   (stab/stagger)
4. We drove up the winding driveway to our new house.
   whine/widow   (wimple/wink)   wise/witness
5. To loosen up my arm, I lobbed the ball to Monk.
   longhand/lore   (llama/loch)   lode/longevity
6. The force of the throw bowled him over.
   (boundary/box)   boxwood/breathe   boon/bough
7. Monk grimaced as he shook his glove hand in pain.
   (grill/grotto)   gratuity/grenadier   gridiron/griffin
8. My dad is a geology professor at the university.
   general/genteel   (gentle/geranium)   gesture/gimlet
9. Wilson Dairy would need a huge rally to win this game.
   radiator/ragged   ragman/rajah   (rake/random)
10. Larry and I were being unreasonable with Mom and Dad that day.
    unvelium   (unpack/unseat)   unseek/unto

Use a dictionary to write the guide words for each of these words.

Name of dictionary _____

squat _____	pronouncement _____	Answers will vary
maneuver _____	fraternity _____	
agenda _____	microphone _____	

Page 73

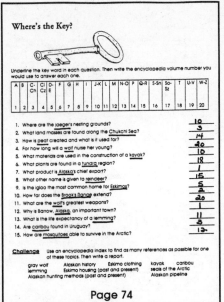

Where's the Key?

Underline the key word in each question. Then write the encyclopedia volume number you would use to answer each one.

A	B	C-Ch	Ci-Cz	D-Dz	E	F	G	H	I	J-K	L	M	N-O	P	Q-R	S-Sn	So-Sz	T	U-V	W-Z
1	2	3		4		5	6	7	8	9	10	11	12	13	14	15	16	17	18	19	20

1. Where are the jaegers nesting grounds? — 10
2. What land masses are found along the Chukchi Sea? — 3
3. How is peat created and what is it used for? — 14
4. For how long will a wolf nurse her young? — 20
5. What materials are used in the construction of a kayak? — 10
6. What plants are found in a tundra region? — 18
7. What product is Alaska's chief export? — 1
8. What other name is given to reindeer? — 15
9. Is the igloo the most common home for Eskimos? — 5
10. How far does the Brooks Range extend? — 2
11. What are the wolf's greatest weapons? — 20
12. Why is Barrow, Alaska, an important town? — 11
13. What is the life expectancy of a lemming? — 8
14. Are caribou found in Uruguay? — 12
15. How are mosquitoes able to survive in the Arctic?

Challenge: Use an encyclopedia index to find as many references as possible for one of these topics. Then write a report.

gray wolf   Alaskan history   Eskimo clothing   kayak   caribou
lemming   Eskimo housing (past and present)   seals of the Arctic
Alaskan hunting methods (past and present)   Alaskan pipeline

Page 74

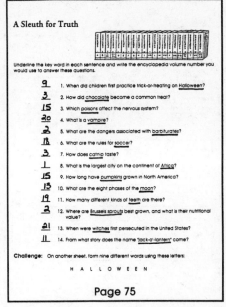

A Sleuth for Truth

Underline the key word in each sentence and write the encyclopedia volume number you would use to answer these questions.

9. 1. When did children first practice trick-or-treating on Halloween?
3. 2. How did chocolate become a common treat?
15. 3. Which poisons affect the nervous system?
20. 4. What is a vampire?
2. 5. What are the dangers associated with barbiturates?
18. 6. What are the rules for soccer?
3. 7. How does catnip taste?
1. 8. What is the largest city on the continent of Africa?
15. 9. How long have pumpkins grown in North America?
13. 10. What are the eight phases of the moon?
19. 11. How many different kinds of teeth are there?
2. 12. Where are Brussels sprouts best grown, and what is their nutritional value?
21. 13. When were witches first persecuted in the United States?
11. 14. From what story does the name "jack-o'-lantern" come?

Challenge: On another sheet, form nine different words using these letters:

H A L L O W E E N

Page 75

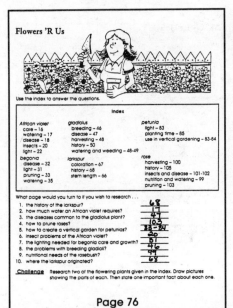

Flowers 'R Us

Use the index to answer the questions.

Index

African violet
care – 16
watering – 17
disease – 18
insects – 20
light – 22

begonia
disease – 32
light – 31
pruning – 33
watering – 35

gladiolus
breeding – 46
disease – 47
harvesting – 48
history – 50
watering and weeding – 48-49

larkspur
coloration – 67
history – 68
stem length – 66

petunia
light – 83
planting time – 85
use in vertical gardening – 83-84

rose
harvesting – 100
history – 105
insects and disease – 101-102
nutrition and watering – 99
pruning – 103

What page would you turn to if you wish to research . . .

1. the history of the larkspur? — 68
2. how much water an African violet requires? — 17
3. the diseases common to the gladiolus plant? — 47
4. how to prune roses? — 103
5. how to create a vertical garden for petunias? — 83-84
6. insect problems of the African violet? — 20
7. the lighting needed for begonia care and growth? — 31
8. the problems with breeding gladioli? — 46
9. nutritional needs of the rosebush? — 99
10. where the larkspur originated? — 68

Challenge: Research two of the flowering plants given in the index. Draw pictures showing the parts of each. Then state one important fact about each one.

Page 76

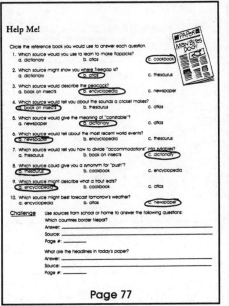

Help Me!

Circle the reference book you would use to answer each question.

1. Which source would you use to learn to make flapjacks?
   a. dictionary   b. atlas   (c. cookbook)
2. Which source might show you where Treegap is?
   a. dictionary   (b. atlas)   c. thesaurus
3. Which source would describe the peacock?
   a. book on insects   (b. encyclopedia)   c. newspaper
4. Which source would tell you about the sounds a cricket makes?
   (a. book on insects)   b. thesaurus   c. atlas
5. Which source would give the meaning of "constable"?
   a. newspaper   (b. dictionary)   c. atlas
6. Which source would tell about the most recent world events?
   (a. newspaper)   b. encyclopedia   c. thesaurus
7. Which source would tell you how to divide "accommodations" into syllables?
   a. thesaurus   b. book on insects   (c. dictionary)
8. Which source could give you a synonym for "push"?
   (a. thesaurus)   b. cookbook   c. encyclopedia
9. Which source would describe what a trout eats?
   (a. encyclopedia)   b. cookbook   c. atlas
10. Which source might best forecast tomorrow's weather?
    a. encyclopedia   b. atlas   (c. newspaper)

Challenge: Use sources from school or home to answer the following questions:
Which countries border Nepal?
Answer: _____
Source: _____
Page #: _____

What are the headlines in today's paper?
Answer: _____
Source: _____
Page #: _____

Page 77

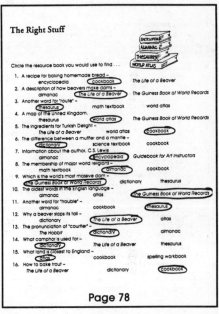

The Right Stuff

Circle the resource book you would use to find . . .

1. A recipe for baking homemade bread – encyclopedia   (cookbook)   The Life of a Beaver
2. A description of how beavers make dams – almanac   (The Life of a Beaver)   The Guiness Book of World Records
3. Another word for "route" – (thesaurus)   math textbook   world atlas
4. A map of the United Kingdom – thesaurus   (world atlas)   The Guiness Book of World Records
5. The ingredients for Turkish Delight – The Life of a Beaver   world atlas   (cookbook)
6. The difference between a muffler and a mantle – (dictionary)   science textbook   cookbook
7. Information about the author, C.S. Lewis – almanac   (encyclopedia)   Guidebook for Art Instructors
8. The membership of major world religions – math textbook   (almanac)   cookbook
9. Which is the world's most massive dam – (The Guiness Book of World Records)   dictionary   thesaurus
10. The oldest words in the English language – almanac   dictionary   (The Guiness Book of World Records)
11. Another word for "trouble" – almanac   cookbook   (thesaurus)
12. Why a beaver slaps its tail – dictionary   (The Life of a Beaver)   atlas
13. The pronunciation of "courrier" – The Hobbit   (dictionary)   almanac
14. What camphor is used for – (dictionary)   The Life of a Beaver   thesaurus
15. What land is closest to England – cookbook   (atlas)   spelling workbook
16. How to bake trout – The Life of a Beaver   dictionary   (cookbook)

Page 78

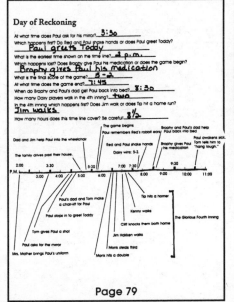

Day of Reckoning

At what time does Paul ask for his mirror? **3:30**

Which happens first? Do Red and Paul shake hands or does Paul greet Toddy?
Paul greets Toddy

What is the earliest time shown on the time line? **2 p.m.**

Which happens last? Does Brophy give Paul his medication or does the game begin?
Brophy gives Paul his medication

What is the final score of the game? **5-2**

At what time does the game end? **7:45**

When do Brophy and Paul's dad get Paul back into bed? **8:30**

How many baseball players walk in the 4th inning? **two**

In the 4th inning which happens first? Does Jim walk or does Tip hit a home run?
Jim walks

How many hours does this time line cover? Be careful! **8½**

[timeline illustration]

Page 79

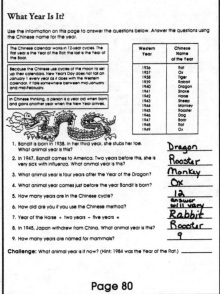

What Year Is It?

Use the information on this page to answer the questions below. Answer the questions using the Chinese name for the year.

The Chinese calendar works in 12-year cycles. The first year is the Year of the Rat. The last is the Year of the Boar.

Because the Chinese use cycles of the moon to set up their calendars, New Year's Day does not fall on January 1 every year as it does with the Western calendar. It falls somewhere between mid-January and mid-February.

In Chinese thinking, a person is a year old when born and gains another year when the New Year arrives.

Western Year	Chinese Name of the Year
1936	Rat
1937	Ox
1938	Tiger
1939	Rabbit
1940	Dragon
1941	Snake
1942	Horse
1943	Sheep
1944	Monkey
1945	Rooster
1946	Dog
1947	Boar
1948	Rat
1949	Ox

1. Bandit is born in 1938. In her third year, she stubs her toe. What animal year is this? — **Dragon**
2. In 1947, Bandit comes to America. Two years before this, she is very sick with influenza. What animal year is this? — **Rooster**
3. What animal year is four years after the Year of the Dragon? — **Monkey**
4. What animal year comes just before the year Bandit is born? — **Ox**
5. How many years are in the Chinese cycle? — **12**
6. How old are you if you use the Chinese method? — **answer will vary**
7. Year of the Horse + two years – five years? — **Rabbit**
8. In 1945, Japan withdrew from China. What animal year is this? — **Rooster**
9. How many years are named for mammals? — **9**

Challenge: What animal year is it now? (Hint: 1984 was the Year of the Rat.)

Page 80

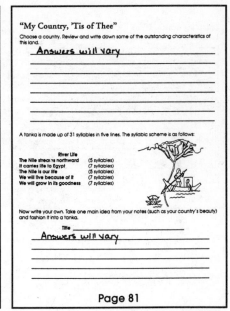

"My Country, 'Tis of Thee"

Choose a country. Review and write down some of the outstanding characteristics of this land.

Answers will vary

A tanka is made up of 31 syllables in five lines. The syllabic scheme is as follows:

River Life
The Nile streams northward (5 syllables)
It carries life to Egypt (7 syllables)
The Nile is our life (5 syllables)
We will live because of it (7 syllables)
We will grow in its goodness (7 syllables)

Now write your own. Take one main idea from your notes (such as your country's beauty) and fashion it into a tanka.

Title
Answers will vary

Page 81

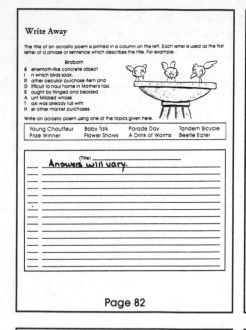

Write Away

The title of an acrostic poem is printed in a column on the left. Each letter is used as the first letter of a phrase or sentence which describes the title. For example:

Birdbath

B ehemoth-like concrete object
I n which birds soak.
R ather peculiar purchase item and
D ifficult to haul home in Mother's taxi.
B ought by fringed and beaded
A unt Mildred whose
T axi was already full with
H er other market purchases.

Write an acrostic poem using one of the topics given here.

Young Chauffeur	Baby Talk	Parade Day	Tandem Bicycle
Prize Winner	Flower Shows	A Drink of Worms	Beetle Eater

(Title)
__Answers will vary.__

Page 82

See the Islands

Research an island of the Caribbean. Then make a travel brochure to convince others that they should visit your island. Include photos or illustrations and descriptions of places to visit, with a map of the island. Last give phone numbers to call for travel information, history and interesting facts.

Tourist Attractions include:

Answers will vary.

COME TO BEAUTIFUL

FOR FURTHER info, call:

Page 83

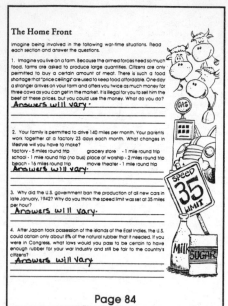

The Home Front

Imagine being involved in the following war-time situations. Read each section and answer the questions.

1. Imagine you live on a farm. Because the armed forces need so much food, farms are asked to produce large quantities. Citizens are only permitted to buy a certain amount of meat. There is such a food shortage that "price ceilings" are used to keep food affordable. One day a stranger arrives on your farm and offers you twice as much money for three cows as you can get in the market. It is illegal for you to sell him the beef at these prices, but you could use the money. What do you do?
Answers will vary.

2. Your family is permitted to drive 140 miles per month. Your parents work together at a factory 23 days each month. What changes in lifestyle will you have to make?
factory - 5 miles round trip   grocery store - 1 mile round trip
school - 1 mile round trip (no bus)   place of worship - 2 miles round trip
beach - 16 miles round trip   movie theater - 1 mile round trip
Answers will vary.

3. Why did the U.S. government ban the production of all new cars in late January, 1942? Why do you think the speed limit was set at 35 miles per hour?
Answers will vary.

4. After Japan took possession of the islands of the East Indies, the U.S. could obtain only about 8% of the natural rubber that it needed. If you were in Congress, what laws would you pass to be certain to have enough rubber for your war industry and still be fair to the country's citizens?
Answers will vary

Page 84

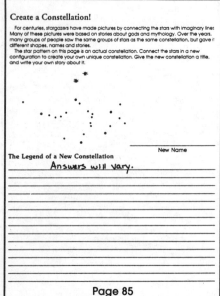

Create a Constellation!

For centuries, stargazers have made pictures by connecting the stars with imaginary lines. Many of these pictures were based on stories about gods and mythology. Over the years, many groups of people saw the same groups of stars as the same constellation, but gave it different shapes, names and stories.

The star pattern on this page is an actual constellation. Connect the stars in a new configuration to create your own unique constellation. Give the new constellation a title, and write your own story about it.

New Name

The Legend of a New Constellation
Answers will vary.

Page 85

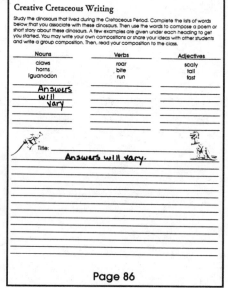

Creative Cretaceous Writing

Study the dinosaurs that lived during the Cretaceous Period. Complete the lists of words below that you associate with these dinosaurs. Then use the words to compose a poem or short story about these dinosaurs. A few examples are given under each heading to get you started. You may write your own compositions or share your ideas with other students and write a group composition. Then, read your composition to the class.

Nouns	Verbs	Adjectives
claws	roar	scaly
horns	bite	tall
Iguanodon	run	fast

Answers will Vary

Title: Answers will vary.

Page 86

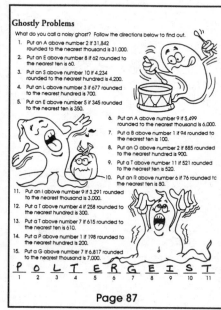

Ghostly Problems

What do you call a noisy ghost? Follow the directions below to find out.

1. Put an A above number 2 if 31,842 rounded to the nearest thousand is 31,000.
2. Put an E above number 8 if 62 rounded to the nearest ten is 60.
3. Put an S above number 10 if 4,234 rounded to the nearest hundred is 4,200.
4. Put an L above number 3 if 677 rounded to the nearest hundred is 700.
5. Put an E above number 5 if 345 rounded to the nearest ten is 350.
6. Put an A above number 9 if 5,499 rounded to the nearest thousand is 6,000.
7. Put a B above number 1 if 94 rounded to the nearest ten is 100.
8. Put an O above number 2 if 885 rounded to the nearest hundred is 900.
9. Put a T above number 11 if 521 rounded to the nearest ten is 520.
10. Put an R above number 6 if 76 rounded to the nearest ten is 80.
11. Put an I above number 9 if 3,291 rounded to the nearest thousand is 3,000.
12. Put a T above number 4 if 258 rounded to the nearest hundred is 300.
13. Put a T above number 7 if 615 rounded to the nearest ten is 610.
14. Put a P above number 1 if 198 rounded to the nearest hundred is 200.
15. Put a G above number 7 if 6,817 rounded to the nearest thousand is 7,000.

P O L T E R G E I S T
1 2 3 4 5 6 7 8 9 10 11

Page 87

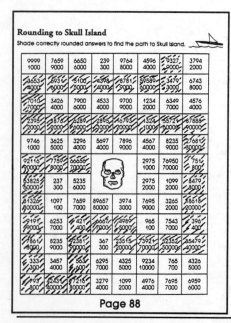

Rounding to Skull Island

Shade correctly rounded answers to find the path to Skull Island.

9999 1000	7659 9000	6650 6000	239 300	9764 8000	4596 4000	9327 9000	3794 2000
3653 4000	693 6000	5100 5000	4398 40000	8781 9000	59589 60000	3479 3000	6743 8000
7010 70000	3426 4000	7900 4000	4533 4000	9700 4000	1234 4000	6349 7000	4576 4000
2395 2000	3876 3000	5284 2000	2895 2000	4679 1000	324 1000	4572 5000	87888 90000
9746 1000	3625 5000	3296 4000	5697 6000	7896 4000	4567 9000	8235 9000	27681 2000
92116 90000	7759 8000	6665 7000			2975 1000	76950 70000	751 800
93825 93000	237 300	5235 6000			2975 2000	1099 2000	8479 8000
81326 80000	1097 100	7659 8000	89657 80000	3974 3000	7695 9000	3265 3000	18618 20000
9191 9000	6253 7000	421 400	6657 7000	4989 5000	965 100	7543 7000	396 400
8861 9000	8235 9000	2381 3000	367 300	23515 23000	73921 74000	52352 52000	85479 80000
333 300	3457 4000	553 500	6295 7000	4325 5000	9234 10000	765 700	4326 5000
8251 800	4243 4000	7218 7000	3279 3000	1099 2000	4976 5000	7695 7000	6959 6000

Page 88

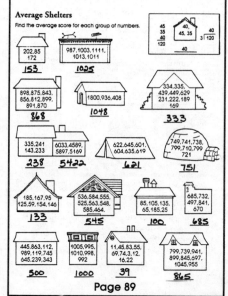

Average Shelters

Find the average score for each group of numbers.

45 35 40 120 / 3 120   40, 35   40   40

202,85 172   __153__

987,1003,1111, 1013,1011   __1025__

898,875,843, 856,812,899, 891,870   __868__

1800,936,408   __1048__

334,335, 439,449,629 231,222,189 169   __333__

335,241 143,233   __238__

6033,4589, 5897,5169   __5422__

622,645,601, 604,635,619   __621__

749,741,738, 799,710,799 721   __751__

185,167,95 125,59,154,146   __133__

536,584,555, 525,563,548, 585,464,   __545__

85,105,135, 65,185,25   __100__

685,732, 497,841, 670   __685__

445,863,112, 989,119,745 645,239,343   __500__

1005,995, 1010,998, 992   __1000__

11,45,83,55, 69,74,3,12, 16,22   __39__

799,739,941, 899,845,697, 1045,955   __865__

Page 89

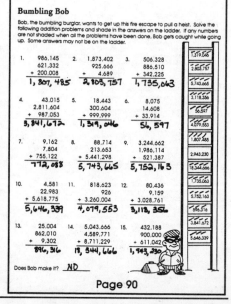

Bumbling Bob

Bob, the bumbling burglar, wants to get up this fire escape to pull a heist. Solve the following addition problems and shade in the answers on the ladder. If any numbers are not shaded when all the problems have been done, Bob gets caught while going up. Some answers may not be on the ladder.

1. 986,145 621,332 + 200,008 = **1,807,485**
2. 1,873,402 925,666 + 4,689 = **2,803,757**
3. 506,328 886,510 + 342,225 = **1,735,063**
4. 43,015 2,811,604 + 987,053 = **3,841,672**
5. 18,443 300,604 + 999,999 = **1,319,046**
6. 8,075 14,608 + 33,914 = **56,597**
7. 9,162 7,804 + 755,122 = **772,088**
8. 88,714 213,653 + 5,441,298 = **5,743,665**
9. 3,244,662 1,986,114 + 521,387 = **5,752,163**
10. 4,581 22,983 + 5,618,775 = **5,646,339**
11. 818,623 926 + 3,260,004 = **4,079,553**
12. 80,436 9,159 + 3,028,761 = **3,118,356**
13. 25,004 862,010 + 9,302 = **896,316**
14. 5,043,666 4,589,771 + 8,711,229 = **18,344,666**
15. 432,188 900,000 + 611,042 = **1,943,230**

Does Bob make it? **NO**

Ladder: 1,319,046 / 2,803,757 / 5,743,665 / 3,118,356 / 56,597 / 4,079,553 / 1,807,485 / 2,943,230 / 18,344,666 / 1,735,063 / 5,752,163 / 896,316 / 3,841,672 / 5,646,339

Page 90

We Can Do It!

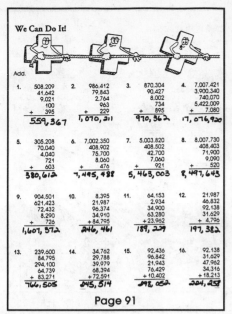

Add.

1. 508,209 + 41,642 + 9,021 + 100 + 395 = **559,367**	2. 986,412 + 79,843 + 2,764 + 963 + 229 = **1,070,211**	3. 870,304 + 90,427 + 8,002 + 734 + 895 = **970,362**	4. 7,007,421 + 3,900,340 + 740,070 + 5,422,009 + 7,080 = **17,076,920**
5. 305,208 + 70,040 + 4,040 + 721 + 603 = **380,612**	6. 7,002,350 + 408,902 + 75,700 + 8,060 + 476 = **7,495,488**	7. 5,003,820 + 408,502 + 42,700 + 7,060 + 921 = **5,463,003**	8. 8,007,730 + 408,403 + 71,900 + 9,090 + 520 = **8,497,643**
9. 904,501 + 621,423 + 72,432 + 8,290 + 726 = **1,607,372**	10. 8,395 + 21,987 + 34,910 + 96,374 + 84,795 = **246,461**	11. 64,153 + 2,934 + 34,900 + 63,280 + 23,962 = **189,229**	12. 21,987 + 46,832 + 92,138 + 31,629 + 4,796 = **197,382**
13. 239,600 + 84,795 + 294,100 + 64,739 + 83,271 = **766,505**	14. 34,762 + 29,788 + 39,979 + 68,394 + 72,591 = **245,514**	15. 92,436 + 96,842 + 21,943 + 76,429 + 10,402 = **298,052**	16. 92,138 + 31,629 + 47,962 + 34,316 + 18,213 = **224,258**

Page 91

TV Time

Tune into this cross number.

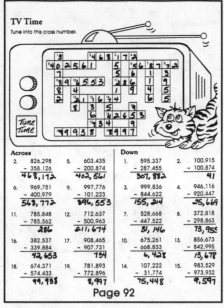

Across

1. 826,298 − 358,126 = **468,172**
5. 603,435 − 200,874 = **402,561**
6. 969,751 − 400,979 = **568,772**
9. 997,776 − 101,223 = **896,553**
11. 785,848 − 785,562 = **286**
12. 712,637 − 500,963 = **211,674**
16. 382,537 − 339,884 = **42,653**
17. 908,465 − 907,731 = **734**
18. 674,371 − 574,433 = **99,938**
19. 781,893 − 772,896 = **8,997**

Down

1. 595,337 − 287,455 = **307,882**
2. 100,915 − 100,874 = **41**
3. 999,836 − 844,622 = **155,214**
4. 946,116 − 920,447 = **25,669**
11. 528,668 − 447,522 = **81,146**
13. 372,818 − 298,863 = **73,955**
15. 675,261 − 668,833 = **6,428**
16. 856,673 − 842,995 = **13,678**
14. 107,222 − 31,774 = **75,448**
15. 983,529 − 973,932 = **9,597**

Page 92

Happy Birthday!

Which cartoon character turned 30 in 1990? To find this answer, solve the following subtraction problems and find the answers in the TV set. Put the letter above the corresponding problem number at the bottom.

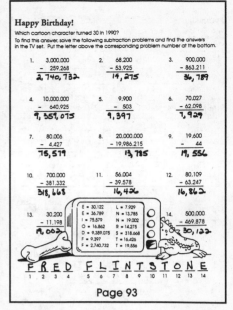

1. 3,000,000 − 259,268 = **2,740,732**
2. 68,200 − 53,925 = **14,275**
3. 900,000 − 863,211 = **36,789**
4. 10,000,000 − 640,925 = **9,359,075**
5. 9,900 − 503 = **9,397**
6. 70,027 − 62,098 = **7,929**
7. 80,006 − 4,427 = **75,579**
8. 20,000,000 − 19,986,215 = **13,785**
9. 19,600 − 44 = **19,556**
10. 700,000 − 381,332 = **318,668**
11. 56,004 − 39,578 = **16,426**
12. 80,109 − 63,247 = **16,862**
13. 30,200 − 11,198 = **19,002**
14. 500,000 − 469,878 = **30,122**

Key: E = 30,122; E = 36,789; I = 75,579; O = 16,862; O = 9,359,075; F = 9,397; F = 2,740,732; L = 7,929; N = 13,785; N = 19,002; R = 14,275; S = 318,668; T = 16,426; T = 19,556

FRED FLINTSTONE

Page 93

Camel Trivia

What kind of camel has two humps? To find out, follow the directions below.

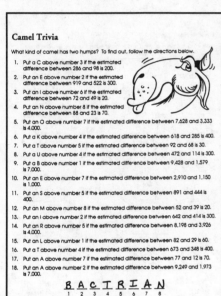

1. Put a C above number 3 if the estimated difference between 286 and 98 is 200.
2. Put an E above number 2 if the estimated difference between 919 and 522 is 300.
3. Put an I above number 6 if the estimated difference between 72 and 49 is 20.
4. Put an N above number 8 if the estimated difference between 88 and 23 is 70.
5. Put an O above number 7 if the estimated difference between 7,628 and 3,333 is 4,000.
6. Put a K above number 4 if the estimated difference between 618 and 285 is 400.
7. Put a T above number 5 if the estimated difference between 92 and 68 is 30.
8. Put a U above number 4 if the estimated difference between 472 and 114 is 300.
9. Put a B above number 1 if the estimated difference between 9,428 and 1,579 is 7,000.
10. Put an E above number 7 if the estimated difference between 2,910 and 1,150 is 1,000.
11. Put an S above number 5 if the estimated difference between 891 and 444 is 400.
12. Put an M above number 8 if the estimated difference between 52 and 39 is 20.
13. Put an I above number 2 if the estimated difference between 642 and 414 is 300.
14. Put an R above number 5 if the estimated difference between 8,198 and 3,926 is 4,000.
15. Put an L above number 1 if the estimated difference between 82 and 29 is 60.
16. Put a T above number 4 if the estimated difference between 673 and 348 is 400.
17. Put an A above number 7 if the estimated difference between 77 and 12 is 70.
18. Put an A above number 2 if the estimated difference between 9,249 and 1,973 is 7,000.

B A C T R I A N

Page 94

Wah! Wah!

Solve the following multiplication problems. Connect the correct problems to make a path from the baby to her bottle.

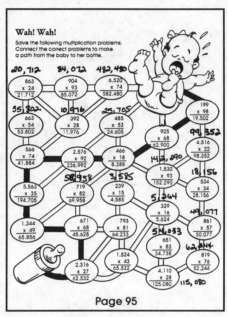

20,712 84,072 482,480
55,802 10,976 25,705
58,958 3,585 99,352
18,156 5,264 49,077
54,033 62,244 115,080

863 × 24 = 20,712
904 × 93 = 84,072
6,520 × 74 = 482,480
663 × 54 = 53,802
392 × 28 = 11,976
485 × 53 = 24,605
199 × 98 = 19,502
566 × 74 = 41,884
2,576 × 92 = 236,992
466 × 18 = 8,388
925 × 68 = 62,900
4,516 × 22 = 98,352
5,563 × 35 = 194,705
719 × 82 = 69,958
239 × 15 = 4,585
1,530 × 93 = 152,290
534 × 34 = 28,156
1,344 × 49 = 65,856
671 × 68 = 45,628
793 × 81 = 64,233
329 × 16 = 5,624
861 × 57 = 50,077
651 × 83 = 34,738
819 × 76 = 52,244
2,316 × 27 = 62,532
1,524 × 43 = 65,532
4,110 × 28 = 125,080

Page 95

Puzzling Cross Number

Dive into this cross number!

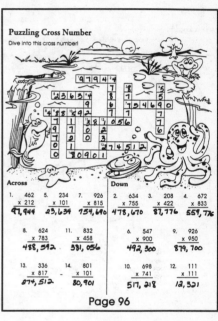

Across

1. 462 × 212 = **97,944**
5. 234 × 815 = **23,634**
7. 926 × 815 = **754,690**
8. 624 × 783 = **488,592**
11. 832 × 458 = **381,056**
13. 336 × 817 = **274,512**
14. 801 × 101 = **80,901**

Down

2. 634 × 755 = **478,670**
3. 208 × 422 = **87,776**
4. 672 × 833 = **559,776**
7. 547 × 900 = **492,300**
9. 926 × 950 = **879,700**
10. 698 × 741 = **517,218**
12. 111 × 111 = **12,321**

Page 96

Happy Remainders

Work problems. Give the clowns with remainders a happy face ☺. Give the clowns without remainders a sad face ☹.

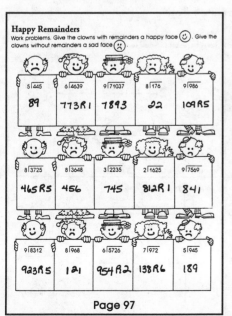

5)445 = **89**
6)4639 = **773 R1**
9)71037 = **7893**
8)176 = **22**
9)986 = **109 R5**
8)3725 = **465 R5**
8)3648 = **456**
3)2235 = **745**
2)1625 = **812 R1**
9)7569 = **841**
9)8312 = **923 R5**
8)968 = **121**
6)5726 = **954 R2**
7)972 = **138 R6**
5)945 = **189**

Page 97

Mousy Maze

Lead the mouse to the trap by connecting the quotients in order starting at 795.

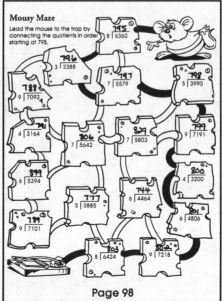

8)6360 = 795
3)2388 = 796
7)5579 = 797
5)3990 = 798
9)7092 = 788
4)3164 = 791
7)5642 = 806
7)5803 = 829
9)7191 = 799
9)5394 = 599
4)3200 = 800
5)3885 = 777
6)4464 = 744
9)7101 = 789
8)6424 = 803
9)7218 = 802
9)4806 = 801

Page 98

Divisors in the Clouds

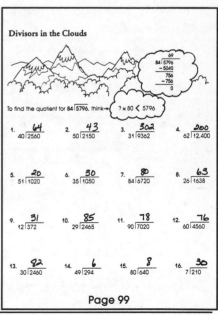

To find the quotient for 84)5796, think ► ? × 80 < 5796

1. 40)2560 = **64**
2. 50)2150 = **43**
3. 31)9362 = **302**
4. 62)12,400 = **200**
5. 51)1020 = **20**
6. 35)1050 = **30**
7. 84)6720 = **80**
8. 26)1638 = **63**
9. 12)372 = **31**
10. 29)2465 = **85**
11. 90)7020 = **78**
12. 60)4560 = **76**
13. 30)2460 = **82**
14. 49)294 = **6**
15. 80)640 = **8**
16. 7)210 = **30**

Page 99

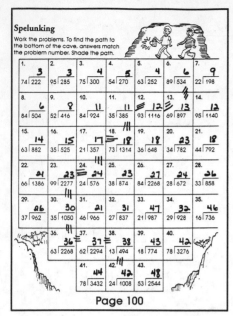

Spelunking

Work the problems. To find the path to the bottom of the cave, answers match the problem number. Shade the path.

Page 100

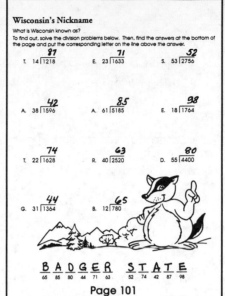

Wisconsin's Nickname

What is Wisconsin known as?
To find out, solve the division problems below. Then, find the answers at the bottom of the page and put the corresponding letter on the line above the answer.

B A D G E R   S T A T E
65 85 80 44 71 63   52 74 42 87 98

Page 101

Prehistoric Problems

Work the problems. Shade in the letters of those problems that have remainders to reveal the "ancient one."

Page 102

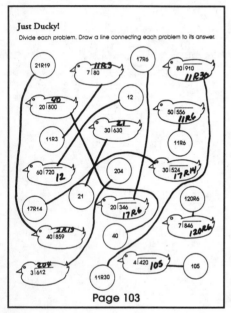

Just Ducky!

Divide each problem. Draw a line connecting each problem to its answer.

Page 103

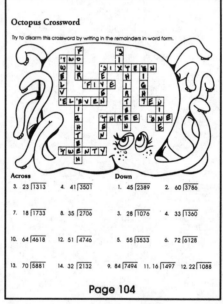

Octopus Crossword

Try to disarm this crossword by writing in the remainders in word form.

Across
3. 23⟌1313   4. 41⟌3501
7. 18⟌1733   8. 35⟌2706
10. 64⟌4618 12. 51⟌4746
13. 70⟌5881 14. 32⟌2132

Down
1. 45⟌2389   2. 60⟌3786
5. 28⟌1076   4. 33⟌1360
5. 55⟌3533   6. 72⟌6128
9. 84⟌7494 11. 16⟌1497 12. 22⟌1088

Page 104

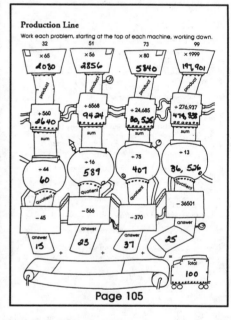

Production Line

Work each problem, starting at the top of each machine, working down.

Page 105

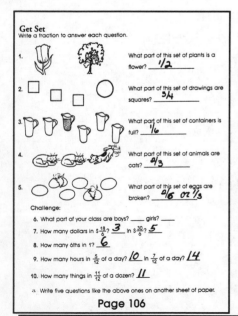

Get Set

Write a fraction to answer each question.

1. What part of this set of plants is a flower? 1/2
2. What part of this set of drawings are squares? 3/4
3. What part of this set of containers is full? 1/6
4. What part of this set of animals are cats? 4/3
5. What part of this set of eggs are broken? 2/6 or 1/3

Challenge:
6. What part of your class are boys? ___ girls? ___
7. How many dollars in $18/6? 3 In $30/6? 5
8. How many 6ths in 1? 6
9. How many hours in 5/12 of a day? 10 In 7/12 of a day? 14
10. How many things in 11/12 of a dozen? 11

☆ Write five questions like the above ones on another sheet of paper.

Page 106

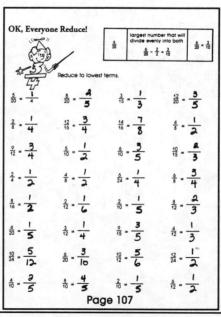

OK, Everyone Reduce!

Reduce to lowest terms.

Page 107

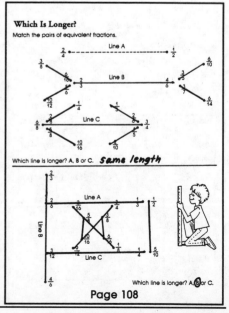

Which Is Longer?

Match the pairs of equivalent fractions.

Which line is longer? A, B or C. same length

Which line is longer? A, B or C.

Page 108

Daily Learning Drills Grade 5

Going for the Gold
Change fractions to mixed numbers. Shade in each answer to find the path to the pot of gold.

Page 109

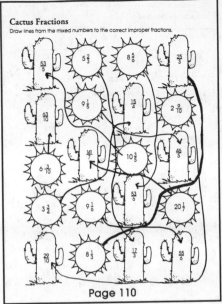

Cactus Fractions
Draw lines from the mixed numbers to the correct improper fractions.

Page 110

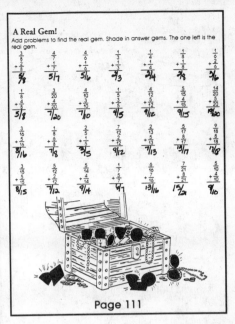

A Real Gem!
Add problems to find the real gem. Shade in answer gems. The one left is the real gem.

Page 111

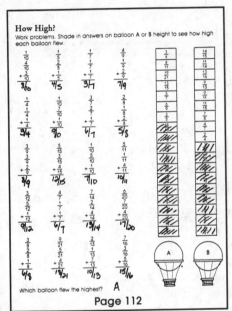

How High?
Work problems. Shade in answers on balloon A or B height to see how high each balloon flew.

Which balloon flew the highest? A

Page 112

Bat Adding
Don't let this crossword puzzle drive you batty!

Across

Down

Page 113

Climbing to New Heights

Page 114

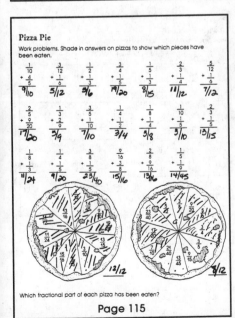

Pizza Pie
Work problems. Shade in answers on pizzas to show which pieces have been eaten.

Which fractional part of each pizza has been eaten?

Page 115

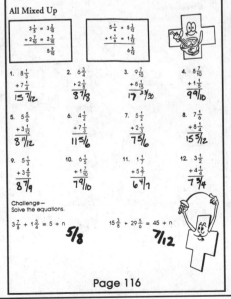

All Mixed Up

Challenge—
Solve the equations.

Page 116

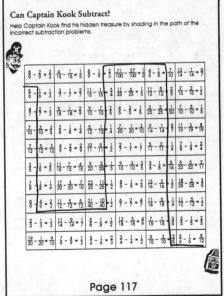

Can Captain Kook Subtract?
Help Captain Kook find his hidden treasure by shading in the path of the incorrect subtraction problems.

Page 117

©McGraw-Hill Children's Publishing

302

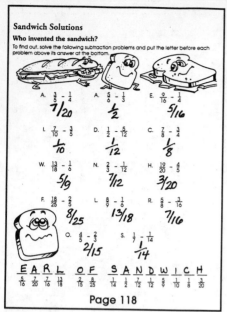

Sandwich Solutions

Who invented the sandwich?

To find out, solve the following subtraction problems and put the letter before each problem above its answer at the bottom.

A. $\frac{3}{5} - \frac{1}{4}$ = $\frac{7}{20}$
A. $\frac{5}{6} - \frac{1}{3}$ = $\frac{1}{2}$
E. $\frac{9}{16} - \frac{1}{4}$ = $\frac{5}{16}$

I. $\frac{7}{10} - \frac{3}{5}$ = $\frac{1}{10}$
D. $\frac{1}{2} - \frac{5}{12}$ = $\frac{1}{12}$
C. $\frac{7}{8} - \frac{3}{4}$ = $\frac{1}{8}$

W. $\frac{13}{18} - \frac{1}{6}$ = $\frac{5}{9}$
N. $\frac{2}{3} - \frac{1}{12}$ = $\frac{7}{12}$
H. $\frac{19}{20} - \frac{4}{5}$ = $\frac{3}{20}$

F. $\frac{18}{25} - \frac{2}{5}$ = $\frac{8}{25}$
L. $\frac{8}{9} - \frac{1}{6}$ = $\frac{13}{18}$
R. $\frac{5}{8} - \frac{3}{16}$ = $\frac{7}{16}$

O. $\frac{4}{5} - \frac{2}{3}$ = $\frac{2}{15}$
S. $\frac{1}{7} - \frac{1}{14}$ = $\frac{1}{14}$

E A R L   O F   S A N D W I C H
$\frac{5}{16}$ $\frac{7}{20}$ $\frac{1}{10}$ $\frac{13}{18}$ | $\frac{8}{25}$ $\frac{3}{20}$ | $\frac{1}{14}$ $\frac{1}{2}$ $\frac{7}{12}$ $\frac{1}{12}$ $\frac{5}{9}$ $\frac{1}{8}$ $\frac{3}{20}$

Page 118

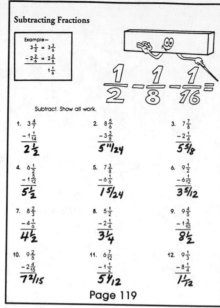

Subtracting Fractions

Example—
$3\frac{1}{2} = 3\frac{3}{6}$
$-2\frac{1}{3} = 2\frac{2}{6}$
$1\frac{1}{6}$

$\frac{1}{2} - \frac{1}{8} - \frac{1}{16} =$

Subtract. Show all work.

1. $3\frac{4}{7}$
$-1\frac{1}{14}$
$2\frac{1}{2}$

2. $8\frac{5}{8}$
$-3\frac{3}{6}$
$5\frac{11}{24}$

3. $7\frac{7}{8}$
$-2\frac{1}{4}$
$5\frac{5}{8}$

4. $6\frac{1}{2}$
$-1\frac{1}{2}$
$5\frac{1}{2}$

5. $7\frac{3}{8}$
$-6\frac{1}{6}$
$1\frac{5}{24}$

6. $9\frac{1}{2}$
$-6\frac{1}{12}$
$3\frac{5}{12}$

7. $8\frac{2}{3}$
$-4\frac{1}{6}$
$4\frac{1}{2}$

8. $5\frac{1}{2}$
$-2\frac{1}{4}$
$3\frac{1}{4}$

9. $9\frac{4}{5}$
$-1\frac{3}{10}$
$8\frac{1}{2}$

10. $9\frac{2}{3}$
$-2\frac{4}{15}$
$7\frac{2}{15}$

11. $6\frac{7}{12}$
$-1\frac{1}{6}$
$5\frac{4}{12}$

12. $9\frac{1}{3}$
$-8\frac{1}{4}$
$1\frac{1}{12}$

Page 119

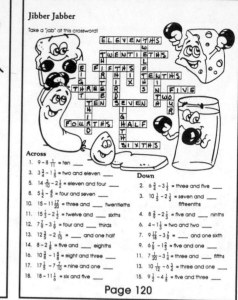

Jibber Jabber

Take a 'jab' at this crossword!

ELEVENTHS
TWENTIETHS
FIFTHS TENTHS
THREE
TEN SEVEN FIVE
THIRD
FOURTHS HALF
SIXTHS

Across

1. $9 - 8\frac{1}{11}$ = ten _____
3. $3\frac{1}{4} - 1\frac{3}{8}$ = two and eleven _____
5. $14\frac{1}{10} - 2\frac{1}{5}$ = eleven and four _____
8. $5\frac{1}{2} - \frac{9}{16}$ = four and seven _____
10. $15 - 11\frac{4}{20}$ = three and _____ twentieths
11. $15\frac{1}{2} - 2\frac{1}{3}$ = twelve and _____ sixths
12. $7\frac{5}{6} - 3\frac{1}{2}$ = four and _____ thirds
13. $12\frac{3}{5} - 2\frac{1}{10}$ = _____ and one half
14. $8 - 2\frac{1}{8}$ = five and _____ eighths
16. $10\frac{3}{8} - 1\frac{3}{5}$ = eight and three _____
17. $17\frac{1}{3} - 7\frac{2}{11}$ = nine and one _____
18. $18 - 11\frac{1}{6}$ = six and five _____

Down

2. $6\frac{3}{4} - 3\frac{1}{5}$ = three and five _____
3. $10\frac{1}{3} - 2\frac{2}{3}$ = seven and _____ fifteenths
4. $8\frac{2}{9} - 2\frac{1}{3}$ = five and _____ ninths
6. $4 - 1\frac{1}{3}$ = two and two _____
7. $9\frac{7}{18} - 3\frac{2}{9}$ = _____ and one sixth
9. $6\frac{1}{2} - 1\frac{1}{5}$ = five and one _____
11. $7\frac{3}{10} - 3\frac{1}{4}$ = three and _____ fifths
13. $10\frac{1}{2} - 6\frac{3}{4}$ = three and one _____
15. $9\frac{1}{2} - 4\frac{1}{5}$ = five and three _____

Page 120

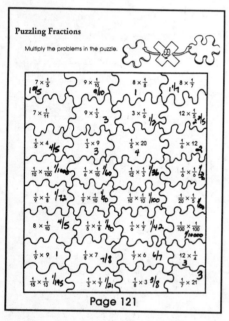

Puzzling Fractions

Multiply the problems in the puzzle.

$7 \times \frac{1}{5}$ = $1\frac{2}{5}$
$9 \times \frac{1}{10}$ = $\frac{9}{10}$
$8 \times \frac{1}{8}$ = 1
$8 \times \frac{1}{7}$ = $1\frac{1}{7}$

$7 \times \frac{1}{11}$
$9 \times \frac{1}{3}$ = 3
$3 \times \frac{1}{6}$ = $\frac{1}{2}$
$12 \times \frac{1}{5}$ = $2\frac{2}{5}$

$\frac{1}{5} \times 4$ = $\frac{4}{5}$
$\frac{1}{3} \times 9$ = 3
$\frac{1}{5} \times 20$ = 4
$\frac{1}{12} \times 12$ = 2

$\frac{1}{10} \times 100$ = 10
$\frac{1}{6} \times \frac{1}{10}$ = $\frac{1}{60}$
$\frac{1}{12} \times \frac{1}{3}$ = $\frac{1}{36}$
$\frac{1}{6} \times \frac{1}{2}$ = $\frac{1}{12}$

$\frac{1}{7} \times \frac{1}{12}$
$\frac{1}{10} \times \frac{1}{10}$ = $\frac{1}{100}$

$8 \times \frac{1}{10}$ = $\frac{4}{5}$
$\frac{1}{5} \times \frac{1}{8}$ = $\frac{1}{40}$
$\frac{1}{6} \times \frac{1}{7}$ = $\frac{1}{42}$
$\frac{1}{100} \times \frac{1}{100}$ = $\frac{1}{10000}$

$\frac{1}{9} \times 9$ = 1
$\frac{1}{8} \times 7$ = $\frac{7}{8}$
$\frac{1}{9} \times 6$ = $\frac{6}{7}$
$12 \times \frac{1}{4}$ = 3

$\frac{1}{15} \times \frac{1}{13}$ = $\frac{1}{195}$
$\frac{1}{3} \times \frac{1}{7}$ = $\frac{1}{21}$
$\frac{1}{8} \times 3$ = $\frac{3}{8}$
$\frac{1}{7} \times 21$ = 3

Page 121

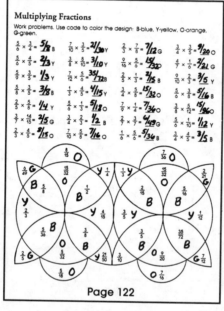

Multiplying Fractions

Work problems. Use code to color the design: B-blue, Y-yellow, O-orange, G-green.

$\frac{5}{6} \times \frac{3}{4}$ = $\frac{5}{8}$ B
$\frac{7}{10} \times \frac{3}{7}$ = $\frac{21}{30}$ Y
$\frac{7}{8} \times \frac{1}{6}$ = $\frac{7}{12}$ G
$\frac{3}{4} \times \frac{3}{5}$ = $\frac{9}{20}$ O

$\frac{5}{6} \times \frac{4}{5}$ = $\frac{2}{3}$ Y
$\frac{3}{8} \times \frac{4}{5}$ = $\frac{3}{10}$ O
$\frac{6}{10} \times \frac{5}{6}$ = $\frac{1}{2}$ O
$\frac{4}{7} \times \frac{1}{6}$ = $\frac{2}{21}$ G

$\frac{5}{6} \times \frac{1}{2}$ = $\frac{5}{12}$ Y
$\frac{7}{12} \times \frac{3}{5}$ = $\frac{35}{72}$ B
$\frac{3}{5} \times \frac{1}{2}$ = $\frac{2}{15}$ B
$\frac{9}{10} \times \frac{3}{5}$ = $\frac{3}{5}$ Y

$\frac{5}{8} \times \frac{3}{5}$ = $\frac{3}{8}$ B
$\frac{1}{3} \times \frac{4}{5}$ = $\frac{4}{15}$ Y
$\frac{5}{8} \times \frac{3}{4}$ = $\frac{15}{32}$ O
$\frac{3}{4} \times \frac{3}{4}$ = $\frac{9}{16}$ B

$\frac{2}{3} \times \frac{4}{5}$ = $\frac{4}{5}$ Y
$\frac{5}{6} \times \frac{3}{5}$ = $\frac{5}{18}$ O
$\frac{7}{9} \times \frac{1}{4}$ = $\frac{7}{36}$ O
$\frac{5}{8} \times \frac{3}{4}$ = $\frac{15}{96}$ O

$\frac{4}{7} \times \frac{14}{15}$ = $\frac{2}{5}$ G
$\frac{3}{4} \times \frac{1}{2}$ = $\frac{2}{5}$ B
$\frac{5}{7} \times \frac{2}{7}$ = $\frac{4}{49}$ O
$\frac{3}{4} \times \frac{1}{10}$ = $\frac{1}{12}$ B

$\frac{2}{3} \times \frac{1}{3}$ = $\frac{2}{15}$ O
$\frac{7}{12} \times \frac{5}{6}$ = $\frac{7}{16}$ G
$\frac{5}{6} \times \frac{1}{3}$ = $\frac{5}{36}$ Y
$\frac{3}{4} \times \frac{3}{5}$ = $\frac{3}{5}$ B

Page 122

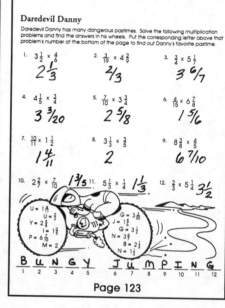

Daredevil Danny

Daredevil Danny has many dangerous pastimes. Solve the following multiplication problems and find the answers in his wheels. Put the corresponding letter above that problem's number at the bottom of the page to find out Danny's favorite pastime.

1. $3\frac{1}{2} \times \frac{4}{6}$ = $2\frac{1}{3}$
2. $\frac{5}{19} \times 4\frac{2}{9}$ = $2/3$
3. $\frac{3}{4} \times 5\frac{1}{7}$ = $3\frac{6}{7}$

4. $4\frac{1}{5} \times \frac{3}{4}$ = $3\frac{3}{20}$
5. $\frac{7}{10} \times 3\frac{3}{4}$ = $2\frac{5}{8}$
6. $\frac{4}{15} \times 6\frac{7}{8}$ = $1\frac{5}{6}$

7. $\frac{10}{11} \times 1\frac{1}{2}$ = $1\frac{4}{11}$
8. $3\frac{1}{3} \times \frac{3}{5}$ = 2
9. $8\frac{3}{8} \times \frac{4}{5}$ = $6\frac{7}{10}$

10. $2\frac{5}{7} \times \frac{?}{?}$ = $1\frac{3}{5}$
11. $5\frac{1}{3} \times \frac{1}{3}$ = $1\frac{1}{3}$
12. $\frac{2}{3} \times 5\frac{1}{4}$ = $3\frac{1}{2}$

U = $1\frac{4}{5}$
U = $\frac{2}{3}$
Y = $2\frac{5}{8}$
P = $6\frac{7}{10}$
M = 2
G = $3\frac{6}{7}$
J = $2\frac{1}{3}$
N = $3\frac{2}{3}$
N = $1\frac{1}{3}$

B U N G Y   J U M P I N G
1 2 3 4 5   6 7 8 9 10 11 12

Page 123

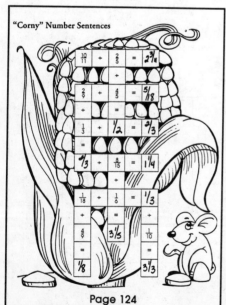

"Corny" Number Sentences

$\frac{10}{11} + \frac{2}{5}$ = $2\frac{7}{11}$

$\frac{2}{9} + \frac{4}{5}$ = $\frac{5}{18}$

$\frac{1}{3} + \frac{1}{2}$ =

$\frac{1}{3} + \frac{8}{15}$ = $1\frac{1}{4}$

$\frac{1}{18} + \frac{1}{6}$ = $\frac{1}{3}$

$\frac{4}{9}$

$3\frac{1}{5}$

$\frac{1}{10}$

=

$\frac{1}{8}$

$3\frac{1}{3}$

Page 124

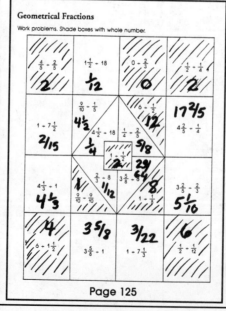

Geometrical Fractions

Work problems. Shade boxes with whole number.

$\frac{4}{5} \div \frac{2}{5}$ = 2
$1\frac{1}{2} \div 18$ = $\frac{1}{12}$
$0 \div \frac{2}{3}$ = 0
$\frac{1}{2} \div \frac{1}{4}$ = 2

$\frac{9}{10} \div \frac{1}{5}$ = $4\frac{1}{2}$
$6 - \frac{1}{2}$ = 12
$17\frac{2}{5}$

$1 \div 7\frac{1}{2}$ = $\frac{2}{15}$
$4\frac{1}{2} \div 18$ = $\frac{1}{4}$
$\frac{1}{4} \div \frac{1}{2}$ = $\frac{1}{2}$
$\frac{5}{8}$
$4\frac{2}{5} \div \frac{1}{4}$

$\frac{2}{3} \div 8$ = $\frac{29}{64}$

$4\frac{1}{3} \div 1$ = $4\frac{1}{3}$
$\frac{3}{8} \div \frac{1}{3}$ = $1\frac{1}{8}$
$3\frac{2}{3} \div \frac{2}{3}$ = $5\frac{1}{10}$
$\frac{9}{10} \div \frac{1}{10}$ = $1\frac{1}{12}$

14
$3\frac{5}{8}$
$3\frac{1}{22}$
6

$6 - 1\frac{1}{2}$
$3\frac{5}{8} \div 1$
$1 \div 7\frac{1}{3}$
$\frac{1}{2} \div \frac{1}{12}$

Page 125

A Mere Fraction

Work problems. Arrange your work this way:

$6 \div \frac{1}{4} = \frac{6}{1} \times \frac{4}{1} = \frac{24}{1} = 24$

$7 \div \frac{1}{3}$ = 21
$8 \div \frac{1}{2}$ = 16

$16 \div \frac{1}{3}$ = 48
$6 \div \frac{1}{2}$ = 12

$5 \div \frac{1}{6}$ = 30
$18 \div \frac{1}{7}$ = 126

$8 \div \frac{1}{5}$ = 40
$7 \div \frac{1}{9}$ = 63

$15 \div \frac{1}{6}$ = 90
$2\frac{1}{2} \div \frac{1}{2}$ = 5

$3\frac{1}{9} \div \frac{1}{3}$ = $9\frac{1}{3}$
$5\frac{1}{4} \div \frac{3}{8}$ = 14

Page 126

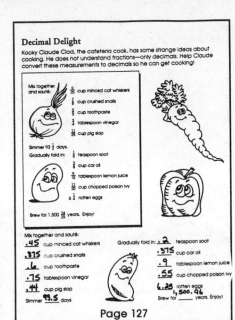

Decimal Delight

Kooky Claude Clod, the cafeteria cook, has some strange ideas about cooking. He does not understand fractions—only decimals. Help Claude convert these measurements to decimals so he can get cooking!

Mix together and sauté:
- cup minced cat whiskers
- cup crushed snails
- cup toothpaste
- tablespoon vinegar
- cup pig slop

Simmer 93½ days.

Gradually fold in:
- teaspoon soot
- cup car oil
- tablespoon lemon juice
- cup chopped poison ivy
- 6¼ rotten eggs

Brew for 1,500 years. Enjoy!

Mix together and sauté:
- .45 cup minced cat whiskers
- .375 cup crushed snails
- .6 cup toothpaste
- .75 tablespoon vinegar
- .44 cup pig slop
- Simmer 93.5 days

Gradually fold in:
- .2 teaspoon soot
- .375 cup car oil
- .9 tablespoon lemon juice
- .55 cup chopped poison ivy
- 6.25 rotten eggs
- Brew for 1,500.96 years. Enjoy!

Page 127

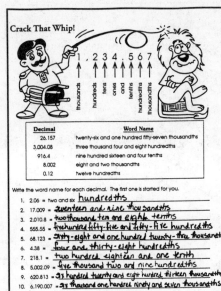

Crack That Whip!

thousands, hundreds, tens, ones and, tenths, hundredths, thousandths

Decimal	Word Name
26.157	twenty-six and one hundred fifty-seven thousandths
3,004.08	three thousand four and eight hundredths
916.4	nine hundred sixteen and four tenths
8.002	eight and two thousandths
0.12	twelve hundredths

Write the word name for each decimal. The first one is started for you.

1. 2.06 = two and six _hundredths_
2. 17.009 = _seventeen and nine thousandths_
3. 2,010.8 = _two thousand ten and eight tenths_
4. 555.55 = _five hundred fifty-five and fifty-five hundredths_
5. 68.123 = _sixty-eight and one hundred twenty-three thousandths_
6. 4.38 = _four and thirty-eight hundredths_
7. 218.1 = _two hundred eighteen and one tenth_
8. 5,002.09 = _five thousand two and nine hundredths_
9. 620.813 = _six hundred twenty and eight hundred thirteen thousandths_
10. 6,190.007 = _six thousand one hundred ninety and seven thousandths_

Page 128

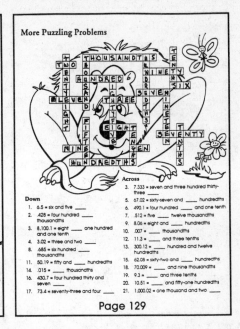

More Puzzling Problems

Across
3. 7.333 = seven and three hundred thirty-three _____
5. 67.02 = sixty-seven and _____ hundredths
6. 490.1 = four hundred _____ and one tenth
7. .512 = five _____ twelve thousandths
9. 8.06 = eight and _____ hundredths
10. .007 = _____ thousandths
12. 11.3 = _____ and three tenths
13. 300.12 = _____ hundred and twelve hundredths
15. 62.08 = sixty-two and _____ hundredths
18. 70.009 = _____ and nine thousandths
19. 9.3 = _____ and three tenths
20. 10.51 = _____ and fifty-one hundredths
21. 1,000.02 = one thousand and two _____

Down
1. .65 = six and five _____
2. .428 = four hundred _____ thousandths
3. 8,100.1 = eight _____ one hundred and one tenth
4. 3.02 = three and two _____
5. .685 = six hundred _____ thousandths
11. 50.19 = fifty and _____ hundredths
14. .015 = _____ thousandths
16. 430.7 = four hundred thirty and seven _____
17. 73.4 = seventy-three and four _____

Page 129

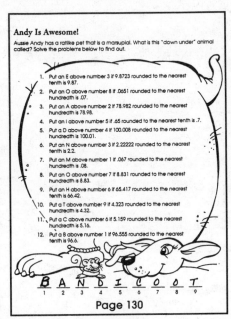

Andy Is Awesome!

Aussie Andy has a ratlike pet that is a marsupial. What is this "down under" animal called? Solve the problems below to find out.

1. Put an E above number 3 if 9.8723 rounded to the nearest tenth is 9.87.
2. Put an O above number 8 if .0651 rounded to the nearest hundredth is .07.
3. Put an A above number 2 if 78.982 rounded to the nearest hundredth is 78.98.
4. Put an I above number 5 if .65 rounded to the nearest tenth is .7.
5. Put a D above number 4 if 100.008 rounded to the nearest hundredth is 100.01.
6. Put an N above number 3 if 2.22222 rounded to the nearest tenth is 2.2.
7. Put an M above number 1 if .067 rounded to the nearest hundredth is .08.
8. Put an O above number 7 if 8.831 rounded to the nearest hundredth is 8.83.
9. Put an H above number 6 if 65.417 rounded to the nearest tenth is 66.42.
10. Put a T above number 9 if 4.323 rounded to the nearest hundredth is 4.32.
11. Put a C above number 6 if 5.159 rounded to the nearest hundredth is 5.16.
12. Put a B above number 1 if 96.555 rounded to the nearest tenth is 96.6.

B A N D I C O O T
1 2 3 4 5 6 7 8 9

Page 130

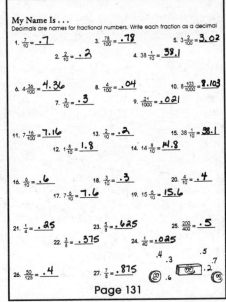

My Name Is . . .

Decimals are names for fractional numbers. Write each fraction as a decimal.

1. 7/10 = .7
2. 2/10 = .2
3. 78/100 = .78
4. 38 1/10 = 38.1
5. 3 2/100 = 3.02
6. 4 36/100 = 4.36
7. 3/10 = .3
8. 4/100 = .04
9. 21/1000 = .021
10. 8 103/1000 = 8.103
11. 7 16/100 = 7.16
12. 1 8/10 = 1.8
13. 2/10 = .2
14. 14 8/10 = 14.8
15. 38 1/10 = 38.1
16. 6/10 = .6
17. 7 6/10 = 7.6
18. 3/10 = .3
19. 15 6/10 = 15.6
20. 4/10 = .4
21. 1/4 = .25
22. 3/8 = .375
23. 5/8 = .625
24. 1/40 = .025
25. 200/400 = .5
26. 50/125 = .4
27. 7/8 = .875

Page 131

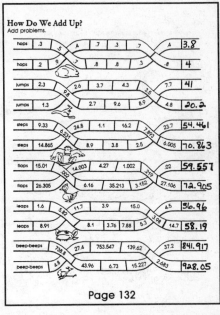

How Do We Add Up?

Add problems.

hops	.3	.5	.1	.3	.7		3.8
hops	.2		.8	.3	.3	.8	4
jumps	2.3		2.6	3.7	4.3		41
jumps	1.3		9.6	8.9		4.8	20.2
steps	9.33		24.8	1.1	16.2	23.7	54.461
steps	14.865		8.9	3.8	2.5	6.005	70.863
flaps	15.01	14.003	4.27	1.002	.02		59.557
flaps	26.305		6.16	35.213	3.152	27.106	72.905
leaps	1.6		11.7	3.9	15.0	4.5	56.96
leaps	8.91		8.1	3.76	7.88	14.7	58.19
beep-beeps		27.4	753.547	139.62	37.2		841.917
beep-beeps		43.96	6.73	15.227	2.683		928.05

Page 132

Blast Off!

Have a blast with this crossnumber! Hint: Decimal points take up their own square.

Down
1. 33.333 + .896 = 34.229
2. 2.587 + 3.191 = 5.778
3. 5.78 + 1.09 = 6.87
7. 22.05 + 15.91 = 37.96
9. 2.057 + .008 = 2.065
10. .531 + .19 = .721
11. 7.852 + 1.489 = 9.341
13. 3.012 + 1.025 = 4.037

Across
3. 1.068 + 5.086 = 6.154
4. .444 + .53 = .974
5. 521.8 + 312.4 = 834.2
6. 7.32 + .99 = 8.31
8. .502 + .191 = .693
12. 40.389 + 38.076 = 78.465
14. 270.85 + 90.57 = 361.42
15. .033 + .066 = .099
16. 8.749 + 3.388 = 12.137

Page 133

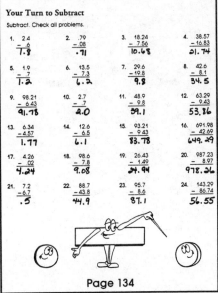

Your Turn to Subtract

Subtract. Check all problems.

1. 2.4 − .6 = 1.8
2. .79 − .08 = .71
3. 18.24 − 7.56 = 10.68
4. 38.57 − 16.83 = 21.74
5. 1.9 − .7 = 1.2
6. 13.5 − 7.3 = 6.2
7. 29.6 − 19.8 = 9.8
8. 42.6 − 8.1 = 34.5
9. 98.21 − 6.43 = 91.78
10. 2.7 − .7 = 2.0
11. 48.9 − 9.8 = 39.1
12. 63.29 − 9.43 = 53.86
13. 6.34 − 4.57 = 1.77
14. 12.6 − 6.5 = 6.1
15. 93.21 − 42.69 = 83.78 [*see note: 9.43]
16. 691.98 − 42.69 = 649.29
17. 4.26 − .02 = 4.24
18. 98.6 − 7.8 = 9.08 [90.8]
19. 26.43 − 1.49 = 24.94
20. 987.23 − 8.97 = 978.26
21. 7.2 − 6.7 = .5
22. 88.7 − 43.8 = 44.9
23. 95.7 − 8.6 = 87.1
24. 143.29 − 86.74 = 56.55

Page 134

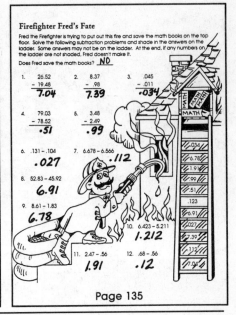

Firefighter Fred's Fate

Fred the Firefighter is trying to put out this fire and save the math books on the top floor. Solve the following subtraction problems and shade in the answers on the ladder. Some answers may not be on the ladder. At the end, if any numbers on the ladder are not shaded, Fred doesn't make it.

Does Fred save the math books? NO

1. 26.52 − 19.48 = 7.04
2. 8.37 − .98 = 7.39
3. .045 − .011 = .034
4. 79.03 − 78.52 = .51
5. 3.48 − 2.49 = .99
6. .131 − .104 = .027
7. 6.678 − 6.566 = .112
8. 52.83 − 45.92 = 6.91
9. 8.61 − 1.83 = 6.78
10. 6.423 − 5.211 = 1.212
11. 2.47 − .56 = 1.91
12. .68 − .56 = .12

Ladder values: .034, 6.78, 1.91, .99, .51, .123, 6.91, .027, 7.39, .112, 7.04

Page 135

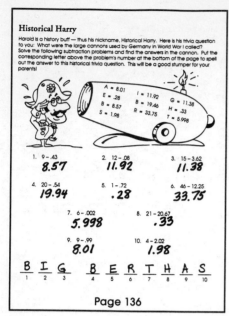

Historical Harry

Harold is a history buff — thus his nickname, Historical Harry. Here is his trivia question to you: What were the large cannons used by Germany in World War I called? Solve the following subtraction problems and find the answers in the cannon. Put the corresponding letter above the problems number at the bottom of the page to spell out the answer to this historical trivia question. This will be a good stumper for your parents!

A = 8.01
E = .28
B = 8.57
S = 1.98
I = 11.92
B = 19.46
R = 33.75
G = 11.38
H = .33
T = 5.998

1. 9 - .43 = **8.57**
2. 12 - .08 = **11.92**
3. 15 - 3.62 = **11.38**
4. 20 - .54 = **19.94**
5. 1 - .72 = **.28**
6. 46 - 12.25 = **33.75**
7. 6 - .002 = **5.998**
8. 21 - 20.67 = **.33**
9. 9 - .99 = **8.01**
10. 4 - 2.02 = **1.98**

B I G   B E R T H A S
1 2 3   4 5 6 7 8 9 10

Page 136

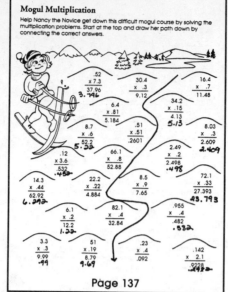

Mogul Multiplication

Help Nancy the Novice get down this difficult mogul course by solving the multiplication problems. Start at the top and draw her path down by connecting the correct answers.

Page 137

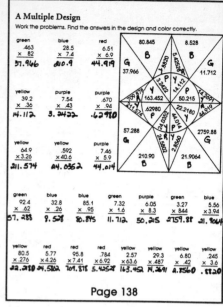

A Multiple Design

Work the problems. Find the answers in the design and color correctly.

green	blue	red
.463 × .82 = **37.966**	28.5 × 7.4 = **210.9**	6.51 × 6.9 = **44.919**

yellow	purple	purple
39.2 × .36 = **14.112**	7.54 × .43 = **3.2422**	.670 × .94 = **.62980**

yellow	yellow	purple
64.9 × 3.26 = **211.574**	.592 × 40.6 = **24.0352**	7.46 × 5.9 = **44.014**

green	blue	blue	green	purple	green	blue
92.4 × .62 = **57.288**	32.8 × .26 = **9.528**	85.1 × .95 = **80.845**	7.32 × 1.6 = **11.712**	6.05 × 8.3 = **50.215**	3.27 × 844 = **2759.88**	5.56 × 3.94 = **21.9064**

yellow	red	red	red	yellow	yellow	yellow	yellow
80.5 × .276 = **22.218**	5.77 × 4.26 = **24.5802**	95.8 × 7.41 = **709.878**	.784 × 6.92 = **5.4528**	2.57 × 63.6 = **163.452**	29.3 × .487 = **14.2691**	6.80 × .42 = **2.7560**	.245 × 3.6 = **.8820**

Page 138

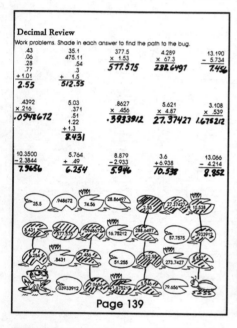

Decimal Review

Work problems. Shade in each answer to find the path to the bug.

.43 .06 .28 .77 + 1.01 = **2.55**	35.1 475.11 .54 .3 + 1.5 = **512.55**	377.5 × 1.53 = **577.575**	4.289 × 67.3 = **288.6497**	13.190 - 5.734 = **7.456**
.4392 × .216 = **.0948672**	5.03 .371 .51 1.22 + 1.3 = **8.431**	.8627 × .456 = **.3933912**	5.621 × 4.87 = **27.37427**	3.108 × .539 = **1.675212**
10.3500 - 2.3844 = **7.9656**	5.764 + .49 = **6.254**	8.879 - 2.933 = **5.946**	3.6 + 6.938 = **10.538**	13.066 - 4.214 = **8.852**

Page 139

The Perfect Sweet-Treat Solution

Solve each division problem. Draw a line from the popcorn (problem) to the correct drink (answer).

Page 140

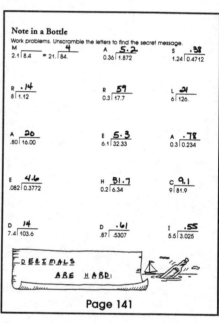

Note in a Bottle

Work problems. Unscramble the letters to find the secret message.

M: 2.1) 8.4 = **4** = 21.) 84.
A: 0.36) 1.872 = **5.2**
S: 1.24) 0.4712 = **.38**

R: 8) 1.12 = **.14**
R: 0.3) 17.7 = **59**
L: 6) 126. = **21**

A: .80) 16.00 = **20**
E: 6.1) 32.33 = **5.3**
A: 0.3) 0.234 = **.78**

E: .082) 0.3772 = **4.6**
H: 0.2) 6.34 = **31.7**
C: 9) 81.9 = **9.1**

D: 7.4) 103.6 = **14**
D: .87) .5307 = **.61**
I: 5.5) 3.025 = **.55**

DECIMALS ARE HARD!

Page 141

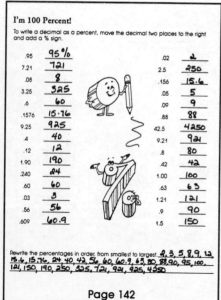

I'm 100 Percent!

To write a decimal as a percent, move the decimal two places to the right and add a % sign.

.95 = **95%**		.02 = **2**
7.21 = **721**		2.5 = **250**
.08 = **8**		.156 = **15.6**
3.25 = **325**		.05 = **5**
.6 = **60**		.09 = **9**
.1576 = **15.76**		.88 = **88**
9.25 = **925**		42.5 = **4250**
.4 = **40**		9.21 = **921**
.12 = **12**		.8 = **80**
1.90 = **190**		.42 = **42**
.240 = **24**		1.00 = **100**
.60 = **60**		.63 = **63**
.03 = **3**		1.21 = **121**
.56 = **56**		.9 = **90**
.609 = **60.9**		1.5 = **150**

Rewrite the percentages in order, from smallest to largest **2, 3, 5, 8, 9, 12, 15.6, 15.76, 24, 40, 42, 56, 60, 60.9, 63, 80, 88, 90, 95, 100, 121, 150, 190, 250, 325, 721, 921, 925, 4250**

Page 142

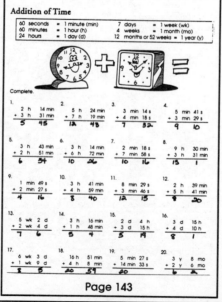

Addition of Time

60 seconds = 1 minute (min)	7 days = 1 week (wk)
60 minutes = 1 hour (h)	4 weeks = 1 month (mo)
24 hours = 1 day (d)	12 months or 52 weeks = 1 year (y)

Complete.

1. 2 h 14 min + 3 h 31 min = **5 45**
2. 5 h 24 min + 7 h 19 min = **12 43**
3. 3 min 14 s + 4 min 18 s = **7 32**
4. 5 min 41 s + 3 min 29 s = **9 10**
5. 3 h 43 min + 2 h 51 min = **6 34**
6. 3 h 14 min + 6 h 72 min = **10 26**
7. 2 min 18 s + 7 min 58 s = **10 16**
8. 9 h 30 min + 3 h 31 min = **13 1**
9. 1 min 49 s + 2 min 27 s = **4 16**
10. 3 h 41 min + 4 h 59 min = **8 40**
11. 8 min 29 s + 3 h 46 min = **12 15**
12. 2 h 39 min + 5 h 41 min = **8 20**
13. 5 wk 2 d + 2 wk 4 d = **7 6**
14. 3 h 14 min + 1 h 48 min = **5 2**
15. 2 d 4 h + 3 d 15 h = **5 19**
16. 3 d 15 h + 4 d 10 h = **8 1**
17. 6 wk 3 d + 1 wk 2 d = **8 5**
18. 16 h 51 min + 3 h 8 min = **20 59**
19. 5 min 27 s + 14 min 33 s = **20**
20. 2 y 8 mo + 2 y 6 mo = **5 2**

Page 143

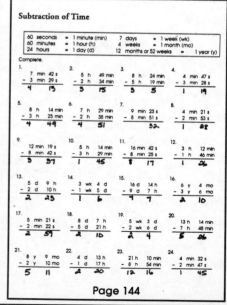

Subtraction of Time

60 seconds = 1 minute (min)	7 days = 1 week (wk)
60 minutes = 1 hour (h)	4 weeks = 1 month (mo)
24 hours = 1 day (d)	12 months or 52 weeks = 1 year (y)

Complete.

1. 7 min 42 s - 3 min 29 s = **4 13**
2. 5 h 49 min - 2 h 34 min = **3 15**
3. 8 h 24 min - 5 h 19 min = **3 5**
4. 4 min 47 s - 3 min 28 s = **1 19**
5. 8 h 14 min - 3 h 25 min = **4 49**
6. 7 h 29 min - 2 h 38 min = **4 51**
7. 9 min 23 s - 8 min 51 s = **32**
8. 4 min 21 s - 2 min 53 s = **1 28**
9. 12 min 19 s - 8 min 42 s = **3 37**
10. 5 h 14 min - 3 h 29 min = **1 45**
11. 16 min 42 s - 8 min 25 s = **8 17**
12. 3 h 12 min - 1 h 46 min = **1 26**
13. 12 min 19 s - 2 d 10 h = **2 23**
14. 8 d 7 h - 1 wk 5 d = **1 6**
15. 16 d 14 h - 9 d 7 h = **7 7**
16. 16 y 4 mo - 3 y 6 mo = **12 10**
17. 5 min 21 s - 2 min 22 s = **2 59**
18. 8 d 7 h - 5 d 21 h = **1 10**
19. 5 wk 3 d - 2 wk 6 d = **2 4**
20. 13 h 14 min - 7 h 48 min = **5 26**
21. 8 y 9 mo - 3 y 11 mo = **5 10**
22. 4 d 13 h - 1 d 17 h = **2 20**
23. 21 h 10 min - 8 h 54 min = **12 16**
24. 4 min 32 s - 1 min 47 s = **2 45**

Page 144

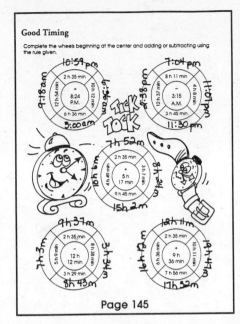

Good Timing

Complete the wheels beginning at the center and adding or subtracting using the rule given.

Page 145

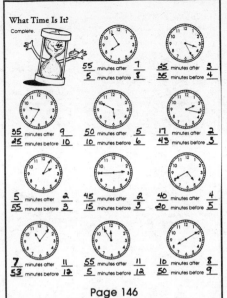

What Time Is It?

Complete.

Page 146

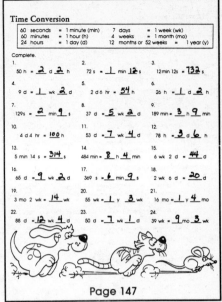

Time Conversion

60 seconds	= 1 minute (min)	7 days	= 1 week (wk)
60 minutes	= 1 hour (h)	4 weeks	= 1 month (mo)
24 hours	= 1 day (d)	12 months or 52 weeks	= 1 year (y)

Complete.

1. 50 h = __2__ d __2__ h
2. 72 s = __1__ min __12__ s
3. 12 min 12 s = __732__ s
4. 9 d = __1__ wk __2__ d
5. 2 d 6 hr = __54__ h
6. 26 h = __1__ d __2__ h
7. 129 s = __2__ min __9__ s
8. 37 d = __5__ wk __2__ d
9. 189 min = __3__ h __9__ min
10. 4 d 4 hr = __100__ h
11. 53 d = __7__ wk __4__ d
12. 78 h = __3__ d __6__ h
13. 5 min 14 s = __314__ s
14. 484 min = __8__ h __4__ min
15. 6 wk 2 d = __44__ d
16. 65 d = __9__ wk __2__ d
17. 369 s = __6__ min __9__ s
18. 2 wk 6 d = __20__ d
19. 3 mo 2 wk = __14__ wk
20. 55 wk = __1__ y __3__ wk
21. 16 mo = __1__ y __4__ mo
22. 88 d = __12__ wk __4__ d
23. 50 d = __7__ wk __1__ d
24. 39 wk = __9__ mo __3__ wk

Page 147

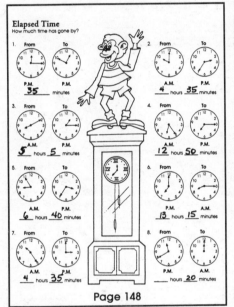

Elapsed Time

How much time has gone by?

Page 148

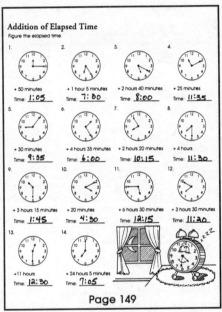

Addition of Elapsed Time

Figure the elapsed time.

Page 149

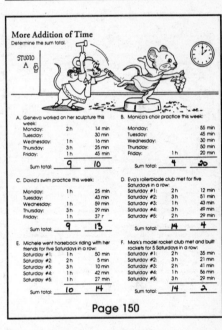

More Addition of Time

Determine the sum total.

STUDIO A 5

A. Geneva worked on her sculpture this week:
Monday:	2h	14 min
Tuesday:		30 min
Wednesday:		16 min
Thursday:	3h	25 min
Friday:	1h	45 min
Sum total:	9	10

B. Monica's choir practice this week:
Monday:		55 min
Tuesday:		45 min
Wednesday:		30 min
Thursday:		50 min
Friday:	1h	20 min
Sum total:	4	20

C. David's swim practice this week:
Monday:	1h	25 min
Tuesday:	1h	43 min
Wednesday:	1h	59 min
Thursday:	3h	29 min
Friday:	1h	37 r
Sum total:	9	13

D. Eva's rollerblade club met for five Saturdays in a row:
Saturday #1:	2h	12 min
Saturday #2:	3h	51 min
Saturday #3:	1h	43 min
Saturday #4:	3h	49 min
Saturday #5:	2h	29 min
Sum total:	14	4

E. Michele went horseback riding with her friends for five Saturdays in a row:
Saturday #1:	1h	50 min
Saturday #2:	2h	5 min
Saturday #3:	3h	10 min
Saturday #4:	1h	42 min
Saturday #5:	1h	27 min
Sum total:	10	14

F. Mark's model rocket club met and built rockets for 5 Saturdays in a row:
Saturday #1:	2h	35 min
Saturday #2:	3h	21 min
Saturday #3:	2h	41 min
Saturday #4:	1h	56 min
Saturday #5:	3h	29 min
Sum total:	14	2

Page 150

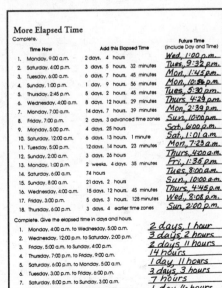

More Elapsed Time

Complete.

	Time Now	Add this Elapsed Time	Future Time (Include Day and Time)
1.	Monday, 9:00 a.m.	2 days, 4 hours	Wed, 1:00 p.m.
2.	Saturday, 4:00 p.m.	3 days, 5 hours, 32 minutes	Tues, 9:32 p.m.
3.	Saturday, 6:00 a.m.	6 days, 7 hours, 45 minutes	Mon, 1:45 p.m.
4.	Sunday, 1:00 p.m.	1 day, 9 hours, 56 minutes	Mon, 10:56 p.m.
5.	Thursday, 2:45 p.m.	5 days, 2 hours, 45 minutes	Tues, 5:30 p.m.
6.	Wednesday, 4:00 p.m.	8 days, 12 hours, 29 minutes	Mon, 2:39 a.m.
7.	Monday, 7:00 a.m.	14 days, 7 hours, 39 minutes	Sun, 10:00 p.m.
8.	Friday, 7:00 p.m.	2 days, 3 advanced time zones	Sat, 6:00 p.m.
9.	Monday, 5:00 p.m.	4 days, 25 hours	Sat, 1:01 a.m.
10.	Saturday, 12:00 a.m.	6 days, 13 hours, 1 minute	Mon, 7:23 a.m.
11.	Tuesday, 5:00 p.m.	12 days, 14 hours, 23 minutes	Thurs, 4:00 a.m.
12.	Sunday, 2:00 a.m.	3 days, 26 hours	Fri, 1:35 p.m.
13.	Monday, 1:00 p.m.	2 weeks, 4 days, 35 minutes	Tues, 8:00 a.m.
14.	Saturday, 6:00 a.m.	74 hours	Sun, 10:00 a.m.
15.	Sunday, 8:00 a.m.	21 days, 2 hours	Thurs, 4:45 p.m.
16.	Wednesday, 4:00 a.m.	15 days, 3 hours, 45 minutes	Wed, 8:05 p.m.
17.	Friday, 3:00 p.m.	5 days, 3 hours, 128 minutes	Sun, 2:00 p.m.
18.	Thursday, 6:00 p.m.	3 days, 4 earlier time zones	

Complete. Give the elapsed time in days and hours.

1. Monday, 4:00 a.m. to Wednesday, 5:00 a.m. — 2 days, 1 hour
2. Wednesday, 12:00 p.m. to Saturday, 2:00 p.m. — 3 days, 2 hours
3. Friday, 5:00 a.m. to Sunday, 4:00 p.m. — 2 days, 11 hours
4. Thursday, 7:00 p.m. to Friday, 9:00 a.m. — 14 hours
5. Saturday, 6:00 a.m. to Monday, 5:00 a.m. — 1 day, 11 hours
6. Tuesday, 3:00 a.m. to Friday, 6:00 a.m. — 3 days, 3 hours
7. Saturday, 8:00 p.m. to Sunday, 3:00 a.m. — 7 hours
8. Monday, 4:00 p.m. to Wednesday, 8:00 a.m. — 1 day, 16 hours

Page 151

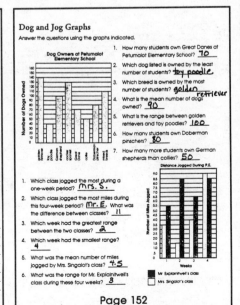

Dog and Jog Graphs

Answer the questions using the graphs indicated.

Dog Owners at Petumalot Elementary School

1. How many students own Great Danes at Petumalot Elementary School? __70__
2. Which dog listed is owned by the least number of students? __toy poodle__
3. Which breed is owned by the most number of students? __golden retriever__
4. What is the mean number of dogs owned? __90__
5. What is the range between golden retrievers and toy poodles? __100__
6. How many students own Doberman pinschers? __80__
7. How many more students own German shepherds than collies? __50__

Distance Jogged During P.E.

1. Which class jogged the most during a one-week period? __Mrs. S.__
2. Which class jogged the most miles during this four-week period? __Mr. E.__ What was the difference between classes? __11__
3. Which week had the greatest range between the two classes? __2__
4. Which week had the smallest range? __4__
5. What was the mean number of miles jogged by Mrs. Singalot's class? __4.5__
6. What was the range for Mr. Explainitwell's class during these four weeks? __4__

Page 152

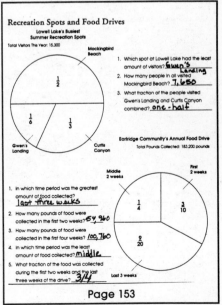

Recreation Spots and Food Drives

Lowell Lake's Busiest Summer Recreation Spots
Total Visitors This Year: 15,300

1. Which spot at Lowell Lake had the least amount of visitors? __Gwen's Landing__
2. How many people in all visited Mockingbird Beach? __7,650__
3. What fraction of the people visited Gwen's Landing and Curtis Canyon combined? __one-half__

Eartridge Community's Annual Food Drive
Total Pounds Collected: 183,200 pounds

1. In which time period was the greatest amount of food collected? __last three weeks__
2. How many pounds of food were collected in the first two weeks? __54,960__
3. How many pounds of food were collected in the first four weeks? __100,760__
4. In which time period was the least amount of food collected? __middle__
5. What fraction of the food was collected during the first two weeks and the last three weeks of the drive? __3/4__

Page 153

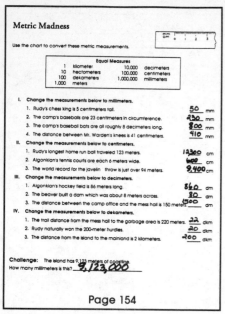

Metric Madness

Use the chart to convert these metric measurements.

Equal Measures			
1	kilometer	10,000	decimeters
10	hectometers	100,000	centimeters
100	dekameters	1,000,000	millimeters
1,000	meters		

I. Change the measurements below to millimeters.
1. Rudy's chess king is 5 centimeters tall. 50 mm
2. The camp's baseballs are 23 centimeters in circumference. 230 mm
3. The camp's baseball bats are all roughly 8 decimeters long. 800 mm
4. The distance between Mr. Warden's knees is 41 centimeters. 410 mm

II. Change the measurements below to centimeters.
1. Rudy's longest home run ball traveled 123 meters. 12300 cm
2. Algonkian's tennis courts are each 6 meters wide. 600 cm
3. The world record for the javelin throw is just over 94 meters. 9,400 cm

III. Change the measurements below to decimeters.
1. Algonkian's hockey field is 86 meters long. 860 dm
2. The beaver built a dam which was about 8 meters across. 80 dm
3. The distance between the camp office and the mess hall is 150 meters. 1500 dm

IV. Change the measurements below to dekameters.
1. The trail distance from the mess hall to the garbage area is 220 meters. 22 dkm
2. Rudy naturally won the 200-meter hurdles. 20 dkm
3. The distance from the island to the mainland is 2 kilometers. 200 dkm

Challenge: The island has 9,123 meters of coastline. How many millimeters is this? 9,123,000

Page 154

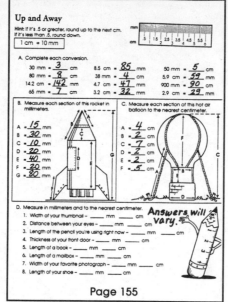

Up and Away

Hint: If it's .5 or greater, round up to the next cm. If it's less than .5, round down.

1 cm = 10 mm

A. Complete each conversion.

30 mm = 3 cm | 8.5 cm = 85 mm | 50 mm = 5 cm
80 mm = 8 cm | 38 mm = 4 cm | 5.9 cm = 59 mm
14.2 cm = 142 mm | 4.7 cm = 47 mm | 900 mm = 90 cm
65 mm = 7 cm | 3.2 cm = 32 mm | 2.9 cm = 29 mm

B. Measure each section of this rocket in millimeters.

A = 15 mm
B = 30 mm
C = 10 mm
D = 20 mm
E = 40 mm
F = 20 mm
G = 80 mm

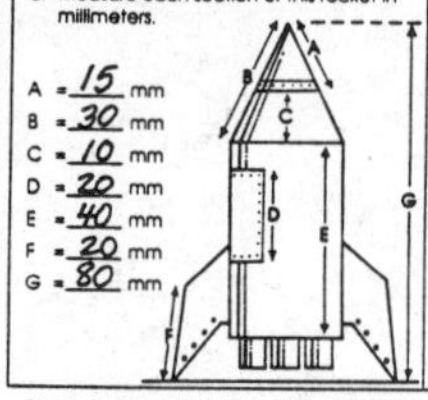

C. Measure each section of this hot air balloon to the nearest centimeter.

A = 4 cm
B = 2 cm
C = 7 cm
D = 2 cm
E = 2 cm
F = .5 cm

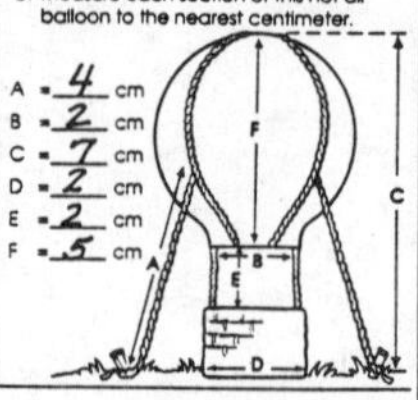

D. Measure in millimeters and to the nearest centimeter.
1. Width of your thumbnail – ____ mm ____ cm
2. Distance between your eyes – ____ mm ____ cm
3. Length of the pencil you're using right now – ____ mm ____ cm
4. Thickness of your front door – ____ mm ____ cm
5. Length of a book – ____ mm ____ cm
6. Length of a mailbox – ____ mm ____ cm
7. Width of your favorite photograph – ____ mm ____ cm
8. Length of your shoe – ____ mm ____ cm

Answers will vary.

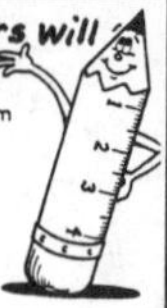

Page 155

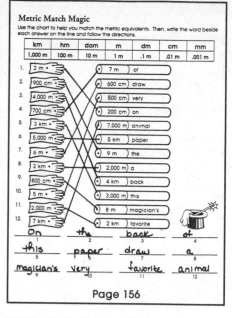

Metric Match Magic

Use the chart to help you match the metric equivalents. Then, write the word beside each answer on the line and follow the directions.

km	hm	dam	m	dm	cm	mm
1,000 m	100 m	10 m	1 m	.1 m	.01 m	.001 m

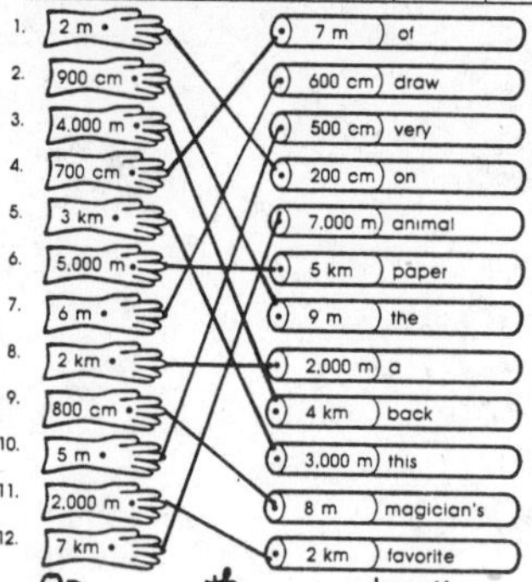

1. 2 m
2. 900 cm
3. 4,000 m
4. 700 cm
5. 3 km
6. 5,000 m
7. 6 m
8. 2 km
9. 800 cm
10. 5 m
11. 2,000 m
12. 7 km
7 m of
600 cm draw
500 cm very
200 cm on
7,000 m animal
5 km paper
9 m the
2,000 m a
4 km back
3,000 m this
8 m magician's
2 km favorite

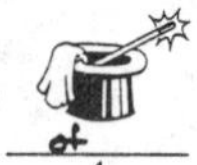

On (1) the (2) back (3) of (4) this (5) paper (6) draw (7) a (8) magician's (9) very (10) favorite (11) animal (12)

Page 156

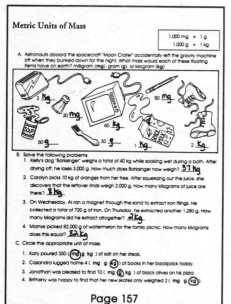

Metric Units of Mass

1,000 mg = 1 g
1,000 g = 1 kg

A. Astronauts aboard the spacecraft "Moon Crater" accidentally left the gravity machine off when they bunked down for the night. What mass would each of these floating items have on earth? milligram (mg), gram (g), or kilogram (kg)

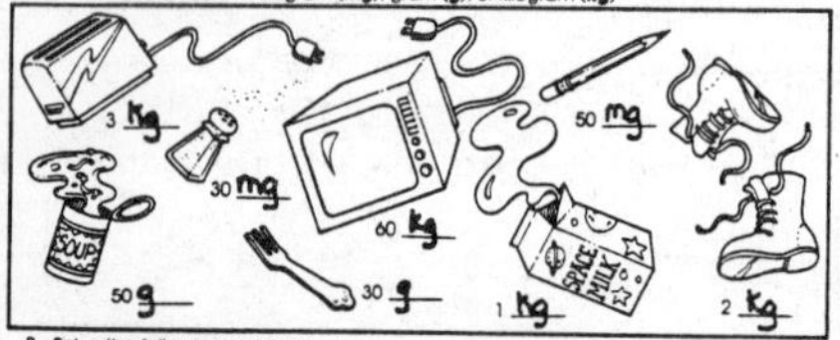

3 kg
30 mg
60 kg
50 mg
50 g
30 g
1 kg
2 kg
SOUP
SPACE MILK

B. Solve the following problems.
1. Kelly's dog "Barksinger" weighs a total of 40 kg while soaking wet during a bath. After drying off, he loses 3,000 g. How much does Barksinger now weigh? 37 kg
2. Carolyn picks 10 kg of oranges from her tree. After squeezing out the juice, she discovers that the leftover rinds weigh 2,000 g. How many kilograms of juice are there? 8 kg
3. On Wednesday, Al ran a magnet through the sand to extract iron filings. He collected a total of 720 g of iron. On Thursday, he extracted another 1,280 g. How many kilograms did he extract altogether? 2 kg
4. Mamie picked 82,000 g of watermelon for the family picnic. How many kilograms does this equal? 82 kg

C. Circle the appropriate unit of mass.
1. Katy poured 350 (mg g kg) of salt on her steak. [mg circled]
2. Casandra lugged home 4 (mg g kg) of books in her backpack today. [kg circled]
3. Jonathan was pleased to find 10 (mg g kg) of black olives on his pizza. [g circled]
4. Brittainy was happy to find that her new skates only weighed 2 (mg g kg). [kg circled]

Page 157

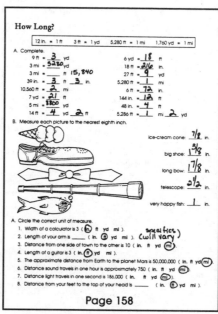

How Long?

12 in. = 1 ft   3 ft = 1 yd   5,280 ft = 1 mi   1,760 yd = 1 mi

A. Complete.

9 ft = 3 yd | 6 yd = 18 ft
3 mi = 5280 yd | 18 ft = 216 in.
3 mi = ____ ft 15,840 | 27 ft = 9 yd
39 in. = 3 ft 3 in. | 5,280 ft = 1 mi
10,560 ft = 2 mi | 6 ft = 72 in.
7 yd = 21 ft | 144 in. = 12 ft
5 mi = 8800 yd | 48 in. = 4 ft
14 ft = 4 yd 2 ft | 5,286 ft = 1 mi 2 yd

B. Measure each picture to the nearest eighth inch.

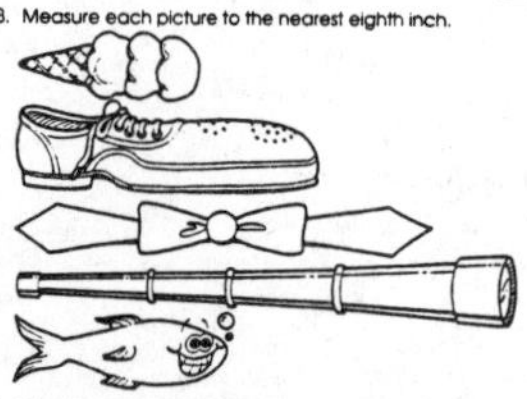

ice-cream cone: 7/8 in.
big shoe: 1 3/8 in.
long bow: 1 7/8 in.
telescope: 2 1/2 in.
very happy fish: 1 in.

A. Circle the correct unit of measure.
1. Width of a calculator is 3 (in. ft yd mi). [in. circled]
2. Length of your arm is ____ (in. ft yd mi). [ft circled] (will vary) specifics
3. Distance from one side of town to the other is 10 (in. ft yd mi). [mi circled]
4. Length of a guitar is 3 (in. ft yd mi). [ft circled]
5. The approximate distance from Earth to the planet Mars is 50,000,000 (in. ft yd mi). [mi circled]
6. Distance sound travels in one hour is approximately 750 (in. ft yd mi). [mi circled]
7. Distance light travels in one second is 186,000 (in. ft yd mi). [mi circled]
8. Distance from your feet to the top of your head is ____ (in. ft yd mi). [ft circled]

Page 158

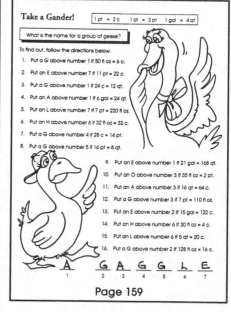

Take a Gander!

1 pt = 2 c   1 qt = 2 pt   1 gal = 4 qt

What is the name for a group of geese?

To find out, follow the directions below.
1. Put a G above number 1 if 50 fl oz = 6 c.
2. Put an E above number 7 if 11 pt = 22 c.
3. Put a G above number 1 if 24 c = 12 qt.
4. Put an A above number 1 if 6 gal = 24 qt.
5. Put an L above number 7 if 7 pt = 220 fl oz.
6. Put an H above number 6 if 32 fl oz = 32 c.
7. Put a G above number 4 if 28 c = 14 pt.
8. Put a G above number 5 if 16 pt = 8 qt.

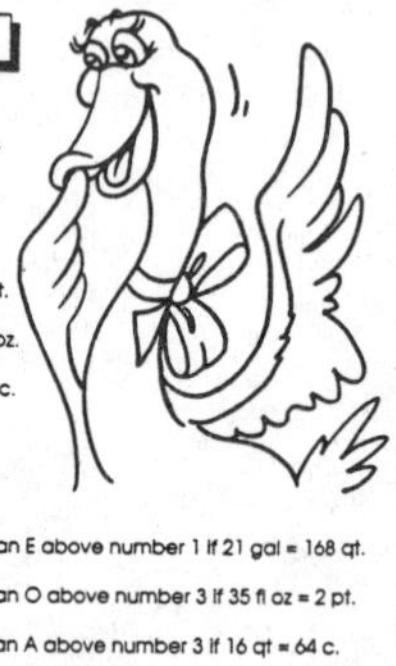

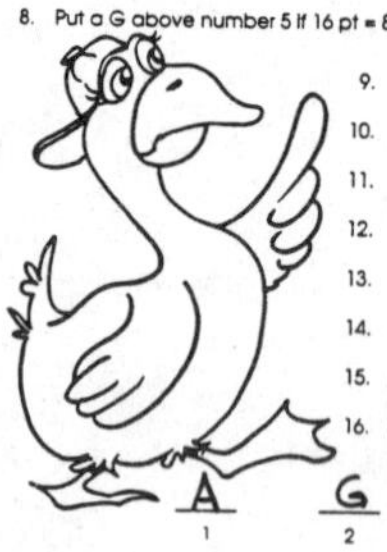

9. Put an E above number 1 if 21 gal = 168 qt.
10. Put an O above number 3 if 35 fl oz = 2 pt.
11. Put an A above number 3 if 16 qt = 64 c.
12. Put a G above number 3 if 7 pt = 110 fl oz.
13. Put an E above number 2 if 15 gal = 122 c.
14. Put an H above number 6 if 30 fl oz = 4 c.
15. Put an L above number 6 if 5 qt = 20 c.
16. Put a G above number 2 if 128 fl oz = 16 c.

A (1) G (2) A (3) G (4) G (5) L (6) E (7)

Page 159

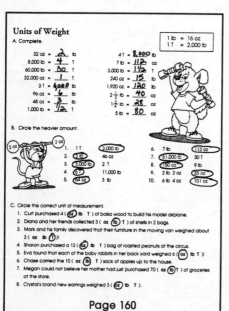

Units of Weight

1 lb = 16 oz
1 T = 2,000 lb

A. Complete.

32 oz = 2 lb | 4 T = 8,000 lb
8,000 lb = 4 T | 7 lb = 112 oz
60,000 lb = 30 T | 3,000 lb = 1 1/2 T
32,000 oz = 1 T | 240 oz = 15 lb
3 T = 6000 lb | 1,920 oz = 120 lb
96 oz = 6 lb | $2\frac{1}{2}$ lb = 40 oz
48 oz = 3 lb | $1\frac{3}{4}$ lb = 28 oz
1,000 lb = 1/2 T | 5 lb = 80 oz

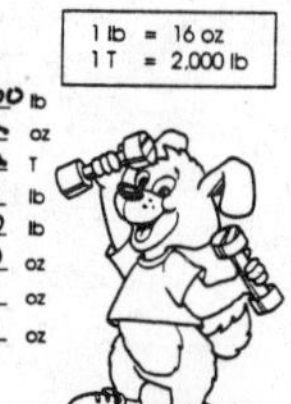

B. Circle the heavier amount.

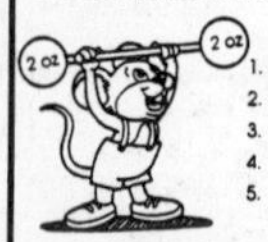

2 oz
2 oz

1. 1 T | 3,000 lb [circled]
2. 3 lb [circled] | 46 oz
3. 5,000 lb [circled] | 2 T
4. 6 T [circled] | 11,000 lb
5. 64 oz [circled] | 3 lb
6. 7 lb | 113 oz [circled]
7. 61,000 lb [circled] | 30 T
8. 150 oz [circled] | 9 lb
9. 2 lb 2 oz | 35 oz [circled]
10. 6 lb 4 oz | 101 oz [circled]

C. Circle the correct unit of measurement.
1. Curt purchased 4 (oz lb T) of balsa wood to build his model airplane. [oz circled]
2. Diana and her friends collected 3 (oz lb T) of shells in 2 bags. [lb circled]
3. Mark and his family discovered that their furniture in the moving van weighed about 3 (oz lb T)! [T circled]
4. Sharon purchased a 12 (oz lb T) bag of roasted peanuts at the circus. [oz circled]
5. Eva found that each of the baby rabbits in her back yard weighed 6 (oz lb T)! [oz circled]
6. Chase carried the 10 (oz lb T) sack of apples up to the house. [lb circled]
7. Megan could not believe her mother had just purchased 70 (oz lb T) of groceries at the store. [lb circled]
8. Crystal's brand new earrings weighed 3 (oz lb T). [oz circled]

Page 160

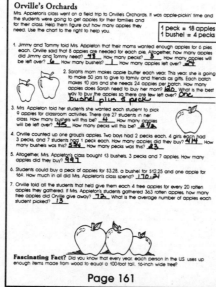

Orville's Orchards

Mrs. Appleton's class went on a field trip to Orville's Orchards. It was apple-pickin' time and the students were going to get apples for their families and for their class. Help them figure out how many apples they need. Use the chart to the right to help you.

1 peck = 18 apples
1 bushel = 4 pecks

1. Jimmy and Tommy told Mrs. Appleton that their moms wanted enough apples for 6 pies each. Orville said that 8 apples are needed for each pie. Altogether, how many apples did Jimmy and Tommy need? 48 How many pecks? 3 How many apples will be left over? 6 How many bushels? 1 How many apples left over? 24

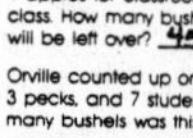

2. Sarah's mom makes apple butter each year. This year, she is going to make 50 jars to give to family and friends as gifts. Each batch makes 10 jars and she needs 24 apples per batch. How many apples does Sarah need to buy her mom? 120 What is the best way to buy the apples so there are few left over? One bushel plus 3 peck

3. Mrs. Appleton told her students she wanted each student to pick 9 apples for classroom activities. There are 27 students in her class. How many bushels will this be? 4 How many apples will be left over? 45 How many pecks will this be? 27/2

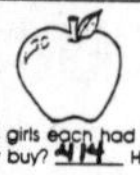

4. Orville counted up one group's apples. Two boys had 2 pecks each, 4 girls each had 3 pecks, and 7 students had 1 peck each. How many apples did they buy? 414 How many bushels was this? 5 3/4 How many pecks was this? 23
5. Altogether, Mrs. Appleton's class bought 13 bushels, 3 pecks and 7 apples. How many apples did they buy? 997
6. Students could buy a peck of apples for $3.28, a bushel for $12.25 and one apple for 16¢. How much in all did Mrs. Appleton's class spend? 170.21
7. Orville told all the students that he'd give them each 4 free apples for every 20 rotten apples they gathered. If Mrs. Appleton's students gathered 363 rotten apples, how many free apples did Orville give away? 72 What is the average number of apples each student picked? 13

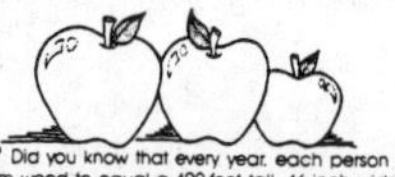

Fascinating Fact? Did you know that every year, each person in the U.S. uses up enough items made from wood to equal a 100-foot tall, 16-inch wide tree?

Page 161

Geometric Figures

Find the perimeter of each figure.

Perimeter is the distance around an area.

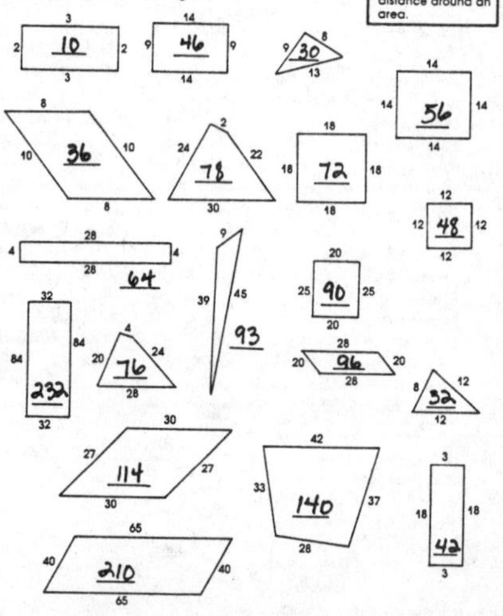

10
46
30
56
36
78
72
48
64
93
90
232
76
96
32
114
140
42
210

Page 162

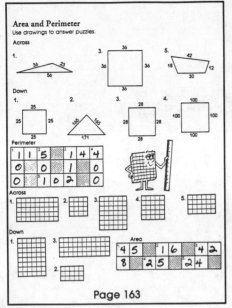

Area and Perimeter
Use drawings to answer puzzles.

Across / Down / Perimeter / Across / Down / Area

Page 163

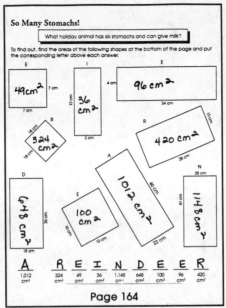

So Many Stomachs!
What holiday animal has six stomachs and can give milk?

To find out, find the areas of the following shapes at the bottom of the page and put the corresponding letter above each answer.

49 cm^2 • 36 cm^2 • 96 cm^2 • 324 cm^2 • 420 cm^2 • 648 cm^2 • 100 cm^2 • $1,012 \text{ cm}^2$ • $1,148 \text{ cm}^2$

A R E I N D E E R

| 1,012 cm² | 324 cm² | 49 cm² | 36 cm² | 1,148 cm² | 648 cm² | 100 cm² | 96 cm² | 420 cm² |

Page 164

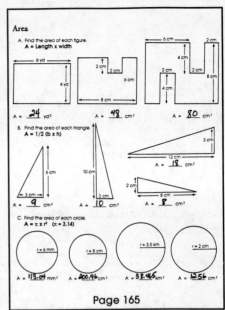

Area
A. Find the area of each figure.
A = Length x width

A = 24 yd²   A = 48 cm²   A = 80 cm²

B. Find the area of each triangle.
A = 1/2 (b x h)

A = 9 cm²   A = 10 cm²   A = 18 cm²   A = 8 cm²

C. Find the area of each circle.
A = π x r² (π = 3.14)

A = 113.04 mm²   A = 200.96 cm²   A = 38.46 km²   A = 12.56 cm²

Page 165

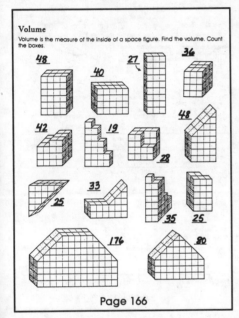

Volume
Volume is the measure of the inside of a space figure. Find the volume. Count the boxes.

48, 27, 36, 40, 42, 19, 48, 28, 33, 25, 35, 25, 176, 80

Page 166

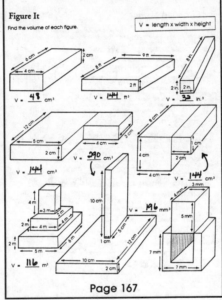

Figure It
Find the volume of each figure.

V = length x width x height

V = 48 cm³   V = 144 ft³   V = 32 in.³
V = 144 cm³   V = 240 cm³   V = 144 cm²
V = 196 mm³   V = 116 m³

Page 167

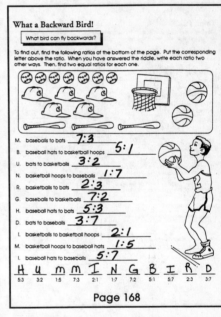

What a Backward Bird!
What bird can fly backwards?

To find out, find the following ratios at the bottom of the page. Put the corresponding letter above the ratio. When you have answered the riddle, write each ratio two other ways. Then, find two equal ratios for each one.

M. baseballs to bats — 7:3
B. baseball hats to basketball hoops — 5:1
U. bats to basketballs — 3:2
N. basketball hoops to baseballs — 1:7
R. basketballs to bats — 2:3
G. baseballs to basketballs — 7:2
H. baseball hats to bats — 5:3
D. bats to baseballs — 3:7
I. basketballs to basketball hoops — 2:1
M. basketball hoops to baseball hats — 1:5
I. baseball hats to baseballs — 5:7

H U M M I N G B I R D

| 5:3 | 3:2 | 1:5 | 7:3 | 2:1 | 1:7 | 7:2 | 5:1 | 5:7 | 2:3 | 3:7 |

Page 168

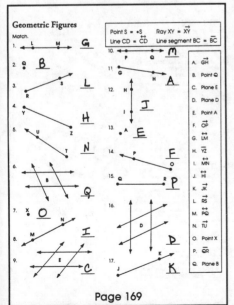

Geometric Figures
Match.

Point S = •S   Ray XY = $\overrightarrow{XY}$
Line CD = $\overleftrightarrow{CD}$ Line segment BC = $\overline{BC}$

1. G   10. M
2. B   11. A
3. L   12. J
4. H   13. E
5. N   14. F
6. Q   15. P
7. O   16. D
8. I   17. K
9. C

A. GH
B. Point Q
C. Plane E
D. Plane D
E. Point A
F. OP
G. LM
H. VZ
I. MN
J. HI
K. JK
L. RS
M. PQ
N. TU
O. Point X
P. QR
Q. Plane B

Page 169

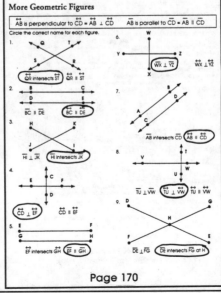

More Geometric Figures
$\overleftrightarrow{AB}$ is perpendicular to $\overleftrightarrow{CD}$ = $\overleftrightarrow{AB} \perp \overleftrightarrow{CD}$ $\overleftrightarrow{AB}$ is parallel to $\overleftrightarrow{CD}$ = $\overleftrightarrow{AB} \parallel \overleftrightarrow{CD}$
Circle the correct name for each figure.

1. QR intersects ST
2. BC ∥ DE
3. HI intersects JK
4. CD ∥ EF
5. EF intersects GH
6. WX ⊥ YZ
7. AB ∥ CD
8. TU ∥ VW
9. DE intersects FG at H

Page 170

Naming Figures
Use this figure to answer the questions below.

Other answers possible.

1. Name the plane in this figure. **X**
2. Point K is inside which angle? **∠LST**
3. Name three triangles in this figure. **LSN, MON, LRP, MQP**
4. Point J is inside which angle? **∠PQC**
5. Name three angles for which Q is the vertex. **∠MQP, ∠RQC, ∠PQC**
6. Which points make up the parallelogram in this figure? **S, R, Q, O**
7. Name the largest triangle in this figure. **LRP**
8. How many other angles can be named inside ∠LNT? **four**
9. Name all the angles that contain a side on LR. **∠LRP, ∠LSN, ∠SRP, ∠RSN, ∠TSR, ∠LST, ∠OSR, ∠LRQ**
10. How many points are on MC? **four** Name them. **M, O, Q, C**
11. Name the point at which LR and NT intersect. **S**
12. Name the vertex for ∠SNL. **N**
13. Are lines TN and RP perpendicular or parallel? **parallel**
14. Are lines LR and MC perpendicular or parallel? **parallel**

Page 171

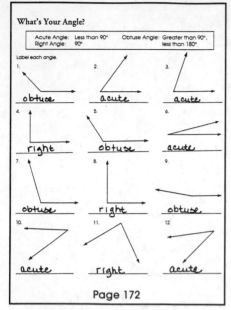

What's Your Angle?

Acute Angle: Less than 90° Obtuse Angle: Greater than 90°,
Right Angle: 90°   less than 180°

Label each angle.

1. obtuse 2. acute 3. acute

4. right 5. obtuse 6. acute

7. obtuse 8. right 9. obtuse

10. acute 11. right 12. acute

Page 172

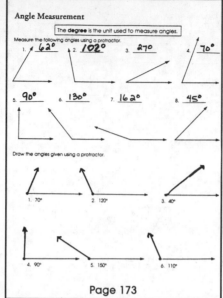

Angle Measurement

The **degree** is the unit used to measure angles.

Measure the following angles using a protractor.

1. 62° 2. 102° 3. 270° 4. 70°

5. 90° 6. 130° 7. 162° 8. 45°

Draw the angles given using a protractor.

1. 70° 2. 120° 3. 40°

4. 90° 5. 150° 6. 110°

Page 173

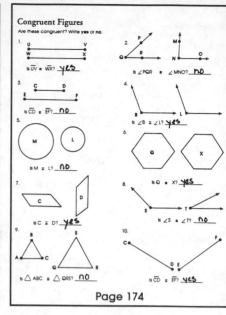

Congruent Figures

Are these congruent? Write yes or no.

1. Is $\overline{UV} \cong \overline{WX}$? yes
2. Is ∠PQR ≅ ∠MNO? no
3. Is $\overline{CD} \cong \overline{EF}$? no
4. Is ∠B ≅ ∠L? yes
5. Is M ≅ L? no
6. Is Q ≅ X? yes
7. Is C ≅ D? yes
8. Is ∠S ≅ ∠T? no
9. Is △ABC ≅ △QRS? no
10. Is $\overline{CD} \cong \overline{EF}$? yes

Page 174

Think Fast!

The time it takes for your ears to send a message to your brain, and your body to respond is called **reaction time**.

Let's try an experiment to test your reaction time. Find a partner and take turns helping one another with the experiment.
Materials: 30 cm metric ruler
Procedure:
1. Place your left arm on a table with your hand over the edge.
2. Space your thumb and index fingers about 4 cm apart.
3. Have a partner hold the "30 cm end" of the ruler, with the other end just above your open thumb and index finger.
4. Your partner will say "set," and drop the ruler.
5. Catch the distance fallen with your thumb and index finger as quickly as possible.
6. Check the distance fallen by taking a reading at the bottom of the index finger.
7. Record your results.
8. Repeat the procedure 10 times with each hand.

Are you right-handed, or left-handed? Which of your hands was the quickest?

Did others find the same results? _____

Form a group of 5 or 6 students. Make a graph depicting your results.

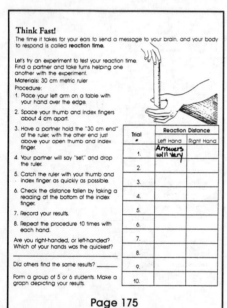

Trial #	Reaction Distance	
	Left Hand	Right Hand
1.	Answers will vary	
2.		
3.		
4.		
5.		
6.		
7.		
8.		
9.		
10.		

Page 175

The Circulatory System

As you read the information given below, underline the two main functions and the main organ of the circulatory system. Then, answer the questions.
The circulatory system is responsible for transporting materials throughout the body and for regulating body temperature.
As a transportation network, the heart is vital to the circulatory system. It pumps blood to all parts of the body. The blood then carries nutrients and other important materials to your cells. Blood also carries waste products away from cells to disposal sites like the liver, lungs and kidneys. The circulatory system also acts as a temperature control for your body. Warmer blood from the center of your body is brought to the surface to be cooled. On a cold day, your blood vessels contract very little allowing little blood to flow through. This is why your skin might appear pale, or even blue. However, in hot weather, blood vessels widen and more blood is able to flow through them, to increase the loss of heat. Thus, your skin looks pinker and feels warmer.

1. What are the two main functions of the circulatory system? transporting materials, regulating temperature
2. The blood carries important nutrients to the cells.
3. Blood carries waste away from cells to the liver, lungs and kidneys.
4. Warmer blood is brought from the center of the body to the surface of the body to be cooled.
5. In cold weather, why does your skin appear pale, or even blue? Blood vessels contract, allowing little blood flow

A "Hearty" Experiment

To learn more about the circulatory system, do the experiment below.
Materials needed: tennis ball   watch with a second hand
- Hold the tennis ball in your strongest hand and give it a hard squeeze. This is about the strength it takes your heart muscle to contract to pump one beat.
- Squeeze the ball as hard as you can and release it 70 times in one minute.
- Record how your hand feels. Answers will vary
Conclusion: _____

Fascinating Fact! Did you know that if your blood vessels were laid end to end, they would encircle the globe twice over?

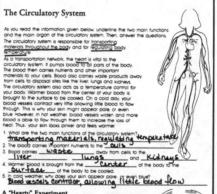

Page 176

Feel the Beat

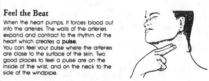

When the heart pumps, it forces blood out into the arteries. The walls of the arteries expand and contract to the rhythm of the heart which creates a **pulse**. You can feel your pulse where the arteries are close to the surface of the skin. Two good places to feel a pulse are on the inside of the wrist, and on the neck to the side of the windpipe.

The type of activity you are doing can greatly affect the rate of your pulse. Try the experiment below and complete the chart by –
1. counting the number of heartbeats in 15 seconds.
2. multiplying that number by 4 to get the pulse rate for one minute.

Study your results. Explain how each type of activity affected your pulse rate.

Activity	Pulse Rate for 15 sec.	X 4 =	Pulse Rate per minute
Sitting still for 10 minutes	Answers will vary		
Running in place for 3 minutes			
Just after finishing your lunch or dinner			
While still in bed in the morning			
Just after getting ready for school			

Fascinating Fact! The heart pumps about 1,250 gallons of blood each day.

Page 177

How Your Digestive System Works

In your digestive system, enzymes, special kinds of chemicals produced by the salivary glands in the walls of your stomach, break food up so it can pass through the wall of your small intestine into your blood. You cannot see inside to watch these enzymes work, but you can do the activity below to help you better understand what they do.
The following experiment will show you the effect enzymes can have on proteins. Enzymes that break down proteins do not become active until the food reaches the stomach.
Materials needed: 4 small bowls, meat tenderizer, small amount of hamburger
Procedure:
1. Mark bowls #1, #2, #3 and #4.
2. Make 4 equal marble-sized pieces of hamburger.
3. Put one piece of hamburger in bowl #1 and another in bowl #3.
4. Break the other 2 pieces of hamburger up into small pieces and put one in bowl #2 and one in bowl #4.
5. Cover the meat in bowl #1 and #2 with meat tenderizer and a few drops of water.
6. Cover the meat in bowls #3 and #4 with the same amount of water only.
7. Let the bowls stand in a warm place for a few days.

Results:
Bowl #1: _____ Answers will vary
Bowl #2: _____
Bowl #3: _____
Bowl #4: _____
Conclusions: _____
_____
_____

Fascinating Fact!
Borborygmi is the rumbling noise your digestive system makes.

Page 178

Enlightening Environmental Information

An **environment** includes all living and nonliving things with which an organism interacts. These living and nonliving things are **interdependent**, that is, they depend on one another. The living things in an environment (plants, animals, etc.) are called **biotic factors** and the nonliving things and factors (soil, light, temperature, etc.) are called **abiotic factors**. **Ecology** is the study of the relationships and interactions of living things with one another and their environment.

Living things inhabit many different environments. A group of organisms living and interacting with each other in their nonliving environment is called an **ecosystem**. The living part of an ecosystem, all the organisms that live together in an area, is called a **community**. In a community, each kind of living thing makes up a **population**.

Follow the directions below. Answers will vary
1. Label two biotic factors and two abiotic factors in the picture.
2. Explain the relationships between the living things in the environment shown in the picture.
3. At the top of the picture, write the type of ecosystem pictured.
4. Circle all the members of the community.
5. Write how the organisms in this environment are dependent on one another.
6. List the types of populations that live in the environment.
7. Define ecology in your own words on the back of the page.

Page 179

Pond Water

Answers will vary

Some of the organisms found in pond water are so small that you need a microscope to see them. To make the following observations, you will need a sample of pond water, a microscope, and a microscope slide. (If you cannot bring in a small container of pond water, your teacher will furnish it.)

1. Put a drop of pond water on your slide. Look at it with your microscope under low power.
2. Mark the circle below which looks like the approximate number of organisms you can see in your sample.

□ □ □ □

3. Turn your microscope to high power and find an organism. Watch it carefully. Make a sketch of it below. If it looks like any of the organisms to the right, write its name in the blank under your sketch.
(If not, try to identify it later by looking in the encyclopedia or biology book.) Does it have any special features such as a tail or hairs to help it move? _____
4. Look for other organisms. Do you see any that are different from your first organism? _____ Sketch two of them on another paper. As time progresses, many of the smaller ones will be eaten by the larger ones, such as the water flea or copepod.

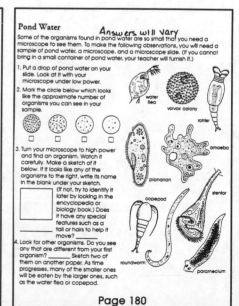

water flea
volvox colony
rotifer
amoeba
planarian
copepod
stentor
roundworm
paramecium

Page 180

File Up, Phylums!

Scientists separate animals according to their differences and group them according to their likenesses.
Draw a line from the phylum in the first column to the correct picture and then to the characteristics. The first one is done for you.

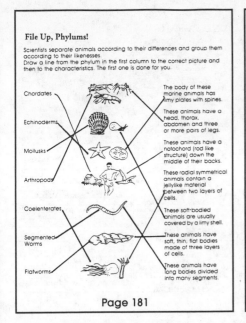

Chordates

Echinoderms

Mollusks

Arthropods

Coelenterates

Segmented Worms

Flatworms

The body of these marine animals has slimy plates with spines.

These animals have a head, thorax, abdomen and three or more pairs of legs.

These animals have a notochord (rod like structure) down the middle of their backs.

These radial symmetrical animals contain a jellylike material between two layers of cells.

These soft-bodied animals are usually covered by a limy shell.

These animals have soft, thin, flat bodies made of three layers of cells.

These animals have long bodies divided into many segments.

Page 181

Mixed-Up Names

What is the name for this cat? Is it a puma, mountain lion, panther, or cougar? Most people use common names when referring to an animal, but it's easy to be confused about what name applies to which animal. Scientists all around the world refer to every animal by its two-part scientific name. This name combines the **genus name** and the **species name**. What is the scientific name for the big cat on this page?

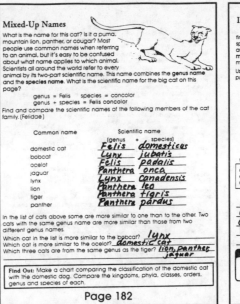

genus = Felis   species = concolor
genus + species = Felis concolor

Find and compare the scientific names of the following members of the cat family. (Felidae)

Common name	Scientific name (genus + species)
domestic cat	Felis domesticus
bobcat	Lynx jubatis
ocelot	Felis padalis
jaguar	Panthera onca
lynx	Lynx canadensis
lion	Panthera leo
tiger	Panthera tigris
panther	Panthera pardus

In the list of cats above some are more similar to one than to the other. Two cats with the same genus name are more similar than those from two different genus names.

Which cat in the list is more similar to the bobcat? **lynx**
Which cat is more similar to the ocelot? **domestic cat**
Which three cats are from the same genus as the tiger? **lion, panther, jaguar**

Find Out: Make a chart comparing the classification of the domestic cat with the domestic dog. Compare the kingdoms, phyla, classes, orders, genus and species of each.

Page 182

Invertebrates

Just three groups of the many kinds of invertebrates are listed below. The first group are arthropods. Arthropods are invertebrates with jointed legs. Insects, spiders, and crustaceans, like lobsters and crabs, belong to this group. Worms are slender, creeping animals with soft bodies and no legs. The last group are mollusks. Mollusks are also soft-bodied, but most have shells for protection. Some mollusks, like the octopus, do not have shells.

Using the words from the word bank, find some examples of invertebrates in the puzzle below. Then list them under the group they belong to.

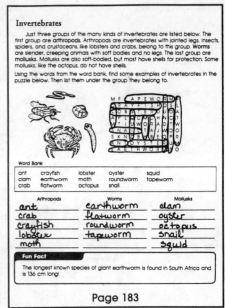

Word Bank

ant	crayfish	lobster	oyster	squid
clam	earthworm	moth	roundworm	tapeworm
crab	flatworm	octopus	snail	

Arthropods	Worms	Mollusks
ant	earthworm	clam
crab	flatworm	oyster
crayfish	roundworm	octopus
lobster	tapeworm	snail
moth		squid

Fun Fact

The longest known species of giant earthworm is found in South Africa and is 136 cm long!

Page 183

Orderly Insects

There are more than 25 different orders of insects. Seven of the most common orders are listed below. Write the name of the insects pictured under the correct order.

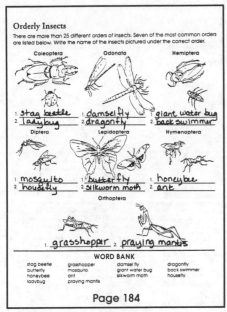

Coleoptera
1. stag beetle
2. ladybug

Odonata
1. damselfly
2. dragonfly

Hemiptera
1. giant water bug
2. back swimmur

Diptera
1. mosquito
2. housefly

Lepidoptera
1. butterfly
2. silkworm moth

Hymenoptera
1. honeybee
2. ant

Orthoptera
1. grasshopper
2. praying mantis

WORD BANK

stag beetle   grasshopper   damsel fly   dragonfly
butterfly   mosquito   giant water bug   back swimmer
honeybee   ant   silkworm moth   housefly
ladybug   praying mantis

Page 184

Friend or Foe?

Insects play a very important role in the balance of nature. Insects eat many kinds of plants and animals, but they also are a source of food for many other kinds of plants and animals. Complete the list of ways that insects can be harmful and helpful.

HELPFUL	HARMFUL
Answers will vary	

Insect Control

Man has used many different methods for insect control. One method is the use of chemicals called insecticides. One such insecticide that is commonly used throughout the world is DDT. DDT is a very effective insecticide, but it was found to also be very harmful to man and the environment. This insecticide has been banned in the United States, but it is still used in many other parts of the world.
Read about the uses and effects of DDT. Pretend that you are writing an editorial in an international newspaper that would convince the other nations of the world that they, too, should ban the use of DDT.

International News Editorial

DDT — Helpful or Harmful?
Answers will vary

Continue on the back of your paper.

Page 185

Worms, Worms, Worms

There are thousands of different kinds of worms. Each kind belongs to one of the four major groups of worms.

Draw a line from each pictured worm to the group to which it belongs.

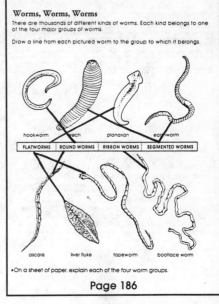

hookworm   perch   planarian   earthworm

FLATWORMS	ROUND WORMS	RIBBON WORMS	SEGMENTED WORMS

ascaris   liver fluke   tapeworm   bootlace worm

• On a sheet of paper, explain each of the four worm groups.

Page 186

Vertebrates

The more than five groups of vertebrates have many characteristics that are similar. Complete the chart below.

	Fish	Amphibians	Reptiles	Birds	Mammals
Warm-blooded or Cold-blooded	cold	cold	cold	warm	warm
Type of Body Covering	scales	moist skin	scales	feathers	skin/hair
Born Alive or Hatched	alive and hatched	hatched	both	hatched	born alive
Feed Young with Milk (Yes/No)	no	no	no	no	yes
Air, Land or Water Habitat	water	water, land	land (some water)	air/land	air, land water
Type of Appendages	fins	legs	legs	wings, feet/legs	legs, wings, arms, tails

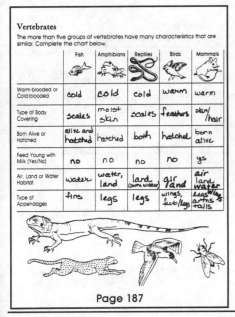

Page 187

Defensive Adaptations

In nature, animals hunt and eat other animals so that they can survive. All animals struggle to stay alive. Some animals hide from predators while others have built-in weapons that other animals fear.

Over the years, each animal has changed to give itself more protection. This is known as defensive adaptation. Some of these adaptations are very strange and unusual.

Identify and explain the adaptation for each vertebrate pictured below.

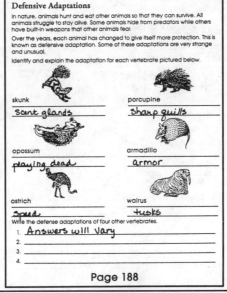

skunk
scent glands

porcupine
sharp quills

opossum
playing dead

armadillo
armor

ostrich
speed

walrus
tusks

Write the defense adaptations of four other vertebrates.
1. Answers will vary
2.
3.
4.

Page 188

Fishy Business

What do a porpoise and a perch have in common? You might answer that they both live in the water, they both have fins and they are both fish. Only two out of your three answers are correct. A porpoise is not a fish. It is a mammal.

Make a comparison between the porpoise and the perch. You can find resource books in your library to help you make this comparison.

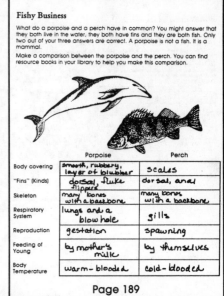

	Porpoise	Perch
Body covering	smooth, rubbery, layer of blubber	scales
"Fins" (Kinds)	dorsal, fluke, flippers	dorsal, anal
Skeleton	many bones with a backbone	many bones with a backbone
Respiratory System	lungs and a blow hole	gills
Reproduction	gestation	spawning
Feeding of Young	by mother's milk	by themselves
Body Temperature	warm-blooded	cold-blooded

Page 189

Marine Life

The ocean is filled with thousands of different kinds of animals. Some of these creatures are so small that they can be seen only with the help of a microscope. Others are over 100 feet long and can weigh over 100 tons. Their habitats, diets, defense systems, and litter size may vary as much as their size.

Use reference books from your library and other sources to research the marine animals listed below.

Name: **White Shark**
Habitat:
What It Eats:
Enemies:
Interesting Facts:

Answers will vary

Name: **Blue Whale**
Habitat:
What It Eats:
Enemies:
Interesting Facts:

Name: **Sea Horse**
Habitat:
What It Eats:
Enemies:
Interesting Facts:

Name:
Habitat:
What It Eats:
Enemies:
Interesting Facts:

Research a marine creature of your choice.

Page 190

A Whale of a Story

Below is information about whales. Make a whale glossary of terms using the words that are in bold. Write a definition of the bold words using the context of the story. Then, use as many of the words as possible to write a poem or story.

Whales belong to a group of animals called **Cetaceans**. There are two major types of whales, **baleen whales** and **toothed whales**. Baleen whales have no teeth. They have hundreds of thin plates made of material similar to human fingernails. These **baleen plates** filter out food from the water. Krill, small, shrimplike animals, are the main food of baleen whales. These are further divided into three groups. One group, the rorquals, have long grooves on their throats and chests and include the largest whale, the blue whale.

There are about 65 kinds of toothed whales that are divided into five groups. One group, the **beluga** and narwhal, measures 10-15 feet long. Belugas are milk-white when fully grown and are often called white whales.

Whales are shaped like torpedoes. They have a **blowhole**, a nostril on top of their head, through which they breathe. Also on top of the body is a **dorsal fin** that stands upright and helps whales steer. **Flippers** also are used for steering and for balance. Whales' **flukes** are two triangular lobes that are part of its tail. The flukes beat up and down to move the whale through the water. Beneath their skin, whales have a layer of fat called blubber. Blubber helps keep whales warm, and when food is scarce whales can live off their blubber for a long time.

Whales are the most intelligent of all animals. They communicate with one another by making a variety of sounds called **phonations**, or whale songs. These songs consist of groans, moans, roars, sighs, high-pitched squeaks, and chirps.

Other interesting facts about whales include: Whales perform impressive leaps from the water called breaching. Many also **migrate**, sometimes thousands of miles every year, to spend the winter in warm water and the summer in cold water. Whales use a method of navigation called **echolocation**. Whales emit sounds and then listen for an echo produced when objects reflect the sounds. From the echoes, they can determine the distance and direction of an object.

Whaling has become so efficient that some whales are **endangered**. Whalers, people who hunt whales, realized that some species were almost extinct. In 1946, the International Whaling Committee (IWC) was formed to protect the whales' future. *Glossary and stories/poems will vary.*

Page 191

Life on a Rotting Log

The forest community is not limited to animals and plants that live in or near living trees. As the succession of the forest continues, many trees will die and fall to the ground. As the "dead" log lies on the forest floor, the actions of plants, animals, bacteria, lichens and the weather help break it down and return its components to the forest soil. Notice the many different varieties of life found on the rotting log.

1. List the different kinds of plant life that are found on the rotting log. *pin cushion moss, pixie cup lichen, pale shield lichen, jack-o-lantern mushroom*
2. How do the small plants help this log to decay? *roots open spaces in the log*
3. What do the plants get from the log? *nutrients (food), place to grow, protection*
4. What kinds of small animals are found in or on the rotting log? *ant larvae, earthworm, red-backed salamander, chipmunk*
5. How do these animals help the log to decay? *They eat and gnaw on the log.*

Find Out — The lichen found on the rotting log is a very interesting kind of plant. It is actually two organisms that are living together. What two organisms form lichen? What does each of these organisms need to live? How do organisms help each other? *Lichen are made of algae and fungus. The fungus absorbs the water that the algae needs to live. The algae makes food by means of photosynthesis.*

Page 192

Endangered

Many of the animals in the grassland community are very rare, and some are in danger of becoming extinct. The American buffalo was once one of those animals. In 1889, only 551 of them could be found. Today, after laws were established to protect them, there are about 15,000 of them in the U.S.

The black-footed ferret, which lives in the western Great Plains of North America, is an endangered species. Complete the chart below and color the picture. You will need to find information from an encyclopedia or other source to help you. When you have finished, complete the activity at the bottom of the page.

Name: **Black-Footed Ferret** (Mustela nigripes) *tail 11-15 cm*
Description:
Size: *weight, 7 kg (1.5 lbs) length 38-46 cm*
Color: *pale yellowish-white head, black area across eyes, brownish-black markings on feet*
Habitat: *North American plains*
Diet: *prairie dog; in captivity - rabbits or poultry*
Conditions causing it to become endangered: *It faces extinction since its main source of food, the prairie dog, has almost disappeared.*

Below is a list of grassland animals that have become rare. Pick one or choose one of your own and do research to find out more about the animal. Then, write a news story voicing your opinion about protecting the animal.

African elephant   white rhinoceros   prairie dog   kangaroo   bald eagle

Page 193

The Great Debate

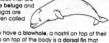

Close to downtown Riverton are 300 acres of wetlands. This area of marshes and ponds is the home of a countless number of species of plants and animals. A group of citizens from the city of Riverton wants to build a new baseball stadium on this land. Riverton has never had a professional baseball team, nor has it ever had any professional sports teams. Riverton is a large city of almost 750,000 people and this is the only open land available near downtown. Some citizens would like to save this wetland and have the ball park made elsewhere, possibly out in the suburbs.

What do you think? What do you want to happen to the wetlands? Make two lists of arguments — one for and one against the building of the new Riverton ball park.

"Riverton should build a new baseball park on the wetlands property."

Pro (for)	Con (against)
1.	1.
2.	2.
3.	3.
4.	4.
5.	5.
6.	6.

Arguments will vary.

Page 194

The Prairie Food Web

In complex prairie communities, like the prairie community, the flow of food and energy cannot be judged by just looking at simple food chains. Instead, you must look at the interlocking of food chains in a community called a food web. The many kinds of producers and consumers available to the prairie community allow animals to select from a wide variety of food sources.

GOPHER   GRASSHOPPER   MOUSE   OWL   BACTERIA   GRASSES   BACTERIA   COYOTE

1. Name at least four relationships shown in the food web pictured above.
   1. *Answers will vary*   3.
   2.   4.
2. If there were no coyotes left in the prairie community, what would happen to the mouse population? Why? *The mouse population would increase there would be fewer predators to eat them.*
3. If there was a decrease in the owl population, what would happen to the gopher population? Why? *The gopher population would increase due to fewer predators.*
4. If the prairie grasses were destroyed by fire what would happen to the coyote population? Why? *The coyote population would decrease, since their prey depend on grasses to live, or they would move.*
5. What does it mean when we say, "The death of one species in a food web upsets the rest of the web"? *All species depend on each other - if one chain link is decreased, the other links are affected.*

Page 195

Bird Watcher's List

Observer _____
Date _____

Almost every bird watcher keeps a list of the birds that he/she sees. Use the chart to record the species, date, time and place of the birds that you see. Accurate identification may also be made by identifying the sound of a bird. If the species are only heard and not seen, place an "H" after the species' name.

SPECIES	DATE	TIME	LOCALITY
Answers			
will			
vary			

What bird did you see?
Look at the following.

1. Size
Is it bigger or smaller than a sparrow? robin? crow?

2. Shape
of head
of wings
of tail

3. Color and Marks
on body
on tail
on head
on wings

4. Habitat and Behaviors
What was it doing?
Where was it?
How does it fly?

Page 196

Adopt a Bird

There are probably more than one hundred different kinds of birds that live in your region. Select one species of bird and become an expert. Research your species of bird and complete the profile below.

Common Name _____
Scientific Name _____

Description	Picture of Male
Size:	
Body shape:	
Wing shape:	
Tail shape:	
Color and field marks:	
Flight pattern:	

Profiles will vary.

Behaviors

Description of Habitat:
Food and Feeding Habits:
Migration (if applicable):

Page 197

Clues from the Past

Fossil clues of dinosaurs and other prehistoric animals are used in forming images of these animals. When only parts of a skeleton have been found, the clues must be pieced together in order to describe the size, habitat, strength, speed and family patterns of the animal. From the clues listed below, make some of your own inferences about the animals.

1. extremely large rib cage and stomach *Answers will vary*
2. long, stiff tails
3. long, hollow nasal bones from snout to back of jaws
4. thousands of tiny, flat teeth in back of jaws
5. moveable spines and plates on back
6. thick, rounded bone on top of skull
7. large, saucer-shaped mud mounds of eggs spaced exact distances apart
8. nostrils on top of skull
9. large, strong hind leg bones; short, weak front leg bones
10. jagged or serrated teeth

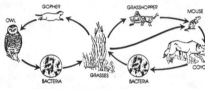

Page 198

Dinosaur Acrostic

Write the answers to the following definitions in the spaces provided. The circled letters are used as clues for your answers.

The middle period of the Age of Dinosaurs — JURA(S)IC
The climate of the middle period — WE(T)
Another name for carnosaur — M(E)AT-EATER
A supercontinent that continued to separate — PAN(G)AEA
One of the largest and longest dinosaurs — DIPL(O)DOCUS
Dinosaur with bony plates on its back — STEG(O)SAURUS
The oldest bird known — ARCH(A)EOPTERYX
A fast, hollow-tailed dinosaur — COEL(U)RUS
One of the first large, meat-eating dinosaurs — ALLOSAU(R)US
A dinosaur better known as Brontosaurus — APATOSAU(R)US
Shallow water that covered much of Europe — (S)EAS

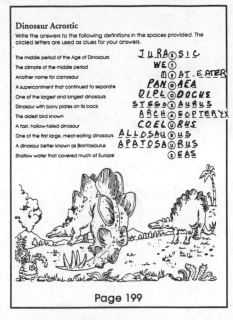

Page 199

Cretaceous Crossword

Solve the crossword puzzle using words found in the Word Bank.

Across
1. Meaning of the word "dinosaur"
3. Dinosaur with three horns on its head
6. Province of Canada in which many fossils of dinosaurs have been found
9. This type of plant flourished during this period.
10. A large group of dinosaurs that traveled together
11. The teeth of this dinosaur were discovered in England by Mary Ann Mantell.
12. A hadrosaurid, or dinosaur with a broad, toothless beak
13. Marine reptiles with flippers; much like dolphins today

Down
1. The third period of time in the Age of Dinosaurs
2. "Tyrant lizard" dinosaur
4. Long-necked marine reptiles
5. "Bird imitator" dinosaur; resembled today's ostrich
7. Dinosaur with massive skull bone used in fighting
8. Flying reptiles such as Pteranodon and Rhamphorhynchus

Word Bank

Terrible Lizard	Ichthyosaurs	Plesiosaurs
Tyrannosaurus	herd	Ornithomimus
Pterosaurs	Triceratops	bonehead
duckbilled	flowering	Alberta
Cretaceous		Iguanodon

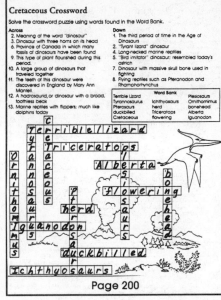

Page 200

Making Fossils

Real fossils of plants and animals are recovered from mud, rock layers and tar pits. In this activity, you will make your own fossil tracks. Read the directions before gathering your supplies.

What to use: small cardboard boxes or milk cartons, plaster of Paris, stirring stick, water, plastic or paper cup, nonstick cooking spray, newspapers, nail, nail file or paper clip

What to do:
1. Select a small box or carton for your fossil mold.
2. Select a small object, such as a shell, bone or leaf, that will fit easily into the box.
3. Fill a cup half full with water. Add plaster of Paris to the water and stir until you have a thin mixture.
4. Pour about half of this mixture into the bottom of the box.
5. Carefully place the object on top of the plaster. Spray a small amount of the nonstick cooking spray on the object.
6. Quickly add the remainder of the plaster mixture to fill the box.
7. Set aside until the next day.
8. After the plaster has hardened, carefully peel the cardboard away from the plaster. Place the hardened plaster on newspaper.
9. Now you are ready to discover your fossil! With an instrument such as a nail, nail file or paper clip, begin to scrape away the top of the plaster carefully until you discover some evidence of a fossil deposit. Continue to work until you have fully uncovered the "fossil."
10. Remove the fossil from the plaster. Examine the depression it has left in the underlying plaster. Is the cast of the object a good copy of the fossil?

Questions to answer: *Answers will vary.*
1. How has this activity demonstrated the actual discovery and removal of fossil remains from a site?
2. Why are the complete skeletons of some animals never found at a site? *Predators carried away parts of bodies, some parts are destroyed or transported by elements*
3. What precautions do paleontologists take to preserve the fossils and remove them from a site without damage? *They use delicate instruments, for example.*
4. What can we learn from the discovered fossils of plants and animals? *Age of rocks they are found in, what kind of life existed in various periods of Earth's history, tell whether rocks were formed on land or under the ocean.*

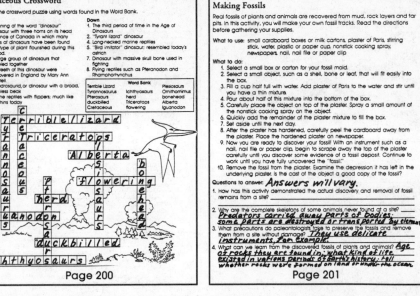

Page 201

Mysteries of the Ice Age

Many of the mysteries of the Pleistocene Epoch are still to be solved. Many of the puzzling questions are still to be answered.
Use reference books to help you form your own hypotheses or answers to these questions. *Answers may vary.*

1. Why have fossils of some animals been found all over the world? *Some animals migrated across ice. Bones were also transported by the ice.*
2. How did animals migrate from one continent to another? *To escape the cold or dry conditions.*
3. What changes in the climate occurred during this epoch? *The temperature of the Earth cooled and warmed four times. Glaciers reached southward.*
4. What changes in the land masses occurred during this epoch? *Lakes were formed, such as Great Lakes. Mounds and ridges were formed when ice melted.*
5. Why did large sheets of ice appear in the Northern Hemisphere? *Temperatures cooled, ice sheets developed and flowed outward; water turned to ice.*
6. Why were there periods of alternating glacial and warm conditions on Earth during the Pleistocene Epoch? *Some scientists believe regularly recurring changes in the shape of the earth's orbit around the sun cause cooling trends that promote formation of huge ice sheets.*

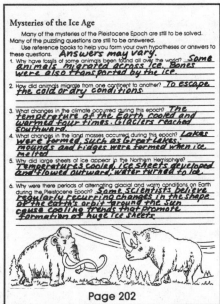

Page 202

Classification of Dinosaurs

Refer to the encyclopedia or a book on dinosaurs to locate the dinosaurs pictured below. Think of the ways in which you could classify these animals under different headings, such as bird-hipped, meat eater, Cretaceous Period.
In the spaces at the bottom of the page, list the Classification Headings and the numbers of the dinosaurs you would place under each of these headings.

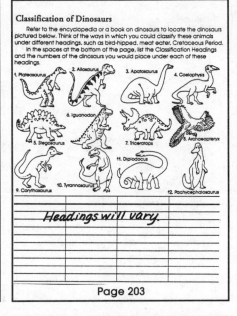

1. Plateosaurus
2. Allosaurus
3. Apatosaurus
4. Coelophysis
5. Stegosaurus
6. Iguanodon
7. Triceratops
8. Archaeopteryx
9. Corythosaurus
10. Tyrannosaurus
11. Diplodocus
12. Pachycephalosaurus

Headings will vary.

Page 203

River System

Using resource materials and the Word Bank below, label the parts of the river system. After labeling each part, write the description of each word in the space provided.

tributary
lake
meander
alluvial fan
waterfall
rapids
flood plain
oxbow lake
delta

Answers will vary. **Word Bank**

waterfall *steep descent of the water of a stream*	meander *a turn or winding of a stream*	rapid: *part of a river where current is fast & broken by obstruction*
flood plain *level land that may be submerged by floodwaters*	delta *deposit at the mouth of a river*	oxbow lake *a lake resembling an oxbow*
tributary *a stream feeding a larger stream or a lake*	lake *a large, inland Body of standing water*	alluvial fan *deposit of a stream where it joins the main stream*

Page 204

The Earth as a Puzzle

Use the Word Bank to complete the word puzzle.

Across
2. Uneven ridges of gravel, sand and rock deposited by a melting glacier
4. Material deposited by wind, water and melting glaciers
7. Molten rock that is deposited on Earth's surface
9. S-shaped loop formed by a river
10. The thin, outermost layer of Earth from where magma flows
11. The action of wearing down Earth's surface by wind and water

Word Bank

erosion	dune	volcano	crust
sediment	delta	meander	waves
moraine	lava	magma	esker

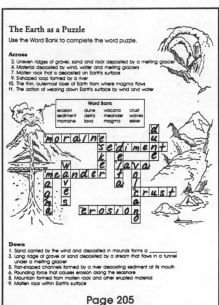

moraine
sediment
lava
meander
magma
crust
erosion
dune

Down
1. Sand carried by the wind and deposited in mounds forms a ___.
3. Long ridge of gravel or sand deposited by a stream that flows in a tunnel in a melting glacier
5. Fan-shaped channels formed by a river depositing sediment at its mouth
6. Pounding force that causes erosion along the seashore
8. Mountain formed from molten rock and other erupted material
9. Molten rock within Earth's surface

Page 205

How the Earth Changes

Earth changes continuously. Some changes, such as an earthquake, take only a few minutes. Others, such as the wearing away of the Grand Canyon, take place over millions of years.
Four kinds of changes affect Earth's surface: weathering, erosion, mass movement and changes in Earth's crust.
With the help of your science book, an encyclopedia or some other source, write a description of each of the four kinds of changes. *Answers will vary.*

Weathering — *the physical disintegration and chemical decomposition of earth materials at or near the earth's surface*

Erosion — *to wear away by the action of water, wind, or glacial ice*

Mass movement — *slipping of large amounts of rock and soil as occurs in a landslide or mudslide, may cause a variety of effects. for example, a landslide may dam a river*

Changes in Earth's crust — *Plate tectonics – Earth's crust and upper mantle are divided into 20 rigid plates that move. These movements fold and reshape Earth's crust and build mountains.*

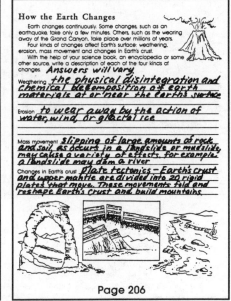

Page 206

The Rock Cycle

With the help of heat, pressure, and weathering, one kind of rock can be changed into a new kind of rock. For example, beautiful marble is formed from limestone, and slate comes from shale and clay.

The changing of rocks is an ongoing cycle. There is no true beginning, but it might be easier to understand by beginning with magma. Complete the rock cycle diagram pictured below.

Rock Cycle

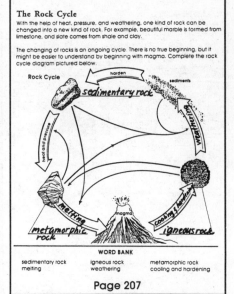

harden
sediments
sedimentary rock
heat and pressure
weathering
melting
cooling & hardening
metamorphic rock
magma
igneous rock

WORD BANK

sedimentary rock	igneous rock	metamorphic rock
melting	weathering	cooling and hardening

Page 207

Classy Rocks

There are three main groups of rock: **igneous rock**, **metamorphic rock**, and **sedimentary rock**. Each of the rocks pictured on this page belongs to one of these groups. Fill in the definitions. Then, in the space below each picture, tell which group each rock belongs to.

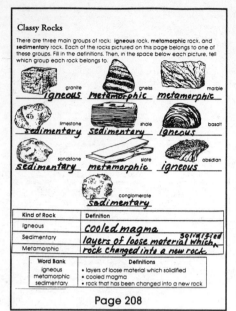

granite — *igneous*
gneiss — *metamorphic*
marble — *metamorphic*

limestone — *sedimentary*
shale — *sedimentary*
basalt — *igneous*

sandstone — *sedimentary*
slate — *metamorphic*
obsidian — *igneous*

conglomerate — *sedimentary*

Kind of Rock	Definition
Igneous	*cooled magma*
Sedimentary	*layers of loose material which solidified*
Metamorphic	*rock changed into a new rock*

Word Bank	Definitions
igneous metamorphic sedimentary	• layers of loose material which solidified • cooled magma • rock that has been changed into a new rock

Page 208

Good News – Bad News

As the edges of Earth's plates bump, grind, slip and slide, they can bring good news and bad news. The good news is that these areas of activity are valuable sources of geothermal energy that man is just beginning to use. The bad news is that great destruction in the forms of earthquakes or volcanic eruptions can also occur in these same areas.

You are the reporter. Using the headlines below, write two news articles that show the good news and the bad news brought about by the forces inside Earth.

Middle Earth News

vol. 2   Thursday, February 20 $1.25

New Unlimited Energy Source

Articles will vary.

Shake, Rattle and Roll

Page 209

Inside Earth

Using the Word Bank below, label the Earth's layers. Then, complete the paragraph. Some words will be used twice.

The structure of Earth is sometimes compared to that of a *peach* . Just like the fruit, Earth also has *three* layers. They are the *crust* , *mantle* , and *core* . The innermost layer of Earth is the *core* . This is the *hottest* part of Earth. Scientists think it is about 1,400 miles thick and is made mostly of *iron* and *nickel* . Beneath the crust is the *mantle* . It is very hot, solid *rock* . The crust is the *first* layer of Earth. This layer is very *thin* and is made of three kinds of *rock* : *igneous* , *sedimentary* , and *metamorphic* .

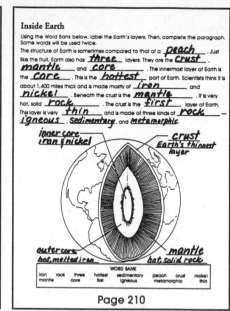

inner core iron & nickel

crust Earth's thinnest layer

outer core hot, melted iron

mantle hot, solid rock

WORD BANK							
iron	rock	three	hottest	sedimentary	peach	crust	nickel
mantle	core	first		igneous		metamorphic	thin

Page 210

How a Volcano Forms

Mount Vesuvius was dormant for hundreds of years before it erupted in 79 A.D. and buried several ancient Roman cities. On August 24, pressure from gases inside the mountain caused its top to blow off. Hot ashes, cinders, and dust shot into the air. Pliny the Younger recorded this disaster in a letter.

Read the paragraph below. Then write the words in bold in the correct place on the diagram.

When the heat in the center of the Earth is so very hot, it melts the rock in the **mantle**, the thick rock layer just below the **crust**. The melted rock is called **magma**. A volcano begins as magma. When rock melts, gases form that mix with magma. Gas-filled magma rises through weakened places in the Earth because it is now lighter than the solid rock around it. It forms a **magma chamber** below the crust. The pressure of the solid rock around the chamber causes the magma to melt a **channel** through the crust up into the mountain. When the gas-filled magma nears the peak and the pressure is too great, it is released through an opening called the **central vent**. Most magma and other volcanic materials like **ashes** and **cinders** fly into the air. When the eruption is over, a **crater** is formed. The central vent is at the bottom of the crater.

Read about another volcano. Write about it. *Answers will vary.*

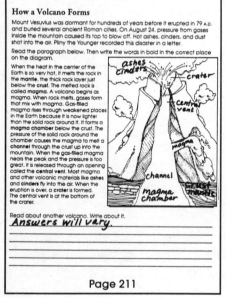

ashes cinders
crater
central vent
magma
channel
crust mantle
magma chamber

Page 211

Volcanic Cones

Volcanic cones can be classified by their shapes. Label the three different kinds of volcanic cones pictured below. Label the parts of the volcanoes.

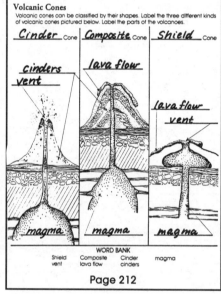

Cinder Cone   *Composite* Cone   *Shield* Cone

cinders vent
lava flow
lava flow vent

magma   *magma*   *magma*

WORD BANK			
Shield vent	Composite lava flow	Cinder cinders	magma

Page 212

Fascinating, Terrifying Eruptions

People have always been fascinated and terrified by the spectacle of volcanic eruptions and their tremendous power. Some of the worst disasters in the world have been caused by volcanic eruptions, which can result in thousands of deaths and entire towns destroyed.

Research a volcanic eruption such as Vesuvius or Mount St. Helens. Write a magazine article about it on another piece of paper as if you were an eyewitness. Include the volcano's location, date of eruption, and other interesting facts. Below, use colored pencils to draw a picture of the volcano erupting. Make a caption for your drawing as if it were the illustration for your article.

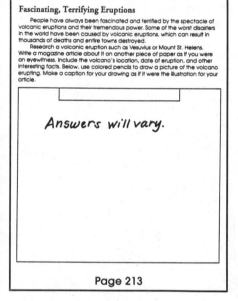

Answers will vary.

Page 213

Majestic Mountains

The word *mountain* means different things to different people. Some people who live on vast, level plains consider a small hill a mountain. Others who live in the mountains would not consider a region mountainous unless it was very high and rugged.

Listed below are eight famous mountains. Graph each mountain's height. On the bottom of the graph, put the mountain's name and on the side of the graph, put its height. When you have finished graphing, use the results to answer the questions below.

Name	Height
Everest	29,028 feet
Lassen Peak	10,457 feet
Kenya	17,058 feet
Pikes Peak	14,110 feet
Fuji	12,388 feet
Mauna Loa	13,677 feet
McKinley	20,320 feet
Mount St. Helens	8,364 feet

Graphs may vary.

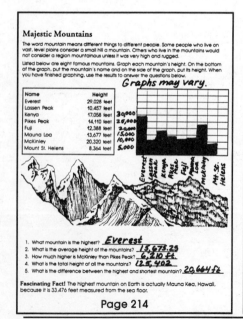

1. What mountain is the highest? *Everest*
2. What is the average height of the mountains? *15,675.25*
3. How much higher is McKinley than Pikes Peak? *6,210 ft.*
4. What is the total height of all the mountains? *125,402*
5. What is the difference between the highest and shortest mountain? *20,664 ft.*

Fascinating Fact! The highest mountain on Earth is actually Mauna Kea, Hawaii, because it is 33,476 feet measured from the sea floor.

Page 214

Soil Profile

Study the soil profile pictured here. Identify the layer or layers where each of the following is found.

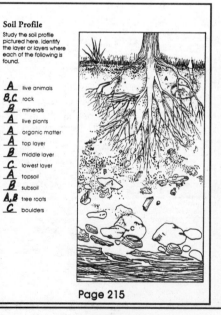

A live animals
B,C rock
B minerals
A live plants
A organic matter
A top layer
B middle layer
C lowest layer
A topsoil
B subsoil
A,B tree roots
C boulders

Page 215

Mysterious Sand

Sand is any earthy material that consists of loose grains of minerals or rocks that are smaller than gravel. Most grains of sand are parts of solid rocks that have been crumbled away by waves battering and grinding down rocky cliffs. Many types of minerals are found in sand, and this determines the color of the sand. Some beaches have a mixture of colors, while others have sand of one color. Some examples are given in the box. Sand has many uses: quartz sand is used to make chemicals and glass, sandpaper is made by gluing loose sand onto heavy paper, and mortar and concrete are also made with sand. Try the experiment below to learn more about sand.

Color	Made of
black	lava
light brown/tan	granite, quartz
yellow	quartz
gold	mica
red	garnet
white	coral, seashells, quartz

Materials Needed:
beach sand or sand from a building supply store
pan
paper
magnifying lens
Popsicle stick
newspaper
measuring cup
hot plate
cornstarch
small milk cartons
milk

Experiment:
1. Spread a few grains of sand on the paper and examine them with a magnifying lens. *Answers will vary.*
2. Sketch some of the grains on the back of this page.
3. Do all the grains look exactly alike?
4. Are all the grains the same color?
5. What were these grains of sand originally?
6. Your teacher will now assist you with the following:
   a. Mix 2 cups of sand, 1 cup of water, and 1 cup of cornstarch with a Popsicle stick. Pour mixture into pan.
   b. Heat mixture slowly until it thickens.
   c. Pour mixture into individual milk cartons to cool and harden.
   d. Peel away the sides of the carton.
   e. Working on newspaper, carve sea animals, plants, shells, coral, or sea sculptures with the Popsicle stick.
   f. Display the work in your class or school media center.

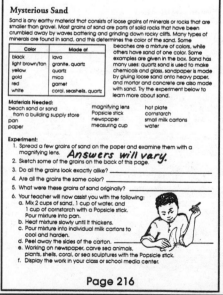

Page 216

What Am I?

The solar system contains many different objects that travel around the sun. Use the encyclopedia and other sources to explore the solar system and solve the following "What Am I?" riddles.

1. I am the largest planet. **Jupiter**
2. I am the planet best known for my rings. **Saturn**
3. I am the planet known for my "Great Red Spot." **Jupiter**
4. I am the smallest planet. **Pluto**
5. I am the planet closest to the sun. **Mercury**
6. I am known as the "Red Planet." **Mars**
7. Voyager 2 discovered new moons and rings around me in 1989. **Uranus**
8. Until 1999, I am the planet farthest from the sun. **Pluto**
9. I am the planet closest in size to Earth. **Venus**
10. I am the planet with the shortest rotation time. **Jupiter**
11. My moon, Titan, is larger than the planet, Mercury. **Saturn**
12. I am the planet with the rotation time most similar to Earth's. **Mars**
13. I am the planet with the most natural satellites. **Saturn**
14. My buddies and I form a belt between Mars and Jupiter. **asteroids**
15. I am the largest object in the solar system. **Sun**
16. I am the brightest planet in the sky. **Venus**
17. I am the only planet known to support life. **Earth**
18. I am the planet that orbits the sun "on my side." **Uranus**
19. I am known as "Earth's Twin." **Venus**
20. People once thought that there were canals on my surface, but they were wrong. **Mars**
21. I am the brightest object in the night sky. **moon**
22. I am often called a "snowball in space." **comet**
23. I am also known as a "shooting star." **meteor**
24. My surface temperature is about 10,000° F. **Sun**
25. I am the most distant planet that can be seen with the unaided eye. **Uranus**

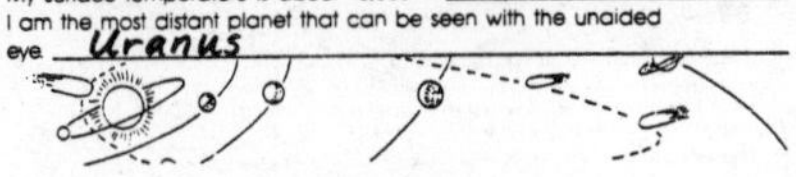

Page 217

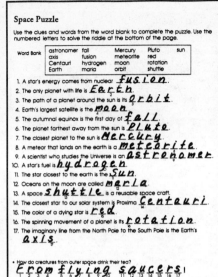

Space Puzzle

Use the clues and words from the word blank to complete the puzzle. Use the numbered letters to solve the riddle at the bottom of the page.

Word Bank

astronomer	fall	Mercury	Pluto	sun
axis	fusion	meteorite	red	
Centauri	hydrogen	moon	rotation	
Earth	maria	orbit	shuttle	

1. A star's energy comes from nuclear **fusion**.
2. The only planet with life is **Earth**.
3. The path of a planet around the sun is its **Orbit**.
4. Earth's largest satellite is the **moon**.
5. The autumnal equinox is the first day of **fall**.
6. The planet farthest away from the sun is **Pluto**.
7. The closest planet to the sun is **Mercury**.
8. A meteor that lands on the earth is a **meteorite**.
9. A scientist who studies the Universe is an **astronomer**.
10. A star's fuel is **hydrogen**.
11. The star closest to the earth is the **Sun**.
12. Oceans on the moon are called **maria**.
13. A space **shuttle** is a reusable space craft.
14. The closest star to our solar system is Proxima **Centauri**.
15. The color of a dying star is **red**.
16. The spinning movement of a planet is its **rotation**.
17. The imaginary line from the North Pole to the South Pole is the Earth's **axis**.

• How do creatures from outer space drink their tea?

From flying saucers!

1 2 3 4 5 6 7 8 9 10 11 12 13 14 15 16 17

Page 218

Mars—Then and Now

Many advances have been made in space exploration, giving scientists new and more accurate information about our solar system. Sixty years ago, our only means of gathering information about distant planets was by observation through a telescope. Today spacecrafts equipped with cameras, such as Mariner and Voyager, send pictures back to Earth. Even robotic space probes, such as Viking I, have been placed on distant planets to transmit high-quality pictures and analyze soil samples.

Early information about the planets was very inaccurate and led people to believe many things that have been proven untrue. An example is the belief that little green men, called Martians, lived beneath the surface of Mars. The Mariner space probe found no evidence to support this idea.

Write two articles that compare our knowledge of the planet Mars. In your first article, pretend that you are a newspaper reporter in the early 1900s reporting on the life and evidence of life on Mars. Your article may refer to the "canals" and intelligent life on the planet. Your second article should reflect what scientists have learned through the most recent space probes.

Use the two headlines below for your articles. Cut out the headlines and paste them on another sheet of paper. Write your articles.

Answers will vary.

The New York Times

Monday, March 5, 1918

Intelligent Life on Mars

The New York Times

Monday, March 5

Space Probe Visits Mars

Page 219

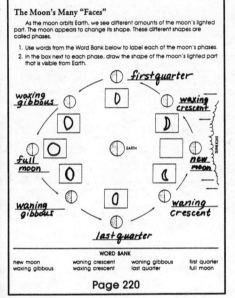

The Moon's Many "Faces"

As the moon orbits Earth, we see different amounts of the moon's lighted part. The moon appears to change its shape. These different shapes are called phases.

1. Use words from the Word Bank below to label each of the moon's phases.
2. In the box next to each phase, draw the shape of the moon's lighted part that is visible from Earth.

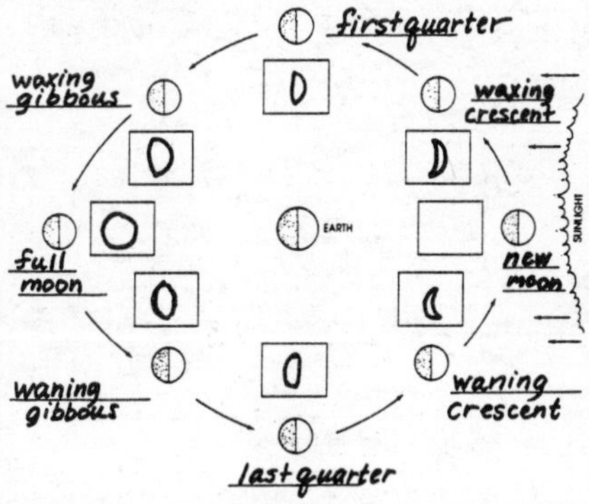

WORD BANK

new moon	waning crescent	waning gibbous	first quarter
waxing gibbous	waxing crescent	last quarter	full moon

Page 220

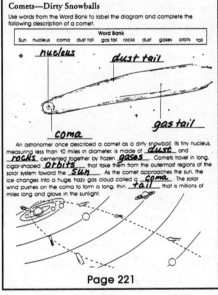

Comets—Dirty Snowballs

Use words from the Word Bank to label the diagram and complete the following description of a comet.

Word Bank

Sun nucleus coma dust tail gas tail rocks dust gases orbits tail

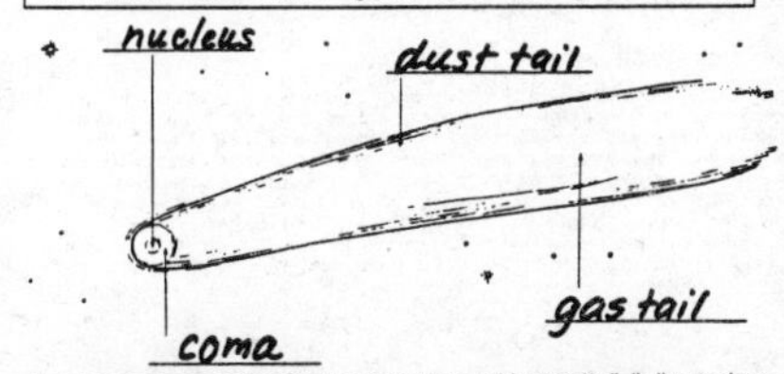

An astronomer once described a comet as a dirty snowball. Its tiny nucleus, measuring less than 10 miles in diameter, is made of **dust** and **rocks** cemented together by frozen **gases**. Comets travel in long, cigar-shaped **orbits** that take them from the outermost regions of the solar system toward the **Sun**. As the comet approaches the sun, the ice changes into a huge, hazy gas cloud called a **coma**. The solar wind pushes on the coma to form a long, thin **tail** that is millions of miles long and glows in the sunlight.

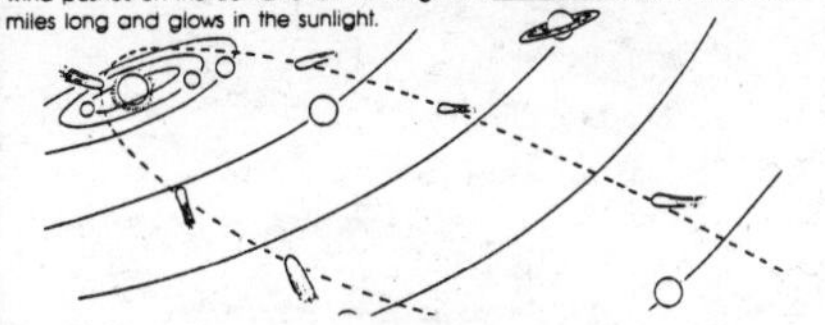

Page 221

Ford and Friction

Model T Ford 1908

Can you imagine if one out of every two people who own cars in the U.S. were driving cars made by the same company? Well, from 1908 to 1927, more than half of the cars sold in the United States were Fords.

In 1903, Henry Ford organized the Ford Motor Company. At first, it produced only expensive cars. However, Ford's invention of the Model T in 1908 helped the average American family afford an automobile not too many years later. Can you imagine life today without cars?

Try the experiment below to learn about one scientific principle Ford may have had to deal with in his quest to make an automobile affordable for many Americans.

Friction is the resistance an object has against being moved when it is in contact with another object or surface. Reducing friction is of great concern to scientists and engineers, especially when they are dealing with the operation of machinery and the movement of heavy objects.

Try the experiment below to see if you can figure out when and why friction is greater or lesser under certain conditions.

Materials Needed: rubber band (Size 32 is ideal.), box of crayons or straws, tape, sheets of sandpaper, ruler

Student Directions

Investigate

1. Wrap a long rubber band around the front cover of a book. Put half of the rubber band against the inside binding and the other half on the outside of the binding.
2. Pull the rubber band just until the book starts to move.
3. Use a ruler to measure the distance the rubber band was stretched just before the book moved. Measure from the spine of the book to the end of the rubber band in your fingers. How many inches did it stretch? **Answers will vary.**

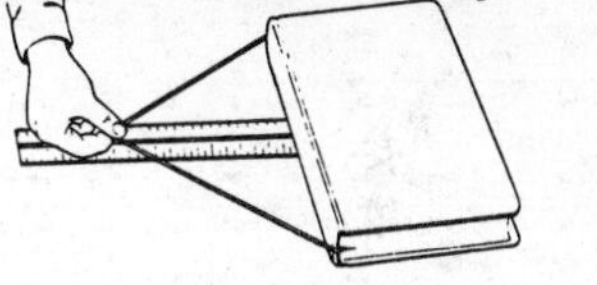

Page 222

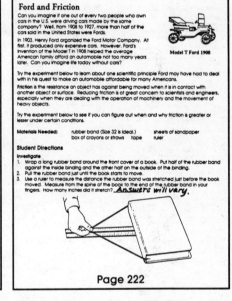

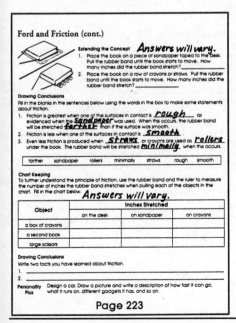

Ford and Friction (cont.)

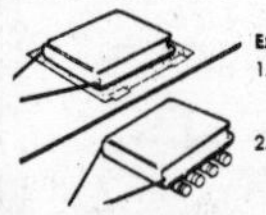

Extending the Concept **Answers will vary.**

1. Place the book on a piece of sandpaper taped to the desk. Pull the rubber band until the book starts to move. How many inches did the rubber band stretch? ______
2. Place the book on a row of crayons or straws. Pull the rubber band until the book starts to move. How many inches did the rubber band stretch? ______

Drawing Conclusions

Fill in the blanks in the sentences below using the words in the box to make some statements about friction.

1. Friction is greatest when one of the surfaces in contact is **rough** as evidenced when the **sandpaper** was used. When this occurs, the rubber band will be stretched **farther** than if the surface was smooth.
2. Friction is less when one of the surfaces in contact is **smooth**.
3. Even less friction is produced when **straws** or crayons are used as **rollers** under the book. The rubber band will be stretched **minimally** when this occurs.

farther sandpaper rollers minimally straws rough smooth

Chart Keeping

To further understand the principle of friction, use the rubber band and the ruler to measure the number of inches the rubber band stretches when pulling each of the objects in the chart. Fill in the chart below. **Answers will vary.**

Object	Inches Stretched		
	on the desk	on sandpaper	on crayons
a box of crayons			
a second book			
large scissors			

Drawing Conclusions

Write two facts you have learned about friction.

1. ______
2. ______

Personality Plus: Design a car. Draw a picture and write a description of how fast it can go, what it runs on, different gadgets it has, and so on.

Page 223

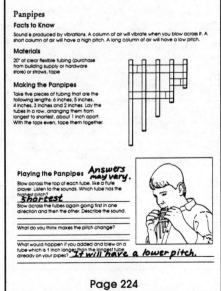

Panpipes

Facts to Know

Sound is produced by vibrations. A column of air will vibrate when you blow across it. A short column of air will have a high pitch. A long column of air will have a low pitch.

Materials

20" of clear flexible tubing (purchase from building supply or hardware store) or straws, tape

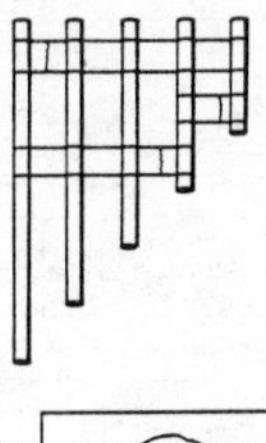

Making the Panpipes

Take five pieces of tubing that are the following lengths: 6 inches, 5 inches, 4 inches, 3 inches and 2 inches. Lay the tubes in a row, arranging them from longest to shortest, about 1 inch apart. With the tops even, tape them together.

Playing the Panpipes **Answers may vary.**

Blow across the top of each tube, like a flute player. Listen to the sounds. Which tube has the highest pitch? **Shortest**

Blow across the tubes again going first in one direction and then the other. Describe the sound. ______

What do you think makes the pitch change? ______

What would happen if you added and blew on a tube which is 1 inch longer than the longest tube already on your pipes? **It will have a lower pitch.**

Page 224

Egg Drop

Facts to Know

Gravity is the force which pulls all objects toward earth. Some materials can insulate and cushion an object from the impact of gravity. Paper, Styrofoam, cloth, and similar materials are good insulators.

Materials

Collect as many of these materials as possible before beginning the project: newspaper, Styrofoam pieces or "peanuts," pantyhose, pieces of cloth, string. In addition, one or more raw eggs and a shoebox or cardboard carton will be needed.

Investigate

The goal of this investigation is to have an egg survive from the highest possible height. Use all of the collected packaging materials to protect the egg inside the cardboard carton or shoe box. Be as creative as you can in wrapping the egg. Let your teacher hold the package as high as possible or use a ladder to stand on. He or she will drop the package. Check your egg. Did it break? ______ If your egg didn't break the first time, have your teacher drop it from a higher point. Did it break this time? ______ From how high do you think it can be dropped before it breaks? ______

Results will vary.

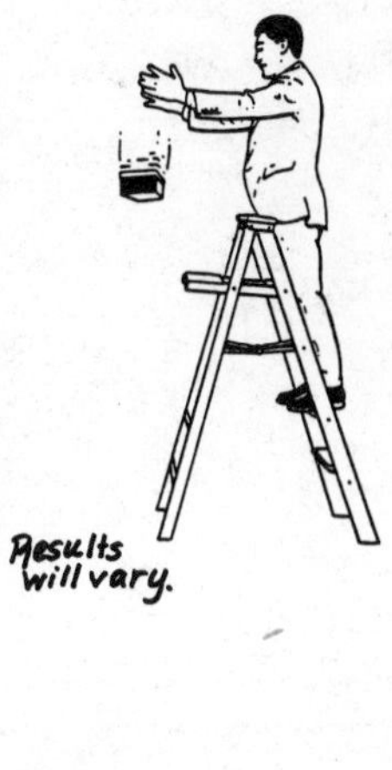

Page 225

Making a Periscope

Facts to Know
Light travels in a straight line. Mirrors reflect light in a straight line. The slanted mirrors in a periscope allow the user to see above a normal field of view.

Materials
shoebox
poster board
two mirrors

Making the Periscope
Stand your box vertically, take the lid off your box and cut a 1-inch-square hole on one side of the top. Cut another hole on the bottom of the box on the opposite side. Fold a long, narrow piece of poster board into fourths. Overlap and tape two of the folded sides to make a triangle. Trim the triangle so that it will fit into the bottom of the box opposite the hole. Make another triangle the same size and shape and fit it into the top of the box opposite the top hole. Use tape or glue to attach both triangles. Attach one mirror onto the slanting side of the bottom triangle and the other mirror onto the top triangle. Make sure each mirror slants at the same angle and that both mirrors face into the box. Place the lid back on your box.

Using the Periscope   *Answers will vary.*
Kneel beside your desk or sit underneath it. Hold the tip of the periscope over the side of your desk. Look through the bottom hole at the mirror. What do you see? _____

Why do you think the periscope works? _____

What do the mirrors do? _____

Draw a picture on the back of this sheet to show one thing you saw through the periscope.

Modifying the Investigation
Change the angle of your triangles. Does this change what you see? _____

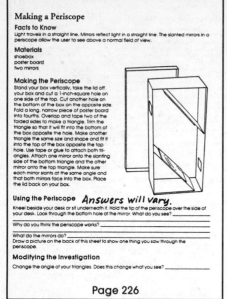

Page 226

Simple Machines

There are six simple machines which are the basic units of all complex machines: the lever, the wheel and axle, the wedge, the pulley, the inclined plane and the screw.

Recognizing Simple Machines
Which simple machines can you find in each of the tools listed below?

hammer	*lever*	scissors	*levers*
doorstop	*wedge*	drill	*wheel, axle, lever*
saw	*wedge*	screwdriver	*lever*
crowbar	*lever, wedge*	monkey wrench	*wheel, axle, lever, wedge*

Bicycle Parts
Study a bicycle carefully. Which simple machines can you find? Fill in the blanks.

tire *wheel & axle*   parking stand *lever, inclined plane*
caliper brakes *pulley, wheel &*   handlebars *lever*
chain and sprocket *pulley, wheel*   gearshift *wheel & axle*
pedal and shaft *wheel & axle*   fork *lever*
other _____

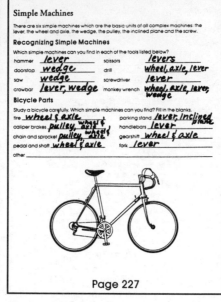

Page 227

Newton's Cradle

Fact to Know
Every action has an equal and opposite reaction.

Materials
ruler   paper clips   beads
pencil or dowel   thread or fish line

Making Newton's Cradle
Use a ruler and measure an unsharpened pencil or dowel at the following points: 1 inch, 2 inches, 3 inches, 4 inches, 5 inches and 6 inches. Use scissors to score a circle around the wood at each mark. Thread an 8-inch piece of fish line through a round bead. Knot one end to a paper clip so that the bead will not slip out. Thread the other fish lines through the other beads and tie them the same way. Tie each of the five fish lines to a mark on the pencil. Then tighten the lines. Line up all the beads so that they hang exactly even.

Using Newton's Cradle
Carefully pull back the farthest bead at one end of the cradle and let it strike the next bead. What happened?
Answers may vary.

Try it again. Did the same thing happen? _____

Why do you think this happens? _____

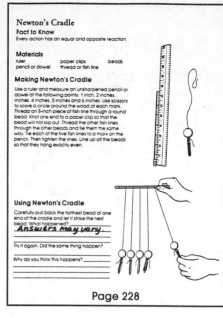

Page 228

Cartesian Diver

Materials
large jar   eyedropper   balloon
rubber band   water

Making the Cartesian Diver
Fill a large clear jar almost full with water. Fill an eyedropper about half full with water. Place the eyedropper in the water. It should barely float. Stretch a piece of balloon across the top of the jar. Use a tight rubber band to hold the rubber balloon firmly in place.

Answers may vary.

Using the Cartesian Diver
Press down on the rubber band. Did the eyedropper sink? _____
If it didn't, put more water in the eyedropper until pressing down on the balloon causes it to sink.

Expanding the Concept
Take out the eyedropper. Put some water in a small cup. Add a few drops of food coloring. Fill the eyedropper with colored water so that it just floats in the jar again. Cover the jar with the rubber again. Press down on the cover. What happened to the water in the eyedropper? _____

Making Hypotheses
What do you think happened to the air when more water went into the eyedropper? _____

What do you think makes the Cartesian Diver work? _____

What could you use instead of an eyedropper? _____

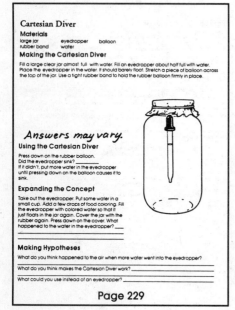

Page 229

Making a Submarine

Facts to Know
A submarine rises by pumping water out of its tanks. It sinks by pumping water into its tanks.

Materials
four crayons   tape   18" thin tubing
plastic packing   small plastic bottle   modeling clay

Building the Submarine
Use plastic packing tape to attach four crayons to the side of a small plastic bottle to form the bottom of your submarine. Tape a piece of stiff plastic to the other side of the bottle to form the "sail" on the deck of your submarine. Insert a flexible straw into the bottle with the flexible end sticking out of the mouth of the bottle and pointing down as shown. Also, insert one end of an 18-inch piece of thin tubing into the bottle. Use modeling clay   thick wad of chewing gum to seal the mouth of the bottle and hold the tubing and straw in place. The other end of the tubing can be held firmly by taping it against the outside of the bottle. Make sure the top tube stays in place. Set the bottle in the water. If necessary, attach additional crayons to improve the sub's balance. Suck gently on the tube. Water should fill the bottle, and the sub should sink. Blow firmly into the tubing. Water should pour out the straw, and the sub should rise.

Making Hypotheses   *Answers may vary.*
How and why does air pressure make the submarine rise and sink?
Because air is lighter than water, a submarine rises when air is pumped into its tanks. When air is pumped out and water admitted, the submarine sinks because the combined weight of water and sub is heavier than the water in which it floats.

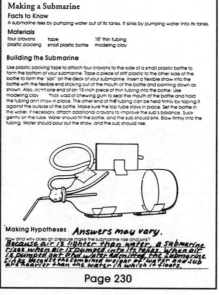

Page 230

Telephone Tactics

Can you imagine life without the telephone? Did you know that our first 17 Presidents ran our country without the use of a telephone? Thanks to Alexander Graham Bell, the telephone was invented in 1876. Try the experiment below to better understand the basics behind this very necessary invention. Note: The project is best done with two people.

Materials Needed: tin cans   paper clips   hammer   nail
30-foot pieces of string or fish line (10 pound test or higher)

Student Directions:
1. Punch a hole in the centers of the bottoms of two tin cans using a hammer and a nail.
2. Thread one end of the string or fish line through the hole in one can. Pull it inside.
3. Tie a paper clip securely to the end of the string on the inside and pull the string until it stops. Do the same with the other end.
4. You and your partner should each take one of the tin cans and walk away from each other until the string is pulled very tight.
5. Have your partner talk into his/her can. You should put your can over your ear. Can you hear what your partner is saying? Now you speak into the can and let your partner listen. Note: String must always be taut and only one person can talk at a time.

Extra: Make a 4-way party line with the tin can telephones. To do this, stretch one pair of phones tight and keep them in place. Have a second pair of phones going the other way at right angles to the first pair of phones. Hook the second pair of phones string around the first pair's string and stretch both strings tight. Remember only one person can talk at a time!

Define the following terms: vibration, diaphragm, molecules, eardrum, party line. Then, on the back of this page, use them to explain the process of the telephone in relation to sound, objects, vibration and distance. *Answers will vary.*

_____

1. What would your life be like today without the telephone? _____

2. How do you think this invention changed the office of the President? _____

Presidential Plus Find another important invention that you think made the role of the President easier. Tell when it was invented, how it changed the role of the President, etc. Share it with the class.

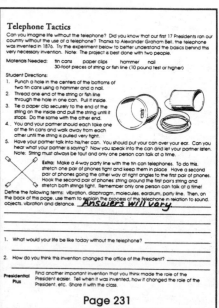

Page 231

What Are You All About?

Create a web on this page that explains who you are.

To start, place your name in the oval. This is the center of the web. Draw three lines branching out from the center and draw a circle at the end of each branch. In each circle, write a word to describe yourself. Draw a branch out from each of these three circles and then draw three larger circles. In each one, write a sentence telling why the word you chose describes you. For example, if one of the words you chose to describe yourself is smart, you might write: I am smart because I study.

Answers will vary.

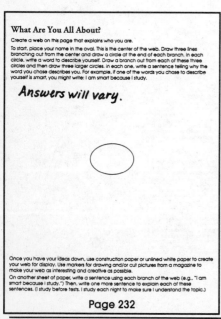

Once you have your ideas down, use construction paper or unlined white paper to create your web for display. Use markers for drawing and/or cut pictures from a magazine to make your web as interesting and creative as possible.

On another sheet of paper, write a sentence using each branch of the web (e.g., "I am smart because I study.") Then, write one more sentence to explain each of these sentences. (I study before tests. I study each night to make sure I understand the topic.)

Page 232

What's Your Slogan?

Write a slogan about yourself and tell why you chose this slogan. It can be a group of words like Encyclopedia Brown's that tell what you can or will do ("No case too small"), or a group of words that tells people what you are best at.

Answers will vary.

Slogan: _____

Now, describe yourself as a sleuth. What might your nickname be? Why?

_____

Jot down several ideas on the lines below to use in creating a poster advertising your sleuthing skills. Then, make your poster.

- _____
- _____
- _____
- _____

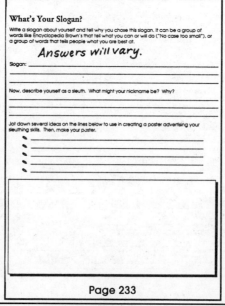

Page 233

"Give Me Your John Hancock"

Below are sentences describing different people. Have someone matching each description sign your sheet in the appropriate space. A person may sign your sheet only once.   *Answers will vary.*

1. _____ is someone who is my height.

2. _____ is someone who is shorter than I am.

3. _____ is someone who has the same hair color as I do.

4. _____ is someone who likes dogs.

5. _____ is someone whose name has been in the newspaper.

6. _____ is someone who loves to read mysteries.

7. _____ is someone who loves to solve mysteries.

8. _____ is someone who has the same number of family members as mine.

9. _____ is someone who can tell a joke. (Let him/her tell it to you.)

10. _____ is someone who loves to play a sport.

11. _____ is someone who plays a musical instrument.

12. _____ is someone who likes to play board games.

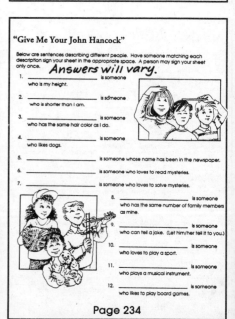

Page 234

Logical Fun

Below is a Venn diagram. Venn diagrams are used to compare and contrast 2 or more subjects. The area in each circle that is not overlapped contains characteristics unique to one subject. The overlapped areas contain characteristics common to 2 or more subjects. Follow the directions to complete the Venn diagram.

1. List the names of the students in your class who have blue eyes in area #1.
2. List the names of the students who wear glasses in area #2.
3. List the names of any students who have blue eyes and wear glasses in area #3.
4. List the names of any students who have brown hair in area #7.
5. List the names of any students who have brown hair and blue eyes in area #4.
6. List the names of any students who have brown hair and wear glasses in area #6.
7. List the names of any students who have blue eyes, wear glasses and have brown hair in area #5.

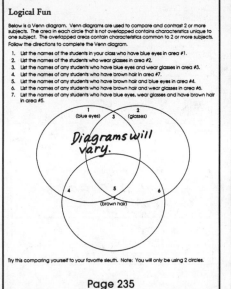

Diagrams will vary.

Try this comparing yourself to your favorite sleuth. Note: You will only be using 2 circles.

Page 235

Social Problems

Look at newspaper articles that tell of various social problems around the world. List what some of these problems are. _Answers will vary._

Select one problem from the articles and answer the following questions:
What is the problem? _____

Where is the problem occurring? _____
Who is affected by the problem? _____
How are they affected? _____

What is being done for the people affected by the problem? _____

What is being done to eliminate the problem? _____

What else do you think should be done, or at least tried, to improve the situation? _____

Unfortunately, no community is without social problems. Find out what one social problem is in your community. Write a few sentences about it.
_____
_____
_____

Who is most affected by this problem? _____
How are they affected? _____

Suggest some things that might be done to help rid your community of this problem. _____

On the back of this paper, compare your community's problem to one of the problems you read about in the newspaper articles.

Page 236

Similarities and Differences

Interpret each of the following sayings. Include an example.
"a chip off the old block" _a child that resembles his parents_

"like night and day" _people (or things, situations etc.) that are as different as night and day_

"two peas in a pod" _two people (or objects) that are very similar, such as twins or siblings or best friends_

Compare yourself to one person. _Answers will vary._
Write the name of the person to whom you will compare yourself.
Write all the similarities that you and that person share. _____
_____
_____

Write the ways in which you and the person are different. _____
_____

Page 237

Getting to Know the Newspaper

Look over a newspaper's flag (headline). Describe what it contains in the box below.

price   day and date   number of pages   name of newspaper

Take a few minutes to look through the paper. List the news articles, features, photographs, and advertisements that interested you the most.
1. _Answers will vary._
2. _____
3. _____
4. _____
5. _____

Answer the following questions about this specific issue of the newspaper.
What is the lead story about? _____

Write the titles for two stories that came from a wire service.
1. _____
2. _____

Write the names of three reporters and the title of each one's article.
Reporter — Title
_____
_____
_____

Write the title of an article that has a dateline. _____
What is its dateline? _the date and place of composition_
On which page will you find the Crossword Puzzle? ___ Obituaries? ___ Television Schedule? ___ Comics? ___ Classified Advertising? ___
Which part of the paper helped you know where to find the above?
Look back at one of the items you listed as interesting you the most. Write which one it is.

Read it thoroughly. On the back of this page, write what it was about or what you liked about it.

Page 238

What Building Am I?

Find out as many facts as you can about one building in your community.

* The building is *

1. Is the building the first to stand on its site? _____ If not, what was there before? _____
2. When was the building built? _____ How old is it? _____
3. Who built the building? _____
4. For what reason was the building built? _____
   For what is the building used now? _____
5. Who are the building's tenants? _____
6. Other information: _____

Answers will vary.

Write 20 facts about the building above without naming it. Write the clues (facts) beginning with the vaguest, or most difficult, and progressing to the easiest, or the "dead giveaway." These clues will be used to play "Get a Clue!"

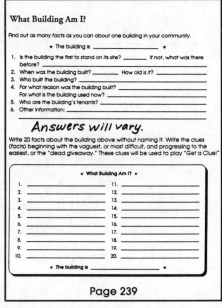

What Building Am I?

1. _____   11. _____
2. _____   12. _____
3. _____   13. _____
4. _____   14. _____
5. _____   15. _____
6. _____   16. _____
7. _____   17. _____
8. _____   18. _____
9. _____   19. _____
10. _____   20. _____

* The building is _____ *

Page 239

The Beginning of Greece

The first major civilization in Greece began on the island of Crete in about 3000 B.C. It is known as the Minoan culture because of its legendary founder, King Minos. It was not the Minoans, however, that settled the mainland of Greece. This area was settled by Greek-speaking peoples from the north who settled in small farming villages around 2000 B.C. By 1600 B.C., fortified towns had been built and the Mycenaean culture had begun. In 1450 B.C., Crete fell into the power of the Mycenaeans. Their power lasted only until about 1200 B.C.

When was your city or town founded? Who were the first people here? Do some research to answer the questions below. Be sure to keep a record of the sources you use. Remember: Senior citizens who grew up in your city are great resources. Include pictures if possible.

Name of city/town _____ Date founded _____
Who founded it? _____
Why was it founded? _____
Why did it grow? _____
Important events in its history:
1. _Answers will vary._
2. _____
3. _____
4. _____
5. _____

Changes you have seen _____

Changes you predict in the future _____

Every city/town has its own flag. To the right is a space in which you can design your own flag for your city or town. On the back of this page, tell why you designed the flag the way you did.

Page 240

Place Poems

Write an acrostic poem about one of the world's major cities. First, do some research on the city. Get to know its attractions, landmarks, and people. To find this information, skim books, magazines, travel brochures, and the encyclopedia, or view a video about the city. After you have gathered the information you need, prepare to write your poem. Study the example below.

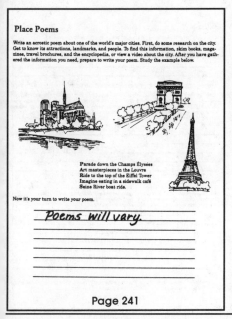

Parade down the Champs Élysées
Art masterpieces in the Louvre
Ride to the top of the Eiffel Tower
Imagine eating in a sidewalk café
Seine River boat ride.

Now it's your turn to write your poem.

Poems will vary.
_____
_____
_____
_____

Page 241

Styles of Dress

Throughout history people in different regions have worn different kinds of clothes. Today, more and more people dress in a similar fashion. They wear what is referred to as Western dress. It is a style of dress common in the United States, Canada, and Western Europe.

In some parts of the world people still prefer to wear traditional clothing. Traditional styles of clothing vary because of climate, available materials, and the customs of a region. Let's examine some different types of clothing.

You will need:
magazines (National Geographic magazines are great!)
2-3 copies per student of Clothing Around the World (page 243)
glue, scissors, markers

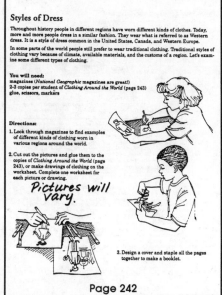

Directions:
1. Look through magazines to find examples of different kinds of clothing worn in various regions around the world.
2. Cut out the pictures and glue them to the copies of Clothing Around the World (page 243), or make drawings of clothing on the worksheet. Complete one worksheet for each picture or drawing.

Pictures will vary.

3. Design a cover and staple all the pages together to make a booklet.

Page 242

Clothing Around the World

(Use with page 242.)

Country _____

Description of clothing: _Answers will vary._

Purpose for wearing this type of clothing: _____

Page 243

"Made in . . ."

Most of the products that we use are not made in our own community. Many are not even made in our own country. Products that are brought into a country are called **imported** products. Products that leave a country are called **exported** products. Most imported products, and the packages in which they are sent, are labeled with the words *Made in . . . .*

Look around your home for imported products. Complete the chart by writing the names of the exporting countries and the products you found that came from each country.

Charts will vary.

The Great Import Hunt

Made in ____________ Made in ____________

Made in ____________ Made in ____________

Made in ____________ Made in ____________

Page 244

Cookbook Geography

Linguini, sukiyaki, burrito—food speaks the languages of the world. Without leaving your own town you can probably sample foods from all around the world.

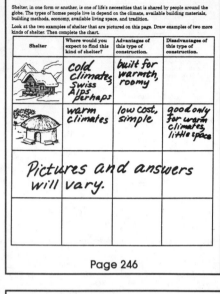

With the help of restaurant menus or ethnic cookbooks, make a list of foods from other countries. (Many families also have favorite recipes that great grandparents brought with them from the "old country" when they immigrated to America.) Write the name of the food and its country of origin.

Foods from Around the World

Food	Country
Foods will vary.	

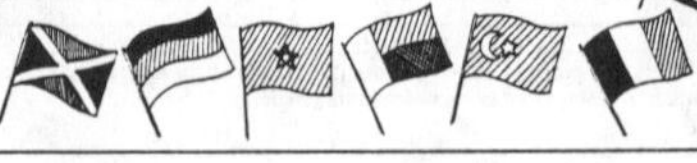

Page 245

Home Sweet Home

Shelter, in one form or another, is one of life's necessities that is shared by people around the globe. The types of homes people live in depend on the climate, available building materials, building methods, economy, available living space, and tradition.

Look at the two examples of shelter that are pictured on this page. Draw examples of two more kinds of shelter. Then complete the chart.

Shelter	Where would you expect to find this kind of shelter?	Advantages of this type of construction.	Disadvantages of this type of construction.
	Cold climates, Swiss Alps perhaps	built for warmth, roomy	
	warm climates	low cost, simple	good only for warm climates, little space
Pictures and answers will vary.			

Page 246

Greek City-States

Ancient Greece was made up of city- states by about the 700's B.C. Most of the citizens in a city-state spoke the same Greek dialect, practiced the same customs and religion and came from common ancestors. The members were like one large family.

Each city-state was governed mainly by a few wealthy men until the 500's B.C. This type of government is called oligarchy. During the 500's, however, some city-states began to move toward democracy.

Did you know that the U.S. government is based on the same type of government the Greek city-states used over 2,300 years ago? However, many countries still do not have a democratic form of government.

Write some advantages and disadvantages of a democracy. Then, choose another type of government to compare it to. Tell which country(s) use this type of government. On a separate sheet of paper, write an essay giving your views on the best type of government for the U.S.

Answers will vary. Democracy	
Advantages: power vested in the people; freedom (to vote; to worship as one pleases; of speech), freedom of enterprise	**Disadvantages:** goods are not held in common – therefore have extremely rich and extremely poor
____________ name of government	
Advantages: Answers will vary.	**Disadvantages:**
country(s):	

Page 247

On the Diplomatic Trail

Eleanor Roosevelt was an unusual President's wife. She worked hard for many human rights programs. As chairman of the United Nations Human Rights Commission, she helped write the Universal Declaration of Human Rights which said, "All people are born free and equal in dignity and rights."

Write a mini Declaration of Human Rights for your school.

Answers will vary.

John Foster Dulles wore many hats. He was a lawyer, diplomat, senator and author. He negotiated several treaties for the United States and helped form the United Nations. He once said that in order to have peace, you must take chances, just as you must take chances in war.

Select one of today's world situations (i.e. the future of the Soviet Union) and tell what chances you might take to solve the problem. ____________

As President Nixon's Secretary of State, Henry Kissinger never stopped traveling around the world. He negotiated secretly with the North Vietnamese to end the war. He made several trips to the Middle East as a negotiator between Israel, Egypt and Syria - the three countries involved in the 1973 Arab-Israeli War. He visited China and Russia and paved the way for the President's visits to the two Communist nations.

Be a diplomat. Whenever sports teams are chosen, Jonathan is always last. After school, a bunch of your classmates are teasing him about it. Write what you would do about the situation. ____________

Page 248

They Were in Command

Three military leaders during World War II are quoted below. After reading the quotes, answer the questions.

Answers will vary.

General Eisenhower had these words for his troops before they invaded Europe. "The hopes and prayers of liberty-loving people everywhere march with you."

What kind of a man do you think he was? ____________

What values/beliefs make you think and act as you do? ____________

When President Roosevelt ordered General MacArthur and his family to leave Corregidor Island in the Philippines in 1942 because they were in great danger, he made a pledge, "I shall return."

How do you think he felt about leaving? ____________

What do you think he said when he did return in 1944 and eventually recaptured the islands in the next nine months? ____________

General George S. Patton, Jr., had a tough approach to war as expressed in the following quote. "Wars may be fought with weapons, but they are won by men."

What do you think he meant by this remark? ____________

What kind of a soldier would do well under Patton? ____________

For which of the above generals would you rather fight? ____________

Why? ____________

If you were a general and were in charge of a battalion of men about to go into a highly dangerous battle situation, what would you say to them? ____________

Personality Plus Write a one-page paper about what you think a day in a battlefield would be like. Include sounds, smells, feelings, etc. Share it with the class.

Page 249

Contributing Factors

The following people played an important role in our country's history. Fill in the blank in front of each event with the correct year from the time line below to learn exactly how these people affected our lives. Hint: Read all the clues before you begin.

1682 1752 1769 1775 1776 1801 1804 1848 1869 1925 1947 1950 1981 1984

1925 Henry Ford's Model T first appeared in 1908. Seventeen years later, it was affordable for the average American family.

1752 Ben Franklin proved lightning was electricity 24 years before Paine published his *Common Sense.*

1804 One hundred eighty years before Geraldine Ferraro was chosen to run for Vice President of the U.S., Aaron Burr killed Alexander Hamilton in a gun duel.

1950 One hundred ninety-eight years after Ben Franklin proved lightning was electricity, Joseph McCarthy gained national attention by accusing the Department of State of harboring communists.

1869 Susan B. Anthony formed the National Woman Suffrage Association 100 years after Daniel Boone journeyed through what is now Kentucky.

1947 George Marshall proposed the European Recovery Program, or Marshall Plan, whereby the U.S. spent billions of dollars to rebuild war-torn western Europe, three years before McCarthy gained great attention for Communism.

1984 Geraldine Ferraro became the first woman chosen as a Vice Presidential candidate by a major American political party 76 years after Henry Ford's Model T first appeared.

1981 Fifty-six years after the average American could afford a Model T, Sandra Day O'Connor became the first woman to serve as an associate justice of the Supreme Court of the U.S.

1682 William Penn saw his colony for the first time 299 years before Sandra Day O'Connor became an associate justice of the Supreme Court.

1776 Thomas Paine published his *Common Sense* one year after Patrick Henry said, "Give me liberty or give me death."

1801 Three years before Aaron Burr killed Alexander Hamilton in a gun duel, John Marshall took office as Chief Justice of the U.S. It was he who established the Supreme Court as an important branch of the federal government.

1848 Twenty-one years before Susan B. Anthony formed the National Woman Suffrage Association in 1869, Elizabeth Cady Stanton and Lucretia Mott called the nation's first Women's Rights Convention.

1769 Daniel Boone journeyed through the Appalachian Mountains in an unexplored area that today is Kentucky 87 years after William Penn first saw his colony in 1682.

1775 Patrick Henry said, "Give me liberty or give me death," urging the Virginia militia to be prepared to defend the colony against England one year before the Declaration of Independence was adopted in 1776.

Page 250

Numbers, Figures, and Graphs

Answer the word problems below to learn more about these American personalities.

1. Benedict Arnold became the most famous traitor in U.S. history when he corresponded with the British during the Revolutionary War. Upon joining the British army, he demanded 20,000 pounds from them. However, he only received 6,315 pounds. If the British pound is worth $1.75, how many dollars would Arnold have received if he had gotten 20,000 pounds? $35,000 How many dollars did he actually receive? $11,051.25
2. Lewis and Clark started up the Missouri River from St. Louis and traveled almost 7,700 miles to the Pacific Coast. If one mile is equal to 1.6 kilometers, approximately how man kilometers did they travel? 12,320 km

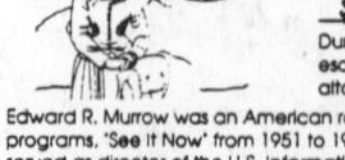

3. During the 1850's, Harriet Tubman helped about 300 slaves escape. If a reward for Tubman totaled $40,000, about how much was offered per slave? $133

   During the Civil War, she helped more than 750 slaves escape. How many slaves did Tubman help free altogether? 1,050
4. Edward R. Murrow was an American radio and TV broadcaster. He narrated the programs, "See It Now" from 1951 to 1958 and "Person to Person" from 1953 to 1959. He served as director of the U.S. Information Agency from 1961 to 1964. On the graph belov shade in the years Murrow narrated 2 programs at the same time.

1951 1952 1953 1954 1955 1956 1957 1958 1959 1960 1961 1962 1963 1964

5. Babe Ruth was the first great home run hitter in baseball history. In 1927, Ruth set a record of 60 home runs in a 154-game season. Since then, Roger Maris of the Yankees h 61 home runs in 1961 in a 162-game season. Ruth hit a total of 714 home runs during his career - a record that wasn't broken until Henry Aaron hit his 715th home run in 1974! Between Aaron and Ruth, how many home runs did they hit? 1429 Who really has a better record, Ruth or Maris? Why? Ruth, because his season was shorter.
6. William Randolph Hearst, a famous American publisher of newspapers and magazines, had one of the most lavish private dwellings in the U.S. It included 240,000 acres of land, 50 miles of ocean frontage, four castles and a priceless art collection. If 2.5 acres is equal to one hectare (metric system), how many hectares of land did Hearst own? 96,000 How many kilometers of ocean frontage did he own? 80 km

Personality Plus Choose 3 famous people. Make up a math word problem concerning them and/or events in their lives. Trade your problems with a friend.

Page 251

What If?

Think about what the world was like before Wilbur and Orville Wright flew the first motor-powered airplane in 1903. List five ways their invention changed the world.

Answers will vary.

Albert Einstein is considered to be one of the fathers of the atom age. When he formed his theory of relativity, $E=mc^2$, he laid the basis for controlling the release of energy (E) from the atom. In 1939, he wrote to President Franklin Roosevelt and urged him to budget monies for studying the release of nuclear energy. He warned that Germany might already be building the atom bomb. Do you think President Roosevelt should have taken Einstein's advice? Why or why not?

Thomas Edison had only three months of formal education, but he had 1,093 inventions patented in his lifetime. Two of his inventions that are very much a part of our lives today are the light bulb and the phonograph. Write a paragraph that tells what life would be like now if Edison had not created his wonderful inventions.

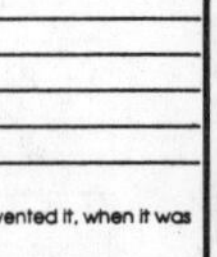

Personality Plus What invention do you think is the best? Write who invented it, when it was invented, etc. and tell why you think it is so great.

Page 252

Inventions

An inventor needs to have an understanding of a problem and an ability to create a device that will alleviate or reduce the problem. Choose and research a problem so you will know all you can about it and it will be better able to answer the questions below and "invent" a device to eliminate or reduce the problem.

Describe precisely what the problem is. _Answers will vary._

What needs to be done about the problem?

Tell how you would do what needs to be done to alleviate or reduce the problem. Tell how your device would work.

Draw a picture of your device to the right. Label its parts.

Page 253

Sorting the Facts

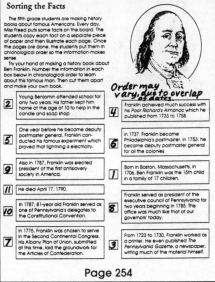

The fifth grade students are making history books about famous Americans. Every day, Miss Freed puts some facts on the board. The students copy each fact on a separate piece of paper and then illustrate each page. Once the pages are done, the students put them in chronological order so the information makes sense.

Try your hand at making a history book about Ben Franklin. Number the information in each box below in chronological order to learn about this famous man. Then cut them apart and make your own book.

Order may vary, due to overlap of dates

2 Young Benjamin attended school for only two years. His father kept him home at the age of 10 to help in the candle and soap shop.

4 Franklin achieved much success with his *Poor Richard's Almanac* which he published from 1733 to 1758.

5 One year before he became deputy postmaster general, Franklin conducted his famous experiment which proved that lightning is electricity.

6 In 1737, Franklin became Philadelphia's postmaster. In 1753, he became deputy postmaster general for all the colonies.

9 Also in 1787, Franklin was elected president of the first antislavery society in America.

1 Born in Boston, Massachusetts, in 1706, Ben Franklin was the 15th child in a family of 17 children.

10 He died April 17, 1790.

8 Franklin served as president of the executive council of Pennsylvania for two years beginning in 1785. This office was much like that of our governors today.

10 In 1787, 81-year old Franklin served as one of Pennsylvania's delegates to the Constitutional Convention.

7 In 1775, Franklin was chosen to serve in the Second Continental Congress. His Albany Plan of Union, submitted at this time, laid the groundwork for the Articles of Confederation.

3 From 1723 to 1730, Franklin worked as a printer. He even published *The Pennsylvania Gazette*, a newspaper, writing much of the material himself.

Page 254

What Would You Say?

When John Tyler's horse died, he wrote the following epitaph for the tombstone on the horse's grave.

"Here lies the body of my good horse, The General. For twenty years he bore me around the circuit of my practice, and in all that time he never made a blunder. Would that his master could say the same."
John Tyler

Write an epitaph for an animal that you know (or knew) for its tombstone.

Epitaphs will vary.

When Coolidge decided not to run again for another term, he called reporters into his summer vacation office in the high school in Rapid City, South Dakota, and surprised them and the nation with the announcement. He had written on it, "I do not choose to run for President in 1928."

If you were President and did not want to run again, how would you handle it and what would you say?

Answers will vary.

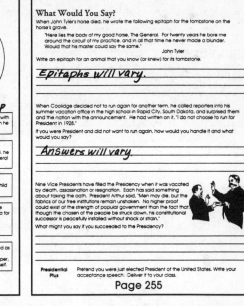

Nine Vice Presidents have filled the Presidency when it was vacated by death, assassination or resignation. Each has said something about taking the oath. President Arthur said, "Men may die, but the fabrics of our free institutions remain unshaken. No higher proof could exist of the strength of popular government than the fact that, though the chosen of the people be struck down, his constitutional successor is peacefully installed without shock or strain."

What might you say if you succeeded to the Presidency?

Presidential Plus — Pretend you were just elected President of the United States. Write your acceptance speech. Deliver it to your class.

Page 255

Hindsight Is 20/20!

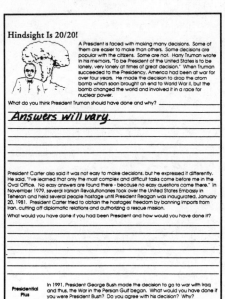

A President is faced with making many decisions. Some of them are easier to make than others. Some decisions are popular with the citizens, some are not. Harry Truman wrote in his memoirs, "To be President of the United States is to be lonely, very lonely at times of great decision." When Truman succeeded to the Presidency, America had been at war for over four years. He made the decision to drop the atom bomb which soon brought an end to World War II, but the bomb changed the world and involved it in a race for nuclear power.

What do you think President Truman should have done and why?

Answers will vary.

President Carter also said it was not easy to make decisions, but he expressed it differently. He said, "I've learned that only the most complex and difficult tasks come before me in the Oval Office. No easy answers are found there - no easy questions come there." In November 1979, several Iranian Revolutionaries took over the United States Embassy in Teheran and held several people hostage until President Reagan was inaugurated, January 20, 1981. President Carter tried to obtain the hostages' freedom by banning imports from Iran, cutting off diplomatic relations and authorizing a rescue mission.

What would you have done if you had been President and how would you have done it?

Presidential Plus — In 1991, President George Bush made the decision to go to war with Iraq and thus, the War in the Persian Gulf began. What would you have done if you were President Bush? Do you agree with his decision? Why?

Page 256

The Presidency

As the chief executive of the United States, the President helps shape and enforce laws, directs foreign policy, is responsible for national defense, presides at ceremonial affairs, and leads his Party. He does not control the Legislative and Judicial Branches, but he can influence law making, and he does appoint justices to the Supreme Court. No one man can assume all the duties of the president, and so he appoints assistants. They form the White House Office. It is their job to keep the President informed about the many departments of the government. They may advise and influence the president in his decisions. The members of the White House office do not need congressional approval, nor must they answer to the Congress. The Cabinet, consisting of thirteen department heads called secretaries, is also appointed by the President to advise and assist him. However, Cabinet members must be approved by Congress and must answer to the Legislative Branch whenever asked.

Label the diagram below to show the various departments and officials running the government. Use the words from the word box to complete the diagram.

PRESIDENT	WHITE HOUSE STAFF	JUSTICES
LEGISLATIVE BRANCH	CABINET	EXECUTIVE BRANCH
SENATE	JUDICIAL BRANCH	CHIEF JUSTICE
HOUSE OF REPRESENTATIVES		SUPREME COURT

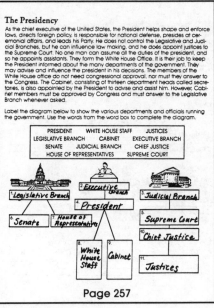

1. Legislative Branch
2. Executive Branch
3. Judicial Branch
4. President
5. Supreme Court
6. Senate
7. House of Representatives
8. White House Staff
9. Cabinet
10. Chief Justice
11. Justices

Page 257

Three Branches of Government

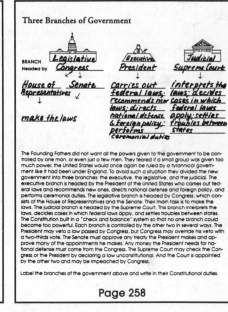

| BRANCH | Legislative | Executive | Judicial |
| Headed by | Congress | President | Supreme Court |

Legislative: House of Representatives, Senate → make the laws

Executive: President → Carries out federal laws; recommends new laws; directs national defense & foreign policy; performs ceremonial duties

Judicial: Supreme Court → interprets the laws; decides cases in which federal laws apply; settles troubles between states

The Founding Fathers did not want all the powers given to the government to be controlled by one man, or even just a few men. They feared if a small group was given too much power, the United States would once again be ruled by a tyrannical government like it had been under England. To avoid such a situation they divided the new government into three branches: the executive, the legislative, and the judicial. The executive branch is headed by the President of the United States who carries out federal laws and recommends new ones, directs national defense and foreign policy, and performs ceremonial duties. The legislative branch is headed by Congress, which consists of the House of Representatives and the Senate. Their main task is to make the laws. The judicial branch is headed by the Supreme Court. This branch interprets the laws, decides cases in which federal laws apply, and settles troubles between states. The Constitution built in a "check and balance" system so that no one branch could become too powerful. Each branch is controlled by the other two in several ways. The President may veto a law passed by Congress, but Congress may override his veto with a two-thirds vote. The Senate must approve any treaty the President makes and approve many of the appointments he makes. Any money the President needs for national defense must come from the Congress. The Supreme Court may check the Congress or the President by declaring a law unconstitutional. And the Court is appointed by the other two and may be impeached by Congress.

Label the branches of the government above and write in their Constitutional duties.

Page 258

Reading the Constitution

We the People

Look at a copy of the entire Constitution. It is only 4,300 words long. After you have looked at it, answer the questions or fill in the blanks below.

The Constitution is divided into **3** main parts. They are the **Preamble, Articles** and **Amendments**.

What is the purpose of the Preamble? _To introduce and explain the reasons for writing the document_

There are **7** Articles in the Constitution. Many of them have several sections. Tell which article provides for the following services or laws.

United States court system **III**

The nation's debts and upholding the Constitution **VI**

The lawmaking body of the government **I**

What must be done for the Constitution to be law **VII** (That process was called _ratification_)

Explains the duties of the President **II**

Allows for changes to be made in the Constitution **V** (That process is called _Amending_)

Tells what the states can do and what the federal government can do **IV**

There are **26** Amendments in the Constitution.

What makes the Constitution a usable document today? _The Bill of Rights and Amendments have kept it up-to-date._

Which Article has allowed it to be an up-to-date document? **V**

Define the following words as they relate to the Constitution.

ARTICLE _sections of the Constitution defining the different powers_

AMENDMENT _Change in the Constitution to reflect changing needs_

RATIFY _To pass & accept the laws proposed in the Constitution_

Page 259

The Preamble

The first sentence of the Preamble to the Constitution could be written simply, "We the people of the United States do ordain and establish this Constitution for the United States of America." But between "We the people of the United States" and "do ordain ....." are six reasons explaining why the Constitution was written. Read the Preamble below and write what each reason for establishment are after each "To" below the Preamble. Then write what each reason means and give an example of why it is included or what it is meant to accomplish or prevent.

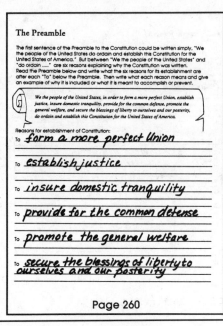

We the people of the United States, in order to form a more perfect Union, establish justice, insure domestic tranquility, provide for the common defense, promote the general welfare, and secure the blessings of liberty to ourselves and our posterity, do ordain and establish this Constitution for the United States of America.

Reasons for establishment of Constitution:

To _form a more perfect Union_

To _establish justice_

To _insure domestic tranquility_

To _provide for the common defense_

To _promote the general welfare_

To _secure the blessings of liberty to ourselves and our posterity_

Page 260

State Fact Sheet

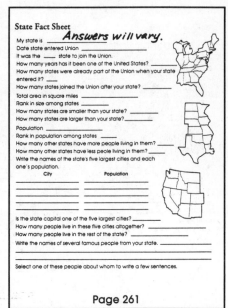

My state is _Answers will vary._

Date state entered Union

It was the ____ state to join the Union.

How many years has it been one of the United States?

How many states were already part of the Union when your state entered it?

How many states joined the Union after your state?

Total area in square miles

How many states are smaller than your state?

How many states are larger than your state?

Population

Rank in population among states

How many other states have more people living in them?

How many other states have less people living in them?

Write the names of the state's five largest cities and each one's population.

City	Population

Is the state capital one of the five largest cities?

How many people live in these five cities altogether?

How many live in the rest of the state?

Write the names of several famous people from your state.

Select one of these people about whom to write a few sentences.

Page 261

Page 262

State Government   *Answers will vary.*

Fill in the names of the people currently holding the elected positions listed below in the executive branch of your state.

Governor _____   Lieutenant Governor _____

Write the names of the people currently representing you (your district) in the legislative branch of the state government.

Senator _____   Representative _____

The executive and legislative branches of the state government make laws that affect every citizen in the state. What kinds of laws can you think of that, if enacted by the legislature, might affect everyone in the state?

What law would you like to see passed that might improve a condition (problem) for everyone in the state?

Write a letter to the governor of your state, your senator or your representative suggesting such a law and giving reasons for it. Write the letter on the stationery below.

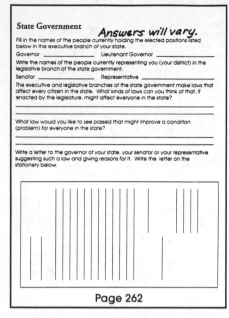

Page 263

From Billings to Boston

Use a U.S. map or an encyclopedia to locate these state stumpers.

1. Which seven letters of the alphabet do not begin the names of any states? *B E Q J, X, Y, Z*
2. Name the nine states with double letters in their names. *Missouri, Mississippi, Illinois, Minnesota Tennessee, Pennsylvania, Massachusetts,*
3. Which state name has only one syllable? *Maine*
4. Name the only letter not used in a state's name. *Q*
5. When listed in alphabetical order, which state comes first? *Alabama*
6. When listed in alphabetical order, which state comes last? *Wyoming*
7. In what state is the letter i used the most? *Mississippi*
8. Which state name has the most o's? *Colorado*
9. Which state name has the most a's? *Alabama*
10. Which state name has the most e's? *Tennessee*
11. Name four states whose names end with o. *Idaho, Ohio, Colorado, New Mexico*
12. Name the ten states that begin with the word "New." *New Jersey, New York, New Mexico, West Virginia, North Dakota, South Dakota, North Carolina, South Carolina, New Hampshire, Rhode Island*
13. Name four states that don't share the same letter. *Ohio, Alabama, Arizona, Alaska*
14. Which two letters are the first letters of more states than any others? *N, M*
15. Which two states have only one consonant in their names? *Ohio, Iowa*
16. Which was the first state to become part of the United States? *Delaware*
17. Which state was last? *Hawaii*

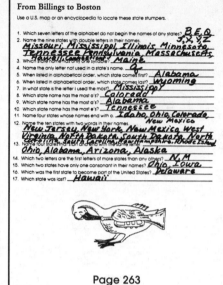

Page 264

What's in a Name?

Over half of the United States' names came from Indian words. Some of the states' Indian names are listed below followed by their postal abbreviations in parentheses. Write the name of each state as we know it today.

Mnishota (MN) *Minnesota*   Teysha (TX) *Texas*
KweEnihtEkot (CT) *Connecticut*   Arizonac (AZ) *Arizona*
Tanasi (TN) *Tennessee*   Illini (IL) *Illinois*
KaNze (KS) *Kansas*   Mitchisawyegan (MI) *Michigan*
alaschka (AK) *Alaska*   Ohiyo (OH) *Ohio*
Mesatuset (MA) *Massachusetts*   kentake (KY) *Kentucky*
Nibaapka (NE) *Nebraska*   miciiibi (MS) *Mississippi*
maugh-wauwame (WY) *Wyoming*   Ookanasa (AR) *Arkansas*

Other states' names were derived from rivers that flowed through them, from people important to the region or from the geography of the region. Read each clue below and write the name of the state you think it is telling about. The postal abbreviation appears in parentheses.

1. It is a Latin word for "mountainous." (MT) *Montana*
2. The state's name might have come from the French word "ouragan" meaning hurricane. (OR) *Oregon*
3. The name of this state honors the King of France, Louis XIV. (LA) *Louisiana*
4. In 1610, Capt. Samuel Argall was blown off-course near this state. He named it for the map, which had sponsored his journey, Thomas West Lord De La Warr. (DE) *Delaware*
5. It was the presence of Indians that caused a land development company to name the area. (IN) *Indiana*
6. In 1602, a Spanish expedition named a stream in the region of this state using a Spanish word to describe the reddish-brown color of the water. The word was later used to name the state and its big river. (CO) *Colorado*
7. This state is named in honor of King George II. (GA) *Georgia*
8. Its green mountains, or "verts monts," as written in slightly incorrect French, give this state its name. (VT) *Vermont*
9. This colony's founder named it after his king's wife, Henrietta Maria. It was known once as Mary's Land. (MD) *Maryland*
10. Its name may have come from several sources. Its size was once described as, "about the bigness of the island of Rhodes," a Greek island. A Dutch sea captain thought the red clay in some of its shoreline made it look fiery and named it "Rooat Eylandt." *Rhode Island* (RI)

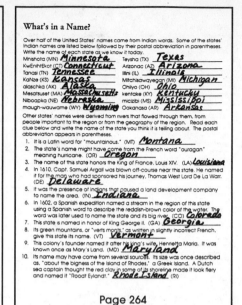

Page 265

The "Maine" Event

Discover facts about Maine by following the instructions below. An encyclopedia or atlas may be used.

1. Label the state capital on the map.
2. Label the four main rivers: Saco, Androscoggin, Kennebec and Penobscot. Color the river lines blue. Write "rivers" on the key.
3. Label the White Mountains. Color them brown and write "mountains" on the key.
4. Label the Atlantic Ocean. Draw blue and green waves.
5. Label all points on the compass rose.
6. Outline the state border in red. Write the state's name in any empty space on the map.

Now travel further into the encyclopedia or atlas and list the following Maine facts.

7. State bird: *Chickadee*
8. State flower: *White Pine Cone ; Tassel*
9. State tree: *White Pine*
10. Date Maine became a state: *March 15, 1820*
11. State motto: *Dirigo (I direct)*
12. State song: *"State of Maine Song"*

Bonus
Make a poster of Maine. Draw the state map as well as pictures of the state bird, flower, etc. Research famous people from Maine, events, and products manufactured by the state.

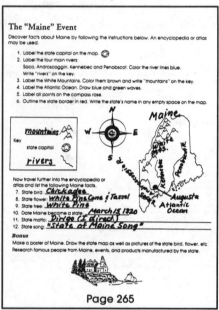

Page 266

U.S. Products and Natural Resources

The United States is one of the world's largest producers of manufactured goods because it is very rich in natural resources.

A study of the *U.S. Products and Natural Resources Map* (p. 267) will indicate which states are the chief suppliers of certain products and natural resources.

For each product and natural resource listed below, use the map on page 267 to name the states that are major suppliers.

Coal	Iron Ore	Oil
Pennsylvania	Michigan	Texas
West Virginia	Minnesota	California
Wyoming		Alaska
Illinois		
Kentucky		

Corn	Wheat	Cotton
Ohio Nebraska	Oklahoma	California
Indiana	Kansas	Texas
Illinois Iowa	Montana	Mississippi
Wisconsin	North Dakota	Arizona
Minnesota	Minnesota	
	Illinois	

Dairy	Lumber	Beef
Wisconsin	Washington	Texas
Pennsylvania	Oregon	Nebraska
New York	California	Kansas
Minnesota		
California		

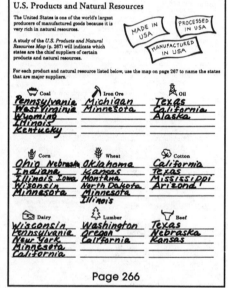

Page 267

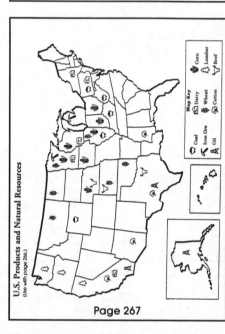

U.S. Products and Natural Resources (Use with page 266.)

Page 268

U.S. Climate Zones

The word climate is used to describe the weather in a particular place over a long period of time. Because the United States covers such a large area, it has a number of different climate zones. Some areas have long, cold winters and short, cool summers, while other areas are always warm in both the summer and the winter.

Choose colors to color-code the Map Key and the climate map. Then, determine the . . .

climate zone you live in. *Answers will vary.*
climate zone of the Northeast. *continental*
climate zone of the Rocky Mountains. *steppe, alpine*
three climate zones found in Alaska. *alpine, tundra subarctic*
climate zones found in Texas. *subtropical, steppe, desert*
climate zones of Florida. *subtropical, tropical*
climate zone of Michigan. *continental*

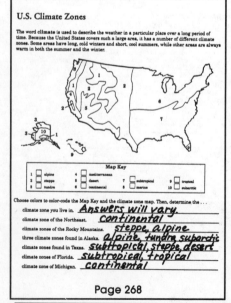

Page 269

Temperature Ranges

What is the average January temperature where you live? The average monthly temperature is figured using the daily temperatures for the whole month. This information can be found in most almanacs and encyclopedias. Why would it be helpful to know the average temperature of a city? *Answers will vary.*

Use an almanac or encyclopedia to find the average high and low temperatures for January and July listed below.

State	City	January High	January Low	July High	July Low
Alaska	*Answers will vary, depending on source.*				
California					
Colorado					
Florida					
Iowa					
Michigan					
New York					
North Dakota					
South Carolina					
Texas					
Wisconsin					
State of your choice:					

Circle the highest temperature in each "high" column and the lowest temperature in each "low" column.

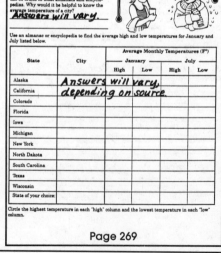

Page 270

Natural Wonders of the U.S.A.

Listed below are ten natural physical features found in the United States.

Use an encyclopedia, atlas, or other source to complete the chart. Write the number of each feature on a copy of the U.S. Political Map (page 271) in its correct location.

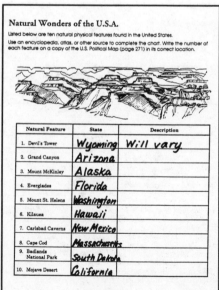

Natural Feature	State	Description
1. Devil's Tower	Wyoming	Will vary
2. Grand Canyon	Arizona	
3. Mount McKinley	Alaska	
4. Everglades	Florida	
5. Mount St. Helens	Washington	
6. Kilauea	Hawaii	
7. Carlsbad Caverns	New Mexico	
8. Cape Cod	Massachusetts	
9. Badlands National Park	South Dakota	
10. Mojave Desert	California	

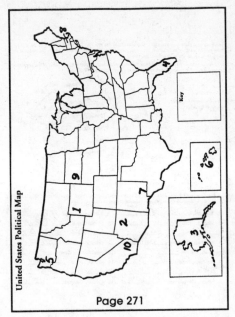

United States Political Map

Key

Page 271

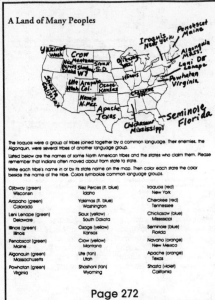

A Land of Many Peoples

The Iroquois were a group of tribes joined together by a common language. Their enemies, the Algonquin, were several tribes of another language group.

Listed below are the names of some North American tribes and the states who claim them. Please remember that Indians often moved about from state to state.

Write each tribe's name in or by its state name on the map. Then color each state the color beside the name of the tribe. Colors symbolize common language groups.

Ojibway (green)
Wisconsin

Arapaho (green)
Colorado

Leni Lenape (green)
Delaware

Illinois (green)
Illinois

Penobscot (green)
Maine

Algonquin (green)
Massachusetts

Powhatan (green)
Virginia

Nez Perces (lt. blue)
Idaho

Yakimas (lt. blue)
Washington

Sioux (yellow)
South Dakota

Osage (yellow)
Kansas

Crow (yellow)
Montana

Ute (tan)
Utah

Shoshoni (tan)
Wyoming

Iroquois (red)
New York

Cherokee (red)
Tennessee

Chickasaw (blue)
Mississippi

Seminole (blue)
Florida

Navaho (orange)
New Mexico

Apache (orange)
Texas

Shasta (violet)
California

Page 272

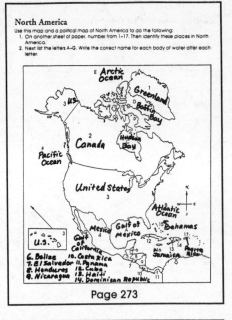

North America

Use this map and a political map of North America to do the following:
1. On another sheet of paper, number from 1–17. Then identify these places in North America.
2. Next list the letters A–G. Write the correct name for each body of water after each letter.

6. Belize
7. El Salvador
8. Honduras
9. Nicaragua
10. Costa Rica
11. Panama
12. Cuba
13. Haiti
14. Dominican Republic

Page 273

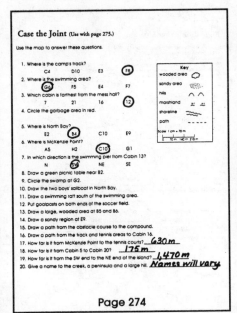

Case the Joint (Use with page 275.)

Use the map to answer these questions.

1. Where is the camp's track?
   C4   D10   E3   **F8**

2. Where is the swimming area?
   G6   F5   E4   F7

3. Which cabin is farthest from the mess hall?
   7   21   16   **12**

4. Circle the garbage area in red.

5. Where is North Bay?
   E2   **B4**   C10   E9

6. Where is McKenzie Point?
   A5   H2   **C10**   G1

7. In which direction is the swimming pier from Cabin 13?
   N   **SW**   NE   SE

8. Draw a green picnic table near B2.

9. Circle the swamp at G2.

10. Draw the two boys' sailboat in North Bay.

11. Draw a swimming raft south of the swimming area.

12. Put goalposts on both ends of the soccer field.

13. Draw a large, wooded area at B5 and B6.

14. Draw a sandy region at E9.

15. Draw a path from the obstacle course to the compound.

16. Draw a path from the track and tennis areas to Cabin 16.

17. How far is it from McKenzie Point to the tennis courts? **630 m**

18. How far is it from Cabin 5 to Cabin 20? **175 m**

19. How far is it from the SW end to the NE end of the island? **1,470 m**

20. Give a name to the creek, a peninsula and a large hill. **Names will vary**

Key
wooded area
sandy area
hills
marshland
shoreline
path

Scale 1 cm = 70 m

Page 274

Case the Joint (cont.)

Page 275

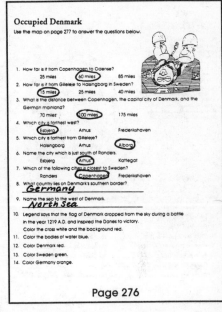

Occupied Denmark

Use the map on page 277 to answer the questions below.

1. How far is it from Copenhagen to Odense?
   25 miles   **60 miles**   85 miles

2. How far is it from Gilleleje to Halsingborg in Sweden?
   15 miles   25 miles   40 miles

3. What is the distance between Copenhagen, the capital city of Denmark, and the German mainland?
   70 miles   **100 miles**   175 miles

4. Which city is farthest west?
   Esbjerg   Arhus   Frederikshaven

5. Which city is farthest from Gilleleje?
   Halsingborg   Arhus   **Alborg**

6. Name the city that is just south of Randers.
   Esbjerg   **Arhus**   Kattegat

7. Which of the following cities is closest to Sweden?
   Randers   **Copenhagen**   Frederikshaven

8. What country lies on Denmark's southern border?
   Germany

9. Name the sea to the west of Denmark.
   North Sea

10. Legend says that the flag of Denmark dropped from the sky during a battle in the year 1219 A.D. and inspired the Danes to victory. Color the cross white and the background red.

11. Color the bodies of water blue.

12. Color Denmark red.

13. Color Sweden green.

14. Color Germany orange.

Page 276

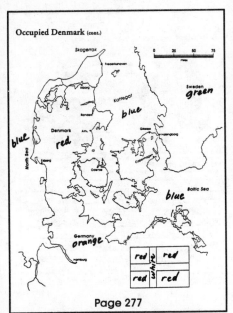

Occupied Denmark (cont.)

Skagerrak

Sweden **green**

Kattegat   **blue**

blue

Denmark   **red**

North Sea

blue   Baltic Sea

Germany **orange**

| **red** | **white** |
| **red** | **red** |

Page 277

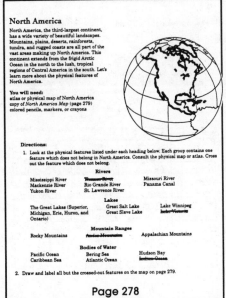

North America

North America, the third-largest continent, has a wide variety of beautiful landscapes. Mountains, plains, deserts, rainforests, tundra, and rugged coasts are all part of the vast areas making up North America. This continent extends from the frigid Arctic Ocean in the north to the lush, tropical regions of Central America in the south. Let's learn more about the physical features of North America.

You will need:
atlas or physical map of North America
copy of North America Map (page 279)
colored pencils, markers, or crayons

Directions:

1. Look at the physical features listed under each heading below. Each group contains one feature which does not belong in North America. Consult the physical map or atlas. Cross out the feature which does not belong.

Rivers

Mississippi River   ~~Thames River~~   Missouri River
Mackenzie River   Rio Grande River   Panama Canal
Yukon River   St. Lawrence River

Lakes

The Great Lakes (Superior, Michigan, Erie, Huron, and Ontario)   Great Salt Lake   Lake Winnipeg
Great Slave Lake   ~~Lake Victoria~~

Mountain Ranges

Rocky Mountains   ~~Andes Mountains~~   Appalachian Mountains

Bodies of Water

Pacific Ocean   Bering Sea   Hudson Bay
Caribbean Sea   Atlantic Ocean   ~~Indian Ocean~~

2. Draw and label all but the crossed-out features on the map on page 279.

Page 278

North America
(Use with page 278.)

Page 279

Landform Regions of the United States

The continental United States can be divided into several major landform regions. Label each region using the list found in the Word Bank.

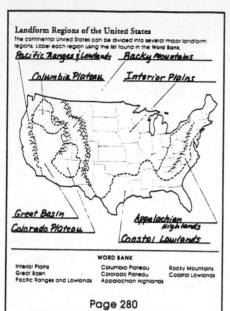

Pacific Ranges & Lowlands   Rocky Mountains

Columbia Plateau   Interior Plains

Great Basin

Colorado Plateau

Appalachian Highlands

Coastal Lowlands

WORD BANK

Interior Plains
Great Basin
Pacific Ranges and Lowlands

Columbia Plateau
Colorado Plateau
Appalachian Highlands

Rocky Mountains
Coastal Lowlands

Page 280

Hemispheres

The earth is a sphere. When the earth is cut in half either vertically or horizontally, hemispheres are created. If the earth is cut in half along the equator, the Northern Hemisphere and the Southern Hemisphere are formed. If the earth is cut in half from the North Pole to the South Pole along the prime meridian, the Eastern Hemisphere and the Western Hemisphere are formed.

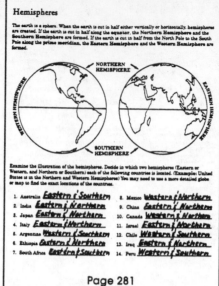

Examine the illustration of the hemispheres. Decide in which two hemispheres (Eastern or Western, and Northern or Southern) each of the following countries is located. (Example: United States is in the Northern and Western Hemispheres.) You may need to use a more detailed globe or map to find the exact locations of the countries.

1. Australia   Eastern & Southern
2. India   Eastern & Northern
3. Japan   Eastern & Northern
4. Italy   Eastern & Northern
5. Argentina   Western & Southern
6. Ethiopia   Eastern & Northern
7. South Africa   Eastern & Southern
8. Mexico   Western & Northern
9. China   Eastern & Northern
10. Canada   Western & Northern
11. Israel   Eastern & Northern
12. Chile   Western & Southern
13. Iraq   Eastern & Northern
14. Peru   Western & Southern

Page 281

Lines of Latitude

The lines on a globe help you find where places are located. The lines that go around the globe from east to west are called lines of latitude, or parallels. The lines of latitude tell you how far north or south of the equator (0°) you are.

All lines of latitude are measured from the equator in degrees. Everything north of the equator is labeled N for north, and everything south of the equator is labeled S for south.

To help remember latitude, think of a ladder.

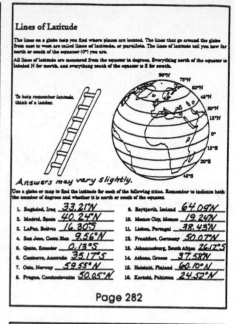

Answers may vary slightly.

Use a globe or map to find the latitude for each of the following cities. Remember to indicate both the number of degrees and whether it is north or south of the equator.

1. Baghdad, Iraq   33.21°N
2. Madrid, Spain   40.24°N
3. LaPaz, Bolivia   16.30°S
4. San Jose, Costa Rica   9.56°N
5. Quito, Ecuador   0.13°S
6. Canberra, Australia   35.17°S
7. Oslo, Norway   59.55°N
8. Prague, Czechoslovakia   50.05°N
9. Reykjavik, Iceland   64.09°N
10. Mexico City, Mexico   19.24°N
11. Lisbon, Portugal   38.43°N
12. Frankfurt, Germany   50.07°N
13. Johannesburg, South Africa   26.12°S
14. Athens, Greece   37.58°N
15. Helsinki, Finland   60.10°N
16. Karachi, Pakistan   24.52°N

Page 282

Lines of Longitude

The lines on a globe help you find where places are located. The lines that go from the North Pole to the South Pole are called lines of longitude, or meridians. The lines of longitude tell you how far east or west of the prime meridian (0°) you are.

All lines of longitude are measured from the prime meridian in degrees. Everything west of the prime meridian is labeled W for west, and everything east of the prime meridian is labeled E for east.

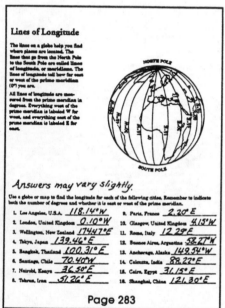

Answers may vary slightly.

Use a globe or map to find the longitude for each of the following cities. Remember to indicate both the number of degrees and whether it is east or west of the prime meridian.

1. Los Angeles, U.S.A.   118.14°W
2. London, United Kingdom   0.10°W
3. Wellington, New Zealand   174.47°E
4. Tokyo, Japan   139.46°E
5. Bangkok, Thailand   100.31°E
6. Santiago, Chile   70.40°W
7. Nairobi, Kenya   36.50°E
8. Tehran, Iran   51.26°E
9. Paris, France   2.20°E
10. Glasgow, United Kingdom   4.15°W
11. Rome, Italy   12.29°E
12. Buenos Aires, Argentina   58.27°W
13. Anchorage, Alaska   149.54°W
14. Calcutta, India   88.22°E
15. Cairo, Egypt   31.15°E
16. Shanghai, China   121.30°E

Page 283

What's My Line?

There are several important lines of latitude on the globe which have special names. Use a map, globe, or other resource to identify the special lines on the illustration of the globe below.

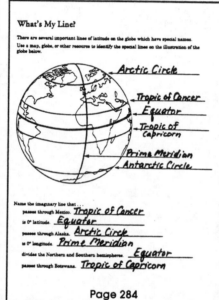

Arctic Circle

Tropic of Cancer

Equator

Tropic of Capricorn

Prime Meridian

Antarctic Circle

Name the imaginary line that . . .

passes through Mexico   Tropic of Cancer
is 0° latitude   Equator
passes through Alaska   Arctic Circle
is 0° longitude   Prime Meridian
divides the Northern and Southern hemispheres   Equator
passes through Botswana   Tropic of Capricorn

Page 284

Pinpointing Your Location

A specific location can be "pinpointed" by using latitude and longitude together. The number of degrees latitude will tell you how far it is north or south of the equator. The number of degrees longitude will tell you how far it is east or west of the prime meridian.

Grand Rapids
43°N 85°W

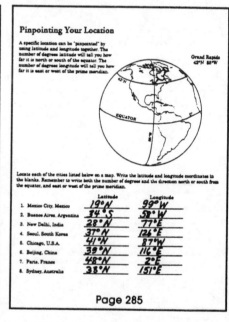

Locate each of the cities listed below on a map. Write the latitude and longitude coordinates in the blanks. Remember to write both the number of degrees and the direction north or south from the equator, and east or west of the prime meridian.

		Latitude	Longitude
1.	Mexico City, Mexico	19°N	99°W
2.	Buenos Aires, Argentina	34°S	59°W
3.	New Delhi, India	28°N	77°E
4.	Seoul, South Korea	37°N	126°E
5.	Chicago, U.S.A.	41°N	87°W
6.	Beijing, China	39°N	116°E
7.	Paris, France	48°N	2°E
8.	Sydney, Australia	33°N	151°E

Page 285

The Story of a River

The river systems of the world provide people with transportation, energy, fertile soil, and water for drinking, washing, and irrigation. The terms below are used when telling the story of a river system. Learn the meanings of these terms, and then label the parts of the river on the illustration.

flood plain	tributary	lake
delta	rapids	levee
mouth	swamp	source

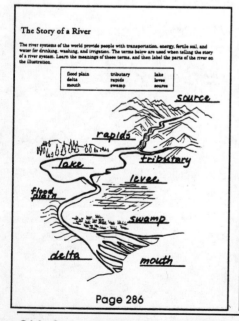

source

rapids

tributary

lake

levee

flood plain

swamp

delta

mouth

Page 286

Famous Rivers of the World

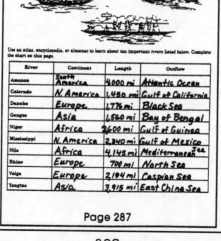

Use an atlas, encyclopedia, or almanac to learn about ten important rivers listed below. Complete the chart on this page.

River	Continent	Length	Outflow
Amazon	South America	4,000 mi	Atlantic Ocean
Colorado	N. America	1,450 mi	Gulf of California
Danube	Europe	1,776 mi	Black Sea
Ganges	Asia	1,560 mi	Bay of Bengal
Niger	Africa	2,600 mi	Gulf of Guinea
Mississippi	N. America	2,340 mi	Gulf of Mexico
Nile	Africa	4,145 mi	Mediterranean Sea
Rhine	Europe	700 mi	North Sea
Volga	Europe	2,194 mi	Caspian Sea
Yangtze	Asia	3,915 mi	East China Sea

Page 287

River Cities

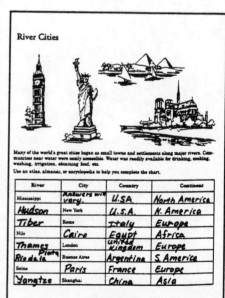

Many of the world's great cities began as small towns and settlements along major rivers. Communities near water were easily accessible. Water was readily available for drinking, cooking, washing, irrigation, obtaining food, etc.
Use an atlas, almanac, or encyclopedia to help you complete the chart.

River	City	Country	Continent
Mississippi	Answers will vary.	U.S.A	North America
Hudson	New York	U.S.A.	N. America
Tiber	Rome	Italy	Europe
Nile	Cairo	Egypt	Africa
Thames	London	United Kingdom	Europe
Rio de la Plata	Buenos Aires	Argentina	S. America
Seine	Paris	France	Europe
Yangtze	Shanghai	China	Asia

Page 288

Daily Learning Drills Grade 5

Name _____

Don't Stress Out!

When a word of two or more syllables is pronounced, usually one of the syllables is stressed. Sometimes there are two ways to pronounce the same word. The accent, or stress, changes as the meaning of the word changes. Example: The detective began to susPECT that the butler was the key SUSpect.

Read each sentence. Then circle the correct pronunciation for the underlined word.

1. At the awards dinner, they will <u>present</u> me with a present.

   PRESent   **preSENT**

2. As you <u>progress</u> through the book, keep track of your progress.

   PROGress   **proGRESS**

3. "I <u>object</u>," shouted the lawyer. "The object of his question was to trick my client."

   obJECT   **OBject**

4. If you are on your best <u>conduct</u>, you can conduct the class on a tour.

   CONduct   **conDUCT**

5. Don't <u>refuse</u> to clean up the refuse from the picnic.

   REFuse   **reFUSE**

6. Without a <u>permit</u>, we cannot permit you to hunt.

   perMIT   **PERmit**

7. This afternoon, I will be at this <u>address</u>. I am giving the main address of the meeting.

   ADdress   **adDRESS**

8. Most <u>conflicts</u> start because differing opinions conflict.

   CONflicts   **conFLICTS**

9. Are you <u>content</u> with the content of your lunch?

   conTENT   **CONtent**

10. Did they <u>convict</u> the convict?

    CONvict   **conVICT**

11. If the air conditioning breaks on the <u>produce</u> truck, it will produce rotten fruit.

    PROduce   **proDUCE**

Name _____

Come on, Goldie!

A **declarative** sentence tells something. It ends with a period. **(.)**
An **interrogative** sentence asks something. It ends with a question mark. **(?)**
An **imperative** sentence gives an order. It ends with a period. **(.)**
An **exclamatory** sentence shows strong feeling. It ends with an exclamation mark. **(!)**

Read each sentence. Write an abbreviation to tell what kind of sentence it is:
    D—declarative   *Int*—interrogative   *Imp*—Imperative   *E*—Exclamatory
Then write the missing punctuation mark.

__Imp__ Goldie, roll over**.**

__Int__ Have you ever tried to train a fish**?**

__D__ I did**.**

__E__ What a disaster**!**

_____ 1. It all started when my friend insulted my fish

_____ 2. Fish are stupid pets

_____ 3. Why do you say that

_____ 4. Look at it

_____ 5. All your fish does is swim and eat

_____ 6. Hmmmph, Goldie is *not* a stupid fish

_____ 7. Teach her some tricks then

_____ 8. OK, I will

_____ 9. How do the trainers at Sea World train the dolphins and whales

_____ 10. They use whistles and rewards, but those are mammals, not fish

_____ 11. Goldie, swim on your side when I blow this whistle

_____ 12. Tweet-tweet

_____ 13. Goldie, didn't you hear me

_____ 14. I'll give you extra food if you do it

_____ 15. Goldie, watch how I do it

Name _____

Animal Armor

The **subject** is the part of a sentence that tells whom or what the sentence is about.

The **predicate** is the part of a sentence that tells what the subject is or does.

Read each sentence. Circle the subject. Underline the predicate.

Examples:

(Many different animals) have armor to protect themselves.

Unlike most mammals, (a pangolin) has scales covering its body.

1. The pangolin's sharp scales are made from a strange, hard form of hair.

2. A pangolin curls up in a ball to escape from danger.

3. An armadillo looks like it is covered in armor.

4. The name *armadillo* means "little armored one" in Spanish.

5. Armadillos have bony plates and very tough skin.

6. A tortoise's hard shell is its armor.

7. Inside its shell, the tortoise can hide from predators.

8. The tortoise beetle is an insect.

9. It has a hard shield that covers its head, legs, and body.

Read these animal sentences. Write **S** if the sentence is missing the subject or **P** if it is missing the predicate.
Finish the sentences, filling in the missing parts.

____ 10. A slow-moving snail _____

_____.

____ 11. Like the crab, _____ is

a shelled animal that lives in the ocean.

____ 12. _____ would

look funny if they were covered with armor.

Name _____

My Favorite Author

The **complete subject** is all the words in a sentence that tell whom or what the sentence is about.

The **simple subject** is the main word that tells whom or what the sentence is about. If a simple subject is a proper noun, it may be more than one word.

A **compound subject** has two or more simple subjects, usually connected with the word *and*.

Read each sentence. Underline the complete subject. Write the simple subject(s).

<u>class</u>

<u>Everyone</u>

<u>Marcus, I</u>

_____

_____

_____

_____

_____

_____

_____

_____

_____

<u>Our class</u> is doing an author study project.

<u>Everyone</u> needs to choose an author.

<u>Both Marcus and I</u> chose Dick King-Smith.

1. Dick King-Smith writes books about animals.

2. I have read five of his books.

3. My favorite one is *Three Terrible Trins*.

4. That book is about mice triplets who befriend a cellar mouse and terrorize a cat.

5. Our assignment has two parts—a report and a project.

6. The report needs to explain themes that are repeated in the author's books.

7. Many of the characters in King-Smith's books want to do more than the others around them.

8. The mice in *Three Terrible Trins* want to have friends in all levels of their farmhouse.

9. The pig in *Pigs Might Fly* learns to swim and hopes to fly.

10. My creative project will be a tape-recorded interview of the different book characters.

11. Marcus and Whitney are going to help me read the parts.

Name _____

A Thank–You Note

A. Read Liz Beth's letter to her grandparents.
   Fill in the missing subject pronouns.

B. Read her grandpa's reply.
   Fill in the missing object pronouns.

Subject Pronoun	Object Pronoun
I	me
you	you
he	him
she	her
it	it
we	us
they	them

Dear Grandma and Grandpa,

    Thank you for the earrings _____ sent me for my birthday. _____ were cool. Dad still thinks ___ am too young to have had my ears pierced. But he said now that _____ is done, he won't complain about it anymore. Last night Michael asked Dad if _____ could get one of his ears pierced. Dad got really mad and said, "___ am going for a long walk!" _____ all started laughing. Mom doesn't think Michael really wants his ear pierced. _____ thinks he just wanted to tease Dad.

    _____ are looking forward to your visit next month. _____ is coming soon. If _____ have time, please write me back.

               Love,
               Liz Beth

Dear Liz Beth,

    We were so happy to get the note you sent _____. Grandma picked out the earrings. We're glad you liked _____. Your poor father—you three are always picking on _____!

    Grandma is at Aunt Yoli's this weekend. She went to visit _____ for a few days.

    I talked to your mom yesterday. She told _____ that you won a mystery award for your computer project. When will you get _____?

    I hope all is well with you and your family. We miss _____.

               Love,
               Grandpa

Name _____

Get in on the Action!

For most verbs, you add *ed* to form the past tense and the past participle. You add *ing* to form the present participle. But for some words, you don't add *ed* or *ing* to show a change in time. These are called **irregular verbs** (example: *catch, caught; buy, bought*). Irregular verb forms are listed in the dictionary.

Write the verb forms that belong on the lines. When you're done, you will have a joke.

Two goats (wander) _____ into an alley behind a
movie theater. They were (look) _____ for their dinner.
They (find) _____ a videotape. One of the goats (eat)
_____ it.
"How was it?" the other goat (ask) _____.
"All right," said the first goat. "But the book was better."

Write the past tense of each verb below.

Verb	Past Tense
1. stop	_____
2. try	_____
3. sing	_____
4. teach	_____
5. go	_____

Use a dictionary to fill in the chart below. The first line is done for you.

Verb	Past Tense	Past Participle (*have* or *has* + verb)	Present Participle
sell	*sold*	*sold*	*selling*
1. go	_____	_____	_____
2. rise	_____	_____	_____
3. sing	_____	_____	_____
4. write	_____	_____	_____
5. tear	_____	_____	_____
6. swim	_____	_____	_____

Name _____

A Bad Fairy Tale

Most verbs name actions. The verb **be** is different.
It tells about someone or something. It can also be a
helping verb that helps with an action verb.

Read this silly fairy tale. Fill in the blanks with a form of
the verb **be**: *be, am, is, are, was, were, being,* or *been*.

Once upon a time, there _____ a sweet, unlucky girl named Mary Badluck. Like

other mothers in fairy tales, her mother _____ gentle, kind, and ill. Unfortunately,

Mary's mother died when Mary _____ only five. Mary and her father _____ quite

sad. "What _____ we going to do?" wept her father.

"I _____ not worried, Father, nor should you be," said Mary. "We will _____ okay."

Mary's father _____ lonely, so he remarried. Mary's stepmother, Lady Grace,

_____ gentle and kind like Mary's own mother had _____. But alas, Lady

Grace _____ ill, too, and she soon died.

"What _____ I going to do?" sobbed her father.

"_____ brave, Father!" admonished Mary.

Once again her father remarried. Mary's new

stepmother, Lady Evila, _____ actually nice. Mary had

_____ expecting an evil stepmother and _____

pleasantly surprised. But guess what? Yes, you _____

right. Lady Evila _____ a sickly creature and died, too.

"What _____ going on around here?" wailed her father.

"I think we are _____ tormented in a bad fairy tale, Father!" realized Mary.

Mary _____ quite right. Her father remarried yet again. This time her new

stepmother, Lady Bullybrains, _____ rough, mean, and healthy.

What _____ Mary and her father going to do? Will they ever _____ happy?
Write an ending to this tale to find out.

Name _____

Noun, Adjective, Adverb

A **noun** is a word that names a person, place, thing, or idea.
An **adjective** is a word that describes a noun.
An **adverb** is a word that modifies a verb, an adjective, or another adverb.

Many nouns, adjectives, and adverbs are variations of the same root word.
<u>Bravery</u> was an important quality for knights. (noun)
The <u>brave</u> knight searched for the dragon. (adjective)
The knight fought <u>bravely</u> when the dragon attacked. (adverb)

Read the words in each row. Write the missing adjective or adverb.

Noun	Adjective	Adverb
intelligence	intelligent	intelligently
kindness		kindly
fearlessness	fearless	
happiness		happily
success		successfully
independence		
arrogance	arrogant	
carelessness		carelessly
possibility		
enthusiasm		enthusiastically
affection	affectionate	
ease		
courtesy		courteously
responsibility		responsibly
stupidity		
wisdom		
anger		
silence		

328   Daily Learning Drills Grade 5

Name _____

LANGUAGE ARTS REVIEW

Watch Out, Goldilocks!

Use **quotation marks** (" ") to show the exact words a speaker says.

> *Papa Bear exclaimed, "Someone's been eating my porridge!"*

Use a **comma** (,) to set off the exact words a speaker says from the rest of the sentence.

> *"Someone's been eating my porridge, too," chimed in Mama Bear.*

> *"Someone's been eating my porridge," sobbed Baby Bear, "and now it's all gone."*

If a speaker's exact words need a **question mark** or **exclamation mark**, write the mark inside the quotation marks.

> *Mama Bear asked, "Do you think the intruder is still here?"*

> *"Watch out, you nasty intruder!" shouted Baby Bear. "We're coming to get you."*

Read this conversation. Write the missing punctuation marks.
Finish the conversation by writing a line each for Baby Bear and Goldilocks.

Let's check the living room   suggested Baby Bear

Hmmph! Someone's been sitting in my chair   growled Papa Bear

Oh, my   gasped Mama Bear. Someone's
been sitting in my chair, too

Quit feeling sorry for yourselves and pay
attention to me   said Baby Bear as he pointed
to his chair. Whoever it was broke my chair

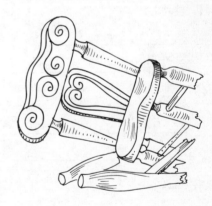

Shall we check the bedroom   asked Papa Bear

Let's go quietly   whispered Mama Bear

Watch out, you nasty intruder   shouted Baby Bear
We're coming to get you

Shh, BB   Mama Bear reprimanded.

Oh, Mom   grumbled Baby Bear

Papa Bear announced   Someone's been sleeping in my bed

Here we go again   sighed Mama Bear   Someone's been sleeping in my bed

_____

_____

_____

Name _____

It's All the Same to Me

Some words mean the same or nearly the same as other words. Two words that mean almost the same are called synonyms. Many dictionary definitions give other words—or **synonyms**—for the words defined.

Read the dictionary entry for the word *talk*. Notice all the synonyms in the definition. Can you think of other synonyms for the word *talk*?

> **talk** (tôk). 1. *v.* use words; speak: *Baby is learning to talk.* 2. *n.* the use of words; spoken words; speech; conversation: *The old friends met for a good talk.* 3. *n.* an informal speech. 4. *v.* discuss: *They talked politics.* 5. *v.* consult; confer: *to talk with one's doctor.* 6. *v.* spread ideas by other means than speech: *to talk by signs.* 7. *v.* bring, influence, etc., by talk: *We talked them into joining the club.* 8. *n.* gossip; report; rumor: *She was the talk of the town.*

A thesaurus is a book of synonyms. Use a thesaurus to find three synonyms for each word below. Compare your answers with other students.

1. avoid

_____

_____

2. border

_____

_____

3. clear

_____

_____

4. effective

_____

_____

5. forbid

_____

_____

6. glorify

_____

_____

7. insane

_____

_____

8. maintain

_____

_____

9. offer

_____

_____

10. period

_____

_____

It's Just the Opposite

Antonyms are words that have opposite meanings. *Guilty* and *innocent* are antonyms. So are *smooth* and *rough*.

Circle the antonym in each group for the boldfaced word on the left.

1. **tired**	weary	sleepy	energetic
2. **help**	assist	hinder	aid
3. **sick**	ailing	healthy	ill
4. **alike**	similar	identical	different
5. **soft**	flexible	rigid	pliable
6. **bright**	vivid	cloudy	brilliant
7. **likeable**	amiable	unpleasant	agreeable
8. **narrow**	slim	wide	thin
9. **incorrect**	erroneous	correct	wrong
10. **wet**	soaked	drenched	arid
11. **huge**	minute	colossal	bulky
12. **risky**	dangerous	safe	hazardous
13. **hostile**	friendly	unsociable	adverse
14. **cheerful**	joyous	lively	glum
15. **active**	sluggish	quick	nimble
16. **irritate**	provoke	rouse	soothe
17. **sharp**	blunt	fine	pointed
18. **timid**	fearful	courageous	afraid

Name _____

Daffy Definitions!

If you know baseball, then you probably know what a *grand slam* is. It's a home run with the bases loaded. But if you like word play, you can come up with a daffy definition: A *grand slam* is someone who slaps $1,000 onto a table. A thousand dollars is sometimes called a *grand*. By using that meaning of *grand*, you can get the daffy definition of *grand slam*.

How daffy are you? See if you can match the expressions below with their crazy definitions. Write your answers on the lines.

rock garden	capital punishment	New Jersey
diamond cutter	net profit	bank balance

1. The person who mows the grass on a baseball field _____

2. A place where outdoor music concerts are held _____

3. Having to stay after school in Washington, D.C. _____

4. What is left after the fishing boat owner pays all expenses _____

5. A replacement for a worn-out turtleneck sweater _____

6. What keeps a building full of money from tipping over _____

Now try the same thing with single words. Think about the sound of each word, as well as its meaning.

bamboo	goblet	cartoon	pharmacy	capsize
Alaska	cantaloupe	watchdog	account	footnotes

7. A school where you learn to be a farmer _____

8. An animal that knows how to tell time _____

9. Music that is written and played for dancing _____

10. A song you might hum while you're driving _____

11. What a girl tells a guy who wants to run away and get married _____

12. A young turkey just learning to make sounds _____

13. A nobleman, like a duke, earl, or lord _____

14. Two loud noises that might frighten you _____

15. What you tell a hat salesperson _____

16. What you say when you want to know a girl's name _____

Name _____

Putting It in Perspective

Cut along the dotted lines to divide the events related to the life of Michelangelo listed below. Then rearrange them in chronological order to put the events in historical perspective. Glue the ordered events to your own paper.

✂

1508–1512 Michelangelo works on the Sistine Chapel Ceiling project.

1564 Having worked on projects until his very last days, Michelangelo dies at the age of 89. His contemporaries describe his death as the passing of a "divine angel."

----

c.1515 Michelangelo completes one of his most famous sculptures, *Moses*.

1386 Donatello is born. His techniques will influence Michelangelo, and one of his former students will serve as Michelangelo's teacher at art school.

1475 Michelangelo Buonarroti is born to a distinguished Florentine family.

1488–1489 Michelangelo apprentices with Domenico Ghirlandaio.

1501–1504 Michelangelo works on the marble figure of *David*.

1452 Leonardo da Vinci is born. His work and Michelangelo's work will be displayed side by side at least once in their lifetimes.

1350 The Renaissance era in art, music, literature, and religion is born. Michelangelo will contribute substantially to the High Renaissance period within this era.

1517 The Reformation is initiated when Martin Luther nails his 95 Theses to the door of a German cathedral, criticizing practices of the Catholic church. The resulting split in the church and beginning of the Protestant faith affects the religious Michelangelo, whose works display more sorrow and disillusionment.

1498–1500 Michelangelo works on the *Pietà*.

1541 Michelangelo completes the *Last Judgment* mural.

1492 Michelangelo's first patron, Lorenzo de Medici, dies, his family falls out of favor in Florence, and Michelangelo finds himself in exile in Bologna two years later.

1505–1516 The Vatican is the primary patron of Michelangelo's work.

1550 Michelangelo begins work on a sculpture many believe he wished to be placed at his own burial site. Out of depression or disappointment in the quality of the work, he destroys his own work, which is later repaired.

Name _____

Figure It Out

When you come across an unfamiliar word, you can usually figure out its meaning by looking for clues in the surrounding words. In each sentence below, guess the meaning of the boldfaced word. Then compare your meaning with the dictionary meaning. Were you close?

1. "This is a **bogus** bill," said the bank teller.

   Bogus probably means _____.

2. The **destitute** family had trouble paying its rent.

   Destitute probably means_____.

3. Her **affable** personality won her many friends.

   Affable probably means _____.

4. The huge ten-story **edifice** dwarfed the other office structures.

   Edifice probably means_____.

5. The team members looked **despondent** after they lost the game.

   Despondent probably means _____.

6. "If you get one more speeding ticket," the judge said, "I will **revoke** your license."

   Revoke probably means _____.

7. After the **altercation**, they kissed and made up.

   Altercation probably means _____.

8. In some states, an accessory to murder is as **culpable** as the actual killer.

   Culpable probably means _____.

9. If you are **loquacious**, you can expect high phone bills.

   Loquacious probably means _____.

10. When Tory cancelled the party a third time, her friends were **irate**.

    Irate probably means_____.

Name _____

Sequence of Events

Fill in this chart with important events from a story you read. The title of the book goes in the center. Then fill in events relating to the story going around the circle.

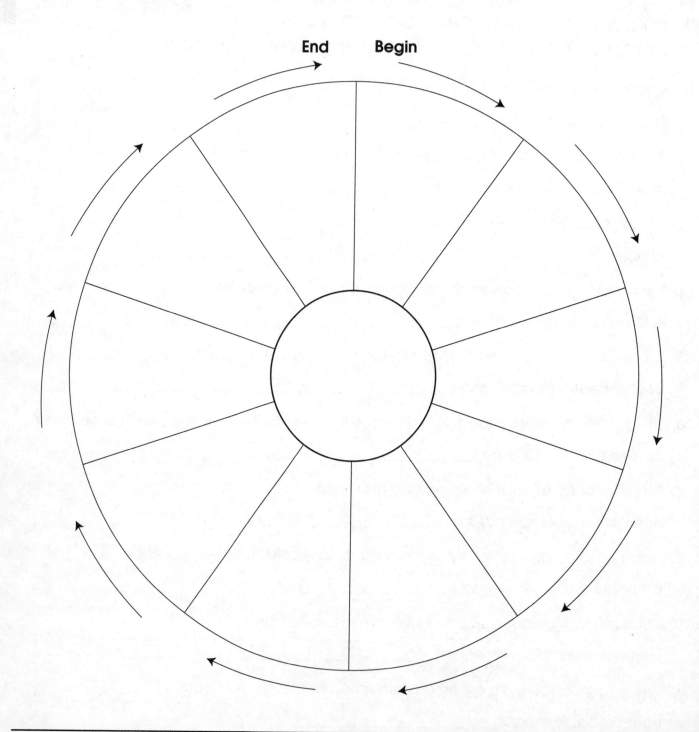

End   **Begin**

Name _____

Many Kinds of Information

Dictionaries provide information on pronunciation, spelling, and word meaning. But that's not all. You can also use dictionaries to find out about people, places, and things—even abbreviations, slang words, and trademarks.

Use a dictionary to answer the questions that follow.

1. Is C.O.D. a kind of fish? _____

2. Did Cleopatra live in Greece? _____

3. Was Kleenex an ancient ruler? _____

4. Would you expect to see a griffin in a zoo? _____

5. Is the Cape of Good Hope something to wear? _____

6. Do Minutemen work in clock factories? _____

7. If you root for a team, are you for or against it? _____

8. If you got an invitation marked R.S.V.P., should you reply? _____

9. Is dragoon a kind of beast? _____

10. Was Prometheus a famous movie star? _____

11. Did Rachel appear in a Greek myth? _____

12. Is hgt. short for height? _____

13. Is HEW a government agency or the name of an author? _____

14. Is Death Valley a real place? _____

15. Does the prefix *deca-* mean *ten*? _____

16. Is Julius Caesar a kind of salad? _____

17. Was Pythagoras a great leader? _____

18. Is Kilimanjaro an island in the South Seas? _____

19. Is Labor Day the day you were born? _____

20. Is KA the abbreviation for Kansas? _____

21. Is Kipling a kind of fish? _____

Name _____

Look It Up!

Most encyclopedias have several volumes. They contain short articles about many different subjects. The articles are arranged alphabetically, according to subjects. An article about airplanes would be in the first volume. One entitled "X-rays" would be in the last volume.

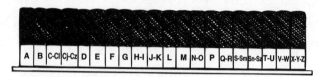

Suppose you wanted to find the answer to each question below. Write the subject you would look up. Then write the volume in which the article would be.

1. What makes sound come from a clarinet?

   Subject _____ **Volume** _____

2. How tall is the Washington Monument?

   Subject _____ **Volume** _____

3. How is a camera similar to the human eye?

   Subject _____ **Volume** _____

4. When was the first transcontinental railroad in the U.S. completed?

   Subject _____ **Volume** _____

5. What is the capital of Alaska?

   Subject _____ **Volume** _____

6. How many different kinds of bears are in North America?

   Subject _____ **Volume** _____

7. What kind of equipment do you need for mountain climbing?

   Subject _____ **Volume** _____

8. What is the meaning of each of the hand signals that a basketball referee uses during a game?

   Subject _____ **Volume** _____

9. How is a suspension bridge built?

   Subject _____ **Volume** _____

10. Who was the 26th President of the United States?

    Subject _____ **Volume** _____

Name _____

Poetry: Recipes for Success

Follow the directions below to create your own poems. Share your works with the class.

> **Spot**
> **Furry, cuddly**
> **Scratching, digging, chewing**
> **Has a nose for trouble**
> **Puppy**

Cinquain

A cinquain is a 5-line poem. A cinquain can take different forms. One form is below.

- Line 1: a noun
- Line 2: two adjectives
- Line 3: three verbs (action words) ending in *ing*
- Line 4: a phrase
- Line 5: a noun (the same as line 1 or different)

_____
_____
_____
_____
_____

Haiku

> *Birds sing in the trees —*
> *melodies like pink flowers*
> *ring in the still air.*

A haiku is a 3-line poem. Each line has a certain number of beats, or syllables.

- Line 1 has 5 syllables. _____
- Line 2 has 7 syllables. _____
- Line 3 has 5 syllables. _____

Diamond Poem

A diamond poem is a 7-line poem that goes from one idea to its opposite. It gets its name from its shape.

Winter   _____
Cold, Icy   _____
Freezing, Snowing, Blowing   _____
Ice, Snow, Sunshine, Flowers   _____
Warming, Blooming, Growing   _____
Hot, Sticky   _____
Summer   _____

Name _____

Prize Pumpkin

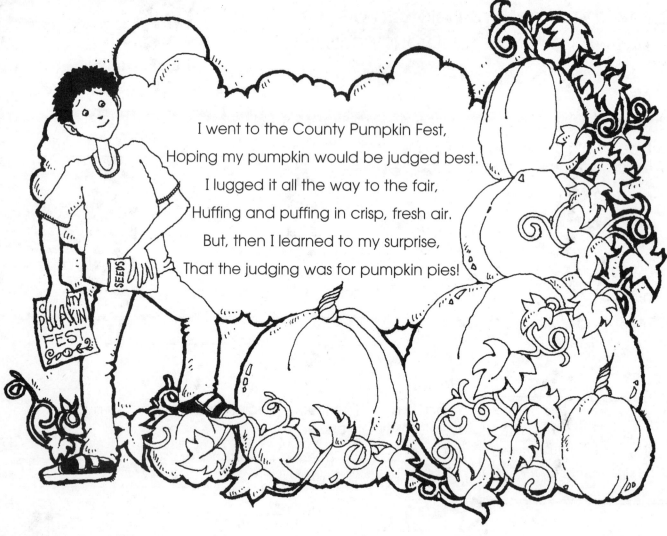

I went to the County Pumpkin Fest,
Hoping my pumpkin would be judged best.
I lugged it all the way to the fair,
Huffing and puffing in crisp, fresh air.
But, then I learned to my surprise,
That the judging was for pumpkin pies!

Complete the following.

1. In what season does this poem take place?_____
   How do you know? _____

2. List 3 adjectives that describe the speaker of the poem.

   _____ _____ _____

3. How big do you think the speaker's pumpkin is?_____
   What clues lead you to this conclusion?_____
   _____

4. Tell what you think happened afterward._____
   _____
   _____

Name _____

If I Were in Charge of the World

Wouldn't it be great to be in charge of the world? Complete the statements below describing what you would do if you were in charge of the world.

If I were in charge of the world, I'd cancel

_____, _____,

and _____.

If I were in charge of the world, there'd be

_____, _____,

and _____.

If I were in charge of the world, everyone could

_____, _____,

and _____.

If I were in charge of the world, these things would be free:

_____, _____,

and _____.

If I were in charge of the world

_____

_____

_____

_____

_____

_____

_____

_____

Name _____

If I Were a. . .

Let your imagination go wild! Complete the phrases below to create a unique, introspective poem.

If I were a color, I'd be

_____ .

If I were a song, I'd be

_____ .

If I were a food, I'd be

_____ .

If I were a car, I'd be

_____ .

If I were an animal, I'd be

_____ .

If I were a place, I'd be

_____ .

If I were a feeling, I'd be

_____ .

If I were a plant, I'd be

_____ .

If I were a climate, I'd be

_____ .

If I were a musical instrument, I'd be

_____ .

If I were a shape, I'd be

_____ .

Name _____

Talk With the Animals

Add or subtract. Use your answers to write and solve a riddle.

O.
  5,038
+ 2,847

W.
  6,034
− 2,993

N.
  7,645
+ 8,397

C.
  57,634
+ 18,906

D.
  9,634
− 5,798

E.
  3,497
+   867

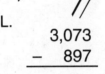

K.
  4,263
− 1,896

H.
  9,156
+ 8,375

P.
  54,375
− 36,693

L.
  3,073
−   897

U.
  5,372
−   439

A.
  23,842
− 1,632

S.
  32,693
+ 41,221

I.
  14,734
− 2,961

F. 1,646 + 1,826 = _____   G. 9,874 − 8,887 = _____   T. 4,419 + 2,987 = _____

___   ___   ___   ___   ___   ___   ___   ___   ___
3,041 17,531 22,210 7,406   3,836 7,885 4,364 73,914   22,210

___   ___   ___   ___   ___   ___   ___   ___   ___   ___   ___   ___
76,540 17,531 11,773 76,540 2,367 4,364 16,042   73,914 17,682 4,364 22,210 2,367   **?**

___   ___   ___   ___   ___   ___   ___   ___   ___   ___   ___   ___
3,472 7,885 3,041 2,176   2,176 22,210 16,042 987 4,993 22,210 987 4,364

Name _____

A Silly Riddle

Find each product. Use the code to solve the riddle.

What has a trunk, two legs, and looks green?

S.   96
x 54

K.   38
x 77

A.   83
x 69

T.   75
x 75

A.   56
x 23

U.   49
x 48

S.   89
x 56

I.   96
x 24

S.   27
x 79

T.   37
x 65

R. 672
x 83

C. 302
x 94

I. 567
x 32

E. 489
x 86

O. 638
x 55

_____   _____ _____ _____ _____ _____ _____ _____
5,727   2,133 42,054 1,288 5,184 2,304 28,388 2,926

_____ _____ _____ _____ _____ _____ _____
2,405 35,090 2,352 55,776 18,144 4,984 5,625

Name _____

Ring Around the Numbers

Circle two numbers in each box whose estimated product would be the amount shown.

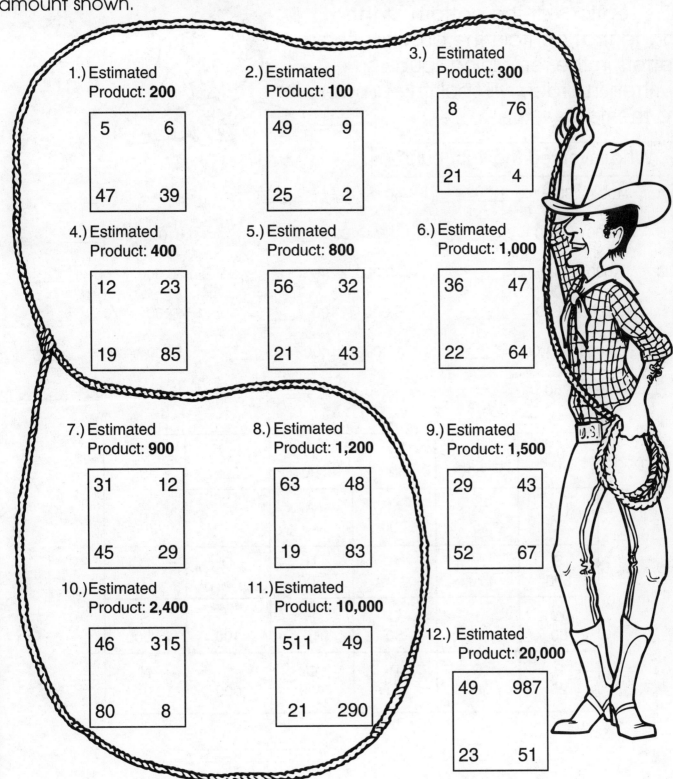

1.) Estimated Product: **200**

5	6
47	39

2.) Estimated Product: **100**

49	9
25	2

3.) Estimated Product: **300**

8	76
21	4

4.) Estimated Product: **400**

12	23
19	85

5.) Estimated Product: **800**

56	32
21	43

6.) Estimated Product: **1,000**

36	47
22	64

7.) Estimated Product: **900**

31	12
45	29

8.) Estimated Product: **1,200**

63	48
19	83

9.) Estimated Product: **1,500**

29	43
52	67

10.) Estimated Product: **2,400**

46	315
80	8

11.) Estimated Product: **10,000**

511	49
21	290

12.) Estimated Product: **20,000**

49	987
23	51

MATH REVIEW

Name _____

Turn on the Light

Find the quotients. Then cross out the sections at the bottom of the page that contain the answers. The letters in the remaining squares, written in order, will spell the answer to the riddle.

Who invented the light bulb?

A. $400 \div 80 =$ _____ $40 \div 10 =$ _____ $420 \div 60 =$ _____

B. $5,000 \div 500 =$ _____ $480 \div 80 =$ _____ $810 \div 90 =$ _____

C. $1,000 \div 10 =$ _____ $32,000 \div 40 =$ _____ $30,000 \div 60 =$ _____

D. $6,000 \div 300 =$ _____ $5,000 \div 100 =$ _____ $4,900 \div 70 =$ _____

E. $60,000 \div 1,000 =$ _____ $12,000 \div 400 =$ _____ $1,000 \div 40 =$ _____

F. $4,000 \div 50 =$ _____ $6,000 \div 30 =$ _____ $45,000 \div 500 =$ _____

T 3	F 60	H 900	K 90	O 300	J 9
Y 30	X 5	M 700	A 40	B 4	Z 200
S 600	V 70	E 1	U 500	D 8	C 7
W 80	I 1,000	Q 50	F 10	K 100	S 2,000
P 25	G 6	P 20	O 400	L 800	N 3,000

___ ___ ___ ___ ___ ___   ___ ___ ___ ___ ___ ___

Name _____

Puzzling Problems

Use the clues to solve the puzzle.

ACROSS

- A. 6,048 ÷ 12 = _____
- C. 14,848 ÷ 16 = _____
- E. 31,680 ÷ 6 = _____
- G. 7,056 ÷ 84 = _____
- I. 0 ÷ 36 = _____
- J. 98,593 ÷ 11 = _____
- M. 5,240 ÷ 10 = _____
- N. 948 ÷ 12 = _____
- Q. 6,630 ÷ 17 = _____
- R. 6,240 ÷ 20 = _____
- S. 13,000 ÷ 25 = _____

DOWN

- A. 11,776 ÷ 2 = _____
- B. 2,070 ÷ 46 = _____
- C. 8,901 ÷ 9 = _____
- D. 1,780 ÷ 89 = _____
- F. 31,276 ÷ 14 = _____
- H. 6,435 ÷ 13 = _____
- K. 68,992 ÷ 11 = _____
- L. 11,376 ÷ 3 = _____
- O. 9,000 ÷ 10 = _____
- P. 2,211 ÷ 67 = _____
- Q. 875 ÷ 25 = _____

Name _____

Fishing for Sums and Differences

Add or subtract. Write the answer in the lowest terms.

A. $\frac{1}{4} + \frac{2}{4} =$ _____ $\frac{3}{4}$ _____

B. $\frac{6}{18} + \frac{2}{18} =$ _____

C. $\frac{2}{3} - \frac{1}{3} =$ _____ $\qquad$ $\frac{2}{8} + \frac{4}{8} =$ _____

D. $\frac{11}{12} - \frac{5}{12} =$ _____ $\qquad$ $\frac{5}{16} + \frac{2}{16} + \frac{5}{16} =$ _____

E. $\frac{5}{16} + \frac{1}{16} + \frac{2}{16} =$ _____ $\qquad$ $\frac{20}{24} - \frac{12}{24} =$ _____

F. $\frac{5}{6} - \frac{3}{6} =$ _____ $\qquad$ $\frac{8}{8} - \frac{3}{8} =$ _____

G. $\frac{2}{18} + \frac{4}{18} + \frac{3}{18} =$ _____ $\qquad$ $\frac{5}{6} - \frac{2}{6} =$ _____

H. $\frac{2}{6} + \frac{3}{6} =$ _____ $\qquad$ $\frac{7}{8} - \frac{3}{8} =$ _____

I. $\frac{8}{15} - \frac{2}{15} =$ _____ $\qquad$ $\frac{7}{15} + \frac{3}{15} =$ _____

J. $\frac{2}{10} + \frac{4}{10} + \frac{3}{10} =$ _____ $\qquad$ $\frac{6}{7} - \frac{3}{7} =$ _____

K. $\frac{12}{14} - \frac{10}{14} =$ _____ $\qquad$ $\frac{5}{16} + \frac{3}{16} =$ _____

L. $\frac{3}{7} + \frac{2}{7} =$ _____ $\qquad$ $\frac{4}{20} + \frac{5}{20} + \frac{7}{20} =$ _____

M. $\frac{5}{5} - \frac{1}{5} =$ _____ $\qquad$ $\frac{7}{8} - \frac{1}{8} =$ _____

N. $\frac{1}{20} + \frac{3}{20} + \frac{1}{20} =$ _____ $\qquad$ $\frac{1}{5} + \frac{3}{5} =$ _____

O. $\frac{12}{10} - \frac{2}{10} =$ _____ $\qquad$ $\frac{3}{12} + \frac{6}{12} =$ _____

P. $\frac{3}{13} + \frac{7}{13} =$ _____ $\qquad$ $\frac{9}{10} - \frac{7}{10} =$ _____

Q. $\frac{8}{9} - \frac{3}{9} =$ _____ $\qquad$ $\frac{11}{16} - \frac{7}{16} =$ _____

Name _____

A Flower Garden
Rename each whole number.

A. $1 = \dfrac{\boxed{}}{8}$ $3 = 2\dfrac{\boxed{}}{6}$ $4 = 3\dfrac{\boxed{}}{10}$ $1 = \dfrac{\boxed{}}{5}$

B. $15 = 14\dfrac{\boxed{}}{9}$ $5 = 4\dfrac{\boxed{}}{4}$ $2 = 1\dfrac{\boxed{}}{2}$ $12 = 11\dfrac{\boxed{}}{7}$

Rename each whole number. Then subtract.

C.
$$\begin{array}{r} 1 = \dfrac{10}{10} \\[4pt] -\ \dfrac{7}{10} = \dfrac{7}{10} \\[2pt] \hline \dfrac{3}{10} \end{array}$$

$$\begin{array}{r} 2 = \\[4pt] -\ 1\dfrac{6}{11} = \\ \hline \end{array}$$

$$\begin{array}{r} 4 = \\[4pt] -\ 2\dfrac{1}{2} = \\ \hline \end{array}$$

D.
$$\begin{array}{r} 7 = \\[4pt] -\ 3\dfrac{1}{4} = \\ \hline \end{array}$$

$$\begin{array}{r} 5 = \\[4pt] -\ 2\dfrac{3}{8} = \\ \hline \end{array}$$

$$\begin{array}{r} 1 = \\[4pt] -\ \dfrac{2}{5} = \\ \hline \end{array}$$

E.
$$\begin{array}{r} 7 = \\[4pt] -\ 3\dfrac{14}{15} = \\ \hline \end{array}$$

$$\begin{array}{r} 5 = \\[4pt] -\ 2\dfrac{9}{10} = \\ \hline \end{array}$$

$$\begin{array}{r} 6 = \\[4pt] -\ 2\dfrac{1}{6} = \\ \hline \end{array}$$

F.
$$\begin{array}{r} 12 = \\[4pt] -\ 8\dfrac{7}{9} = \\ \hline \end{array}$$

$$\begin{array}{r} 20 = \\[4pt] -\ 13\dfrac{1}{4} = \\ \hline \end{array}$$

$$\begin{array}{r} 16 = \\[4pt] -\ 3\dfrac{5}{7} = \\ \hline \end{array}$$

G.
$$\begin{array}{r} 9 = \\[4pt] -\ 8\dfrac{13}{20} = \\ \hline \end{array}$$

$$\begin{array}{r} 14 = \\[4pt] -\ 11\dfrac{5}{24} = \\ \hline \end{array}$$

MATH REVIEW

Name _____

Mix It Up

Add or subtract. Write the answers in lowest terms.

 A.

$$3 \frac{3}{5}$$
$$+ 2 \frac{1}{5}$$
___

$$1 \frac{5}{9}$$
$$+ 4 \frac{3}{9}$$
___

$$2 \frac{8}{14}$$
$$- 1 \frac{5}{14}$$
___

$$6 \frac{8}{9}$$
$$- 3 \frac{3}{9}$$
___

B.

$$11 \frac{12}{15}$$
$$- 5 \frac{8}{15}$$
___

$$7 \frac{1}{6}$$
$$+ 3 \frac{2}{6}$$
___

$$21 \frac{19}{14}$$
$$- 18 \frac{16}{24}$$
___

$$8 \frac{1}{4}$$
$$+ 8 \frac{2}{4}$$
___

C.

$$7 \frac{1}{16}$$
$$+ 1 \frac{3}{16}$$
___

$$11 \frac{9}{10}$$
$$- 6 \frac{3}{10}$$
___

$$8 \frac{1}{15}$$
$$+ 10 \frac{2}{15}$$
___

$$15 \frac{17}{20}$$
$$- 9 \frac{11}{20}$$
___

D.

$$5 \frac{7}{12}$$
$$- 2 \frac{5}{12}$$
___

$$3 \frac{2}{4}$$
$$+ 2 \frac{1}{4}$$
___

$$9 \frac{7}{8}$$
$$- 8 \frac{1}{8}$$
___

$$7 \frac{1}{5}$$
$$+ 8 \frac{3}{5}$$
___

E.

$$4 \frac{3}{4}$$
$$- 2 \frac{1}{4}$$
___

$$6 \frac{7}{10}$$
$$+ 1 \frac{1}{10}$$
___

$$4 \frac{5}{12}$$
$$+ 3 \frac{1}{12}$$
___

$$8 \frac{3}{9}$$
$$- 2 \frac{1}{9}$$
___

Name _____

Fraction Product Riddle

Multiply. Use your answers to break the code and solve the following riddle:

Why did Sam take a hammer to bed?

B. $\frac{1}{8} \times \frac{1}{7} =$ _____

H. $\frac{1}{3} \times \frac{4}{7} =$ _____

W. $2 \times \frac{3}{5} =$ _____

T. $\frac{5}{9} \times \frac{2}{3} =$ _____

H. $\frac{2}{7} \times \frac{2}{7} =$ _____

T. $\frac{5}{6} \times 4 =$ _____

H. $\frac{1}{3} \times 6 =$ _____

E. $\frac{8}{9} \times \frac{1}{3} =$ _____

E. $\frac{2}{5} \times \frac{4}{7} =$ _____

A. $\frac{1}{4} \times \frac{2}{3} =$ _____

O. $\frac{2}{5} \times \frac{1}{4} =$ _____

I. $\frac{3}{8} \times \frac{1}{2} =$ _____

H. $\frac{1}{6} \times 8 =$ _____

A. $8 \times \frac{3}{5} =$ _____

C. $\frac{4}{5} \times \frac{1}{4} =$ _____

N. $\frac{2}{7} \times \frac{7}{8} =$ _____

T. $\frac{4}{5} \times \frac{1}{6} =$ _____

E. $\frac{1}{10} \times 5 =$ _____

Y. $\frac{5}{12} \times \frac{1}{3} =$ _____

A. $\frac{2}{3} \times \frac{5}{8} =$ _____

T. $7 \times \frac{1}{3} =$ _____

U. $\frac{2}{3} \times \frac{2}{5} =$ _____

E. $9 \times \frac{2}{3} =$ _____

S. $\frac{5}{8} \times \frac{4}{9} =$ _____

						E			
$\frac{1}{56}$	$\frac{8}{27}$	$\frac{1}{5}$	$\frac{1}{6}$	$\frac{4}{15}$	$\frac{5}{18}$			$\frac{4}{21}$	$\frac{8}{35}$

		D				
$1\frac{1}{5}$	$4\frac{4}{5}$	$\frac{1}{4}$	$\frac{10}{27}$	$\frac{1}{2}$	$3\frac{1}{3}$	$\frac{1}{10}$

$\frac{4}{49}$	$\frac{3}{16}$	$\frac{2}{15}$	$2\frac{1}{3}$	2	6	$1\frac{1}{3}$	$\frac{5}{12}$	$\frac{5}{36}$

Name _____

Focus on Fractions

Multiply.

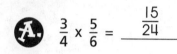

Multiply the numerators. Then multiply the denominators.

A. $\frac{3}{4} \times \frac{5}{6} = \frac{15}{24}$

B. $\frac{3}{8} \times \frac{2}{3} = $ _____

C. $\frac{3}{5} \times \frac{7}{8} = $ _____

D. $\frac{11}{12} \times \frac{3}{4} = $ _____ $\qquad \frac{1}{2} \times \frac{3}{4} = $ _____ $\qquad \frac{1}{10} \times \frac{2}{3} = $ _____

E. $\frac{2}{5} \times \frac{2}{5} = $ _____ $\qquad \frac{1}{6} \times \frac{3}{4} = $ _____ $\qquad \frac{1}{5} \times \frac{1}{5} = $ _____

F. $\frac{1}{3} \times \frac{3}{4} = $ _____ $\qquad \frac{2}{3} \times \frac{2}{3} = $ _____ $\qquad \frac{1}{6} \times \frac{2}{5} = $ _____

G. $\frac{2}{3} \times \frac{7}{8} = $ _____ $\qquad \frac{3}{4} \times \frac{3}{8} = $ _____ $\qquad \frac{2}{5} \times \frac{3}{8} = $ _____

H. $\frac{1}{5} \times \frac{2}{4} = $ _____ $\qquad \frac{5}{6} \times \frac{3}{4} = $ _____ $\qquad \frac{7}{10} \times \frac{1}{4} = $ _____

I. $\frac{1}{6} \times \frac{5}{6} = $ _____ $\qquad \frac{1}{2} \times \frac{7}{9} = $ _____ $\qquad \frac{1}{9} \times \frac{9}{10} = $ _____

J. $\frac{1}{4} \times \frac{5}{6} = $ _____ $\qquad \frac{1}{4} \times \frac{1}{2} = $ _____ $\qquad \frac{5}{8} \times \frac{2}{3} = $ _____

K. $\frac{1}{3} \times \frac{1}{2} = $ _____ $\qquad \frac{4}{5} \times \frac{7}{8} = $ _____ $\qquad \frac{1}{3} \times \frac{3}{8} = $ _____

L. $\frac{8}{9} \times \frac{1}{9} = $ _____ $\qquad \frac{9}{10} \times \frac{5}{6} = $ _____ $\qquad \frac{2}{5} \times \frac{5}{6} = $ _____

M. $\frac{1}{4} \times \frac{1}{6} = $ _____ $\qquad \frac{1}{2} \times \frac{2}{3} = $ _____ $\qquad \frac{1}{5} \times \frac{1}{4} = $ _____

N. $\frac{2}{5} \times \frac{2}{3} = $ _____ $\qquad \frac{3}{4} \times \frac{2}{5} = $ _____ $\qquad \frac{1}{4} \times \frac{3}{5} = $ _____

O. $\frac{3}{4} \times \frac{2}{7} = $ _____ $\qquad \frac{1}{3} \times \frac{3}{10} = $ _____ $\qquad \frac{11}{12} \times \frac{1}{2} = $ _____

P. $\frac{1}{10} \times \frac{10}{10} = $ _____ $\qquad \frac{1}{6} \times \frac{2}{3} = $ _____ $\qquad \frac{5}{8} \times \frac{2}{4} = $ _____

Q. $\frac{3}{4} \times \frac{1}{4} = $ _____ $\qquad \frac{5}{6} \times \frac{3}{5} = $ _____ $\qquad \frac{2}{6} \times \frac{4}{5} = $ _____

R. $\frac{1}{8} \times \frac{1}{4} = $ _____ $\qquad \frac{2}{3} \times \frac{4}{5} = $ _____ $\qquad \frac{5}{12} \times \frac{1}{3} = $ _____

Name _____

Tic-Tac Products

Use the tic-tac-toe board to find the factors and write each
multiplication equation. Then write the products in lowest
terms.

$3\frac{1}{3}$	$\frac{4}{5}$	$2\frac{1}{2}$
$5\frac{1}{4}$	$\frac{3}{4}$	$1\frac{1}{2}$
$2\frac{3}{4}$	$2\frac{2}{5}$	$\frac{2}{3}$

A. ⌞ x ⌟

  $2\frac{1}{2} \times \frac{4}{5}$

B. ⌐ x ⌐

C. ⌐ x ⌐

D. ⌐ x ⌐

E. ⌞ x ⌞

F. ⌐ x ⌞

G. ⌞ x ⌐

H. ⌐ x ⌐

I. ⌐ x ⌞

J. ⌐ x ⌞

K. ⌐ x ⌐

L. Which two factors will make the greatest product? Write the factors and solve the equation.

M. Which two factors will make the smallest product? Write the factors and solve the equation.

Name _____

Thousandths of Leaves

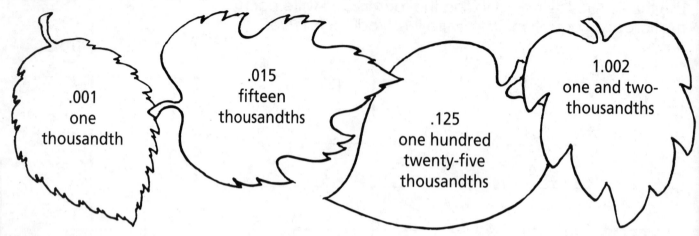

.001
one
thousandth

.015
fifteen
thousandths

.125
one hundred
twenty-five
thousandths

1.002
one and two-
thousandths

Write each decimal in words. Remember to use *and* for decimals greater than one.

A. 0.008   eight thousandths _____

B. 0.072   _____

C. 0.276   _____

D. 41.103   _____

E. 2.084   _____

Write a decimal for each exercise.

F. four thousandths   .004

G. six and forty-seven thousandths _____

H. two thousandths _____

I. three hundred two thousandths _____

J. sixty-two thousandths _____

K. seventy-three thousandths _____

L. five hundred thirty thousandths _____

M. one and three thousandths _____

Name _____

Round Up

To round a number:

1. Find the place to be rounded.
2. Look at the number to its right.

   If the number is 5 or more, add 1 to the digit in the rounding place.

   If the number is less than 5, the digit in the rounding place stays the same.

Round each number to the nearest tenth.

A. 56.82 = __56.8__   246.76 = _____

B. 149.49 = _____   1.87 = _____

C. 87.19 = _____   467.63 = _____

D. 529.72 = _____   36.19 = _____

Round each number to the nearest whole number.

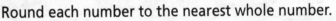

E. 43.24 = __43__   67.84 = _____

F. 1.976 = _____   1,927.59 = _____

G. 296.148 = _____   98.43 = _____

H. 0.986 = _____   653.27 = _____

Round each number to the nearest hundredth.

I. 8.355 = __8.36__   289.986 = _____

J. 462.992 = _____   117.007 = _____

K. 76.046 = _____   45.373 = _____

L. 0.671 = _____   338.017 = _____

Name _____

What's Missing?

Find the missing numbers.

A.

7.3 + 2.1 − 6.26 + 5.1 =

B.

+ 2.8 − 4.02 − 1.08 = 7.04

C.

1.25 − 0.8 + − 2.1 = 2.14

D.

7.93 + 1.08 − 3.09 + = 8.62

E.

5.35 − 1.16 + − 0.61 = 13.4

F.

12.24 − + 5.2 − 3.9 = 5.38

G.

3.46 + 8.7 + − 3.7 = 18.46

H.

48.9 − 24.25 + 16.1 − 0.4 =

I.

+ 17.46 − 4.7 + 8.02 = 32.89

Name _____

Where's the Decimal?

To determine the decimal point in the product, count the number of decimal places in the factor.

Multiply.

There is one decimal place in the factor, so the product has one decimal place.

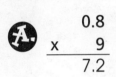

A.
```
  0.8
x   9
-----
  7.2
```

```
  0.05
x    7
```

```
  7.4
x   4
```

B.
```
  6.5
x   5
```

```
  7.07
x    9
```

```
  3.2
x  44
```

```
  3.87
x    6
```

C.
```
  4.32
x    3
```

```
  5.24
x    8
```

```
  4.07
x   68
```

```
  0.802
x     9
```

D.
```
  5.63
x    4
```

```
  8.3
x   6
```

```
  3.03
x    6
```

```
  0.34
x    6
```

MATH REVIEW

Name _____

Count the Places

To place the decimal point in the product, count the number of decimal places in both factors.

Multiply.

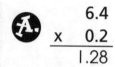
A.
```
    6.4
  x 0.2
  -----
   1.28
```

Each factor has one decimal place. 1 + 1 = 2, so the product must have two decimal places.

```
    0.4
  x 0.87
  ------
```

```
   9.12
  x 0.32
  ------
```

B.
```
   23.7
  x 0.12
  ------
```

```
   3.047
  x 5.01
  -------
```

```
   0.25
  x 65.1
  ------
```

```
   34.1
  x  0.3
  ------
```

C.
```
   56.1
  x 2.2
  -----
```

```
   23.9
  x 0.2
  -----
```

```
    8.4
  x 0.6
  -----
```

```
   7.014
  x  .15
  -------
```

Name _____

Exploring Division

Divide.

A.
```
    4.3
2 ) 8.6
   -8 ↓
    0 6
     -6
      0
```

B. 3) 7.2

Remember to put the decimal point in the quotient directly above the decimal point in the dividend.

C. 5) 23.25

D. 3) 20.4

E. 3) 3.69

F. 8) 27.2

G. 9) 310.5

H. 8) 73.6

I. 7) 40.6

J. 6) 56.28

K. 5) 41.5

L. 6) 14.94

M. 4) 6.08

N. 7) 3.864

Name _____

Making the Grade

Find the percentage for each student's test. Write it beside the word *score*. Then give each test a grade based on the scale shown to the right.

90–100	A
80–89	B
70–79	C
60–69	D

1. Erica 18/20

   Score: _____

   Grade: _____

2. Lamont 20/25

   Score: _____

   Grade: _____

3. Cathy 9/12

   Score: _____

   Grade: _____

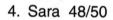

4. Sara 48/50

   Score: _____

   Grade: _____

5. Rick 17/25

   Score: _____

   Grade: _____

6. Matthew 12/15

   Score: _____

   Grade: _____

7. Judith 23/25

   Score: _____

   Grade: _____

8. Uma 30/40

   Score: _____

   Grade: _____

9. Penny 66/75

   Score: _____

   Grade: _____

10. Hector 17/20

    Score: _____

    Grade: _____

11. Mary 46/50

    Score: _____

    Grade: _____

12. Holly 81/90

    Score: _____

    Grade: _____

13. Victoria 38/50

    Score: _____

    Grade: _____

14. Ed 186/200

    Score: _____

    Grade: _____

15. Ben 33/55

    Score: _____

    Grade: _____

Name _____

In the Ballpark

Estimate the answer. Then solve each problem.

A. Mrs. North takes Rachel and two of her friends to the ballpark. Tickets cost $3.50. Juice costs $1.50 and popcorn costs $2.00. Tax on the juice and the popcorn is 7%. Mrs. North plans to buy one ticket, one juice, and one popcorn for each girl and herself. How much money will she spend?

Estimate: _____   Actual: _____

B. Mr. Bell wants to be sure that the chairs at the baseball store will fit at his table at home. Each chair is 42 cm wide. He needs 6 chairs. What is the least amount of space the chairs require to fit around the table?

Estimate: _____   Actual: _____

C. A snack table at the ballpark is 103 cm long and 89 cm wide. What is the perimeter of the snack table?

Estimate: _____   Actual: _____

D. The perimeter of a buffet table at the ballpark is 55 ft. The length is 15¼ ft. What is the width of the table?

Estimate: _____   Actual: _____

E. At the ballpark, 25% of the regular ticket holders bring guests. One day 3,720 regular ticket holders went to the game. How many brought guests?

Estimate: _____   Actual: _____

F. The ballpark charges $1.20 per hour for parking. How much is collected for 11 cars staying in the ballpark 3 hours?

Estimate: _____   Actual: _____

G. Irma purchased 6 program books. She paid $47.34 for them. How much did each program book cost?

Estimate: _____   Actual: _____

MATH REVIEW

Name _____

Can You Measure Up?

Solve each problem.

12 in. = 1 ft.
3 ft. = 1 yd.

A. Marcia needs 100 inches of ribbon. She bought a roll of 9 feet of ribbon. Does she have enough ribbon? If so, how much will she have left over?

_____

B. Luther is 4 feet 5 inches tall. He needs to be 48 inches tall to ride the roller coaster. Is he tall enough to ride the roller coaster?

C. Rachel has an oak tree in her front yard that is 660 inches tall. She wants to know how tall the tree is in feet. What is her answer?

_____

D. Paul built a frame for a pond. He cut a board $34\frac{1}{2}$ inches long from a board that was 4 feet long. How long was the leftover piece of board?

E. Joe had a piece of lumber 3 feet 5 inches long. He sawed off a $\frac{3}{4}$ foot long piece for a sign. How long was the piece of lumber that was left?

_____

F. Randy is on the track team. He does the long jump. His longest jump was 5 feet $\frac{3}{4}$ inches long. He thinks it sounds longer in inches. How many inches did Randy jump?

G. Chris' older brother is 6 feet 6 inches tall. Chris' height is 4 feet 2 inches tall. Chris would like to be as tall as his older brother. How many more inches does Chris need to grow?

_____

H. Marlin built a deck that was 21 feet 2 inches x 14 feet 10 inches. What was the perimeter of the deck in yards?

_____

Name _____

Pool-Side Perimeters

Find the perimeters of the pools and the pool-side objects below.

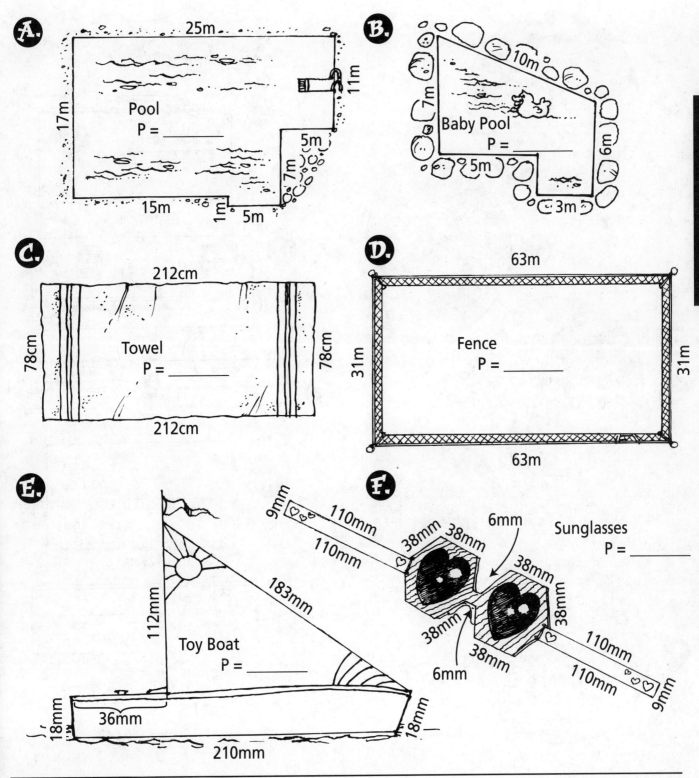

A. Pool P = _____
25m, 17m, 11m, 5m, 7m, 15m, 1m, 5m

B. Baby Pool P = _____
10m, 7m, 6m, 5m, 3m

C. Towel P = _____
212cm, 78cm, 78cm, 212cm

D. Fence P = _____
63m, 31m, 31m, 63m

E. Toy Boat P = _____
112mm, 183mm, 18mm, 36mm, 18mm, 210mm

F. Sunglasses P = _____
9mm, 110mm, 110mm, 38mm, 38mm, 6mm, 38mm, 38mm, 38mm, 38mm, 6mm, 110mm, 110mm, 9mm

Name _____

Turn up the Volume!

Calculate the volume of the objects in the column on the left. Match each to its corresponding player on the right. All measurements are in centimeters.

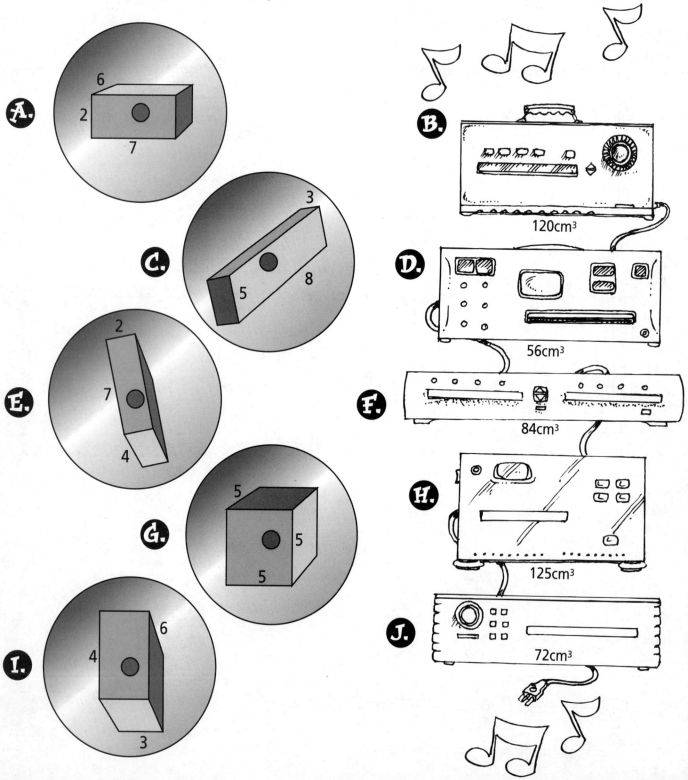

A. 6, 2, 7

B. 120cm³

C. 3, 5, 8

D. 56cm³

E. 2, 7, 4

F. 84cm³

G. 5, 5, 5

H. 125cm³

I. 6, 4, 3

J. 72cm³

Name _____

Does This Joke "Measure" Up?

When it rains cats and dogs, what do you step into?

To find out, measure the angles below. Put their measurements in order from least to greatest. The letters in the angles will spell out the answer.

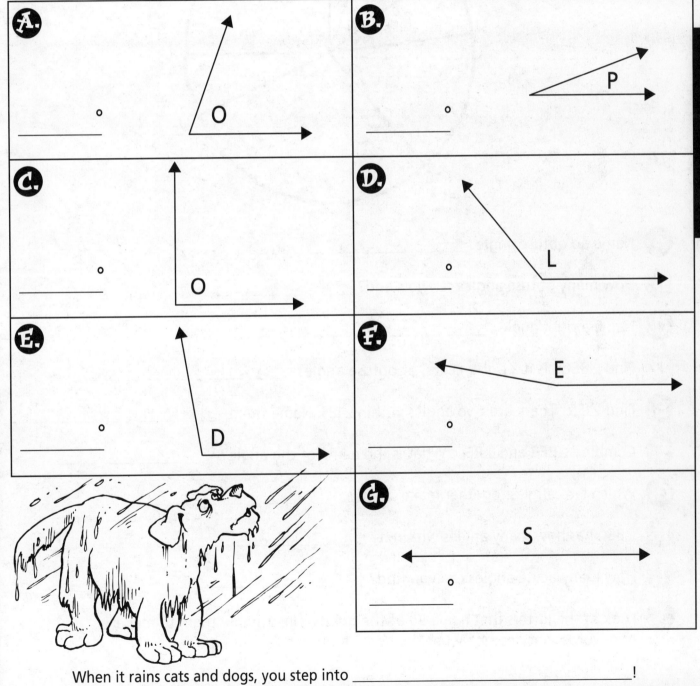

A. _____ O

B. _____ P

C. _____ O

D. _____ L

E. _____ D

F. _____ E

G. _____ S

When it rains cats and dogs, you step into _____!

Name _____

"Angles" in the Outfield

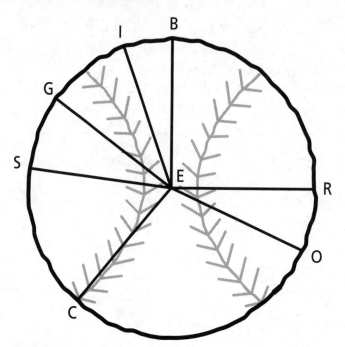

A. Name an obtuse angle. _____

B. How many obtuse angles can you find? _____

C. Name a right angle. _____

D. Find ∠BEG. Is it a right, acute, or obtuse angle? _____

E. Find ∠IES. There are two angles within ∠IES. Name them. _____

F. Combine ∠BER and ∠REO. What is the name of the angle? _____

G. Which two angles together make ∠BEG? _____

H. ∠BEC has how many angles within it? _____

I. How many acute angles can you find? _____

J. Look at the letters that name all of the points. Unscramble them to make two words that describe what the home team fans are hoping for.

____ ____ ____ ____   ____ ____ ____

Name _____

Concept Mapping and the Human Body

A **concept map** is a graphic representation of the key terms or ideas that relate to a central theme. Branches and sub-branches are used to show how the terms are organized into different groups.

On a separate sheet of paper, construct your own concept map following the diagram. With the term HUMAN BODY as the central theme, identify the five terms below that represent five subtopics. Cut them out and glue those five terms to the five branches. Then cut out and glue the other terms to their subtopics. Lines may be drawn to show the connections.

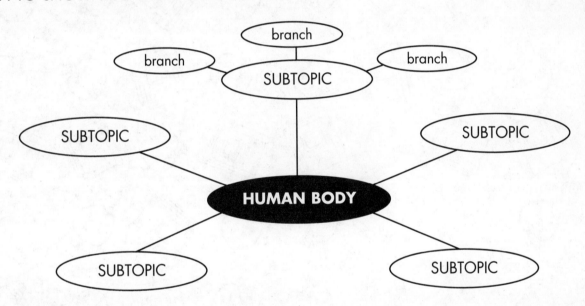

collar bones	intestines	testes	skeletal system	organs
circulation	smallpox	diseases	endocrine system	skull
pelvis	liver	adrenal gland	shoulder blades	legs
spinal column	measles	movement	body functions	rabies
stomach	thyroid	respiration	hepatitis	hands
parathyroid	influenza	excretion	thymus	neck
heart	digestion	tetanus	colds	feet
tuberculosis	lungs	arms	reproduction	sternum
nerve reactions	pituitary	esophagus	gall bladder	ovaries

SCIENCE REVIEW

Name _____

The Human Digestive System

Important parts of the human digestive system are hidden in the maze below. From the starting letter, skip every other letter and write the words in the spaces.

1. __ __ __ __ __ __

2. __ __ __ __ __ __ __ __

3. __ __ __ __ __ __ __

4. __ __ __ __ __ __ __ __
   __ __ __ __ __ __ __

5. __ __ __ __ __ __ __
   __ __ __ __ __ __ __

6. __ __ __ __ __ __

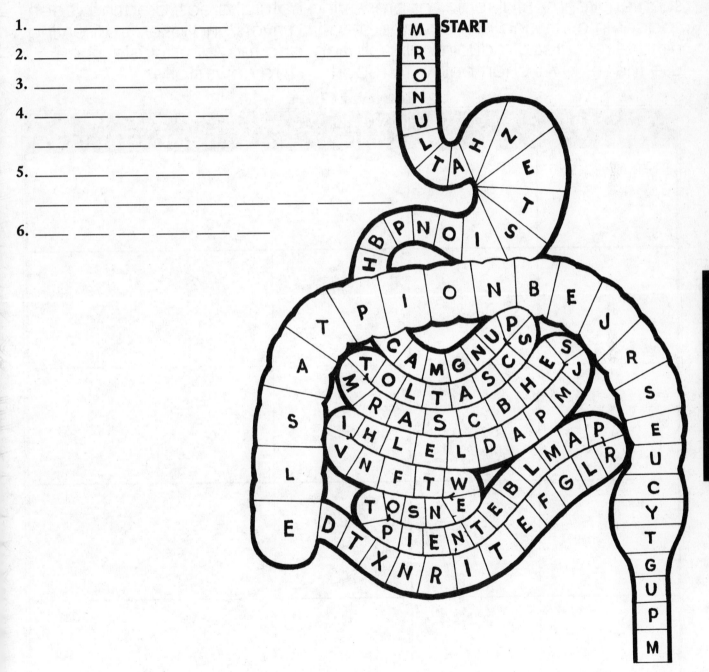

SCIENCE REVIEW

Name _____

Environmental Issues

On April 22, 1970, the first Earth Day was celebrated. Since then, much has been done to protect Earth's environment. But there is still much more to do to save Earth from destruction.

Look for news stories, both locally and from around the world, involving the environment. Among the stories you might find, include those on such environmental topics as preserving natural areas, creating green spaces in cities and along roads, cleaning rivers and lakes, conserving natural resources, reducing air pollution, and recycling waste. Then use the retrieval chart below to report on five news stories.

Retrieval Chart

NEWS STORY TOPIC	WHEN DID IT HAPPEN?	WHERE DID IT HAPPEN?	WHAT HAPPENED?

Name _____

The World of Arthropods

The largest percentage of animals in the world are arthropods. **Arthropods** are animals with exoskeletons and jointed appendages. They live in all parts of the world and in every type of habitat.

Look at the list of arthropods below. Print the names of insects in the square, the names of arachnids in the triangle, and the names of crustaceans in the circle.

TARANTULA	BEE	MITE	CRAB
LOBSTER	BUTTERFLY	SCORPION	WASP
BEETLE	SHRIMP	HORNET	FLY
GRASSHOPPER	CRICKET	CRAYFISH	TICK
GARDEN SPIDER	BROWN RECLUSE	BLACK WIDOW	CICADA
BARNACLE	LOUSE	WATER FLEA	APHID
TERMITE	ANT	GNAT	FLEA
MOTH	FIREFLY		MAYFLY

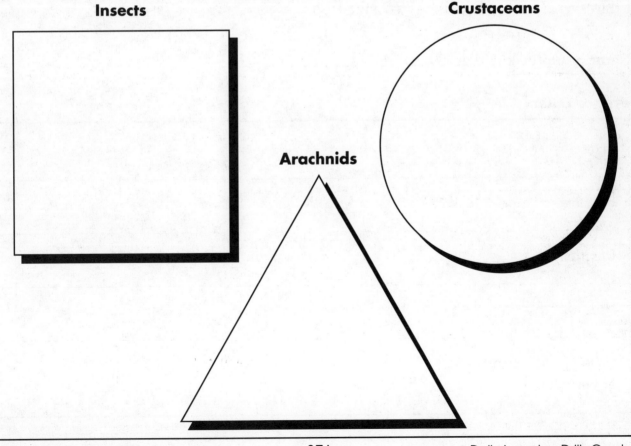

Insects

Crustaceans

Arachnids

SCIENCE REVIEW

Name _____

Mollusks

Mollusks are animals with soft, boneless bodies. Most of them have shells. Three of the most common classes of mollusks are bivalves, gastropods, and cephalopods.

Choose one of the mollusks below to research. Data collected on each example could include the following: size, habitat, description, uses of, and unusual characteristics or behaviors. Write the data in the chart below.

BIVALVES:	GASTROPODS:	CEPHALOPODS:
oyster, clam, scallop, mussel, cockle, ark, angel wing, jewel box, jingle, ox heart	land snail, abalone, conch, slug, sea slug, limpet, sea snail, moon snail, cone shell, murex, olive, cowrie, whelk, bonnet, periwinkle	squid, octopus, nautilus, cuttlefish

Mollusk I will research (Circle one):

BIVALVE   GASTROPOD   CEPHALOPOD

Name of mollusk: _____

Type of Data:

Size:	
Habitat:	
Description:	
Uses of:	
Unusual Characteristics or Behaviors:	

Name _____

Marine Life

The oceans are teeming with living things. Complete the word grid below to learn the names of some marine life.

CONCH   EEL   LOBSTER   OCTOPUS   SHRIMP   STARFISH
CORAL   HERMIT CRAB   MANATEE   SCALLOP   SPONGE   TRITON
DOLPHIN   LIMPET   MUSSEL   SEAL   SQUID   WHALE

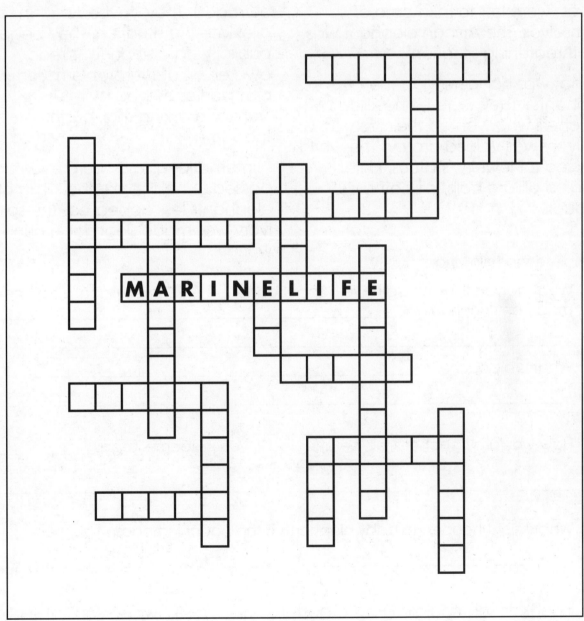

M A R I N E L I F E

       Daily Learning Drills Grade 5

SCIENCE REVIEW

Name _____

Save the Elephants

During the 1980's, the African elephant population was a casualty of human desires. The number of elephants declined from well over one million to about 600,000. It is estimated that more than 270 elephants were killed each day! Thousands of baby elephants, called calves, were left to take care of themselves. The African elephant was in a threatening situation.

What was happening to the elephants? They were being killed by poachers who wanted their ivory tusks. The ivory was valued around the world. It is used for jewelry, statues, knife handles, billiard balls, plus other products.

Organizations that protect animals and look out for their welfare were outraged. They devised a plan to alleviate the situation. They began a publicity campaign to spread awareness of the problem. Some large companies helped by refusing to buy ivory and asking their customers to do the same.

International laws were eventually passed to help make the killing of elephants less appealing. The sale of ivory was made illegal all around the world.

Complete the following.

1. What do you think would have happened to the African elephant if no one had made any changes? _____

   _____

2. What is a poacher?_____

   _____

3. How would a poacher's job be affected if ivory became illegal? _____

   _____

4. What might happen to baby elephants if the poaching doesn't cease? _____

   _____

Join a publicity campaign! Draw a poster to help raise awareness of the plight of an endangered animal in the twenty-first century.

Name _____

Pandas

Read the article. Then match the cause and effect statements by drawing a line.

The giant panda is an Asian mammal that lives on the mountain slopes of China. Pandas eat only bamboo, which grows extensively in the Chinese highlands. In order to get enough nutrients, a panda must eat as much as 85 pounds (39 kg) of bamboo a day. The rampant destruction of the panda's habitat has endangered this creature. The government of China has tried to save the panda's food supply by setting up reserves of bamboo-rich land. Large reserves are necessary to ensure adequate food for the pandas. Because bamboo plants take so long to grow into mature plants, there have been shortages in the past. These periodic shortages have led to the deaths of hundreds of pandas. Only about 1,000 giant pandas remain in the wild.

Cause

1. Many pandas die each year.

2. Pandas must get enough nutrients.

3. Bamboo takes a long time to mature.

4. There is rampant destruction of the panda habitat.

5. There have been bamboo shortages.

Effect

a. Pandas are endangered.

b. Hundreds of pandas have died.

c. They must eat huge amounts of bamboo.

d. Periodic bamboo shortages occur.

e. China has set up bamboo reserves.

SCIENCE REVIEW

Name _____

Tectonic Plates of the Earth

Earth's surface consists of about 20 rigid plates that move slowly past one another. Label the tectonic plates of Earth on the map below.

EURASIAN PLATE   INDIAN PLATE   PHILIPPINE PLATE

PACIFIC PLATE   NORTH AMERICAN PLATE   NAZCA PLATE

SOUTH AMERICAN PLATE   AFRICAN PLATE   ANTARCTIC PLATE

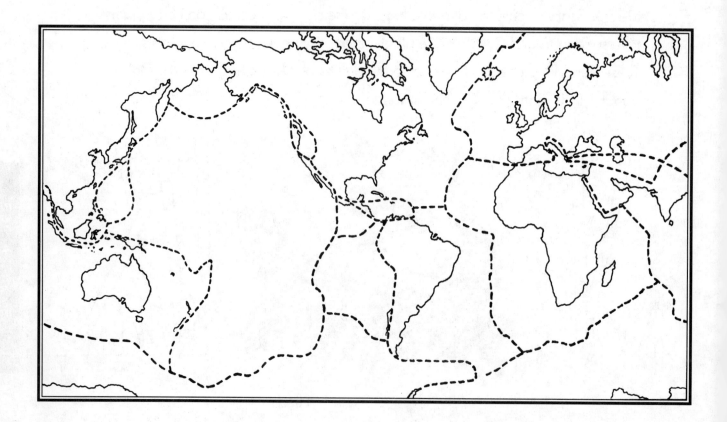

Write what you think (or know) an earthquake would do to your city/town.

_____

_____

_____

Name _____

The World's Most Destructive Earthquakes

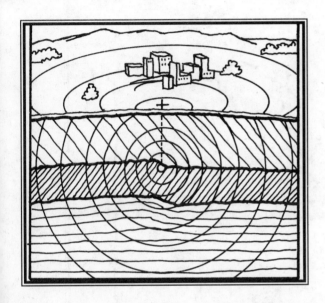

Earthquakes have been recorded on Earth for thousands of years. In addition to the damage to buildings, highways, and land, millions of people have been killed.

For this activity, you will need a copy of the World Map on the next page and a globe or an atlas. Locate the countries in which the earthquakes below occurred. The estimated number of deaths from the earthquakes and the dates of the earthquakes are recorded. Place the number of the earthquake in its correct location on the map.

Earthquake	Date of occurrence	Number of estimated deaths
1. Syria	526	250,000
2. Iraq	847	50,000
3. Iran	856	200,000
4. India	893	180,000
5. Egypt	1201	1,000,000
6. Italy	1456	60,000
7. China	1556	830,000
8. Japan	1703	200,000
9. Ecuador-Peru	1797	41,000
10. Java	1883	100,000
11. Chile	1906	20,000
12. Turkey	1939	30,000
13. Nicaragua	1972	10,000
14. Guatemala	1976	23,000
15. Mexico	1985	4,200

SCIENCE REVIEW

Name _____

Map of the World

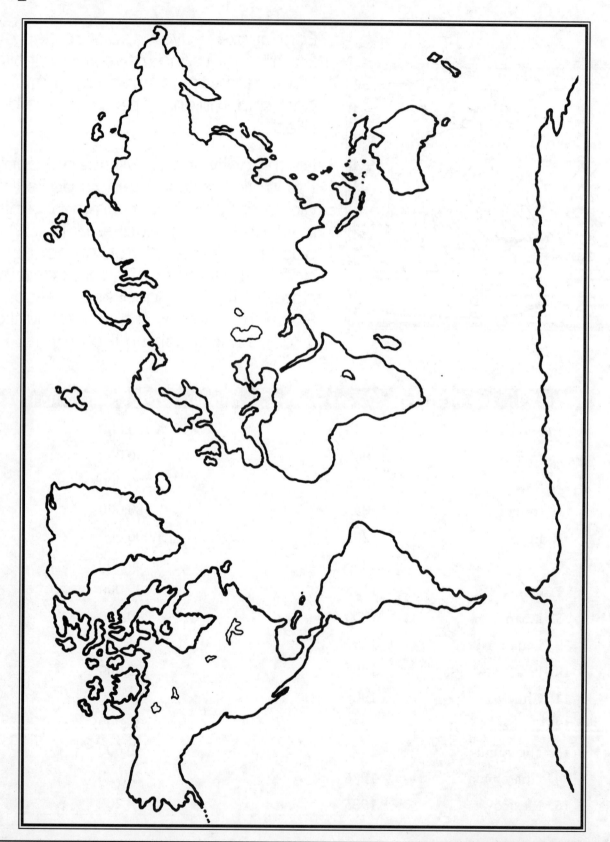

Name _____

Which Rocks Are These?

The hard, solid part of Earth is rock. Three main kinds of rocks are igneous, sedimentary, and metamorphic. To learn more about rocks, match the names of the rocks to their definitions.

1. _____ SANDSTONE

2. _____ SHALE

3. _____ CONGLOMERATE

4. _____ BRECCIA

5. _____ LIMESTONE

6. _____ SEDIMENTARY ROCKS

7. _____ BITUMINOUS COAL

8. _____ GEODES

9. _____ GNEISS

10. _____ SCHIST

11. _____ ANTHRACITE COAL

12. _____ MARBLE

13. _____ QUARTZITE

14. _____ SLATE

15. _____ METAMORPHIC ROCKS

A. a metamorphic rock which can be formed from limestone

B. a sedimentary rock of plant origin

C. the most common metamorphic rock made from granite

D. a metamorphic rock made from sandstone

E. a sedimentary rock made from cemented sand

F. rocks changed in form from sedimentary or igneous rocks

G. hard metamorphic rock made from soft coal

H. cemented mud, clay, or silt

I. coarse sedimentary rock made up of pebbles or boulders

J. metamorphic rock made from shale

K. sedimentary rock composed of rough and angular fragments of rock

L. metamorphic rock made from schist

M. sedimentary rock made from the shells and skeletons of plants and animals

N. hollow spheres in limestone

O. layered rocks made from sediments

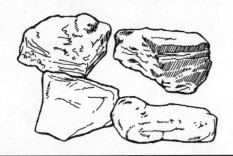

metals

Name _____

Metals From Minerals

Metal forms a large part of Earth. Earth's crust is made up of certain metals. Identify the metals below from the clues given.

1. I am obtained from the mineral bauxite.
I am shiny and often seen as rolls of thin sheets.
Many soft drink cans are made from me.
I am used to make canoes, chairs, windows, and siding for houses.
My chemical symbol is Al.
What metal am I?

_____

2. I am found in the minerals limonite, hematite, and magnetite.
I am used in the manufacture of steel.
I rust easily.
I am also found in "fool's gold," or pyrite.
My chemical symbol is Fe.
What metal am I?

_____

3. I am found in the mineral galena.
I am used in pipes, batteries, and glass.
I was once used in many paints.
I am used to protect people from the effects of X-rays.
My chemical symbol is Pb.
What metal am I?

_____

4. I am found in the mineral cinnabar.
I remain liquid over a wide range of temperatures.
I am shiny.
I am used in many thermometers.
My chemical symbol is Hg.
What metal am I?

_____

5. I am found in the mineral chalcopyrite and in others.
I am used in most electrical wires.
I am used in many coins.
I am mixed with other metals to make bronze.
My chemical symbol is Cu.
What metal am I?

_____

6. I am found in the mineral chromite.
I am used in cars and bathroom fixtures.
I am very shiny and one of the hardest substances.
I am used to make stainless steel.
My chemical symbol is Cr.
What metal am I?

_____

7. I am found in the mineral cassiterite.
I am used in welding solder.
I was once widely used as roofing material for houses and barns.
I am mixed with copper to make bronze.
My chemical symbol is Sn.
What metal am I?

_____

Name _____

Our Solar System

There is so much to know about our solar system. To learn a little about it, solve the crossword puzzle below. Use the terms in the box and the clues under the box to help you.

ASTEROIDS	EMIT	LOWELL	MOON	SATURN	TRITON
CERES	HALLEY'S	MARS	NEPTUNE	SPOT	URANUS
COMET	IO	MERCURY	PLUTO	SUN	VENUS
EARTH	JUPITER	METEORS	RINGS	TAIL	WAY

ACROSS

1. rocky particles which orbit the sun mainly between Mars and Jupiter

4. another name for a satellite of a planet

8. the center of our solar system

9. the seventh planet from the sun

11. Planets do not _____ light energy of their own.

13. one of the moons of Neptune

14. sometimes called "the red planet"

15. consists of a head and tail

18. a comet that appears every 76 years

20. known as Earth's twin

21. Saturn is probably best known for its _____.

22. Our solar system is in the galaxy called "The Milky _____."

23. usually the most distant planet from the sun

DOWN

2. the sixth planet from the sun

3. one of the moons of Jupiter

5. the planet discovered in 1846

6. planet covered with dark and light bands

7. planet whose atmosphere is mostly oxygen and nitrogen

10. The Great Red _____ is a prominent feature of Jupiter.

12. often called "falling stars" or "shooting stars"; results when a meteoroid enters Earth's atmosphere from space

15. the largest asteroid

16. planet closest to the sun

17. The _____ of a comet may be over 100 million miles long.

19. American astronomer who began the search for Pluto in 1905

SCIENCE REVIEW

Name _____

Constellations of the Zodiac

Astronomers have divided the sky into 88 constellations. The letters in the blocks below will spell out the names of 12 constellations found in the sky. The beginning letter of each constellation is in the star. Draw straight lines between the letters to find the name of each constellation. No lines will cross. Write the name of each constellation at the bottom of the page.

1. T R
T A I
   U   S
     S
  G I
      A
	2. U A
	    Q R
	      I
	  A U
	       S
		3. G
		E
		   M
		  I
		N I

4. C
   I C
A   O
  P R
R U   N
   S I
	5. O R
	  C
	   O S
	    I P
		6. E C
		   P
		  S I
		       S

7. S   A
  T
   U
U   R
	8. C E C
	     N
	  R
	    A
		9. I
		  O
		  V
		G
		     R

10. L
I
    B
A R
	11. A R
	  E
	S I
		12. L
		E
		     O

1. _____   7. _____

2. _____   8. _____

3. _____   9. _____

4. _____   10. _____

5. _____   11. _____

6. _____   12. _____

Name _____

Friction on a Rolling Sphere

Friction is the property that objects have that makes them resist being moved across one another.

To learn more about friction, try the activity below. For this activity, you will need a meterstick, a piece of corrugated cardboard, masking tape, four books, a large marble, a sheet of wax paper, a sheet of aluminum foil, sandpaper, a piece of scrap carpet, cotton cloth, and wool cloth.

You may complete this activity individually or in groups.

1. Cut a piece of corrugated cardboard 10 centimeters by 30 centimeters. Fold it down the middle to make a trough. Use the masking tape to hold the trough in place. *(See illustration.)*

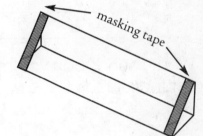
masking tape

2. Prop the trough on a stack of four books. Use more masking tape to hold the trough in place.

3. Place a large piece of wax paper at the base of the trough.

4. Place a large marble at the top of the trough and release it. Use the meterstick to measure the distance the marble rolls. Record your results in the chart below.

5. Repeat Steps 3 and 4 by replacing the wax paper with aluminum foil, sandpaper, carpet, cotton cloth, and wool cloth. Measure the distance in each trial.

MATERIAL	DISTANCE MARBLE ROLLED IN CENTIMETERS
wax paper	
aluminum foil	
sandpaper	
carpet	
cotton cloth	
wool cloth	

6. How did the friction created by the different materials affect the results?

_____
_____
_____
_____

Daily Learning Drills Grade 5

SCIENCE REVIEW

Name _____

Sound All Around Us

You will need: small piece of bubble wrap, metal pie plate, other sound-making materials, piece of wax paper, spoon

Use the materials to produce a variety of sounds. Can you combine materials to come up with something new? When you make a sound, try to find (or invent) a word to describe it.

_____   _____
_____   _____
_____   _____

What sounds can you make with your mouth, hands, and feet?
List the sounds.

_____   _____
_____   _____
_____   _____

Close your eyes and listen to the sounds around you right now. List the sounds that you hear now.

_____   _____
_____   _____
_____   _____

Draw a picture of a noisy place and label all the sounds you might hear there.

Name _____

Newton's Three Laws of Motion

All moving objects on Earth are governed by Sir Isaac Newton's three laws of motion. These laws are as follows:

1st Law: Objects at rest stay at rest and objects in motion stay in motion unless acted on by a force.

2nd Law: Acceleration of an object depends on its mass and the size and direction of the force acting on it.

3rd Law: Every action has an equal and opposite reaction force.

Write an example of how each of the laws is applied in the following events:

bowling	skating
baseball	biking
football	skiing
canoeing	sailing
archery	sledding
rocketry	swimming

SCIENCE REVIEW

Name _____

Why Integrity Counts

It is no fun to lose to a cheater, but integrity does more than keep the game fun. It is so important to our interactions with each other as human beings that we demand it of our business contacts, our teachers, our politicians, and our families and friends. In complete sentences, indicate below why it is important to be able to trust people in the situations described below.

1. Your doctor says that you need a life-saving operation. Why is it important that he be a trustworthy man? _____

   _____

2. Your banker handles all the money in your checking and savings accounts. Why is it important for you to be able to trust a banker?_____

   _____

3. Your teacher assures you that by following the assignment sheet she provides, you will complete the course for a full credit. Why is it important that you be able to trust your teacher?_____

   _____

4. Your best friend confidentially tells you something about himself that would make your classmates laugh at him. Why is it important that you keep your friend's secret?

   _____

   _____

5. You want your mother to give you more freedoms. Why is it so important to your mother that she can trust you before giving you the freedoms you want?

   _____

   _____

6. Your classmate offers to complete a poster for a group project if you will complete a required survey. Why is it important that you be able to trust each other?

   _____

   _____

7. A car dealer is attempting to convince you to buy a used car. Why is it important that the salesman be trustworthy?_____

   _____

8. A newspaper reporter writes stories about your local community. Why is it important that the newspaper reporter be honest?_____

   _____

9. A politician makes promises to voters. Why is it important that he live up to the promises?

   _____

   _____

Masks

Decorate the mask to look like you. Glue the mask onto thick paper. Cut out the face and create holes for the eyes. Attach a craft stick along one side of the mask to use as a holder.

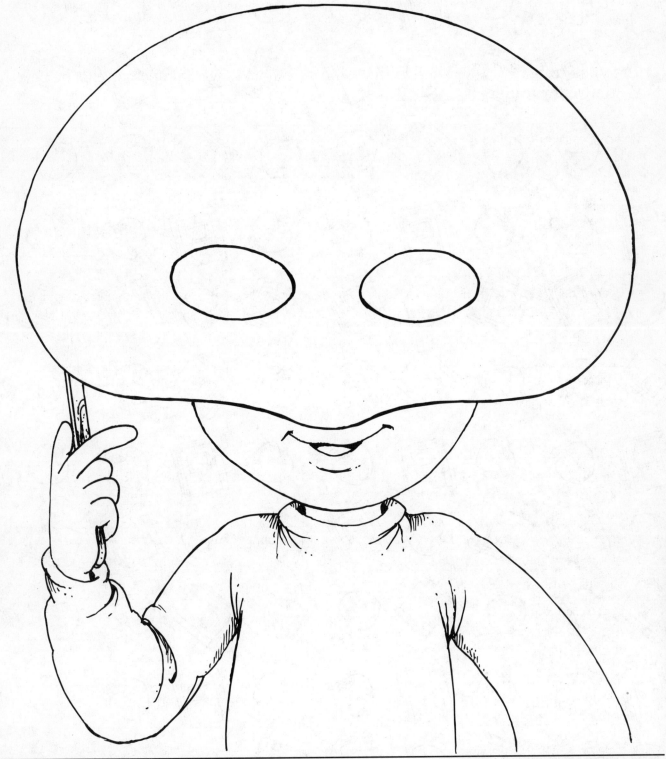

SOCIAL STUDIES REVIEW

Name _____

Have I Got a Job for You

Read the five job opportunities below. Match each job applicant with a job or jobs below by writing the correct numbers on each line.

1. **Bakers Wanted.** Must know flour from powdered sugar. Ability to read is required. Must be 18 years or older. Call Bun in the Oven at 267-1010. Ask for Rose.

2. **Yard Work.** Like to work up a sweat? Eager to work with loud machines? We've got many positions for hardworking men. Call Hulk at 268-8760.

3. **Candy Sales.** Sugar-N-Spice is looking for door-to-door sales reps willing to work strictly on commission. Must be at least 16 years old. $100 deposit on first order of candy. Call 1-800-GOCANDY.

4. **Child Care.** Looking for a 12- to 16-year-old girl to care for my precious 3-year-old. Must love children and ferrets. Need for evening care. Call Mommy at 264-9800.

5. **Photogenic?** We need students ages 7–14 to model for our Fall Series Clothing Sale. Must have no police record. For the required parental permission form write: P.O. Box 9009, Good Pose, IA 50014.

_____ Tad: 14-year-old boy; has no money

_____ Blanche: 16-year-old girl; hates noise

_____ Anselm: 19-year-old man; cannot read

_____ Zoe: 18-year-old woman; won't work door-to-door

_____ Perry: 17-year-old female; doesn't know baking ingredients

SOCIAL STUDIES REVIEW

Name _____

Unscrambling Script

The interpretation of ancient texts presents a challenging mystery to both literary scholars and general historians. Literary scholars learn about the development of ancient and modern languages by unscrambling script, while historians gain invaluable information about all aspects of ancient cultures by solving the same mystery.

Egyptian Hieroglyphics

Although pictorial characters were used to represent common objects by several ancient peoples including the Greeks, Hittites, Cretans, and Maya, Egyptian hieroglyphs are the most frequently studied pictograms. Egyptians communicated through the use of hieroglyphs from around 3000 B.C. until about 394 A.D. Eventually, a more cursive-like script replaced the pictograms, although hieroglyphs continued to be applied to some religious texts until the early fourth century A.D.

The decipherment of Egyptian hieroglyphs presented an unsolved mystery to historians until the nineteenth century. Hieroglyphic inscriptions were sometimes written horizontally and sometimes vertically. They were usually transposed from right to left, but not always. The pictograms seemed to be symbolic and allegorical, but some argued that they could be interpreted phonetically. All suggestions about the interpretation of Egyptian hieroglyphs were purely theoretical until Napoleon's army discovered the Rosetta Stone in Egypt in 1799.

The stone, which states a decree from Ptolemy V in three different languages, enabled French Egyptologist Jean François Champollion and others to interpret many different hieroglyphics from two different eras by comparing them to the Greek words on the stone. Champollion discovered that hieroglyphic inscriptions represented both ideograms and phonograms, as well as rebus-style symbols. The ideogram symbols pictorially represented objects; the phonogram symbols denoted specific sounds; and the rebus symbols employed pictures of objects to stand for homonyms of the pictured word. Many hieroglyphs, Champollion discovered, combined an ideogram and a phonogram.

Egyptologists and linguists have studied the fascinating ancient script to such a degree that little remains a mystery about hieroglyphics. Complete dictionaries have been composed for scholars, shorter versions have been made available to lay enthusiasts, and common hieroglyphs now grace stamps, stickers, magnets, and various other decorative and craft-oriented merchandise.

Name _____

Writing a Rebus

Use the following key to a few common Egyptian hieroglyphs to help you complete the statements below.

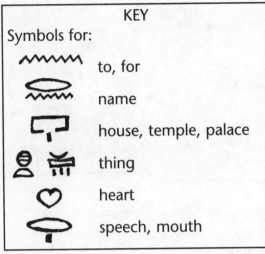

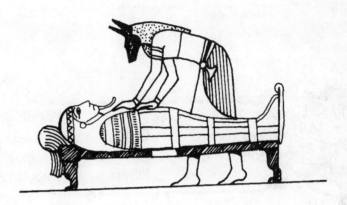

1. I ran _____ my _____ after school.

2. Since I was new to the class, the teacher asked me my _____.

3. The king in his _____ had a _____ full of joy.

4. What kind of _____ is that?

5. Thomas Clark's _____ convinced me to give him my vote.

Now create a reasonable character to symbolize each of the words listed here:

Man	School	Study
Woman	Child	Work
Eat	Play	Book

Using your newly created symbols, write a paragraph interspersing standard English with your new signs. Challenge a classmate to interpret your rebus through context clues and the logic of the shapes of your symbols.

_____

_____

_____

Daily Learning Drills Grade 5

Name _____

Kids Around the World

Are kids the same around the world? The reporters at Kidsworld
Television wanted to find out. They traveled around the globe,
interviewing young people about their lives. Read these segments
of their interviews. Then, using the Word Bank for additional clues,
fill in the blanks.

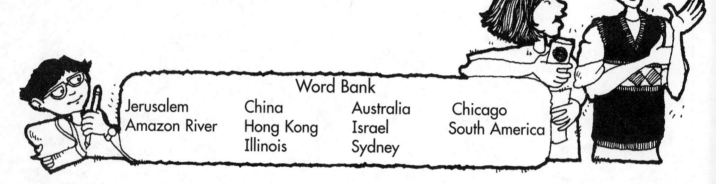

Word Bank

Jerusalem	China	Australia	Chicago
Amazon River	Hong Kong	Israel	South America
	Illinois	Sydney	

1. Malik lives in a small town on the edge of a jungle. Sometimes after school, he visits the spider monkeys and macaws in their natural habitat. His favorite sport is soccer. Malik and his friends play barefoot much of the time. Once, a jaguar prowled around the outskirts of their game!

   Malik could live near the _____ on the continent of _____.

2. Ari lives in a city many people consider holy. Sometimes after school, he visits the places where people from 2000 years ago were said to have lived. He and his friends speak Hebrew. Ari plays soccer on the dry, dirty ground. Occasionally, small whirlwinds come and whip the dirt up!

   Ari could live in the city of _____ in the country of _____.

3. Luisa lives in a large urban area near a body of water. Sometimes, on weekends, she visits a famous skyscraper or the aquarium. Luisa's favorite sport is soccer; she plays it on the high-school practice field. Once, local basketball hero Michael Jordan walked by and waved at Luisa and her teammates!

   Luisa could live in the city of _____ in the state of _____.

4. Wei-yan lives in a crowded city that recently reverted to Chinese rule. Sometimes after school, he visits the bustling financial district. Wei-yan's favorite sport is soccer, but he does not get to play often. There are few undeveloped areas of land large enough for a field. So, he watches the sport on TV and cheers for his favorite teams.

   Wei-yan could live in the city of _____ in the country of _____.

5. Maddy lives Down Under in a seaside city. Sometimes after school she visits a bird sanctuary which houses many of the 700 species native to her area. Maddy loves to attend soccer games. The city's harborside opera house is a famous landmark.

   Maddy could live in the city of _____ in the country of _____.

Religious Customs Trackdown

American society is influenced by the customs of many religious traditions. Listed on the left below are some key religious concepts, symbols, and ceremonies. Each item listed is associated with one of the following religions: Judaism, Christianity, Islam, Hinduism, and Buddhism. Use resource books to help you match the religions listed on the right with the items associated with them on the left. Write the correct letters in the blanks.

Religious Concepts, Symbols, and Ceremonies

_____ 1. Shiva

_____ 2. kosher

_____ 3. Ramadan

_____ 4. "the Enlightened One"

_____ 5. Noble Eightfold Path

_____ 6. cross

_____ 7. Star of David

_____ 8. Festival of Sacrifice

_____ 9. Hanukkah

_____ 10. Christmas

_____ 11. synagogue

_____ 12. mosque

_____ 13. church

_____ 14. Kaaba

_____ 15. menorah

_____ 16. Torah

_____ 17. Koran

_____ 18. nirvana

_____ 19. The Vedas

Religions

A. Christianity

B. Judaism

C. Islam

D. Hinduism

E. Buddhism

Name _____

Food–Societies Connection

Many factors contributed to the development of the world's earliest societies. Two of the most important factors were these:

- a lush environment suitable for agriculture, and
- a staple food crop to feed a growing population.

The staple food crops differed across early societies. The early Mesopotamian civilization in the Middle East depended on wheat. In East Asia, rice was the staple crop. And in the Americas, maize, or corn, was the main food of the Maya and Aztec, while the potato was one of the primary staples of the Inca. Make a list of foods below that contain wheat, rice, corn, or potatoes as the main ingredient.

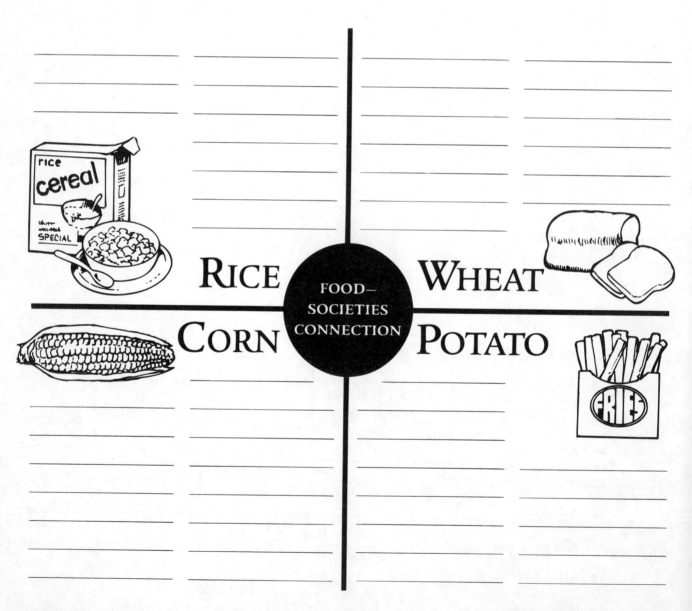

Name _____

All That Jazz

Work with a partner to research the jazz musicians in
the box below. Fill in each blank with the name of the
musician who matches the information.

Earl "Fatha" Hines   Ella Fitzgerald

Louis Armstrong   Charlie Parker

Count Basie   Dizzy Gillespie

Fats Waller   Lester Young

1. I was a great alto saxophonist and played in Missouri, Kansas City, and New York City.

   I am _____.

2. I played the trumpet and cornet. I was also a singer and bandleader. I am known for

   creating a musical style called swing. I am

   _____.

3. I was a jazz pianist and had my own nightly radio broadcast, which featured my band's

   music. I am _____.

4. I played jazz trumpet and was popular for nearly 60 years. I composed many songs,

   including "Salt Peanuts," and "Bebop." I am

   _____.

5. I was a jazz pianist and was known for combining my music with slapstick comedy.

   I am _____.

6. I was one of the greatest tenor saxophone players of all times. My nickname was

   "Prez." I am _____.

7. I was a well-know jazz bandleader and piano player. I began studying jazz with my

   mother. I am _____.

8. I was known as a jazz singer. I was raised in an orphanage and was discovered while

   singing in a talent show in Harlem. I am _____.

Daily Learning Drills Grade 5

SOCIAL STUDIES REVIEW

Name _____

Just Like a Rockwell Painting

Norman Rockwell, arguably the most recognized artist in America for over 60 years, was a storyteller. In an art world of surrealism and post-Impressionistic works of abstraction, Rockwell's paintings remained representational. Viewers could not only identify the people and objects in his paintings, they could even interpret a tale created by Rockwell's brush strokes. Rockwell liked it that way. Although he agreed with his critics that storytelling might not be the highest of art forms, he also recognized that relating anecdotes through art is what he did best.

Norman Rockwell was determined from childhood to paint pictures. At 14, he enrolled in an art school part time. By 16, he was attending as a full-time student. Rockwell was a quick learner. He thrived at The Art Student's League, which focused on teaching students the technical skills of drawing and painting. His talents did not go unnoticed. Rockwell received his first commission to illustrate four Christmas cards at age 15. At 18, he illustrated his first book, *Tell Me Why Stories*. A year later, while still a teen and art student, he accepted the post of art director for *Boys' Life* magazine.

In 1916, at the young age of 22, Rockwell made the big time. He was commissioned to paint the cover illustration for a *Saturday Evening Post* edition. In 1916, the *Post* found its way into one in every nine American households. Creating its cover was a tremendous honor—one which Rockwell would accept another 321 times over the next 47 years, giving him an audience larger than any other artist has had in history. Every time he contributed a cover, the magazine's circulation jumped by as much as 250,000.

In addition to his popular *Saturday Evening Post* covers, Rockwell designed 53 Boy Scout calendars, painted famous posters illustrating Franklin Roosevelt's Four Freedoms speech, illustrated scenes of the 1960s' Civil Rights Movement, and painted portraits of three American presidents and several other heads of state. He created advertising campaign art for countless products and contributed illustrations to popular books and magazines from the *Ladies' Home Journal* to *McCall's*. Rockwell wrote and illustrated an autobiography with one of his sons.

Rockwell received numerous awards for his work, including two important national prizes: 1957's Great Living American Award and 1977's Presidential Medal of Freedom. Rockwell earned such high national honors because his works captured the American spirit. Children, dogs, and adults in every occupation smile and grimace, gesture, and pose in Rockwell's paintings to tell a story of hope and innocence. Rockwell's paintings feel so warm and homespun that Americans continue to refer to scenes that exemplify the American dream as "Rockwellian."

Although Rockwell worked hard to tell his tales of the folks next door, arranging his own backgrounds, posing his models, painstakingly drawing his subjects from life, and revising his works as many as 20 times per painting, the resulting illustration was always fresh, alive, and undeniably American.

Name _____

Name That Scene

Norman Rockwell's paintings illustrated America at its best. They were often humorous and always thought- and emotion-provoking. Match the following Rockwell paintings with their descriptions below. To view prints of the paintings listed, look up "Norman Rockwell" on the Internet.

In which painting will you see . . .

____ 1. . . . the backs of a boy and girl as they sit on a sagging bench watching a large, round sun in the background.

____ 2. . . . a mother with her child over her knee, one hand raised and holding a hairbrush, as the other hand holds a book which the mother is consulting for her best next move.

____ 3. . . . a young girl and an old storekeeper looking at puppets together in an incredibly cluttered shop.

____ 4. . . . three schoolgirls: one opening her mouth wide as two look inside to see the work a dentist has completed.

____ 5. . . . the back of Norman Rockwell's head as he looks past the side of a canvas on which he is painting a portrait of himself to a mirror beyond the canvas.

____ 6. . . . a police officer and a young boy sitting at a soda fountain counter.

____ 7. . . . a nervous rookie about to go to bat as the crowd and his teammates in the dugout show signs of doubt.

____ 8. . . . a young soldier being welcomed home by his father as his mother and siblings look on excitedly from the stairwell.

____ 9. . . . a boy in a cowboy hat petting a dog who looks up to him with puppies surrounding her.

____10. . . . the backs of boys dressed in sports gear and huddled in a circle arguing as one boy holds a basketball and the others shout and point in various directions.

____11. . . . a black boy and girl standing beside a moving truck and furniture as three white kids stare on pensively.

____12. . . . a smiling grandpa and a young boy reeling in a big fish.

A. *The Runaway*

B. *New Kids in the Neighborhood*

C. *The Curiosity Shop*

D. *Triple Self-portrait*

E. *Homecoming*

F. *A Boy and His Dog: Parenthood*

G. *Child Psychology*

H. *Check-up*

I. *Sporting Boys: Oh Yeah!*

J. *The Dugout*

K. *Catching the Big One*

L. *Sunset*

SOCIAL STUDIES REVIEW

International Temperatures

Use the weather section of the newspaper to check the temperature for your local area and the temperatures for the five cities identified on the graph below.

Complete the bar graph showing the temperatures for each city. Then use the graph and a world atlas to answer the questions.

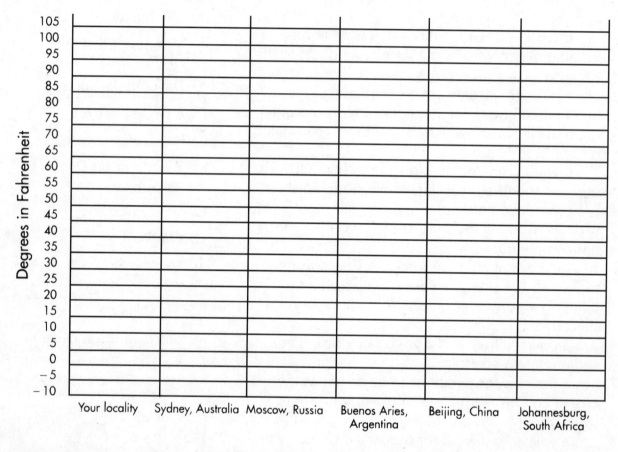

1. On what date did you record the temperatures for all six places? _____

2. Which place was the coldest? _____

3. Which place was the warmest? _____

4. What might account for the temperature difference between the coldest and

warmest places? _____

5. Which place is farthest away from the equator? _____

6. Which of the five international cities would you like to visit the most? Why?

_____

_____

Around the World

Below are facts about Ferdinand Magellan's famous explorations.
Connect each cause with its matching effect.

Cause

____ 1. Trading would make investors rich.

____ 2. The Portuguese controlled the sea route to the East Indies.

____ 3. Seamen prepared to ward off enemies.

____ 4. The crew's food supplies ran out.

____ 5. The Spanish ships had a long journey across the Pacific.

____ 6. Magellan's own men were loyal to him.

____ 7. The mapmakers had underestimated the size of the Pacific Ocean.

____ 8. Magellan offered to help an island ruler warring with another.

____ 9. The shores the ships passed were illuminated by the fires of the natives.

____ 10. The Portuguese controlled the African Cape of Good Hope.

____ 11. The Victoria was caught in a vicious storm.

____ 12. The surviving ships took on a cargo of cloves.

Effect

a. Spanish explorers dared not travel south around Africa.

b. The ship returned to Spain with its sails in tatters.

c. Ships were sent to the Far East to trade.

d. Magellan was killed in the conflict.

e. Magellan was able to squelch a mutiny by some of the crew.

f. They were forced to eat sawdust, leather sail rigging, and rats.

g. Magellan named this land Tierra del Fuego (land of fire).

h. Seamen suffered from thirst, malnutrition, and starvation while crossing the ocean.

i. The Spanish hoped to discover a different route to the Spice Islands by traveling west.

j. Food and water supplies were quickly used up.

k. Despite the loss of ships, the voyage earned a profit.

l. The ships were armed with guns and cannons.

Name _____

Ancient Farming

Read the article. Then answer the questions on the next page.

Three ancient civilizations from the Americas were the Incan, the Aztec, and the Mayan. The Maya thrived in the area we now know as Mexico's Yucatan peninsula and Central America. The Incan Empire was located along the west coast of South America in what are known today as Peru and Chile. The Aztec lived in the area we know today as Mexico. Their capital city was in the same place as modern-day Mexico City. Agriculture was very important to all of these civilizations.

For the Aztecs, the common agricultural tool was a pointed stick used for digging. In areas covered with dense forest, farmers practiced slash-and-burn agriculture, in which they burned a section of forest and planted in the cleared areas. In this way, the ashes from the burn produced highly fertile soil. In hilly or mountainous regions, the farmers cut terraces into the hills to increase the amount of flat farmland on which to plant. Farmers also built island-gardens, called *chinampas*. They scooped up mud from lake bottoms and made islands that were suitable for planting. The chinampas yielded huge crops.

The Inca used a variety of farming methods. Along the coastal desert, they built networks to help irrigate the land. In mountainous areas, they cut terraces into the hillsides as the Aztecs did. Their farm fields were divided into three groups. One field was dedicated to the needs of local people. The other two supported state and religious activities.

Mayan farmers built raised fields similar to the chinampas of the Aztecs. They used swampy lowlands and drained the soil to unearth fields on which to grow their crops. They combined this technique with terracing to provide food to feed large populations.

Name _____

1. Why do you think agriculture may have been so important to these ancient civilizations?

_____

_____

2. Why did slash-and-burn agriculture produce highly fertile soil?

_____

_____

3. Why do you think the chinampa farms of the Aztecs yielded large crops?

_____

_____

4. List one other reason why terracing might have been helpful to these ancient civilizations.

_____

_____

5. The farming techniques of all three civilizations are similar even though the people lived in different areas. List two reasons why this might be.

_____

_____

_____

_____

_____

SOCIAL STUDIES REVIEW

Name _____

Create an Island Culture

Human activity on Earth is influenced by geographic features. Below is a blank map of an island. On it, show how geographic features influence an imaginary culture on an imaginary island. To create an environment and human settlement patterns for the island, you need to do the following:

1. Select and write the latitude and longitude coordinates of your island to establish the influence of latitude on your island's climate. _____

2. On the map, draw symbols and use combinations of colors to show major natural and man-made features (bays, rivers, lakes, vegetation, mineral deposits, mountains, hills, swamps, plains, bridges, roads, cities, dams, etc.). Create a map key to explain the symbols and colors.

3. Label the geographic features you created.

4. Draw a compass rose to show cardinal directions.

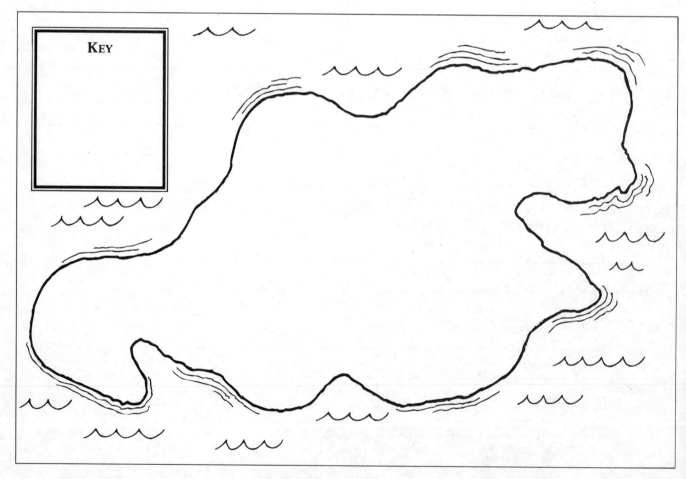

On another sheet of paper, answer the following question:

How have the geographic features of your island influenced the way of life of its inhabitants?

Name _____

America's Rivers

Ten of America's rivers are highlighted on the map below. Use an atlas to identify each one. Then write the name of the river on the appropriate line.

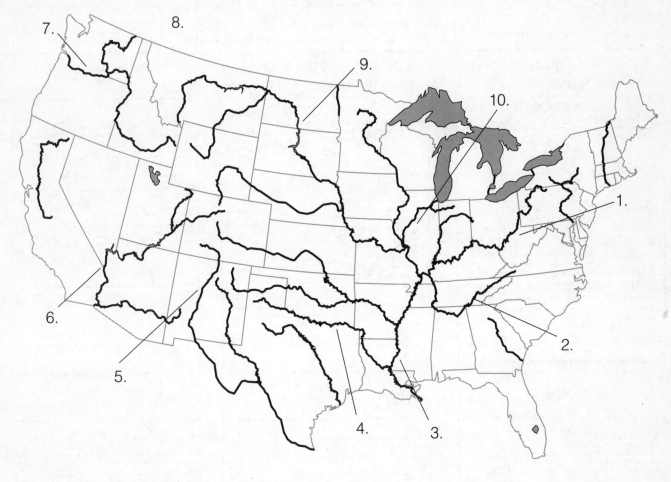

1. _____   6. _____

2. _____   7. _____

3. _____   8. _____

4. _____   9. _____

5. _____   10. _____

Review Answer Key

Don't Stress Out!

When a word of two or more syllables is pronounced, usually one of the syllables is stressed. Sometimes there are two ways to pronounce the same word. The accent, or stress, changes as the meaning of the word changes. Example: The detective began to susPECT that the butler was the key SUSpect.

Read each sentence. Then circle the correct pronunciation for the underlined word.

1. At the awards dinner, they will present me with a present.
   PRESent (preSENT)
2. As you progress through the book, keep track of your progress.
   PROGress (proGRESS)
3. "I object," shouted the lawyer. "The object of his question was to trick my client."
   (obJECT) OBject
4. If you are on your best conduct, you can conduct the class on a tour.
   (CONduct) conDUCT
5. Don't refuse to clean up the refuse from the picnic.
   REFuse (reFUSE)
6. Without a permit, we cannot permit you to hunt.
   perMIT (PERmit)
7. This afternoon, I will be at this address. I am giving the main address of the meeting.
   (ADdress) adDRESS
8. Most conflicts start because differing opinions conflict.
   (CONflicts) conFLICTS
9. Are you content with the content of your lunch?
   (conTENT) CONtent
10. Did they convict the convict?
    CONvict (conVICT)
11. If the air conditioning breaks on the produce truck, it will produce rotten fruit.
    (PROduce) proDUCE

321

Come on, Goldie!

A **declarative** sentence tells something. It ends with a period. (.)
An **interrogative** sentence asks something. It ends with a question mark. (?)
An **imperative** sentence gives an order. It ends with a period. (.)
An **exclamatory** sentence shows strong feeling. It ends with an exclamation mark. (!)

Read each sentence. Write an abbreviation to tell what kind of sentence it is:
D—declarative *Int*—interrogative *Imp*—Imperative *E*—Exclamatory
Then write the missing punctuation mark.

Imp Goldie, roll over.
Int Have you ever tried to train a fish?
D I did.
E What a disaster!
D 1. It all started when my friend insulted my fish.
D or E 2. Fish are stupid pets . or !
Int 3. Why do you say that?
Imp 4. Look at it.
D 5. All your fish does is swim and eat.
E 6. Hmmmph, Goldie is *not* a stupid fish!
Imp 7. Teach her some tricks then.
D or E 8. OK, I will . or !
Int 9. How do the trainers at Sea World train the dolphins and whales?
D 10. They use whistles and rewards, but those are mammals, not fish.
Imp 11. Goldie, swim on your side when I blow this whistle.
E 12. Tweet-tweet!
Int 13. Goldie, didn't you hear me?
D 14. I'll give you extra food if you do it.
Imp 15. Goldie, watch how I do it.

322

Animal Armor

The **subject** is the part of a sentence that tells whom or what the sentence is about.
The **predicate** is the part of a sentence that tells what the subject is or does.

Read each sentence. Circle the subject. Underline the predicate.

Examples:

(Many different animals) have armor to protect themselves.
Unlike most mammals, (a pangolin) has scales covering its body.

1. (The pangolin's sharp scales) are made from a strange, hard form of hair.
2. (A pangolin) curls up in a ball to escape from danger.
3. (An armadillo) looks like it is covered in armor.
4. (The name *armadillo*) means "little armored one" in Spanish.
5. (Armadillos) have bony plates and very tough skin.
6. (A tortoise's hard shell) is its armor.
7. Inside its shell, (the tortoise) can hide from predators.
8. (The tortoise beetle) is an insect.
9. (It) has a hard shield that covers its head, legs, and body.

Read these animal sentences. Write **S** if the sentence is missing the subject or **P** if it is missing the predicate. Finish the sentences, filling in the missing parts.

P 10. A slow-moving snail Sentences will vary.
S 11. Like the crab, ______ is a shelled animal that lives in the ocean.
S 12. ______ would look funny if they were covered with armor.

323

My Favorite Author

The **complete subject** is all the words in a sentence that tell whom or what the sentence is about.
The **simple subject** is the main word that tells whom or what the sentence is about. If a simple subject is a proper noun, it may be more than one word.
A **compound subject** has two or more simple subjects, usually connected with the word *and*.

Read each sentence. Underline the complete subject. Write the simple subject(s).

class — Our class is doing an author study project.
Everyone — Everyone needs to choose an author.
Marcus, I — Both Marcus and I chose Dick King-Smith.
Dick King-Smith — 1. Dick King-Smith writes books about animals.
I — 2. I have read five of his books.
one — 3. My favorite one is *Three Terrible Trins*.
book — 4. That book is about mice triplets who befriend a cellar mouse and terrorize a cat.
assignment — 5. Our assignment has two parts—a report and a project.
report — 6. The report needs to explain themes that are repeated in the author's books.
characters — 7. Many of the characters in King-Smith's books want to do more than the others around them.
mice — 8. The mice in *Three Terrible Trins* want to have friends in all levels of their farmhouse.
pig — 9. The pig in *Pigs Might Fly* learns to swim and hopes to fly.
project — 10. My creative project will be a tape-recorded interview of the different book characters.
Marcus, Whitney — 11. Marcus and Whitney are going to help me read the parts.

324

A Thank-You Note

A. Read Liz Beth's letter to her grandparents. Fill in the missing subject pronouns.
B. Read her grandpa's reply. Fill in the missing object pronouns.

Subject Pronoun	Object Pronoun
I	me
you	you
he	him
she	her
it	it
we	us
they	them

Dear Grandma and Grandpa,

Thank you for the earrings you sent me for my birthday. They were cool. Dad still thinks I am too young to have had my ears pierced. But he said now that it is done, he won't complain about it anymore. Last night Michael asked Dad if he could get one of his ears pierced. Dad got really mad and said, "I am going for a long walk!" We all started laughing. Mom doesn't think Michael really wants his ear pierced. She thinks he just wanted to tease Dad.

We are looking forward to your visit next month. It is coming soon. If you have time, please write me back.

Love,
Liz Beth

Dear Liz Beth,

We were so happy to get the note you sent us. Grandma picked out the earrings. We're glad you liked you. Your poor father—you three are always picking on him!

Grandma is at Aunt Yoli's this weekend. She went to visit her for a few days.

I talked to your mom yesterday. She told me that you won a mystery award for your computer project. When will you get it?

I hope all is well with you and your family. We miss you.

Love,
Grandpa

325

Get in on the Action!

For most verbs, you add *ed* to form the past tense and the past participle. You add *ing* to form the present participle. But for some words, you don't add *ed* or *ing* to show a change in time. These are called **irregular verbs** (example: *catch, caught; buy, bought*). Irregular verb forms are listed in the dictionary.

Write the verb forms that belong on the lines. When you're done, you will have a joke.

Two goats (wander) wandered into an alley behind a movie theater. They were (look) looking for their dinner. They (find) found a videotape. One of the goats (eat) ate it.

"How was it?" the other goat (ask) asked.

"All right," said the first goat. "But the book was better."

Write the past tense of each verb below.

Verb	Past Tense
1. stop	stopped
2. try	tried
3. sing	sang
4. teach	taught
5. go	went

Use a dictionary to fill in the chart below. The first line is done for you.

Verb	Past Tense	Past Participle (have or has + verb)	Present Participle
sell	*sold*	*sold*	*selling*
1. go	went	gone	going
2. rise	rose	risen	rising
3. sing	sang	sung	singing
4. write	wrote	written	writing
5. tear	tore	torn	tearing
6. swim	swam	swum	swimming

326

A Bad Fairy Tale

Most verbs name actions. The verb **be** is different. It tells about someone or something. It can also be a helping verb that helps with an action verb.

Read this silly fairy tale. Fill in the blanks with a form of the verb **be**: *be, am, is, are, was, were, being, or been.*

Once upon a time, there was a sweet, unlucky girl named Mary Badluck. Like other mothers in fairy tales, her mother was gentle, kind, and ill. Unfortunately, Mary's mother died when Mary was only five. Mary and her father were quite sad. "What are we going to do?" wept her father.

"I am not worried, Father, nor should you be," said Mary. "We will be okay."

Mary's father was lonely, so he remarried. Mary's stepmother, Lady Grace, was gentle and kind like Mary's own mother had been. But alas, Lady Grace was ill, too, and she soon died.

"What am I going to do?" sobbed her father.

"Be brave, Father!" admonished Mary.

Once again her father remarried. Mary's new stepmother, Lady Evila, was actually nice. Mary had been expecting an evil stepmother and was pleasantly surprised. But guess what? Yes, you are right. Lady Evila was a sickly creature and died, too.

"What is going on around here?" wailed her father.

"I think we are being tormented in a bad fairy tale, Father!" realized Mary.

Mary was quite right. Her father remarried yet again. This time her new stepmother, Lady Bullybrains, was rough, mean, and healthy.

What are Mary and her father going to do? Will they ever be happy? Write an ending to this tale to find out.

327

Noun, Adjective, Adverb

A **noun** is a word that names a person, place, thing, or idea.
An **adjective** is a word that describes a noun.
An **adverb** is a word that modifies a verb, an adjective, or another adverb.

Many nouns, adjectives, and adverbs are variations of the same root word.
Bravery was an important quality for knights. (noun)
The brave knight searched for the dragon. (adjective)
The knight fought bravely when the dragon attacked. (adverb)

Read the words in each row. Write the missing adjective or adverb.

Noun	Adjective	Adverb
intelligence	intelligent	intelligently
kindness	kind	kindly
fearlessness	fearless	fearlessly
happiness	happy	happily
success	successful	successfully
independence	independent	independently
arrogance	arrogant	arrogantly
carelessness	careless	carelessly
possibility	possible	possibly
enthusiasm	enthusiastic	enthusiastically
affection	affectionate	affectionately
ease	easy	easily
courtesy	courteous	courteously
responsibility	responsible	responsibly
stupidity	stupid	stupidly
wisdom	wise	wisely
anger	angry	angrily
silence	silent	silently

328

Watch Out, Goldilocks!

Use **quotation marks** (" ") to show the exact words a speaker says.
Papa Bear exclaimed, "Someone's been eating my porridge!"
Use a **comma** (,) to set off the exact words a speaker says from the rest of the sentence.
"Someone's been eating my porridge, too," chimed in Mama Bear.
"Someone's been eating my porridge," sobbed Baby Bear, "and now it's all gone."

If a speaker's exact words need a **question mark** or **exclamation mark**, write the mark inside the quotation marks.
Mama Bear asked, "Do you think the intruder is still here?"
"Watch out, you nasty intruder!" shouted Baby Bear. "We're coming to get you."

Read this conversation. Write the missing punctuation marks.
Finish the conversation by writing a line each for Baby Bear and Goldilocks.

"Let's check the living room," suggested Baby Bear.
"Hmmph! Someone's been sitting in my chair," growled Papa Bear.
"Oh, my!" gasped Mama Bear. "Someone's been sitting in my chair, too."
"Quit feeling sorry for yourselves and pay attention to me," said Baby Bear as he pointed to his chair. "Whoever it was broke my chair!"
"Shall we check the bedroom ?" asked Papa Bear.
"Let's go quietly," whispered Mama Bear.
"Watch out, you nasty intruder!" shouted Baby Bear. "We're coming to get you!"
"Shh, BB!" Mama Bear reprimanded.
"Oh, Mom ," grumbled Baby Bear.
Papa Bear announced "Someone's been sleeping in my bed."
"Here we go again," sighed Mama Bear . "Someone's been sleeping in my bed."

Final lines will vary.

329

It's All the Same to Me

Some words mean the same or nearly the same as other words. Two words that mean almost the same are called synonyms. Many dictionary definitions give other words—or **synonyms**—for the words defined.

Read the dictionary entry for the word *talk*. Notice all the synonyms in the definition. Can you think of other synonyms for the word *talk*?

> **talk** (tôk). 1. *v.* use words; speak: *Baby is learning to talk.* 2. *n.* the use of words; spoken words; speech; conversation: *The old friends met for a good talk.* 3. *n.* an informal speech. 4. *v.* discuss: *They talked politics.* 5. *v.* consult; confer: *to talk with one's doctor.* 6. *v.* spread ideas by other means than speech: *to talk by signs.* 7. *v.* bring, influence, etc., by talk: *We talked them into joining the club.* 8. *n.* gossip; report; rumor: *She was the talk of the town.*

A thesaurus is a book of synonyms. Use a thesaurus to find three synonyms for each word below. Compare your answers with other students.

1. avoid
bypass, dodge, duck

2. border
brink, edge, margin

3. clear
brighten, disengage, hurdle

4. effective
efficient, forceful, operative

5. forbid
outlaw, ban, profit

6. glorify
exalt, honor, praise

7. insane
cracked, bedtime, bonkers

8. maintain
assert, claim, defend

9. offer
attempt, go, propose

10. period
age, time, end

330

It's Just the Opposite

Antonyms are words that have opposite meanings. *Guilty* and *innocent* are antonyms. So are *smooth* and *rough*.

Circle the antonym in each group for the boldfaced word on the left.

1. **tired** — weary — sleepy — (energetic)
2. **help** — assist — (hinder) — aid
3. **sick** — ailing — (healthy) — ill
4. **alike** — similar — identical — (different)
5. **soft** — flexible — (rigid) — pliable
6. **bright** — vivid — (cloudy) — brilliant
7. **likeable** — amiable — (unpleasant) — agreeable
8. **narrow** — slim — (wide) — thin
9. **incorrect** — erroneous — (correct) — wrong
10. **wet** — soaked — drenched — (arid)
11. **huge** — (minute) — colossal — bulky
12. **risky** — dangerous — (safe) — hazardous
13. **hostile** — (friendly) — unsociable — adverse
14. **cheerful** — joyous — lively — (glum)
15. **active** — (sluggish) — quick — nimble
16. **irritate** — provoke — rouse — (soothe)
17. **sharp** — (blunt) — fine — pointed
18. **timid** — fearful — (courageous) — afraid

331

Daffy Definitions!

If you know baseball, then you probably know what a *grand slam* is. It's a home run with the bases loaded. But if you like word play, you can come up with a daffy definition: A *grand slam* is someone who slaps $1,000 onto a table. A thousand dollars is sometimes called a *grand*. By using that meaning of *grand*, you can get the daffy definition of *grand slam*.

How daffy are you? See if you can match the expressions below with their crazy definitions. Write your answers on the lines.

rock garden   capital punishment   New Jersey
diamond cutter   net profit   bank balance

1. The person who mows the grass on a baseball field   diamond cutter
2. A place where outdoor music concerts are held   rock garden
3. Having to stay after school in Washington, D.C.   capital punishment
4. What is left after the fishing boat owner pays all expenses   net profit
5. A replacement for a worn-out turtleneck sweater   New Jersey
6. What keeps a building full of money from tipping over   bank balance

Now try the same thing with single words. Think about the sound of each word, as well as its meaning.

bamboo   goblet   cartoon   pharmacy   capsize
Alaska   cantaloupe   watchdog   account   footnotes

7. A school where you learn to be a farmer   pharmacy
8. An animal that knows how to tell time   watchdog
9. Music that is written and played for dancing   footnotes
10. A song you might hum while you're driving   cartoon
11. What a girl tells a guy who wants to run away and get married   cantaloupe
12. A young turkey just learning to make sounds   goblet
13. A nobleman, like a duke, earl, or lord   account
14. Two loud noises that might frighten you   bamboo
15. What you tell a hat salesperson   capsize
16. What you say when you want to know a girl's name   Alaska

332

Putting It in Perspective

Cut along the dotted lines to divide the events related to the life of Michelangelo listed below. But that's not all. Then rearrange them in chronological order to put the events in historical perspective. Glue the ordered events to your own paper.

1508–1512 Michelangelo works on the Sistine Chapel Ceiling project.   10

1564 Having worked on projects until his very last days, Michelangelo dies at the age of 89. His contemporaries describe his death as the passing of a "divine angel."   15

c.1515 Michelangelo completes one of his most famous sculptures, *Moses*.   11

1386 Donatello is born. His techniques will influence Michelangelo, and one of his former students will serve as Michelangelo's teacher at art school.   2

1475 Michelangelo Buonarroti is born to a distinguished Florentine family.   4

1488–1489 Michelangelo apprentices with Domenico Ghirlandaio.   5

1501–1504 Michelangelo works on the marble figure of *David*.   8

1452 Leonardo da Vinci is born. His work and Michelangelo's work will be displayed side by side at least once in their lifetimes.   3

1350 The Renaissance era in art, music, literature, and religion is born. Michelangelo will contribute substantially into the High Renaissance period within this era.   1

1517 The Reformation is initiated when Martin Luther nails his 95 Theses to the door of a German cathedral, criticizing practices of the Catholic church. The resulting split in the church and beginning of the Protestant faith affects the religious Michelangelo, whose works display more sorrow and disillusionment.   12

1498–1500 Michelangelo works on the *Pietà*.   7

1541 Michelangelo completes the *Last Judgment* mural.   13

1492 Michelangelo's first patron, Lorenzo de Medici, dies, his family falls out of favor in Florence, and Michelangelo finds himself in exile in Bologna two years later.   6

1505–1516 The Vatican is the primary patron of Michelangelo's work.   9

1550 Michelangelo begins work on a sculpture many believe he wished to be placed at his own burial site. Out of depression or disappointment in the quality of the work, he destroys his own work, which is later repaired.   14

333

Figure It Out

When you come across an unfamiliar word, you can usually figure out its meaning by looking for clues in the surrounding words. In each sentence below, guess the meaning of the boldfaced word. Then compare your meaning with the dictionary meaning. Were you close?

1. "This is a **bogus** bill," said the bank teller.
   Bogus probably means   fake

2. The **destitute** family had trouble paying its rent.
   Destitute probably means   poor, without money

3. Her **affable** personality won her many friends.
   Affable probably means   pleasant, friendly

4. The huge ten-story **edifice** dwarfed the other office structures.
   Edifice probably means   building

5. The team members looked **despondent** after they lost the game.
   Despondent probably means   sad, heartbroken

6. "If you get one more speeding ticket," the judge said, "I will **revoke** your license."
   Revoke probably means   take back

7. After the **altercation**, they kissed and made up.
   Altercation probably means   fight

8. In some states, an accessory to murder is as **culpable** as the actual killer.
   Culpable probably means   guilty

9. If you are **loquacious**, you can expect high phone bills.
   Loquacious probably means   talkative

10. When Tory cancelled the party a third time, her friends were **irate**.
    Irate probably means   very angry

335

Sequence of Events

Fill in this chart with important events from a story you read. The title of the book goes in the center. Then fill in events relating to the story going around the circle.

End   Begin

Events and stories will vary.

336

Many Kinds of Information

Dictionaries provide information on pronunciation, spelling, and word meaning. But that's not all. You can also use dictionaries to find out about people, places, and things—even abbreviations, slang words, and trademarks.

Use a dictionary to answer the questions that follow.

1. Is C.O.D. a kind of fish?   no
2. Did Cleopatra live in Greece?   no
3. Was Kleenex an ancient ruler?   no
4. Would you expect to see a griffin in a zoo?   no
5. Is the Cape of Good Hope something to wear?   no
6. Do Minutemen work in clock factories?   no
7. If you root for a team, are you for or against it?   for
8. If you got an invitation marked R.S.V.P., should you reply?   yes
9. Is dragoon a kind of beast?   no
10. Was Prometheus a famous movie star?   no
11. Did Rachel appear in a Greek myth?   no
12. Is hgt. short for height?   yes
13. Is HEW a government agency or the name of an author?   government agency
14. Is Death Valley a real place?   yes
15. Does the prefix deca- mean ten?   yes
16. Is Julius Caesar a kind of salad?   no
17. Was Pythagoras a great leader?   no
18. Is Kilimanjaro an island in the South Seas?   no
19. Is Labor Day the day you were born?   no
20. Is KA the abbreviation for Kansas?   no
21. Is Kipling a kind of fish?   no

337

Look It Up!

Most encyclopedias have several volumes. They contain short articles about many different subjects. The articles are arranged alphabetically, according to subjects. An article about airplanes would be in the first volume. One entitled "X-rays" would be in the last volume.

Suppose you wanted to find the answer to each question below. Write the subject you would look up. Then write the volume in which the article would be.

1. What makes sound come from a clarinet?
   Subject   clarinet   Volume   Cj-Cz

2. How tall is the Washington Monument?
   Subject   Washington Monument   Volume   V-W

3. How is a camera similar to the human eye?
   Subject   camera   Volume   C-Ci

4. When was the first transcontinental railroad in the U.S. completed?
   Subject   railroad   Volume   Q-R

5. What is the capital of Alaska?
   Subject   Alaska   Volume   A

6. How many different kinds of bears are in North America?
   Subject   bears   Volume   B

7. What kind of equipment do you need for mountain climbing?
   Subject   Mountain climbing   Volume   M

8. What is the meaning of each of the hand signals that a basketball referee uses during a game?
   Subject   basketball   Volume   B

9. How is a suspension bridge built?
   Subject   bridge   Volume   B

10. Who was the 26th President of the United States?
    Subject   president   Volume   P

338

Poetry: Recipes for Success

Follow the directions below to create your own poems. Share your works with the class.

> Spot
> Furry, cuddly
> Scratching, digging, chewing
> Has a nose for trouble
> Puppy

Cinquain
A cinquain is a 5-line poem. A cinquain can take different forms. One form is below.

- Line 1: a noun
- Line 2: two adjectives
- Line 3: three verbs (action words) ending in *ing*
- Line 4: a phrase
- Line 5: a noun (the same as line 1 or different)

Poems will vary.

Haiku

> Birds sing in the trees —
> melodies like pink flowers
> ring in the still air.

A haiku is a 3-line poem. Each line has a certain number of beats, or syllables.
- Line 1 has 5 syllables.
- Line 2 has 7 syllables.
- Line 3 has 5 syllables.

Diamond Poem
A diamond poem is a 7-line poem that goes from one idea to its opposite. It gets its name from its shape.

Winter
Cold, Icy
Freezing, Snowing, Blowing
Ice, Snow, Sunshine, Flowers
Warming, Blooming, Growing
Hot, Sticky
Summer

339

Prize Pumpkin

I went to the County Pumpkin Fest.
Hoping my pumpkin would be judged best.
I lugged it all the way to the fair,
Huffing and puffing in crisp, fresh air.
But, then I learned to my surprise,
That the judging was for pumpkin pies!

Complete the following.
1. In what season does this poem take place? __autumn__
   How do you know? __crisp air ; pumpkins in basket__
2. List 3 adjectives that describe the speaker of the poem.
   Suggestions: __tired__ __embarrassed__ __disappointed__
3. How big do you think the speaker's pumpkin is? __very large__
   What clues lead you to this conclusion? __He lugged it to the fair, huffing and__
   __puffing.__
4. Tell what you think happened afterward. __Answers will vary.__

340

If I Were in Charge of the World

Wouldn't it be great to be in charge of the world? Complete the statements below describing what you would do if you were in charge of the world.

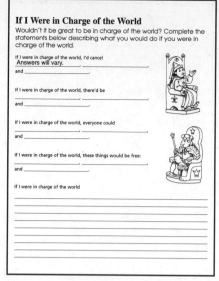

If I were in charge of the world, I'd cancel __Answers will vary.__
and _____

If I were in charge of the world, there'd be _____
and _____

If I were in charge of the world, everyone could _____
and _____

If I were in charge of the world, these things would be free:
and _____

If I were in charge of the world _____
_____
_____
_____
_____
_____

341

If I Were a. . .

Let your imagination go wild! Complete the phrases below to create a unique, introspective poem.

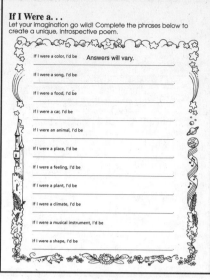

If I were a color, I'd be __Answers will vary.__

If I were a song, I'd be _____

If I were a food, I'd be _____

If I were a car, I'd be _____

If I were an animal, I'd be _____

If I were a place, I'd be _____

If I were a feeling, I'd be _____

If I were a plant, I'd be _____

If I were a climate, I'd be _____

If I were a musical instrument, I'd be _____

If I were a shape, I'd be _____

342

Talk With the Animals

Add or subtract. Use your answers to write and solve a riddle.

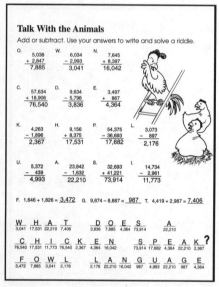

O. 5,038 + 2,847 = 7,885	W. 6,034 − 2,993 = 3,041	N. 7,645 + 8,397 = 16,042
C. 57,634 + 18,906 = 76,540	D. 9,634 − 5,798 = 3,836	E. 3,497 + 867 = 4,364
K. 4,263 − 1,896 = 2,367	H. 9,156 + 8,375 = 17,531	P. 54,375 − 36,693 = 17,682
		3,073 − 897 = 2,176
U. 5,372 − 439 = 4,993	A. 23,842 − 1,632 = 22,210	S. 32,693 + 41,221 = 73,914
		I. 14,734 − 2,961 = 11,773

F. 1,646 + 1,826 = __3,472__   G. 9,874 − 8,887 = __987__   T. 4,419 + 2,987 = __7,406__

W H A T   D O E S   A
3,041 17,531 22,210 7,406   3,836 7,885 4,364 73,914   22,210

C H I C K E N   S P E A K ?
76,540 17,531 76,540 2,367   4,364 16,042   73,914 17,682 4,364 22,210 2,367

F O W L   L A N G U A G E
3,472 7,885 3,041   2,176 22,210 16,042 987 4,993 22,210 987 4,364

343

A Silly Riddle

Find each product. Use the code to solve the riddle.

What has a trunk, two legs, and looks green?

S. 96 × 54 = 5,184	K. 38 × 77 = 2,926	A. 83 × 69 = 5,727
T. 75 × 75 = 5,625	A. 56 × 23 = 1,288	U. 49 × 48 = 2,352
S. 89 × 56 = 4,984	I. 96 × 24 = 2,304	S. 27 × 79 = 2,133
T. 37 × 65 = 2,405	R. 672 × 83 = 55,776	C. 302 × 94 = 28,388
I. 567 × 32 = 18,144	E. 489 × 86 = 42,054	O. 638 × 55 = 35,090

A   S E A S I C K
5,727   2,133 42,054 1,288 5,184 2,304 28,388 2,926

T O U R I S T
2,405 35,090 2,352 55,776 18,144 4,984 5,625

344

Ring Around the Numbers

Circle two numbers in each box whose estimated product would be the amount shown.

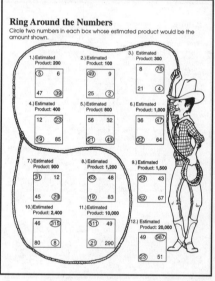

1.) Estimated Product: 200 — 5, 6, 47, 39
2.) Estimated Product: 100 — 49, 9, 25, 2
3.) Estimated Product: 300 — 8, 76, 21, 4
4.) Estimated Product: 400 — 12, 23, 19, 85
5.) Estimated Product: 800 — 56, 32, 21, 43
6.) Estimated Product: 1,000 — 36, 47, 22, 64
7.) Estimated Product: 900 — 31, 12, 45, 29
8.) Estimated Product: 1,200 — 63, 48, 19, 83
9.) Estimated Product: 1,500 — 29, 43, 52, 67
10.) Estimated Product: 2,400 — 46, 315, 80, 8
11.) Estimated Product: 10,000 — 511, 49, 21, 290
12.) Estimated Product: 20,000 — 49, 987, 23, 51

345

Turn on the Light

Find the quotients. Then cross out the sections at the bottom of the page that contain the answers. The letters in the remaining squares, written in order, will spell the answer to the riddle.

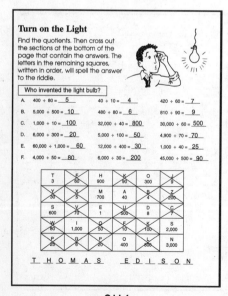

Who invented the light bulb?

A. 400 ÷ 80 = 5	40 ÷ 10 = 4	420 ÷ 60 = 7
B. 5,000 ÷ 500 = 10	480 ÷ 80 = 6	810 ÷ 90 = 9
C. 1,000 ÷ 10 = 100	32,000 ÷ 40 = 800	30,000 ÷ 60 = 500
D. 6,000 ÷ 300 = 20	5,000 ÷ 100 = 50	4,900 ÷ 70 = 70
E. 60,000 ÷ 1,000 = 60	12,000 ÷ 400 = 30	1,000 ÷ 40 = 25
F. 4,000 ÷ 50 = 80	6,000 ÷ 30 = 200	45,000 ÷ 500 = 90

T 3	F 80	H 900	K 90	O 300
X 30	Y 100	M 700	A 40	Z 200
S 600	V 70	E 500	U 7	C 5
W 80	I 1,000	C 10	L 100	S 2,000
P 20	G 8	O 400	O 600	N 3,000

T H O M A S   E D I S O N

346

Puzzling Problems

Use the clues to solve the puzzle.

ACROSS
A. 6,048 ÷ 12 = __504__
C. 14,848 ÷ 16 = __928__
E. 31,680 ÷ 6 = __5,280__
G. 7,056 ÷ 84 = __84__
I. 0 ÷ 36 = __0__
J. 98,593 ÷ 11 = __8,963__
M. 5,240 ÷ 10 = __524__
N. 948 ÷ 12 = __79__
Q. 6,630 ÷ 17 = __390__
R. 6,240 ÷ 20 = __312__
S. 13,000 ÷ 25 = __520__

DOWN
A. 11,776 ÷ 2 = __5,888__
B. 2,070 ÷ 46 = __45__
C. 8,901 ÷ 9 = __989__
D. 1,780 ÷ 89 = __20__
F. 31,276 ÷ 14 = __2,234__
H. 6,435 ÷ 13 = __495__
K. 68,992 ÷ 11 = __6,272__
L. 11,376 ÷ 3 = __3,792__
O. 9,000 ÷ 10 = __900__
P. 2,211 ÷ 67 = __33__
Q. 875 ÷ 25 = __35__

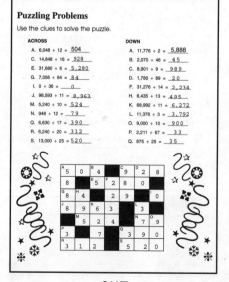

347

Fishing for Sums and Differences

Add or subtract. Write the answer in lowest terms.

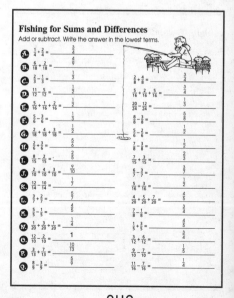

A. $\frac{3}{4} + \frac{3}{4} =$ _____ $\frac{2}{4} + \frac{3}{4} =$ _____
B. $\frac{6}{18} + \frac{2}{18} =$ _____ $\frac{3}{4} + \frac{2}{4} =$ _____
C. $\frac{2}{3} - \frac{1}{3} =$ _____ $\frac{5}{16} + \frac{2}{16} + \frac{5}{16} =$ _____
D. $\frac{11}{12} - \frac{5}{12} =$ _____ $\frac{20}{24} - \frac{12}{24} =$ _____
E. $\frac{5}{12} + \frac{11}{12} + \frac{2}{12} =$ _____ $\frac{8}{24} + \frac{2}{24} =$ _____
F. $\frac{6}{8} - \frac{3}{8} =$ _____ $\frac{5}{8} - \frac{2}{8} =$ _____
G. $\frac{2}{18} + \frac{4}{18} + \frac{3}{18} =$ _____ $\frac{6}{8} + \frac{1}{8} =$ _____
H. $\frac{4}{5} - \frac{1}{5} =$ _____ $\frac{7}{8} - \frac{3}{8} =$ _____
I. $\frac{2}{15} + \frac{7}{15} =$ _____ $\frac{7}{15} + \frac{5}{15} =$ _____
J. $\frac{2}{10} + \frac{4}{10} + \frac{3}{10} =$ _____ $\frac{5}{7} - \frac{2}{7} =$ _____
K. $\frac{12}{14} - \frac{1}{14} =$ _____ $\frac{5}{16} + \frac{5}{16} =$ _____
L. $\frac{3}{7} + \frac{2}{7} =$ _____ $\frac{6}{20} + \frac{7}{20} + \frac{2}{20} =$ _____
M. $\frac{5}{5} - \frac{1}{5} =$ _____ $\frac{5}{8} + \frac{2}{8} =$ _____
N. $\frac{5}{20} + \frac{2}{20} + \frac{3}{20} =$ _____ $\frac{1}{5} + \frac{3}{5} =$ _____
O. $\frac{6}{10} + \frac{4}{10} =$ _____ $\frac{6}{12} + \frac{4}{12} =$ _____
P. $\frac{6}{13} + \frac{4}{13} =$ _____ $\frac{7}{10} + \frac{3}{10} =$ _____
Q. $\frac{8}{9} - \frac{3}{9} =$ _____ $\frac{11}{16} + \frac{5}{16} =$ _____

348

Daily Learning Drills Grade 5

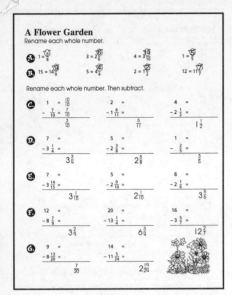

A Flower Garden
Rename each whole number.

A. 1 = 8/8   3 = 6/6 (2 6/6)   4 = 10/10 (3 10/10)   1 = 5/5

B. 15 = 14 9/9   5 = 4 4/4   2 = 1 2/2   12 = 11 7/7

Rename each whole number. Then subtract.

C. 1 = 10/10   2 =   4 =
   − 7/10 = 7/10   − 6/11   − 2 1/2
   _____   _____   _____
    3/10   5/11   1 1/2

D. 7 =   5 =   1 =
   − 3 1/4   − 3/8   − 5/8
   _____   _____   _____
    3 3/4   2 5/8   3/8

E. 7 =   5 =   6 =
   − 3 14/15   − 2 9/10   − 2 1/6
   _____   _____   _____
    3 1/15   2 1/10   3 5/6

F. 12 =   20 =   16 =
   − 8 7/9   − 13 1/4   − 3 5/7
   _____   _____   _____
    3 2/9   6 3/4   12 2/7

G. 9 =   14 =
   − 6 13/20   − 11 5/24
   _____   _____
    7/20   2 19/24

Mix It Up
Add or subtract. Write the answers in lowest terms.

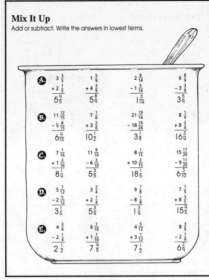

A. 3 3/5   1 5/9   2 8/14   6 8/9
   + 2 1/5   + 4 3/9   − 1 5/14   − 3 3/9
   _____   _____   _____   _____
    5 5/5   5 5/9   1 7/14   3 3/9

B. 11 12/15   7 1/6   21 19/14   8 1/4
   − 5 4/15   + 3 2/4   − 18 16/24 + 8 2/4
   _____   _____   _____   _____
    6 4/5   10 2/4   3 3/8   16 1/4

C. 7 1/16   1 5/16   15 17/20   15 7/10
   + 1 2/16   − 6 3/16   + 10 2/5   − 9 21/20
   _____   _____   _____   _____
    8 1/16   5 3/5   18 5/5   6 5/10

D. 5 7/12   3 2/4   9 7/8   8 3/9
   − 2 5/12   + 2 1/4   − 8 1/4   + 8 2/9
   _____   _____   _____   _____
    3 3/5   5 3/4   1 3/4   15 5/5

E. 4 3/4   6 7/10   4 5/12   8 3/9
   − 2 1/4   + 1 3/10   + 3 1/12   − 2 2/9
   _____   _____   _____   _____
    2 2/2   7 5/5   7 2/2   6 3/9

Fraction Product Riddle
Multiply. Use your answers to break the code and solve the following riddle:
Why did Sam take a hammer to bed?

B. 1/8 × 1/7 = 1/56   H. 1/3 × 4/7 = 4/21   W. 2 × 3/5 = 1 1/5

T. 5/9 × 2/3 = 10/27   H. 2/7 × 2/3 = 4/21   T. 5/6 × 4 = 3 1/3

H. 1/3 × 6 = 2   E. 8/9 × 1/3 = 8/27   E. 2/5 × 4/7 = 8/35

A. 1/4 × 2/3 = 1/6   O. 2/5 × 1/4 = 1/10   I. 3/5 × 1/2 = 3/10

H. 1/8 × 8 = 1 1/3   A. 8 × 3/5 = 4 4/5   C. 4/5 × 1/4 = 1/5

N. 2/7 × 7/8 = 1/4   T. 1/5 × 1/6 = 1/15   E. 1/10 × 5 = 1/2

Y. 5/12 × 1/3 = 5/36   A. 2/3 × 5/8 = 5/12   T. 7 × 1/3 = 2 1/3

U. 2/5 × 2/5 = 4/25   E. 9 × 2/3 = 6   S. 5/4 × 4/9 = 5/18

B E C A U S E   H E
W A N T E D   T O
H I T   T H E   H A Y

Focus on Fractions
Multiply.

Multiply the numerators. Then multiply the denominators.

(multiplication problems A–R in columns)

Tic-Tac Products
Use the tic-tac-toe board to find the factors and write each multiplication equation. Then write the products in lowest terms.

3 1/3	4/5	2 1/2
5 1/4	3/4	1 1/2
2 3/4	2 2/5	2/3

A. 2 1/2 × 4/5 = 2
B. 2 2/5 × 2/3 = 1 3/5
C. 1 1/2 × 5 1/4 = 7 7/8
D. 3/4 × 2 3/4 = 2 1/6
E. 2 1/3 × 2 3/4 = 9 1/6
F. 2/3 × 2 1/2 = 1 2/3
G. 4/5 × 2 2/5 = 1 23/25
H. 3/4 × 5 1/4 = 3 15/16
I. 2 2/5 × 5 1/4 = 12 3/5
J. 2 3/4 × 2 1/2 = 6 7/8
K. 2 2/5 × 1 1/2 = 3 3/5

L. Which two factors will make the greatest product? Write the factors and solve the equation.
   3 1/3 × 5 1/4 = 17 1/2

M. Which two factors will make the smallest product? Write the factors and solve the equation.
   2/3 × 3/4 = 1/2

Thousandths of Leaves

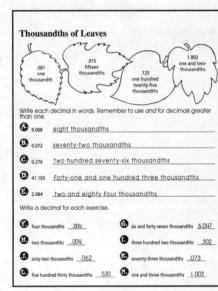
.001 one thousandth   .015 fifteen thousandths   .125 one hundred twenty-five thousandths   1.002 one and two thousandths

Write each decimal in words. Remember to use and for decimals greater than one.

A. 0.008   eight thousandths
B. 0.072   seventy-two thousandths
C. 0.276   two hundred seventy-six thousandths
D. 41.103   forty-one and one hundred three thousandths
E. 2.084   two and eighty four thousandths

Write a decimal for each exercise.

F. four thousandths .004   G. six and forty-seven thousandths 6.047
H. two thousandths .004   I. three hundred two thousandths .302
J. sixty-two thousandths .062   K. seventy-three thousandths .073
L. five hundred thirty thousandths .530   M. one and three thousandths 1.003

Round Up

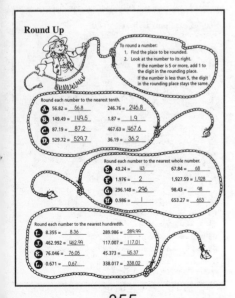

To round a number:
1. Find the place to be rounded.
2. Look at the number to its right.
   If the number is 5 or more, add 1 to the digit in the rounding place.
   If the number is less than 5, the digit in the rounding place stays the same.

Round each number to the nearest tenth.
A. 56.82 = 56.8   246.76 = 246.8
B. 149.49 = 149.5   1.87 = 1.9
C. 87.19 = 87.2   467.63 = 467.6
D. 529.72 = 529.7   36.19 = 36.2

Round each number to the nearest whole number.
E. 43.24 = 43   67.84 = 68
F. 1.976 = 2   1,927.59 = 1,928
G. 296.148 = 296   98.43 = 98
H. 0.986 = 1   653.27 = 653

Round each number to the nearest hundredth.
I. 8.355 = 8.36   289.986 = 289.99
J. 462.992 = 462.99   117.007 = 117.01
K. 76.046 = 76.05   45.373 = 45.37
L. 0.671 = 0.67   338.017 = 338.02

What's Missing?
Find the missing numbers.

A. 7.3 + 2.1 − 6.26 + 5.1 = 8.24
B. 9.34 − 2.8 − 4.02 + 1.08 = 7.04
C. 1.25 + 0.8 − 3.79 + 2.1 = 2.14
D. 7.93 + 1.08 − 3.09 − 2.7 = 8.62
E. 5.35 + 1.16 − 9.82 + 0.61 = 13.4
F. 12.24 − 8.16 + 5.2 − 3.9 = 5.38
G. 3.46 + 8.7 + 10 − 3.7 = 18.46
H. 48.9 − 24.25 + 16.1 − 0.4 = 40.35
I. 12.11 + 17.46 − 4.7 + 8.02 = 32.89

Where's the Decimal?

To determine the decimal point in the product, count the number of decimal places in the factor.

Multiply.

A. 0.8   0.05   7.4
   × 9   × 7   × 4
   ____   ____   ____
   7.2   0.35   29.6
There is one decimal place in the factor, so the product has one decimal place.

B. 6.5   7.07   3.2   3.87
   × 5   × 9   × 44   × 6
   ____   ____   ____   ____
   32.5   63.63   140.8   23.22

C. 4.32   5.24   4.07   0.802
   × 3   × 8   × 68   × 9
   ____   ____   ____   ____
   12.96   41.92   276.76   7.218

D. 5.63   8.3   3.03   0.34
   × 4   × 6   × 6   × 6
   ____   ____   ____   ____
   22.52   49.8   18.18   2.04

---

349   350   351
352   353   354
355   356   357

Count the Places

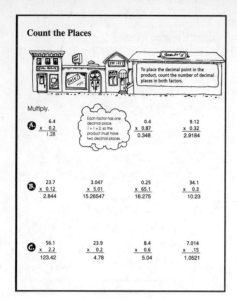

To place the decimal point in the product, count the number of decimal places in both factors.

Multiply.

A.
Each factor has one decimal place. 1 + 1 = 2, so the product must have two decimal places.

6.4	0.4	9.12
x 0.2	x 0.87	x 0.32
1.28	0.348	2.9184

B.
23.7	3.047	0.25	34.1
x 0.12	x 5.01	x 65.1	x 0.3
2.844	15.26547	16.275	10.23

C.
56.1	23.9	8.4	7.014
x 2.2	x 0.2	x 0.6	x .15
123.42	4.78	5.04	1.0521

358

Exploring Division

Divide.

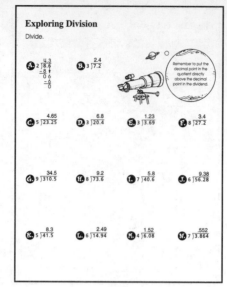

A. 2)8.6 4.3
8
-6
6
-6
0

B. 3)7.2 2.4

Remember to put the decimal point in the quotient directly above the decimal point in the dividend.

C. 5)23.25 4.65
D. 3)20.4 6.8
E. 3)3.69 1.23
F. 8)27.2 3.4

G. 9)310.5 34.5
H. 8)73.6 9.2
I. 7)40.6 5.8
J. 6)56.28 9.38

K. 5)41.5 8.3
L. 6)14.94 2.49
M. 4)6.08 1.52
N. 7)3.864 .552

359

Making the Grade

Find the percentage for each student's test. Write it beside the word *score*. Then give each test a grade based on the scale shown at the right.

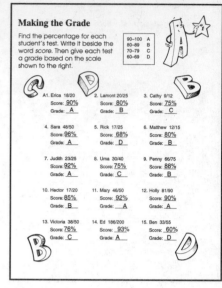

90–100	A
80–89	B
70–79	C
60–69	D

A1. Erica 18/20 Score: 90% Grade: A
2. Lamont 20/25 Score: 80% Grade: B
3. Cathy 9/12 Score: 75% Grade: C

4. Sara 48/50 Score: 96% Grade: A
5. Rick 17/25 Score: 68% Grade: D
6. Matthew 12/15 Score: 80% Grade: B

7. Judith 23/25 Score: 92% Grade: A
8. Uma 30/40 Score: 75% Grade: C
9. Penny 66/75 Score: 88% Grade: B

10. Hector 17/20 Score: 85% Grade: B
11. Mary 46/50 Score: 92% Grade: A
12. Holly 81/90 Score: 90% Grade: A

13. Victoria 38/50 Score: 76% Grade: C
14. Ed 186/200 Score: 93% Grade: A
15. Ben 33/55 Score: 60% Grade: D

360

In the Ballpark

Estimate the answer. Then solve each problem.

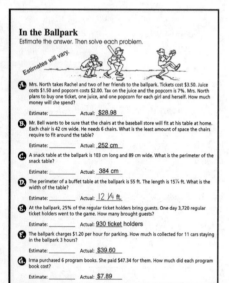

Estimates will vary.

A. Mrs. North takes Rachel and two of her friends to the ballpark. Tickets cost $3.50. Juice costs $1.50 and popcorn costs $2.00. Tax on the juice and the popcorn is 7%. Mrs. North plans to buy one ticket, one juice, and one popcorn for each girl and herself. How much money will she spend?

Estimate: _____ Actual: $28.98

B. Mr. Bell wants to be sure that the chairs at the baseball store will fit at his table at home. Each chair is 42 cm wide. He needs 6 chairs. What is the least amount of space the chairs require to fit around the table?

Estimate: _____ Actual: 252 cm

C. A snack table at the ballpark is 103 cm long and 89 cm wide. What is the perimeter of the snack table?

Estimate: _____ Actual: 384 cm

D. The perimeter of a buffet table at the ballpark is 55 ft. The length is 15¼ ft. What is the width of the table?

Estimate: _____ Actual: 12 ¼ ft.

E. At the ballpark, 25% of the regular ticket holders bring guests. One day 3,720 regular ticket holders went to the game. How many brought guests?

Estimate: _____ Actual: 930 ticket holders

F. The ballpark charges $1.20 per hour for parking. How much is collected for 11 cars staying in the ballpark 3 hours?

Estimate: _____ Actual: $39.60

G. Irma purchased 6 program books. She paid $47.34 for them. How much did each program book cost?

Estimate: _____ Actual: $7.89

361

Can You Measure Up?

Solve each problem.

12 in. = 1 ft.
3 ft. = 1 yd.

A. Marcia needs 100 inches of ribbon. She bought a roll of 9 feet of ribbon. Does she have enough ribbon? If so, how much will she have left over?

Yes, 8 inches

B. Luther is 4 feet 5 inches tall. He needs to be 48 inches tall to ride the roller coaster. Is he tall enough to ride the roller coaster?

yes

C. Rachel has an oak tree in her front yard that is 660 inches tall. She wants to know how tall the tree is in feet. What is her answer?

55 feet

D. Paul built a frame for a pond. He cut a board 34½ inches long from a board that was 4 feet long. How long was the leftover piece of board?

13 ½ inches

E. Joe had a piece of lumber 3 feet 5 inches long. He sawed off a ¾ foot long piece for a sign. How long was the piece of lumber that was left?

2 feet 8 inches

F. Randy is on the track team. He does the long jump. His longest jump was 5 feet ¾ inches long. He thinks it sounds longer in inches. How many inches did Randy jump?

60 ¾ inches

G. Chris' older brother is 6 feet 6 inches tall. Chris' height is 4 feet 2 inches tall. Chris would like to be as tall as his older brother. How many more inches does Chris need to grow?

28 inches

H. Marlin built a deck that was 21 feet 2 inches x 14 feet 10 inches. What was the perimeter of the deck in yards?

24 yards

362

Pool-Side Perimeters

Find the perimeters of the pools and the pool-side objects below.

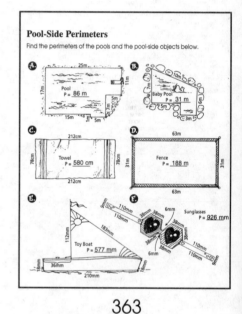

A. Pool P = 86 m (25m, 17m, 15m, 5m)

B. Baby Pool P = 31 m (10m, 11m, 3m)

C. Towel P = 580 cm (212cm, 78cm, 212cm)

D. Fence P = 188 m (63m, 31m, 63m, 31m)

E. Toy Boat P = 577 mm (110mm, 183mm, 112mm, 36mm, 210mm, 18mm)

F. Sunglasses P = 926 mm (110mm, 38mm, 6mm)

363

Turn up the Volume!

Calculate the volume of the objects in the column on the left. Match each to its corresponding player on the right. All measurements are in centimeters.

A. (6, 2, 7)

B. 120cm³

C. (3, 5, 8)

D. 56cm³

E. (2, 7, 4)

F. 84cm³

G. (5, 5, 5)

H. 125cm³

I. (4, 6, 3)

J. 72cm³

364

Does This Joke "Measure" Up?

When it rains cats and dogs, what do you step into?

To find out, measure the angles below. Put their measurements in order from least to greatest. The letters in the angles will spell out the answer.

A. 70° O

B. 20° P

C. 90° O

D. 130° L

E. 100° D

F. 170° E

G. 180° S

When it rains cats and dogs, you step into _poodles_ !

365

"Angles" in the Outfield

A. Name an obtuse angle. Answers will vary.

B. How many obtuse angles can you find? 9; ∠BEO, ∠IER, ∠GER, ∠SER, ∠BEC, ∠IEC, ∠SEO, ∠CEO, ∠CER

C. Name a right angle. ∠BER

D. Find ∠BEG. Is it a right, acute, or obtuse angle? acute

E. Find ∠IES. There are two angles within ∠IES. Name them. ∠IEG and ∠GES

F. Combine ∠BER and ∠REO. What is the name of the angle? ∠BEO

G. Which two angles together make ∠BEG? ∠BEI and ∠GEI

H. ∠BEC has how many angles within it? 10

I. How many acute angles can you find? 8

J. Look at the letters that name all of the points. Unscramble them to make two words that describe what the home team fans are hoping for.
B I G S C O R E

366

Concept Mapping and the Human Body

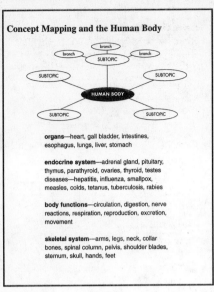

organs—heart, gall bladder, intestines, esophagus, lungs, liver, stomach

endocrine system—adrenal gland, pituitary, thymus, parathyroid, ovaries, thyroid, testes
diseases—hepatitis, influenza, smallpox, measles, colds, tetanus, tuberculosis, rabies

body functions—circulation, digestion, nerve reactions, respiration, reproduction, excretion, movement

skeletal system—arms, legs, neck, collar bones, spinal column, pelvis, shoulder blades, sternum, skull, hands, feet

367

The Human Digestive System

Important parts of the human digestive system are hidden in the maze below. From the starting letter, skip every other letter and write the words in the spaces.

1. M O U T H
2. E S O P H A G U S
3. S T O M A C H
4. S M A L L   I N T E S T I N E
5. L A R G E   I N T E S T I N E
6. R E C T U M

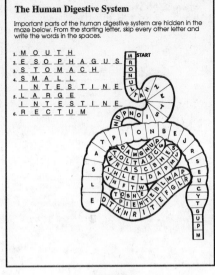

369

Environmental Issues

On April 22, 1970, the first Earth Day was celebrated. Since then, much has been done to protect Earth's environment. But there is still much more to do to save Earth from destruction.

Look for news stories, both locally and from around the world, involving the environment. Among the stories you might find, include those on such environmental topics as preserving natural areas, creating green spaces in cities and along roads, cleaning rivers and lakes, conserving natural resources, reducing air pollution, and recycling waste. Then use the retrieval chart below to report on five news stories.

Retrieval Chart

News Story Topic	When Did It Happen?	Where Did It Happen?	What Happened?

Answers will vary.

370

The World of Arthropods

The largest percentage of animals in the world are arthropods. **Arthropods** are animals with exoskeletons and jointed appendages. They live in all parts of the world and in every type of habitat.

Look at the list of arthropods below. Print the names of insects in the square, the names of arachnids in the triangle, and the names of crustaceans in the circle.

TARANTULA	BEE	MITE	CRAB
LOBSTER	BUTTERFLY	SCORPION	WASP
BEETLE	SHRIMP	HORNET	FLY
GRASSHOPPER	CRICKET	CRAYFISH	TICK
GARDEN SPIDER	BROWN RECLUSE	BLACK WIDOW	CICADA
BARNACLE	LOUSE	WATER FLEA	APHID
TERMITE	ANT	GNAT	FLEA
MOTH	FIREFLY		MAYFLY

Insects
bee, butterfly, wasp, beetle, hornet, fly, grasshopper, cricket, cicada, aphid, termite, ant, flea, moth, firefly, gnat, mayfly, louse

Crustaceans
crab, lobster, shrimp, crayfish, barnacle, water flea

Arachnids
mite, tarantula, scorpion, tick, garden spider, brown recluse, black widow

371

Mollusks

Mollusks are animals with soft, boneless bodies. Most of them have shells. Three of the most common classes of mollusks are bivalves, gastropods, and cephalopods.

Choose one of the mollusks below to research. Data collected on each example could include the following: size, habitat, description, uses of, and unusual characteristics or behaviors. Write the data in the chart below.

BIVALVES:	GASTROPODS:	CEPHALOPODS:
oyster, clam, scallop, mussel, cockle, ark, angel wing, jewel box, jingle, ox heart	land snail, abalone, conch, slug, sea slug, limpet, sea snail, moon snail, cone shell, murex, olive, cowrie, whelk, bonnet, periwinkle	squid, octopus, nautilus, cuttlefish

Mollusk I will research (Circle one):

BIVALVE   GASTROPOD   CEPHALOPOD

Name of mollusk: _____

Type of Data:

Size:	
Habitat:	
Description:	
Uses of:	
Unusual Characteristics or Behaviors:	

Answers will vary.

372

Marine Life

The oceans are teeming with living things. Complete the word grid below to learn the names of some marine life.

CONCH	EEL	LOBSTER	OCTOPUS	SHRIMP	STARFISH
CORAL	HERMIT CRAB	MANATEE	SCALLOP	SPONGE	TRITON
DOLPHIN	LIMPET	MUSSEL	SEAL	SQUID	WHALE

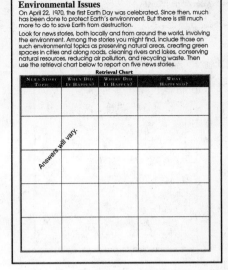

373

Save the Elephants

During the 1980's, the African elephant population was a casualty of human desires. The number of elephants declined from well over one million to about 600,000. It is estimated that more than 270 elephants were killed each day! Thousands of baby elephants, called calves, were left to take care of themselves. The African elephant was in a threatening situation.

What was happening to the elephants? They were being killed by poachers who wanted their ivory tusks. The ivory was valued around the world. It is used for jewelry, statues, knife handles, billiard balls, plus other products.

Organizations that protect animals and look out for their welfare were outraged. They devised a plan to alleviate the situation. They began a publicity campaign to spread awareness of the problem. Some large companies helped by refusing to buy ivory and asking their customers to do the same.

International laws were eventually passed to help make the killing of elephants less appealing. The sale of ivory was made illegal all around the world.

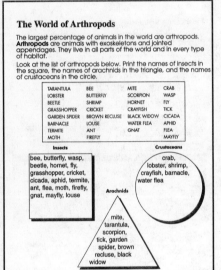

Complete the following.

1. What do you think would have happened to the African elephant if no one had made any changes? **They might have become extinct.**

2. What is a poacher? **Someone who kills animals illegally for money.**

3. How would a poacher's job be affected if ivory became illegal? **No one would buy the ivory.**

4. What might happen to baby elephants if the poaching doesn't cease? **They might be orphaned or die.**

Join a publicity campaign! Draw a poster to help raise awareness of the plight of an endangered animal in the twenty-first century.

374

Pandas

Read the article. Then match the cause and effect statements by drawing a line.

The giant panda is an Asian mammal that lives on the mountain slopes of China. Pandas eat only bamboo, which grows extensively in the Chinese highlands. In order to get enough nutrients, a panda must eat as much as 85 pounds (39 kg) of bamboo a day. The rampant destruction of the panda's habitat has endangered this creature. The government of China has tried to save the panda's food supply by setting up reserves of bamboo-rich land. Large reserves are necessary to ensure adequate food for the pandas. Because bamboo plants take so long to grow into mature plants, there have been shortages in the past. These periodic shortages have led to the deaths of hundreds of pandas. Only about 1,000 giant pandas remain in the wild.

Cause
1. Many pandas die each year.
2. Pandas must get enough nutrients.
3. Bamboo takes a long time to mature.
4. There is rampant destruction of the panda habitat.
5. There have been bamboo shortages.

Effect
a. Pandas are endangered.
b. Hundreds of pandas have died.
c. They must eat huge amounts of bamboo.
d. Periodic bamboo shortages occur.
e. China has set up bamboo reserves.

375

Tectonic Plates of the Earth

Earth's surface consists of about 20 rigid plates that move slowly past one another. Label the tectonic plates of Earth on the map below.

EURASIAN PLATE	INDIAN PLATE	PHILIPPINE PLATE
PACIFIC PLATE	NORTH AMERICAN PLATE	NAZCA PLATE
SOUTH AMERICAN PLATE	AFRICAN PLATE	ANTARCTIC PLATE

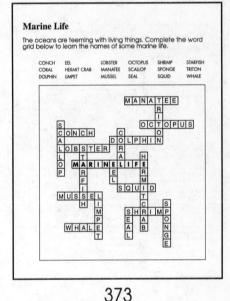

Write what you think (or know) an earthquake would do to your city/town.

Answers will vary.

376

Map of the World

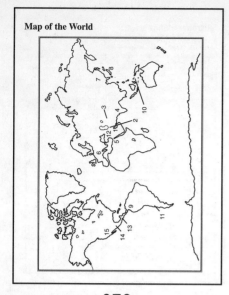

378

Which Rocks Are These?

The hard, solid part of Earth is rock. Three main kinds of rocks are igneous, sedimentary, and metamorphic. To learn more about rocks, match the names of the rocks to their definitions.

1. E SANDSTONE
2. H SHALE
3. I CONGLOMERATE
4. K BRECCIA
5. M LIMESTONE
6. O SEDIMENTARY ROCKS
7. B BITUMINOUS COAL
8. N GEODES
9. C GNEISS
10. J SCHIST
11. G ANTHRACITE COAL
12. A MARBLE
13. D QUARTZITE
14. L SLATE
15. F METAMORPHIC ROCKS

A. a metamorphic rock which can be formed from limestone
B. a sedimentary rock of plant origin
C. the most common metamorphic rock made from granite
D. a metamorphic rock made from sandstone
E. a sedimentary rock made from cemented sand
F. rocks changed in form from sedimentary or igneous rocks
G. hard metamorphic rock made from soft coal
H. cemented mud, clay, or silt
I. coarse sedimentary rock made up of pebbles or boulders
J. metamorphic rock made from shale
K. sedimentary rock composed of rough and angular fragments of rock
L. metamorphic rock made from schist
M. sedimentary rock made from the shells and skeletons of plants and animals
N. hollow spheres in limestone
O. layered rocks made from sediments

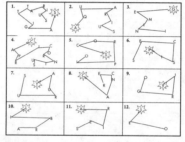

379

Metals From Minerals

Metal forms a large part of Earth. Earth's crust is made up of certain metals. Identify the metals below from the clues given.

1. I am obtained from the mineral bauxite.
   I am shiny and often seen as rolls of thin sheets.
   Many soft drink cans are made from me.
   I am used to make canoes, chairs, windows, and siding for houses.
   My chemical symbol is Al.
   What metal am I?
   aluminum

2. I am found in the minerals limonite, hematite, and magnetite.
   I am used in the manufacture of steel.
   I rust easily.
   I am also found in "fool's gold," or pyrite.
   My chemical symbol is Fe.
   What metal am I?
   iron

3. I am found in the mineral galena.
   I am used in pipes, batteries, and glass.
   I was once used in many paints.
   I am used to protect people from the effects of X-rays.
   My chemical symbol is Pb.
   What metal am I?
   lead

4. I am found in the mineral cinnabar.
   I remain liquid over a wide range of temperatures.
   I am shiny.
   I am used in many thermometers.
   My chemical symbol is Hg.
   What metal am I?
   mercury

5. I am found in the mineral chalcopyrite and in others.
   I am used in most electrical wires.
   I am used in many coins.
   I am mixed with other metals to make bronze.
   My chemical symbol is Cu.
   What metal am I?
   copper

6. I am found in the mineral chromite.
   I am used in cars and bathroom fixtures.
   I am very shiny and one of the hardest substances.
   I am used to make stainless steel.
   My chemical symbol is Cr.
   What metal am I?
   chromium

7. I am found in the mineral cassiterite.
   I am used in welding solder.
   I was once widely used as roofing material for houses and barns.
   I am mixed with copper to make bronze.
   My chemical symbol is Sn.
   What metal am I?
   tin

380

Our Solar System

There is so much to know about our solar system. To learn a little about it, solve the crossword puzzle below. Use the terms in the box and the clues under the box to help you.

ASTEROIDS	EMIT	LOWELL	MOON	SATURN	TRITON
CERES	HALLEY'S	MARS	NEPTUNE	SPOT	URANUS
COMET	IO	MERCURY	PLUTO	SUN	VENUS
EARTH	JUPITER	METEORS	RINGS	TAIL	WAY

ACROSS
1. rocky particles which orbit the sun mainly between Mars and Jupiter
4. another name for a satellite of a planet
8. the center of our solar system
9. the seventh planet from the sun
11. Planets do not _____ light energy of their own.
13. one of the moons of Neptune
14. sometimes called "the red planet"
15. consists of a head and tail
18. a comet that appears every 76 years
20. known as Earth's twin
21. Saturn is probably best known for its _____
22. Our solar system is in the galaxy called "The Milky _____"
23. usually the most distant planet from the sun

DOWN
2. the sixth planet from the sun
3. one of the moons of Jupiter
5. the planet discovered in 1846
6. planet covered with dark and light bands
7. planet whose atmosphere is mostly oxygen and nitrogen
10. The Great Red _____ is a prominent feature of Jupiter.
12. often called "falling stars" or "shooting stars"; results when a meteoroid enters Earth's atmosphere from space
15. the largest asteroid
16. planet closest to the sun
17. The _____ of a comet may be over 100 million miles long.
19. American astronomer who began the search for Pluto in 1905

381

Constellations of the Zodiac

Astronomers have divided the sky into 88 constellations. The letters in the blocks below will spell out the names of 12 constellations found in the sky. The beginning letter of each constellation is in the star. Draw straight lines between the letters to find the name of each constellation. No lines will cross. Write the name of each constellation at the bottom of the page.

1. Sagittarius
2. Aquarius
3. Gemini
4. Capricornius
5. Scorpio
6. Pisces
7. Taurus
8. Cancer
9. Virgo
10. Libra
11. Aries
12. Leo

382

Friction on a Rolling Sphere

Friction is the property that objects have that makes them resist being moved across one another.

To learn more about friction, try the activity below. For this activity, you will need a meterstick, a piece of corrugated cardboard, masking tape, four books, a large marble, a sheet of wax paper, a sheet of aluminum foil, sandpaper, a piece of scrap carpet, cotton cloth, and wool cloth.

You may complete this activity individually or in groups.

1. Cut a piece of corrugated cardboard 10 centimeters by 30 centimeters. Fold it down the middle to make a trough. Use the masking tape to hold the trough in place. (*See illustration.*)
2. Prop the trough on a stack of four books. Use more masking tape to hold the trough in place.
3. Place a large piece of wax paper at the base of the trough.
4. Place a large marble at the top of the trough and release it. Use the meterstick to measure the distance the marble rolls. Record your results in the chart below.
5. Repeat Steps 3 and 4 by replacing the wax paper with aluminum foil, sandpaper, carpet, cotton cloth, and wool cloth. Measure the distance in each trial.

MATERIAL	DISTANCE MARBLE ROLLED IN CENTIMETERS
wax paper	
aluminum foil	
sandpaper	*Answers will vary.*
carpet	
cotton cloth	
wool cloth	

6. How did the friction created by the different materials affect the results?
   Answers will vary.

383

Sound All Around Us

You will need: small piece of bubble wrap, metal pie plate, other sound-making materials, piece of wax paper, spoon

Use the materials to produce a variety of sounds. Can you combine materials to come up with something new? When you make a sound, try to find (or invent) a word to describe it.

Sample answers: pop, clang, crackle, etc.

What sounds can you make with your mouth, hands, and feet? List the sounds.

Sample answers: pop, clang, crackle, etc.

Close your eyes and listen to the sounds around you right now. List the sounds that you hear now.

Answers will vary.

Draw a picture of a noisy place and label all the sounds you might hear there.

Pictures will vary.

384

Newton's Three Laws of Motion

All moving objects on Earth are governed by Sir Isaac Newton's three laws of motion. These laws are as follows:

1st Law: Objects at rest stay at rest and objects in motion stay in motion unless acted on by a force.

2nd Law: Acceleration of an object depends on its mass and the size and direction of the force acting on it.

3rd Law: Every action has an equal and opposite reaction force.

Write an example of how each of the laws is applied in the following events:

bowling	skating
	Answers will vary.
baseball	biking
football	skiing
canoeing	sailing
archery	sledding
rocketry	swimming

385

Why Integrity Counts

It is no fun to lose to a cheater, but integrity does more than keep the game fun. It is so important to our interactions with each other as human beings that we demand it of our business contacts, our teachers, our politicians, and our families and friends. In complete sentences, indicate below why it is important to be able to trust people in the situations described below.

1. Your doctor says that you need a life-saving operation. Why is it important that he be a trustworthy man?
   Answers will vary.

2. Your banker handles all the money in your checking and savings accounts. Why is it important for you to be able to trust a banker?

3. Your teacher assures you that by following the assignment sheet she provides, you will complete the course for a full credit. Why is it important that you be able to trust your teacher?

4. Your best friend confidentially tells you something about himself that would make your classmates laugh at him. Why is it important that you keep your friend's secret?

5. You want your mother to give you more freedoms. Why is it so important to your mother that she can trust you before giving you the freedoms you want?

6. Your classmate offers to complete a poster for a group project if you will complete a required survey. Why is it important that you be able to trust each other?

7. A car dealer is attempting to convince you to buy a used car. Why is it important that the salesman be trustworthy?

8. A newspaper reporter writes stories about your local community. Why is it important that the newspaper reporter be honest?

9. A politician makes promises to voters. Why is it important that he live up to the promises?

386

Masks

Decorate the mask to look like you. Glue the mask onto thick paper. Cut out the face and create holes for the eyes. Attach a craft stick along one side of the mask to use as a holder.

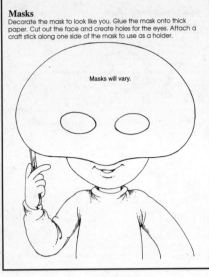

Masks will vary.

387

Have I Got a Job for You

Read the five job opportunities below. Match each job applicant with a job or jobs below by writing the correct numbers on each line.

1. **Bakers Wanted**. Must know flour from powdered sugar. Ability to read is required. Must be 18 years or older. Call Bun in the Oven at 267-1010. Ask for Rose.
2. **Yard Work**. Like to work up a sweat? Eager to work with loud machines? We've got many positions for hardworking men. Call Hulk at 268-8760.
3. **Candy Sales**. Sugar-N-Spice is looking for door-to-door sales reps willing to work strictly on commission. Must be at least 16 years old. $100 deposit on first order of candy. Call 1-800-GOCANDY.
4. **Child Care**. Looking for a 12- to 16-year-old girl to care for my precious 3-year-old. Must love children and ferrets. Need for evening care. Call Mommy at 269-9800.
5. **Photogenic?** We need students ages 7–14 to model for our Fall Series Clothing Sale. Must have no police record. For the required parental permission form write: P.O. Box 9009, Good Pose, IA 50014.

2, 5	Tad: 14-year-old boy; has no money
3, 4	Blanche: 16-year-old girl; hates noise
2, 3	Anselm: 19-year-old man; cannot read
1	Zoe: 18-year-old woman; won't work door-to-door
3	Perry: 17-year-old female; doesn't know baking ingredients

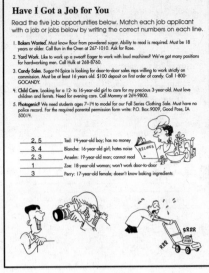

389

Writing a Rebus

Use the following key to a few common Egyptian hieroglyphs to help you complete the statements below.

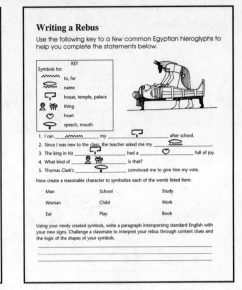

KEY

Symbols for:
- 〰 — to, for
- 〜 — name
- ⛫ — house, temple, palace
- ♥ — thing
- ♡ — heart
- 👄 — speech, mouth

1. I ran 〰 my 👄 after school.
2. Since I was new to the class, the teacher asked me my 〜.
3. The king in his ⛫ had a ♡ full of joy.
4. What kind of ♥ is that?
5. Thomas Clark's 👄 convinced me to give him my vote.

Now create a reasonable character to symbolize each of the words listed here:

Man	School	Study
Woman	Child	Work
Eat	Play	Book

Using your newly created symbols, write a paragraph interspersing standard English with your new signs. Challenge a classmate to interpret your rebus through context clues and the logic of the shapes of your symbols.

391

Kids Around the World

Are kids the same around the world? The reporters at Kidsworld Television wanted to find out. They traveled around the globe, interviewing young people about their lives. Read these segments of their interviews. Then, using the Word Bank for additional clues, fill in the blanks.

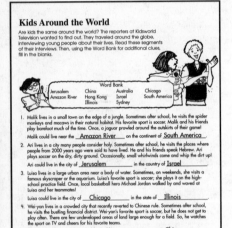

Word Bank
Jerusalem	China	Australia	Chicago
Amazon River	Hong Kong	Israel	South America
	Illinois	Sydney	

1. Malik lives in a small town on the edge of a jungle. Sometimes after school, he visits the spider monkeys and macaws in their natural habitat. His favorite sport is soccer. Malik and his friends play barefoot much of the time. Once, a jaguar prowled around the outskirts of their game!
   Malik could live near the _Amazon River_ on the continent of _South America_.

2. Ari lives in a city many people consider holy. Sometimes after school, he visits the places where people from 2000 years ago were said to have lived. He and his friends speak Hebrew. Ari plays soccer on the dry, dirty ground. Occasionally, small whirlwinds come and whip the dirt up!
   Ari could live in the city of _Jerusalem_ in the country of _Israel_.

3. Luisa lives in a large urban area near a body of water. Sometimes, on weekends, she visits a famous skyscraper or the aquarium. Luisa's favorite sport is soccer; she plays it on the high-school practice field. Once, local basketball hero Michael Jordan walked by and waved at Luisa and her teammates!
   Luisa could live in the city of _Chicago_ in the state of _Illinois_.

4. Wei-yan lives in a crowded city that recently reverted to Chinese rule. Sometimes after school, he visits the bustling financial district. Wei-yan's favorite sport is soccer, but he does not get to play often. There are few undeveloped areas of land large enough for a field. So, he watches the sport on TV and cheers for his favorite teams.
   Wei-yan could live in the city of _Hong Kong_ in the country of _China_.

5. Maddy lives Down Under in a seaside city. Sometimes after school Maddy visits a bird sanctuary which houses many of the 700 species native to her area. Maddy loves to attend soccer games. The city's harborside opera house is a famous landmark.
   Maddy could live in the city of _Sydney_ in the country of _Australia_.

392

Religious Customs Trackdown

American society is influenced by the customs of many religious traditions. Listed on the left below are some key religious concepts, symbols, and ceremonies. Each item listed is associated with one of the following religions: Judaism, Christianity, Islam, Hinduism, and Buddhism. Use resource books to help you match the religions listed on the right with the items associated with them on the left. Write the correct letters in the blanks.

Religious Concepts, Symbols, and Ceremonies

D	1. Shiva
B	2. kosher
C	3. Ramadan
E	4. "the Enlightened One"
E	5. Noble Eightfold Path
A	6. cross
B	7. Star of David
B	8. Festival of Sacrifice
B	9. Hanukkah
A	10. Christmas
B	11. synagogue
C	12. mosque
A	13. church
C	14. Kaaba
B	15. menorah
B	16. Torah
C	17. Koran
E	18. nirvana
D	19. The Vedas

Religions

A. Christianity
B. Judaism
C. Islam
D. Hinduism
E. Buddhism

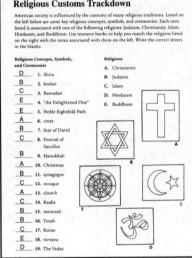

393

Food–Societies Connection

Many factors contributed to the development of the world's earliest societies. Two of the most important factors were these:
- a lush environment suitable for agriculture, and
- a staple food crop to feed a growing population.

The staple food crops differed across early societies. The early Mesopotamian civilization in the Middle East depended on wheat. In East Asia, rice was the staple crop. And in the Americas, maize, or corn, was the main food of the Maya and Aztec, while the potato was one of the primary staples of the Inca. Make a list of foods below that contain wheat, rice, corn, or potatoes as the main ingredient.

Answers will vary.

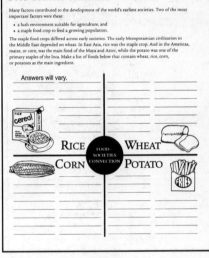

RICE — WHEAT
CORN — POTATO
FOOD–SOCIETIES CONNECTION

394

All That Jazz

Work with a partner to research the jazz musicians in the box below. Fill in each blank with the name of the musician who matches the information.

Earl "Fatha" Hines	Ella Fitzgerald
Louis Armstrong	Charlie Parker
Count Basie	Dizzy Gillespie
Fats Waller	Lester Young

1. I was a great alto saxophonist and played in Missouri, Kansas City, and New York City.
   I am _Charlie Parker_

2. I played the trumpet and cornet. I was also a singer and bandleader. I am known for creating a musical style called swing. I am
   Louis Armstrong

3. I was a jazz pianist and had my own nightly radio broadcast, which featured my band's music. I am _Earl "Fatha" Hines_

4. I played jazz trumpet and was popular for nearly 60 years. I composed many songs, including "Salt Peanuts," and "Bebop." I am
   Dizzy Gillespie

5. I was a jazz pianist and was known for combining my music with slapstick comedy.
   I am _Fats Waller_

6. I was one of the greatest tenor saxophone players of all times. My nickname was "Prez." I am _Lester Young_

7. I was a well-know jazz bandleader and piano player. I began studying jazz with my mother. I am _Count Bessie_

8. I was known as a jazz singer. I was raised in an orphanage and was discovered while singing in a talent show in Harlem. I am _Ella Fitzgerald_

395

Name That Scene

Norman Rockwell's paintings illustrated America at its best. They were often humorous and always thought- and emotion-provoking. Match the following Rockwell paintings with their descriptions below. To view prints of the paintings listed, look up "Norman Rockwell" on the Internet.

In which painting will you see . . .

L	1. . . . the backs of a boy and girl as they sit on a sagging bench watching a large, round sun in the background.
G	2. . . . a mother with her child over her knee, one hand raised and holding a hairbrush, as the other hand holds a book which the mother is consulting for her best next move.
C	3. . . . a young girl and an old storekeeper looking at puppets together in an incredibly cluttered shop.
H	4. . . . three schoolgirls: one opening her mouth wide as two look inside to see the work a dentist has completed.
D	5. . . . the back of Norman Rockwell's head as he looks past the side of a canvas on which he is painting a portrait of himself to a mirror beyond the canvas.
A	6. . . . a police officer and a young boy sitting at a soda fountain counter.
J	7. . . . a nervous rookie about to go to bat as the crowd and his teammates in the dugout show signs of doubt.
E	8. . . . a young soldier being welcomed home by his father as his mother and siblings look on excitedly from the stairwell.
F	9. . . . a boy in a cowboy hat petting a dog who looks up to him with puppies surrounding her.
I	10. . . . the backs of boys dressed in sports gear and huddled in a circle arguing as one boy holds a basketball and the others shout and point in various directions.
B	11. . . . a black boy and girl standing beside a moving truck and furniture as three white kids stare on pensively.
K	12. . . . a smiling grandpa and a young boy reeling in a big fish.

A. The Runaway
B. New Kids in the Neighborhood
C. The Curiosity Shop
D. Triple Self-portrait
E. Homecoming
F. A Boy and His Dog: Parenthood
G. Child Psychology
H. Check-up
I. Sporting Boys: Oh Yeah!
J. The Dugout
K. Catching the Big One
L. Sunset

397

International Temperatures

Use the weather section of the newspaper to check the temperature for your local area and the temperatures for the five cities identified on the graph below.

Complete the bar graph showing the temperatures for each city. Then use the graph and a world atlas to answer the questions.

Degrees in Fahrenheit

Answers will vary.

Your locality | Sydney, Australia | Moscow, Russia | Buenos Aires, Argentina | Beijing, China | Johannesburg, South Africa

1. On what date did you record the temperatures for all six places? _____
2. Which place was the coldest? _Answers will vary._
3. Which place was the warmest? _____
4. What might account for the temperature difference between the coldest and warmest places? _location and elevation_
5. Which place is farthest away from the equator? _Moscow_
6. Which of the five international cities would you like to visit the most? Why?
   Answers will vary.

398

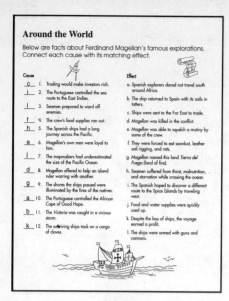

Around the World

Below are facts about Ferdinand Magellan's famous explorations. Connect each cause with its matching effect.

Cause

- c 1. Trading would make investors rich.
- i 2. The Portuguese controlled the sea route to the East Indies.
- l 3. Seamen prepared to ward off enemies.
- f 4. The crew's food supplies ran out.
- h 5. The Spanish ships had a long journey across the Pacific.
- e 6. Magellan's own men were loyal to him.
- j 7. The mapmakers had underestimated the size of the Pacific Ocean.
- d 8. Magellan offered to help an island ruler warring with another.
- g 9. The shores the ships passed were illuminated by the fires of the natives.
- a 10. The Portuguese controlled the African Cape of Good Hope.
- b 11. The Victoria was caught in a vicious storm.
- k 12. The surviving ships took on a cargo of cloves.

Effect

- a. Spanish explorers dared not travel south around Africa.
- b. The ship returned to Spain with its sails in tatters.
- c. Ships were sent to the Far East to trade.
- d. Magellan was killed in the conflict.
- e. Magellan was able to squelch a mutiny by some of the crew.
- f. They were forced to eat sawdust, leather sail rigging, and rats.
- g. Magellan named this land *Tierra del Fuego* (land of fire).
- h. Seamen suffered from thirst, malnutrition, and starvation while crossing the ocean.
- i. The Spanish hoped to discover a different route to the Spice Islands by traveling west.
- j. Food and water supplies were quickly used up.
- k. Despite the loss of ships, the voyage earned a profit.
- l. The ships were armed with guns and cannons.

399

---

1. Why do you think agriculture may have been so important to these ancient civilizations?
   It was one of the only ways to get food.

2. Why did slash-and-burn agriculture produce highly fertile soil?
   The ashes from the burn fertilized the soil.

3. Why do you think the chinampa farms of the Aztecs yielded large crops?
   The mud from the bottom of the lake was very fertile and rich.

4. List one other reason why terracing might have been helpful to these ancient civilizations.
   Terraces helped reduce erosion.

5. The farming techniques of all three civilizations are similar even though the people lived in different areas. List two reasons why this might be.
   Answers will vary.

401

Create an Island Culture

Human activity on Earth is influenced by geographic features. Below is a blank map of an island. On it, show how geographic features influence an imaginary culture

on an imaginary island. To create an environment and human settlement patterns for the island, you need to do the following:

1. Select and write the latitude and longitude coordinates of your island to establish the influence of latitude on your island's climate. _____

2. On the map, draw symbols and use combinations of colors to show major natural and man-made features (bays, rivers, lakes, vegetation, mineral deposits, mountains, hills, swamps, plains, bridges, roads, cities, dams, etc.). Create a map key to explain the symbols and colors.

3. Label the geographic features you created.

4. Draw a compass rose to show cardinal directions.

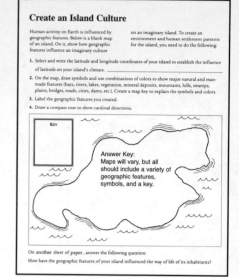

KEY

Answer Key:
Maps will vary, but all should include a variety of geographic features, symbols, and a key.

On another sheet of paper, answer the following question:

How have the geographic features of your island influenced the way of life of its inhabitants?

402

America's Rivers

Ten of America's rivers are highlighted on the map below. Use an atlas to identify each one. Then write the name of the river on the appropriate line.

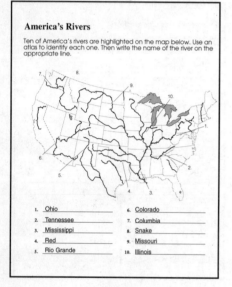

1. Ohio
2. Tennessee
3. Mississippi
4. Red
5. Rio Grande
6. Colorado
7. Columbia
8. Snake
9. Missouri
10. Illinois

403